A Dick Francis Companion

A Dick Francis Companion

Characters, Horses, Plots, Settings and Themes

STEPHEN SUGDEN

McFarland & Company, Inc., Publishers
Jefferson, North Carolina, and London

Library of Congress Cataloguing-in-Publication Data

Sugden, Stephen, 1950–
A Dick Francis companion : characters, horses, plots, settings and
themes / Stephen Sugden.
p.   cm.
Includes bibliographical references and index.

ISBN 978-0-7864-2944-8
softcover : 50# alkaline paper ∞

1. Francis, Dick—Dictionaries.   2. Detective and mystery stories,
English—Dictionaries.   I. Title.
PR6056.R27Z67   2008   823'.914—dc22   2008033622

British Library cataloguing data are available

Cover photograph ©2007 Corbis Images

Manufactured in the United States of America

*McFarland & Company, Inc., Publishers
Box 611, Jefferson, North Carolina 28640
www.mcfarlandpub.com*

For my wife Sheila,
whose patience has been infinite;
my daughter Jeanna;
and my sons Jamie, Jonnie and Peter

Acknowledgments

I am grateful to Graham Lord for the meticulous research he undertook for his biography of Dick Francis, *Dick Francis: A Racing Life* (Little, Brown & Company 1999). I have relied upon it particularly for information about where Francis got the ideas for his novels.

I am also indebted to the following writers and publications for providing details of locations mentioned in the novels: *Great Britain* (Dorling Kindersley Travel Guides 1995, reprinted 2000); Stephen Cartmell: *Racing Around Britain* (Aesculus Press 2002); John Tyrrel: *Chasing Around Britain* (The Crowood Press 1990); Alan Lee: *An Inspector Calls* (racecourse reviews on *www.timesonline.co.uk*).

Finally, I found the discussions on plot construction and other elements of fiction writing in Raymond Obstfeld's book *Fiction First Aid* (Writers Digest Books 2002) extremely useful.

Contents

Preface

Few authors have had such a long career as ex-champion steeplechase jockey Dick Francis. After retiring from the saddle in 1957 Francis wrote his autobiography, *The Sport of Queens*, and worked as a racing journalist for the *Sunday Express* newspaper. Five years passed, and Francis was in his early forties before he published his first novel, *Dead Cert*, in 1962. Between that date and 2000 he produced a biography of legendary Flat jockey Lester Piggott, a collection of short stories and a further thirty-seven novels. In 2006, following a five year hiatus, he published *Under Orders*. In 2007 he collaborated with his son Felix in the writing of a fortieth novel, *Dead Heat*. Over this period of time Francis's popularity as a writer of crime novels, many with a horse racing background, has been immense. Through his fiction he has given us a series of contemporary snapshots of almost five decades of British racing.

Over the years there have been academic studies of Francis as a writer, and untold numbers of articles about his individual books. However, such a substantial body of work as Francis's, whose novels and short stories include well over a thousand characters—not to mention the horses—requires a reference work which can provide a comprehensive survey of his oeuvre. This Companion volume aims to do just that. All Francis's novels are written from a first person perspective, and central to the action are the thirty-seven main characters whose motivations drive the plots. Each of them has an essay devoted to him, detailing his role, physical appearance, family background, relationships, and personal strengths and weaknesses. Though many share similarities in temperament and professional background, the most successful main characters are complex, independent and have their own unique view of the world. The entries include an assessment of the character's success or otherwise as a credible and memorable protagonist.

Crucial to any crime novel is the interaction between the main characters and the villains. A first person perspective can make it difficult for the writer to develop the villain as fully as the hero, and Francis's strategies for doing so are explored. Does the villain avoid being stereotypical? Is he sufficiently complex to involve the reader? Are his actions unpredictable? These are some of the questions that are addressed.

Minor and peripheral characters are similarly considered. If well-drawn, they can add color and texture to the plot; they have interesting lives of their own which transcend the storyline; and they help to define the profiles of the principal players through their relationships with them. Every one of these minor characters has its own entry, its length dependent upon its importance in a particular scene or in the plot as a whole. In addition, there are extended essays on different categories of characters, including Trainers, Jockeys, Owners, Stable Staff, Bookmakers, Police, and Women. Other thematic entries cover various sorts of crimes perpetrated by Francis's villains, such as Murder, Fraud, Arson and Blackmail.

The quality of each novel's plot is considered with reference to a range of criteria. To what extent is suspense created by conflict within the plot itself or between the characters? Is the development of the characters sufficient to allow the reader to care what happens to them? Does the plot intensify the suspense by providing increasingly difficult problems for the main character to solve in order to achieve his goal? Is the dénouement appropriate and memorable?

An important element in any novel is its geographical setting, which must be convincing and interesting without submerging the plot in irrelevant detail. This book describes every significant location in Francis's books, including no fewer than 55 racecourses, real and fictional.

Francis writes about horses with affection and deep understanding, and in many ways they are the stars of the show; in *Dead Cert*, for example, the brilliant hunter-chaser Admiral plays a crucial part in the plot. In his descriptions of horses Francis brings out their individual characters, so that the reader cares as much about what happens to them as to their human counterparts. For example, North Face (*Break In* 1975) is a tough, moody steeplechaser and the winner of 38 races: "an unpredictable rogue and as clever a jumper as a cat"; the stallion Chrysalis (*Blood Sport* 1967), stolen en route to stud duties in Lexington, Kentucky, is subsequently identified by his liking for sardines. Every horse merits a mention in this Companion, and these entries, taken as a whole, help the reader to gain an appreciation of the animal whose athleticism and marvelous spirit are the cause, directly or indirectly, of many of the events—inspirational, courageous or downright evil—that take place in the novels.

Throughout the book a cross-referencing system is used whereby the reader can check any character, plot, horse or location that is mentioned. **Bold** lettering is used for all cross-references (with *bold italics* for book titles). A reference is highlighted in bold only the first time it is cited in an entry; any subsequent mention is in roman type.

My interest in Dick Francis's work stems from a lifelong love of horses—in particular, the thoroughbred racehorse—and a fascination with the literature of the Turf. I have worked in racing stables—Flat, jumping and trotting—and for many years I have practiced as an equine chiropractor. Seeing racing from the inside has been of value in interpreting and commenting on what goes on in the hearts and minds of racing people, and has impressed upon me just how brilliantly Francis, at his best, evokes that vibrant, absorbing and sometimes arcane world.

Introduction

To reach the top in one's chosen career is a notable achievement. For a person to do so in two entirely disparate professions is rare indeed, but Dick Francis is one of the few who can claim that distinction. From the standpoint of breeding Francis's first profession, that of a steeplechase jockey, was easier to predict than his subsequent reincarnation as a writer. With a grandfather and a father who were both jockeys it was perhaps inevitable that the young Dick Francis would have no other ambition but to emulate them. But before he could find himself a job in racing stables the Second World War intervened, and Francis joined the Royal Air Force. At first they wouldn't take him as a pilot, and he spent three frustrating years as an aircraft fitter before his repeated application to fly was finally accepted. After completing his training Francis was initially posted to fighter escort duty during the Allied invasion of Europe. However, the RAF had trained too many Spitfire pilots, so he soon found himself transferred to Wellington bombers, in a squadron that made diversionary sorties in support of bombers attacking the principal targets in Europe. Towards the end of the war Francis joined Coastal Command, shepherding surrendering enemy craft into Allied ports.

Francis returned to civilian life as determined as ever to become a jockey. But he was now 25 years old, and it had begun to look as though the opportunity may have passed him by. He resolved to start as an amateur and see where it led him. His first job in racing was as a secretary and stable amateur with farmer and ex-jockey George Owen in Cheshire, in the north-west of England. In the spring of his first season with Owen Francis rode his first winner, a hunter-chaser called Wrenbury Tiger at Bangor-on-Dee. That summer he married Mary, whom he had met in late 1945 at the wedding of his cousin Nesta.

A busy and successful second season with Owen saw Francis up before the Stewards of the National Hunt Committee. They told him he was riding too many horses as an unpaid amateur, and taking the rides from professionals who needed the money. Stick to amateur races, they told him, or turn professional. It was not a decision that Francis agonized over: he immediately joined the professional ranks.

Francis's career really took off when he was retained to ride for the prominent owner Lord Bicester whenever his lordship's first jockey, Martin Molony, was riding in Ireland. In the Grand National at Aintree Francis partnered Lord Bicester's good chestnut horse Roimond into second place behind Russian Hero; ironically the winner was trained by George Owen, and Francis had won on him several times. By now Francis's ability was being noticed by the top National Hunt trainers. As well as riding for Lord Bicester's trainer George Beeby, Francis was getting the leg up on plenty of horses for Ken Cundall and Gerald Balding. In the spring of 1949 he moved south, from Cheshire to Berkshire, to be closer to his retaining stables. But there was a second, more worrying reason for his relocation. Mary had been hospitalized in London with poliomyelitis, and was, initially, unable to breathe without the help of an artificial respirator. Mary slowly recovered, though long after

3

leaving hospital she continued to suffer from muscular weakness. Francis himself was no stranger to the medical profession. He had already broken various bones, and suffered continual problems with his shoulders, which dislocated easily.

In the 1953-54 season Francis began to ride for Peter Cazalet, who trained for the Royal Family. This connection coincided with a wonderful run of luck when everything Francis rode seemed to win, and he finished the season as champion jockey. Two years later he had great hopes for Queen Elizabeth the Queen Mother's Devon Loch, a strapping Irish-bred gelding that looked an ideal type for the Grand National. In the race itself almost everything went according to plan; Francis jumped the last fence in front, still going sweetly and with the race at his mercy. As Devon Loch galloped alone up the long run-in at Aintree, with the huge crowd cheering home a Royal winner, he suddenly, inexplicably, collapsed. Francis could only watch in disbelief as the rest of the field galloped past him. At first Francis believed that Devon Loch had suffered cramp in his hind legs, but later he thought it more likely that the horse had simply been terrified by the deafening noise of the crowd.

Devon Loch's defeat hastened the end of Francis's career in the saddle. His body, punished by years of falls, was beginning to cry "enough"; in ten years he'd broken his collarbone alone twelve times. As he grew older his injuries were taking longer to heal, and there was pressure on him to retire from friends in high places, including those close to the Queen Mother. Soon after the Devon Loch incident Francis had begun to write his autobiography, but when he retired in January 1957—after 2300 races and almost 350 winners—he had no clear idea of how he was going to make a living. A lifeline appeared in the form of an offer from a popular newspaper, the *Sunday Express*, to write a weekly racing article. His first attempts—written, according to Francis's biographer, Graham Lord, with not a little help from his well-educated wife Mary—were well received, and Francis's literary career was

out of the gate and running. Meanwhile, publishing firm Michael Joseph had accepted Francis's autobiography, *The Sport of Queens*; when it came out in December 1957 the first edition sold out within a week. By that time Francis, though desperately missing his old life as a jockey, had found his stride as a columnist, and he proved to have the blood of a stayer: he continued to produce an article every week for the next sixteen years.

Francis's income from journalism, however, was not enough to pay the bills, and in 1960 he decided to try his hand at writing a full length crime novel. He may have been influenced by the doping of favorites that was prevalent in racing at the time—in May of that year the three-year-old colt Pinturischio, well-fancied for the Derby, had been given a powerful drug which ensured that he never saw a racecourse again.

In January 1962 Francis's first novel, *Dead Cert*, was published by Michael Joseph. It is the story of an amateur jump jockey's quest for justice for his friend, killed when his horse is deliberately brought down during a race. *Dead Cert*'s inspired evocation of English steeplechasing and its criminal elements represented a stunning debut for a novice writer. Reviews were positive and hardback sales promising. *Dead Cert* set a standard that Francis maintained for several years. His third book, *For Kicks* (1965), won the Crime Writers' Association Silver Dagger Award though, by now, publishers Holt Rinehart, who had published *Dead Cert*, had decided to sever connections with Francis and had been replaced by Harper and Row. This was an error almost on the scale of that made by music company Decca Records, who in 1962 had turned down the Beatles. *For Kicks* was snapped up by New York editor Joan Kahn on behalf of Harper and Row, heralding the start of a long and lucrative association between author and publisher. Kahn's instinct was immediately proved correct: Francis's fourth book, *Odds Against*, also published in 1965, is in plotting terms relatively straightforward, but is notable for its depiction of Sid Halley, its main character. Ex-jump jockey Halley has overcome a tough upbringing to reach the peak of his profession; now he is disabled, his marriage has fallen apart and he is in a job he hates. Then he is shot in the stomach. Halley's battle with his demons makes *Odds Against* an absorbing read, and confirmed Francis's growing reputation.

From the mid 1960's until the publication in 2000 of *Shattered*, Dick Francis wrote one book a year. In the first decade of his writing career he produced crime novels that were not only thrillers with tense, action-filled plots, but also psychological studies of human motivation. *Bonecrack* (1971), for example, describes life in a Newmarket racing stable so vividly that you can almost smell the sweat of the horses as the string jig-jogs back through the streets after exercise. But beneath the surface of the day-to-day routines of trainer Neil Griffon's life there are terrifying choices to be made, forced upon him by the murderous obsession of a father to see his son become a top jockey. Parallel with this runs Neil's difficult relationship with his own father; how Francis weaves the thread of conflict between these characters and, ultimately, resolves them demonstrates his skill in exploring the human psyche.

Francis is at his best when writing about racing and, in particular, racing in England. When he strays from this world he knows so well, problems soon surface. The action in *Blood Sport* (1967) takes place in Wyoming and California, and the novel was well reviewed, though its strength is in the psychological study of troubled investigator Gene Hawkins rather than in its locations. However, *Smokescreen* (1972) is little more than a South African travel brochure and only marginally more interesting. *Slay-Ride* (1973), set in Norway, is more convincing, but Francis's world tour reached a nadir in 1976 with the desperately disappointing *In the Frame*. Set in Australia, the novel has a tedious plot, unsympathetic characters and fails utterly to convey that country's vibrancy. *Trial Run* (1978) is not much better; Communist Russia was a gloomy place, and it required something more edifying than an upper-class, asthmatic Englishman bumbling around in dark alleys to convey its sinister atmosphere.

Side by side with these aberrations Francis continued to turn out novels of real quality, with well-crafted plots and strong characterization: *Knock Down* (1974), set in the unscrupulous world of bloodstock dealing; *Risk* (1977) with its superb opening that causes incipient panic to tighten the reader's stomach; and *Whip Hand* (1979) in which investigator Sid Halley makes a successful return. In peak form, Francis followed this with the excellent *Reflex* (1980), the first of his novels to be chosen in the USA by the Reader's Digest Book Club. Reflex's main character, Philip Nore, is a disillusioned jump jockey with a dysfunctional family background, whose interest in photography draws him into a web of blackmail and murder. Like Sid Halley, Nore is a flawed but decent man, whose inner conflict is as absorbing and intractable as the crimes he's struggling to solve.

The retirement of Joan Kahn at publishers Harper and Row coincided with Francis transferring his allegiance to Putnam, whose editor, Phyllis Grann, saw huge potential in promoting Francis aggressively in the USA, not merely as a thriller writer but as a serious novelist. Grann, however, would have had her work cut out promoting the disappointing *Twice Shy* (1981). There are too many unconvincing characters in this story about a thug in pursuit of a computer program that picks winners at the race track, and any suspense generated in the first half of the book is dissipated by the 14-year time lag in the middle. Indeed, several of Francis's novels written in the 1980's suffer from plotting problems, or characterization that at times lacks credibility: *Banker* (1982), *The Danger* (1983), *Break In* (1985), *Bolt* (1986), *Hot Money* (1987) and *The Edge* (1988) all have their merits but are far from flawless. *Straight* (1989), an otherwise excellent story set in the world of diamond trading, is marred by the weakness of its villains. Only *Proof* (1984), which has foul play in the wine trade as its theme, and a vintage Francis hero in Tony Beach, rivals the quality of *Reflex*.

Over the years Francis moved ever further away from horse racing as the main theme of his novels. Seventeen of his first 19 books, written between 1962 and 1980, have racing as either central to the plot or as an important element in it. But in 13 of the following 19 books (1981–2000), racing plays only a minor role in the plot. In fact, in the last three novels of that period—*10 lb. Penalty*, *Second Wind* and *Shattered*—racing has virtually no part to play at all. Significantly, the two novels of the 1990's that stand out from the rest for their convincing plots and believable characters are *Driving Force* (1992) and *Decider* (1993). In both of these racing provides a background that Francis handles with a confidence that derives from intimate knowledge and experience.

 Decider is Francis's last novel of real quality. *Wild Horses* (1994) and *To the Hilt* (1996) are competent, but from that point on, Francis's writing has much in common with a patched-up old steeplechaser, once a star of Aintree and Cheltenham, but now struggling in modest company round the leaky-roof tracks. Following the publication of the dismal *Shattered* in 2000, Francis appeared to have opted for an honorable retirement. But after a six year break, at the age of 85, he produced his 39th novel, *Under Orders*. Its horse racing milieu, however, is not enough to compensate for weaknesses in characterization and plotting. In 2007 Francis, with the not inconsiderable help of his son Felix, wrote *Dead Heat*, a pedestrian tale allegedly written partly to keep the Francis back catalogue in the bookshops. It is difficult to quantify Dick Francis's input into this novel.

In 2000 Dick Francis's wife Mary, whose health had been uncertain for most of her life, died, and this may well have been a crucial factor in Francis's initial decision, later reconsidered, to retire. There had long been speculation about how great a part Mary Francis played in the writing of the novels, a question Graham Lord considered at length in his 1999 biography, *Dick Francis: A Racing Life*. He was of the opinion that Mary's role was not confined solely to the extensive research and advice on English grammar that both Dick and Mary freely acknowledged. Whereas Dick had left school at 15 and had shown neither interest in nor aptitude for academic study, Mary had taken a degree in French and English at London University. There she had written short stories, published in her college magazine, in a style which, according to Lord, bore marked similarities to that adopted by Dick Francis in his novels twenty years later. For his part, Francis was quick to acknowledge Mary's contribution, though he stopped short of publicly admitting that she did any of the actual writing. He always stressed, however, that the books were a result of teamwork, and Lord believed that he would have liked to go further by crediting Mary with co-authorship; Mary, though, would not hear of it. Whatever the truth of the matter—and it seems certain that Mary's input was considerable—it is Dick Francis's name that appears on the cover of the novels, and it is to the work of Dick Francis that this book is a Companion.

Characters, Horses, Plots, Settings and Themes, A–Z

A

Abbott, Norris (*Whip Hand* 1979)

Fraudster Norris Abbott is also known as **Nicholas Ashe** and **Ned**. He involves **Sid Halley's** ex-wife, **Jenny Halley**, in one of his scams, and is known to the police for committing other frauds. A cousin of eccentric hot air balloonist **John Viking**, Abbott is similar in age and appearance to Sid himself. This is possibly why Jenny became attached to him in the first place.

Abduction

In Francis's novels of the 1960's, and up to the early 1980's, the crime of abduction is a not uncommon occurrence. After 1983, however, there are no more successfully perpetrated abductions, either in the novels or the short stories.

Nerve (1964): Hero **Rob Finn** is abducted by a man who is insanely jealous of Rob's growing success as a jockey.

Forfeit (1968): Investigative racing reporter **James Tyrone** is abducted in an attempt to make him reveal the whereabouts of a racehorse.

Bonecrack (1971): A deranged criminal sends henchmen to abduct a racehorse trainer but they take the wrong man. Only a spot of quick thinking on **Neil Griffon's** part saves him from a quick death. Later, when the criminal is displeased with what he perceives as Neil's obstructive attitude, he has Neil abducted again and, for good measure, subjects him to a vicious assault.

Smokescreen (1972): Film star **Edward Lincoln** finds life imitating art in a seriously life-threatening way. His abductor recreates a scene from Edward's last film which threatens to lead to his death in terrifying circumstances.

In the Frame (1976): Painter **Charles Todd** is abducted from his hotel in New Zealand by a gang of burglars. They believe that Charles has a list of names that implicates them in a particularly horrific murder.

Risk (1977): The opening scenes, in which accountant and amateur jockey **Roland Britten** is abducted and imprisoned in a confined space, represent Francis's writing at its best. When Roland escapes, the man responsible organizes a second abduction. His motive is to prevent Roland from discovering a major and long-running fraud.

Whip Hand (1979): The reason for the abduction of ex-champion jockey, now racing investigator, **Sid Halley** is intimidation pure and simple. The perpetrator intends to harm a valuable racehorse, and wants no interference from Sid.

The Danger (1983): Francis makes abduction the central theme of *The Danger*, reflecting the prevalence at the time of a crime commonly perpetrated by left-wing terrorist groups in Europe. Members of such organizations were often from comfortable middle-class backgrounds but had rejected the ballot box as a means of seeking political change in favor of violence. Their preferred method of raising funds for the cause was kidnapping. In *The Danger* the leader of a criminal gang is pursued relentlessly by **Andrew Douglas**, an expert in kidnapping. The man is forced to abduct Andrew, an error of judgment that leads ultimately to violence and death.

Aberezzio, Phillip (*Field of 13* 1998: "The Gift")

Aberezzio is an American jockey who rides in

the last race on Kentucky Derby day at **Churchill Downs**. Unbeknown to him, the race is fixed.

Abseil (*Bolt* 1986)

An eight-year-old grey steeplechaser owned by **Princess Casilia**, Abseil is a kind, intelligent horse and a bold jumper but is one-paced at the business end of a race and has stamina limitations. He starts second favorite for a chase at **Sandown Park** and, ridden by **Kit Fielding**, just lasts home up the stiff finishing straight. Abseil is deliberately killed in his box at the stables of trainer **Wykeham Harlow**.

Adams, Annette (*Straight* 1989)

Adams is personal assistant to **Greville Franklin**, a dealer in semi-precious stones. She is competent but lacks initiative. After recovering from the shock of Greville's death, she familiarizes Greville's brother, **Derek Franklin**, with the business. Adams takes it personally when Derek tells her that someone in the office has been listening in to Greville's conversations. She is unwilling to believe that Greville had bought diamonds, something he'd never done before. She is appointed office manager by Derek.

Adams, Paul James (*For Kicks* 1965)

Adams is the owner of several horses in a small racing stable in the north-east of England. None of them is much good, at least until Adams and his trainer, **Hedley Humber**, persuade them to run faster than they would from choice. A cruel and barbaric method is used to terrify the horses into responding in the way their tormentors want.

The stewards of the **National Hunt Committee**, steeplechasing's governing body, are aware of malpractice but have no hard evidence. They recruit Australian **Daniel Roke** to investigate. Daniel lands a job at Humber's racing yard, where conditions make the Gulags look welcoming. Adams, broad-shouldered and over six feet tall, is a borderline psychopath who derives pleasure from knocking the lads around. He is immediately suspicious of Daniel and singles him out for special treatment. Daniel takes the hint and leaves, but he has already discovered the nature of Adam's cruel scheme.

Fearful, with good reason, for the safety of a friend, Daniel returns to Humber's yard. There Daniel has to fight for his life against a combined assault from Adams and Humber. It is only later that the extent of Adams's psychopathic nature is revealed. As a boy he'd avoided being sent to a school for delinquents only by the influence of his wealthy parents. Subsequently expelled from **Eton College**, he was later suspected of murdering his widowed mother by pushing her from a bedroom window.

Admiral (*Dead Cert* 1962)

Admiral, a chestnut steeplechaser, is the best hunter-chaser in England. He loses his first race for two years when deliberately brought down at **Maidenhead** races, a fall that results in the death of amateur jockey **Major Bill Davidson**. His wife, **Scilla Davidson**, gives Admiral to his friend and fellow amateur **Alan York**. Escaping an attempted abduction at **West Sussex racecourse**, Alan rides Admiral over open fields and Forestry Commission enclosures.

Aintree racecourse

Situated in a suburb of Liverpool in north-west England, Aintree is the home of the world-famous Grand National steeplechase, first run in 1837. The winner of the inaugural race, Lottery, ended up as a carthorse in London. The racecourse itself has had a chequered history, suffering neglect and financial mismanagement along the way; it is now the property of the **Jockey Club** and on a sound footing. The Grand National has thrived, producing excitement, drama and mystery over the years to equal anything that has flowed from the pen of Dick Francis. The writer himself, when he was jockey to Queen Elizabeth the Queen Mother, was involved in perhaps the greatest of these mysteries. In 1956 the Queen Mother's Devon Loch, ridden by Francis, was well clear on the run-in and about to win the great race when he inexplicably collapsed. Why it happened no-one knows. Francis initially thought that the horse had suffered from a cramp; later he favored the theory that Devon Loch had been startled by the noise of the huge crowd.

The 1970's were dominated by the achievements of the incomparable Red Rum, a moderate two year old sprinter on the Flat who became the most successful and best-loved of all Grand National runners. "Rummy" won the race in 1973, 1974 and 1977, and was second in 1975 and 1976. More recently, an unacceptable number of equine fatalities has led to changes designed to make the race safer. The most daunting of the fences have been modified and horses of limited ability disqualified from running.

Bonecrack (1971): At Aintree's spring flat meeting, apprentice jockey **Alessandro Rivera** finishes third on **Buckram** for trainer **Neil Griffon**.

Come to Grief (1995): **Sid Halley**, investigating cases of cruelty to horses, asks journalist **Kevin Mills** to help him follow up a lead involving race sponsors **Topline Foods** at **Aintree** on the day before the Grand National.

Field of 13 (1998): In "The Day of the Losers," banknotes stolen in an armed robbery are circulated on the racecourse on Grand National day.

Akkerton, Vince (*Twice Shy* 1981)

Akkerton is an overweight kitchen employee of **Angels Kitchens**, a food production business in **Newmarket, Suffolk**. He gives **Jonathan Derry** information about a former colleague, **Chris Norwood**.

d'Alban, The Honorable James (*Proof* 1984)

James d'Alban is secretary to racehorse trainer **Jack Hawthorn**. His insouciant exterior belies the quality of his work, though it was said of him that he wasn't clever enough to work in the City of London's financial district. He asks **Tony Beach** if he can distinguish between different whiskies; he suspects that one of Hawthorn's owners is implicated in the fraudulent sale of cheap whisky. D'Alban sustains broken ribs, concussion and a punctured lung when a horse van rolls down the hill during a party at Hawthorn's stables.

Aldridge, Detective Superintendent (*Under Orders* 2006)

Aldridge is an officer with London's Metropolitan police. After **Marina van der Meer** suffers injury, Aldridge interviews **Sid Halley** at the hospital. He is pleased when Sid tells him she is making a good recovery but warns that he doesn't have the resources to allocate a team to investigate further. Subsequently Aldridge is sent a videotape by Sid relating to race fixing.

Alec (*Banker* 1982)

Alec is an employee in the Banking department of merchant bankers **Paul Ekaterin Ltd**. In his early thirties, he has a first class degree in Law from **Oxford**, and a highly developed sense of humor. He begins to show signs of dissatisfaction with his job which, he feels, is not stretching him. When Alec is discovered by **Tim Ekaterin** to be guilty of disloyalty to his employer he has to quit his job; he isn't unhappy about it though, having been offered employment elsewhere.

Alexis, Mrs. (*Proof* 1984)

Large and voluptuous, Mrs. Alexis is the landlady of the Peverill Arms, a pub near **Reading, Berkshire**. She has a husband, Wilfred, but she wears the trousers. According to **Sergeant Ridger** of the local police, the pub has been the subject of complaints about the quality of the whisky on sale. Mrs. Alexis tells **Tony Beach** that she'd bought both wine and whisky from a new supplier in good faith, and gives Tony the phone number of her supplier.

Alf (*Flying Finish* 1966)

Alf is a deaf old stableman who works for **Yardman** Transport and is involved in his nefarious activities. He gives **Lord Henry Gray** a drink of coffee when Henry is being held captive, but doesn't care whether Henry lives or dies. Alf resignedly accepts the situation when Henry tells him to bury a dead body.

Alfie (*Straight* 1989)

Alfie, an elderly employee of **Greville Franklin** in his business importing semi-precious stones, parcels up the orders into cardboard boxes. He is cynical about the honesty of the average jockey. **Derek Franklin** appoints Alfie to the post of shipment manager.

Alice (*Flying Finish* 1966)

Alice is **Lord Henry Gray**'s sister, and fifteen years older than him. She is unmarried, plain, and intelligent. She runs the house and looks after her elderly parents as if they were her children. Largely responsible for Henry's upbringing, Alice is keen to get him married off to a rich girl.

Alice Springs, Australia

Alice Springs is a remote town in Central Australia's Northern Territory. It has a population of around 28,000, twenty per cent of whom are aboriginal. The town, which has a rich cultural and sporting life, attracts half a million tourists annually.

In the Frame (1976): Painter **Charles Todd**, with friend **Jik Cassavetes** and Jik's wife **Sarah Cassavetes**, visits the Yarra River art gallery in Alice Springs. While he is there Charles is the subject of an unprovoked assault.

Allardeck, Bobby (*Break In* 1985)

Newmarket racehorse trainer Bobby Allardeck is thirty-two years old, tall and blond. He is married to **Holly Allardeck**, twin sister of champion steeplechase jockey **Kit Fielding**. According to Kit, Bobby is a natural horseman, and of middling intelligence. Occasionally vacillating, he has the strength of character to stand up to his domineering father, **Maynard Allardeck**, when necessary. Bobby's family have been bitter enemies of the Fieldings for more than three hundred years, and Bobby had defied Maynard's threat of disinheritance to marry Holly.

Bobby is jealous of the close, telepathic relationship between Kit and Holly. He feels an antagonism towards the Fieldings which he tries to control but which surfaces when he is angry or worried. He tells Kit that when he was a small boy his father had taught him to hit things and to imagine he was hitting Kit. When Maynard gives Bobby a gun and urges him to shoot Kit, Bobby has to make a snap decision that will decide the course of his life.

Allardeck, Holly (*Break In* 1985)

Holly is the twin sister of champion steeplechase jockey **Kit Fielding**. She is thirty years old; she has, like Kit, dark hair and brown eyes. She was orphaned at the age of two when her parents were killed in a skiing accident, and was brought up by her paternal grandparents. She developed a telepathic understanding with Kit which strengthened as they got older; however this understanding has weakened during Holly's four year marriage to **Newmarket** racehorse trainer **Bobby Allardeck**.

Holly's family have been enemies of the Allardecks since the time of Queen Anne. Holly's grandfather and Bobby's, both Newmarket trainers, had hated each other. In Bobby's opinion, Holly is unlike her family, being unambitious, placid and gentle.

Holly's anxiety about Bobby's financial situation is picked up telepathically by Kit, who goes immediately to reassure her. She confirms to Kit, who has already guessed, that she is pregnant.

Allardeck, Maynard (*Break In* 1985; *Bolt* 1986)

Wealthy **Jockey Club** member Maynard Allardeck's handsome figure—he's tall, well-groomed and good-looking—belies a deeply unpleasant character. He is a man who, according to jockey

Kit Fielding, "could hold a grudge implacably for ever." In this he is conforming to family type—his relatives had been holding grudges since the seventeenth century, most notably against the Fieldings, their bitter rivals in the racing town of **Newmarket**. When his son, **Bobby Allardeck**, marries Kit's twin sister **Holly**, Allardeck sees it as an act of betrayal, and vows to disinherit him. Not that he has ever treated his son with an ounce of generosity: he had made Bobby, a racehorse trainer, take out a crippling mortgage in order to buy the family stables.

Allardeck is livid when a Sunday newspaper publishes a damning exposé of his unscrupulous business methods. His temper is not improved when he learns that Kit Fielding has collected evidence of his wrongdoings and is prepared to use that information against him.

In *Bolt*, the sequel to *Break In*, Allardeck's detestation of Kit Fielding intensifies, and he uses what malign influence he can to make Kit's life awkward. In his capacity as **Jockey Club** steward at several important race meetings, Allardeck scrutinizes Kit's riding, and looks for the slightest infringement of the rules for which Kit can be punished.

When Allardeck finds one of his lifelong ambitions thwarted as a result of Kit's investigations into his unsavory business practices, he exacts a cruel and callous revenge upon Kit. But, in a bizarre turn of events, Allardeck has the tables turned on him in a way that he couldn't have anticipated.

Allegheny (*Break In* 1985)

Allegheny is a chasing mare owned by **Princess Casilia**, and is a moderate old plodder. At **Ascot**, ridden by **Kit Fielding**, she tears a suspensory ligament in a hind joint. As Allegheny is from a good family, Kit suggests to the Princess to get her sound and sell her on as a broodmare.

Allyx (*Blood Sport* 1967)

After his racing career was over the French horse Allyx had become one of the best young sires in Europe. At the age of nine he was sold to a syndicate in the USA headed by **Dave Teller**. During a fire at Teller's stud farm Allyx had apparently escaped and insurers Buttress Life had to pay out. Though the circumstances were suspicious, no evidence of arson was found. Allyx's disappearance is investigated by **Gene Hawkins**.

Amber Globe (*Reflex* 1980)

Amber Globe is a racehorse trained by **Mr. Morton**. In place of Amber Globe, Morton had run a substitute, known as a "ringer," at **Southwell** races. Amber Globe had subsequently won a race at **Fontwell Park**. This serious infringement of the Rules of Racing was subsequently discovered by racecourse photographer **George Millace**.

Ambrose, Dobson (*Rat Race* 1970)

Dobson is an unpleasant owner of racehorses trained by **Jarvis Kitch**. He hires a **Derrydown** plane, piloted by **Matt Shore**, to fly to **Haydock Park** races. Treating Matt like a chauffeur, Dobson tells him to go and fetch his hat from the racecourse cloakroom.

When Ambrose discovers, on the return flight, that Matt is searching for a missing plane, he is angry that Matt had not asked his permission, and refuses to pay any extra expenses incurred. He is subsequently killed in a traffic accident near **Newmarket** along with Jarvis Kitch.

Ambrose, John (*Comeback* 1991)

Known as "Brose," John Ambrose is Deputy Director of Security Services for the **Jockey Club**, and a big, physically powerful man. He tells **Peter Darwin** that he knows racehorse owner **Wynn Lees**, and is aware of his reputation. Ambrose agrees to meet Peter Darwin at **Cheltenham** races to discuss the suspicious circumstances surrounding the death of a mare. He introduces Peter to equine insurance expert **Mr. Higgins**.

Amhurst, Lucy (*Comeback* 1991)

Amhurst is a partner in Hewett and Partners, veterinary surgeons, of Cheltenham, **Gloucestershire**. She specializes in small animals, sheep and ponies. Unmarried, Ambrose lives with her sister in the village of Riddlecombe. She is middle-aged, practical and competent.

Amy (*10 lb. Penalty* 1997)

Amy is a middle-aged widow who runs a charity shop next door to **George Juliard's** constituency offices in **Hoopwestern, Dorset**. Well-meaning but rather dim, Amy is very upset when her charity shop is burnt down in an arson attack which destroys the constituency offices.

Andrews, Thomas (*Odds Against* 1965)

In the course of breaking into premises, petty criminal Thomas Andrews is disturbed and, panicking, uses a gun. A few weeks later his decomposing body is found in Epping Forest, near London.

Andy (*Bonecrack* 1971)

Andy is a middle-aged stable lad employed by **Newmarket** trainer **Neville Griffon**. He is an excellent work rider, but his lack of tactical awareness meant that he was unable to make it as a jockey.

Andy-Fred (*High Stakes* 1975)

The oddly-named Andy-Fred works as a horse van driver for trainer **Jody Leeds**. As he is leaving the racecourse car park at **Sandown Park** he is involved in a crash with a stationary trailer, owing to the intervention of owner **Steven Scott**. Leeds, furious with Andy-Fred, fires him on the spot.

Angel Kitchens (*Twice Shy* 1981)

Angel Kitchens is a **Newmarket**-based food production company where petty criminal **Chris Norwood** was employed.

Anglia Bloodstock Agency (*Flying Finish* 1966)

Lord Henry Gray works at this London-based firm. One day Henry goes out for lunch and doesn't go back; instead he takes a job with **Yardman** Transport as a traveling head groom.

Angus (*The Edge* 1988)

Angus, a chef on the Great Transcontinental Mystery Race Train, is employed by the catering firm which is providing food for the journey. He is well thought of by both railway staff and passengers.

Anna (*Trial Run* 1978)

Anna is one of two Russian Intourist guides provided for **Randall Drew** whilst he is in Moscow. She is squat, and has something of the Gulag prison guard about her, but is amiable enough so long as Randall is prepared to bend to her will. She is unhappy when Randall declines her offer of a guided tour of the Kremlin, but mollified when he accepts a bus tour of the city.

Arcady, Paul (*Twice Shy* 1981)

Paul Arcady is a pupil at East Middlesex Comprehensive School in London. In **Jonathan Derry's** physics class, he puts an apple on his head as a joke for Jonathan to shoot off with the rifle which Jonathan is using to demonstrate the law of momentum.

Archangel (*Bonecrack* 1971)

Archangel, a classy three-year-old colt trained by **Neil Griffon** at **Newmarket**, is due to run in the Two Thousand Guineas Guineas, a Classic race for colts over one mile. The decision as to who will ride Archangel in the race is at the centre of the dispute involving Neil, **Alessandro Rivera** and Alessandro's father **Enso Rivera**.

Archie (*Enquiry* 1969)

Archie is head lad to trainer **Dexter Cranfield**; according to **Kelly Hughes**, he is excellent at his job and responsible for much of Cranfield's success. He has just taken out a mortgage on a new bungalow and is extremely worried when his future employment with Cranfield becomes uncertain.

Arknold, Greville (*Smokescreen* 1972)

Arknold is a racehorse trainer in South Africa. He trains **Nerissa Cavesey**'s horses, which are running unaccountably badly. He is a cold-eyed, acne-scarred, stocky man, and devoid of a sense of humor. He claims to have no idea why the horses are so out of form, but **Edward Lincoln** is unconvinced.

Arkwright, Mr. (*Blood Sport* 1967)

Arkwright, a **Yorkshire** racehorse trainer, is a neighbor of **Gene Hawkins**' father. He had trained **Chrysalis**, a horse that, after his racing career was over, was destined for stud duties in America but disappeared in transit to Kentucky.

Arkwright, Vernon (*Field of 13* 1998: "Haig's Death")

Vernon Arkwright is a steeplechase jockey who is always ready to cheat, especially when riding horses trained by his brother **Villiers Arkwright**. Just such an opportunity presents itself while he is riding **Fable** in a valuable race at **Winchester**. However, things do not go according to plan.

Arkwright, Villiers (*Field of 13* 1998: "Haig's Death")

Villiers Arkwright is a **National Hunt** trainer, and the elder brother of jockey **Vernon Arkwright**. Like Vernon, he is of dubious reputation. He trains a hurdler, **Fable**, for his cousin, and runs the horse in a valuable hurdle race at **Winchester**.

Arletti, Russell (*Bonecrack* 1971)

Arletti is the boss of Arletti International, a firm of financial troubleshooters for whom **Neil Grif-** fon works. He is exasperated to learn that Neil intends to take a break of at least three months to run his father's **Newmarket** racing stables.

Armadale, Ken (*Whip Hand* 1979)

Armadale is a research vet at the Equine Research Establishment, **Newmarket**; he is in his mid-thirties. He carries out a post-mortem on **Gleaner**, a young stallion who collapsed and died after covering a mare on a hot day. Armadale is surprised by the results.

Arnold (*Second Wind* 1999)

Arnold is chauffeur, bodyguard and general assistant to the **Unified Traders**.

Arson

The crime of arson features only four times in Francis's novels, and not at all in his short stories.

Knock Down (1974): bloodstock agent **Jonah Dereham**'s stables and house near **Gatwick** are torched; **Crispin Dereham**, Jonah's alcoholic brother, is almost killed owing to smoke inhalation.

Reflex (1980): the house of **Mrs. Marie Millace** is the subject of an arson attack while she is in hospital.

Comeback (1991): the office block of a veterinary practice in Cheltenham, **Gloucestershire**, is burnt to the ground.

10 lb. Penalty (1997): a fire is deliberately started during the night at the constituency offices of election candidate **George Juliard** in **Hoopwestern**, **Dorset**.

Arthur Robins (*Shattered* 2000)

This is the trading name of a racecourse bookmaking firm whose partners include **Norman Osprey** and **Rose Payne**.

Ascot Bloodstock Sales

Established in 1946, Ascot Bloodstock Sales take place monthly at Ascot Racecourse Stables in **Berkshire**. Brightwells are the official auctioneers.

Knock Down (1974): Bloodstock agent **Jonah Dereham** buys a horse named **Hearse Puller** at Ascot sales for American client **Kerry Sanders**.

Ascot racecourse

Racing at Ascot dates back to the reign of Queen Anne (1702–1714), who hunted with the Royal Buckhounds. The first race meetings catered for horses owned by members of the Royal Hunt, and the names of races at Royal Ascot recall former Masters of the Buckhounds—Lords Coventry,

Ribblesdale, Hardwicke and Cornwallis among others.

Racing at Ascot was limited to the four day royal meeting on the flat until King George VI decided that the course was being underused. In 1965 **National Hunt** racing was introduced successfully to Ascot, though some have reservations about the position of the jump course inside the flat track, which contributes to a lack of atmosphere. By 2004 Ascot was in need of a facelift; the following year the royal meeting was transferred to **York** and the course closed for major renovations, including the construction of a new grandstand. It reopened in 2006, but the improvements did not meet with universal approval; in particular the viewing areas of the grandstand were roundly criticized, and further work had to be carried out.

Nerve (1964): At Ascot **Rob Finn** is handed a telegram asking him to pick a friend up at a pub that evening; it proves to be a bogus request. At a subsequent Ascot race meeting Rob rides **Template** in Ascot's Midwinter Gold Cup.

Reflex (1980): Jockey **Philip Nore** hears racecourse gossip that newly elected **Jockey Club** member **Ivor den Relgan** is to head a committee to appoint new stewards.

Banker (1982): Merchant banker **Tim Ekaterin** goes to Royal Ascot with a colleague from work. They leave the course with equine healer **Calder Jackson,** who is the subject of an assault.

Break In (1985): At Ascot races jump jockey **Kit Fielding**'s twin sister **Holly Allardeck** updates him on the problems faced by her husband, trainer **Bobby Allardeck.** At the next Ascot meeting Kit rides two winners for trainer **Wykeham Harlow.**

Bolt (1986): **Kit Fielding** is introduced at Ascot to the English wife of a French trainer, who gives him information about French businessman **Henri Nanterre.**

Come to Grief (1995): **Ellis Quint** asks **Sid Halley** how his investigation into the mutilation of horses is going; Quint comments that the perpetrator might not be able to help himself.

Field of 13 (1998) "Blind Chance": a betting fraud is perpetrated at Ascot races involving horses contesting photo-finishes.

Ashe, Nicholas (*Whip Hand* 1979)

Nicholas Ashe is a pseudonym used by fraudster **Norris Abbott.**

Assiniboia Downs racecourse

Assiniboia Downs, in Winnipeg, Manitoba,

Canada, is a 6½ furlong oval track which stages thoroughbred racing between May and September.

The Edge (1988): At Assiniboia Downs, Australian horse **Upper Gumtree** owned by **Mr. and Mrs. Harvey Unwin,** wins the Jockey Club Race Train Stakes.

Aston, Caroline (*Dead Heat* 2007)

Caroline Aston is a viola player with the Royal Philharmonic Orchestra. She performs with a string quartet at **Newmarket racecourse** on the evening before the first Classic race of the season, the Two Thousand Guineas, is run. After eating a meal prepared by **Max Moreton** she suffers food poisoning. Subsequently she instructs her lawyer to sue Max. She is annoyed when Max, in the course of a telephone conversation, pretends to be a double glazing salesman. She rings him back and agrees to meet him at an expensive London restaurant. She and Max get on well; they discuss his theory about the food poisoning being linked to a bombing at the racecourse on Two Thousand Guineas day that resulted in numerous fatalities. However, she still intends to sue Max, on the advice of her agent.

Visiting Max in hospital after someone tampers with the brakes of his car, Caroline tells Max that she doesn't want to lose him when she's only just found him. She flies to Chicago to perform with her orchestra; when Max goes out to join her she says she loves him. Back in England, Caroline accompanies Max to his **Newmarket** restaurant, **The Hay Net,** where, he is led to believe, there is a staff shortage. When Max is tied up by criminals Caroline manages to avoid detection. She saves Max's life by knocking out the most dangerous of the criminals with her viola.

When Max opens his new restaurant in London's Mayfair, he proposes to Caroline. Caroline says yes and, as settlement for being poisoned, she accepts another viola from Max.

Axminster, James (*Nerve* 1964)

Tall, well-built James Axminster is a trainer of sixty **National Hunt** horses. He puts **Rob Finn** up on some of his better horses after Rob wins on a no-hoper at **Cheltenham.** Soon afterwards he gives Rob the job of second stable jockey. When first stable jockey **Pip Pankhurst** breaks his leg, Axminster allows Rob to take his place. According to Rob, Axminster is an extremely good trainer but always puts his own interests first.

When Rob rides a succession of losers Axminster is inclined to believe rumors that Rob has lost his nerve, and looks for another jockey. However, subsequent events persuade him to change his mind. He books Rob to ride his good horse **Template** in the Midwinter Cup at **Ascot**.

Axwood Stables Ltd. (*Risk* 1977)

Axwood Stables Ltd. is an expensive complex, complete with Victorian mansion, owned by an American family, the **Nantuckets**. They employ a salaried trainer, **William Finch**.

Aynsford, England

Aynsford is a fictional village in West **Oxfordshire** where retired **Rear Admiral Charles Roland**, **Sid Halley**'s ex-father-in-law, lives. Sid stays at Aynsford with Roland when he needs a refuge or when his spirits are low.

B

Ballerton, John (*Nerve* 1964)

Ballerton, a Steward at **Dunstable** races, is an ill-tempered, aggressive bully. On **Maurice Kemp Lore**'s TV show he takes pleasure in denigrating struggling jockeys, and is angered at **Rob Finn**'s impassioned defense of race riding for its own sake.

Baltzersen, Lars (*Slay-Ride* 1973)

Baltzersen is Chairman of **Øvrevoll racecourse**, Oslo. A merchant banker and mortgage bank chief, he is a civilized and serious man. He has a Dutch wife and lots of children. He telephones English **Jockey Club** Head of Security **David Cleveland** and asks him to send over an investigator to look into the disappearance of English jockey **Bob Sherman** and 16,000 kroner, the day's takings at the course.

Banff, Canada

Banff, in the province of Alberta, is situated in the Banff National Park, west of the city of Calgary. Banff is believed to be named after the town in Aberdeenshire, Scotland.

The Edge (1988): Great Transcontinental Mystery Race Train conductor **George Burley** tells **Tor Kelsey** that he had seen a suspicious character, whom he recognized from a photograph that Tor had taken, at the horse car in Banff, asking for **Lenny Higgs**.

Banker (1982)

Young merchant banker **Tim Ekaterin**, great grandson of the bank's founder, loans the owner of a stud farm a large sum of money to buy a top class racehorse to stand as a stallion. But events take a sinister turn when a local vet is found dead, and the stallion's first crop of foals is born with limb deformities. Worse is to follow: the stud owner's teenage daughter, in the wrong place at the wrong time, is killed; and Tim, whose private life is complicated by his strong feelings for the wife of a colleague, finds himself in mortal danger.

Because the action takes place over a period of three years, *Banker* has a disjointed feel to it. There are long stretches during which nothing very interesting happens. An example of this is the slow, somewhat dull progress of Tim's clandestine romance. Both parties behave in an infuriatingly decent, middle-class way by stifling the rampant passion they feel for each other—except that the middle classes don't really behave like that. Another instance of *Banker*'s meandering development is the violent death of a minor character, a disturbing enough event at the time of its perpetration but which takes a good sixteen months to solve. It's a pity that the time-span of *Banker* weakens the unity of the plot, because the central idea is interesting and original.

Barbo, Minty (*High Stakes* 1975)

Minty Barbo is **Allie Ward**'s cousin, and lives on Garden Island, **Miami**. She entertains **Steven Scott** when he visits Miami. The next day, Minty goes to **Hialeah** races with husband **Warren**, Allie and Steven. Later, at the sales, she stops Warren bidding for a colt that sells for $25,000.

Barbo, Warren (*High Stakes* 1975)

Warren Barbo is the husband of **Minty Barbo**, **Allie Ward**'s cousin. He sells retirement homes for a living. He already has horses in training in North Carolina, but is keen to buy another colt at **Hialeah** sales; however he is dissuaded by Minty. He buys a moderate black gelding on behalf of **Steven Scott**.

Barnes, Chico

Odds *Against* (1965): Chico Barnes, in his early twenties, is an employee of **Hunt Radnor Associates** detective agency. A judo expert, Chico is clever and hyperactive. He was abandoned as a toddler on the steps of a police station. Chico and

Sid Halley mount a guard at Seabury racecourse to prevent the race meeting being sabotaged. Later Sid, in grave danger, manages to alert Chico to his predicament by sending a covert message via an unsuspecting criminal.

Whip Hand (1979): Chico is no longer working for the detective agency; he is now a judo teacher at a north London comprehensive school, and helping Sid Halley when required. He goes to Newmarket to trace the whereabouts of ex-race-horses Gleaner, Zingaloo and Bethesda. He is worried when Sid disappears for six days but doesn't press him to explain. He is attacked in a London car park by Scottish hard men and knocked unconscious with a truncheon; with Sid, he is held captive and whipped with a length of chain.

Barnet, Fred (*Banker* 1982)

Barnet trains a few jumpers at Exning, near Newmarket. He has a son, Ricky. Barnet's blood-stock agent, Ursula Young, considers him impulsive and unable to deal equably with setbacks. He is the former owner of a good horse, Indian Silk, which had completely lost its form while in his care. Later, in different ownership, Indian Silk had gone on to win the Cheltenham Gold Cup.

Barnet, Ricky (*Banker* 1982)

Ricky is the seventeen-year-old son of jumping trainer Fred Barnet. Believing that his father had been cheated over the sale of a potentially top class horse, Indian Silk, Ricky takes the law into his own hands. The stress of the situation causes Ricky to fail most of his exams; however, he resits and passes them, and is now working for an electrical engineering firm near Cambridge.

Barnette, Major (*Bonecrack* 1971)

Barnette is the elderly co-owner, with trainer Neville Griffon, of racehorse Pease Pudding. He is persuaded by the hospitalized Griffon to expect the horse to run badly in the Lincoln Handicap at Doncaster, the first important race of the flat season, and regrets running him. He is insulted when Griffon's son Neil offers him half of his £100 ante-post bet at odds of 20/1. When Pease Pudding wins the Lincoln Neil hears Barnette telling his friends that he knew the horse was good enough to win.

Barowska, Lance K. (*Twice Shy* 1981)

Barowska is Director of Selection in the Science faculty at the University of Eastern California. He writes to Jonathan Derry to tell him that his application for a teaching post there has been successful.

Barty (*Smokescreen* 1972)

Barty is head lad to South African trainer Greville Arknold. He is suspected by Edward Lincoln of complicity in stopping Nerissa Cavesey's horses.

Bath racecourse

Hosting flat racing only, Bath racecourse is set high on a hill overlooking the Georgian city of Bath in the county of Avon in the south-west of England. Bath caters for mainly moderate horses.

Rat Race (1970): At Bath, jockey Kenny Bayst accuses owner Eric Goldenberg of having him beaten up at Redcar racecourse for winning a race he was meant to lose.

Baudelaire, Bill (*The Edge* 1988)

Baudelaire is Director of Security for the Canadian Jockey Club. He asks his British counterpart, Val Catto, to put an investigator on the Great Transcontinental Mystery Race Train to keep an eye on a known criminal. He arranges to make regular contact with Tor Kelsey via his bedridden mother, and supports Tor throughout his week posing as a waiter on the train.

Baudelaire, Mrs. (*The Edge* 1988)

Mrs. Baudelaire is the mother of Bill Baudelaire, the Canadian Jockey Club's Director of Security. She acts as an intermediary between her son and Tor Kelsey, passing on messages between the two. Though bedridden and in poor health, she is efficient and knowledgeable about racing form. She consistently declines to answer Tor's polite enquiries about her health. Tor's concerns prove to be well-founded.

Baxter, Lloyd (*Shattered* 2000)

Baxter is a millionaire racehorse owner. He had sold his shares in a shipping company and bought a 1,000 acre estate in Northumberland, in the north-east of England. He is physically unattractive, with a personality to match. On 31 December 1999 his horse, Tallahassee, falls at Cheltenham, crushing jockey Martin Stukely to death. Baxter's reaction is one of annoyance. After the racing he stays at a hotel in the village of Broadway. He takes a bottle of champagne over to Gerard Logan's workshop to celebrate the millennium. There he suffers an epileptic fit; he is found unconscious by Gerard and taken to hospital. Baxter subsequently decides to sack his trainer, blaming him for not having schooled Tallahassee adequately.

Bayst, Kenny (*Rat Race* 1970)

Australian Kenny Bayst is stable jockey to trainer **Annie Villars**. He is one of **Matt Shore**'s air-taxi passengers on a flight to **Haydock Park** races. Bayst appears to be on bad terms with owner **Eric Goldenberg**. He argues with Annie Villars after the horse he rides at Haydock Park is beaten, and doesn't travel back with the rest of the party. At **Redcar** races Bayst is attacked by two men near the plane. He is grateful to Matt for coming to his assistance.

Bayst is a passenger in the car which racehorse owner **Dobson Ambrose** is driving when he crashes head-on with a truck; Bayst breaks both legs, and his face is cut by flying glass.

Beach, Tony (*Proof* 1984)

When it comes to parents, Francis's heroes have not, on the whole, chosen wisely. Their moms and dads are generally deranged, bankrupt, or dead. Tony Beach's father was a war hero who suffered a fatal fall in a steeplechase; his mother, fanatical in her pursuit of the fox, had viewed her pregnancy with irritation since it interrupted her hunting season. Despite being an only child, Tony was never his mother's favorite. That Tony grew up uninterested in pursuing the fox merely confirmed to her that having children was time sadly misspent.

But his mother's indifference caused Tony fewer psychological difficulties than the spectre of his dead father. Beach senior had been a career soldier who, on the field of battle, had won medals for valor and on the racecourse a Military Gold Cup. By breaking his neck at **Sandown Park** he had died a man's death and enhanced his reputation as a dashing blade. His devil-may-care attitude was inherited from his own father, Tony's grandfather, who had won a Victoria Cross in the Great War and had finished second in a Grand National. By contrast Tony didn't much enjoy riding, and despite being educated at Wellington—a boarding school with strong military connections—didn't like marching either. Leaving school with an inferiority complex and no clear idea of what he wanted to do, other than to put a safe distance between himself and his mother, Tony ended up in Bordeaux. Staying as a paying guest with the family of **Henri Tavel**, a wine shipper, he found that he was blessed with a discerning palate. More importantly he actively enjoyed learning about the wine trade, and after a year's tuition from M. Tavel he had his future career mapped out. Back in England his mother, only too pleased that her errant son had stumbled upon something he was vaguely good at, loaned him the money to open a wine shop.

The next few years were the happiest of Tony's life. He met and married his wife Emma, who helped him to run the shop. They were much in love, and when Emma fell pregnant, they were overjoyed. Then, tragically, a sub-arachnoid hemorrhage killed Emma. Tony blamed himself, believing that Emma's raised blood pressure during pregnancy had caused the faulty blood vessel in her brain to burst. Six months on, the satisfaction he once derived from his business has evaporated. He is going through the motions, but he doesn't really care anymore.

One evening Tony delivers drinks for a racehorse trainer's party in a marquee at his stables and stays on as an invited guest. While getting extra supplies of drink from his car he sees a horse van roll down the hill behind the tables and smash into the marquee. Carnage and death result, and the tragedy is a catalyst for a police investigation into serious crimes committed in the wine trade. Inevitably Tony becomes involved, and the dangers he faces lead him to question whether he possesses the strength and courage of his forebears. But when he is able to save a colleague from a terrifying death at the hands of sadistic criminals, Tony proves to himself that he is not a coward and is proud that he has not failed the memory of his dead wife.

Beckett, Colonel (*For Kicks* 1965)

Beckett, a Steward of the **National Hunt Committee**, is thin, with an unhealthy complexion and a limp handshake. He briefs **Daniel Roke**, on his arrival in England, about Daniel's investigation into the suspicious running of a number of racehorses. He buys a useful hurdler for Daniel to look after at **Inskip**'s yard so that he can go to race meetings on overnight stops and meet lads from other yards. When Daniel needs detailed information on the horses involved, Beckett sets it as an initiative exercise to some army officer cadets, who do a good job.

Bedford, England

Bedford is the county town of Bedfordshire, in the south-east of England. The county lies about seventy miles to the north of London, and is essentially rural.

Dead Heat (2007): **Max Moreton** is taken to hospital in Bedford after he injures his knee when a bomb explodes at **Newmarket racecourse**.

Beecher, Chris (*Under Orders* 2006)

Beecher, in his mid-forties, is a racing journalist on *The Pump* newspaper. He is a bully, who doesn't care whom he wounds or ridicules in print. He rudely asks Sid whom he's sleeping with, and writes a libelous article about him in *The Pump*. After a *Pump* photographer snaps Sid and **Marina van der Meer** outside Sid's apartment, Beecher e-mails Sid to taunt him about it. Subsequently, after a partial rapprochement between the two men, Beecher agrees to help Sid with his investigation into a murder in return for an exclusive story.

Bell, Jiminy (*Knock Down* 1974)

Bell, an ex-steeplechase jockey, is down on his luck and has lost his self-respect. He sponges drinks off **Jonah Dereham**. At **Ascot Bloodstock Sales**, Bell tries to find out which horse Jonah is going to bid for, so that he can bid the price up for the vendor and earn himself a commission. At **Newmarket Sales**, Jonah asks Bell to start the bidding for **Antonia Huntercombe**'s chestnut yearling colt. Bell, however, is warned by another bloodstock agent not to bid.

Bellbrook, Arthur (*Hot Money* 1987)

Bellbrook is an elderly gardener at **Malcolm Pembroke**'s house, **Quantum**. He challenges **Ian Pembroke** with a shotgun when Ian goes to collect Malcolm's passport. Bellbrook is suspected—with no good reason—by **Joyce Pembroke** of involvement in a murder; in fact he is, according to Ian, honest and reliable.

Ben (*The Edge* 1988)

Ben is a character in the mystery play staged on the Great Transcontinental Mystery Race Train; he plays an unpleasant old groom. His role requires him to leave the train in fear because he knows that **Giles** killed **Angelica Standish**.

Benchmark, Patsy (*To the Hilt* 1996)

In her early thirties, Patsy Benchmark is the manipulative daughter of **Sir Ivan Westering**. She is tall, attractive and able to turn the charm off and on at will. Her main concern is to ensure that her father doesn't alter his will after his heart attack,

and that he leaves his money to her, and not to **Alex Kinloch**'s mother. She is also anxious to discover the whereabouts of the King Alfred Cup, and will stop at nothing to do so.

Benchmark, Surtees (*To the Hilt* 1996)

The husband of **Patsy Benchmark**, Surtees is deceptively harmless but is capable of spiteful behavior, and he hates **Alex Kinloch**. He regularly visits a prostitute for sadomasochism. Informed that the **King Alfred Brewery**'s racehorse **Golden Malt** is back at **Emily Cox**'s yard in **Lambourn**, Benchmark and his daughter, **Xenia Benchmark**, make an unsuccessful attempt to remove him.

Benchmark, Xenia (*To the Hilt* 1996)

Xenia is the pretty, spoilt nine-year-old daughter of **Surtees** and **Patsy Benchmark**. She goes with her father when he tries to take **Golden Malt** from **Emily Cox**'s yard.

Bergen, Clare (*Reflex* 1980)

Clare Bergen is the twenty-two-year-old daughter of **Samantha Bergen**, who had often looked after **Philip Nore** as a child. A publisher's assistant, she is energetic and good at her job. She is interested when Philip says he lives in **Lambourn**; she rings her boss, who is publishing a book on life in British villages, and arranges for the writer and photographer to visit Philip. When she sees Philip's own photos of Lambourn and his life as a jockey, she is amazed at their quality. Clare is keen to publish a book that will establish her reputation, and thinks that Philip's photos will do just that.

Clare is appointed to the Board of Directors of her publishing house. Finding Philip after he's been beaten up, she insists that he is not moved; Philip is impressed by her understanding. She is amused when Philip, out of the blue, asks her if she will live with him. She and Philip stay for two nights in a pub by the Thames.

Bergen, Samantha (*Reflex* 1980)

Samantha Bergen, a friend of **Philip Nore**'s feckless mother, had looked after Philip on several occasions when he was a child. She is a kind, warm woman with whom Philip always felt secure. Philip traces her to London, where she is still living in the same house. She is writing a cookery book. She lets Philip stay with her when he is having physiotherapy after he is beaten up. Philip tells Samantha and her daughter, **Clare Bergen**, everything, subtly strengthening his relationship with them. Samantha goes to the cinema, leaving Clare and Philip together; she senses that something is going to happen between them.

Berit (*Slay-Ride* 1973)

Berit, an old nurse who had looked after **Per Bjorn Sandvik** as a child, lives in **Finse**, in the Norwegian mountains. She speaks with a Scots accent even though she is Norwegian. **David Cleveland** visits Berit when he is searching for Sandvik's son, **Mikkel Sandvik**; she is able to give him the information he needs.

Berkeley, Mrs. (*The Danger* 1983)

Mrs. Berkeley, a **Jockey Club** employee, takes a phone call from kidnappers who say that they are holding a senior member of the Jockey Club and are demanding a ransom.

Berkshire, England

The county of Berkshire (also known as Royal Berkshire) lies to the west of London. The county town is **Reading**, but Windsor, with its famous castle, is better known and certainly visited more often by tourists.

Flying Finish (1966): **Lord Henry Gray** was educated at **Eton**, near Windsor in Berkshire. **Simon Searle's Aunt Edna** lives in Potter's Green, Berkshire.

Smokescreen (1972): Film actor **Edward Lincoln** lives in Berkshire with his wife, **Charlie** and three children. Edward has a steeplechaser in training with **Bill Tracker**, whose stables are in Berkshire.

Risk (1977): Roland Britten is a junior partner in a firm of accountants in **Newbury**, Berkshire.

Hot Money (1987): **Alicia Pembroke**, third of **Malcolm Pembroke's** five wives, lives in Windsor, Berkshire. The sons of **Donald** and **Helen Pembroke** are at **Eton**.

Straight (1989): Brad, an unemployed welder who works as a driver for **Derek Franklin**, lives in Hungerford, Berkshire.

Longshot (1990): Writer **John Kendall** accepts a commission to write the biography of racehorse trainer **Tremayne Vickers**, whose yard is in Berkshire.

Bernie (*To the Hilt* 1996)

Bernie is one of four hired thugs from the East End of London whose actions lead to the death of one man and the torture of another.

Bernina

Break In (1985): Bernina is a four-year-old mare, owned by **Princess Casilia** and named after an Alpine mountain. As a hurdler she is no world beater but capable at her own level; however, she has her off days when she races unenthusiastically. At **Devon and Exeter races** she has a "going day" and wins a two mile hurdle race, ridden by **Kit Fielding**.

Bolt (1986): In good form, Bernina wins a race at **Newton Abbot**, ridden by Kit.

Berrick, Detective Sergeant (*To the Hilt* 1996)

In his late thirties, Berrick is a stout, if somewhat bigoted, upholder of the law in Scotland; he doesn't care for Englishmen, Celtic football club or the Conservative Party. **Alex Kinlock** promises to paint Berrick's wife's portrait if he finds Alex's stolen golf paintings.

Bert (*Dead Cert* 1962)

Bert is a taxi driver employed by **Marconicars, Brighton**. He is leading a horse around in a roadside rest area where a horse van, apparently broken down, is parked. Jockey **Alan York**, passing in his car, stops, which proves not to be a good idea.

Bert (*For Kicks* 1965)

Bert, one of **Hedley Humber's** stable lads, is deaf, owing to his father hitting him when he was a child. He is also a bed-wetter.

Bess (*Risk* 1977)

Bess is an eighteen-year-old secretary at King and Britten (Accountants), **Newbury**. Her mind is focused more on her sex life than her work.

Bessie (*Twice Shy* 1981)

Bessie is an efficient barmaid at **Bananas Frisby's** pub and restaurant in **Six Mile Bottom**, near **Newmarket**.

Bethany, Miss (*Come to Grief* 1995)

Miss Bethany is the joint owner, with **Miss Richardson**, of Windward Stud Farm, Northamptonshire. Of the two, Miss Bethany is the real horsewoman, knowledgeable and sympathetic. A yearling colt on the pair's farm is the subject of a sickening attack.

Bethesda (*Whip Hand* 1979)

A classy two-year-old filly trained by **George Caspar**, Bethesda had been favorite for the following year's fillies' Classic races, the One Thousand Guineas and the Oaks. She had flopped badly in the Guineas, but all tests had proved negative. Retired to stud in **Gloucestershire**, Bethesda dies while foaling; the surprising reason for her death is discovered at a later date.

Bethune, Isobel (*10 lb. Penalty* 1997)

Isabel is the wife of **Paul Bethune**, an opponent of **George Juliard** in the **Hoopwestern, Dorset,** by-election. She has an unhappy home life with her adulterous husband and awkward teenage sons. Finally tiring of his philandering, she goes to live with her sister in Wales. When **Benedict Juliard** visits her some years later she is thriving and happy.

Bethune, Paul (*10 lb. Penalty* 1997)

Local councilor Paul Bethune opposes **George Juliard** in the **Hoopwestern, Dorset,** by-election. He is balding, physically unattractive, bombastic and an unfaithful husband. Though politically astute, he takes a career nosedive, and his wife leaves him.

Betsy (*Bolt* 1986)

Betsy is the wife of a **Lambourn** trainer whom **Kit Fielding** rides for; she had made friends with **Danielle de Brescou** while she was at the races with Kit.

Betty (*Twice Shy* 1981)

Betty works as a cook for **Bananas Frisby** at his pub and restaurant in **Six Mile Bottom**, near Newmarket. According to Frisby, she can be awkward, and makes up her own rules.

Betty (*Wild Horses* 1994)

Betty is mentioned by **Dorothea Pannier** as being a neighbor to whom her brother **Valentine Clark**, dying and confused, had expressed the wish to receive absolution from a priest. She goes to sit with Dorothea after Valentine dies. It is Betty who finds Dorothea at home, gravely in need of medical help after suffering an assault.

Billington Innes, Jasper (*Field of 13* 1998: "Haig's Death")

Billington Innes is a wealthy landowner until unwise investments on the stock market cause the loss of his entire fortune and that of his wife, **Wendy Billington Innes**. He is essentially decent, if not very bright and an unsuccessful gambler.

When he is told of his stock market losses he is determined at least to pay his gambling debts. However, his arrangements to do so are muddle-headed and dishonest. When his plans fail miserably Billington Innes considers suicide, but a message from his wife on his car phone appears to give him a second chance to sort out his life.

Billington Innes, Wendy (*Field of 13* 1998: "Haig's Death")

Aged thirty-seven, Wendy is the wife of **Jasper Billington Innes** and the mother of his four children. Wealthy in her own right, she lives on a large estate with numerous staff. She is appalled to learn that Jasper had lost not only his own money but hers as well through unwise investments on the stock market. Unable to contact Jasper, Wendy is anxious that he might be intending to harm himself. She leaves a message on his car phone which proves instrumental in saving her husband's life.

Billyboy (*Field of 13* 1998: "Spring Fever")

Billyboy, a steeplechaser owned by **Mrs. Angela Hart**, trained by **Clement Scott** and ridden by jockey **Derek Roberts**, finishes fourth at **Cheltenham**. He is sold out of Scott's yard when Mrs. Hart discovers that the trainer has defrauded her.

Binsham, Mrs. Marjorie (*Decider* 1993)

The widowed sister of the late **William Lord Stratton**, Mrs. Binsham is a formidable octogenarian. She is energetic, strong-willed, manipulative, and a born leader. She is on the Board of Directors of **Stratton Park racecourse**. Marjorie does not believe, as some directors do, that the racecourse needs new stands. She apologizes to architect **Lee Morris**, a shareholder in the racecourse, for behaving badly towards Lee's mother after she had left her violent husband, **Keith Stratton**, Marjorie's nephew. She tells Lee that she wants the racecourse to be successful.

Marjorie is supportive of Lee in his stand against the more awkward members of her family, and acts on his advice as a builder and architect. When Stratton Park holds a race meeting despite the lack of a grandstand, she is very impressed by the tented accommodation that Lee has organized.

Birmingham, England

Birmingham, in the West Midlands, is England's second largest city. In the nineteenth century Birmingham was at the forefront of the industrial revolution, with all the benefits and problems which that entailed. Much of the poor housing and many of the ugly factories have now gone, and the city has reinvented itself as an important cultural centre, with a world-renowned orchestra, a ballet company, and a state-of-the-art conference and exhibition center. Birmingham's extensive canal system, built to transport the products of the mills, factories and mines, is now a valuable part of the tourism and leisure industry.

Forfeit (1968): Crooked bookmaker **Charlie Boston** owns a string of betting shops in Birmingham.

Enquiry (1969): Unscrupulous enquiry agent **David Oakley** has his office in Birmingham. **Teddy Dewar**, the landlord of the Great Stag Hotel in Birmingham, is an acquaintance of **Kelly Hughes**.

Bisley, Surrey

Bisley is a village in the county of **Surrey** in the south-east of England. It is the home of the National Rifle Association of the United Kingdom, with extensive rifle and pistol ranges.

Twice Shy (1981): **Jonathan Derry**, a member of the British Rifle Team, goes to Bisley to practice.

Black Fire (*High Stakes* 1975)

Black Fire is a five-year-old black gelding bought by **Warren Minty** for $4600 on behalf of **Steven Scott** at **Hialeah** Sales, **Miami**. He has not won since his three-year-old season. Steven wants him because of his striking resemblance to a horse that he owns. Black Fire is transported to England and initially stabled at Hantsford Manor Riding School, **Hampshire**. Subsequently Black Fire's life is cut cruelly short at the hands of criminals.

Blackett, Mrs. (*The Danger* 1983)

Formerly manager of the Villa Francese in Italy for **Paolo Cenci**, Mrs. Blackett had taught Cenci's daughters English. A widow, she is now back in Britain, living with her brother in **Sussex**.

Blackmail

Blackmail is a crime that features in four of Francis's books, but not at all in his short stories.

Forfeit (1968): A foreign criminal, in order to discover the whereabouts of the ante-post favorite for a forthcoming race, threatens to blackmail **James Tyrone** over an extra-marital relationship.

Enquiry (1969): The sexual proclivities of a sen-

ior figure in racing's hierarchy lay him open to blackmail from within the racing community. He is compelled to abuse his not inconsiderable powers over the livelihood of trainers and jockeys in order to ensure the blackmailer's silence.

Reflex (1980): Several dishonest members of the racing community find themselves the subject of blackmail from an unexpected source.

The Edge (1988): A known criminal is traveling across Canada on the Great Transcontinental Mystery Race Train. His preferred method of acquiring racehorses is by means of threats, intimidation and blackmail.

"Blind Chance" (*Field of 13* 1998)

Arnold Roper has won a lot of money from a horserace betting fraud he considers foolproof. Elsewhere blind teenager **Jamie Finland**, listening to aircraft and police broadcasts on the numerous radios in his house, picks up an item of racing information which proves lucrative. But the suspicions of racecourse bookmaker **Billy Hitchens**, who also owns the local betting shop, are aroused.

Blood Sport (1967)

Gene Hawkins, in a permanent trough of depression, gloomily contemplates three weeks leave from his job as a counter-espionage agent in a secret department of the British Civil Service. Gene's boss, concerned at his state of mind, invites him to spend a day on the Thames on his motor launch. He shows Gene a newspaper article about the disappearance of a valuable stallion in America. Gene, tired not just through overwork but of life itself, shows no interest—until an attempted murder, and an incipient friendship with his boss's daughter, cause him to change his mind about getting involved.

Gene's investigations in America are as fraught with danger as anything he has encountered in his day job. His fatalistic mindset is not appreciated by American **Walt Prensela**, who is delegated to work with Gene in his hunt for the missing stallion.

"With your kind," Walt comments, "dying comes easy. It's living takes the guts."

Francis wrote *Blood Sport* in an era when tight controls over the identification of stallions and the provenance of foals were not yet in place, and it is conceivable that frauds of this nature went undetected. But it is not so much the storyline that lifts *Blood Sport* above the average as the psychological study of a man's battle with himself. Gene Hawkins functions competently in the pursuance of a dangerous task yet he is at the same time tormented by a mental state that threatens to drive him to suicide. Paradoxically, the freedom to end his own life whenever he wants to is what keeps him alive: so many opportunities to die present themselves that he has the luxury of choosing when and where it should happen. Salvation comes in the form of a teenage girl's love for him which makes him think that life might just be worth living. He has reservations about her age, but she says that she is willing to wait for him until she is twenty-one.

Blue Clancy (*Hot Money* 1987)

A four-year-old colt, Blue Clancy had been second in the **Epsom** Derby and had won the King Edward VII Stakes at Royal **Ascot**. Owner **Ramsey Osborn** sells a half-share to **Malcolm Pembroke** just days before he runs in the Prix de L'Arc de Triomphe at Longchamp. He is third in the Arc, and then wins the Breeders Cup Turf at Santa Anita. Blue Clancy is then retired to stud.

Bluecheesecake (*Longshot* 1990)

A steeplechaser trained by **Tremayne Vickers**, Bluecheesecake wins narrowly at **Windsor**, ridden by stable jockey **Sam Yaeger**.

Bob (*Come to Grief* 1995)

Bob is an employee of Teledrive, a London-based chauffeur-driver car hire firm sometimes used by **Sid Halley**.

Bobbie (*Enquiry* 1969)

The son of Lord Iceland, Bobbie is blond, and in his forties. He is with **Roberta Cranfield** at the Jockeys' Fund dance. He welcomes jockey **Kelly Hughes** to their table, offers him a drink and admires his courage—since tongues are wagging about Kelly's suspension—in coming to the dance. Bobbie is seen by **Dexter Cranfield** as an ideal son-in-law, an opinion not shared by Roberta.

Bogside racecourse

Bogside was a **National Hunt** racecourse in Ayrshire, Scotland. It closed in the mid–1960's.

For Kicks (1965): Journalist **Tommy Stapleton** had died in an unexplained car accident in **Yorkshire** when returning to London from Bogside races.

Boles, Piper (*Field of 13* 1998: "The Gift")

Boles is a veteran American jockey who is struggling to keep his weight down. He is not averse to taking a bribe to fix a race or to stop his horse from winning, even at the highest level.

Bolingbroke, Oliver (*Field of 13* 1998: "Song for Mona")

Bolingbroke, a Gold medal–winning Olympic rider, employs **Mona Watkins** as a groom for his show jumpers. He is married to glamorous American country and western singer **Cassidy Lovelace Ward**.

Bologna, Italy

Bologna is a city in northern Italy, lying between the Po River and the Apennine mountains. Though it suffered from extensive bombing during World War II, Bologna still has much medieval and Renaissance architecture. The city has a reputation for left-wing politics—one of its nicknames is "Bologna the red," referring to both the red brick buildings and its political persuasions. The University of Bologna, founded in 1088, is the oldest university in Europe.

The Danger (1983): A jockey is kidnapped in Bologna by terrorists, who demand a large ransom.

Bolt (1986)

Champion steeplechase jockey **Kit Fielding**, stable jockey to veteran trainer **Wykeham Harlow**, rides all the horses owned by European aristocrat **Princess Casilia**. When the Princess finds herself the subject of threats and intimidation Kit doesn't hesitate to give whatever help and support he can. The situation pits Kit against an opponent determined to bend the Princess and her frail, elderly husband to his will. At the same time Kit is depressed because his fiancée **Danielle de Brescou**—Roland's niece—is apparently becoming keen on **Prince Litsi**, the nephew of Princess Casilia. And Kit also has his implacable enemy, **Maynard Allardeck**, to deal with; the Fieldings and the Allardecks have been at each others' throats since the reign of Queen Anne, and Allardeck hates Kit with a passion.

Kit Fielding is the only one of Francis's heroes, apart from **Sid Halley**, to make a reappearance in a second novel. Indeed, several of the characters in *Break In* (1985) feature in *Bolt*. There was unfinished business between Kit and Maynard Allardeck left over from *Break In*, and Francis continues the enmity as a subplot in *Bolt*. Francis saw, too, that there was more mileage to be had from Kit's relationship with Danielle de Brescou. Like many of Francis's heroes, Kit keeps his emotions on a tight rein, suffering in silence for most of the book until Danielle finally realizes what a gem he is despite his predilection for dangerous sports. In *Bolt* Francis promotes Princess Casilia from the minor part she played in *Break In* to a more central role, weaving the plot around the machinations of a ruthless businessman.

Essentially, the storyline is straightforward, with few of the unexpected twists and turns that distinguish Francis's best novels. Of the two villains, one is rich and stupid, and acts in a wholly predictable way throughout. The other is irredeemably nasty but lacks the depth and complexity to make him truly interesting.

Bolt, Ellis (*Odds Against* 1965)

Bolt is a stockbroker with the firm Charing, Street and King. He has a smug manner, and acts patronizingly towards **Sid Halley**. He is an associate of **Howard Kraye**; he thinks that Kraye is wrong in considering Sid to be stupid, pointing out that everything has gone wrong since Sid appeared on the scene. Subsequently Bolt has a physically uncomfortable meeting with Sid's colleague **Chico Barnes**.

Bonecrack (1971)

A case of mistaken identity catapults **Newmarket** trainer's son **Neil Griffon** into a terrifying scenario in which he is seconds away from a violent death. As a result Neil is forced into a situation that compels him to tread a fine line between asserting his authority and accommodating the demands of a deranged and volatile Italian criminal, **Enso Rivera**. Their battle of wills is fought out over **Alessandro Rivera**, Enso's son, whose desire to be a top jockey creates a dangerous and highly charged emotional maelstrom from which none of those involved emerges unscathed.

Though a jumping man through and through, Francis brilliantly evokes in **Bonecrack** the sights, sounds and smells of Newmarket, the **Suffolk** town that is the Headquarters of flat racing. Background apart, Bonecrack is well-plotted and maintains its pace throughout. The action is driven by the behavior of the chillingly unhinged Enso Rivera on behalf of his arrogant yet bewildered son.

The novel's strength lies in its exploration of the father-son relationship: that of Enso Rivera with Alessandro and, parallel with it, Neil Griffon's own loveless, fragile bond with his father, **Neville Griffon**. Enso's relationship with Alessandro is proprietorial and primal: whatever his son wants he shall have, and nothing will stand in the way of that. But Enso cannot give Alessandro what he needs—a father who will listen to him and guide him through the insecurities of his youth.

In many ways Neville Griffon is a worse father: cold and indifferent, he had callously shut Neil out of his life for years, and had accepted Neil's attempt to harmonize relationships with bad grace. By contrast, the relationship between Neil and Alessandro grows from that of an unwilling employer and a sullen, arrogant youth to one of mutual respect and incipient affection. Gradually Neil assumes the paternal role that Enso had failed to fulfill, providing for Alessandro the structure of stability that he desperately needs.

Bookmakers

In the UK it is legal for bookmakers to bet both on and off the racecourse. A familiar sight on course is the rows of bookmakers' boards advertising the prices on offer, with the bookmaker shouting the odds to attract business and his clerk recording the bets as they are taken—until a few years ago in a ledger, but now on computer. The well-known names of the bookmaking profession, the ones prepared to lay the bigger bets, can be found on the rails between the Members' and the less exclusive Tattersall's enclosures. Here also are the representatives of the big off-course firms such as Corals, William Hills and Ladbrokes, whose betting shops are a feature of high streets all over the UK. Bookmaking in the USA does not feature in Francis's writing, except for one character—**Marius Tollman**, an illegal bookmaker in "The Gift."

In Francis's novels and short stories the bookmaking profession has, on the whole, a tarnished reputation. Of the twelve bookies whose roles are big enough for them to have a name, eight are of dubious character:

Forfeit (1968): **Birmingham** betting shop owner **Charlie Boston** has an interest in ensuring that heavily-backed horses do not run. Facing huge losses, Boston's clumsy attempt to prevent a horse from taking part in a race is doomed to fail.

High Stakes (1975): **Ganser Mays** has built up a string of betting shops, mainly by dubious means. Now he is colluding with trainer **Jody**

Leeds to swindle racehorse owners. When things go wrong, Mays' crazed pursuit of vengeance ends horrifically.

Whip Hand (1979): Bookmaker **Trevor Deansgate** is also an owner, whose horses are with **Newmarket** trainer **George Caspar**. Urbane and well-groomed, he has, superficially, come a long way from his upbringing in the slums of Manchester. But there is little he won't do to ensure that the money keeps rolling in.

Field of 13 (1998): In Francis's short story, "Carrot for a Chestnut," bookie **Henry Buskins'** favored modus operandi is to bribe stable employees. Another who offers financial inducement as a means of fixing races is illegal American bookmaker **Marius Tollman** in "The Gift."

Shattered (2000): Thuggish racecourse bookie **Norman Osprey** is one of several unsavory characters who trade under the name **Arthur Robins**. When not taking bets Osprey spends much of his time assaulting people.

Under Orders (2006): Francis introduces a new kind of bookmaker, but retains the old kind of corruption. **George Lochs** runs an internet betting exchange, and profits from information about horses that aren't trying.

Borodino (*The Danger* 1983)

A hurdler trained by **Popsy Teddington** at Lambourn, Borodino jumps well in a schooling session when watched by **Alessia Cenci** and **Andrew Douglas**.

Boston, Charlie (*Forfeit* 1968)

Boston is a **Birmingham** bookmaker who owns a string of betting shops. Until a year ago he had only a few shops and a reasonable reputation. Lately he has expanded his business significantly, and has hired two ex-boxers to collect unpaid debts. Boston is in league with a criminal, laying horses in the certain knowledge that he and his accomplice can't lose. When their plans are thwarted, Boston is left with massive liabilities over a well-fancied horse. Desperate, Boston tries to stop the horse from running. His failure to do so verges on the farcical.

Bowes, Buddy (*Come to Grief* 1995)

Bowes, a television news reporter; announces the discovery of a body in a car in the **New Forest, Hampshire.**

Bracken, Mrs. Betty (*Come to Grief* 1995)

Mrs. Bracken is the sister of **Archie Kirk**. Tall, thin and about fifty years old, she lives at Combe Bassett, near Hungerford, **Berkshire**. She phones **Sid Halley** to tell him that a young thoroughbred colt, for which she'd paid £¼ million, has been deliberately injured. She hasn't insured the colt.

Brad (*Straight* 1989)

An unemployed welder, Brad does odd jobs in the Hungerford area of **Berkshire**. He is about thirty years old but looks older; he is taciturn, awkward and stubborn. Brad works as a driver for **Derek Franklin** while Derek is on crutches. He is embarrassed but pleased when Derek praises him. He realizes that Derek is in danger but is nevertheless happy to continue to drive him, and tells Derek that he's having the time of his life.

Bradbury racecourse

Bradbury is a fictional racecourse in the south of England.

Bolt (1986): **Prince Litzi** and **Danielle de Brescou** go with jockey **Kit Fielding** to Bradbury races. On his way to the parade ring Kit hears a cry for help, and sees Litzi, at the top of the grandstand, in serious trouble.

Bradley, Saul (*Break In* 1985)

Bradley, a former sports editor of the *Sunday Towncrier* newspaper, lives at Selsey, **Sussex**. He is a friend of **Lord Vaughnley**. When Vaughnley throws his son, **Hugh Vaughnley**, out, Hugh goes to stay with Bradley.

Breadwinner (*Enquiry* 1969)

Breadwinner is an unprepossessing chestnut, but a chaser of great promise. Ridden by **Kelly Hughes**, he wins the **Cheltenham** Gold Cup, beating **Squelsh** by a nostril.

Break In (1985)

Champion steeplechase jockey **Kit Fielding's** twin sister, **Holly Allardeck**, seeks him out at **Cheltenham** races, untypically troubled. She shows him an article in the *Daily Flag*, a national newspaper, alleging that her husband, **Newmarket** racehorse trainer **Bobby Allardeck**, is unable to pay his debts. Holly is worried that their own grandfather had given the newspaper information about Bobby's financial affairs. He had never forgiven Holly for marrying an Allardeck, the Fieldings and Allardecks having been bitter enemies for over three hundred years. Holly's grandfather denies any involvement; instead he points the finger at Bobby's obnoxious father, **Maynard Allardeck**, who is still furious that his son had married a Fielding.

Kit Fielding does what he can to help his brother-in-law, both financially and by using his contacts to get the *Daily Flag* off Bobby's back. For his part Bobby, who finds it hard to ignore the pull of his family genes, is half-hearted in his gratitude. In Bobby, Maynard's nastiness is diluted but still likely to reveal itself in stressful situations. Meanwhile Kit is collecting evidence of Maynard Allardeck's unscrupulous business practices, which have also been the subject of hostile coverage by another newspaper, the *Sunday Towncrier*. Kit also discovers the reasons behind the newspaper's vendetta against Maynard Allardeck. The knowledge that Kit acquires threatens to cost him his life. They say that the business world is a jungle, and in *Break In* there is no shortage of dangerous beasts lurking in the undergrowth. Apart from Maynard Allardeck, *Break In* harbors a surfeit of unpleasant types, several of whom are journalists apparently devoid of professional ethics.

Fans of Dick Francis whose primary interest is in horseracing will have welcomed the return of a racing professional as the main character, the first since **Philip Nore** in *Reflex* five years previously. Though not as multi-faceted as Nore, Kit Fielding still has enough about him to make him interesting: his close bond with twin sister Holly, his determination to contain the enmity between his family and Bobby's, and his perceptiveness about his tiny but significant contribution to the history of horseracing in Britain. As a main character Kit is, in most respects, a standard example of his genre: intelligent, self-effacing, generous and courageous. These qualities are not lost on pretty young American **Danielle de Brescou**, the niece of elderly racehorse owner **Princess Casilia**, whose horses Kit rides. Romance blossoms while Kit manfully strives to steer to a satisfactory conclusion a plot which, at times, struggles to remain realistic.

Brecon, Wales

Brecon is a market town on the northern edge of the Brecon Beacons National Park in mid-Wales.

Under Orders (2006): **Evan Walker**, father of jockey **Huw Walker**, is from Brecon.

Bredon, John (*Bonecrack* 1971)

Bredon, a recently-retired **Newmarket** trainer, is asked by **Neil Griffon** to take over temporarily his father **Neville Griffon's** racing stable while Neville is in hospital. Bredon asks for time to think it over. When he calls Neil back to say he will do it, Neil tells him he's decided to stay on himself.

Breezy Palm (*Proof* 1984)

Breezy Palm is a two-year-old chestnut colt with three white socks owned by **Orkney Swayle** and trained by **Jack Hawthorn**. He finishes fourth in a race at **Martineau Park**. Swayle is not pleased; Breezy Palm was entered in the Sales and he'd wanted the colt to win to boost his value.

De Brescou, Danielle

Break In (1985): Danielle de Brescou is the young, attractive, American niece of racehorse owner **Princess Casilia**; the Princess's husband, **Roland de Brescou**, is the elder brother of Danielle's father. An only child, she lives with her uncle and aunt in London. She has recently been appointed to a post in a news-gathering agency. She meets **Kit Fielding**, her aunt's jockey, at **Devon and Exeter racecourse** and accepts a lift back to London with him. As they get to know each other better, Danielle and Kit become romantically involved. Some time later, Danielle has a strong feeling that Kit is in danger, and makes her aunt drive to **Newmarket** to see if he is all right. Her sense of danger is accurate.

Bolt (1986): Danielle is engaged to be married to Kit Fielding but is spending a lot of time with **Prince Litsi**, nephew of Princess Casilia. She goes away with Litsi for a cultural weekend in the **Lake District** in the north-west of England. On her return she is lukewarm in her greeting to Kit, and generally acts as though she is no longer in love with him.

Kit, concerned about their relationship, asks Danielle what's wrong. She replies that she is always afraid that Kit is going to be killed or injured in a fall and that with Litsi she feels safe and calm. She knows, though, that she can't ask Kit to give up race-riding.

Danielle goes with Kit to **Windsor** races; afterwards she asks Kit if he wants to marry her. She explains that being with Kit so much had helped her change her mind, as well as the obvious respect that Prince Litsi had for Kit. Most important, though, had been a conversation she'd had with the wife of a jockey who'd been badly injured in a fall at **Sandown Park**. She had told Danielle that she'd always choose to have her husband and the fear that went with it over not having him at all.

De Brescou, Roland (*Bolt* 1986)

De Brescou is the aristocratic French husband of **Princess Casilia**. He is old, frail and wheelchair-bound, but still mentally sharp. Cautious and reserved, he has a highly developed sense of honor. He lives in Eaton Square, London. He owns a half-share, together with business partner **Henri Nanterre**, in a construction company. He strongly disagrees with Nanterre's future plans for the company, and his refusal to comply puts both himself and his family in danger.

De Brescou Bunt, Beatrice (*Bolt* 1986)

Beatrice is the sister of **Roland de Brescou**; she lives in Palm Beach, Florida, but comes to stay with Roland in London. She is the widow of an American businessman. She expects to get her own way, and dislikes **Kit Fielding** intensely. She attempts, unsuccessfully, to make her brother change his mind about his refusal to agree to fundamental changes in the company that he owns in partnership with Frenchman **Henri Nanterre**.

Brevett, Constantine (*Knock Down* 1974)

Brevett, a tough, wealthy businessman and the father of top amateur jockey **Nicol Brevett**, lives in a large country house in **Gloucestershire**; he is about to marry American, **Mrs. Kerry Sanders**. He is building up a string of expensive horses, and is a client of bloodstock agent **Vic Vincent**.

Brevett, Nicol (*Knock Down* 1974)

Nicol, the son of businessman **Constantine Brevett**, is a top amateur jockey. He is given the racehorse **River God** as a birthday present by **Kerry Sanders**, his father's fiancée, as a replacement for **Hearse Puller**. Nicol is unpopular with other jockeys because of his wealthy background, his ruthless will to win and his volatile temper. He meets **Jonah Dereham** at the races and the two men, somewhat unexpectedly, like each other. Nicol says that he learned from Jonah, when he used to ride against him, "not to go around squealing when things weren't fair." Never one to accept advice, Nicol gets angry when Jonah suggests he should become a professional jockey. But his uncompromising tactics when winning a race at

Cheltenham are not those of an amateur, and Jonah's advice gives Nicol food for thought.

Brevity (*Forfeit* 1968)

Owned by **Charles Dembley**, and trained by **Norton Fox**, Brevity was the ante-post favorite for the Champion Hurdle at **Cheltenham**. He was withdrawn from the race by Dembley without Fox's knowledge.

Brewer, John (*Nerve* 1964)

Brewer is the owner of the horse that **Art Matthews** is booked to ride at **Dunstable** races prior to events taking a tragic turn.

Brewer, John (*Field of 13* 1998: "The Gift")

An American veterinary surgeon, Brewer is reported to have denied rumors that Kentucky Derby entrant **Salad Bowl** was running a temperature prior to the race.

Brian (*Nerve* 1964)

Brian is the boyfriend of **Joanna**, **Rob Finn's** cousin. Joanna, however, terminates the relationship.

Brian (*Proof* 1984)

Brian is the nephew of **Mrs. Palissey**; like his aunt, he works in **Tony Beach's** wine shop. He is quiet, not very bright, and employed by Tony as a favor to Mrs. Palissey. Though good at the physical side of the job, he is apprehensive of anything requiring him to think. However, Brian makes a discovery that proves significant.

Brickell, Angela (*Longshot* 1990)

Aged seventeen, Angela Brickell is employed as a groom for trainer **Tremayne Vickers**. She is considered "moody" by workmates. Her absence from work without explanation causes concern, which proves to be justified. Her body is subsequently found in a nearby wood.

Bricknell, Mavis and Walter (*The Edge* 1988)

These are the stage names of a couple, married in real life, playing racehorse owners in a mystery play on the Great Transcontinental Mystery Race Train.

Briggs, Victor (*Reflex* 1980)

Briggs is a racehorse owner. In his forties, he is unfriendly, tight-lipped and known to like a big bet. His horses are trained by **Harold Osborne** and ridden by **Philip Nore**. Briggs's inconsistent approach to the way he wants his horses to be ridden puzzles Philip, and is a source of disagreement between them. Later, Philip discovers the true reason behind Briggs's behavior.

Brighton, Sussex

Brighton is a popular south coast resort in East Sussex, England. In the late 1700's the Prince Regent, later King George IV, spent much of his leisure time in the town; he was responsible for the building of the Royal Pavilion, the town's best-known landmark. Today the city has a large gay community; it is cosmopolitan in nature and attracts large numbers of visitors from London. Graham Greene's novel *Brighton Rock*, first published in 1938, is a thriller set in the town.

Dead Cert (1962): The rival taxi-drivers who fight in the car park at **Plumpton** races are from Brighton.

The Danger (1983): **Andrew Douglas** takes a phone call from his employers, kidnap negotiators **Liberty Market Ltd.**: a crime has been committed on a beach near Brighton.

10 lb. Penalty (1997): After he is sacked from his job at **Sir Vivian Durridge**'s stables, **Benedict Juliard** meets his father, **George Juliard**, in Brighton.

Brighton racecourse

Run-down and neglected until 1998, Brighton racecourse has benefited from an upgrade of facilities by new owners. It is now a venue which values its customers, and has a lot more of them as a result. Brighton is an undulating track which turns continuously left-handed until straightening up three furlongs from the winning post. It's a course which, from a jockey's point of view, takes a bit of knowing.

The Danger (1983): At Brighton races **Lambourn** trainer **Mike Noland** asks Italian jockey **Alessia Cenci** to come and ride out for him. **Andrew Douglas** is at Brighton races with **Alessia** when he receives a call from **Liberty Market Ltd.** telling him of an incident on a nearby beach.

"Bright White Star" (*Field of 13* 1998)

On a freezing cold Christmas Eve a tramp, who had made a makeshift home in woods on private land, is moved on by the landowner and people from the local council. On the same day, at **Jockey Club** headquarters in London, a wealthy racehorse owner is complaining that a dark bay colt with a white star on its forehead that he'd bought at the Sales is not the same colt that had been delivered to his trainer. Behind these two apparently unconnected incidents lies a tale of criminality, well-planned and on the point of success but foiled by a seemingly trivial act of meanness.

Brinton, Mervyn (*Odds Against* 1965)

Mervyn is the elderly brother of the late William Brinton, former Clerk of the Course at **Dunstable racecourse**. After a life spent abroad, Mervyn retired on a small pension to **Reading**, west of London. His discovery of an unposted letter in William's effects, and the decision he makes as a result, lead to serious problems for himself and others.

Bristol, England

At the mouth of the river Avon, Bristol is the largest city in the south-west of England. From the thirteenth century onwards Bristol was an important trading centre, and was granted city status by Henry VIII in 1542. Bristol merchants grew wealthy through trading in tobacco, wine and slaves. Today the dock area has a thriving mix of shops, bars and art galleries.

Whip Hand (1979): **Sid Halley** follows the trail of fraudster **Nicholas Ashe** to Bristol.

Bristol racecourse

Bristol is a fictional racecourse in the south-west of England.

Dead Cert (1962): Jockey **Alan York**'s mount **Palindrome** is deliberately brought down at Bristol.

For Kicks (1965): Undercover investigator **Daniel Roke** takes a horse to run at Bristol, and stays in the stable lads' hostel overnight.

British Horseracing Board

The British Horseracing Board, until 2007, was the governing authority for British horseracing. It was formed in 1993, when it took over responsibilities for governance and regulation previously held by the **Jockey Club**. In 2007 a new body, the Horseracing Regulatory Authority, was created to take over these functions from the B.H.B.

Come to Grief (1995): **Charles Roland** tells his ex-son-in-law, **Sid Halley**, that the B.H.B. wants him to do some work for them.

Britt, Miss (*Blood Sport* 1967)

Miss Britt is a middle-aged lady who works for a Kentucky horse journal. Possessed of a formidable memory, she helps **Gene Hawkins** in his search for two missing stallions.

Britten, Roland (*Risk* 1977)

The first chapter of *Risk* is very short but immensely powerful in the way it instantly allows the reader to empathize with the terrifying ordeal that its hero, Roland Britten, is faced with. He wakes up in the pitch dark, totally disorientated, a battery of noise assaulting his ears, feeling sick and cold, with no idea of how he got there, and unable to move. Roland is a chartered accountant and, stringent though the training for that profession might be, it tends not to include strategies for combating mental torture. Roland fights against a rising tide of panic. He wants to scream but is frightened that if he does, there'll be no-one listening.

For the last six years Roland has been the junior partner in a firm of accountants in **Newbury, Berkshire**, many of whose clients have racing connections. His motivation to become an accountant lay in the tragic circumstances that had led to his mother's death. Mrs. Britten, a widow, brought up Roland on her own while running a small hotel in Ryde, **Isle of Wight**. A poor head for business combined with bad advice from her accountant led her into financial difficulties. She became depressed and Roland, upset, promised her that when he grew up he'd become an accountant and sort out her affairs for her. Sadly, before Roland qualified, she took her own life.

He works flexible hours to allow him to satisfy his fifteen-year obsession with race riding. At the age of thirty-one, and with his workload increasing, he is finding it harder both to keep fit and to make time to go racing. But amazingly, just a few short hours before waking up in a nightmare, Roland had attained the summit of an amateur steeplechase jockey's personal mountain, a victory in the **Cheltenham** Gold Cup. Now, though, he feels so wretched that he just wants to die. Roland's prolonged confinement brings him close to the limits of endurance, but in the end his mutinous streak sees him through, and he engineers his escape. In this he is aided by a virginal, unmarried headmistress with a hunger for carnal knowledge. It's impossible not to feel sympathy for Roland; how many of us would survive a prolonged period of sensory deprivation, then summon up the enthusiasm to have sex with a woman old enough to remember the invasion of Poland?

Roland suspects that he had been abducted because of his accountancy work in the murkier end of the business pool, and resolves to probe the reasons behind it. The consequences are far-reaching, for both Roland and those with something to hide.

Broadway, Cotswolds, England

Broadway is situated in the Cotswold Hills, between **Oxford** and Worcester. It is a pretty, unspoilt village in one of the most beautiful parts of England.

Shattered (2000): Glass blower **Gerard Logan** has a workshop in the village of Broadway.

Brook, Roger (*Come to Grief* 1995)

Brook is Sales Manager at English Sporting Motors, **Oxford**. He is smarmy, and running to fat. For a financial inducement, he gives **Sid Halley** information about customers who have bought cars from him.

Brothersmith, Mr. (*Whip Hand* 1979)

Brothersmith is a young **Newmarket** veterinary surgeon who numbers trainer **George Caspar** among his clients. He is interested, to **Sid Halley's** discomfort, in Sid's electronic hand. He gives Sid information about the possible effect of a hard race on a young racehorse's heart.

Brown, Leslie (*The Edge* 1988)

Leslie Brown is an ultra-officious lady in charge of the horse car on the Great Transcontinental Mystery Race Train. She refuses to let **Tor Kelsey** into the horse car until reluctantly obliged to on the conductor's instructions. She sleeps in the horse car, and considers the security of the horses to be paramount, but gives the impression of being stubborn and intransigent.

Brunelleschi (*The Danger* 1983)

An awkward Italian colt trained by **Silvio Lucchese**, Brunelleschi runs well in the **Epsom** Derby; then, ridden by **Alessia Cenci**, he wins the Washington International at **Laurel Park racecourse**, Maryland.

Bubbleglass (*High Stakes* 1975)

Bubbleglass is a late-maturing colt owned by **Steven Scott** and trained by **Jody Leeds**; he is subsequently transferred to **Newmarket** trainer **Trevor Kennet**. He ran once unplaced as a two-year-old but has done well physically over the winter.

Buckingham, England

Buckingham is a market town in north Buckinghamshire, about sixty miles north of London. There is an old Royal Air Force airfield at Little Horwood, near Buckingham, which is owned by developers who are presently considering building new homes on the site. This plan is opposed by villagers from Great and Little Horwood.

Rat Race (1970): Small air-taxi firm **Derrydown** is based at an old R.A.F. airfield near Buckingham.

Buckram (*Bonecrack* 1971)

Buckram is a horse in training at **Rowley Lodge** Stables, **Newmarket**; he is owned by trainer **Neville Griffon**. A deliberate attempt is made to injure Buckram. At **Aintree**, Alessandro Rivera finishes third on the horse.

Burghley Horse Trials

Burghley, near Stamford, **Lincolnshire**, is one of England's great stately homes, built between 1555 and 1587 by William Cecil, Lord High Treasurer to Queen Elizabeth I. It is the setting for the Burghley Horse Trials, a Three Day Event comprising the disciplines of dressage, cross-country and jumping.

Trial Run (1978): In Moscow, amateur jockey **Randall Drew** meets a Russian named **Chulitsky**, who had been an observer at the recent Burghley Horse Trials.

Burley, George (*The Edge* 1988)

Middle-aged, well-built and wryly humorous, Burley is the conductor in charge of the Great Transcontinental Mystery Race Train. His family has a long history of service to the railways in Canada. He suffers a serious assault in the course of protecting his train.

Burns, Juliet (*Under Orders* 2006)

About twenty-five years old, Burns is assistant trainer to **Bill Burton**. Her father is a blacksmith; she has four older brothers, and as a child had no choice but to be a tomboy. This is her first assistant trainer's job after working as a groom in **Lambourn** racing stables since leaving school. She tells **Sid Halley** that Burton would never do anything dishonest. She subsequently applies, successfully, for an assistant's job with Lambourn trainer **Andrew Woodward**. However, she soon has more to worry about than which brand of horse cubes to feed.

Burton, Bill (*Under Orders* 2006)

Burton is an ex-jockey turned moderately successful racehorse trainer, and a former weighing-room colleague of **Sid Halley**. As a jockey, he was not entirely honest; he was willing to stop a horse and rumored not to have changed now he's a trainer. He has a wife, **Kate**, and four young children. His horse **Candlestick** wins the Triumph Hurdle at the **Cheltenham** Festival. But despite his success Burton's life is unraveling. The police are keen for him to help them with their enquiries, and his owners are taking their horses away. If Burton thinks that things can't get much worse, he's wrong.

Burton, Daphne (*Under Orders* 2006)

Daphne is **Kate Burton's** mother. When Kate leaves her husband, **Bill Burton**, Daphne takes her and her four children in. She does not get on with Bill, considering him not good enough for her daughter; she tells Kate that she is better off without him.

Burton, Kate (*Under Orders* 2006)

Aged thirty-four, Kate is the wife of trainer **Bill Burton**, and the elder daughter of a trainer whom Burton had ridden for as a jockey. She has been married to Burton for twelve years, and has four children. The pressures of training racehorses has put a strain on the marriage, and recently rows have been frequent. After a brief affair Kate leaves Burton and goes back to her mother's house, taking the children with her.

Burton, William (*Under Orders* 2006)

William is the eleven-year-old son of trainer **Bill Burton**, and the eldest of Burton's four children.

Buskins, Harry (*Field of 13* 1998: "Carrot for a Chestnut")

Buskins is a racecourse bookmaker, trading under the name of Alexander McGrant. He is middle-aged, and from the East End of London. He is always prepared to break the law if he can make some money. He sees an opportunity to indulge in a spot of bribery with a view to stopping a horse.

C

Cal (*Bonecrack* 1971)

Cal is one of two hired thugs who break into a **Newmarket** stable and abduct the wrong man. Deranged Italian crime boss **Enso Rivera** orders Cal, a marksman with a rifle, to shoot a jockey who is exercising a horse on the gallops. Believing, mistakenly, that Cal has shot dead his son, **Alessandro Rivera**, in error, Rivera shoots Cal. Though mortally injured, Cal shoots Rivera dead.

Calculator (*The Edge* 1988)

In the mystery play on the Great Transcontinental Mystery Race Train, one of the characters, **Walter Bricknell**, is being blackmailed. He gives his horse, Calculator, to the blackmailer.

Calder, Dave and Sally (*Hot Money* 1987)

The Calders are bloodstock breeders and owners of Dogwood Drift Farm, near **Lexington**, Kentucky. They are friends of **Ramsey Osborn**, who arranges for **Malcolm Pembroke** to stay with them en route to the Breeders' Cup at Santa Anita, California.

Calgary, Canada

Calgary is a city of one million inhabitants in the province of Alberta, Canada. It lies about fifty miles east of the Rocky Mountains. Calgary is the centre of the country's petroleum industry. It also attracts many tourists who come for the winter sports.

The Edge (1988): Canadian racehorse owner **Daffodil Quentin** leaves the Great Transcontinental Mystery Race Train at Calgary.

Cambridge, England

Cambridge is a beautiful city, famous for its ancient and world-renowned university, in the East Anglia region of England. Sited on the first navigable point on the River Cam, Cambridge has been an important town since Roman times. The university was founded in the thirteenth century by a group of scholars who moved from Oxford. The thirty-one colleges of the university are spread throughout the city, many of the older ones backing onto the River Cam.

Twice Shy (1981): Two men threaten **Jonathan Derry** with a pistol, demanding to know the whereabouts of certain computer tapes. Jonathan says he will send the tapes to Cambridge post office, where they can collect them.

Hot Money (1987): After surviving an attempt to kill him, wealthy gold trader **Malcolm Pembroke** moves out of his home and into a Cambridge hotel.

Wild Horses (1994): Firm director **Thomas Lyon** goes to a Cambridge hospital to check on his friend **Dorothea Pannier**, an elderly lady who has been brutally assaulted. Some time later he returns to Cambridge to visit knife expert **Professor Derry**.

Dead Heat (2007): Twenty-four people are treated for food poisoning at Addenbrooke's hospital, Cambridge, after a dinner prepared by **Max Moreton** at **Newmarket racecourse**.

Cambridge Airport, England

Cambridge city airport is a regional airport three miles from the centre of **Cambridge**, in the county of **Cambridgeshire**, East Anglia.

Flying Finish (1966): **Lord Henry Gray**, who has recently joined a bloodstock transport firm, flies from Cambridge airport to **Chantilly**, near Paris, with two consignments of racehorses.

Cambridgeshire, England

Cambridgeshire, together with **Essex**, **Norfolk** and **Suffolk**, is one of the counties in the east of England which together make up the agricultural region of East Anglia. Until the seventeenth century much of Cambridgeshire, known as The Fens, was a swamp. It was drained by Dutch engineers, and remains dry today with the help of electric pumps.

Twice Shy (1981): Mrs. O'Rorke, the widow of professional gambler **Liam O'Rorke**, lives in Stetchworth, Cambridgeshire.

Dead Heat (2007): Health and Safety Inspector **James Ward** works for Cambridgeshire County Council.

Cameron, Donald (*To the Hilt* 1996)

Cameron is a dour old man who runs a post office in the Scottish Highlands. He is suspected by **Alexander Kinloch** of vandalizing the public telephone so that customers would have to pay extra to use his phone. He offers to collect Alexander's pipes, which are being repaired, from Inverness while he is there.

Candlestick (*Under Orders* 2006)

A four-year-old hurdler trained by **Bill Burton**, Candlestick wins the Triumph Hurdle by a head at the **Cheltenham** Festival, ridden by **Huw Walker.**

Canterfield, Charlie (*High Stakes* 1975)

Canterfield is a merchant banker and a friend of **Steven Scott.** He is from a working class background but was educated at **Eton College** on a scholarship. Now he is a successful businessman and lives in a big house in **Surrey.** He has a private box at **Sandown Park** racecourse. Steven Scott is one of his guests at Sandown when Steven sacks his trainer, **Jody Leeds.** When Steven asks for help in organizing a sting against Leeds Canterfield is ready and willing.

Carlisle, Detective Chief Inspector (*Under Orders* 2006)

Carlisle, of **Gloucestershire** CID, is in charge of the investigation into the death of **Huw Walker.** He arrests **Bill Burton** on suspicion of murder and of race fixing. After Burton's apparent suicide, he is visited by **Sid Halley,** who doesn't believe that Burton killed himself.

Carlo (*Bonecrack* 1971)

Carlo is **Enso Rivera's** Italian chauffeur, and one of two thugs who break into a **Newmarket** stable and abduct the wrong man. Acting on Rivera's orders, Carlo returns to the yard and breaks the leg of **Indigo,** an old horse used as a schoolmaster for the apprentices. When Carlo returns to the stables to repeat the treatment on another horse, he is surprised by **Neil Griffon** and knocked unconscious.

Carlo is with **Cal** on the gallops when Cal tries to shoot a jockey as he is riding work. Rivera, mistakenly thinking that Cal has killed his son, shoots both Carlo and Cal. Carlo dies instantly.

Carol (*Twice Shy* 1981)

Carol works in the office of Angel Kitchens, a **Newmarket** food production company. She tells **Jonathan Derry** that **Mrs. O'Rorke** had turned up, complaining that **Chris Norwood,** a former employee of Angel Kitchens, had stolen things from her house. She tells Jonathan where Mrs. O'Rorke lives.

"Carrot for a Chestnut" (*Field of 13* 1998)

A bookmaker bribes a young stable groom and occasional jockey to dope a talented steeplechaser

in the racing stable where he works. At **Cheltenham** races the following day, the groom's handiwork has far-reaching consequences for both the horse and himself.

Carteret (*Decider* 1993)

Carteret is an old friend of **Lee Morris's** from his time at the Architectural Association's school; he is of mixed British-Thai parentage. Lee asks for Carteret's help when he is looking for information about another graduate of the school, **Wilson Yarrow.** Carteret loans Lee the diaries he kept as a student. Like Lee, he is unimpressed by Yarrow's plans for a new stand at **Stratton Park racecourse.**

Carthy-Todd, Charles (*Rat Race* 1970)

Sitting in the bar at **Haydock Park racecourse,** fraudster Carthy-Todd sings the praises of The Racegoers Accident Fund, which appears to offer generous insurance cover. The genial but dim **Duke of Wessex** has been procured as a guarantor of the Fund. When air-taxi pilot **Matt Shore** becomes suspicious and begins to delve into Carthy-Todd's involvement in the Fund, Carthy-Todd resolves to rid himself of Matt and to cash in by arranging an accident for the Duke. His plans backfire, and his attempt to flee the scene of his attempted crime results in a fitting dénouement.

Cartier, Canada

Cartier is a small town in north-eastern Ontario, situated to the north-west of the city of Sudbury. It is known as the "Nickel City" because of its nickel and copper mines.

The Edge (1988): The Great Transcontinental Mystery Race Train stops briefly at Cartier. There the **Lorrimores'** private car is deliberately unhitched from the train, which pulls away without it.

Cascade (*Bolt* 1986)

Cascade is a two-mile chaser owned by **Princess Casilia;** he is not a great thinker, even for a horse, but has won a lot of races. He is given a very hard ride by **Kit Fielding** at Newbury, winning narrowly. He is a brave horse who gives all he has but communicates nothing to his rider. Cascade is deliberately killed in his stable.

Cashless (*Longshot* 1990)

A jumper trained by **Tremayne Vickers,** Cashless is a trier but one-paced. He finishes fourth at **Windsor** ridden by stable jockey **Sam Yaeger.**

Casilia, Princess

Break In (1985): Casilia is a middle-aged princess from a European aristocratic family, long dethroned. She has employed jockey **Kit Fielding** to ride her horses for the last ten years. Her relationship with Kit is much less formal on the racecourse than off it. The Princess maintains private boxes at her favorite racecourses, where she entertains her friends. She is married to an elderly, wealthy Frenchman, **M. Roland de Brescou**. She loves her **National Hunt** horses, and watches them run whenever possible. She is delighted when Kit rides two winners for her at **Towcester**. As she is leaving the course her chauffeur sees Kit with two men and suspects he is in trouble. The Princess stops the car and opens the rear door for Kit to dive in and escape his would-be abductors.

Princess Casilia watches the burgeoning romance between Kit and her niece **Danielle de Brescou** without comment but with tacit approval. After a race sponsors' lunch in London she responds to Danielle's strong feeling that Kit is in danger by driving to **Newmarket** to see if he is all right.

Bolt (1986): At **Newbury** races, the Princess breaks her invariable habit of going down to the parade ring before the race, and afterwards to the unsaddling enclosure. She is dazed and upset by a conversation she has in her box with Frenchman **Henri Nanterre**, her husband's business partner. She accepts Kit Fielding's offer to travel back to London with her, and asks him to witness a document preventing her husband—with his full consent—from making any business decisions without the assent of herself, **Prince Litsi** and her niece Danielle.

The Princess is horrified when three of her horses, trained by veteran **Wykeham Harlow**, are deliberately killed. She is deeply grateful to Kit for the help he gives her in resolving her problems, and is delighted when Kit tells her that he and Danielle are to be married.

Caspar, George (*Whip Hand* 1979)

Caspar is a leading **Newmarket** racehorse trainer. According to journalist **Bobby Unwin**, Caspar is brilliant with racehorses but totally insensitive when dealing with people. He had trained two top class two-year-olds, **Gleaner** and **Zingaloo**, which had subsequently failed to train on as three-year-olds. Now he is training the previous season's best juvenile, **Tri-Nitro**. He is married to **Rosemary** but is rumored to fancy anything in a skirt. At **Kempton Park** races Caspar introduces **Sid Halley** to owner **Trevor Deansgate**.

Caspar, Rosemary (*Whip Hand* 1979)

The wife of **Newmarket** trainer **George Caspar**, Rosemary is about forty-five years old, thin and elegant. In a state of extreme anxiety, she disguises herself to go and see **Sid Halley**. In the past, when Sid was a jockey, she had treated him in a peremptory manner. Now she's doubtful that Sid, as an investigator, can help her, but she has no-one else to turn to. She is desperate that **Tri-Nitro**, her husband's best two-year-old last season, doesn't flop as a three-year-old as others have done in recent years. She pleads with Sid to guard Tri-Nitro, but without George's knowledge.

She meets Sid again and agrees to get George to take precautions when Tri-Nitro does his final gallop before the Two Thousand Guineas. She insists that Sid accept a bundle of cash.

When Tri-Nitro finishes last in the Guineas, she storms round to Sid's flat. She blames Sid for "disgracing" them and demands her money back. Later, seeing Sid at **Chester** races, she is rude and dismissive towards him.

Cass (*For Kicks* 1965)

Cass is head lad at **Hedley Humber's** racing stables in **County Durham**. He refuses to tell **Daniel Roke** the racing names of the horses he looks after. He advises stable lads who stay too long to move on before Humber gets even nastier with them. Cass is involved with Humber, owner **Paul J Adams** and traveling head lad **Jud Wilson**, in making the horses run faster by terrifying them.

Cassavetes, Jik (*In the Frame* 1976)

An old art school friend of **Charles Todd**, with whom he used to share an apartment, Cassavetes lives on his boat in Sydney, Australia. He is bearded, mercurial and extrovert, and holds liberal, leftist political views. He is a first class sailor and a talented artist who paints powerful abstracts which, through choice, he rarely sells. His money derives from a family trust fund. Cassavetes has recently married **Sarah** who, in Charles's opinion, has curbed his adventurous spirit. Be that as it may, Cassavetes provides loyal support to Charles in his efforts to track down the killers of his cousin's wife.

Cassavetes, Sarah (*In the Frame* 1976)

An Australian, Sarah has been married for three weeks to **Jik Cassavetes**; she has a face somewhere between plain and pretty. She is protective of her new husband and not happy when **Charles Todd** involves Jik in his investigations into the death of his cousin's wife. Satisfied that her husband will do nothing to displease her, she declares an unspoken truce with Charles. Gradually, though, Sarah's opposition to Jik's support for Charles softens.

Sarah tells Charles that there is a side to Jik she doesn't know. She says that Jik hasn't painted anything since they met, but she is sure that his urge to paint will return after Charles is gone. Sarah is apparently unaware of Charles's growing attraction towards her.

Castle Houses (*Longshot* 1990)

This is a hotel chain which sponsors **National Hunt** races. It also arranges the award dinner at which trainer **Tremayne Vickers** receives a Lifetime Award.

Cathcart, India (*Come to Grief* 1995)

Young and attractive, India Cathcart is a well-known columnist on *The Pump* newspaper. Her articles are incisive and heartless to the point of cruelty, but not without a touch of humor. She meets **Sid Halley** when colleague **Kevin Mills** is called away to another story. She asks Sid about **Mrs. Bracken**'s mutilated colt but Sid won't tell her anything. She invites Sid to have dinner with her and secures a promise from him—which he knows he can't keep—that he will give Kevin Mills an exclusive story in a couple of days. Subsequently India vilifies Sid in *The Pump* but, according to Mills, she is not in control of what goes into her column. She agrees to have dinner with Sid; when she arrives at the restaurant she is horrified to find Sid lying outside with a gunshot wound. She had innocently given away Sid's whereabouts at *The Pump*. India visits Sid in hospital and apologizes. She asks Sid if she can help him put on his artificial hand; she tells Sid, who thinks she feels only pity for him, that he has got it completely wrong. Sid kisses her, leaving open the possibility of future romance.

Cathy (*The Edge* 1988)

Cathy is a dining car waitress on board the Great Transcontinental Mystery Race Train.

Catterick racecourse

Racing over jumps began at Catterick in North **Yorkshire** in the mid-nineteenth century and,

from the outset, attracted decent crowds even though facilities were rudimentary and it was 1906 before a grandstand was built. Today the course is well-patronized by trainers seeking opportunities for their less talented inmates, both over jumps and on the flat. Stephen Cartmell, visiting the track while researching his book *Racing Around Britain* (Aesculus Press 2002), was underwhelmed by the view from the grandstand and decided to try the cheap enclosure in the centre of the course: "The Silver Ring," he says, "is never a bad indicator of how a course intends to treat the small punter." In the case of Catterick it turned out to be an unpleasant revelation: "A Victorian workhouse would have been more palatial."

For Kicks (1965): **Jockey Club** investigator **Daniel Roke**, at Catterick races and pretending to be a scruffy and dishonest unemployed stable lad, is offered a job at **Hedley Humber**'s **County Durham** racing yard.

Bonecrack (1971): **Pullitzer**, trained by **Neil Griffon** and ridden by **Alessandro Rivera**, wins a race at Catterick.

Catto, Brigadier Valentine (*The Edge* 1988)

Catto, the **Jockey Club**'s Director of Security, is intellectually sharp and good at his job. He is also a cricket fanatic. On the recommendation of solicitor **Clement Cornborough** he offers **Tor Kelsey** a job as an undercover investigator. He gives support to Tor during the week that he poses as a waiter on the Great Transcontinental Mystery Race Train. Subsequently Catto flies to Vancouver to confront the criminal that Tor has been tracking with evidence of his attempt to sabotage the race train.

Cavesey, Danilo (*Smokescreen* 1972)

Danilo Cavesey appears to be the archetypal American golden boy—blue-eyed, clean-cut, straight white teeth, a student at Berkeley. He is heir to his terminally ill aunt's considerable fortune. But he also acutely aware that his aunt, **Nerissa Cavesey**, has made bequests that will reduce the value of his inheritance. Neither is he keen on the idea of paying death duties on the assets that will soon be his. Included among these is a string of racehorses, currently being trained in South Africa.

One of the bequests that Nerissa intends to make—a share in a South African goldmine—is to film actor **Edward Lincoln**, her friend and godson. Edward's arrival in South Africa to look into the reasons for the horses' current lack of form is the cue for Danilo to make plans which don't include an assiduous concern for Edward's health and safety.

Cavesey, Nerissa (*Smokescreen* 1972)

Nerissa is an unofficial aunt-cum-godmother to **Edward Lincoln**. She had horses in the racing yard where Edward's father was head lad; she has always been kind to Edward and interested in what he is doing—unlike Edward's stepmother. From an old aristocratic family, Nerissa lives in the Cotswold Hills; she is only in her fifties but is dying of Hodgkin's disease and has aged alarmingly. She asks Edward to go to South Africa to see why the eleven racehorses left to her in her sister's will are running badly. Nerissa wants to leave them to her nephew **Danilo Cavesey**, the son of her late husband's brother, and doesn't want them to be valueless, having been expensive as yearlings. She thinks Edward will be good at investigation since he often played such roles in his films.

Cawdor-Jones, Major Kevin (*Field of 13* 1998: "The Raid at Kingdom Hill")

Cawdor-Jones is the manager of **Kingdom Hill racecourse**. He is ex-army, and was not the racecourse's first choice for manager. He is personable, idle, courageous and fundamentally dishonest. When, during a race meeting, he has to have the course evacuated after a bomb warning, his lack of scruples becomes apparent.

Cecil (*For Kicks* 1965)

Cecil is a stable lad at **Hedley Humber**'s racing yard in **County Durham**. He is a replacement for **Jimmy**, who left after Humber hit him with a stick. A thirty-five-year-old alcoholic, Cecil has in the past been sacked from several stables.

Cenci, Alessia (*The Danger* 1983)

Alessia, twenty-three years old, is the leading female jockey in Italy. Her mother is dead; her father, **Paolo Cenci**, is a wealthy businessman. Alessia is kidnapped in **Bologna**; when she is finally set free she is handed over drugged and naked except for a plastic raincoat. Alessia is surprised, then relieved, that kidnap negotiator **Andrew Douglas** understands the emotions she had felt while kidnapped—humiliation, guilt, and fear—and now, having been found, shame. She

handles the subsequent television interview calmly, impressing Andrew with her courage.

Alessia decides to go to England to stay with racehorse trainer **Popsy Teddington**. She is reluctant, though, to ride out because she feels that people will be looking at her; she knows that the kidnappers had watched her sleeping naked. She tells Andrew that she wants him, not a doctor, to help her through the aftermath of her ordeal.

Alessia's confidence in her riding ability soon returns, and she goes back to Italy. She meets Andrew in America, where she has been offered a ride in the Washington International. When he suggests that they become lovers, Alessia says she has lost interest in physical love. The next day she wins the Washington International on **Brunelleschi**. She is unaware that there is a link, through the horse, to her kidnap. She subsequently tells **Kent Wagner** that she didn't realize how much she loved Andrew, and that she regretted saying no to him in Washington.

Cenci, Ilaria (*The Danger* 1983)

Ilaria is the elder daughter of **Paolo Cenci**, a wealthy Italian businessman. She doesn't work, and is spoilt, petulant and rude. She lives a life of shopping, lunching and playing tennis. Ilaria shows no concern for her sister Alessia when she is being held by kidnappers; instead, she is angry that Alessia should have got herself into that situation.

Ilaria refuses to take **Andrew Douglas**'s advice to change her routine. When Paolo tells her that he has to raise more ransom and that money would be much tighter she is shocked. Despite her jealousy of her sister's popularity, Ilaria's relief at Alessia's release from captivity seems genuine.

Cenci, Paolo (*The Danger* 1983)

A rich Italian businessman, Cenci heads an international leather trading company; he lives near **Bologna**. When his daughter **Alessia**, a leading jockey, is kidnapped, he hires **Andrew Douglas** of **Liberty Market Ltd.** to advise on negotiations with the kidnappers. Cenci is a tough man, but he is finally reduced to tears by his daughter's plight. He can't keep his mind on his work, and his business is starting to be adversely affected. Even when Alessia is set free, Cenci remains stressed. He worries that the media will publicize the fact that his daughter was held without clothes on.

Cenci agrees to offer a reward for the return of the ransom money. He doesn't see Andrew again until they meet five months later at **Laurel racecourse** for the Washington International. By then Cenci has largely recovered from his ordeal.

Centaur Care (*Driving Force* 1992)

This is a dubious charity for old horses, based in Scotland and run by **John Tigwood**.

Centigrade (*Blood Sport* 1967)

Centigrade is a stallion standing at **Culham James Offen**'s stud farm in California. In reality, however, Centigrade is not the horse that he appears to be.

Cervano, Ed (*Break In* 1985)

Cervano is a news reporter employed by London-based American news-gathering agency where **Danielle de Brescou** works.

Chainmail (*Reflex* 1980)

Chainmail is a four-year-old hurdler owned by **Victor Briggs** and trained by **Harold Osborne**. He is immature and a hard ride, but fast and courageous. Jockey **Philip Nore** refuses to stop Chainmail in his races because it will sour him. The horse finishes third of fourteen in a race at **Ascot**.

The Chairman (*The Danger* 1983)

Referred to only as The Chairman, he is the founder of **Liberty Market Ltd.**, a firm specializing in negotiating the release of kidnap victims. He is about sixty, ex–Army, and an effective leader and decision maker. He is mildly critical of **Andrew Douglas** at a weekly conference for taking too personal an involvement in the negotiations to secure **Alessia Cenci**'s release.

Chambers, Sally (*Dead Heat* 2007)

Sally is the wife of racehorse trainer **Toby Chambers** and the sister-in-law of **Max Moreton**. In the past she has not got on well with Max. She is unhappy that Max is staying with them, fearing that her family is being endangered. However, when a criminal that Max has been investigating is finally arrested, her relationship with Max improves.

Chambers, Toby (*Dead Heat* 2007)

Chambers, **Max Moreton**'s half-brother, is a racehorse trainer. He lives in the Moretons' family home in East Hendred, **Oxfordshire**. He has a wife, **Sally**. He suggests to Max that the metal ball that Max got from Mrs. Schumann could be

used to smuggle drugs in an unusual way. Chamber's relationship with Max has not been a close one, but after the arrest of a criminal that Max has been pursuing, it becomes warmer.

Chance, Mrs. (*Proof* 1984)

Mrs. Chance is a regular customer at **Tony Beach**'s wine shop. A near-alcoholic, she is middle-aged and apprehensive. She buys a bottle of cheap gin every day.

Chanter (*Rat Race* 1970)

An irritating art teacher from Liverpool, Chanter is a former art school acquaintance of **Nancy Ross**, and pesters her whenever she goes racing at **Haydock Park**. He is a stereotypical hippie type who has to be prevented by **Matt Shore** from pawing Nancy at every available opportunity. Matt thinks Chanter is in love with Nancy; Nancy thinks he's in love with himself, but she is not displeased with the attention he shows her.

Chantilly, near Paris

The Château de Chantilly is one of France's largest estates. It is twenty miles north of Paris, on the confluence of the Seine and Oise rivers. Within the environs of the sixteenth century château are stables, training grounds and racecourse. Chantilly is the largest training centre in France, with over 2,500 horses in training. The racecourse is the home of the Prix du Jockey Club and the Prix de Diane.

Flying Finish (1966): **Lord Henry Gray**, in his capacity as traveling groom with **Yardman** Transport, flies from **Cambridge airport** to Chantilly with two consignments of racehorses.

Charlie (*For Kicks* 1965)

A stable lad at **Hedley Humber**'s racing yard in **County Durham**, Charlie is a tough ex-prisoner. He is a bully and a liar.

Charlie (*Reflex* 1980)

Charlie is a gay photographer who, with partner Duncan, had brought up **Philip Nore** between the ages of twelve and fifteen at the request of Philip's errant mother **Caroline Nore**. When Duncan leaves Charlie, Caroline takes Philip away. Not long afterwards, Charlie takes an overdose of sleeping pills and dies. In his will he leaves his cameras and darkroom equipment to Philip.

Charter, Kenneth (*Proof* 1984)

Charter is the owner of a fleet of trucks which specialize in transporting liquids. He is a tall, thin, teetotal Scot. He has had three tankers of whisky stolen in the past six months. He has his own suspicions about who is responsible for passing information about tanker schedules to the criminals. Charter tells **Tony Beach** that his tankers are no longer insured to carry whisky and that his business can carry on for only two more weeks before running out of money. However, after the crime is solved, Charter's insurers agree to reinstate his cancelled insurance cover, and he is able to continue in business.

Charter, Kenneth Jnr. (*Proof* 1984)

Kenneth Jnr. is the son of tanker fleet owner **Kenneth Charter**. He is considered ill-tempered and idle by his father. Charter goes on holiday to Australia; on his way to the airport he drops a notebook in his father's car which contains information not guaranteed to endear him to his father. He does not return from Australia; later, he writes to his father asking for money. He sends it, but warns his son to stay away until he feels more kindly disposed towards him.

Chaud, Dr. Ravi (*Second Wind* 1999)

An Indian from Uttar Pradesh, Chaud is a highly regarded medical specialist working in a London private hospital. He diagnoses **Perry Stuart**'s illness as a rare form of paratuberculosis, contracted by drinking unpasteurized milk.

Checkov, Bert (*Forfeit* 1968)

Checkov is a veteran **Fleet Street** racing journalist. He is an alcoholic and a scruffy dresser. He is already drunk when **James Tyrone** walks with him back from the Devereux pub to his office. Before he leaves James, Checkov advises him not the "sell" his column. Then he takes the elevator up to his office on the seventh floor. After drinking from a whisky bottle, Checkov staggers against the window and falls to his death.

Cheltenham racecourse

Steeplechasing on the Prestbury Park course at Cheltenham began in 1902, though there had been jump racing in the area since 1834. The Cheltenham Gold Cup, steeplechasing's most prestigious race, was first run in 1924, and its future was assured when Dorothy Paget's superb chaser Golden Miller won the race five times in the 1930's. After the Second World War Irish-trained horses dominated the race, and Arkle, the best ever Irish chaser, won three times in the 1960's.

Cheltenham racecourse stages a four-day **National Hunt** festival in March, providing championship races for every kind of National Hunt horse—steeplechasers and hurdlers, novices and experienced handicappers, the best that England, Scotland, Wales, France and Ireland can produce. The crowds are massive, and the scale of betting unparalleled. Over the four days, close on 150,000 pints of Guinness will be sold at the racecourse's bars.

Flying Finish (1966): **Lord Henry Gray** speaks to the pilot and engineer who had flown to Milan with his colleague **Simon Searle**, who has gone missing.

Risk (1977): Accountant and amateur jockey **Roland Britten** wins the Cheltenham Gold Cup on the unfancied **Tapestry**. Later, he is abducted from the racecourse.

Break In (1985): Champion jockey **Kit Fielding** wins the valuable *Sunday Towncrier* Trophy on **North Face**, owned by **Princess Casilia**. Kit's twin sister **Holly Allardeck** tells him that her husband's **Newmarket** racing stable is the subject of a scurrilous article in a national newspaper.

Hot Money (1987): Amateur steeplechase jockey **Ian Pembroke** rides at Cheltenham.

Field of 13 (1998): "Carrot for a Chestnut": Crooked jockey **Chick Morrison** is badly injured in a fall at Cheltenham.

Shattered (2000): Glass blower **Gerard Logan** is at Cheltenham races when his friend, jockey **Martin Stukeley**, is killed in a fall from his horse.

Under Orders (2006): Jockey **Huw Walker** is found murdered, with three bullets in his chest, at Cheltenham racecourse during the Festival meeting.

The Chequers Hotel (*Straight* 1989)

After an attempt on his life **Derek Franklin** stays the night in The Chequers Hotel in Newbury, deeming it potentially unsafe to spend it at home or at his late brother **Greville Franklin**'s house in London.

Cherry Pie (*Enquiry* 1969)

Cherry Pie is the unfancied winner of the Lemonfizz Crystal Cup Steeplechase at **Oxford**, beating favorite **Squelsh**, his stable companion, into second place. It is alleged at the subsequent enquiry that Cherry Pie was backed by an anonymous punter on behalf of trainer **Dexter Cranfield**.

Chester, John (*Field of 13* 1998: "Haig's Death")

Well-built, forthright racehorse trainer John Chester is currently in second place in the stakes-won trainers' list and desperate to be champion. He tells jockey **Moggie Reilly** to win a valuable hurdle race at **Winchester** at all costs on his horse **Storm Cone**. He is furious when Storm Cone appears to have won in a tight finish but the race is declared void because the judge had suffered a fatal heart attack before Storm Cone crossed the line.

Chester racecourse

Chester is in the county of Cheshire in northwest England. The racecourse is not far from the city centre. In Roman times Chester had a thriving harbor on the River Dee, and the racecourse, known as the Roodee, is on the site of the harbor. The course is very sharp—only one mile round, with tight bends. However the standard of racing is high and the course is very popular with the public.

Whip Hand (1979): At Chester, **Rosemary Caspar** is rude to **Sid Halley**, blaming him for failing to stop **Tri-Nitro** being "got at" before the Two Thousand Guineas. Sid tells **Lord Friarly** to withdraw from the dubious racehorse syndicates of which he is a member. Later, in the Stewards' box, bookmaker **Trevor Deansgate** threatens Sid.

Chickweed (*Longshot* 1990)

A chestnut with a white blaze, Chickweed is a hunter-chaser owned by **Julia Goodhaven** and trained by **Tremayne Vickers**. After winning a race Chickweed is found to have been given a stimulant. It is suspected that stable girl **Angela Brickell** had given the horse chocolate. Brickell subsequently disappears and, months later, is found dead in a nearby wood. A photo of Chickweed is in her handbag. Chickweed wins a hunter chase at **Sandown Park** under an inspired ride from **Nolan Everard**.

Child, Raymond (*High Stakes* 1975)

Child is a journeyman jump jockey; he rides all the horses that **Steven Scott** has with **Jody Leeds**. Steven suspects Child of stopping the horses, and tells him that in future **Energise** will be ridden by another jockey. Child comments that he can't really blame Steven—which Steven construes as an admission of guilt.

Chinchee, Mrs. (*Decider* 1993)

Mrs. Chinchee is a cleaner employed at the home of **Conrad, Lord Stratton**.

Chink (*Smokescreen* 1972)

Chink is a racehorse owned by **Nerissa Cavesey** and trained by **Greville Arknold** in South Africa. He had cost 25,000 rand as a yearling, and had won first time out as a two-year-old. At **Newmarket (South Africa)** racecourse, Chink looks well in the parade ring before his race; however, he weakens quickly and is beaten a long way out. Afterwards he is sweating and looks exhausted.

Christopher (*Flying Finish* 1966)

Christopher works with **Lord Henry Gray** at the **Anglia Bloodstock Agency**, London; it is his first job after leaving **Cambridge** University, where he had spent much of his time playing cricket and had failed his final exams. A genial soul, Christopher has given up trying to make a friend of Henry, who is irritated by his habit of practicing his bowling in the office.

Chrysalis (*Blood Sport* 1967)

A thoroughbred stallion part-owned by **Dave Teller**, Chrysalis is stolen in Ohio en route from Kennedy Airport to Teller's stud farm in **Lexington**, Kentucky. **Gene Hawkins** is hired to track him down. Chrysalis has a liking for sardines.

Chrysos (*Hot Money* 1987)

Chrysos is a chestnut yearling colt bought for £2 million at **Newmarket Bloodstock Sales** by **Malcolm Pembroke**. He subsequently wins the Futurity, a race for potentially top class horses, at **Doncaster**.

Chulitsky, Yuri Ivan (*Trial Run* 1978)

A Russian architect, Chulitsky acts as an observer at the International Horse Trials, **Burghley**. He is about forty, clever, and running to fat. At the request of **Nikolai Kropotkin**, Chulitsky meets **Randall Drew** and tells him what he knows about the relationship between **Jonnie Farringford** and Hans Kramer.

Churchill Downs racecourse, Louisville, Kentucky

On the first Saturday of May every year Churchill Downs hosts America's most famous race, the Kentucky Derby, known also as the Run for the Roses. Churchill Downs racecourse was established in 1874 in order to improve the local horse breeding industry, which was still feeling the adverse effects of the Civil War. The first Kentucky Derby was run in 1875, with a crowd of ten thousand people turning up to see it. It was another twenty-five years, however, before the meeting showed a profit. Throughout the twentieth century the race's reputation steadily grew, helped by marvelous performances that live on in the memory, such at the 1978 duel between Affirmed and Alydar and the record-breaking time set by Secretariat in 1973. Today the Kentucky Derby attracts crowds of 150,000 to Churchill Downs, many enjoying their picnics and mint julep drinks as much as the racing.

Field of 13 (1998): "The Gift": Alcoholic journalist **Fred Collyer** has his wallet stolen on Kentucky Derby day at Churchill Downs.

Cibber (*Wild Horses* 1994)

Cibber is a character in the film *Unstable Times*, which is being shot by director **Thomas Lyon** in Newmarket. Cibber is based on **Jockey Club** member **Rupert Visborough**, whose wife's sister, **Sonia**, died in mysterious circumstances when married to trainer **Jackson Wells**. According to his newspaper obituary, Visborough's political ambitions were compromised by the resulting scandal. In Thomas Lyon's film, Cibber murders **Yvonne** (Sonia) who had mocked him when he tried to seduce her.

Cinders (*Driving Force* 1992)

Cinders is **Freddie Croft's** daughter. She lives with her mother, **Susan Palmerstone** and her husband **Hugo**, whom Cinders believes to be her real father.

Cirencester, England

Cirencester is a market town in **Gloucestershire**, in the heart of the Cotswold Hills. As its name suggests, the town is of Roman origin. In Roman times, Cirencester was well-known for producing fine mosaics.

Knock Down (1974); Bloodstock agent **Jonah Dereham**, at the request of **Sophie Randolph**, goes to see her aunt, **Antonia Huntercombe**, who runs an ailing stud farm near Cirencester.

Clark, Derry (*Forfeit* 1968)

Derry Clark is a racing journalist on the *Sunday Blaze* newspaper. In the drawers of his desk he keeps alcohol, illegal drugs and pornography, but they are only for show; in reality he is a quiet, conventional man. Clark remarks that most of **Bert Checkov's** ante-post tips for favorites in big races turn out to be non-runners.

Clark, Valentine (*Wild Horses* 1994)

Valentine Clark, an elderly ex–Newmarket farrier and self-taught racing journalist, is blind and dying of bone cancer. Mistaking his young friend **Thomas Lyon** for a priest, he begs for absolution for killing "the Cornish boy," despite not being a practicing Roman Catholic. At Thomas's instigation, Clark receives absolution from a priest before he dies. Clark's friend, **Professor Derry**, confirms to Thomas that he had left a knife with him for safe-keeping. Clark leaves his books to Thomas, who finds in them marked references to autoeroticism and paraphilia. Thomas subsequently discovers that Clark's plea for divine forgiveness was not misplaced.

Clayton, Gerry (*The Danger* 1983)

Clayton is a partner and insurance specialist in the firm of **Liberty Market Ltd.** He is overweight, middle-aged and bald. He phones **Andrew Douglas** at **Brighton** races to tell him that a child has been kidnapped at **West Wittering, Sussex**.

Clem (*Dead Cert* 1962)

An elderly racecourse valet, Clem looks after jockey **Alan York**. He has the physical stature of an ex-jockey.

Clem (*Knock Down* 1974)

Clem is a horse van driver sent from **Devon** with **River God** to deliver him to **Jonah Dereham** in a roadside rest area in **Gloucestershire**. He is threatened by two thugs who want River God.

Cleveland, David (*Slay-Ride* 1973)

Jockey Club chief investigating officer **David Cleveland** is thirty-three years old, unmarried, and a graduate of **Cambridge** University, where he read psychology. Physically he is tall and thin, and doesn't look his age. David has been invited to go to Norway to look into the simultaneous disappearance of a sum of money from a racecourse and an English jockey working there. His youthful appearance and lack of gravitas work against him, however, when it comes to inspiring confidence in the chairman of the racecourse.

It is not long before David gets a closer look at the Norwegian fjords than he would have pre-

ferred, but he emerges unscathed, as does his opposite number in Norway, **Arne Kristiansen**.
David likes Arne, but likes his wife **Kari** more. He
is too much of a gentleman to reveal this to her,
and tortures himself by having supper with her
and Arne. Despite David's attempts at dissimula-
tion Kari realizes that he's like a sex-starved stallion in her company, and she is not averse to milk-
ing the situation. Soon after supper David makes
his excuses and leaves in case Kari's husband notices his interest—though if he hasn't, he must suffer from serious sensory deprivation.

David is a man who likes and is liked by women.
He demonstrates the caring side of his nature
when dealing with **Emma Sherman**, the pregnant
young wife of missing jockey **Bob Sherman**.
Emma, who has traveled to Norway to look for
her husband, is understandably upset at his disappearance, but David is kind and sympathetic towards her. He suggests that she go home, saying
that there is no more she can do in Norway. Soon
afterwards a body is discovered, hidden on the
racecourse, by a small child, who says, chillingly,
"I've found a hand."

Not long afterwards David has reason to be
thankful for his quick reactions when surviving a
knife attack. Asked by a Norwegian colleague why
he doesn't give up investigation while he is still
healthy, David replies, "Natural bloody obstinacy."

David's hormones are another aspect of his
physiology that is functioning at full capacity. He
meets Kristiansen with her husband Arne for dinner at his hotel in Oslo; when Arne goes outside
for some air, David asks Kari to dance. Kari holds
him close and slowly, deliberately, achieves orgasm, leaving David, not unsurprisingly, aroused
and unsatisfied.

David demonstrates that his physical courage, in
evidence when fighting off his knife-wielding assailant, borders on the foolhardy when a second
attempt is made on his life, this time involving an
explosive device. Later, David uses his skill at
prompting the memory of witnesses to draw out
information from a four-year-old girl who had witnessed the incident.

When next in England, David calls to see
Emma, who is beginning to get over the trauma
she had suffered. He realizes that he is attracted to
her; when she tells him to call again, he doesn't
need telling twice.

David is adept at tuning in to young people's
wavelengths and, as the plot of *Slay-Ride* reaches
its dénouement, he is called upon to show sympa-

thy and understanding toward a young man who
had witnessed a murder and is now fearful for his
own life.

Clip-Clop (*Bonecrack* 1971)

Clip-clop is a racehorse trained at **Newmarket**
by **Neville Griffon**, and subsequently by his son
Neil Griffon while Neville is in hospital. Italian
apprentice **Alessandro Rivera** rides work on Clip-
Clop; instead of going a half-speed gallop as **Etty
Craig**, the head lass, had told him, he works the
horse flat out, earning a rebuke from Neil.

Clive, Matt (*Blood Sport* 1967)

Matt Clive is a young, fit American who, with
his sister **Yola**, runs a dude ranch in Wyoming. He
and Yola, however, have a dark side to their characters, and have been involved for years in criminal activity.

After a stallion disappears from their ranch
Clive questions the guests and recognizes English
investigator **Gene Hawkins**, who is staying there
under an alias. His attempt to arrange an accident
for Hawkins is unsuccessful.

Later Clive tries again to shorten Hawkins' life,
this time at his farm in Arizona. The encounter
ends tragically, but not for Hawkins.

Clive, Yola (*Blood Sport* 1967)

Yola is the young, tough sister of **Matt Clive**; together they run a dude ranch in Wyoming. Yola
is very efficient, and friendly to her guests in a
wholly impersonal way. She also has no compunction about breaking the law. When she realizes
that a stallion is missing, Yola's calm competence
is quickly replaced by panic and impulsive anger.
Suspecting English undercover investigator **Gene
Hawkins** to be the culprit, she helps Matt to organize an unpleasant end for Hawkins. Their
plans, however, are thwarted.

Yola is distraught when she finds out that her
house in Las Vegas has been trashed. But it's nothing compared with her devastation when she learns
what has happened to her brother.

Clobber (*Flying Finish* 1966)

Clobber is an eight-year-old thoroughbred
chestnut hunter; he finishes fourth in the **Cheltenham** Gold Cup, exceeding expectations, after
Lord Henry Gray allows him to make the
running. His previous inconsistency may have
been due to being held up in his races against his
will.

Cloud-Cuckoo-Land (*Bonecrack* 1971)

Cloud-Cuckoo-Land is the horse that **Neil Griffon** uses as a hack on the **Newmarket** gallops; he is a strong five-year-old handicapper.

Clutter, Basil (*Bolt* 1986)

Clutter is a **Lambourn** racehorse trainer. He tells **Kit Fielding** that **Henri Nanterre** is a racehorse owner in France. At Ascot, Clutter introduces Kit to his French owners, the **Roquevilles**, whose friend, **Madeleine Darcy**, knows Nanterre.

Coconut (*Longshot* 1990)

Coconut is a fourteen-year-old friend of **Gareth Vickers**. He goes on an afternoon's survival course with **John Kendall** and Gareth on **Tremayne Vickers'** land; a few days later, he goes on a similar trip in the woods, again with John and Gareth.

Col (*Bolt* 1986)

A steeplechaser owned by **Princess Casilia** and trained by **Wykeham Harlow**, Col is a bright chestnut with a white blaze and three white socks. He is a talented horse and is being trained for the **Cheltenham** Gold Cup, but needs to be brought with a late run. Just short of peak fitness, Col is beaten narrowly at **Ascot** two weeks before Cheltenham. He is deliberately killed in his box.

"Collision Course" (*Field of 13* 1998)

Bill Williams, a young newspaper editor, has had his contract terminated by the paper's new owners, and is due to leave his job in a few days. He sends out his CV to potential employees and receives an offer to meet for dinner from the owners of another newspaper conglomerate. Meanwhile, he asks his racing journalist to follow up a story about a man, **Dennis Kinser**, who is selling shares in a syndicated racehorse which he intends to train himself. The racing journalist interviews Kinser and concludes that his ego, ambition and self-confidence far outweigh his ability to deliver results.

Williams is not happy with the service he receives at the restaurant where he meets his potential employers. Discovering that the restaurant is run by a relative of Dennis Kinser, Williams uses the information to his advantage.

Collyer, Fred (*Field of 13* 1998: "The Gift")

Collyer is a forty-six-year-old racing journalist on the *Manhattan Star*. An alcoholic, Collyer fiddles his expenses, and is close to being sacked.

He flies out to Louisville to cover the Kentucky Derby. At the Turfwriters' Association dinner he gets blind drunk and collapses outside the building. There he hears two men arranging to fix one race and to stop a horse in another. At **Churchill Downs** on Derby day he remembers enough of what he heard to profit financially from the information. Collyer realizes that he has the makings of a big story for his newspaper, one that will restore his former reputation as a hard-hitting journalist. True to form, however, Collyer blows it.

Come to Grief (1995)

Investigator **Sid Halley** has accused a good friend, TV personality **Ellis Quint**, of committing sickening crimes against defenseless animals. Quint, an ex-champion amateur jockey, is a popular man; no-one wants to believe Sid, who is vilified in the press. The more evidence that Sid collects, the greater is the outcry against him. Then a similar atrocity occurs when Quint is hundreds of miles away, and Sid's case seems shot to pieces. But he continues to dig, and soon discovers that there are powerful businessmen who have a vested interest in Quint's being acquitted in a court of law. These men are prepared to stop at nothing to achieve their ends, and Sid's life is immaterial to them. But it is from within Quint's own family that the greatest threat to Sid emerges.

In *Come to Grief* Sid Halley struggles against impossible odds with a plot that is mediocre, lacks credibility and, worst of all, is repellent. Sadly, cases of unspeakable cruelty to animals are not uncommon, but Francis's decision to base a story around this phenomenon is questionable. To add insult, Francis chooses to bring back his most convincing character, sixteen years after his last appearance, to investigate this catalogue of depravity. That *Come to Grief* does not develop Sid's character or focus on its potentially fascinating complexity is an opportunity that Francis could ill afford to spurn.

Comeback (1991)

Diplomat **Peter Darwin**, en route from Mexico City to take up a new post in London, stops off in **Miami** to visit consul **Fred Hutchings**. There he meets Fred's friends, singers **Vicky Larch** and **Greg Wayfield**, and goes to their aid when they are mugged outside a restaurant. The next day Peter flies to England with Vicky and Greg; persuaded by Fred, he travels with them to **Gloucestershire**, where he spent his childhood and where

Vicky's self-centered daughter, **Belinda**, and her fiancé, **Ken McClure**, work in a veterinary surgeon's practice.

That night the office block and all the practice's records are destroyed by fire. Ken—the practice's horse specialist—tells Peter that he's had four horses die under anesthetic recently. Peter recalls that, in his youth, there were similar unsavory goings-on in the local racing community, and is immediately suspicious. He's right to be: an unidentified body is found in the burnt-out office block, and not long afterwards an employee of the practice suffers a horrific death.

Peter's snooping into the possible reasons for the deaths, both human and equine, does not go unnoticed. Before he can give the police the names of the men responsible for a well-planned series of crimes he is forced to put up a desperate fight for his own life.

The main problem with *Comeback* is that too many strands of the plot are not really tied up. Peter has plausible theories but there are few clear-cut answers. The death of the veterinary practice's employee is not satisfactorily explained. The apparent suicide of Ken McClure's father may have been murder, but we don't find out. Of the principal villain's motivations, some are clear whilst others are baffling. Francis's device of using Peter's memories of his childhood to allow him to theorize about the crimes now being committed is confusing. And it is stretching credibility to have the same crime repeated by the same people a generation later. Whilst *Comeback* is interesting on the work of an equine veterinary practice, the novel is weakened both by the shortcomings of the plot and by a protagonist whose role is little more than that of an amateur detective.

Compass, Greg (*Wild Horses* 1994)

Compass is a paddock commentator on a TV racing show, and a friend of **Thomas Lyon**. An ex-jump jockey, he is good-looking, fit, and has a sense of humor. In return for seats at the premier of Thomas's film, he agrees to do a TV interview with Thomas and actor **Nash Rourke** at **Doncaster** races, allowing Nash to refute newspaper allegations that he is not happy with the way the film is going. Later, Compass accepts a fee to appear in Thomas's film, interviewing Nash Rourke's character at the races.

Conker (*Flying Finish* 1966)

Conker works for **Yardman** Transport; he is an ex-stud farm employee and the father of seven unruly children. He tells **Henry Gray** that he should have had his terms and conditions of work clearly defined when he started work for Yardman.

Conrad (*Smokescreen* 1972)

Conrad was the Director of Photography on the film *Man in a Car*, which was shot in Spain with **Evan Pentelow** and **Edward Lincoln**. He is an Oscar winner. In South Africa to make a film with Pentelow, Conrad turns up at Edward's press conference in Johannesburg. Conrad tells Edward that the rushes of the desert scene in *Man in a Car* are good, but that Edward wouldn't like them as they reveal too much of Edward's own personality. He accompanies Pentelow to film elephants in **Kruger National Park**. He helps Pentelow to search for Edward when he goes missing, partly because Edward has some of his photographic equipment in his car.

Cook, Thomas (*Dead Cert* 1962)

This is the false name given by an employee at **Maidenhead racecourse** who was responsible for the death of **Major Bill Davidson**.

Cooper (*Flying Finish* 1966)

Cooper is an elderly employee of the **Anglia Bloodstock Agency**, dealing with insurance. He dislikes **Christopher**'s and **Maggie**'s messy habits; he wishes aloud that they were as organized as **Lord Henry Gray**, thus causing Maggie to be scathing about Henry's character.

Copeland, Jack (*Odds Against* 1965)

Copeland is Head of the Bona Fides section at detective agency **Hunt Radnor Associates**; his department undertakes checks on people for clients. Large, bald and scruffily dressed, he is nevertheless very thorough and good at his job. He is influential within the Hunt Radnor organization, but apparently unaware of it and therefore well-liked.

Coral Key (*Reflex* 1980)

Coral Key is a six-year-old novice chaser owned by **Victor Briggs** and trained by **Harold Osborne**. He is a promising young horse which **Philip Nore** intended to refuse to stop if asked to by Briggs; however, Briggs never asks him to do so. Philip finishes second on Coral Key at **Sandown Park**.

"Corkscrew" (*Field of 13* 1998)

In South Carolina, American-based English bloodstock agent **Sandy Nutbridge** sells a two-year-old filly to fellow-countryman **Jules Harlow**, a wealthy inventor and entrepreneur. Soon afterwards Nutbridge is arrested on suspicion of tax evasion and laundering drug money. He appoints a lawyer friend, **Patrick Green**, to represent him. Though the charges prove to be groundless, Nutbridge's association with Green brings him nothing but grief. Harlow is caught up in the aftermath, but is adept at playing a waiting game, and eventually justice—both rough and otherwise—prevails.

Cornborough, Clement (*The Edge* 1988)

A senior partner in law firm Cornborough, Cross and George, Clement Cornborough administers trust funds on behalf of **Tor Kelsey**. He suggests Tor as a possible undercover investigator to the Director of **Jockey Club** Security **Val Catto**.

Cornish, Chief Inspector (*Odds Against* 1965)

Cornish is a middle-aged policeman who is keen on racing. He handles the investigation into **Thomas Andrews's** death; later, he reports to **Sid Halley** that Andrews was shot in the back by the same gun that Andrews had used on Sid.

Corunna, Carl (*Field of 13* 1998: "Corkscrew")

Corunna is a crooked South Carolina–based lawyer who shares office space with equally corrupt colleague **Patrick Green**. Aged about fifty, he is bearded and well-built. He reports to Green that **Jules Harlow** appeared to be the timid sort of man who could easily be swindled. In this, Corunna's judgement is sadly flawed.

Cotopaxi (*Bolt* 1986)

Cotopaxi is an eight-year-old steeplechaser, owned by **Princess Casilia** and trained by **Wykeham Harlow**; a big, angular liver chestnut, Cotopaxi is being aimed at the Grand National. Not fully fit, he finishes third under a sympathetic ride from **Kit Fielding** at Newbury. The horse is deliberately killed at Harlow's stables.

County Durham *see* **Durham, England**

Course, Tom (*Twice Shy* 1981)

Course is a young doctor at the hospital where **Angelo Gilbert** is taken after his car crash. He tells **William** and **Jonathan Derry** that Gilbert has suffered permanent loss of memory.

Coventry racecourse

Coventry is a fictional racecourse in or near the city of Coventry in the West Midlands.

Rat Race (1970): Fraudster **Charles Carthy-Todd**, having failed in his attempt to commit murder in the parking lot at Coventry racecourse, runs out in front of the runners in the last race.

Cox, Emily Jane (*To the Hilt* 1996)

Emily Jane Cox, a **Lambourn** racehorse trainer, is the estranged wife of painter **Alexander Kinloch**. Straightforward, energetic and a born leader, Emily Jane trains for **Sir Ivan Westering** and Alex's uncle, **Robert, Earl of Kinloch**. Emily Jane and Alex had married when both were twenty-three years old. Alex had found it impossible to paint in Lambourn, and when Emily Jane refused to leave the racing village, Alex had left her after only four months. She was very hurt by Alex's departure but the two have remained on good terms. She helps Alex with his plans for the **King Alfred Brewery** horse **Golden Malt**, and even allows herself to be persuaded to sleep with Alex.

Craig, Etty (*Bonecrack* 1971)

Etty is head groom at **Neville Griffon's** **Newmarket** racing stable. She is from a wealthy background, and is expensively educated; her parents are unhappy that she has chosen to work with horses instead of marrying someone rich and eligible. Now middle-aged, Etty much prefers the company of horses to men, and is content with her lot. An excellent horsewoman, Etty copes well after her employer has an accident, but she knows she can't do all the jobs a trainer has to do. She is horrified when **Neil Griffon** tells her he is staying on as temporary trainer, considering him completely unqualified.

Etty is also unhappy when Neil takes on **Alessandro Rivera** as an apprentice. She puts Alessandro up on **Traffic**, a very difficult, colt, to teach him a lesson. She is unsympathetic when Traffic bucks Alessandro off and he is knocked unconscious. When, contrary to her instructions, Alessandro works a horse flat out instead of at half speed, Etty tells Neil that Alessandro must go.

Lacking confidence in her own judgment, Etty asks Neil his opinion on how to work Lincoln Handicap runner **Pease Pudding**. She grows more tense as the flat season approaches, but Neil leaves her to make more of the decisions. She is delighted when Pease Pudding wins the Lincoln.

When Alessandro starts winning races for the stable, Etty begins to warm to him.

Cranfield, Dexter (*Enquiry* 1969)

Racehorse trainer Dexter Cranfield inherited vast wealth from his father, a social climber who had passed on his snobbish attitudes to his son. He is a useful trainer, but has the advantage of rich friends who can afford to buy good horses. Cranfield is a mean-spirited man who is interested only in people who may be socially useful to him. His license to train is withdrawn indefinitely by the Stewards of the **Jockey Club** when his horse **Squelsh**, hot favorite for the Lemonfizz Gold Cup at **Oxford**; is beaten into second place by an outsider, also trained by Cranfield. **Kelly Hughes**, Cranfield's jockey, also has his license withdrawn.

Cranfield sinks into a depression verging on the suicidal. He resists Kelly's attempts to make him snap out of it and fight back, insisting that it is hopeless.

When Kelly tells Cranfield that he'll be getting his training license back he is delighted, but only mildly interested in how and why. He is much more concerned with making plans for his horses. On **Cheltenham** Gold Cup day, Cranfield is back to his usual snooty, arrogant self, especially towards Kelly. He doesn't believe it when his daughter, **Roberta**, tells him that Kelly was responsible for the restoration of his license.

Cranfield, Mrs. (*Enquiry* 1969)

The plain, dowdy wife of **Dexter Cranfield** is the daughter of an Irish baron, Lord Codihan. She blames **Kelly Hughes** for her husband losing his license to train. When Kelly comes to her door, looking for **Grace Roxford**, Mrs. Cranfield says that Grace has gone and that Kelly should go away too. When she says that the car outside the house is her gardener's, not Grace's, Kelly knows that she is lying; she is too much of a snob to let the gardener park his car outside the house.

Cranfield, Roberta (*Enquiry* 1969)

Roberta, the nineteen-year-old daughter of trainer **Dexter Cranfield**, is pretty, spoilt, snobbish and difficult. Like her father, she is used to treating jockey **Kelly Hughes** as a servant. She is surprised to discover that Kelly has a luxurious flat, though she refuses to believe that he decorated it himself; she is similarly taken aback at Kelly's intelligence and self-confidence.

Roberta shows courage when attending the Jockeys' Fund dance after her father has lost his license to train, calmly weathering the stares and whispers. When three jockeys at the dance are friendly towards her, she realizes that she is judging people by the wrong standards. When she dances with Kelly, Roberta maintains a strict formality, but her expression betrays a physical attraction.

Roberta finds herself cast in the role of ministering angel after Kelly ends up in hospital and then suffers a serious assault on his return home. She is delighted when Kelly tells her that he and her father have their licenses back. She confides that she was "scared stiff" of Kelly a week ago, considering him stand-offish and unapproachable, but now she sees him in a different light.

Soon it is Roberta's turn to face extreme danger at the hands of a deranged knife-wielder. She shows immense courage to confront her assailant and then to save Kelly from grave injury or worse.

Afterwards, Roberta tells Kelly that she fell in love with him when she was twelve years old, but it wore off. Her father wants her to marry her friend **Bobbie**, the son of an Earl, but she says she isn't going to, to Kelly's intense satisfaction.

Cratchet, Paul (*Shattered* 2000)

Detective Constable Cratchet is a colleague of **Catherine Dodd**. According to Catherine, Cratchet is a good policeman, though known as "Pernickety Paul" owing to his painstaking approach to report writing. He is separated from his wife. He helps Catherine to patrol the village of **Broadway**. Entering **Gerard Logan**'s workshop, Cratchet is killed when accidentally struck by molten glass.

Creggan, Earl of (*Flying Finish* 1966)

The Earl is the octogenarian father of **Lord Henry Gray**. He dies soon after Henry takes a job as traveling head groom with **Yardman** Transport.

Creggan, Lady (*Flying Finish* 1966)

Lady Creggan is **Lord Henry Gray's** mother. Now seventy-three years old, she was forty-seven when Henry was born. She lives in the past and is more than a little eccentric. She had raised Henry at arm's length, and their relationship is one of duty and politeness, not love. Lady Creggan is appalled at Henry's change of occupation and worries what her friends will think.

Following her husband's death, she assumes that

Henry will immediately give up his horse transport job. When he refuses she and the rest of the family are furious.

Cressie, Harbourne (*Field of 13* 1998: "The Gift")

Cressie is an American racehorse trainer; his horse, **Pincer Movement**, wins the Kentucky Derby at **Churchill Downs**.

Crest, Denby (*Risk* 1977)

Crest is a solicitor, and a client of accountant **Trevor King**; he requires an audit of his cash and securities held on behalf of his client for his six-monthly Solicitor's Certificate. **Roland Britten**, doing the checking because King is on holiday, can't get the figures to tally. This does not surprise Crest, who knows full well that his accounts are a work of fiction and is desperate to prevent Roland from finding out.

Crinkle Cut (*Field of 13* 1998: "The Gift")

Crinkle Cut is an American racehorse trained by **George Highbury**; he is ridden in the Kentucky Derby by **Piper Boles**, who has been bribed to stop the horse winning. Boles steers Crinkle Cut into another horse, causing him to fall back and eventually finish in twelfth place.

Crispin, Chief Superintendent (*Field of 13* 1998: "The Day of the Losers")

Crispin is the local police chief in Aintree, Liverpool. When bank notes from a recent violent bank robbery turn up at **Aintree racecourse** on Grand National day, Crispin asks the Stewards to fix the result of the race, so that the police can arrest the man who used the notes to place a bet with the Tote when he goes to collect his winnings. Crispin, not a racing man, considers that fixing the Grand National is a small price to pay for catching one of the perpetrators of a robbery during which several people were killed. However the Stewards refuse, on practical and moral grounds, to accede to his request.

Croft, Freddie (*Driving Force* 1992)

Retired jump jockey Freddie Croft runs a fleet of horse vans in the village of **Pixhill, Hampshire**. He enjoys his work but still yearns for the life of danger and excitement that he's lost. Close to top class, Freddie had consistently finished among the top jockeys each year in races won, though he'd never been champion. But he'd been retained by a top stable yard and, from the age of twenty to thirty-two, he'd ridden in four hundred jump races a year. The loss of that adrenalin rush was hard to take.

Freddie had driven horse vans as a young man for his late father, a jumping trainer. Freddie has brought to his new career the determination and hard work that had made him a successful jockey. His horse transport business is thriving, helped in large part by his ability to provide an efficient and courteous service to his customers. The courteous bit comes easy to Freddie, who possesses an equable and conciliatory temperament.

Unusually for a Francis hero, Freddie has a child. However, his daughter **Cinders** is peripheral to the plot and only glimpsed at a distance. She is not even aware that Freddie is her father, her mother having married someone else and persuaded him that he was the father. Freddie admits that he is not paternal, but things are complicated; Freddie continues to live not far from his ex-lover **Susan Palmerstone** and her husband, **Hugo Palmerstone** who, as Cinders grew up, came to realize that she was not his child, since she bore no resemblance to him whatsoever. Meeting socially presents problems since Hugo hates Freddie with a passion.

At the moment though, Freddie has other things on his mind, not least the appearance of mysterious containers on the underside of his horse vans and the murder of one of his employees. In the course of protecting his business Freddie narrowly avoids a watery grave. He is also compelled to confront an irrational phobia of his own, discovering in the process that there is nothing he won't do for those he loves.

Croft, Lizzie (*Driving Force* 1992)

Lizzie is the unmarried elder sister of **Freddie Croft**. She is a physicist at **Edinburgh University**. Her lovers tend to be intense academics like herself; her present boyfriend is an organic chemist, **Professor Quipp**. As a child Lizzie had been both bossy and protective towards Freddie and her other brother, Roger; she is still inclined to mother Freddie. She has a quarter-share in a helicopter, which she pilots herself down to **Pixhill** to see Freddie and find out about the problems he is having in his business. She uses her contacts at the university to analyze the contents of tubes found in one of the horse vans.

Croft Raceways (*Driving Force* 1992)

Croft Raceways is a racehorse transport firm, owned by **Freddie Croft** and based in **Pixhill**, Hampshire.

Cross, Mrs. (*Odds Against* 1965; *Come to Grief* 1995; *Under Orders* 2006)

Mrs. Cross is **Charles Roland**'s housekeeper and cook. She is of quiet demeanor, and excellent at her job. Despite **Sid Halley**'s request for her to call him Sid, she continues to address him as Mr. Halley.

Crossmead, Rufus (*10 lb. Penalty* 1997)

Crossmead is the editor of gossip magazine *SHOUT!* which prints malicious and untrue allegations that **Benedict Juliard** had taken drugs while working for **Sir Vivian Durridge**. He is threatened with libel action by Benedict. When Sir Vivian writes a letter of reference confirming Benedict's good character, Crossmead agrees to settle out of court and print a retraction.

Curtiss, Robin (*Bolt* 1986)

Curtiss is a veterinary surgeon who looks after **Wykeham Harlow**'s racehorses. He is unsentimental and efficient. Called out to see two dead horses, **Cotopaxi** and **Cascade**, Curtiss confirms that the horses had been deliberately killed. When a third horse, **Col**, dies, Curtiss tells **Kit Fielding** that he had been killed in the same way.

Curzon, Ronnie (*Longshot* 1990)

Curzon is an author's agent, with an office in **Kensington** High Street, London; he works hard and successfully on behalf of his clients. He advises **John Kendall** against writing **Tremayne Vickers**' biography. When John decides to take the job, he negotiates reasonable terms with Vickers for John. Later, he phones John to tell him that an American colleague likes John's novel and is sure that he can find a publisher for it.

D

Dace, J.L. (*Dead Cert* 1962)

Dace is the Clerk of the Course at **Maidenhead** racecourse.

Daily Flag (*Break In* 1985)

The *Daily Flag* is a national newspaper; an irreverent scandal sheet and no respecter of persons, the newspaper is increasing its readership steadily. It runs an article suggesting that trainer **Bobby Allardeck** is heavily in debt. *The Flag* is the subject of an unsuccessful takeover bid by **Maynard Allardeck**, whom the *Flag*'s owner, **Nestor Pollgate**, subsequently sets out to discredit.

Daily Planet (*Whip Hand* 1979)

Racing journalist **Bobby Unwin** works for the *Daily Planet*, a national newspaper. He writes an article about **Newmarket** trainer **George Caspar**.

Dainsee (*Bonecrack* 1971)

Dainsee, **Neville Griffon**'s vet, is called out to put down **Moonrock** and **Indigo**. At Neville's request, he x-rays Indigo's broken pastern and takes blood to be tested at the Equine Research Laboratory. He suggests to **Neil Griffon** that Moonrock's smashed hock may have been an accident as it would have needed a heavy blow to smash it, unlike a pastern. Dainsee later confirms, on receiving the results of the blood tests, that Indigo was doped.

Daisy (*Longshot* 1990)

A receptionist for authors' agent **Ronnie Curzon**, Daisy is black and well spoken. She is helped in the office by her sister Alice, who keeps the accounts.

Dan (*Twice Shy* 1981)

A jovial friend of **Liam O'Rorke**, Dan was formerly a farrier from Wexford in the Irish Republic. He worked as O'Rorke's gardener and helped him put on his bets in various towns, since the bookmakers at the races wouldn't take O'Rorke's bets. When Dan died, O'Rorke decided to sell his system.

The Danger (1983)

In Italy, kidnappers are holding **Alessia Cenci**, a top female jockey. After several days of tense negotiation **Andrew Douglas**, whose firm, **Liberty Market Ltd.**, has been employed by Alessia's father, **Paolo**, to mediate with the kidnappers, secures Alessia's release. Alessia flies to England with Andrew and stays with a friend who trains racehorses in **Lambourn**. She wants to continue to see Andrew, who understands her state of mind better than doctors would. She tells him everything she can remember that might be helpful. Soon afterwards Andrew is called upon to investigate the kidnapping of a child from a beach on the south coast. He and a colleague manage to release the child, who identifies one of the kidnappers as the same man that was involved in Alessia's kidnapping.

At **Laurel Park racecourse**, at the running of the Washington International, a senior figure in the administration of British racing is the next victim to be snatched. Andrew flies to Washington to negotiate with the kidnappers but is himself abducted from his hotel room and finally comes face to face with his quarry.

Racing plays only a minor role in the plot of *The Danger*, a novel with a strong didactic function. We learn much about how kidnappers work, how the authorities try to deal with them, and the effects on the victim. Andrew Douglas is not a dominant protagonist; in fact he's rather dull. Of course, flamboyancy is hardly a prerequisite of carrying out painstaking negotiations for the safe release of hostages, but even Andrew's friends find him hard work. The novel's strength is not in Andrew Douglas as a character but in the cat and mouse game he engages in with the kidnappers. Francis undertook meticulous research into the crime of kidnapping, a common tactic of terrorist organizations in the 1970's and 1980's. Prominent politicians and the children of wealthy parents were the typical targets of such groups as the notorious Baader-Meinhoff gang, the Symbionese Liberation Army and the Red Brigades. The latter group, many of whose members were young and middle class, was responsible in 1978 for the kidnap and subsequent murder of Italian Prime Minister, Aldo Mori. Thus the theme of *The Danger* would have given the novel a topical, contemporary feel when it was published in 1983, and even today, when kidnapping is less prevalent in Western Europe, the writing is still fresh and gripping.

Darcy, Evelyn (*Second Wind* 1999)

Evelyn is the wife of **Robin Darcy**. About fifty years old, she lives in Sand Dollar Beach, Florida. Evelyn dominates conversations with her loud voice. She is a guest at a lunch party given by **Caspar Harvey**. She pays for a helicopter to search for **Kris Ironside** and **Perry Stuart** after their plane crashes during a hurricane. One of the **Unified Traders**, Evelyn threatens Perry with a gun on both occasions that he goes to the Darcys' house. She is warned by her husband not to shoot Perry. She is apparently unaware of the true nature of the game that her husband is playing.

Darcy, Mme. Madeleine (*Bolt* 1986)

Mme. Darcy is the English wife of a French racehorse trainer. At **Ascot** races she is introduced by trainer **Basil Cutter** to **Kit Fielding** because she knows **Henri Nanterre**. M. Darcy, she tells Kit, used to train Nanterre's horses. He had forced her husband to sell him a yearling filly that he wanted on the threat of removing his horses. When M. Darcy sold him the filly, Nanterre had removed his horses anyway.

Darcy, Robin (*Second Wind* 1999)

An American, Darcy lives at Sand Dollar Beach, Florida, and is married to **Evelyn**. He is small of stature, wears glasses and is physically unremarkable. Mentally, however, he is very sharp, and his quiet self-confidence derives from his intellectual capacity. Darcy and Evelyn are guests at a lunch party given by **Caspar Harvey**. Evelyn says that Robin makes his money by selling mushrooms and turf. Darcy prevaricates when **Perry Stuart** asks him about **Trox Island**. When Perry, staying at the Darcys' home, sets off alarms when swimming at night in their pool, Darcy points a gun at him, thinking he is an intruder. Perry doesn't believe everything that Darcy says; when Perry asks why **Amy Ford** had sold him her plane, Darcy suggests that she wanted to buy a diamond necklace with the proceeds.

Darcy organizes a helicopter search for Perry and **Kris Ironside** after their plane is lost in a hurricane. Darcy, however, is not all he seems, and Perry suspects him of trading in a dangerous and illegal market. Darcy's role, though, proves to be complex and shrouded in mystery.

Darnley, Noel George (*Proof* 1984)

Darnley, the new landlord of an old coaching inn, had carried out alterations to the inn which had not improved its atmosphere. He is the subject of complaints from the public that his whisky and gin are watered down; however, these suspicions have proved to be without foundation. Darnley is visited by **Tony Beach** and **Sergeant Ridge** to sample his whisky, which is found to be genuine.

Darwin, Mrs. (*Comeback* 1991)

Mrs. Darwin is the mother of **Peter Darwin**. When Peter was a baby, his mother was widowed, at the age of twenty, when husband Paul, an aspiring jump jockey, was killed in a road accident while riding out. A trained secretary, she is helped by the **Injured Jockeys Fund** to find a job at **Chelten-ham** racecourse. Later, when Peter was twelve years old, she married a diplomat, John Darwin. She tells Peter over the telephone that, as a young widow, she had a brief affair with **Kenny McClure**.

Darwin, Peter (*Comeback* 1991)

Peter is a career diplomat and the adopted son of a diplomat. His life might have been very different had his natural father survived. But jump jockey Paul Perry was killed in a car accident when he was twenty-one and Peter just a baby. Peter's mother, though working as secretary to the manager of **Cheltenham racecourse** for the next ten years, was adamant that her only son would not follow his late father's dangerous occupation. Peter's heartfelt desire to be a jockey was frustrated when she remarried. When he was twelve years old the family embarked on a series of overseas diplomatic postings. Peter took his stepfather's name and grew to like the regular change of domicile that the diplomat's life entailed. Throughout his teens he developed his facility for languages and when he was old enough he joined the diplomatic service. Now aged thirty-two, Peter is "rootless and nomadic, well used to it and content." He has never married, and saying goodbye to girlfriends before moving on has been more of a relief than a cause for sadness.

Peter is between postings and revisiting the part of rural **Gloucestershire** where he was brought up when a suspicious fire damages the veterinary surgery where he is staying. One of the vets who work there, **Ken McClure**, has had several of his equine patients die unexpectedly. Peter's involvement in the investigation into the problems surrounding the practice uncovers forgotten paths back to his childhood. Many characters from the past emerge, but Francis's device of using Peter's memories of growing up in the same area and around the same families is not convincing. While it allows Peter to theorize about the motivation for crimes currently being committed, it is hard to believe that the same crimes would be perpetrated by the same people a generation later.

This is only one of several unrealistic elements in the plot that detract from Peter as a strong central character. Another example is when he phones his mother for information about events that took place twenty years ago. She immediately makes a shocking confession about her behavior at that time that a woman would hesitate to tell her best friend about, let alone her son.

The romantic interest is supplied by **Annabel Nutbourne**, a young and pretty employee of the **Jockey Club**, whom Peter meets at **Stratford** races. She is struggling to communicate with two members of the Japanese Jockey Club in her charge and Peter offers his services as a translator. Dinner follows, and it is not long before he is explaining to her what a diplomat's life entails—"an odd way to tell her I was ... interested in her future."

For a while, though, it is debatable whether either of them has a future. The criminal responsible for various acts of mayhem is bent on eliminating them both, and Peter has to engineer an unlikely escape.

Despite his name Peter Darwin in no way represents a significant step along the evolutionary path trodden by Francis's heroes. Indeed, he is a mediocre example of the species. The main reason is that Peter is not directly involved in the storyline; he is an outsider called upon to shed light on the nefarious goings-on at a veterinary practice. A first person narrator who is not central to the action is up against it from the start. Working in the diplomatic service, Peter must have been called upon to smooth over potentially awkward situations; even his skills, though, are insufficient to paper over the improbabilities of this plot, and his character suffers as a consequence.

Datepalm (*Straight* 1989)

Datepalm, a seven-year-old gelding trained by **Milo Shandy**, is a bay with black points and good conformation. He is a former winner of the **Cheltenham** Gold Cup. When Datepalm's lady owner leaves England to live abroad, she sells him to Americans **Harley** and **Martha Ostermeyer**.

Davidson, Major Bill (*Dead Cert* 1962)

Davidson is the leading amateur steeplechase jockey in England when he is killed in a fall at **Maidenhead racecourse**; his horse, **Admiral**, is brought down through an act of deliberate and premeditated malice. He was **Alan York**'s best friend. A friendly, warm and reliable man, Davidson was not, intellectually, out of the top drawer. He was, however, methodical in his habits.

Davidson, Henry (*Dead Cert* 1962)

Henry is the eight-year-old son of **Major Bill Davidson**. He is highly intelligent, and an excellent poker player. Henry overhears a telephone conversation between his father and an unknown man. The man warns Davidson to stop his horse **Admiral** from winning a race.

Davidson, Polly (*Dead Cert* 1962)

Polly is the eleven-year-old daughter of **Major Bill Davidson**.

Davidson, Scilla (*Dead Cert* 1962)

Scilla is the wife, and subsequently the widow, of **Major Bill Davidson**. She is a small, dark-eyed woman with a loving and compassionate nature.

Davidson, William (*Dead Cert* 1962)

William is the youngest son of **Major Bill Davidson**.

Davies, Mr. (*Break In* 1985)

Davies is a **Sussex** farmer, and one of trainer **Wykeham Harlow**'s owners; **Kit Fielding** wins narrowly at **Ascot** on his horse. Davies is impressed, describing Kit as "a bloody demon."

Davis, Nurse (*Wild Horses* 1994)

Nurse Davis is mentioned by **Dorothea Pannier** as nursing her brother, **Valentine Clark**, during his last days.

Davis, Sue (*Forfeit* 1968)

Sue Davis is a neighbor of **James** and **Elizabeth Tyrone** in a mews behind Grays Inn Road, London. She is happy to sit with Elizabeth if James is suddenly called away. She worries Elizabeth one day by reading James's article in the *Sunday Blaze* about non-starting favorites and commenting that his quiet personality belies his forthright journalistic style.

Dawkins, Mrs. Robin (*Field of 13* 1998: "Collision Course")

Mrs. Dawkins, the co-owner of and majority shareholder in Lionheart News Group, dislikes the other owners, and because of constant arguments the Group is not doing well. She interviews editor **Bill Williams** at a restaurant near **Oxford** for a job with the Group. She is not impressed with either Williams or the service she receives at the restaurant. Later, owing to wily tactics employed by colleague **Harold F. Field**, she changes her mind about Williams.

Dawson (*Bolt* 1986)

Dawson is a butler, and reminiscent of P.G. Wodehouse's creation Jeeves (though Jeeves was a valet, not a butler). He is employed by **Princess Casilia** and **M. Roland de Brescou**, and lives with his wife in the basement of the Princess's house.

"The Day of the Losers" (*Field of 13* 1998)

Austin Dartmouth Glenn goes to **Aintree racecourse** for the Grand National, his pockets stuffed with stolen banknotes—his share for his part in successfully springing a bank robber from jail. Also traveling to **Aintree** on the same train, steeplechase jockey **Jerry Springwood** is dreading his participation in the Grand National. Aged thirty-two, his nerve has gone, and it is only his instinctive skill that gets him through a race.

On arrival at the racecourse Glenn goes straight to the Tote window and bets £100 on **Haunted House**, Springwood's mount in the National. A sharp-eyed Tote employee, primed to look out for stolen banknotes, checks the serial numbers and alerts the police.

The local police chief tries, unsuccessfully, to persuade the Aintree Stewards to fix the Grand National so that Haunted House wins and the police can arrest the man who had placed the bet when he collects his winnings.

Jerry Springwood, a quivering wreck inside, goes out to ride Haunted House, unaware of how important his performance as a jockey is to the police's hopes of arresting Glenn.

Daylight (*Reflex* 1980)

Daylight is a useful steeplechaser trained by **Harold Osborne**, and a fluent jumper. He is hot favorite for a handicap chase at **Sandown Park** but, on the orders of owner **Victor Briggs**, jockey **Philip Nore** causes the horse to fall, losing a race he would have easily won. Next time out at **Ascot**, Philip is trying his best to win, but Daylight makes jumping errors and finishes second.

Dead Cert (1962)

Top amateur steeplechase jockey **Major Bill Davidson**, riding his champion hunter chaser **Admiral**, is killed at **Maidenhead** races. **Alan York**, his close friend, is also riding in the race, and knows immediately that there was something odd about the fall. He informs the Jockey Club and the police, who treat Alan's suspicions with skepticism. But the slow fuse of Alan's anger has been lit, and he is determined to discover the truth.

Alan's search leads him down dangerous paths; he encounters a beautiful girl with an enigmatic guardian; gangs of taxi drivers at war with each other; corrupt jockeys; and criminals prepared to commit murder to protect their vested interests.

Following the murder of a jockey at the racecourse the perpetrators target Alan, who finds himself hunted down like an animal. But Alan, turning the tables, tracks down the evil mastermind behind the crime wave.

Dead Cert is a remarkable debut novel. Francis shows a sureness of touch worthy of an experienced crime writer in plotting, in characterization and in setting. The sharpness of Francis's depiction of racing life is maintained from the first page to the last. In fact Francis based the opening episode, in which Davidson is killed, on an incident that actually happened to him; he was nearly brought down during a race by a length of chicken wire stretched across a fence to stop golf balls from the local driving range getting caught in the birch. Graham Lord, Dick Francis's biographer, has identified other autobiographical references in the book: Alan York comes from near Bulawayo in Southern Rhodesia, where Francis was sent by the RAF to train as a pilot in 1943; and in the equine hero, Admiral, there are resonances of Lord Bicester's top-class chaser Finnure, on whom Francis won the King George VI chase at **Kempton** in 1949, and of prolific winner Crudwell, one of Francis's favorite horses.

Dead Heat (2007)

Michelin-starred chef **Max Moreton** provides the catering for two hundred and fifty guests at a function at **Newmarket racecourse** on the evening before the running of the Two Thousand Guineas, the first major flat race of the season. Along with Max himself, many of the guests suffer acute food poisoning. The following day Max, despite feeling awful, organizes lunch in the racecourse hospitality boxes hired by the race sponsors, an American tractor manufacturing company. Just after lunch a huge explosion rips through the boxes; dozens of guests are killed or seriously injured.

Max strives to reestablish the reputation of **The Hay Net**, his Newmarket restaurant, which is temporarily closed following adverse publicity due to the food poisoning incident. He is convinced that the ingredients which had been responsible for the poisoning had been added deliberately. More disturbingly, Max begins to suspect a link between the poisoning and the racecourse explosion, which proves to have been caused by a bomb. Max is aided in his investigations by musician **Caroline**

Aston, one of the victims of food poisoning, whose initial resolve is to sue Max for loss of earnings. Romance soon blossoms between them but, following attempts on his life, Max's ability to survive long enough to enjoy the relationship is debatable.

Max's determination to get at the truth takes him to the United States to follow up a possible connection with the world of international polo. He returns to England, certain that he knows who planted the bomb at Newmarket racecourse, and why. But the perpetrator of the crime has no intention of letting Max live long enough to do anything about it.

Dead Heat was written by Dick Francis and his son Felix with the alleged aim, in part at least, of ensuring that bookstores continue to stock the Francis brand. If a new Dick Francis novel doesn't come out every year, then Francis's previous novels are less likely to remain on the shelves. This may make sound commercial sense but it is futile to pretend that *Dead Heat* bears the hallmark of a vintage Dick Francis novel. It is a pleasant enough read, but the plot is pedestrian and its resolution by hero Max Moreton depends upon him seeing connections between disparate events and making inferences from these connections that stretch credibility to the limit. But *Dead Heat*'s principal weakness lies in its lack of a properly developed villain. The man that Max suspects of the Newmarket racecourse bombing does not make an appearance until the penultimate chapter. For the reader, the villain holds no interest as a character because he materializes far too late to establish his credentials.

Leaving aside this major flaw, there are other small irritations, one example of which will suffice. Professional musician Caroline Aston is a viola player with the Royal Philharmonic Orchestra. Discussing music with Max Moreton, she says that she *thinks* the composer Sibelius is Finnish, but isn't sure. That's like Hillary Clinton expressing doubt as to whether or not George W. Bush is a Republican.

"Dead on Red" (*Field of 13* 1998)

A professional hit-man crosses the Channel to carry out a commission. He does his job successfully but, for the man who hired him, plans do not pan out as expected. To solve his problems he turns again to the hit-man, who once again boards the cross-Channel ferry. This time, however, it is the assassin's luck that runs out.

Deansgate, Trevor (*Whip Hand* 1979)

Deansgate is the sanitized, more socially accept-able name that **Trevor Shummuck**, born in the back streets of Manchester, has adopted in order to oil the wheels of his ascent in the hierarchy of the racing world. His bookmaker's business, trad-ing under the name of Billy Bones, is thriving, and he has accumulated sufficient wealth to own horses in **George Caspar**'s top **Newmarket** yard. Along the way Deansgate has shed, superficially at least, the rough coat that his upbringing had endowed him with; he is immaculately groomed, urbane, the epitome of the self-made man.

But if the poverty of Deansgate's childhood had forged the determination to escape it, it has also left him with the savage instincts of the street fighter. Scornful of the ethical standards of the world he has chosen to inhabit, Deansgate is prepared to use any means at his disposal to achieve his ends. When he finds that **Sid Halley** has been hired to prevent that eventuality, Deansgate ruthlessly ex-ploits Sid's greatest fear, causing him to plum the depths of guilt and despair. But, having reached rock bottom, Sid resolves never again to submit to threats. His investigations reveal vital evidence of Deansgate's criminal activities. He presents this evidence to the **Jockey Club** Stewards who, in turn, inform the police.

Deansgate's career as a bookmaker and owner is ruined. He plots revenge against Sid but, in the end, even that satisfaction is denied him.

Deb, Aunt (*Dead Cert* 1962)

Aunt Deb is **Uncle George**'s wife, and **Kate Ellery-Penn**'s aunt. Seventy years old, elegant and well-preserved, she lacks human warmth and has a keen sense of what she sees as her social posi-tion. She is very old-fashioned in her attitudes and, essentially, a snob. She has no idea about George's double life. After his death, she suffers four heart attacks, of which the last is fatal.

Debbie (*Risk* 1977)

Debbie is an assistant at the **Newbury** firm of accountants King and Britten. She is unambitious, but is painstaking and good at her job. She tells **Roland Britten** that he could be making better use of her talents.

Decider (1993)

Roger Gardner, manager of **Stratton Park** racecourse in **Wiltshire**, and Clerk of the Course **Oliver Wells**, go to see architect and builder **Lee Morris**, who is a shareholder in the racecourse, and whose mother's first husband, **Keith Strat-ton**, is the son of the recently deceased Lord Strat-ton. They tell Lee that Lord Stratton's heirs are feuding over the course, some of whom want to sell the racecourse to developers. Gardner and Wells want Lee to use his voting shares to vote against selling. Soon afterwards Lee receives a let-ter inviting him to a shareholders' meeting at Stratton Park.

Lee's presence at the shareholders' meeting is generally resented, particularly by Keith Stratton, who is rumored to be heavily in debt Soon after-wards an explosion destroys the old stands; Lee and his son Toby narrowly avoid serious injury or worse.

Lee's wife **Amanda**, with whom he has a prob-lematic relationship, is angry with Lee for putting their children in danger. The next day Lee gets more grief, this time of a physical nature, from Keith Stratton and various unpleasant Stratton rel-atives.

The more Lee gets to know the Strattons, the more he realizes that "within the family there were levers and coercions." All secrets were "assimilated ... into the family pool" and used for "internal fam-ily blackmail." When, finally, Lee discovers the shocking truth about Keith Stratton's past, he puts himself and his children in mortal danger.

Francis's departure from his usual practice of avoiding the depiction of children in his novels could have been risky; writing about the reactions and emotions of juveniles, not to mention their speech rhythms and their usage of words and phrases unintelligible to many adults, is a special-ist area strewn with pitfalls. However, despite going over the top somewhat with the size of Lee Morris's family, Francis handles the relationship between Lee and his sons with sensitivity, and Lee's own role in the novel is enhanced by it. Life in the Morris family is given a sharp dose of real-ity by the awkward relationship between Lee and his wife Amanda.

The plot of *Decider* arises from the human re-lationships within the Stratton family, and here too the characterization is sharp and multi-lay-ered. The novel explores the machinations of a wealthy, unpleasant family divided into warring factions. How they behave is largely dependent upon the secrets each knows about the others. As a study of conflict within a family, *Decider* is a suc-cessful and well-crafted story.

Dee Dee (*Longshot* 1990)

Dee Dee is trainer **Tremayne Vickers'** secretary. In her mid-thirties, she is feline in movement and with a cat's reserve. She has been badly treated by her ex-boyfriend and is still suffering. According to Vickers, Dee Dee is indispensable. At first, she is cool towards **John Kendall**, considering him not well enough known to be writing Vickers' biography. When she finds out how John had helped **Fiona Goodhaven** and the others after their car crash, she is better disposed towards him.

Deglets (*Proof* 1984)

Deglets is a detective agency specializing in services to commercial clients. **Gerard McGregor** is the manager of Deglets.

Delafield Industries Inc. (*Dead Heat* 2007)

This is an American company, based in Wisconsin, which manufactures tractors. The company sponsors the Two Thousand Guineas, the first of the Classic races for three-year-olds, at **Newmarket racecourse**. However the company is in financial trouble, and one third of the workers have recently been laid off. Three months after the bombing at Newmarket the Wisconsin factory closes down.

Dell, Larry (*Driving Force* 1992)

Dell is a racehorse trainer and a client of **Freddie Croft**. He rings Freddie to cancel a proposed trip to **Southwell** for one of his horses who has got cast in his box and injured himself.

Dembley, Charles (*Forfeit* 1968)

Dembley is the ex-owner of **Brevity**, the ante-post favorite for the Champion Hurdle at **Cheltenham**. Dembley withdrew Brevity from the race without telling **Norton Fox**, his trainer. He reluctantly tells **James Tyrone** that he had received threats that his fifteen-year-old daughter would be raped if he did not withdraw Brevity. Dembley did so and, sickened with racing, later sold his horses.

Denny (*Proof* 1984)

Denny is one of the men who break into **Tony Beach's** shop to recover the falsely-labeled wine removed by Tony from the **Silver Moondance restaurant**. They are caught in the act by Tony and **Gerard McGregor**. Either Denny or his accomplice shoots Gerard, and both escape. Denny catches Tony and Gerard in the bottling plant owned by **Paul Young** and threatens Gerard with a shotgun. Tony turns a hose containing red wine on Denny; half-blinded, Denny can't stop Tony taking his shotgun. Tony knocks him unconscious and ties him up.

Dereham, Crispin (*Knock Down* 1974)

Crispin, the alcoholic elder brother of **Jonah Dereham**, lives with Jonah near **Gatwick** airport. He was orphaned at the age of seventeen and left without money, owing to his parents' profligacy. Forced to leave his boarding school, he had tried careers in stockbroking and insurance without success. He is abusive and self-pitying.

When arsonists set fire to the house, Jonah finds Crispin unconscious in the bathroom of the burning house. A fireman and Jonah revive Crispin; later, Jonah finds empty gin bottles in the bathroom and in Crispin's room. Visited by Jonah in hospital, Crispin tells Jonah not to expect him to be grateful.

Later, Crispin is depressed, and blames Jonah for not letting him die in the fire. He admits that his life is a disaster. But Jonah knows it will be his fault when Crispin starts drinking again.

Crispin dies a violent death in tragic circumstances, but his final act is a courageous one. Minutes later there is a phone call: it is Alcoholics Anonymous for Crispin, who, earlier that evening, had phoned them, asking for help.

Dereham, Jonah (*Knock Down* 1974)

Jonah Dereham's early life had been privileged and comfortable, but the big house and expensive boarding school had been funded by his parents' borrowings, second mortgages and generally feckless financial juggling. When a riding accident claimed his mother's life and, soon afterwards, a blood clot killed his father, Jonah was left, aged sixteen, with nothing. He promptly left school and found a job as a stable lad. Discovering a talent for race riding, Jonah eventually graduated to being a fully-fledged steeplechase jockey. He loved the life, but it was hard and unforgiving. After breaking his back in a heavy fall he was forced to retire. As a legacy of his time in the saddle he is left with a shoulder joint that falls apart if left to its own devices and has to be permanently strapped into place.

Casting around for alternative employment in the racing industry, Jonah sets himself up as a bloodstock agent, a profession whose trustworthiness, in the public's perception, is on the same rung as a politician's. Jonah, however, chooses the path of righteousness and, after two years in business, is starting to make it pay. His riding career had allowed him to pay off the mortgage on his house, with paddock and stabling, near **Gatwick** airport. Success had come at a price; Jonah mentions a "busted marriage," though there is no further reference to the circumstances of the break-up. And there's a ball and chain in the shape of his brother **Crispin Dereham**, an abusive alcoholic, who lives with him.

A chance meeting with a girl who is involved in a car crash outside his home, caused by one of Jonah's horses escaping, leads to an unexpected relationship developing between them. Revealing the impulsive side of his nature, Jonah has known **Sophie Randolph** for only twenty-four hours before he's asking her to marry him. Sensibly, Sophie declines the offer.

Increasing pressure on Jonah to conform to the culture of scams and kickbacks that permeates the bloodstock business leads to violent confrontation after two thugs try to snatch a colt that he had bought on behalf of a client. Without stopping to think he picks up a tree branch and lays into them, breaking arms and bloodying heads. Jonah may have prevailed this time, but the bloodstock agents see him as a real threat to their lucrative swindles. Jonah returns from **Newmarket Bloodstock Sales** one evening to find his house on fire and the stables already destroyed.

The comments of an amateur jockey, **Nicol Brevet**, shed light on Jonah's approach to life: "I learned [from you] not to go squealing when things weren't fair ... to shrug off small injustices and get on with the next things and put my energies in the future."

Forward-looking he may be, but Jonah is also bloody-minded. Far from frightening him off, the arson attack makes him more determined to resist the criminals. Meanwhile Jonah's softly-softly wooing of Sophie pays dividends when she offers him a bed for the night, with her in it. But the better that Jonah gets to know Sophie, who prefers her own company, the clearer it becomes that there is no long-term future in their relationship.

Jonah closes in on the prime mover behind the fraudulent practice. His instinctive, almost reckless, courage is in evidence when he tries to stop his quarry, who has added murder to his litany of crimes, from driving away. His arm is wrenched from its socket; in agony, he persuades Sophie to put it back. Afterwards he admits to a less heroic side to his nature; that he'd run a mile rather than face another operation on his shoulder.

The surgeon's knife may rattle Jonah a bit, but he displays typical sang-froid when staring down the barrel of a gun. He knows he is about to die, but he can't bring himself to plead for mercy. As it turns out, he doesn't have to; his brother Crispin blunders in, gin bottle in hand, and becomes, posthumously, a hero.

Derek (*Enquiry* 1969)

Derek, a mechanic at **Kelly Hughes'** local garage, looks after Kelly's sports car. After Kelly's car accident, Derek suspects foul play, and his examination of the wreckage proves his instincts reliable.

Derek (*Under Orders* 2006)

Derek is a security guard on the front desk of the London apartment block where **Sid Halley** lives. He gives Sid an envelope that has been delivered by taxi, which proves to contain a threat against **Marina van der Meer**.

Derry, Jonathan (*Twice Shy* 1981)

"I liked teaching physics ... how could anyone think it was dull?" Quite easily is the answer to that one, but, to Jonathan Derry, Newtonian principles matter. Jonathan's aim in life is to make them matter to the skeptical adolescents at the North London comprehensive where he is head of department. At the age of thirty-three, Jonathan enjoys his job, but his personal life is more problematic. His wife Sarah can't have children, but instead of stoically accepting the inevitable, is compelled to make everyone around her as miserable as she is. Top of her list of targeted victims is husband Jonathan. Meanwhile **Donna Keithley**, a friend of Sarah's who is similarly childless, steals a baby from a pram whilst the balance of her mind is disturbed. Sarah rushes to **Norwich** to look after her, Jonathan reluctantly in tow. When she insists on staying indefinitely, Jonathan's sigh of relief is heartfelt. Before Jonathan makes his escape Donna's husband, **Peter Keithley**, hands him some cassette tapes to look after, which prove to be copies of a computer program for handicapping horses. At this point Jonathan's life becomes a good deal more complicated. A thug, scenting easy money, threatens to harm both Jonathan and Sarah if he isn't given the computer tapes. Fortunately the villain isn't many rungs above plant life, and soon ends up in secure accommodation.

With the thug safely behind bars, Jonathan could have been forgiven for thinking that life might improve. Instead, Donna comes to stay with Sarah. By the time Donna leaves (as mad as ever, her welcome thoroughly outstayed) Jonathan has come to a decision. He's going to the States and he's not coming back. Still, he's unwilling to give up on his marriage completely (he might have a point—it's hard not to feel that they deserve each other) and he asks Sarah if she wants to keep trying. Disappointingly, she does.

Derry, Professor Meredith (*Wild Horses* 1994)

Derry is a retired lecturer in medieval history; a former fellow of Trinity College, **Cambridge**, he still lives in the city in genteel poverty. An expert on knives, Derry is frail of body, but his mind is still sharp.

Newmarket farrier **Valentine Clark** claimed on his deathbed to have left a knife with Derry. Subsequently the police consult Derry about a knife found by film director **Thomas Lyon** on **Newmarket** Heath.

Later, Derry receives a visit from Thomas, and gives him information about a knife that someone had sent him as a threat and also about one that he had been stabbed with. Derry tells Thomas that he had known Valentine Clark for thirty years and shows him a knife that Clark had made and had given him to look after.

Derry, Sarah (*Twice Shy* 1981)

Sarah is the wife of **Jonathan Derry**; they've been married for eight years. She is blonde and slim, but her prettiness is marred by a permanently dissatisfied demeanor, caused by her inability to have children. She and Jonathan no longer love each other. She doesn't get on with Jonathan's younger brother **William Derry**. On learning that her friend **Donna Keithley** has stolen a baby, Sarah insists on going immediately to comfort her. When Donna's husband, **Peter Keithley**, is killed in an accident Sarah stays on to look after her.

Angry and scared, Sarah rings Jonathan to tell him that thugs have broken into Donna's house and have tied her and Donna up. When Jonathan arrives with the computer tapes that they are demanding, Sarah is relieved, but furious with Jonathan.

Donna goes to stay with Sarah until she outstays her welcome and goes home. From that point on there is a change in Sarah's habitual state of resentment. One night she tells Jonathan that Donna's experience—the baby she had stolen cried incessantly and dirtied itself, so that she began to hate it—had made her reconsider her own feelings about her childlessness. Sarah doesn't react when Jonathan tells her he is thinking of going to live in America. When he asks her if she is willing to try to save their marriage, she agrees.

Derry, William (*Twice Shy* 1981)

In Part Two of *Twice Shy* the focus switches away from **Jonathan Derry** to his younger brother William. In Part One William is fifteen years old and at boarding school thanks to the generosity of a wealthy, deceased godfather. He is the sort of boy of whom the more cerebral teachers would have despaired: he likes a joke, he doesn't like being told what to do, and he doesn't really see the point of books. So long as he can ride horses during the holidays, William is perfectly happy. All he wants is to become a jockey; university is for wimps.

Fourteen years later William's brief career as a jump jockey lives on only in the form books. A badly broken leg and a body that wouldn't stop growing had extinguished any hopes of long-term success. Accepting the inevitable, William had tried his hand at a variety of jobs in racing, including bloodstock agent, assistant trainer, and sales representative for a horse feed company. Then, at the age of twenty-nine, he landed a job looking after the English and Irish racing interests of wealthy American racehorse owner **Luke Houston**, whom his brother Jonathan, now teaching at a university in California, had met at a party.

William is living in a rented cottage in **Six Mile Bottom**, near **Newmarket**, with his feisty girlfriend, **Cassie Morris**. Meanwhile a lunatic is back on the streets after fourteen years in jail, still pursuing the computer tapes containing a racing system. Surviving a violent assault only with Cassie's help, William makes it his goal to find the tapes and pass them on to his assailant. But the system has been tampered with, and the consequences of this are life-threatening, for both William and the villain.

Derrydown Air Transport (*Rat Race* 1970)

This is an air taxi and flying instruction firm, with three aircraft, based on an old RAF airstrip near **Buckingham**. It is not a prosperous business; apart from its owner, **Harley**, Derrydown has one elderly mechanic, a part-time boy helper, one full-time taxi pilot, **Matt Shore**, and one part-time pilot. Harley's niece, **Honey Harley**, does the secretarial work.

Devon, England

Devon is a rural county in the south-west of England. It has a spectacular coastline with small fishing villages and hidden beaches as well as popular resorts. Inland, Devon is a county of rich farmland criss-crossed with narrow lanes. Dartmoor National Park—the setting for Arthur Conan Doyle's novel The Hound of the Baskervilles—can be bleak and forbidding, but also has pretty, sheltered valleys and thatched cottages. The Roman city of **Exeter** is the county's capital, built on a plateau above the River Exe.

Knock Down (1974): Bloodstock agent **Jonah Dereham** buys a horse, **River God**, on behalf of an American client, **Kerry Sanders**. He arranges for a horse transport firm to pick the horse up in Devon and meet him in **Gloucestershire** near the home of the new owner, Kerry's future son-in-law.

Bolt (1986): Princess Casilia's horse **Bernina** wins a race at **Newton Abbot** in Devon.

To the Hilt (1996): Alexander Kinloch, worried about the safety of his mother, his estranged wife **Emily Cox** and **Norman Quorn**'s sister **Audrey Newton**, persuades them to go away to Devon for a few days.

Shattered (2000): Glass blower **Gerard Logan** visits the nursing home in Devon where corrupt medical researcher **Dr. Force** works.

Devon and Exeter racecourse

Devon and Exeter is the former name of **Exeter** racecourse.

(*Break In* 1985): **Kit Fielding** wins a hurdle race on **Bernina** for **Princess Casilia**, who has a box at the course.

Dewar, Teddy (*Enquiry* 1969)

Dewar, the landlord of the Great Stag Hotel, **Birmingham**, is an acquaintance of **Kelly Hughes**, who had stayed there several times. Kelly asks Dewar if he will put feelers out among his contacts in the city for information about who might recommend private investigator **David Oakley** for a job, Dewar says he knows a man who might help but he can't promise results. Subsequently, he sends Kelly a letter with the information he requires.

Dhaulagiri (*Break In* 1985)

Dhaulagiri is a novice chaser trained by **Wykeham Harlow**, and owned by **Princess Casilia**. He wins at **Towcester**, ridden by **Kit Fielding**.

Dial (*High Stakes* 1975)

Dial is a novice hurdler owned by **Steven Scott**. He is trained by **Jody Leeds** until transferred to **Rupert Ramsey** after Steven sacks Leeds. Dial wins a hurdle race for four-year-olds at **Newbury**.

Diarist (*Banker* 1982)

Diarist, a fifteen-year-old stallion standing at **Oliver Knowles'** stud farm in **Hertfordshire**, has bred plenty of useful winners, though none has been outstanding.

Didi (*Enquiry* 1969)

Didi is **David Oakley**'s secretary at his private enquiry agent's office in **Birmingham**. In her early twenties, she is tall, strong, and loyal to her employer. When summoned by Oakley she threatens Kelly with a silenced pistol. She tells Kelly not to come back as she shows him the door.

The Diving Pelican (*Comeback* 1991)

This is a restaurant on 18th Street, North **Miami**. **Fred Hutchings**, the British Consul in Miami, invites **Peter Darwin** to have dinner with him there. Fred's friends, singers **Vicky Larch** and **Greg Wayfield**, are attacked and robbed outside the restaurant.

Dodd, Catherine (*Shattered* 2000)

Detective Constable Dodd investigates the theft of money and a videotape from **Gerard Logan**'s workshop. She comes to check on Gerard after he is attacked outside his workshop. She allows Gerard to do a portrait of her in glass; afterwards, she is not displeased when he kisses her. Catherine's relationship with Gerard deepens and they sleep together. In the absence of clear plotting, Francis has Gerard bouncing ideas and theories off Catherine so that the reader has some notion of what is going on.

Dolly (*Odds Against* 1965)

Dolly is the head of the Racing Section at **Hunt Radnor Associates**. She is around forty years old and twice divorced. An excellent worker with unbounded energy, Dolly can drink as much as any of her male colleagues. She has an inner sadness at her inability to have children, and tries unsuccessfully to mother **Chris Barnes**. She is **Sid Halley's** immediate boss.

Donald (*Twice Shy* 1981)

Donald—his first name—is Governor of Albany prison, Parkhurst, **Isle of Wight**. He writes to his friend, the Governor of Wakefield prison in West Yorkshire, to tell him that **Angelo Gilbert** is due to be released on parole after fourteen years, and to express his reservations about Gilbert's mental stability.

Doncaster Bloodstock Sales

Doncaster Bloodstock Sales, based in South Yorkshire, is one of the United Kingdom's two biggest thoroughbred sales companies. Its sales include those for yearlings, two-year-olds, horses in training, foals, broodmares and fillies. The company conducts around a dozen auctions a year, selling about 3,000 horses for both flat and **National Hunt** racing.

Proof (1984): **Flora**, wife of racehorse trainer **Jack Hawthorn**, tells **Tony Beach** that **Harry Trent**, one of their owners who had been killed by a runaway horse van, had bought a horse the previous year at **Doncaster Sales** for £30,000. The horse had never been put into training, which Fiona thought odd.

Doncaster racecourse

Doncaster racecourse is the home of the St Leger, first run in 1776 and the oldest Classic race for three-year-olds in Britain. The course also stages the Lincoln Handicap, an early season flat race over a mile and formerly run at the now defunct Lincoln racecourse. The racecourse is situated in South **Yorkshire** and is owned by the local council. Though a grade one course, Doncaster's facilities had compared badly with **Sandown Park**, **York** and **Haydock Park**. Doncaster reopened in 2007 after a temporary closure while a £55 development was carried out. It is generally agreed that this money has been well spent.

Bonecrack (1971): Stable jockey **Tommy Hoylake** wins the Lincoln Handicap at Doncaster by a short head on Pease Pudding for trainer **Neil Griffon**.

Knock Down (1974): Racehorse owner **Wilton Young** and **Fynedale**, his bloodstock agent, have a public row at Doncaster races. Young sacks Fynedale and asks **Jonah Dereham** to buy a horse for him.

Twice Shy (1981): **William Derry** goes to the Doncaster St Leger meeting where he sees **Angelo Gilbert**, who has been bragging about winning a lot of money using **Liam O'Rorke's** system. **Genotti** wins the St. Leger.

Banker (1982): While talking to bloodstock agent **Ursula Young** at Doncaster races, merchant banker **Tim Ekaterin** meets equine healer **Calder Jackson**, whom he had saved from a knife attack at Royal **Ascot**.

Wild Horses (1994): Film director **Thomas Lyon** and actor **Nash Rourke** go to Doncaster to watch the Lincoln Handicap.

Second Wind (1999): Meteorologist **Perry Stuart** flies with his friend **Kris Ironside** to Doncaster. There Perry speaks with trainer's wife **Glenda Loricroft**, who complains to Perry that her husband is cheating on her.

Donna (*The Edge* 1988)

Donna is a character in the mystery play on board the Great Transcontinental Mystery Race Train; she is the daughter of racehorse owners, the **Bricknells**. In love with gambler **Pierre**, Donna steals her mother's jewels to pay Pierre's gambling debts.

Donny (*High Stakes* 1975)

Donny is a young, unsmiling stable lad at **Rupert Ramsey's** yard. He looks after **Steven Scott's** horse **Dial**. He accepts five pounds from Steven with the bare minimum of gratitude.

Doone, Detective Chief Inspector (*Longshot* 1990)

D.C.I. Doone, of Thames Valley police, is idiosyncratic and not a team player but is a proven thief-taker. He is in charge of the investigation into the discovery of the remains of a young woman found in a wood near **Tremayne Vickers'** racing stables. After **John Kendall** is shot with arrows fired from a crossbow Doone questions John, who refuses to tell him what happened. Doone is unhappy that John has "closed ranks" with the Vickers clan, but is unable to prove anything.

Dorset/Dorset County racecourse

Dorset County is a fictional racecourse in the south-west of England. In the Dark Ages Dorset, together with the neighboring counties of Wiltshire and Somerset, formed the ancient Saxon Kingdom of Wessex. Dorset is famous for its connection with the nineteenth century writer Thomas Hardy, who used the county town of Dorchester as the backdrop to his novel *The Mayor of Caster-bridge*.

10 lb. Penalty (1997): **Benedict Juliard**, at the racecourse with his father **George** as a guest of the Stewards, is asked by the Chief Steward to entertain **Orinda Nagle**, wife of the recently deceased Member of Parliament for **Hoopwestern, Dorset**.

Doug (*Come to Grief* 1995)

An acquaintance of **Sid Halley**, Doug is a computer expert who had set up Sid's computer for him. He gives Sid advice on changing his insecure analogue cell phone for a secure digital phone.

Douglas, Andrew (*The Danger* 1983)

In *The Danger* the focus is not on Andrew Douglas but on his job, which is, it has to be said, considerably more interesting than he is. Andrew is a partner in a firm, **Liberty Markets Ltd.**, that advises its clients how to avoid being kidnapped. If a client fails to follow the firm's advice and is abducted, Liberty Market negotiates with the kidnappers for his or her release.

Quite how Andrew acquired the kind of CV which qualified him for his present career is not entirely clear. All we are told of his provenance is that he previously had a boring job in a Lloyds underwriting firm and that his father, who was half–Spanish, was an Andalucian hotelier. Now here Andrew is acting as an advisor to a rich Italian, **Paolo Censi**, whose twenty-three-year-old daughter **Alessia**, a leading female jockey, has been kidnapped. Showing cool judgment throughout, Andrew ensures Alessia's return unharmed.

Andrew himself accepts that he's a bit of a bore. When Alessia asks him why he is so sensible he blames it on his Scottish ancestry: "the dour sort, not the firebrands." Still, he thinks it a bit harsh when **Popsy Teddington**, the friend Alessia is staying with in England, professes surprise at how someone as cold as he is can have cheered Alessia up.

But beneath that controlled exterior there beats a passionate heart. Without admitting it even to himself, Andrew has fallen for Alessia. When she tells him it's time for her to pick up her career once more, their friendly kiss turns intimate. He knows, though, that Alessia is almost ready to look after herself. She goes back to Italy and Andrew feels a strong sense of loss.

Some time later Andrew sees Alessia at a racecourse in Washington D.C., where she's riding in a big race. Meeting her again crystallizes his feelings for Alessia: "Want a lover?" he asks her flippantly. She laughs, and doesn't reply. But later she tells him that since the kidnap she's lost interest in physical love.

The iron in Andrew's soul is tested to the full when he suffers the embarrassment of being kidnapped himself. Face to face with his kidnapper, Andrew sees a man with many of the same qualities as himself, whose satisfaction in the taking of victims mirrored Andrew's in securing their release. Andrew views the kidnapper's subsequent fate with unexpected regret: the grudging recognition of a fighter on the opposite side of the same battle.

Dove, Mrs. (*Come to Grief* 1995)

Mrs. Dore is the office manager in the Customer Relations Department at **Topline Foods**, Frodsham, near Liverpool. She is middle-aged, experienced and efficient. **Sid Halley** breaks into her office and transfers secret computer files to his own computer. Mrs. Dove acts calmly when Sid is caught on Topline Foods premises. She advises **Owen Yorkshire** to let Sid go on the grounds that he is no threat.

Dozen Roses (*Straight* 1989)

Dozen Roses is a five-year-old flat racehorse owned by the late **Greville Franklin** and trained by **Nicholas Loder**. After a useful three-year-old career he had disappointed at four, but had won three times as a five-year-old. **Derek Franklin** suspects that Loder had been cheating in some way with Dozen Roses. The horse was named for Greville's lover **Lady Knightwood**, to whom he often sent roses. Dozen Roses is gelded by Loder contrary to Greville's instructions, accounting for his improved form. At **York** he finishes second but gets the race on an objection. He is sold by Derek to the **Ostermeyers** to go jumping with trainer **Milo Shandy**. He seems too docile when he arrives at Shandy's yard and is dope-tested. The test proves negative for barbiturate but further tests reveal the existence of a prohibited substance.

"The Dragon" (*Shattered* 2000)

This is the nickname of the formidable lady manager of the Wychwood Dragon Hotel in **Broadway**, in the Cotswold Hills. She flirts with **Gerard Logan** despite a thirty year age difference.

The Dream (*Bolt* 1986)

An ex-flat horse, The Dream has his first run over hurdles at **Newbury**. He is fast but hasn't yet learned to jump. Ridden by **Kit Fielding**, he falls at the fourth hurdle.

Drew, Randall (*Trial Run* 1978)

From today's perspective *Trial Run* has, inevitably, a dated feel to it. The novel is set in Communist Russia at a time when Mikhail Gorbachev is still a party apparatchik oppressing the downtrodden proletariat, glasnost not even a twinkle in his eye. Upper-class Englishman **Randall Drew** comes with the same musty, anachronistic smell. Men like Randall Drew may still exist in time-warped corners of rural England, but even by the standards of the 1970's Randall is humorless and stuffy. Nor do his family connections with the British royal family exactly help to make him normal, with an equerry for a grandfather, a lady-in-waiting for an aunt and the **Prince** more than a nodding acquaintance.

Randall has got to know the heir to the throne through his obsession with race riding—as an amateur, naturally, since his countless acres of rolling Warwickshire countryside don't farm themselves. To Randall's chagrin, however, he has recently had to hand in his jockey's license, the **Jockey Club** having decreed that wearing glasses to help steer a semi-wild animal weighing a thousand pounds over fences at high speed might be construed as dangerous. A sensible precaution, but Randall feels hard done by despite having worse eyesight than a Mongolian fruit bat. But myopia isn't Randall's only health concern: he can't breathe either. All his life he's been plagued with wheeziness and chest infections.

A bit heartless of the Prince, then, to ask Randall as a favor to go to Moscow, a city where the weather could not easily be mistaken for that of South Florida. His brief is to investigate rumors of a sexual peccadillo concerning the Prince's chinless brother-in-law, **Johnny Farringford**. Randall is none too keen but manfully accepts the commission; as his terrifying girlfriend, **Lady Emma Louders-Allen-Croft** (three girlfriends for the price of one, but not the bargain it appears to be) witheringly points out, "It's all too ingrained in you. Service to the sovereign and all that."

The Prince clearly appreciates Randall's fine qualities, of which courage is not the least. In Moscow he manages to resist when attacked in the street and make it back to the relative safety of his Intourist hotel, where the principal danger to his life is the food. The next day he survives a second assault, but he knows that he won't be able to cheat death indefinitely. An involuntary immersion in a freezing river has seriously damaged his lungs, which were already more congested than the London Underground in rush hour.

Having struggled his way through an unconvincing and largely tedious plot enlivened only by the attempts on his life, Randall returns to England. What he desperately needs is a sympathetic girlfriend to tuck him up in bed with a hot water bottle and a bottle of brandy. What he gets is Emma.

"Why did you want me to come here?" she demands. "You usually tell me to stay away when you're ill."

In mild desperation Randall suggests marriage. Disdainfully, Emma tells him it wouldn't work, and Randall is forced to concede that she's not wrong. In a downbeat ending to the novel, Francis leaves us to speculate upon whether Randall will ever recover his vitality. You wouldn't bet your mortgage on it.

Driffield, Percy (*Field of 13* 1998: "Haig's Death")

Driffield, a **Lambourn** racehorse trainer, is currently champion jumps trainer judged on prize money won. He runs a promising hurdler, **Lilyglit**, owned by **Jasper Billington Innes**, in a valuable race at **Winchester**. He is concerned when Lilyglit, his favorite horse, takes a crashing fall at the last hurdle, but the horse is only winded.

Driffield, Sarah (*Field of 13* 1998: "Haig's Death")

Sarah is the attractive daughter of champion racehorse trainer **Percy Driffield**. She lives in the racing village of **Lambourn**. After a party, she goes to the house of jockey **Moggy Reilly** and sleeps with him. She is impressed by Reilly's riding ability in a hurdle race at **Winchester**.

Drifter (*Longshot* 1990)

Drifter is a jumper trained by **Tremayne Vickers**. **John Kendall**, not concentrating after a fight with **Nolan Everard** the previous day, falls off Drifter on the gallops when the horse swerves. A day or two later, the horse goes well when John rides work on him.

Driving Force (1992)

Ex-jump jockey **Freddie Croft** runs a fleet of horse vans out of **Pixhill, Hampshire**. One morning **Jogger**, the company mechanic, finds an empty metal box underneath the chassis of one of the vans, stuck on by a magnet. When Jogger subsequently discovers containers hidden under two more horse vans, and Freddie finds a thermos flask in a van that had picked up a hitchhiker, Freddie suspects that his vans may be being used for drug running. Then Jogger is found dead in mysterious circumstances, and Freddie knows he has a major problem. His own investigations, concentrating on the unidentified substances found in the thermos flask, lead to an attempt on his life and compel him, finally, to confront a personal dread that has haunted him for years.

The "driving force" of the novel's title is twofold: malice and a desire for revenge. These incentives to break the law combine to produce a catalogue of nefarious practices sufficiently off-beat and original to keep the reader guessing. Familiar elements of Francis's technique are here too: his mission to educate, this time in the day-to-day running of a horse transport firm; and the violence, often shocking, sometimes gratuitous. The novel is strengthened by the main character; Freddie Croft is an ex-jockey, and Francis's knowledge of such men allows the reader to get inside the character's skin. Francis's own motivation to write *Driving Force* came from within his own family. His son Merrick had recently given up trying to make a living training racehorses, and was running a horse transport firm in the racing village of **Lambourn** in **Berkshire**.

The Duke (*10 lb. Penalty* 1997)

The Duke—of where we aren't told—is Chief Steward at **Dorset County racecourse**. He is about sixty years old, businesslike and approachable. He meets **Benedict Juliard** at a lunch in the Stewards' room on race day, and remembers that Benedict rode against his son in amateur races. He asks Benedict to look after fellow-guest **Orinda Nagle** and show her the horses.

Duke, Joe (*10 lb. Penalty* 1997)

Joe Duke is a Detective Sergeant based in **Hoopwestern, Dorset**. He investigates the attempted shooting of **George Juliard** and the fire at the constituency offices.

Duke, Johnnie (*Field of 13* 1998: "Nightmare")

Johnnie Duke is a young American police officer who goes undercover to catch a horse thief.

Duncan (*Reflex* 1980)

Duncan was the gay partner of **Charlie**, a photographer. He and Charlie acted as guardians to **Philip Nore** when he was young at the request of his mother, **Caroline Nore**. When Duncan left, Charlie committed suicide.

Dunstable racecourse

Dunstable is a fictional racecourse in Bedfordshire. The modern town of Dunstable is on the site of a former Roman settlement at the crossroads of the Roman Watling Street and the prehistoric Icknield Way. Industries which have established themselves in the town include engineering, printing and the motor trade.

Nerve (1964): Jockey **Art Matthews** shoots himself in the head in the paddock of Dunstable racecourse soon after being sacked by trainer **Corin Kellar**. **Rob Finn** finishes last on **Shantytown**, a gelding owned by **John Ballerton**; the horse is later found to have been doped.

Odds Against (1965): Dunstable racecourse has recently closed, having been procured for building land by fraudster **Howard Kraye**. Kraye had blackmailed the Clerk of the Course into deliberately running down the course until it was no longer financially viable.

Durham, England

County Durham is in the north-east of England, between North **Yorkshire** and Northumberland. For centuries the region was ruled by the powerful Bishops of Durham, almost as an independent state, with their own army, courts and currency. The landscape is rich and varied, from the North Pennine hills in the east to the North Sea coast in the west. At the heart of the region is Durham City, with its magnificent Norman Castle and its cathedral, shrine of St Cuthbert. Within the walls of Durham Castle is University College, the foundation college of Durham University. There are sixteen colleges spread around the city.

For Kicks (1965): Hedley Hunter's racing stable is situated in County Durham. **Elinor Tarren**, elder daughter of **National Hunt Committee** member **Lord October**, is studying at Durham University.

Durridge, Sir Vivian (*10 lb. Penalty* 1997)

Sir Vivian is a racehorse trainer and a wealthy establishment figure. He accuses stable lad/amateur jockey **Benedict Juliard** of drug taking and sacks him. Years later, after Benedict graduates from university, Durridge hears that he has applied for a job with **Weatherbys**, racing's administrators. Durridge writes to Benedict, apologizing for his false accusation; he says that the allegation was made at the instigation of Benedict's father, who didn't want Benedict wasting his time trying to be a jockey. Durridge gives Benedict a glowing reference. Five years later he has a stroke, goes senile and has to retire to an old people's home. He is visited by **Usher Rudd** who is looking for dirt on Benedict; confused, Durridge tells Rudd that Benedict had taken drugs.

Dusty (*Break In* 1985; *Bolt* 1986)

Dusty is traveling head lad to veteran trainer **Wykeham Harlow**. As Harlow grows older and more vague he relies increasingly on Dusty. Dusty's attitude towards **Kit Fielding** varies between grudging respect and unwarranted prickliness. In *Bolt*, Dusty is annoyed with Kit for giving **Cascade** a hard race and tells Harlow about it. After **Hillsborough** runs badly, Dusty tells Harlow that Kit was interviewed by the stewards. He rejects Kit's attempts to be friendly at **Plumpton** races. When Kit has a bad fall at **Sandown Park** Dusty goes to see if he's all right, but only because he doesn't want an unfit jockey on Harlow's horses.

Duveen, Pete (*High Stakes* 1975)

Duveen is a cheerful young man who runs a horse transport business with a single horse van. At **Sandown Park** races, **Steven Scott** hires Duveen to take **Energise** back to his transit yard. When Duveen discovers that the horse left in the racecourse stables is not Energise, he waives his cancellation fees. Steven hires Duveen again when he is putting his sting against the men who had defrauded him into operation.

E

Eagler, Detective Superintendent (*The Danger* 1983)

Eagler, of the **Sussex** police force, is called in when a small boy is kidnapped from a beach near **Brighton**. He is quiet, unobtrusive and willing to listen to other people's opinions. He is supportive of **Andrew Douglas**'s plans to rescue the child.

Eaglewood, Izzy (*Comeback* 1991)

Izzy is a former girlfriend of **Ken McClure**. Her mother, **Russett Eaglewood**, is remembered by **Peter Darwin** as having a loose reputation. Born out of wedlock, Izzy is, according to her mother, an impressionable girl; she has gone off on a music course in the company of a guitarist.

Eaglewood, J. Rolls (*Comeback* 1991)

Eaglewood, a veteran racehorse trainer based in **Gloucestershire**, is the father of **Russett Eaglewood**. At **Stratford** races he accuses **Ken McClure** of killing his horse; in all, two of his horses had died during surgery, and another in its box. He insists that McClure must never attend his horses again. It subsequently transpires that Eaglewood is far from being an innocent victim of veterinary negligence.

Eaglewood, Russett (*Comeback* 1991)

Russett is the daughter of racehorse trainer **J. Rolls Eaglewood**. She's a "tart" according to **Josephine McClure**, and has an illegitimate daughter, **Izzy**. Russett assists her father at his stables, acting as his business manager. She is willing to answer **Peter Darwin**'s questions about the horses in her father's yard that had died. She fancies Peter, and is happy to accept his offer of a casual sexual liaison.

East Ilsley, Berkshire

East Ilsley is a village in West **Berkshire**, to the north of **Newbury**. The village, and its neighbor West Ilsley, have long been associated with racehorse training.

To the Hilt (1996): **Alexander Kinloch** rides racehorse **Golden Malt** away from his estranged wife's **Lambourn** yard and spends the night with him in a farmer's hut on the **Berkshire** Downs. Next morning he follows a string of horses back to their yard in East Ilsley and pays the trainer to look after Golden Malt.

Ecurie Bonne Chance (*Driving Force* 1992)

This is a small racing yard near Belley, Southern France, owned by English owner-trainer **Benjy Usher**.

Ed (*Wild Horses* 1994)

Ed is an assistant to film director **Thomas Lyon**; he is working on the filming of *Unstable Times*.

Eddy (*Twice Shy* 1981)

Eddy is **Angelo Gilbert's** cousin; their mothers were twins. He is Italian by descent. In Part One of *Twice Shy* Eddy assists Gilbert in his various criminal activities. In Part Two Eddy looks after **Harry Gilbert**, who has multiple sclerosis, but is treated with contempt by Harry. Eddy is both resentful and afraid of Harry, but is dependent on him. When **William Derry** goes to see Harry, Eddy brags to William that Angelo has bought a gun.

The Edge (1988)

Julius Apollo Filmer, recently acquitted of conspiracy to murder and known to be an unsavory character on the English racing scene, is to be a passenger on the Great Transcontinental Mystery Race Train for wealthy owners intending to race their horses on various tracks across Canada. At the request of the Canadian Jockey Club, English **Jockey Club** Director of Security **Valentine Catto** sends **Tor Kelsey**, one of his operatives, to keep an eye on Filmer.

Filmer has bought a half-share in one of the horses on the race train, giving him access to the horse car. Tor decides to travel on the train as a waiter. A troupe of actors, who are staging a mystery play as on-board entertainment, co-opt Tor as an actor. They explain the plot of the mystery to him, which involves the attempted kidnap of a horse and a murder.

After the train makes a brief stop during its journey across Canada a private car, which is the last one on the train, is deliberately unhitched with potentially disastrous consequences. During another stop Tor sees Filmer in heated conversation with a man that Tor doesn't recognize. At **Calgary, Daffodil Quentin**, a rich widow who had sold a half-share in her horse to Filmer, leaves the train after a serious disagreement with her co-owner.

The actors, having a problem with the script of the play, ask Tor for suggestions. Tor revises the script in such a way that Filmer is made aware that his actions have not gone unnoticed, and potential victims are forewarned.

Further problems with the train ensue. First, the heating system is deliberately drained while the train is in a siding. Then the horse car is found to have a hot axle, and Tor manages to avert a major disaster with seconds to spare. Before the train finally arrives in Vancouver, its final destination, there is a death on board which is directly related to Filmer's criminal activities. In Vancouver, however, Filmer's multifarious misdeeds catch up with him.

Francis describes the plot of *The Edge* as a "two horse race" between Filmer and Tor Kelsey in which, according to Tor's boss Valentine Catto, "our horse had the edge." Two horse races can be thrilling and full of drama, like the epic 1938 duel between top class horses War Admiral and Seabiscuit; or they can be dull, plodding affairs, staged between two cheap claimers on rock hard ground when all the other horses have been withdrawn for fear of breaking down. *The Edge* lies somewhere between the two; Filmer and Kelsey are a pair of handicappers, attempting to negotiate a tricky, switchback circuit. Just as a first time visitor to **Epsom** might wonder how a world-class race like the Derby can be run on such a course, so the reader might have similar doubts about the setting of *The Edge*—a transcontinental train on which actors construct a mystery for the entertainment of the passengers. Francis chose this background as a result of a similar trip across Canada that he and Mary had made. His descriptions of the terrain through which the train passes rise above the travelogue-type prose of which he has been guilty in other books. But the plot is contrived and in parts unlikely, in particular the role of the mystery play by means of which Tor lets a fellow-passenger know how Filmer intends to harm him. And why should professional, experienced actors rely on Tor to write the script for them?

As for the two horses themselves, Tor is a standard specimen of the breed exhibiting the behavior patterns expected of a Francis hero, whilst Filmer is a nasty piece of work but doesn't exude the tangible physical menace of Francis's best villains. They are adequate characters in a barely adequate plot.

Edinburgh/Edinburgh University, Scotland

Edinburgh is one of the United Kingdom's foremost universities. Founded over 400 years ago, the university has over 20,000 students. Scotland's capital, Edinburgh is its second largest city. It is situated in the south-east of the country, in the central lowlands. Edinburgh's annual performing arts festival is the largest in the world.

Driving Force (1992): **Freddie Croft's** sister **Lizzie** is a physicist at Edinburgh University. **Guggenheim**, an American research scientist and expert on ticks, works for the McPherson Foundation in Edinburgh.

Edna (*To the Hilt* 1996)

Edna works as a cook for **Sir Ivan** and **Lady Westering**; she is the sister of a cleaner, **Lois**, formerly employed by **Patsy Benchmark**.

Edna, Aunt (*Flying Finish* 1966)

Simon Searle's aunt Edna lives in Potters Green, **Berkshire**. She is stout, wheezy and smells of cough pastilles. She tells **Lord Henry Gray** that Simon was considerate, always bringing her small gifts. Aunt Edna has two daughters, one of whom lives in Canada. She says that Simon had given her £100 for her birthday for the last three years.

Edward (*Under Orders* 2006)

Edward is the Managing Director of **Cheltenham** racecourse. The character is presumably based on Edward Gillespie, the actual supremo of Cheltenham, whom Francis thanks, among others, for his help on the dedication page of the novel. Edward clears it with the security guard for Sid to go up to the private boxes during the Cheltenham Festival to see **Lord Enstone**; he promises to send Sid a pass to give him access to all parts of the racecourse.

Egocentric (*Forfeit* 1968)

Egocentric is a steeplechaser owned by **Harry** and **Sarah Hunterson**, who won him in a raffle. He is entered in Lamplighter Gold Cup Steeplechase at **Heathbury Park**. He finishes fourth in a prep race at **Leicester**; the jockey is unimpressed with Egocentric's jumping. The horse injures a leg in the Lamplighter and finishes lame.

Ekaterin, Tim (*Banker* 1982)

Merchant banker Tim Ekaterin is the only child of rich parents whose main aim in life was to rid themselves of their inherited wealth as quickly as was decent. Tim's workshy father had died when Tim was nineteen. His mother, like Lady Godiva, had put all she had on a horse, or rather on a succession of them. She may have been betting on the right horses, but the wrong ones kept winning. Worse, she insisted that Tim went with her to the races to watch her lose his inheritance. Half a million pounds later she was made bankrupt, by which time Tim was working for a bookmaker.

Tim was hugely unimpressed when the bailiffs, sent to clear his mother's house, helped themselves to his collection of Beatles LP's. Nor was he pleased when his uncle **Freddie**, vice-chairman of merchant bankers **Paul Ekaterin Ltd.**, blackmailed him into coming to work for the bank, guaranteeing to clear Tim's mother's debts if he did so. Rather to his surprise, Tim found that he enjoyed the work. Eight years on, when Tim's boss, **Gordon Michaels**, is taken ill, the chairman of the bank asks Tim to do Gordon's job until he's well enough to return to work. Flattered, Tim jumps at the chance.

It's not only Gordon's job that Tim covets; it's his wife, **Judith Michaels**, as well. Judith reciprocates Tim's feelings but, out of respect and affection for Gordon, they both make valiant efforts to stifle the ferment of emotion seething behind their rigidly controlled middle class exteriors.

Tim and Judith are together at Royal **Ascot**, observing the social niceties as best they can, when an attempt is made on the life of one of their party. Tim, regardless of his own safety, jumps between the assailant and his intended victim, and saves the day.

Performing acts of unthinking bravery is second nature to Tim, and he's soon in action once more. **Sandcastle**, a stallion recently purchased with the bank's help by a local stud farm, gets free of his handler and bolts. As Sandcastle hurtles past Tim grabs the rope attached to horse's head collar. Though dragged along by Sandcastle and suffering grazes and bruising, Tim is otherwise unscathed.

For stud farm owner **Oliver Knowles**, however, life soon becomes a succession of business and personal disasters. Tim, closely involved, investigates the sinister motives behind them; his enquiries invite something nasty to happen to him, and it does.

Elena (*Trial Run* 1978)

Elena is the sister of **Misha**, who is a groom with the Russian Olympic Three Day Event Team. Asked by Misha to deliver a package to **Randall Drew**, Elena meets him clandestinely in GUM department store, Moscow. She asks Randall not to cause any trouble for her brother.

Ellery-Penn, Kate (*Dead Cert* 1962)

Kate is the young, beautiful and vivacious niece of **Uncle George**. She has been brought up by George and **Aunt Deb** after her parents divorced and more or less abandoned her. Kate is given a racehorse by her uncle and aunt as a birthday present. Kate's presence on the racecourse raises the temperature among the jockeys in the weighing room. Kate is horrified and disbelieving when she discovers the truth about her uncle, and initially blames her boyfriend, amateur jockey **Alan York**, for his death. Soon, however, she sees that Alan had acted correctly, and accepts his proposal of marriage.

Elroy, Sticks (*Risk* 1977)

Elroy is a jockey and an ex-client of accountant and amateur jockey **Roland Britten**. Elroy's father had set up a tax-dodging scheme. When Roland discovered this and refused to connive at it, Elroy senior had verbally abused Roland one evening in a restaurant. Subsequently Sticks Elroy tells Roland that he has decided not to go along with the tax avoidance scheme, which has infuriated his father.

Emerald (*Nerve* 1964)

Emerald is an Irish mare brought over to England to contest the Midwinter Cup at **Ascot**. She has a huge reputation in Ireland, but is beaten into second place by **Rob Finn** on **Lord Tirrold's Template**.

Emil (*The Edge* 1988)

Frenchman Emil is the head steward on the Great Transcontinental Mystery Race Train. He is good-natured, courteous and helpful to **Tor Kelsey** when he is learning to be a waiter.

Enders, Jim (*Enquiry* 1969)

Steeplechase jockey Jim Enders is a friend of **Kelly Hughes**. He phones Kelly to sympathize when he learns that Kelly has lost his license to ride. He tells Kelly that he'd once lost his license and had eventually got it back at a postponed enquiry. Before attending the enquiry Enders had read in the Racing Calendar that his license had been restored—the result of the enquiry had been published before it had even taken place.

Energise (*High Stakes* 1975)

Energise is a good-looking, brave and useful hurdler owned by **Steven Scott** and trained by **Jody Leeds**. Following a parting of the ways between Scott and Leeds, Energise is apparently sent to another trainer; however it transpires that Leeds has sent a substitute in place of Energise. With the help of his friends Steven manages to recover Energise. The horse is subsequently given by Steven as a gift to his friends; he is beaten a short

head into second place in the Champion Hurdle at **Cheltenham**.

England, Martin (*Whip Hand* 1979)

England is a **Newmarket** racehorse trainer and a friend of **Sid Halley**. He asks Sid if he'd like to ride out one morning for him; he lets Sid exercise his Derby prospect, **Flotilla**, due to run in the Dante Stakes at **York**.

English, Marigold (*Driving Force* 1992)

Racehorse trainer Marigold English hires **Freddie Croft**'s horse transport firm to move her string from Salisbury Plain, **Wiltshire**, to new stables in **Pixhill, Hampshire**. A forthright lady in her fifties, Marigold conceals a kind heart under a hard exterior. At Freddie's request, she gives elderly retired racehorse **Peterman** a home when **John Tigwood** asks her to help. She later rings Freddie to say she's not happy with Peterman's health, and that she'd found ticks on him; she asks Freddie to find Peterman another home.

Enquiry (1969)

Top jump jockey **Kelly Hughes** and trainer **Dexter Cranfield** have been banned indefinitely from all racecourses by the Stewards of the **Jockey Club** after an enquiry finds them guilty of cheating. From the outset the chairman of the stewards, **Lord Gowery**, had seemed convinced of their guilt, and only one of the other three stewards had raised any objection to his handling of the enquiry.

Cranfield cannot cope with the shock of being warned off, and it is left to Kelly, supported by **Roberta Cranfield**, the trainer's nineteen-year-old daughter, to try to clear their names. Kelly's persistence eventually pays off, but not before he avoids certain death by a matter of seconds, and then suffers a vicious assault with one of his own crutches.

Central to the plot of *Enquiry* is the justice meted out by the disciplinary stewards of the all-powerful Jockey Club to jockeys and trainers deemed to have transgressed the rules of racing. In the 1960's this justice could be very rough indeed, and a man could be "warned off"—have his livelihood taken away—for an indefinite period without recourse to appeal. That Stewards' Enquiries were invariably held behind closed doors added to the sense of unfairness that many jockeys felt. In addition, the enquiry system was overshadowed by social assumptions which, forty years later, seem archaic. The Stewards were the ruling class—expensively educated, wealthy men from aristocratic, land-owning or military backgrounds who were used to telling people what to do. Though things were slowly changing, jockeys were still largely perceived as the paid servants of the owners and trainers, expected to follow instructions and not to have ideas above their station. If they were the subject of a Stewards' Enquiry, the done thing was to tell the press that they had a fair hearing and take the punishment without whining.

The plot of *Enquiry* calls, in places, for an over-optimistic suspension of disbelief on the part of the reader, in particular where the villains are too quick to admit to their misdemeanors. Minor flaws apart, *Enquiry* works well as an exposé of the potential injustices inherent in an essentially unfair disciplinary system.

Enstone, Lord (*Under Orders* 2006)

Born Jonnie Enstone in Newcastle-upon-Tyne in the north-east of England, Lord Enstone had worked his way up from being an apprentice bricklayer to owning J. W. Best, a nationwide construction firm. He had been knighted for services to industry, and then elevated to the House of Lords. He has a son, **Peter Enstone**, an amateur jockey who resents the fact that his father won't put him up on his horses. Lord Enstone asks **Sid Halley** to investigate why his racehorses, which are trained by **Bill Burton** and ridden by **Huw Walker**, are running badly. Subsequently Enstone tells Sid he has moved his horses to **Andrew Woodward's** yard, and asks Sid to drop his investigation.

According to Peter, Enstone was a cruel father who had inflicted physical punishment on him as a boy and had bullied him emotionally when Peter had grown too big to be beaten. Enstone had also been violent towards his wife, forcing her to leave him, and had denied her money to live on. Peter accuses him of responsibility for the death of his mother, who had walked out in front of a bus.

Enstone, Peter (*Under Orders* 2006)

Peter is the son of **Lord Enstone**; he is in his early thirties, and is a competent amateur jockey. He resents the fact that his father won't let him ride the horses he owns in case he gets injured. At **Newbury** races, he tells **Sid Halley** that he's due to ride **Roadtrain**, a horse that he says has no chance. Peter wins easily on Roadtrain at long odds.

Sid discovers that Enstone, while at **Harrow**

School, had been disciplined, along with **George Lochs**, for taking bets from other boys. As an adult Enstone has graduated to considerably more serious misdemeanors. A final showdown with Sid Halley ends, ironically, with Enstone inflicting upon himself a disability similar to Sid's own.

Epsom racecourse

Epsom racecourse, the home of the Derby, is on Epsom Downs in **Surrey**, a few miles south of London. The course is idiosyncratic: the runners in the Derby have to negotiate a twelve furlong, left-handed circuit which rises sharply over the first five furlongs before an equally marked descent to Tattenham Corner. The three and a half furlong finishing straight has a final climb to the winning post.

The first race meeting on Epsom Downs took place in 1661. In 1778 the twelfth Earl of Derby established a race over twelve furlongs for three-year-old fillies, and named it The Oaks, after his estate. The following year a new race over the same distance was added for colts and fillies. Lord Derby and his friend, Sir Charles Bunbury, flipped a coin to decide which of them the race should be named after. Lord Derby won.

Bonecrack (1971): At Epsom, **Enso Rivera** tells trainer **Neil Griffon** that he has disobeyed his instructions in refusing to let his son **Alessandro** ride the best horses in the stable, and insists that Alessandro ride **Archangel** in the Two Thousand Guineas at **Newmarket**.

Erik (*Slay-Ride* 1973)

Erik is the elder brother of **Knut**, the Oslo policeman investigating the disappearance of **Bob Sherman**. An impecunious writer, Erik is hired by **David Cleveland** as a driver. He is about fifty-five years old, scruffy, genial and slightly shambolic; he drives an old Volvo badly. Erik has a faithful Great Dane, **Odin**, who accompanies him everywhere. He had worked on a London newspaper, speaks fluent English and holds left-wing political views.

When David suspects that Erik's car has been rendered even more dangerous than it usually is, Erik's first thoughts are for Odin, who has been left in the car. He wants to rescue the dog but Knut won't let him. When David opens the car door Erik whistles and Odin jumps out. David's suspicions about the car prove accurate, but Odin is not injured.

Erik insists on continuing to drive David in a hired car, though Knut disapproves.

Erskine, Jay (*Break In* 1985)

Erskine is an employee of the *Daily Flag* newspaper. He was formerly a crime reporter on another newspaper, the *Towncrier*. Erskine has cold eyes and a propensity for violence; he has served a prison sentence for conspiring to obstruct the course of justice. He plants a bug on the roof of **Bobby Allardeck's** house, attached to the telephone wires. He is surprised by Bobby and **Kit Fielding** one night when either removing the bug or changing its battery. Erskine falls off the ladder but manages to escape after a struggle, leaving behind his jacket containing his ID.

In **Sam Leggatt's** office at the *Daily Flag*, Erskine attacks Kit for refusing to return his possessions, but Kit throws him over his shoulder. At a race sponsors' lunch in London, Erskine employs a more effective method to make Kit return the bug and his belongings.

Essex, England

To the north of the Thames estuary, Essex is the southernmost of the counties, along with **Cambridgeshire**, **Suffolk** and **Norfolk**, which make up the East Anglia region. The south of the county is urban, forming part of the Greater London conurbation, whilst the central and northern parts are agricultural. The county town is Chelmsford.

Forfeit (1968): **Tiddely-Pom**, ante-post favorite for the Lamplighter Gold Cup at **Heathbury Park**, is owned and trained by Essex farmer **Victor Roncey**.

Eton College

Eton College is a famous independent boarding school for boys near Windsor, **Berkshire**. It was founded by King Henry VI in 1440. The boys wear a uniform of black tailcoat and waistcoat, and pin-striped trousers. Eton has educated nineteen British prime ministers, and its alumni include several members of the Royal Family, James Bond author Ian Fleming, economist John Maynard Keynes and poet Percy Bysshe Shelley.

Flying Finish (1966): **Lord Henry Gray** was educated at Eton College.

Bonecrack (1971): Neil Griffon was at Eton until the age of sixteen.

Hot Money (1987): The sons of **Donald** and **Helen Pembroke** are at Eton. Donald struggles to pay the fees and is desperate to inherit some money from father **Malcolm**, a multi-millionaire gold trader.

Evan (*10 lb. Penalty* 1997)

Evan is **Benedict Juliard's** boss in the insurance department at **Weatherbys**. He is in his late twenties, and lanky. He is efficient and well thought of at Weatherbys. When he leaves to become managing director of an insurance company, Benedict succeeds him.

Evans, Mr. (*Break In* 1985)

Evans is a lawyer who works in the legal department of London newspaper the *Daily Flag*. He advises editor **Sam Leggatt** to print an apology for the newspaper's attack on **Bobby Allardeck**, since **Kit Fielding** has in his possession proof that two *Flag* journalists were responsible for bugging Bobby's house.

Everard, Lewis (*Longshot* 1990)

Lewis is the brother of **Nolan Everard**, and the cousin of **Fiona Goodhaven**. At a party at **Tremayne Vickers'** house, Nolan had been involved in the death of a girl named **Olympia**. Lewis was present but said he was drunk and couldn't remember anything. Unlike Nolan, Lewis is chubby and unfit; he is brighter than Nolan but jealous of his brother's success with horses and women; Lewis drinks too much.

At **Sandown Park** races he tells Fiona that Nolan is in his debt—meaning that he had perjured himself at Nolan's trial when claiming to be too drunk to notice anything. He tells **John Kendall** to steer clear of Nolan, who dislikes John.

Everard, Nolan (*Longshot* 1990)

Nolan Everard is an amateur jockey; he is the brother of **Lewis Everard** and cousin of **Fiona Goodhaven**. He is in his late thirties, with a dark complexion. He delivers a constant flow of obscenities in an upper-class accent. Nolan is believed to have caused the death of a girl, **Olympia**, at a party at **Tremayne Vickers'** house, but maintains that it was an accident. However, Olympia's father brings a private case against him.

Nolan often rides Fiona's horses; he has aspirations to become a member of the **Jockey Club**. He was once briefly engaged to **Mackie Vickers**, who called off the wedding because of his moodiness and uncertain temper. He is generally considered to be a brave and talented jockey, but not very bright and envious of his brother's brains. Nolan doesn't get on with Tremayne Vickers' stable jockey **Sam Yaeger** whom he considers his rival for both rides and women.

At **Windsor** races, Nolan rides a winner on **Telebiddy**; he is angry when the owners don't give him a cash present. He rides a brilliant race to win a hunter chase at **Sandown Park** on **Chickweed**. At Vickers' award dinner, he warns **John Kendall** to leave **Shellerton**; he is angry that Vickers is going to give John rides. He comes to blows with Sam Yaeger; when John intervenes Nolan turns on him. After they are separated Nolan threatens to kill John.

Exeter, Devon

Exeter is the largest city in the county of **Devon** in the south-west of England. The city suffered a good deal of damage from bombing in World War II but has nevertheless retained much of its character. Overlooking the river Exe, Exeter lies within Roman and medieval walls, and is a bustling, vibrant city.

10 lb. Penalty (1997): On **Benedict Juliard's** eighteenth birthday his father sends a car to **Hoopwestern, Dorset,** to take him to Exeter. From there he is taken to meet a racehorse trainer who sells him a horse, **Sarah's Future**. Benedict later studies at Exeter University.

Exeter racecourse, Devon

Formerly known as **Devon and Exeter**, the racecourse is at Haldon, seven miles south-west of Exeter, on the edge of Dartmoor. Racing began here in 1738, though a steeplechase course wasn't in place until 1898. Today the two-mile oval circuit, with its pronounced undulations, is considered a tough test. Exeter stages **National Hunt** racing only.

Bolt (1986): **Kit Fielding** wins a race at Exeter on hurdler **Bernina** for **Princess Casilia**.

10 lb. Penalty (1997): Amateur jockey **Benedict Juliard** rides his horse **Sarah's Future** to win at Exeter.

Exhibition Park (*The Edge* 1988)

Exhibition Park is a complex in Vancouver, Canada, which includes **Hastings Park racecourse**.

F

Fable (*Field of 13* 1998: "Haig's Death")

Fable is a hurdler trained by **Villiers Arkwright**. At **Winchester** races Fable is ridden in the valuable Cloister Handicap Hurdle by Villiers' brother **Vernon Arkwright**, who is more interested in preventing one of the other runners from winning than winning himself. Fable finishes unplaced.

Fahrden, K.L. (*Smokescreen* 1972)

Fahrden is stable jockey to **Greville Arnold**. He is cautious and defensive when talking to **Edward Lincoln** about **Nerissa Cavesey's** horses, and refuses to tell Edward his theory about why they are running badly.

Fairchild Smith, Mrs. (*High Stakes* 1975)

Mrs. Fairchild-Smith is an elderly lady who, with her sister **Miss Johnson**, runs Hantsford Manor, a dilapidated riding school and livery yard in **Hampshire** which also offers accommodation. The sisters look after **Black Fire** for **Steven Scott**, unwitting participants in Steven's complicated plans. **Allie Ward** stays at Hantsford Manor on the evening before the sting is put into operation, and takes Black Fire away in a horse van when Steven needs him.

Faith (*10 lb. Penalty* 1997)

Faith is a volunteer worker for **George Juliard** in the **Hoopwestern** by-election. She helps with canvassing door-to-door.

Falmouth, P.G. (*Wild Horses* 1994)

Falmouth, known as "Pig"; was stable jockey to **Jackson Wells** at Newmarket. His relationship with **Sonia**, Wells' wife, ends tragically for both of them.

Farringford, Johnny (*Trial Run* 1978)

Johnny's title is the Earl of Farringford; he is the twenty-two-year-old brother-in-law of **The Prince**, who is the Monarch's cousin. His inherited wealth is controlled by trustees until he is twenty-five. Farringford wants to buy a good horse in order to have a chance of selection for the Three Day Event team due to compete in the Moscow Olympics. However, Farringford is involved in a potential scandal, and the Prince, concerned that Farringford's indiscretions may compromise both Farringford himself and the Royal Family, asks **Randall Drew** to investigate.

Farway, Dr. Bruce (*Driving Force* 1992)

Farway is a doctor in **Pixhill**, a racing village in **Hampshire**. He has recently arrived in the village, and is considered arrogant and cold. His patronizing manner has already upset many of his patients. He considers racing a waste of time, and is unsympathetic towards injured jockeys.

Faulds, Penelope (*Decider* 1993)

Penelope is the eighteen-year-old daughter of **Stratton Park racecourse** shareholder **Perdita Faulds**. Tall, slim, and fair, Penelope strongly reminds **Lee Morris** of his wife, **Amanda Morris**, when she was young. Penelope works in one of her mother's hairdressing salons; she cuts the hair of Lee's sons when Lee goes to see her mother.

Faulds, Perdita (*Decider* 1993)

Perdita Faulds is a shareholder in **Stratton Park racecourse**. She is about sixty years old, is sensible and friendly and has an eighteen-year-old daughter, **Penelope**. Perdita had inherited her father's hairdressing businesses on the Stratton Hays estate and elsewhere. Perdita was a friend of **Lee Morris**'s mother and mistress of old Lord Stratton, who had given her the shares in the racecourse as a present.

Perdita reads in the newspapers about the grandstand being destroyed in an explosion, and goes along to the race meeting to meet Lee. She agrees with Lee that the racecourse should remain open. Having been Lord Stratton's confidante for many years, she tells Lee of various Stratton family scandals that have been hushed up.

Ferns, Linda (*Come to Grief* 1995)

Linda is the slim, pretty mother of leukemia sufferer **Rachel Ferns**, whose pony, **Silverboy**, had suffered a horrific assault. She is divorced and apparently well-off. She phones **Sid Halley** to ask for his help in finding out who had attacked the pony, because Rachel suffers from nightmares about it. She has a son, Pegotty (Peter), conceived by artificial insemination using ex-husband Joe's sperm. Linda was hoping for a tissue match so that Rachel could have a bone marrow transplant, but Pegotty doesn't match Rachel's tissue type. When Sid tells her who had injured Silverboy Linda reacts with disbelief and anger, and tells Sid to leave. Later in the week she apologizes by letter, though still insisting that Sid is mistaken. She gradually comes round to believing Sid, but doesn't tell Rachel. She phones Sid to tell him that the doctors have found a bone marrow donor for Rachel.

Ferns, Rachel (*Come to Grief* 1995)

Rachel is a nine-year-old leukemia sufferer. She has nightmares about her pony, **Silverboy**, which had been cruelly attacked. She has a baby brother, Pegotty (Peter). Rachel gets on well with **Sid Halley**; she is interested in his artificial hand. Chemotherapy had put Rachel's disease into remission but after two years it has returned. She needs a bone marrow transplant but so far the doctors have not found a tissue match. When a bone marrow donor is eventually found and Rachel is preparing for the transplant, she talks to Sid about dying, and asks him how to be brave. Sid tells her that the courage will come from within her.

Ferryboat (*High Stakes* 1975)

Ferryboat is a jumper, owned by **Steven Scott** and trained by **Jody Leeds** until transferred to **Rupert Ramsey**. During the previous season Ferryboat had won three races from seven runs. He had been given a hard race by jockey **Raymond Child** when winning his last race, which had soured him; now he is not inclined to try his best.

Ferth, Lord (*Enquiry* 1969)

Lord Wykeham, Baron Ferth, is a tall, thin, forceful man. As a disciplinary Steward of the **Jockey Club**, Ferth sits on the enquiry into the running and riding of **Squelsh** in the Lemonfizz Gold Cup at **Oxford**. Ferth is disturbed by the way that **Lord Gowery** conducts the enquiry at which trainer **Dexter Cranfield** and jockey **Kelly Hughes** lose their licenses. However, he had agreed to say nothing during proceedings.

At the Jockeys' Fund dance Ferth listens to Kelly Hughes' complaints about the enquiry He is impressed by Kelly's obvious intelligence and is astonished to hear that Kelly was educated at the London School of Economics.

After conducting his own revealing interview with Gowery, Ferth tells Kelly that his and Cranfield's licenses will be restored in a few days. Ferth wants Kelly to take his license back and keep quiet, believing that a scandal would be harmful to racing. Kelly refuses, but agrees not to call in the police to investigate an attempt on his life.

Field, Harold F. (*Field of 13* 1998: "Collision Course")

Field, a co-owner of Lionheart News Group, doesn't like his two co-owners. Arguments between them have led to financial difficulties. Field interviews editor **Bill Williams** for a post within their organization. He sees qualities in Williams that the others miss. Using wily tactics, he persuades them that Williams should be employed. At **Marlborough** races, after reading a hard-hitting article that Williams has written about **Dennis Kinser**, Field decides to give him a job as editor of one of the Group's newspapers.

Field of 13 (1998)

In 1998 Dick Francis published a collection of thirteen short stories with the title *Field of 13*. Of these, eight had been previously published in magazines or newspapers, whilst five were new. Reviews of *Field of 13* were decidedly mixed, oscillating between ecstatic and excoriating. The pendulum, in the UK at least, skewed towards the critical, with reviewers citing a lack of depth and credibility in both plotting and character development. A departure from Francis's usual modus operandi was his use of third person narrative in all thirteen stories. He is clearly much more at ease when employing the first person, as he does in his novels. Like the novels, the more successful short stories are those in which horseracing is central, rather than peripheral, to the plot. Amongst the better ones are "**Carrot for a Chestnut**," "**The Gift**" and "**Spring Fever**."

Below is a list of the thirteen stories and, where applicable, the magazine or newspaper in which they first appeared. A brief discussion of each story can be found in the individual alphabetical entries: **Raid at Kingdom Hill** (*The Times* 1975), **Dead on Red, Song for Mona, Bright White Star** (*Cheshire Life* 1979), **Collision Course, Nightmare** (*The Times* 1974), **Carrot for a Chestnut** (*Sports Illustrated* 1970), **The Gift** (*Sports Illustrated* 1973; renamed "The Day of Wine and Roses"), **Spring Fever** (*Women's Own* 1980; previously published by Faber & Faber in 1979 as "Twenty-One Good Men and True" in an anthology entitled "Verdict of 13"), **Blind Chance** (*Women's Own* 1979), **Corkscrew, The Day of the Losers** (*Horse and Hound* 1977), **Haig's Death**.

Fielder, Mr. (*Dead Cert* 1962)

In his mid-forties, Fielder is the manager of **Brighton** taxi firm **Marconicars**. He is well-dressed and impeccably groomed, but has unsmiling eyes.

Fielding, Grandfather (*Break In* 1985)

Aged eighty-two, Fielding is still training a few horses in **Newmarket**. His life-long hatred of the Allardeck family has not mellowed with age, and he has never forgiven his granddaughter **Holly Allardeck** for marrying **Bobby Allardeck**. He had brought up Holly and her twin brother, **Kit Fielding**, after their parents were killed in a skiing accident.

Stubborn and awkward, Grandfather Fielding is a perfectionist who has never learned to accept that those around him are never likely to live up to his impossibly high standard; as a result, irritation is his normal state of mind.

Fielding, Kit

Break In (1985): Twins Kit Fielding and **Holly Allardeck** (née Fielding) were still in diapers when their parents were killed in a skiing accident. Their father's parents, who trained racehorses in **Newmarket**, had brought them up. Even for twins they were unusually close; they had spoken to each other in a private language, and developed a telepathic understanding which allowed each to know what the other was thinking. They were aware, when apart, when the other was in danger or difficulty.

At the age of thirty Kit is leading an enviable, action-man lifestyle. His ruggedly handsome features have avoided the involuntary rearrangement that his profession—steeplechase jockey—so often bestows. Currently champion jockey, Kit is at the pinnacle of his career, though he is not spared the bane of a jockey's life, the never-ending battle to control his weight.

Holly meanwhile had, in the eyes of her grandparents, committed an unutterable crime in marrying **Bobby Allardeck**, a young **Newmarket** trainer. Since the reign of Charles II in the seventeenth century a bitter feud had raged between the Fieldings and the Allardecks which, despite the union of Holly and Bobby, showed no sign of abating. For Holly's sake, Kit does his best to be polite to Bobby. He has to put up with larger doses of Bobby's company than he would prefer when Holly, worried about malicious press reports concerning Bobby's training business, seeks his help.

Kit had given up a university place to study veterinary science in order to become a professional jockey. There are strong echoes of Francis's own childhood in Kit's explanation: "I was born to it ... I can't remember not being able to ride." The same quote is used to explain Francis's subsequent career in the saddle in the preface to many of his early novels. As for Kit, being a jockey is what he loves most. He knows that one day he'll be expected to take over from his grandfather and train at Newmarket, but he desperately wants to keep riding for another four or five years.

He dreads his grandfather, now in his early eighties, dying or having to give up through ill health before he, Kit, is ready. Kit's main employer, trainer **Wykeham Harlow**, is almost as old as his grandfather, and his close contact with the pair has given Kit a perspective on racing's place in history: "I was coming to see the whole of racing as a sort of stream that rolled onwards through time..."

Up till now Kit's romantic life has consisted of a few casual liaisons that were never going to go anywhere because of his love for his twin sister. He adds, for the sake of propriety, that he hadn't wanted to marry Holly or to sleep with her. Then he meets **Danielle de Brescou**, the American niece of **Princess Casilia**, and he soon realizes that she is different from his previous girlfriends. He invites Danielle to visit the house which he's currently having built in **Lambourn**. There, lying on dust sheets on the floor, they make love.

Considerably less cordial is Kit's relationship with brother-in-law Bobby, who finds the burden of past enmities difficult to shed despite Kit's willingness to help Bobby combat those who bear him ill-will. At one point Bobby turns on Kit with all the hatred that Allardecks had had for Fieldings for centuries. Kit, though, refuses to fight with Bobby. Later, when Bobby has calmed down, he tells him, "What I fight is being brainwashed. Why should we still jump to that old hate?"

After Kit galvanizes a horse to win narrowly at **Ascot**, the owner comments, "You're a bloody demon, lad ... hard as bloody nails." He has to be, because Bobby's enemies are playing dirty and see Kit as an obstacle that needs to be removed. So does Bobby's father **Maynard Allardeck**, a wealthy, unscrupulous businessman who hates all Fieldings with a passion. He urges Bobby to shoot Kit, who is afraid but calmly turns his back on Bobby. At the moment he thinks he is going to die, Kit thinks of Danielle; and Danielle, fifty miles away, is instantly aware that Kit is in danger. Bobby, though sorely tempted to kill Kit, has the sense to resist.

Bolt (1986): Apart from **Sid Halley**, Kit Fielding is the only protagonist to appear in more than one novel. In *Bolt*, Kit is engaged to be married to Danielle de Brescou, but he is having doubts about Danielle's commitment to their relationship, and about his own ability to provide her with what he thinks she needs. Kit leads a hectic life as a jump jockey; Danielle's interests are music, art and literature. Kit worries that he is not sufficiently cerebral for her and is alarmed at the amount of time she is spending with Princess Casilia's nephew, the urbane **Prince Litsi**.

Kit's unhappiness affects the way he rides, and he starts taking unnecessary risks in his races. Trainer Wykeham Harlow is annoyed when Kit gives Princess Casilia's horse **Cascade** a particularly hard ride to win at **Newbury**. Kit's implacable enemy, Maynard Allardeck, is stewarding at the meeting and tries to get Kit suspended for improper use of the whip, but there are no marks on Cascade.

Kit temporarily forgets his own troubles when Princess Casilia is physically threatened by her husband's business partner, **Henri Nanterre**, who wants to change fundamentally the nature of their construction company. Kit agrees to help the Princess resist Nanterre's pressure.

Danielle's return from a trip to the **Lake District** with Prince Litsi serves only to renew Kit's anxieties about her feelings for him. Her greeting is more sisterly than passionate, and Kit has to confront the unpalatable possibility that he is losing her.

When Kit's uncertainty finally compels him to have it out with Danielle, her explanation is not what he had expected. Danielle tells him that she lives in constant fear that Kit is going to be killed or maimed. With Litsi, she says, she at least feels calm and safe.

Kit's understanding of Danielle's misgivings is deepened when he narrowly escapes serious injury in a fall at **Sandown Park**. For Kit, though, falls are an inevitable consequence of doing a job he loves, and he thinks of them as no more than a minor inconvenience. Kit's insouciance angers Danielle; his lack of fear for his own safety somehow mocks her own fear for him. But Danielle has grown to realize that she would rather be with Kit, fear and all, than without him. When she tells Kit that she'll marry him, he's overjoyed.

His romantic difficulties settled, Kit throws all his energies into dealing with Henri Nanterre. His ongoing problem with Maynard Allardeck, whose cordial hatred of Kit threatens to unhinge him completely, is resolved in a bizarre and unexpected way. Kit feels that, finally, the feud between the Fieldings and the Allardecks may be over.

Filmer, Julius Apollo (*The Edge* 1988)

From a wealthy criminal family based on the Isle of Man off the north-west coast of England,

Filmer is a racehorse owner who prefers to succeed in the racing world by illegal means. For years the **Jockey Club** has been trying unsuccessfully to gather enough evidence against Filmer to warn him off. Filmer had been tried on a charge of conspiracy to murder but was acquitted.

The Canadian Jockey Club's suspicions are aroused when Filmer books a place on the Transcontinental Mystery Race Train, a trip designed for wealthy racehorse owners to run their horses at racetracks across Canada, and featuring an on-board entertainment in which actors would stage a mystery involving the passengers.

The journey across Canada is interrupted by a succession of criminal acts, including sabotage, intimidation and blackmail. Filmer's involvement is closely monitored by **Tor Kelsey**, a **Jockey Club** investigator working as a waiter on the train.

Tor uses the mystery murder play which has been enacted each day to give Filmer a taste of his own medicine. Filmer is horrified when the plot of the play mirrors his own criminal activity. He is confident, however, that none of the disruption to the train's schedule can be traced back to him. He goes to **Hastings Park racecourse**, Vancouver, to collect the paperwork for transferring ownership of a horse he has acquired by dubious means. Instead he finds a welcoming committee, comprising the Directors of Security of the English and Canadian Jockey Clubs, Tor Kelsey and members of the Vancouver Jockey Club. Confronted with evidence of his wrongdoing that Tor has collected, Filmer reacts furiously, knowing that a jail term is inevitable.

Finch, Desmond (*To the Hilt* 1996)

Finch is second-in-command to **Sir Ivan Westering** at the **King Alfred Brewery**. He is an energetic fifty-year-old who, according to **Tobias Tollright**, is an efficient executive but not a decision-maker. Finch is furious that power of attorney has been given to **Alex Kinloch**. He bursts into a meeting between Alex and the insolvency practitioner, **Mrs. Morden** and demands, unsuccessfully, that Alex leave. He says he is the acting managing director of the brewery and in charge of the brewery's affairs, a claim at which Mrs. Morden demurs. He tears up the power of attorney document. He is motivated partly by **Patsy Benchmark**'s assertion that Alex is after Sir Ivan's fortune.

Finch, Jossie (*Risk* 1977)

Jossie is the pretty daughter of racehorse trainer **William Finch**. She is sensible, amusing and competent. She goes to **Towcester** races with **Notebook**, a horse that **Roland Britten** is going to ride for her father. Jossie teases Roland when he is unseated by Notebook. She tells Roland over dinner that she hasn't seen her mother, an anthropologist, for years. She dislikes her father's girlfriend, **Lida**.

Jossie goes to the **Isle of Wight** with Roland when he goes to see boat builder **Johnnie Frederick**; on their return to her house she sees Lida's car outside and complains that she might soon be moving into her home. Roland invites her to move in with him, taking her by surprise. Jossie, however, doesn't commit herself.

When her father decamps to France Jossie is annoyed that he had taken Lida with him instead of her.

Finch, William (*Risk* 1977)

Tall, authoritative and around fifty years old, Finch is a top racehorse trainer with ninety horses, flat and jumping, housed in a luxury stable complex near **Newbury, Berkshire**. Years of success and the respect of his peers have given Finch an appearance of wealth and stature, but it is only a veneer: **Axwood Stables** belong not to him but to his principal employers, the American **Nantucket** family, whose horses he trains. He is their paid employee, and as such is never going to make the kind of money he feels is his due. Unable to build-up the capital he wants legally, Finch turns to crime to achieve his ends.

Discovering that accountant **Roland Britten** is about to inspect the Axwood Stables accounts, Finch adopts desperate measures to prevent him doing so. When, finally, Finch realizes that the game is up, he absconds to France.

Fingall, Jamie (*Bolt* 1986)

Jump jockey Jamie Fingall is a colleague of **Kit Fielding**: he rides for **Lambourn** trainer **Basil Clutter**. He tells Kit that **Henri Nanterre** owns horses in France, but otherwise knows nothing about him.

Finland, Jamie (*Field of 13* 1998: "Blind Chance")

Jamie Finland is a fifteen-year-old blind boy who lives with his mother near **Ascot racecourse**. His hobby is listening to local radio broadcasts from aircraft and police. One day, while listening to Ascot races on TV, he hears a number on the radio minutes before the horse of the same number is announced the winner of a photo-finish. When this happens again at the next meeting, Jamie realizes that he is privy to valuable information. He gets his mother to set up a credit account at the local bookmakers. The next time he hears a number while waiting for the result of a photo-finish at Ascot he backs the horse, which wins. Later in the afternoon he repeats the winning formula.

Finn, Caspar (*Nerve* 1964)

A world-renowned oboist, Caspar Finn is **Rob Finn**'s father. He treats Rob with polite friendliness but has no real interest in him or his career.

Finn, Rob (*Nerve* 1964)

National Hunt jockey Rob Finn is not the son his parents wanted. For two professional musicians to produce a tone-deaf son who would have struggled to hold down a place as triangle player in the school band is, to them, ignominious. Accordingly, Rob is dispatched to boarding school as soon as is decent. During the holidays he finds himself exiled to a farm in the country where he learns to ride. When he chooses to make riding horses his career, his parents are unimpressed but, with their own musical commitments paramount, they shrug their shoulders and let him get on with it.

Rob decamps to Australia and South America, where he works in rodeos and as a stockman. On his return to England he begins to ride in jump races, where he finds total fulfillment. His love life doesn't go quite so smoothly. He only has eyes for his cousin, **Joanna**, whom he loves unreservedly. Joanna, unfortunately, has grave reservations about getting involved with a blood relation.

Rob attracts media attention in the form of **Maurice Kemp-Lore**, who invites Rob onto his popular TV racing show. Kemp-Lore, from a well-known racing family but unable to ride owing to an allergy to horses, is keen to portray Rob as a "fringe" jockey who is struggling to make a living riding bad horses around the smaller tracks. Rob doesn't quite fit the bill; since accepting Kemp-Lore's offer he's ridden a few winners and has just been appointed second jockey to a successful stable. On the show Rob surprises Kemp-Lore, first when revealing his unusual background and then by his impassioned defense of race-riding for its own sake: "I don't care if I don't earn much money, or if I break my bones, or if I have to starve to keep my weight down. All I care about is racing ... and winning, if I can."

But following his TV appearance, winning becomes a foreign land as far as Rob's concerned. Every horse he rides runs like it's carrying a sumo wrestler, and Rob is so devoid of luck that he couldn't have ridden the winner of a walkover. As his losing run lengthens, the rumors gather momentum that Rob has lost his nerve. This sometimes happens to jump jockeys nearing the end of their career whose battered bodies have endured one fall too many, but rarely to young, fit men like Rob.

The public perception of Rob as a coward is almost too much for him to bear, but he clings to the certainty that his nerve is intact and he resolves to find out who is spreading the lie, and why. At **Stratford** races he gives a ride to a novice chaser that proves beyond any doubt his physical courage. As he delves deeper into the reasons for his persecution and comes closer to the truth, Rob needs to draw on every ounce of that courage.

Through all Rob's tribulations Joanna is in the background offering support, and the physical agonies he endures are matched by the emotional torment caused by Joanna's steadfast refusal to treat him as anything other than a favorite cousin. But Rob doesn't give up easily; by the time he has the man who had tried to ruin his life backed into a corner, he has also managed to persuade Joanna that suspicions of incest should not obstruct the path of true love.

Finnegan, Dermot (*Forfeit* 1968)

Irish jockey Dermot Finnegan rides mostly no-hopers and is content with his extremely moderate success rate. He is unambitious, except for a desire to have a ride in the Grand National. Given a chance on **Rockville**, his trainer's first string in the Lamplighter Gold Cup at **Heathbury Park**, Finnegan rides like a demon to win the race.

Finse, Norway

Finse is the highest village on the railway line connecting Bergen and Oslo. It has one hotel, a railway station and not much else. Finse is on the highland plateau of Hardangervidda, which separates Norway into western and eastern regions. It has snow for eight months of the year.

Slay-Ride (1973): **David Cleveland** travels by train to Finse, where he believes that **Per Bjorn Sandvik**'s son, **Mikkel Sandvik**, has gone to stay with his father's old nurse **Berit**.

Fisher, Val (*Banker* 1982)

Fisher is Head of Banking at merchant bank **Paul Ekaterin Ltd**. He is a smooth operator and good at his job. When **Tim Ekaterin** consults him about possibly loaning money to a cartoonist, Fisher has a word with chairman **Henry Shipton**, and then tells Tim that the decision is his alone. Fisher receives a request from stud owner **Oliver Knowles** to borrow several million pounds to buy the racehorse **Sandcastle**; he asks Tim to look into it.

Fitzwalter (*Comeback* 1991)

Fitzwalter, a scrap metal merchant, is the owner-trainer of a horse that had died unexpectedly after being treated by veterinary surgeon **Ken McClure**. According to McClure, Fitzwalter had accepted the horse's death philosophically and assured McClure that he would still use the veterinary practice. However, Fitzwalter is by no means as good-natured as he appears to be.

Fleet Street, London

Named after the River Fleet, a tributary of the Thames which flows beneath London's streets, Fleet Street was until the 1980's the home of Britain's national daily and Sunday newspapers. From 1500, when an assistant of William Caxton set up his printing presses in Fleet Street, many of London's writers and playwrights frequented the local taverns, including William Shakespeare, Ben Johnson and Samuel Pepys. In 1702 *The Daily Courant*, the first newspaper, was published in Fleet Street, and for the next 380 years the street was the centre of the publishing industry. But by 1985 News International, publishers of *The Times*, had become frustrated by the restrictive practices of the print unions, and decided to transfer production to Wapping, East London. One by one every other publisher followed suit, and today not a single newspaper business remains in Fleet Street.

Forfeit (1968): **James Tyrone** is an investigative racing reporter on the *Sunday Blaze*, whose offices are in Fleet Street.

Fletcher (*Dead Cert* 1962)

Fletcher is the driver of the horse van used to trap **Alan York** on the Maidenhead road; he is a taxi-driver employed by **Marconicars** of **Brighton**.

Flokati (*The Edge* 1988)

Flokati, an American racehorse on board the Great Transcontinental Mystery Race Train, runs unplaced in the Jockey Club Racetrain Stakes at **Assiniboia Downs, Winnipeg**.

Florida Everglades

The Florida Everglades are an area of subtropical marshland extending from Lake Okeechobee in the north to Florida Bay in the south. The Everglades National Park, preserving the southern section of the Everglades, covers 1.5 million acres. About half of the original Everglades has been lost to agriculture.

Second Wind (1999): Unified Trader **Michael Ford** shoots an intruder at his home. The bullet matches one found in a corpse in the Everglades.

Floyd, Yvonne (*Comeback* 1991)

Floyd is a partner in Hewett and Partners, veterinary surgeons of Cheltenham, **Gloucestershire**. A small animal specialist, Floyd is about thirty years old, and married with two step-children. One morning she finds a body in the operating theatre; the shock makes her vomit.

Flying Finish (1966)

Lord Henry Gray arrives one Monday morning at his boring, unloved job at the London-based **Anglia Bloodstock Agency**, brooding on his sister's description of him as a "spoilt, bad-tempered bastard." Contacting **Yardman** Transport to arrange the shipment of four yearlings to Argentina, Henry finds that a delay is likely; **Peters**, their travelling head groom has, without explanation, failed to return from his last trip.

In turmoil inside, and smarting at his elderly mother's attempts at matchmaking on his behalf, Henry goes for lunch and does not go back to Anglia Bloodstock afterwards. Instead he goes to Yardman Transport and talks himself, despite Yardman's reluctance, into Peters' job. Three weeks later he flies his first consignment of horses to Argentina. Despite his family's disapproval, Henry at first enjoys his new job, which still allows him time to ride as an amateur jockey.

On a trip to Paris, however, a member of his team of grooms called **Billy Watkins**, who is a replacement for a groom on leave, is overtly antagonistic towards Henry. Over the next few weeks a pattern of intimidation and violence by Watkins causes Henry serious problems. The one bright spot is when, on a stopover in Milan, Henry meets an Italian girl, **Gabriella**. She works at the airport and is involved in the smuggling of birth control pills into Italy, where their use is illegal. Using

French as a common language Henry and Gabriella talk for hours, falling in love straight away. When snow at **Gatwick** airport delays Henry in Milan for an extra day, he and Gabriella make love in the airplane.

Already suspecting that something illegal is going on within Yardman Transport, Henry has further cause for concern when a colleague goes missing after a flight to Milan. The stakes are raised again when an attempt is made on Gabriella's life. By now Henry has discovered that horses are not the only commodity that Yardman transports, but it is clear that Watkins is not going to allow Henry to live long enough to divulge this information. Watkins, though, has seriously underestimated Henry.

Though elements of the plot of *Flying Finish* inevitably have a dated feel to them today, they accurately reflect the social and political conditions of Europe in the 1960's. Then, birth control pills were a relatively recent medical advance, and in a staunchly Catholic country like Italy, there was no possibility of obtaining them legally. Yet many young Italian women were questioning the strict codes of morality that they had increasingly come to see as an infringement of their rights as individuals.

Politically, the Cold War was at its height; the capitalist countries of Western Europe viewed the Communist bloc with deep distrust, while the people of Soviet-controlled countries behind the Iron Curtain were prevented from traveling to the West in case they were seduced by its false gods. Against that background, intelligence gathering was conducted on both sides by a network of spies and agents, and there were instances of minor government officials or civil servants going over to the enemy.

The sexual attraction between Henry and Gabriella is immediate and powerful. Gabriella's role in the plot allows the reader to care what happens to her and to sympathize with the depths of Henry's devastation when she is the victim of violence. Though Francis suggests that Gabriella survives we are told no more about her. This is a weakness; as readers we don't want to choose the ending. We want to know what happened.

Flynn, David (*The Edge* 1988)

Flynn is an actor on board the Great Transcontinental Mystery Race Train. In the mystery play he is **Zac**, an investigator. He gives **Tor Kelsey** the name "Tommy" to use while he is pretending to

be a waiter. Flynn writes all the plays for travel company **Merry & Co.**'s trips which have a mystery element included. When he has a problem with the plot of the mystery owing to an injury to an actor, he is happy to accept Tor's idea for a solution; it works well, and he asks Tor to think up more ideas for the plot. When Flynn realizes that Tor is using the script to provoke a reaction from certain people on the train, he is concerned that the actors may be sued for slander.

Folk, Jeremy (*Reflex* 1980)

Folk is a young solicitor from the firm of Folk, Langley, Son and Folk, **St Albans, Hertfordshire**. Physically Folk is tall and thin; in character he is unassertive but persistent. Folk is sent to **Sandown Park** to speak to jockey **Philip Nore**; he is acting on behalf of Philip's grandmother, whom Philip has never met. Folk tells Philip his grandmother is dying and wants to see him; Philip is reluctant but Folk perseveres until Philip agrees.

Folk comes to see Philip at his home in **Lambourn** to persuade him to look for his half-sister, **Amanda Nore**. Later, at **Kempton Park** races, he tells Philip that his grandmother will tell him who his father is if looks for Amanda.

At Philip's house Folk suffers serious harm when he is the victim of an insidious attack meant for Philip. Though critically ill, Folk gradually recovers.

Folkestone racecourse

When racing began at Westenhanger Park, four miles from Folkestone, Kent, in 1898, there was speculation in the local press that, since it was the nearest racecourse to France, it might attract the French aristocracy in considerable numbers. Such optimism was ill-founded. In his book *Chasing Around Britain* John Tyrrel wryly comments that "not even Horatio Nelson could have spotted a Frenchman in the grandstand."

If Folkestone racecourse did not exactly thrive, at least it survived. Dick Francis rode many winners at the track, mostly for Queen Elizabeth the Queen Mother's trainer, Peter Cazalet. Today the racing is of modest quality and, up to a few years ago, the facilities were dire. Recently, though, the track's owners have invested money in upgrading bars and restaurants, and in generally giving the place a facelift. Reporting for *The Times* newspaper in 2003, racing journalist Alan Lee offered cautious praise: "Suddenly, it is not a place a man would be ashamed to bring a woman."

Rat Race **(1970):** Flat jockey **Colin Ross** cancels his flight to Folkestone racecourse with **Derrydown**, his usual air-taxi firm, and flies with rivals **Polyplane** instead.

Bolt **(1986):** Champion steeplechase jockey **Kit Fielding** is at Folkestone when he is given information as to the whereabouts of Frenchman **Henri Nanterre** on the night that **Princess Casilia's** horse, **Col**, was deliberately killed.

Fontwell Park racecourse

Fontwell Park is located on the **Sussex** downs, between Arundel and Chichester. It was once part of the gallops used by trainer Alfred Day, who designed the figure-of-eight steeplechase course which opened in 1924. The fixture was popular from the start, and continues today to have an elegant, rustic charm that is quintessentially English, though the standard of racing is moderate.

Trial Run **(1978):** Amateur jockey **Randall Drew** meets the **Prince** and the Prince's brother-in-law, **Johnny Farringford**, for lunch at Fontwell Park.

For Kicks (1965)

While visiting racing and breeding centers in Australia, **National Hunt Committee** member **Lord October** visits **Daniel Roke's** stud farm. He'd heard about an English groom there who was homesick, and thinks that he might be able to recruit him to help investigate a serious problem of horses that are apparently being doped. The groom turns out to be unsuitable for undercover work, but October sees immediately that Daniel himself would be ideal. Since the death of his parents in an accident nine years before, Daniel has worked without a break to pay for the education of his brother and two sisters. He feels trapped by his responsibilities, and the opportunity to do something different, together with the offer of a large sum of money, is too tempting to ignore.

Once in England, Daniel goes undercover, pretending to be a shifty and unreliable groom. A malicious and untrue accusation of sexual assault besmirches Daniel's reputation even further.

Through intense study of the form of the doped horses James establishes a common thread linking several of them, at some point in their miserable lives, to a racing stable in the north of England. Taking a job there, James comes into contact with men whose ruthlessness, immorality and cruelty to horses know no bounds. In confronting these men Daniel is all too aware of the risks to his own life. What he hasn't bargained for is the danger that an innocent girl will face through her friendship with him.

Graham Lord, in *Dick Francis: A Racing Life*, tells us that Francis was watching dog trials before the races at Cartmel, in the north-west of England, and saw the shepherds using whistles, whose frequency the sheep collies could hear but which to humans were silent. Testing out a dog whistle on his own ponies at home, he found that they responded to it, and the plot of *For Kicks* was hatched.

Daniel Roke has many of the qualities that define the Francis hero; he is self-effacing, equable, courageous, and motivated by a desire to do the decent thing. In *For Kicks*, his third novel, Francis begins to explore a dimension which he develops in his main characters through the 1960's, largely abandons during the 1970's and returns to in the early 80's: the difficulties in their personal circumstances that color their views, affect their decisions, or alter their lives altogether. For Daniel, it is his feelings of entrapment in a way of life offering no mental stimulation which cause him to leave his stud farm for an alternative that promises only discomfort, danger or worse.

Another strand of characterization which is strong in *For Kicks* and is a notable element in many of the later books is the brutal side of human nature. The quasi-psychopathic addiction to cruelty of the principal villain is graphically described, as is his violent death. He represents an embodiment of the evil tendencies of the human psyche, and is thus a worthy foe for the protagonist to strive against.

Force, Dr. Adam (*Shattered* 2000)

Force is middle-aged, well-groomed and cultivated, with a track record of outstanding medical research behind him. He is also unscrupulous and dishonest. After being caught selling medical information to a middleman, he is initially allowed to keep his job. When he attempts to sell confidential data on his latest research project, he is sacked. This data Force has recorded on videotape; when it goes missing Force is desperate to get it back. He enlists the aid of a bunch of dubious friends, most of whom are associated with the racecourse bookmaking firm **Arthur Robins**. Their efforts, bordering on farce at times, do not meet with success, and Force's misdeeds finally catch up with him.

Ford, Amy (*Second Wind* 1999)

The wife of **Michael Ford**, Amy lives on **Grand Cayman Island**. She sells her private plane to **Robin Darcy** for **Kris Ironside** and **Perry Stuart** to use. Amy had owned a chain of video stores in the USA. Now she is one of the **Unified Traders** who buy and sell radioactive material. On her husband's behalf, she returns the lists of client contacts to the safe on **Trox Island**. When Perry returns to Robin Darcy's house to confront him about his activities, Amy encourages Michael to assault Perry.

She claims in court that Trox Island is her property; she says she is experimenting with improved pasteurization techniques on a herd of cows. Her claim, however, is unsuccessful.

Ford, Bonnington (*Reflex* 1980)

Ford is an ungifted and dishonest racehorse trainer. He is the subject of blackmail for having a warned-off person at his training stables, in contravention of **Jockey Club** regulations.

Ford, Michael (*Second Wind* 1999)

Originally from **Berkshire**, England, Ford is a resident of **Grand Cayman Island** who had worked in the gymnasium business in the USA. He is short in stature but powerfully built. According to **Perry Stuart**, Ford and his wife Amy, though outwardly sociable, are practiced liars.

Ford, together with his wife, is a **Unified Trader**, dealing in radioactive material. At **Robin Darcy's** house Ford physically attacks Perry. The police are called; when they arrive Ford claims it was only a game, and the police don't take the matter any further. Subsequently Ford shoots an intruder at his house; the bullet is found to be identical with one used in a previous fatal shooting.

Fordham, Mary-Lou (*Dead Heat* 2007)

Mary-Lou Fordham works as a marketing executive for **Delafield Industries Inc.** of Wisconsin. She arranges for chef **Max Moreton** to provide dinner for the company's guests at **Newmarket racecourse** on the night before the Two Thousand Guineas, and lunch on the day of the race. She is rather bossy in her dealings with Max, but deferential towards her boss, **Rolf Schumann**. When a bomb explodes in the Grandstand boxes during the running of the Guineas, Mary-Lou loses both her legs.

Forfeit (1968)

James Tyrone, investigative racing reporter on Fleet Street's *Sunday Blaze*, is offered the chance to write a freelance magazine article on the forthcoming Lamplighter Gold Cup Steeplechase at **Heathbury Park**. Later that day James chats in a pub with **Bert Checkov**, a drunken old newspaperman. Checkov gives James some puzzling advice, the significance of which does not become clear to James until later. Checkov returns to his office on the seventeenth floor, staggers against the window and falls out, killing himself on the street below.

In the course of researching his article James interviews the **Huntersons**, racehorse owners whose stunning niece **Gail Pominga** immediately makes it clear that she fancies James. Left alone together, they make love. Afterwards James is wracked with guilt for betraying his wife, **Elizabeth Tyrone**, who is almost totally paralyzed after contracting polio and requires twenty-four hour care.

James discovers that Checkov had often tipped horses in his racing column that had been heavily backed in the ante-post market but subsequently declared non-runners; as a result the backers had lost their money without even getting a run. James is determined to ensure that **Tiddely-Pom**, favorite for the Lamplighter Gold Cup, arrives safely at the post. It soon becomes clear that others are equally determined to prevent the horse's participation. The result, for both James and Elizabeth, is terrifying and ultimately life-threatening.

In *Forfeit* James Tyrone's relationship with his polio-stricken wife is crucial. Criminals try to use James's infidelity to exert pressure on him; when that fails they attempt a more direct line of attack by putting Elizabeth's life in jeopardy. Elizabeth's helplessness whilst being used as a pawn is touching; her fear of losing her main carer is greater than her hurt at James's sexual betrayal. In her miserable situation—not uncommon in Britain before the polio vaccine was universally available—a secure and happy relationship is more a luxury than a priority. As for James Tyrone, he is a man who is not wholly good, and it is his humanity that lends credibility to the depiction of his character.

Forfeit provides evidence of Francis's skill in depicting scenes of violent confrontation. He has been criticized for his graphic portrayal of violence, but this is one of his strengths as a crime writer. The infliction of pain, whether gratuitous or for a purpose, is something that criminals do, and Francis's books merely reflect this.

Many of Francis's novels contain autobiographical elements, a fact that he has readily acknowledged. In *Forfeit* Francis used his own wife's experiences as a polio sufferer—though Mary's affliction was of a comparatively minor nature—to color his depiction of Elizabeth Tyrone. He also drew on his own work as a columnist for the *Sunday Express* to describe the routines of a racing journalist's life.

Forlorn Hope (*Dead Cert* 1962)

Forlorn Hope is a five-year-old, strongly-built brown gelding, owned and ridden by **Alan York** and trained by **Pete Gregory**. A novice hurdler, he is inexperienced and very green when sixth at **Plumpton**. Alan is riding Forlorn Hope in a race at **Maidenhead** when rival jockey **Sandy Mason** tries to put Alan over the rails.

Fornebu, Norway

Fornebu is a peninsular area in the suburban municipality of Bærum, close to Oslo. Fornebu was the site of Oslo's main airport until 1998, when it was moved inland to Gardermoen. Today Fornebu is a centre for information technology and the telecommunications industry.

Slay-Ride (1973): Oslo policeman **Knut** plants a drilling chart in a locker at Fornebu airport; the man who comes to collect it is arrested.

Fotherton (*Odds Against* 1965)

Fotherton is Clerk of the Course at **Seabury racecourse**. He is also in charge at **Bristol**, a much more successful course and in the city where Fotherton lives; for that reason he doesn't give Seabury the attention it requires. After **Sid Halley** foils an attempt to sabotage Seabury, Fotherton asks Sid if he'd be interested in becoming Clerk of the Course. Sid asks for time to think it over.

Fox, Norton (*Forfeit* 1968)

Fox is a racehorse trainer based in **Berkshire**. He trains **Zig Zag**, an entry for the Lamplighter Gold Cup at **Heathbury Park**. He was furious when, eight months previously, an owner had withdrawn **Brevity**, ante-post favorite for the Champion Hurdle at **Cheltenham**, without his knowledge two days before the race. Fox had told the owner to take his horses away.

Fox willingly agrees to train **Tiddely Pom** during the week before the Lamplighter. Only he and **James Tyrone** knew the horse's real identity. When Tiddely Pom develops violent colic Fox, unable to contact anyone at the *Sunday Blaze*, phones **Victor Roncey**, who tells his son **Pat Roncey** where the horse is. When James insists that Tiddely Pom must be moved again Fox is not happy but loans James a horse van. He is even less happy when he is told by the police that the van has been involved in a crash, but calms down when he learns the circumstances.

Foxhill, Wiltshire

Foxhill is a village in the county of **Wiltshire**, west of London.

To the Hilt (1996): Alexander Kinloch rides **Sir Ivan Westering's** chaser **Golden Malt** along the **Ridgeway** to a livery yard at Foxhill.

Franklin, Derek (*Straight* 1989)

A trait that many of Francis's heroes share is a temperament that is almost unnaturally equable. Neither verbal abuse nor physical indignity seems to ignite their wrath, and they have a biblical ability to turn the other cheek. In this respect, ex-champion jump jockey Derek Franklin is a refreshing change. Derek swears, and means it. No tongues are bitten—metaphorically at least—when his dead brother's lover hits him with a cosh. "Bitch!" he exclaims, and contained in that word is a wealth of pain and anger.

Nor is Derek conciliatory in the face of doubts on the part of his dead brother's former employees that a mere jockey can keep his gemstone business going: if he doesn't run the business, he tells them bluntly, they can kiss goodbye to their jobs. Derek's relations with the trainers who employ him are not always cordial either; he freely admits to the odd yelling match.

This all adds massively to Derek's credibility. In most other ways, he conforms to type: mid-thirties, unmarried, lean, dark hair, good teeth, parents dead—not of misadventure, merely old age. They'd had Derek late in life, and after his mother died, Derek had lived with his aged father "in tolerant mutual non-comprehension." One of the things that Derek's dad had failed to comprehend was why, after taking a degree at **Lancaster** University, he had abandoned academia completely and taken paid employment in a racing stable. Discovering an inborn talent for race-riding, Derek's hard work and single-minded determination pay dividends when he eventually tops the list of winning jockeys. His philosophy—and here we recognize the authentic voice of Francis himself—is simple: "I rode races, as every jump jockey did, from a different impetus than making money, though the money was nice enough and thoroughly earned besides." It may be more than coincidence that Derek shares the same initials as the writer.

Derek isn't earning any riding fees at the moment, though. Nearing the end of his career and no longer champion jockey, he's on crutches nursing an ankle injury when he receives bad news. Brother **Greville**, nineteen years older than Derek, has been critically injured by falling scaffolding in **Ipswich**. Derek makes the journey from his home in Hungerford, **Berkshire**, to find Greville brain dead, and his permission requested by the doctors to switch off the life support machine. Shocked and depressed, Derek is just leaving the hospital when he is attacked and a bag containing Greville's clothes is stolen.

Owing to the age difference between them Derek and Greville had not been particularly close but, reading Greville's diary, in which he has chronicled Derek's victory in a **Cheltenham** Gold Cup, Derek feels his loss acutely and wishes that he had known Greville better.

Derek learns that Greville has recently borrowed $1½ million to buy diamonds, the whereabouts of which are unknown. Greville's racing interests—he had two horses in training in his company's name—are no more straightforward: Derek suspects that the trainer, **Nicholas Loder**, has been cheating with the horses.

At his brother's funeral, Derek is acutely aware of how he now seems to be living Greville's life rather than his own. The feeling of filling Greville's shoes extends even to his dead brother's love life. Derek had met **Clarissa Williams**, Greville's lover, in painful circumstances. Finding Derek in Greville's home and thinking him a burglar, she had whacked him with a cosh. A few days later, at **York** races, Derek is astonished to meet Clarissa again, this time as **Lady Knightwood**, the youngish wife of an elderly peer. She tells Derek that she'd known he'd be at the races, and Derek immediately knows why she's come. He warns her not to think of him as Greville.

Clarissa acknowledges the truth in Derek's words, but tells him that to be near him gives her comfort. Derek recognizes an odd kind of bond between them, and doesn't actively discourage it. His acquiescence, ultimately, leads to their making love in Greville's flat.

Trying to unravel the complex threads of Greville's life proves not only difficult for Derek, but also bad for his health. Twice villains try to murder him; on the second occasion Derek fights back desperately, using his crutches as a weapon, but it is only the arrival of Clarissa with her trusty cosh that saves the day. Eventually a fortuitous discovery brings Derek's tribulations to a satisfactory conclusion.

Franklin, Greville Saxony (*Straight* 1989)

Greville is the elder brother, by nineteen years, of **Derek Franklin**. He is walking along a street in **Ipswich** when scaffolding falls on his head, leaving him critically injured. The next day, with Derek's permission, Greville's life support machine is switched off. Greville and Derek had not been close until an unplanned meeting, when Derek was almost thirty years old, had strengthened their relationship. Greville had been brought up in a grand house on a large estate managed by his father. Greville himself owned a firm, **Saxony Franklin**, which imported and sold semi-precious stones. A pillar of the community, Greville served as a Justice of the Peace and owned racehorses. He was a private person, considered exceptionally clever by those who knew him. His hobby was collecting gadgets of all sorts. In his will he left everything to Derek.

Greville had borrowed $1½ million to buy diamonds; tracing the whereabouts of these precious stones proves problematic for Derek. Greville had a lover, **Clarissa Williams**, who is the wife of **Lord Knightwood**.

Fraser Canyon, Canada

Fraser Canyon, in British Columbia, is a series of gorges in the Coast Mountains where the Fraser River passes from the interior plateau of British Columbia to the Fraser Valley. The Canadian National and Pacific railways, and the Trans-Canada Highway, trace a route across the Canyon's rock faces by means of tunnels, bridges and trestles.

The Edge (1988): As the Great Transcontinental Mystery Race Train passes through Fraser Canyon, **Sheridan Lorrimore** falls to his death from the rear platform of his family's private car into the Fraser River one hundred feet below.

Fraud

After murder, attempted murder and violent assaults, the crime that is perpetrated most often in Francis's novels is fraud, in all its ingenious manifestations. In *Under Orders* (2006), a jockey is involved in race fixing, an issue which in Britain has recently exercised the collective mind of the Horseracing Regulatory Authority. In December 2007 a high-profile case heard in the High Court and involving ex-champion flat jockey Kieron Fallon was thrown out due to lack of hard evidence. Nevertheless, stopping horses from winning is a common fraud on the betting public which has gone on since horseracing began, and is a crime that Francis explores in several novels and short stories. In *Dead Cert* (1962) a villain runs an off-course bookmaking business whose profits derive from his bribing of jockeys to stop their horses. A psychopathic owner in *For Kicks* (1965) prefers to speed up habitually slow horses in order to pull off betting coups. To do so he conditions the wretched animals to bolt in terror in the final stages of their races. In *High Stakes* (1975) a trainer and a bookmaker conspire to stop the horses of a wealthy owner whenever he has had a large bet. This is only one of several fraudulent practices by which the trainer, over the years, has conned his owners. Claiming traveling expenses for horses that haven't traveled and jockeys' expenses for schooling sessions that haven't taken place are minor fiddles; more serious is his habit of substituting an owner's good horse for a bad one, then selling the good one at a profit under another name. In *Risk* (1977) a trainer benefits by falsifying the accounts of his wealthy employers.

Substitution of horses is a fraud that an American stud owner works in *Blood Sport* (1967). Two top class stallions are standing on his farm under false names. Their progeny have been successful on the racetrack, and the fees that the stud owner charges for covering a mare have risen steadily.

The sheer range of frauds that the crooked ring of bloodstock agents employ in *Knock Down* (1974) is breathtaking. Most common is the practice of demanding "kickbacks" from sellers; an agent will ask for a share of the profit in return for bidding the horse up to a good but unrealistic price. If the seller refuses the agent spreads a false rumor that the horse has a problem, which deters buyers from bidding. One agent had charged an owner the cost of sending horses abroad by air when they'd gone, much more cheaply, by sea. Another had shipped an apparently valuable stallion abroad by air; it had died in transit and the insurance company had had to pay up. But the agent had already switched the stallion for another, less valuable one, that had been showing signs of illness. He had then sold on the original stallion.

Twenty-five years on from *Knock Down*, not much had changed in the bloodstock world. In 1999 a High Court judge awarded an owner £51,000 damages after two British trainers were found guilty of "collusive bidding." The **Jockey Club** fined the trainers £4000 each for bringing racing into disrepute. In 2003, a code of conduct was introduced whereby owners can ask for full disclosure of financial details of a purchase or sale.

In *Comeback* (1991), a villain defrauds insurance companies by claiming on horses that he has deliberately killed. There is another insurance scam in *Rat Race* (1970); a fund is set up to pay out in the event of injuries incurred on the racecourse, but the villain behind the fraud plans to benefit financially by murdering the fund's wealthy guarantor.

In *Smokescreen* (1972) a racehorse trainer is bribed to stop horses which form part of an estate, thus minimizing potential death duties payable on them. A fraudster in *Driving Force* (1992) fiddles money from a charity for old horses. Another to exploit horses for financial gain is a bogus healer in *Banker* (1982).

Non-racing frauds are, unsurprisingly, much less common in Francis's books. The owner of a bottling plant (*Proof* 1984) enhances his profits by selling cheap wine and whisky under expensive labels. Selling fake paintings as genuine is the preferred scam of a villain in *In the Frame* (1976).

Fred (*Odds Against* 1965)

Fred, a big, balding Londoner, is an associate of **Howard Kraye**. He is suspected by **Sid Halley** of sabotaging **Dunstable racecourse** by digging false drains to cause injury to horse and jockeys, and of setting fire to the stable block. At **Seabury racecourse**, he is suspected of using a tractor to pull over a tanker, causing a chemical spillage on the course.

Fred is a judo expert, and carries a gun, which he is not afraid to use. When the police have collected sufficient evidence against him, he is arrested and charged with murder.

Freddie, Uncle (*Banker* 1982)

Freddie is the uncle of **Tim Ekaterin**, and the ex-vice chairman of merchant bank **Paul Ekaterin Ltd.** When Tim's mother was bankrupted, Freddie had blackmailed Tim into going to work at the bank by offering to clear her debts and arranged an allowance for her. Though retired, Freddie still wields considerable influence at the bank due to his large shareholding. He is a good judge of character, but delivers his judgments bluntly. He tells Tim that he had closely followed his career and had always known that he would make a good banker. He says that it is time that Tim is made a director of the bank.

Frederick, Johnny (*Risk* 1977)

Johnny Frederick is a former school friend of **Roland Britten**; he is now running the family boat-building business on the **Isle of Wight**, taking over after his father was injured. He is a skilled craftsman, and the business is thriving. He looks at Roland's photos of the boat that Roland was abducted on, and of a man that Roland suspects of involvement; he promises to make enquiries. The next day he phones Roland with information about the boat and the suspect's telephone number.

Freemantle, Morgan (*The Danger* 1983)

Freemantle, a Senior Steward of the **Jockey Club**, is clever and forceful, but lacks warmth. He discusses with **Andrew Douglas** the problem of kidnapping and extortion within the racing world and how racehorse owners might insure against it. He offers the help of the Jockey Club to **Liberty Market Ltd.** if needed.

Freemantle goes to Washington D.C. as a guest of honor of the President of **Laurel racecourse**, and is himself kidnapped. On a tape sent to the Jockey Club by the kidnappers, Freemantle says that they will kill him if a ransom is not paid, but does not sound afraid. He is subsequently freed by Andrew and police officer **Kent Wagner**.

Friarly, Lord (*Whip Hand* 1979)

Lord Friarly is an old-fashioned, aristocratic landowner for whom **Sid Halley** used to ride. His main priorities in life are to preserve his country seat in **Shropshire** and to enjoy his racehorses. He asks Sid to investigate some racehorse syndicates he's involved in, suspecting that the horses are not being allowed to run to form. As a result, Friarly takes Sid's advice to dissociate himself from the syndicates.

Fringe (*Longshot* 1990)

Fringe is a jumper trained by **Tremayne Vickers**, who has a half-share in him. He is schooled over hurdles by **John Kendall**, whose first attempt at schooling it is. John does not school the horse brilliantly but he tells Vickers that he'll learn from it.

Frisby, Bananas (*Twice Shy* 1981)

Frisby is an old friend of **William Derry**; he helps William to find a cottage to rent in the village of **Six Mile Bottom**, near **Newmarket**, where Frisby runs a pub and restaurant. He is unmarried, overweight and eccentric; his real name is John James Frisby, but is nicknamed Bananas after one of his puddings. He is a jovial companion but plagued with depression about the human condition. He closes the pub during the winter months and decamps to the West Indies.

Frisby finds William after he is attacked and knocked semi-conscious. Despite reservations, he helps William to imprison the perpetrator in the cellar of William's cottage while he locates some computer tapes. Frisby is again first on the scene after William is shot in the chest, and drives him to hospital in **Cambridge**.

Frodsham, Cheshire

Frodsham is a market town with a population of about 9,000 in the county of Cheshire in the north west of England. The town overlooks the estuary of the River Mersey.

Come to Grief (1995): Race sponsors **Topline Foods** are based at Frodsham.

Frost, Detective Inspector (*In the Frame* 1976)

Frost is a **Shropshire** policeman who conducts the investigation into the murder of **Regina Stuart** and the theft of antiques and paintings from her and husband **Donald Stuart**'s home. His questioning of Donald suggests that he suspects him of complicity in the crime.

Frost takes a phone call from **Charles Todd** in Australia, who passes on vital information connected with the crime. Frost alerts police in other countries. He tells Charles that he will arrange for the criminal named by Charles to be detained, and that Donald is no longer a suspect.

Fynedale (*Knock Down* 1974)

Fynedale is a dishonest bloodstock agent whose main client is **Wilton Young**, a wealthy **Yorkshire** businessman. Fynedale is defrauding Young by conspiring with other agents to drive up the cost of yearlings and splitting the extra commission. His other frauds include transporting horses abroad by sea and charging Young the cost of air freight.

When **Jonah Dereham** tells Young about Fynedale's scams, Young has a public row with Fynedale at **Doncaster** races and sacks him. At **Ascot Sales** Fynedale follows Jonah into a horse's box and tries to kill him with a pitchfork. Fynedale is arrested and held in custody. Jonah visits him and says he won't press charges in exchange for information about another crooked agent. Fynedale co-operates, and the police reluctantly release him.

G

Gabriella (*Flying Finish* 1966)

Gabriella is a tall, dark-haired Italian girl; she has pale olive skin and flawless bone structure. Whilst working at Milan airport selling trinkets to tourists, Gabriella receives birth control pills smuggled in by British pilots and cabin crew, and passes them on to needy Italian women. She falls in love with **Henry Gray** on their first meeting. She doesn't speak English, so she talks with him in French. Gabriella lives with her sister, her husband and their seven children. The day after meeting him, she makes love with Henry in his airplane. Three weeks later, on Henry's next visit to Milan, they spend the weekend together. Gabriella helps Henry to search for a missing colleague without success, but the shared effort strengthens the bond between them. Gabriella wonders how Henry can afford hotel bills and train fares on what he earns as a groom, but Henry doesn't immediately tell her of his aristocratic background. When, eventually, Henry asks her if she would mind being a countess, Gabriella says she could bear it.

While returning to the airport Gabriella is shot in the back; the bullet passes through a lung and smashes a rib on the way out. An ambulance gets her to hospital in time for a successful emergency operation, and the doctors are hopeful that she will recover.

Gardner, Brett (*Driving Force* 1992)

Brett Gardner is a probationary employee of **Croft Raceways** horse transport firm. He is with **Dave Yates** when Yates picks up a hitchhiker, who dies during the journey. Gardner is a good driver, but a moaner and unwilling to accept responsibility for mistakes; he is not popular with the firm's clients. He leaves the firm voluntarily the day after picking up the hitchhiker, knowing that **Freddie Croft** was not going to keep him on.

Gardner, Roger (*Decider* 1993)

Roger Gardner is an ex-army officer, and is now manager of **Stratton Park racecourse**, near Swindon, **Wiltshire**. He is married, with two grown-up daughters. He goes, with Clerk of the Course, **Oliver Wells**, to see **Lee Morris**; he asks Lee to use his voting shares to vote against those of the late Lord Stratton's heirs who want to sell the racecourse for building land. Gardner is worried about his chances of finding another job if made redundant. He is also concerned that plans to build a new grandstand have been entrusted to an architect who knows nothing about racing. With untypical cynicism, Gardner dismisses a fatality at Stratton Park when a horse runs out and kills a racegoer, commenting that a dead horse is more harmful to racing's image that a dead person.

Gardner is showing Lee the architect's plans of the original stands when the stands are destroyed by an explosion. He and his wife look after Lee's children while Lee receives treatment in hospital. He gratefully takes the credit, rather than Lee whose idea it was, for locating and hiring a big tent as temporary accommodation for the next race meeting; he is anxious to secure his job, since **Rebecca Stratton** and **Keith Stratton** want him sacked.

Garvey, Tom (*Whip Hand* 1979)

Garvey, a **Gloucestershire** stud farmer, is sixty years old and powerfully built. He is loud, self-important, and not averse to sailing close to the wind. He is a hard man, but his understanding of horses has made him successful. He tells Sid that the mare **Bethesda**, who had been retired from racing with a heart murmur, had died whilst foaling a month before.

Gary (*Dead Heat* 20007)

Gary is the sous-chef at **The Hay Net**, a **Newmarket** restaurant run by **Max Moreton**. He is an associate of **Pyotr Komarov**. He entices Max back to the restaurant so that Komarov can kill him. He ties Max to a chair, then goes outside to look for **Caroline Aston**. There he meets a violent end. It later transpires that Gary knew more about a food poisoning incident at **Newmarket racecourse** than he should.

Gatwick, Surrey

Gatwick is a village in **Surrey**, about twenty-five miles south of London. Britain's second largest airport is situated close by.

Flying Finish (1966): **Lord Henry Gray**'s flight from Milan is delayed due to snow at Gatwick airport.

Knock Down (1974): Bloodstock agent **Jonah Dereham** lives near Gatwick. His house is the subject of an arson attack.

Gemstones (*Straight* 1989)

Gemstone is a flat racehorse owned by the late **Greville Franklin** and trained by **Nicholas Loder**.

Genotti (*Twice Shy* 1981)

Genotti, a three-year-old colt trained by **Mort Miller** for wealthy American **Lake Houston**, wins the St Leger, the final Classic race of the season, at **Doncaster** by four lengths.

George (*Bonecrack* 1971)

George—known as "Old" George—is the yardman at **Rowley Lodge**, **Neville Griffon**'s Newmarket stables. He was formerly deputy head gardener at the Viceroy's palace in India. He uses his horticultural knowledge to keep Rowley Lodge looking attractive.

George (*Smokescreen* 1972)

George is a black South African guide who accompanies **Edward Lincoln** when he hires a horse for a day. He is quiet, pleasant and a good rider. Edward enjoys George's undemanding company and gives him a tip considered excessive by George's employers.

George (*Hot Money* 1987)

George is a successful, highly-regarded Newmarket trainer for whose wife, **Jo**, **Ian Pembroke** rides as an amateur. He is delighted when Jo's horse **Young Higgins**, ridden by Ian, wins at long odds at **Kempton Park**.

George, Uncle (*Dead Cert* 1962)

Uncle George and his wife, **Aunt Deb**, have brought up their niece, **Kate Ellery-Penn**, ever since the divorce of Kate's parents, who no longer wanted her. Uncle George seems harmless, but his interest in the violent tendencies of primitive peoples hints strongly at his sinister side. His physical appearance, too, is suggestive of a person in whose company you may not feel entirely at ease: running to fat, a soft, moist handshake, and a bland smile that never reaches the eyes. Uncle George and Aunt Deb don't appear to be short of money, the provenance of which Kate never thinks to question. Unbeknown to her, Aunt Deb's ex-

pensive tastes have so eroded George's savings that he has turned to crime to restore his fortunes. When, finally, George's double life is about to be exposed, he is persuaded to do the decent thing and shoot himself, thus protecting Aunt Deb and Kate from the publicity of a trial. Since George was a man who, though fascinated by violence, much preferred to experience it vicariously, his messy suicide doesn't quite ring true. But this is the only blemish on an otherwise convincing character.

Germiston, South Africa

Germiston is in the Gauteng region of South Africa on the Witwatersrand, one of the world's richest gold-mining areas. Racing at Germiston takes place at **Gosforth Park racecourse**, a triangular right-handed track which favors horses which can lie up with the pace rather than those which need time to find their stride.

Smokescreen (1972): Film actor **Edward Lincoln** goes to **Germiston** races, where he introduces **Danilo Cavesey** to **Quentin Van Huren**.

Gerry (*Driving Force* 1992)

Gerry is a driver for **Croft Raceways** horse transport firm. He is considered reliable.

"Ghost" (*Second Wind* 1999)

A frail, elderly man, "Ghost" is a text-book publisher who is also a civil servant in a clandestine department involved with anti-terrorists activities. **Perry Stuart** passes on to him lists of nuclear materials that the **Unified Traders** are currently dealing in. "Ghost" undertakes to pass them on to colleagues who will prevent the deals; however, the Traders will be allowed to continue so that the anti-terrorist section can acquire more information.

Gibbons, Major Colly (*Forfeit* 1968)

Gibbons, a **Jockey Club** handicapper, is very good at his job and knows the form book backwards. When **James Tyrone** visits him to talk about non-starting ante-post favorites, Gibbons' wife has just run off with an American colonel and he is in the process of drowning his sorrows. At first reluctant to divulge any information, Gibbons tells James that the Jockey Club is aware of something going on but lack the evidence to prove it.

A few days later, at **Newcastle** races, Gibbons asks James if he could swap James's train ticket for his plane ticket, since he has to attend a meeting on the course after the last race and will miss his plane. He wants to be back in London that evening; his wife had contacted him to say she was coming home that day and he wanted to be there in case she left again.

Gideon, Ezra (*The Edge* 1988)

The late Ezra Gideon was a wealthy and well-respected racehorse owner. He loved his horses, and surprised everyone when he sold two of his best two-year-olds to **Julius Apollo Filmer**. It was suspected at the time by the **Jockey Club** security service that Filmer had somehow forced the sale. Gideon was not seen on a racecourse again, and subsequently shot himself.

"The Gift" (*Field of 13* 1998)

Washed-up, alcoholic racing journalist **Fred Collyer** flies out to Louisville to cover the Kentucky Derby for his newspaper, *The Manhattan Star*. He is unaware that his unreliability is close to costing him his job. That evening he has too much to drink at the annual dinner of the Turfwriters' Association and collapses outside the building. There he hears two men planning to fix a race in which one of them is riding; the jockey also arranges to stop his horse in another race.

Two days later Collyer goes to **Churchill Downs** for the Derby. When he sees the plan that he had overheard actually carried out, Collyer realizes that he has a story for his newspaper which could redeem his tarnished reputation.

Gilbert, Angelo (*Twice Shy* 1981)

Greed, limited intelligence, an absence of conscience and a frightening capacity for reckless behavior are attributes which, taken together, are liable to make unpleasant things happen. In Angelo Gilbert just such a potent combination occurs, and mayhem is the result. Gilbert knows of the existence of a horse race betting system that will make him rich, and he wants it. He has already committed murder in pursuance of the system when he discovers that a teacher, **Jonathan Derry**, has a copy. When his attempts to extort the computer tapes on which the system is written are thwarted, Gilbert threatens to kill Jonathan. But before he can do so he is arrested, convicted of murder, and receives a life sentence.

A lengthy incarceration in no way rehabilitates Gilbert; he re-emerges into society fourteen years later with his criminal urges fully intact and still looking for the cassette tapes. Jonathan having

moved abroad, Gilbert focuses his energies on Jonathan's younger brother **William Derry**. Surviving Gilbert's violent onslaught, William obtains a copy of the system, passes it on to Gilbert and prays that that is the last he will hear of it.

Gilbert wastes no time in using the betting system. A few initial successes convince him that the bookmakers will soon be crying for mercy. But, when things go badly wrong, Gilbert looks for a scapegoat, and William Derry fits the bill. He is by now out of control, all the constraints of civilized behavior forgotten in his single-minded determination to seek revenge. He almost succeeds, but ultimately it is Gilbert, not William, who pays the price of his obsession.

Gilbert, Harry (*Twice Shy* 1981)

Gilbert, a bingo hall owner, is the father of **Angelo Gilbert**. In manner he is cold and blunt. He offers to buy **Liam O'Rorke**'s betting system; when O'Rorke dies, **Jonathon Derry** offers the system to him on behalf of **Mrs. O'Rorke**. When Angelo adopts a challenging stance towards his father, Harry, initially at least, is tough enough to stand up to him. But before long Harry sees for himself that Angelo's days of doing what his father says are well and truly behind him.

In Part Two of *Twice Shy*, fourteen years have elapsed and Harry Gilbert is confined to a wheelchair, suffering from multiple sclerosis. His speech is slightly slurred but his mind is unaffected. Gilbert is supplying the funds for Angelo to use O'Rorke's system. When Jonathan visits him and tells him that Angelo is losing money using the system, he blames it on Jonathan. When he sees Jonathan and William Derry at the hospital where Angelo is a patient, Gilbert accuses them of destroying his son.

Giles (*The Edge* 1988)

Giles is a character in the mystery play on board the Great Transcontinental Mystery Race Train; he is a bloodstock agent. **Tor Kelsey** suspects that he is gay in real life. In the play, Giles murders **Angelina Standish** and her lover **Steve** to prevent them revealing that he had cheated them. Then Giles murders **Ricky**, a groom, who had seen him disposing of evidence. He blackmails **Walter Bricknell** after seeing his daughter **Donna** stealing her mother's jewels. He tries to shoot Donna; he shoots **Pierre** instead, and is arrested.

Gill, Robbie (*Wild Horses* 1994)

Gill is a doctor in **Newmarket**. He is Scottish, ginger-haired and overly abrupt with his patients, one of whom, ex-farrier and journalist **Valentine Clark**, is dying of bone cancer. He tells Valentine's sister, **Dorothea Pannier**, not to phone him in the middle of the night if Valentine dies. When Valentine does die during the night and his son **Paul Pannier** phones, Gill tells him he will come at 7am.

Gill is called out by **Betty**, a neighbor, who finds Dorothea in a serious condition after being assaulted. He patches **Thomas Lyon** up after he is attacked at **Huntingdon** *racecourse*, and subsequently discovers a murder victim in Dorothea's house.

Gillie (*Bonecrack* 1971)

Gillie is the tenant of **Neil Griffon**'s London flat, and also his long-term partner. In her mid-thirties, Gillie has an attractive face and no hang-ups about not being fashionably thin. Her mother and father had died in a Moroccan earthquake and left her a valuable wine cellar; she and Neil are gradually drinking their way through it. She has a legacy from her grandmother, which has left her well off. Gillie is divorced; her eight-year old daughter had been killed by a youth on a motorbike, and soon afterwards her husband had left her for someone else. She would quite like to marry Neil but doesn't want to pressurize him, and so is content to leave things as they are. She works part-time for an adoption society; her politics are vaguely left of centre.

Gillie wants to come and stay with Neil at **Rowley Lodge**; when Neil says not just now she realizes there's a serious problem but doesn't pry. She senses that Neil won't go back to his previous job as a financial troubleshooter.

Gleaner (*Whip Hand* 1979)

Gleaner is a top class two-year-old colt trained by **George Caspar** at **Newmarket**. He is winter favorite for the following season's Two Thousand Guineas and Derby. However, Gleaner flops in the Guineas and is subsequently found to have a heart murmur. According to Caspar's head lad, Gleaner also suffers from arthritis. He is retired to **Henry Thrace**'s stud outside Newmarket. Thrace says that Gleaner tires easily. The horse collapses and dies after covering a mare, and tests show that he died of a disease that horses do not normally suffer from.

Glenn, Austin Dartmouth (*Field of 13* 1998: "The Day of the Losers")

Glenn is about forty years old; he is slightly built, self-important and unpopular. He goes to the Grand National at **Aintree** with a thick wad of stolen bank notes, a recent reward for helping to spring a murderer and bank robber from jail. Unbeknown to Glenn, a lady selling Tote tickets spots that the notes are stolen and informs the police. When the horse he backs in the Grand National finishes second, Glenn tears up his ticket. But the winner is disqualified, and the horse that Glenn backed is promoted to first place. Meanwhile the police are waiting to arrest Glenn when he cashes his ticket.

Glitberg (*Risk* 1977)

Glitberg has recently been released from jail after serving a six-year sentence—reduced for good behavior—for embezzlement, a crime discovered by **Roland Britten**. A local councilor, Glitberg had authorized and received payments for buildings that were never built, keeping the money for himself. Together with **Connaught Powys** and **Ownslow**, Glitberg meets Roland at **Vivian Iverson**'s gambling club and warns him that he will never feel safe from retribution. Subsequently Glitberg proves as good as his word.

Gloucestershire, England

Gloucestershire is a county in the "heart of England," essentially rural yet close to the industrial conurbations of **Birmingham** and the Potteries. The villages of Gloucestershire's Cotswold Hills are amongst the most picturesque in the country. The region also has some lovely towns, including Cheltenham with its elegant Regency architecture and the market town of **Cirencester**, founded by the Romans.

Enquiry (1969): Warned-off jockey **Kelly Hughes** goes to Gloucestershire to speak to fellow-jockey **Charlie West**, who had lied at the enquiry into Kelly's riding of beaten favorite **Squelsh** at **Oxford** races.

Knock Down (1974): Wealthy businessman and racehorse owner **Constantine Brevett** lives in Gloucestershire.

Risk (1977): Fraudster **Connaught Powys** is a former inmate of **Leyhill Prison** in Gloucestershire

Comeback (1991): Diplomat **Peter Darwin** goes to Gloucestershire, where he'd spent his childhood. Veterinary surgeons **Ken McClure** and Lucy

Amhurst work for Hewett and Partners, a practice based in Cheltenham.

Shattered (2000): Gerard Logan's glass-blowing business is in the Cotswold village of **Broadway** in Gloucestershire.

Godbar, George (*Come to Grief* 1995)

Godbar is the editor of *The Pump* newspaper. He instructs columnist **India Cathcart** to write articles discrediting **Sid Halley**.

Golden Lion, Bletchley (*Break In* 1985)

This is a hotel in **Shropshire**. On his way to ride at **Towcester** races, **Kit Fielding** books a room at the Golden Lion and leaves there articles belonging to journalists **Owen Watts** and **Jay Erskine**.

Goldenberg, Eric (*Rat Race* 1970)

Goldenberg, an ill-tempered racehorse owner, is a passenger on **Matt Shore**'s air-taxi flight to **Haydock Park racecourse**. He argues with another passenger, jockey **Kenny Bayst**, apparently over whether or not Bayst is going to stop a horse in the 3.15pm race. When Bayst tells him not to waste his money on the race, Goldenberg is furious and raises his fists to hit Bayst, but is checked by trainer **Annie Villars**.

After the race, in which Bayst gets his horse boxed in and finishes third, Goldenberg has a less than cordial conversation with **Major Tydeman**, the nature of which is unclear. Returning to the plane, Goldenberg complains loudly about Bayst. He is not happy when Matt lands the plane at **Nottingham Airport** to have it checked over. Fortunately for Goldenberg, Matt's instincts are accurate.

Goldenberg hires two thugs to beat up Bayst at **Redcar** races; he denies it, albeit unconvincingly, when Bayst accuses him of it at **Bath** races.

Goldenwave Marine (*Risk* 1977)

A shipyard based in **Lymington**, Hampshire, Goldenwave Marine specializes in building "miniliners" for wealthy Arabs and ocean-going racing yachts. The firm had built a Golden Sixty Five yacht for **Arthur Robinson**, on which **Roland Britten** was held against his will.

Goldoni, Bruno and Beatrice (*The Danger* 1983)

The Goldonis are the Italian owners of **Brunelleschi**, winner of the Washington International at **Laurel Park racecourse** when ridden by **Alessia Cenci**. Unaware of her son **Pietro**'s criminality, Beatrice meets him in Washington and tells him that Alessia is in town.

Goldoni, Pietro (*The Danger* 1983)

Goldoni is the son whom every middle-class Italian family must have dreaded spawning. In the 1970's and early 1980's young men like Goldoni were not content with ingesting recreational drugs and trashing their parents' houses at all-night parties. Their chosen narcotic was politics: groups such as the Red Brigades and the Bader-Meinhoff gang were extreme left wingers whose political agenda was terrorism. Like the terrorists of today, they organized themselves into small, effective cells of highly-committed zealots for whom the ends justified the means.

Goldoni, the son of a wealthy racehorse owner, had been a left-wing student activist at Milan University until his expulsion for passing dud checks. He soon becomes involved with hard-line communist extremists and shows leadership qualities, chief of which are meticulous planning and a total lack of conscience. Kidnapping is his preferred modus operandi, and his success soon brings him to the attention of **Liberty Market Ltd.**, a firm that specializes in negotiating or otherwise effecting the release of kidnap victims. When **Andrew Douglas**, one of their agents, targets him, Goldoni takes steps to neutralize the threat. Violent death is the result.

Goodboy, Collie (*The Edge* 1988)

Collie Goodboy is the trading name of a racecourse bookmaker, whose real name is Les Morris. Goodboy is seen by **Tor Kelsey** at **Nottingham** races receiving information, via his clerk, from an apprentice jockey, and adjusting his odds accordingly.

Goodhaven, Erica (*Longshot* 1990)

Erica Goodhaven is the aunt, by marriage, of **Harry Goodhaven**. She is a literary novelist, writing under the name of **Erica Upton**, and is highly regarded in the literary world. She is sharp, to the point of cruelty, in her criticisms of others. Not impressed with the theme of **John Kendall**'s novel—survival—Goodhaven is disparaging about what she sees as his literary pretensions. She attends **Tremayne Vickers**' Lifetime Award dinner, where she discusses with John the attack on her nephew Harry. By doing so she helps him to focus on the significance of certain facts.

Goodhaven, Fiona (*Longshot* 1990)

Fiona is the wife of **Harry Goodhaven**; she and Harry are the owners of a horse in **Tremayne Vickers'** yard. In her forties, Fiona is tall, blonde, sensible and reliable. She is a passenger in the jeep driven by **Mackie Vickers** when it skids into a water-filled ditch, and is rescued by **John Kendall**. Fiona is angry at **Detective Chief Inspector Doone**'s suspicion that her husband is implicated in the death of a stable girl.

Goodhaven, Harry (*Longshot* 1990)

Goodhaven is the owner, with his wife **Fiona**, of a horse in **Tremayne Vickers'** yard. He is of fair complexion, and good-natured. He is in the jeep driven by **Mackie Vickers** when it skids on an icy road into a water-filled ditch. He is pulled out of the car by **John Kendall**.

Items belonging to Goodhaven are found near the body of a stable girl in nearby woods. He denies all knowledge of how they got there, but can't remember where he was on the day she disappeared. **Detective Chief Inspector Doone** suspects him of murder. Goodhaven himself believes he will be tried for the murder and convicted. Then an unknown person phones to say he has information which might clear him, and to meet him in **Sam Yaeger**'s boathouse on the Thames. Goodhaven goes, taking John Kendall with him. There he falls through rotten floorboards into the dock beneath, impaling his leg on a spike beneath the surface. He is saved from drowning by John, who pulls him out of the river and gives him artificial respiration. He soon recovers in hospital.

Gosforth Park racecourse, South Africa

Gosforth Park is the name of the racecourse at **Germiston**, in the Gauteng region of South Africa.

Smokescreen (1972): Film actor **Edward Lincoln** goes to the races at Gosforth Park whilst visiting South Africa to find out why **Nerissa Cavesey**'s horses are running badly.

Gowery, Lord (*Enquiry* 1969)

Lord Gowery, the Senior Disciplinary Steward of the **Jockey Club**, conducts the enquiry at which **Kelly Hughes** and **Dexter Cranfield** lose their licenses for allegedly stopping **Squelsh**, favorite for the Lemonfizz Crystal Cup at **Oxford**. In Kelly's opinion, Gowery has made up his mind that they are guilty even before the enquiry gets under way, and that the evidence against them appears to be rigged.

Gowery is severely rattled when Kelly approaches him at a charity dance. He refuses to answer Kelly's questions and storms off. Later, Gowery has a taped conversation with **Lord Ferth**, who had also sat on the enquiry but had agreed to say nothing. Gowery insists that Kelly and Cranfield are guilty and that he had no option but to warn them off. Eventually, however, he admits that he had acted solely on a package of evidence from an anonymous source sent through the post. His reasons for doing so prove to be dishonorable.

Grand Cayman Island

Grand Cayman is the largest of the three Cayman Islands, a largely self-governing territory of the United Kingdom in the Western Caribbean Sea. In 2004 the island was severely damaged by Hurricane Ivan, the worst to hit the islands for almost one hundred years.

Second Wind (1999): Meteorologists **Perry Stuart** and **Kris Ironside** plan to fly through the eye of a hurricane. They fly to Grand Cayman, where they stay with **Amy Ford**, who has recently sold to **Robin Darcy** the plane that they will use.

Granger (*For Kicks* 1965)

Granger, a racehorse trainer based in North Yorkshire, employs dishonest stable lad **Thomas Nathaniel Tarleton**.

Grant, Sister (*Come to Grief* 1995)

Sister Grant is a nurse on the children's ward in the Kent hospital where nine-year-old **Rachel Ferns** is being treated for leukemia.

Grantchester, Oliver (*To the Hilt* 1996)

Grantchester is a middle-aged solicitor who has, as one of his clients, the **King Alfred Brewery** near Wantage, **Oxfordshire**. Grantchester, however, does not have the best interests of the brewery at heart. For some time he has abused his privileged position and, in concert with a trusted employee of the brewery, has acted dishonestly in order to line his own pockets. Having fallen out with his accomplice, Grantchester is responsible for the man's death.

Grantchester is alarmed when **Alexander Kinloch**, stepson of the brewery's owner, **Sir Ivan Westering**, is appointed a director with power of attorney. He views Alex's presence as a threat, and conspires to have him removed. Despite his lack of compunction about using a frightening level of violence, Grantchester's vendetta against Alex does not have the outcome he desires.

Graves, Jasper (*Break In* 1985)

Jasper is the teenage nephew of **Jermyn Graves**, an owner of **Bobby Allardeck**'s who wants to remove his horses from the stable. He has been prevented from doing so by **Kit Fielding** because he owes money for training fees. Jasper goes with his uncle in the middle of the night to try to get the horses but Kit and Bobby, woken by an alarm bell, stop them. When his uncle finally pays the fees, Jasper helps him to collect the horses.

Graves, Jermyn (*Break In* 1985)

Groves is an unpleasant racehorse owner with horses in **Bobby Allardeck**'s yard. One night he tries to remove them despite owing a huge amount in training fees. He is furious when **Kit Fielding** and Bobby prevent him, and shouts obscenities. He is forced by Kit to write a check for the fees but not allowed to take the horses until the check is cleared. Graves threatens to stop the check; Kit says he will have Graves put on the forfeit list and thus barred from all racecourses. With his nephew **Jasper**, Graves again goes to the stables in the middle of the night to get his horses, but Kit and Bobby stop him. When his check clears Graves, still angry and abusive, collects his horses.

Gray, Lord Henry (*Flying Finish* 1966)

Henry is in his early thirties; his father, the **Earl of Creggan**, is an octogenarian and his mother a not-so-sprightly seventy-three. He had been sent away to prep school when barely out of diapers, then on to **Eton College**—in those days not the liberal, touchy-feely place it is today. It is not a total surprise, then, that he's grown into a man who could have given the KGB a tip or two about repression.

Henry's childhood was an emotional desert; up to now his way of dealing with it has been to grow a protective shell. That means no outward revelation of his feelings, conformity to the behavior expected of his class and, above all, self-control. Affection for another human being is, for Henry, virgin territory.

He has a job in London which he considers sterile and unexciting, but so far obedience and an innate sense of duty have kept him at his desk. Henry though, has a consuming passion. He lives for riding racehorses over jumps. It's a temporary escape from the straitjacket of his everyday existence.

Lately, Henry has questioned the relevance of his way of life, and has found it wanting. One day he goes to lunch and, instead of returning to his job at the **Anglia Bloodstock Agency**, persuades a horse transport firm to take him on as a traveling head groom. There, Henry plays down his aristocratic background, preferring to be judged on his own merits.

Not everyone at **Yardman** Transport is prepared to grant Henry the level playing field he asks for. **Billy Watkins**, a young groom with psychopathic tendencies, baits Henry at every opportunity. Henry has had a lot of practice at controlling his temper, but having boxed for Eton, knows how to use his fists. When Billy gets physical Henry beats him into submission.

Henry's family is appalled at his change of career, but Henry doesn't care. He cares even less about his mother's unsubtle attempts to engineer meetings with the kinds of girls whom she considers suitable for a man of Henry's class. Henry treats them as if they had foot and mouth disease. His reserve in social situations does not prepare him for the *coup de foudre* that awaits him. Flying a consignment of broodmares to Milan, he has to stay there overnight owing to bad weather. The pilot introduces him to **Gabriella**, a local girl who, under the cover of selling cheap jewelry at the airport, acts as a conduit for the smuggling of birth control pills into Italy. The attraction between them is instantaneous and intense; within twenty-four hours they are having sex in the back seat of the airplane.

Their relationship, however, proves bad for Gabriella's health. Helping Henry in his search for a missing colleague, she is shot in the back. Henry, distraught, gets her to hospital. Close to death, Gabriella survives an emergency operation while Henry, his defenses breached at last, is reduced to tears.

Henry, too, comes close to suffering a gruesome fate at the hands of the same maniac. When he gets the opportunity to turn the tables Henry displays a calculated ruthlessness in dispensing summary justice, adding a disconcerting dimension to his personality that is no less credible for being unexpected.

Green, Patrick (*Field of 13* 1998: "Corkscrew")

A member of the South Carolina Bar Association, Green is a crooked lawyer. His friend, English bloodstock agent **Sandy Nutbridge**, asks for his help in raising $100,000 bail money when he is arrested on tax and drugs charges. Green, however, had engineered Nutbridge's arrest; when the charges against Nutbridge are dropped for lack of evidence, Green refuses to return the bulk of the money. He reasons that the guarantors will write the money off rather than pursue a long and costly legal battle through the courts. He's wrong.

Greene, Mr. (*In the Frame* 1976)

Found by **Maisie Matthews** poking around the ruins of her recently burnt-down house in Hastings, **Sussex**, Greene tells her, falsely, that he is from the insurers. Greene is working at **Yarra River Fine Arts** gallery, Melbourne, Australia, when he recognizes **Charles Todd**. He temporarily detains Charles behind a steel mesh gate. With two accomplices, Greene goes to **Jik** and **Sarah Cassavetes**' hotel room. They threaten to harm Sarah if Jik doesn't get Charles to come to the room. However, Jik and Sarah manage to escape.

In New Zealand Greene and two others abduct Charles and take him to a lonely beach. However their plans to deal with Charles once and for all come to nothing.

Greening, Gerald (*Bolt* 1986)

Greening is solicitor to **Princess Casilia** and **M. Roland de Brescou**. He is middle-aged, bald and overweight. He draws up a document, which **Kit Fielding** witnesses, preventing M. de Brescou making business decisions without the assent of the Princess, **Prince Litsi** and **Danielle de Brescou**. He is initially skeptical of Kit's ability to help the Princess. When **Henri Nanterre**, M. de Brescou's business partner, tears up the assent document, Greening prepares another. A few days later he draws up two copies of a watertight contract binding under French law and signed by the Princess, Roland, Litsi and Danielle.

Gregory, Peter (*Dead Cert* 1962)

Racehorse trainer Peter Gregory trains horses for **Alan York** and **Kate Ellery-Penn**. He is an ex-jockey, who has trained a winner of the Champion Hurdle at **Cheltenham**.

Griffon, Neil (*Bonecrack* 1971)

Bubbling away beneath the surface of *Bonecrack*'s main storyline—the obsessive determination of Italian crime boss **Enso Rivera** to get his son appointed stable jockey to a top **Newmarket** yard—there is a powerful subtext. Through the eyes of Neil Griffon, Francis looks at the difficult emotional issues arising from the filial relation-

ship. Do sons ever truly get to know their fathers? Do fathers ever know what their sons really want? Neil is forced to consider the implications of such questions from two angles: that of the Italian's blind steamrollering of any obstacles in his path to ensure that his son **Alessandro Rivera** becomes a jockey; and Neil's own awkward, loveless relationship with his father, **Neville Griffon**. As the story unfolds, Neil begins to find himself in the role of the parent and to appreciate how bonds between father and son are forged or shattered.

As a child Neil Griffon had feared his father, a **Newmarket** racehorse trainer; as a teenager he had hated him. Though not physically abused, he had suffered mean and petty punishments. Packed off to **Eton College**, he had run away at sixteen and, for the next fourteen years while pursuing a successful business career, he had had no contact with his father. Finally resolving to make peace, Neil went to see Neville, who didn't recognize him. An uneasy truce prevailed, and Neil was permitted to visit three or four times a year, though not to stay overnight.

Now thirty-four, Neil had spent years building up a chain of antique shops. Then he sold the lot, and he now works as a financial trouble-shooter for an international company. Except, at the moment, he doesn't. He is in Newmarket, having taken three months off to look after eighty-five blue-blooded thoroughbreds for his father, who is in hospital after breaking a leg in a car crash. Not that Neville feels the slightest gratitude; he dismisses the possibility that his son may be capable of overseeing a racing stable and tells him to find someone competent.

Neil's intention had been to deal with the yard's finances and leave the training of the horses to a more experienced horseman. But events dictate otherwise, and Neil, to ensure his own survival, is obliged not just to train the horses, but to employ Alessandro Rivera.

Mistaken for his father, Neil is abducted by armed men and taken to the home of Rivera who, discovering the error, prepares to kill him. Neil narrowly avoids death by telling Rivera that he is training the horses. His life is spared only on condition that he employs Rivera's son Alessandro as stable jockey.

Though acutely aware that Rivera is unpredictable and possibly unhinged, Neil shows Alessandro no favor, treating him like he would any other apprentice. Alessandro admits to Neil that his father gives him anything he wants, but that he can't talk to him. Neil is shocked by this revelation; the parallel with his own situation is too strong. He too has a father with whom the channels of communication are virtually closed.

Soon, Neil and Alessandro are seeing unexpected sides to each other's personalities. Alessandro cannot believe that anyone would have the courage to disobey his father, whilst Neil is beginning to feel excited at the young Italian's potential as a jockey. Driving to racecourses together, Neil and Alessandro talk naturally just as a father and son should.

But the deepening of his relationship with Alessandro comes at a heavy price. Enso is insanely jealous of Neil and resorts to extreme violence to exact vengeance. In doing so he puts his own son in grave danger. Ultimately it takes the unexpected deaths of two inadequate parents to free their sons; from two unhealthy relationships has grown one that works.

Griffon, Neville Knollys (*Bonecrack* 1971)

Neville Griffon, a **Newmarket** racehorse trainer, is the father of **Neil Griffon**. He breaks a leg in a car crash and is hospitalized, necessitating his son's taking over the training until he recovers. Disapproval is Griffon's habitual mindset; as a father he had been unable to love Neil, and had been consistently unkind to his son as he grew up. He would punish Neil for minor misdemeanors by locking him in his bedroom for days at a time. He had never forgiven Neil for running away from **Eton** at the age of sixteen, and did not speak to or make contact with Neil for fourteen years. When Neil finally went to see him, Griffon did not recognize his son. Unbending slightly, he now allowed Neil to call on him occasionally but continued to be distant, harsh and critical.

Unaware of the situation with **Enso Rivera**, Griffon treats with contempt Neil's suggestion that he should look after the stables until Griffon himself is well enough to return. He tells Neil to find someone else as soon as possible, but is in no position to ensure that Neil accedes to his demands.

Griffon is angry when Neil tells him he has taken on a new apprentice; however, he knows that the stable's financial position is precarious, and grudgingly accepts that the father is paying for his son to be there. Reluctant to relinquish control of the stable, Griffon tells Neil that he will continue to enter horses in races. He insists that Neil take **Pease Pudding** out of the Lincoln Handicap; he

retains a half-share, and is afraid that a poor run will reduce the colt's value. He is shocked that Neil has discovered that the stable is in trouble owing to his practice of retaining an interest in many of the horses he trains, thus reducing the amount of training fees he can charge. With bad grace, he agrees to sell some of the shares.

When Neil declares Pease Pudding for the Lincoln, Griffon informs the press that the horse has no chance. Pease Pudding wins the race by a short head, and Griffon is not pleased. He gives Neil no credit, saying that the jockey had ridden a brilliant race. Griffon feels threatened by Neil's success, and sees his authority slipping away; in addition, his leg is slow to mend and he remains bedridden.

When he learns of the serious incidents, involving Neil and the Riveras, that have taken place on the gallops, Griffon places the blame squarely on Neil's shoulders. He is dismissive when **Archangel**, the stable's best colt, wins the Two Thousand Guineas; he tells Neil to do no more work with Archangel, and to make no more entries. That evening he dies suddenly of a pulmonary embolism.

Grits (*For Kicks* 1965)

Grits, a stable lad at **Inskip**'s racing stables, is a gawky boy of eighteen. He tries to be friendly with **Daniel Roke**, who has to pretend to be untrustworthy and a whinger, thus earning Grits' disapproval.

Gross, Nick (*Come to Grief* 1995)

Gross is the account manager at **Intramind Imaging Ltd.** He deals in a rude and overbearing manner with **Sid Halley**, who is pretending to be an employee of **Topline Foods**. Gross appears to have a low opinion of that company.

Groundsel (*Longshot* 1990)

Groundsel is a steeplechaser owned by **Fiona Goodhaven** and trained by **Tremayne Vickers**. Ridden by **Nolan Everard**, he finishes second in an amateur chase at **Newbury**, beaten one length.

Grundy, John (*Bolt* 1986)

Grundy is a male nurse employed by wheelchair-bound **Roland de Brescou**, husband of **Princess Casilia**; he is a sixty-year-old widower. He guards Roland the day after the Princess has been threatened with a gun.

Gudrun (*Trial Run* 1978)

Gudrun is a pleasant West German girl from Bonn; she is an exchange student at Moscow University, and a friend of **Stephen Luce**. She speaks perfect English and good Russian. She helps Stephen to translate the notes in **Misha's** Matrushka doll. Reading the information on Hans Kramer, Gudrun realizes that he'd been at a school for troubled children, and in a clinic where the theory of terrorism was preached to the patients by a Dr. Huber.

Guggenheim (*Driving Force* 1992)

Guggenheim, a young American research scientist, works in **Edinburgh** for the McPherson Foundation, researching into obscure illnesses. He is an authority on ticks, and his expertise is used by **Freddie Croft**.

Guirlande, Emil Jacques (*Field of 13* 1998: "Dead on Red")

Guirlande, a French assassin, is based in Paris. He is thirty-seven years old, of quiet demeanor and unobtrusive. He is terrified of flying. He has killed sixteen people. Guirlande was brought up in orphanages, and had learned to shoot in the army. In December 1986 he is hired by to kill a jockey, a commission he carries out successfully. In February 1987 he is contacted again, this time to assassinate a racehorse trainer. He takes the ferry from Zeebrugge on March 6th; it is a fateful journey.

Gypsy Joe (*Field of 13* 1998: "Dead on Red")

Gypsy Joe's real name is **John Smith**. He is a successful trainer of steeplechasers. He surprises the racing community by offering a job as stable jockey to an inexperienced, if talented, amateur, **Red Millbrook**. His instinct proves correct, and Millbrook rides a lot of winners for him. When Millbrook is murdered in London a few months later, Gypsy Joe has strong suspicions about who was responsible. Gypsy Joe never finds out how close he came to suffering a similarly violent death.

H

Haagner (*Smokescreen* 1972)

Haagner is a ranger in the **Kruger National Park**, South Africa. He guides **Evan Pentelow**, **Conrad** and **Edward Lincoln** when they are filming elephants in the park. An Afrikaner, Haagner speaks only halting English. He is understandably irritated with Pentelow when he tries to throw a plastic bag out of the station wagon window, and again when he throws food out. When Pentelow complains about Haagner driving away from an angry elephant while Conrad is filming, Haagner stops the car. The elephant begins to charge, and Pentelow urgently demands that Haagner drive away. Having made his point, the ranger complies.

Hagbourne, Viscount (*Odds Against* 1965)

Hagbourne, the Senior Steward of the **National Hunt Committee**, is somewhat cold and reserved; he has not been a great success as Senior Steward owing to his disinclination to make decisions. He is concerned to hear from **Sid Halley** of suspicious dealing in **Seabury racecourse**'s shares but is surprised at Sid's suggestion that Seabury's bad luck could be more than just coincidence. With some hesitation, Hagbourne agrees to **Hunt Radnor Associates** carrying out an investigation on behalf of the National Hunt Committee. Taken to see the racecourse by Sid, Hagbourne is shocked at Seabury's state of disrepair. He is doubtful about its long-term chances of survival.

Loaned Sid's photos of **Howard Kraye**'s share certificates by **Radnor** to show to the Seabury racecourse executive, Hagbourne puts them down on a table, from where they are stolen.

Haig, Christopher (*Field of 13* 1998: "Haig's Death")

Haig is an animal feed consultant and a part-time racecourse judge. Aged forty-two, he is separated from his wife. Competent and popular, Haig enjoys his judging but is beginning to wish he'd led a more adventurous life, and is planning to change direction soon. He is acting as judge at **Winchester racecourse** when, as a race nears its climax, he suffers a massive heart attack.

"Haig's Death" (*Field of 13* 1998)

Christopher Haig arrives at **Winchester** races to perform his duties as racecourse judge. He checks that he knows the colors of the runners in the day's big race. Unbeknown to Haig, attempts are being made by the connections of certain of the runners to influence the result of the race. Their machinations prove fruitless when the judge suffers a massive heart attack and the race is declared void.

Hall, Connie (*To the Hilt* 1996)

Connie Hall is the elderly caretaker of the house next door to **Sir Ivan** and **Lady Westering** in London. She is invited to a gathering after Sir Ivan's death by Lady Westering. There she tells **Alex Kinloch** that she saw Sir Ivan searching for a tissue box in the rubbish bags outside the house on the night of his death.

Halley, Jenny

Whip Hand (1979): Jenny is the ex-wife of **Sid Halley**. She is pretty but waspish, and their marriage break-up—due mainly to Sid's obsession with his career—was acrimonious. Whenever Jenny sees Sid she verbally rips him to shreds. Stupidly, Jenny has fallen for a fraudster, **Nicholas Ashe**, and has unwittingly become involved in his scam. Jenny runs the risk of being charged with fraud, but she is annoyed that her father has asked Sid to help clear her name. Attempting to justify her relationship with Ashe, Jenny says that he made her laugh. Sid thinks that Jenny doesn't want Ashe found; Jenny doesn't deny it. Bitterly, Jenny berates Sid for the way he treated her during their marriage with racing first and her nowhere. She tries to provoke a reaction from Sid by disparaging his disabled hand, but Sid refuses to respond. She is jealous of Sid's relationship with her father, **Charles Roland**, saying that Charles only puts up with Sid because he pities him.

When Sid suggests to Jenny that Nicholas Ashe reminds her of him, and that she was trying to relive the early years of their marriage. Jenny denies it, but unconvincingly. When Sid shows her a photo of Ashe with his new girlfriend she is reluctantly convinced that Ashe no longer cares about her, and tells Sid to give it to the police. She tries to justify her scathing tongue by telling Sid it was his fault she left him: he always had to win, and never asked for, or needed, her support.

Come to Grief (1995): Jenny is now **Lady Wingham**, having recently married **Sir Anthony Wingham**. She meets Sid at her father's house. At first, she speaks to Sid in her habitually scornful way. She complains that **India Cathcart** had tried to pump her for information about him; later, Cathcart had written that not only was Sid crippled, but he was unable to satisfy Jenny physically. Then, Jenny's attitude towards Sid softens; she tells him that she had never said that, and urges Sid not to let Cathcart get to him. Smiling, she says goodbye to Sid, who recognizes that Jenny has

finally rid herself of the anger and resentment that their failed marriage had caused her.

Under Orders (2006): See **Wingham, Lady**

Halley, Sid

Odds Against (1965): Once, Sid had been at the top of his profession: champion **National Hunt** jockey, in constant demand, living in the public gaze, admired and envied. Like most jockeys, he had closed his mind to the possibility that the bad fall, the one that cuts short a career in the blink of an eye, could happen to him. Then a horse galloped over him; its racing plate, sharp and vicious, cut through his wrist like a slicer through bacon. The surgeons had left Sid's hand on, but it is withered and useless.

Sid's obsession with race-riding had already alienated his wife. Now, lacking the one thing that he needs most to pursue his career—a whole body—Sid is failing miserably to adapt to altered circumstances. He had drifted into a job with **Hunt-Radnor Associates**, a detective agency which investigated racing's seedy underbelly. Not given much to do, for two years Sid had hung around the office, an embarrassment to himself and his colleagues. Then, sent on a routine surveillance operation, Sid is shot in the stomach by a petty criminal.

Though separated from his wife, **Jenny Halley**, Sid has maintained a good relationship with her father. Retired Rear Admiral **Charles Roland** had deplored his daughter's decision to marry a mere jockey. But when, on a rare visit to Roland's house, Sid beat him at chess, he began to see his son-in-law in a different light. Their friendship grew, as did Roland's interest in racing. He discovers that **Seabury racecourse** is under threat from unscrupulous property developers. Concerned about Sid's mental state, Roland resolves to get Sid involved in saving the racecourse on his release from hospital.

Sid Halley could scarcely have had a less auspicious start in life. His teenage father, a window cleaner, fell off his ladder and killed himself before Sid was born. His unmarried mother worked in a biscuit factory. Fifteen years later and dying from kidney failure, she had removed her bright, scrawny son from his state grammar school and apprenticed him to a **Newmarket** racing trainer so that he would at least have a job and somewhere to live when she died.

His mother's foresight served Sid well. He found he had a natural talent for race-riding and he had forged a brilliant career. But his estrangement from his wife, though he sees it as permanent, haunts him because he feels that he forced her into it. Jenny, a party animal, needed a husband who would dance and drink with her till dawn. With horses to school in the early morning and to race in the afternoon, Sid wasn't that man. If compromises were to be made, they had to be Jenny's. Jenny tried compromise, and found it not to her taste. So she left. Six months later, beneath a maelstrom of pounding hooves, Sid's life as a jockey is over.

Charles Roland's ploy to rekindle the spark of motivation in his son-in-law is successful; Sid comes out of hospital determined to start earning his pay at Hunt Radnor. Not that Sid needs the money; he has for years speculated shrewdly on the stock market, an interest dating from when he was a Newmarket apprentice, nurtured by the far-sighted trainer to whom he was indentured.

As **Radnor**, his boss, comments, Sid is like "a zombie waking up." Sid, put in charge of the Seabury investigation, wastes no time in tracking down the perpetrators of the fraudulent attempts to take over the racecourse. His success comes at a price; the villain-in-chief uses a poker in imaginative ways to vent his spleen on Sid's withered hand. When he has finished, amputation is the only option.

The injuries Sid has suffered working for Hunt Radnor, far from deterring him from continuing as an investigator, have the opposite effect; he decides to buy a partnership in the business.

Whip Hand (1979): Fourteen years after *Odds Against*, Francis brings Sid Halley back in *Whip Hand*. Sid isn't fourteen years older; only a year or so has past since Sid lost his hand. Now he has an electronic hand, which works via the nerve impulses in his forearm. Sid has a recurring dream that he is still a jockey, and wakefulness always brings a churning regret for the life he has lost.

Nor has Sid got over the break-up of his marriage. Even though he and Jenny are now divorced, five minutes in each other's company still generate the urge to spill blood. But he shows he still cares for her by getting angry about her involvement with a fraudster, **Nicholas Ashe**. Jenny doesn't appreciate Sid's concern; she's more interested in belittling him at every opportunity, if only to get him to react.

Sid refuses to react to Jenny's taunts about his crippled hand, but his disability undoubtedly disturbs his peace of mind. Having only one good hand is bad enough; having none is unthinkable. Sid has proved his physical courage countless times, but when a criminal threatens to remove his good hand with a shotgun blast, Sid discovers the true meaning of terror.

But though fear has beaten him once, Sid is determined not to let it tighten its grip. He soon gets the chance to prove to himself that his nerve is intact. A near-death experience in a hot air balloon in the company of a semi-lunatic leaves Sid grinning with exhilaration. When Sid investigates the reasons behind a number of top class two-year-olds flopping as three-year-olds, he knows he is inviting retribution, but is doing so with his eyes open.

As a favor to his father-in-law, Sid has been delving into the murky background of Nicholas Ashe, who has embroiled Jenny in his schemes. Jenny is unrepentant, telling Sid defiantly that Ashe was fun to be with. Sid remembers that he and Jenny had been like that in the beginning, before his career had taken precedence. Now all Jenny wants to do is hurt Sid for never putting her first, for never really needing her.

Finally the moment arrives when Sid has to confront his demons. Looking down the barrel of a shotgun, Sid is terrified, but can't bring himself to beg for mercy. "I'd forgotten what you're like," snarls the man holding the gun. "You've no bloody nerves."

Come to Grief (1995): Francis's decision to resurrect Sid Halley fully sixteen years after his appearance in *Whip Hand* is questionable. Certainly, Halley is one of Francis's most successful characters combining, as he does, strength with vulnerability, self-belief with self-doubt, an indomitable will with human weakness. But the unconvincing plot of *Come to Grief* is an unworthy vehicle for Sid, and the only significant developments are in his relationships with the female characters in the book. In *Whip Hand*, Sid met **Louise McInnes**, a friend and former flat mate of Jenny's, who had surprised herself by fancying him. They have sex in a hotel room, but the liaison is peripheral to the plot and seems to be going nowhere. Sure enough, it has petered out at the opening of *Come to Grief*.

Come to Grief revolves around Sid's investigation into incidents of sickening and gratuitous cruelty to horses. One of the victims is a pony owned by nine-year-old **Rachel Ferns**, a leukemia sufferer who is desperately in need of a bone marrow transplant. One of the more plausible themes of *Come to Grief* is the growing attachment between Sid and the gravely ill little girl, bound together by a love of horses and troubles shared.

Sid's exposure of the perpetrator brings him into contact with **India Cathcart**, a feisty journalist who extracts from Sid a promise—which he knows he won't be able to keep—of an exclusive story. When she visits Sid in hospital after he is shot, an undeclared, possibly unacknowledged, mutual affection suddenly manifests itself.

It is a beginning, maybe, with India, but finally an end for Sid and Jenny. So long as they felt a mutual need to snipe at each other there was a bond, however hurtful. Antagonism was the cement of their relationship, corrosive and yet drawing them together. In *Come to Grief* though, the fight has gone out of Jenny. Perhaps it is because she has recently remarried and is now **Lady Wingham**, wife of a baronet. Meeting Sid at her father's house, she makes a half-hearted attempt to be nasty to him, but the bitterness she had nurtured for so long has died in her. Sid's feelings are ambivalent: he is conscious not of relief, but of a sense of loss.

Under Orders (2006): If Francis's decision to bring Sid Halley back in *Come to Grief* failed to show Sid in the best light, wheeling him out once again for the deeply disappointing *Under Orders* further diminished him as a character. On the face of it, using Halley at least had the merit of introducing readers unfamiliar with Francis's work to a character whose complex personality, admirable yet flawed, reveals the essential nature of what it is to be human. For long-standing devotees, Halley should have been a welcome and familiar reference point connecting *Under Orders* with Francis's best-loved novels of the 60's and 70's. None of this, unfortunately, is the case, because Sid Halley is not the man he was. Once dynamic and unpredictable, now he's living in the comfort zone and, at the age of thirty-eight, sinking fast into middle-aged complacency. Halley himself admits that he no longer seeks out the dangerous assignments, preferring to potter about doing unthreatening surveillance work. He doesn't even argue any more with his vituperative ex-wife Jenny, now **Lady Wingham**, consolidating a rapprochement that had begun at the end of *Come to Grief*. A sure sign of his retreat from action man to paragon of domesticity is his harmonious relationship with Dutch girlfriend **Marina van der Meer**; by the end of the novel they're married and, no doubt, thinking of decorating the spare room as a nursery.

In *Under Orders* Halley spends a lot of time sharing information—mostly irrelevant to the plot—with the reader. We are given the benefit of his opinions on such diverse topics as cork removers, computer spam, London buses, the ability of criminals to retain their seats in the House of Lords, the pressures on the countryside caused by building new houses in the south of England, and the distribution of National Lottery funds. None of this advances the plot by one iota. At the height of his violent struggle with a murderer in his flat, Halley reflects on the moral dilemma of whether he would use a knife if he could manage to reach one in the kitchen. This does little to heighten the scene's dramatic tension, but it does neatly sum up the problems inherent in Francis's portrayal of Sid Halley in *Under Orders*.

Hamlet (*Field of 13* 1998: "Spring Fever")

Hamlet is a steeplechaser owned by **Mrs. Angela Hart** and trained by **Clement Scott**. He is sold out of Scott's yard when Mrs. Hart discovers that Scott has defrauded her.

Hampshire, England

Hampshire is a county on the south coast of England. Its county town is Winchester. Southampton and Portsmouth are important ports. Hampshire was the birthplace of writers Charles Dickens and Jane Austen. The **New Forest** National Park lies mainly in Hampshire.

High Stakes (1975): **Black Fire**, a gelding bought at bloodstock sales in Miami, is stabled at Hantsford Manor Riding School in Hampshire.

Risk (1977): A boat was built at **Lymington**, Hampshire, for a client named **Arthur Robinson**.

To the Hilt (1996): **Alexander Kinloch**'s wife **Emily Cox** gives him the name of a friend of hers in **Hampshire** who trains racehorses. Emily says that her friend will look after **Golden Malt**, a racehorse belonging to the **King Alfred Brewery**.

Driving Force (1992): **Freddie Croft**'s racehorse transport business is based in **Pixhill**, Hampshire. Trainer **Michael Watermead**'s yard is also in Pixhill.

Come to Grief (1995): A body is discovered in a car in the **New Forest**, Hampshire.

Hampstead, London

Hampstead is a fashionable area of north-west London. Many actors, musicians, artists and writers have homes there. Hampstead Heath is one of London's biggest and most beautiful parks.

Bonecrack (1971): **Neil Griffon** owns a flat in Hampstead. His girlfriend **Gillie**, who is also his tenant, lives there.

High Stakes (1975): Young American **Alexandra Ward** borrows money from **Steven Scott** for her taxi fare home to Hampstead.

Harding, Clare (*Dead Heat* 2007)

Clare Harding is the News Editor on the *Cambridge Evening News*. She goes, at **Max Moreton**'s invitation, to interview him at **The Hay Net**, Max's **Newmarket** restaurant. She is initially skeptical of Max's assurances that the food poisoning incident was not his fault, but leaves more or less convinced. She accepts an invitation to dine at The Hay Net with her husband as Max's guests.

Harley (*Rat Race* 1970)

Harley is the owner of **Derrydown Air Transport**, a small air-taxi firm working out of a former RAF airfield near **Buckingham** in south-east England. He is irritable and bossy; according to his niece, **Honey Harley**, he is jealous of pilot **Matt Shore**'s flying experience. When Matt saves the lives of **Colin Ross** and **Nancy Ross** by guiding them home after the instruments of their plane are tampered with, Harley is angry that Matt had contravened the rules of the Air Navigation Order. He says he will state in court that Derrydown dissociated itself from Matt's actions, and that if Matt is fined he will have to pay it himself.

Harley complains to Matt that he's flying too quickly and so Derrydown has to charge its clients less. Then he says he's taking on another pilot because of the increased taxi work. He's affronted when Matt suggests there is a connection between the two.

Harley, Crystal (*10 lb. Penalty* 1997)

Crystal Harley is **Mervyn Teck**'s secretary, and **George Juliard**'s political agent. Her outwardly testy manner belies an unexpectedly generous nature. She loans a car to Juliard to tour the constituency while his own is checked out for possible sabotage. When **Benedict Juliard** visits **Hoopwestern** a few years later she is less edgy, and has settled down to married life.

Harley, Honey (*Rat Race* 1970)

Honey is the niece of the owner of **Derrydown Air Transport**. She works as a secretary and air traffic controller, and makes a habit of seducing the pilots. She propositions **Matt Shore**, who isn't interested. Without being asked, she leaves a bag of groceries for Matt in his caravan, noticing that he has nothing to eat there.

Harlow, Jules Reginald (*Field of 13*: "Corkscrew")

Jules Harlow is a wealthy English inventor and entrepreneur. He lives in America, and is about fifty years old. He buys a two-year-old filly as an engagement present for his wife-to-be from bloodstock agent **Sandy Nutbridge**. When Nutbridge is arrested on tax evasion charges Harlow stands bail for him to the tune of $10,000. When Nutbridge is cleared of the charges his crooked lawyer, **Patrick Green**, refuses to return Harlow's bail money. Green thinks Harlow will just write it off, but he has badly underestimated Harlow.

Harlow, Wykeham (*Break In* 1985; *Bolt* 1986)

Wykeham Harlow is a veteran racehorse trainer who has stables on the **Sussex** Downs, and trains for **Princess Casilia**. He hates traveling, and mysteriously develops a migraine headache which prevents him from watching his horses run at racecourses furthest from his stables. Harlow is a top class trainer who loves and understands his horses, and is an expert at getting them to the track fit to run for their lives. In his old age he has become forgetful of the names of both horses and jockeys. He races his horses regularly between October and New Year's Day. Then he gives them a break during the cold weather, bringing them out again in March. As a young man, Harlow had been a successful amateur rider and a magnet for the ladies too. As a trainer he had won the **Aintree** Grand National on two occasions. Ten years ago he had spotted **Kit Fielding**'s potential as a young amateur and had appointed him stable jockey.

Harlow is annoyed with Kit when he gives **Cascade** a hard ride at **Newbury**, fearing that the horse may not recover in time for the **Cheltenham** festival. He is devastated when he finds two of the Princess's horses dead in their boxes, deliberately killed. He hires a dog patrol to keep his other horses safe, but early one morning he phones Kit in distress; another horse has been killed. When the perpetrator returns for a third time Harlow surprises him; his intervention is shocking but decisive.

Harris, Mr. (*Blood Sport* 1967)

Mr. Harris is an elderly man who works for a leading horse journal in Kentucky, compiling the annual stallion register. He helps **Gene Hawkins** to track down two missing stallions via the journal's database.

Harrison (*The Edge* 1988)

An ex-policeman, Harrison is employed by the **Jockey Club's** Security Service; he is close to retirement.

Harrow School

Harrow is a famous boarding school for boys in Harrow-on-the-Hill, north-west London. Founded in 1572, Harrow has roughly 800 pupils, each of whom pays around £25,000 a year. The school's alumni include Sir Winston Churchill, actors Edward and James Fox, Jawaharlal Nehru and novelist Anthony Trollope. In 2007 the school received unwelcome publicity when a violent crime, which wouldn't have been out of place in a Dick Francis novel, occurred in one of the staff houses. The beautiful and talented daughter of a member of Harrow's teaching staff was brutally murdered by the drug-addicted son of another teacher.

Under Orders (2006): **Sir Anthony Wingham**, **Peter Enstone** and **George Lochs** are all former pupils of Harrow School.

Hart, Mrs. Angela (*Field of 13* 1998: "Spring Fever")

Mrs. Hart, a widow, is a racehorse owner in her early fifties. She is kind and good-natured. She develops a schoolgirl crush on the jump jockey who rides her two horses. In order to see more of him, she decides to buy another horse. She accompanies the jockey to **Yorkshire**, where he apparently pays a considerable sum on her behalf for **Magic**, a nondescript gelding. When she discovers that the jockey, in collusion with her trainer, has defrauded her, she deals with it in her own way.

Harvey (*Driving Force* 1992)

Harvey is the head driver at **Croft Raceways** racehorse transport firm. In his previous career as a racecourse valet Harvey had looked after **Freddie Croft**. In his mid-thirties and reliable, Harvey has a skeptical view of life tempered with a sense of humor. With his wife and four children, he lives next door to the farmyard used as offices and workshop by Croft Raceways. Harvey finds another of Croft Raceways' employees dead, his neck broken, in the inspection pit.

Harvey, Belladonna (*Second Wind* 1999)

Belladonna, known as "Bell," is the blonde, attractive daughter of wealthy farmer and racehorse owner **Caspar Harvey**. She is the former lover of **Kris Ironside** and is still friendly with Ironside, though their relationship is awkward. She takes a job as assistant trainer to **George Loricroft**. When Ironside asks Bell to marry him, she says yes.

Harvey, Caspar (*Second Wind* 1999)

Harvey, a wealthy farmer and racehorse owner; lives near **Newmarket** and runs a lucrative business selling birdseed. He throws a Sunday lunch party, and invites **Kris Ironside** and **Perry Stuart**. He asks Perry to discourage Ironside from seeing his daughter **Belladonna Harvey**, who used to go out with Ironside and has not got over him; Perry declines to help. Harvey is shocked when his best two-year-old filly is found ill and distressed in her box. He transfers his horses to trainer **George Loricroft**, where Bell is working as Loricroft's assistant. It transpires that Harvey is one of the **Unified Traders**, who act as middlemen in the buying and selling of radioactive material.

Harwich, England

Harwich is a coastal town and port on the estuary of the Rivers Stour and Orwell in north-east **Essex**.

Straight (1987): **Greville Franklin**, a dealer in precious and semi-precious stones, had been on his way to Harwich to collect some cut diamonds from a partner in a firm of Antwerp diamond cutters who was arriving on the ferry. His car had broken down in **Ipswich** and he was killed by falling scaffolding in the street.

Hastings Park racecourse

Hastings Park racecourse is part of a larger complex, known as **Exhibition Park**, in Vancouver, Canada.

The Edge (1988): **Julius Apollo Filmer** goes to Hastings Park to collect, as he thinks, accreditation as the sole owner of racehorse **Laurentide Ice**. Instead he faces an enquiry into his criminal activities.

Mercer Lorrimore's horse **Voting Right** wins the Jockey Club Race Train Stakes at Hastings Park.

Haunted House (*Field of 13* 1988: "The Day of the Losers")

Steeplechaser Haunted House is third favorite for the **Aintree** Grand National. In the race he is ridden by jockey **Gerry Springwood** who has lost his nerve and gives the horse no help from the saddle. However, Haunted House has run over the Aintree fences before and knows what to do. He runs a steady race and finishes second. The winner, though, has carried the wrong weight and is disqualified, so Haunted House is promoted to first place.

Hawkins, Gene (*Blood Sport* 1967)

In *Blood Sport* Francis shows us a life lived within the confines of despair. Gene Hawkins is thirty-eight years old and has no desire to see thirty-nine. His job—to prevent foreign powers from insinuating their agents into sensitive government departments—involves sleeping with a gun under his pillow. He derives comfort from having readily to hand the means either to defend his life, or to take it. When he is called upon to save a man from drowning in the Thames, Gene is tempted to allow the strength of the current to kill them both.

His mental state is due in large part to the departure of Caroline, his partner for six years. Alone and lonely, Gene sees a void that no-one else can fill. When he does meet a girl who stirs his interest, it is someone with whom a relationship of any kind, let alone a sexual one, is likely to be problematic—**Lynnie Keeble**, the seventeen-year-old daughter of his boss.

Gene flies to America to search for a missing thoroughbred stallion, engaging the reader's sympathy through his vulnerability and his meticulous approach to an unwanted task. He doggedly follows up wafer-thin leads and eventually finds the stolen stallion, as well as the villains responsible. Narrowly foiling an attempt on his life, Gene reflects on the irony of the situation; the villains were trying to kill him, an outcome he himself would welcome, and yet he was, by avoiding it, disappointing all concerned. Later his American colleague, **Walt Prensela**, tells him he doesn't enjoy working with people like Gene: "With your kind, dying comes easy. It's living that takes the guts."

Gene continues to brood on the breakdown of his relationship with Caroline. Being free and single, considered a state of bliss by many for whom it is a distant memory, is for him a prison without bars. A walk on a California beach with Lynnie allows a sliver of light to penetrate his curtain of despair, but he knows that it would be dangerous to let anything develop between them.

Gene undertakes a thirty-hour solitary surveillance operation in the Arizona desert. To die by his own hand in such a desolate place is an inviting prospect, but eventually he draws back from the ultimate solution to his troubles. When Prensela is killed, the anguish that Gene feels is tinged with anger that Prensela had somehow cheated him: "Walt had taken what I'd wanted, stolen my death..."

And yet, finally, a glimmer of hope struggles free of the gloom. He flies back to England with Lynnie, who is reluctant to leave him at the airport. Because of the difference in their ages, Gene can see no future for them. But when Lynnie tells him she will still be there for him when she is twenty-one, it jolts Gene out of his morbid self-pity. He realizes he cannot waste this chance of happiness.

Hawthorn, Flora (*Proof* 1984)

Flora is the wife of racehorse trainer **Jack Hawthorn**. Quiet and good natured, she has three children from her first marriage. When a horse van crashes into the marquee at Jack's owners' party, Flora is rescued, relatively unscathed, by **Tony Beach**. The next day, when her husband is in hospital with a broken leg, she asks Tony to go round evening stables with her, feeling unable to cope without support. She also asks Tony to go with her to the races as she's worried about dealing with a difficult owner. Later, she buys Tony a silver penknife as a token of her gratitude for his help.

Hawthorn, Jack (*Proof* 1984)

Hawthorn is a **Berkshire** racehorse trainer; he is about sixty years old, successful and perennially busy. At the annual owners' party at his stables, a horse van careers down the hill and crashes into a marquee, killing eight guests. Hawthorn is taken to hospital with a broken leg. According to his wife **Flora** his enforced rest does nothing to improve his temper.

Haydock Park racecourse

Haydock Park is situated at Newton-le-Willows, Merseyside, in the north-west of England. It is a well-run racecourse which stages top class racing both over jumps and on the flat. Its stiff fences provide a stern test for steeplechasers.

Rat Race (1970): Air taxi pilot **Matt Shore**

ferries a group of racing professionals from London to Haydock Park races.

The Hay Net (*Dead Heat* 2007)

The Hay Net is a successful restaurant in **Newmarket** run by chef **Max Moreton**. It is popular with the town's racing fraternity. Its reputation is temporarily sullied after a food poisoning incident at **Newmarket racecourse** at a dinner prepared by Max.

Hearse Puller (*Knock Down* 1974)

Hearse Puller is a five-year-old hurdler bought by **Jonah Dereham** for **Mrs. Kerry Sanders** as a birthday present for **Nicol Brevett**. He is leggy, with wayward eyes and not an easy ride, but a good prospect nonetheless, and had never fallen. Jonah pays £3400 for him at **Ascot Sales**. In the car park he is threatened with serious injury by two men and is forced to sell the horse on at a small profit.

Heathbury Park racecourse

Heathbury Park is a fictional racecourse in the south of England.

Forfeit (1968): Journalist **James Tyrone** has been commissioned to write a magazine article on the forthcoming Lamplighter Gold Cup Steeplechase at Heathbury Park. Ante-post favorite **Tiddely-Pom**, stabled at Heathbury Park prior to the race, has to be moved to avoid being "got at" by criminals.

Helikon (*Bolt* 1986)

Helikon, a novice hurdler owned by **Princess Casilia**, is fairly talented but nervous and wayward. He is brought down at the fourth hurdle at **Sandown Park**; jockey **Kit Fielding** is thrown off and another faller lands on top of him.

Hengelman, Sam (*Blood Sport* 1967)

Hengelman, a horse van driver; works for **Dave Teller** at his stud farm in Kentucky. He accompanies **Sam Kitchens** and **Walt Prensela** to the Teton Mountains to collect **Chrysalis** from **Gene Hawkins**. Later, he drives from Kentucky to Kingman, Arizona to meet Gene in order to rescue two stolen stallions.

Henry (*Decider* 1993)

Henry is **Lee Morris**'s friend, who hires out big tents. He provides a circus big top for **Stratton Park racecourse** as temporary accommodation for racegoers after the stands are destroyed. Henry forcibly detains bogus animal rights protester **Harold Quest** when he catches him eating a hamburger.

Hermes (*High Stakes* 1975)

Hermes is a colt owned by **Steven Scott** and trained by **Jody Leeds** until transferred to **Trevor Kennet**. He is unremarkable to look at but very useful. Hermes had won several races but lost every time Steven had backed him. It later transpires that it was not Hermes, but a substitute that was sent to Kennet. The trainer later phones Steven to say that the horse has broken down.

Heroes

"The world's made up of individuals who don't want to be heroes."

Brian Moore, Irish-born Canadian novelist, quoted in the *Sunday Times* April 15th 1990.

The heroes of Dick Francis's novels are considered under the following headings: physical appearance; age; marriage; girlfriends/partners; children; vulnerability; equanimity; courage; and the duds.

(a) Physical appearance: In *Wild Horses* (1994) film director **Thomas Lyon** describes himself as physically "unremarkable." It is a description—or lack of it—that would fit a healthy proportion of Francis's heroes. Indeed, in over half of his novels Francis sees no need for his narrators—all his books are written from a first person perspective—to supply any details at all. This is in keeping with their general reluctance to draw attention to themselves. Of the characters that do provide information about themselves, most have dark hair and brown eyes. In complexion they are sallow rather than ruddy. If they are handsome it is in an unconventional or understated way.

Although many of the heroes are or have been jockeys, none is small in stature. Jump jockeys tend, in any case, to be of similar size to the general population, only thinner. In *Dead Cert* (1962) **Alan York** describes himself as being of average height; ex-champion jump jockey **Derek Franklin**, the hero of *Straight* (1989) is five feet nine. Others—not jockeys—are six feet or more, including **Jockey Club** Security Service agent **Tor Kelsey** (*The Edge* 1988), toy inventor **Steven Scott** (*High Stakes* 1975), and Jockey Club Chief Investigating Officer **David Cleveland** (*Slay-Ride* 1973). Tallest at six feet three is ex-jockey and now racing manager **William Derry** (*Twice Shy* 1981), whose incipient riding career was, unsurprisingly, curtailed by increasing weight.

(b) Age: Of the thirty heroes whose ages we know, seven are in their late twenties and eighteen in their early thirties. Four of the remaining five fall just outside this age range. They are mature enough to know what they want out of life, if not how best to achieve it. They are experienced enough to have had hopes dashed and illusions shattered, but still have enough energy to bounce back from whatever vicissitudes fate has dealt them.

That Francis was sensible to impose an age limitation on his heroes is proven by the one exception, the protagonist of *10 lb. Penalty* (1997). Seventeen-year-old **Benedict Juliard** is a youth for whom the word callow could have been personally coined. On the other hand the next youngest, **Alan York**, at twenty-four the hero of Francis's first novel, *Dead Cert*, is one of his most convincing characters, and the maturity of his reactions to the problems that confront him belie his comparatively tender years.

At the other end of the age scale are **Gene Hawkins** (*Blood Sport* 1967) and Sid Halley (*Under Orders* 2006). Hawkins, thirty-eight, works for a clandestine government department arranging accidents for perceived enemies of the state. Old before his time, Hawkins is a man whose years of living an essentially anti-social existence on the periphery of civilized life have gradually eroded in him the will to observe the conventions of normal social interaction. Since his girlfriend walked out on him six years before, he has continually fought against depression. It's debatable whether he'll reach the end of the book without finding a way to organize a terminal accident for himself.

Francis brings back his greatest hero, **Sid Halley**, in *Under Orders*; he is, at thirty-eight, four years older than he was in *Come to Grief* (1995). Sadly, those years have not been kind to him. Once a complex and dynamic man of action, Sid is now in serious danger of preferring an evening at home with his pipe and slippers to catching villains.

(c) Marriage: Among Francis's heroes, marriage is not a popular institution. Only four of the thirty-seven are living with their wives, and three of them have troubled marriages. In *Forfeit* (1968) **James Tyrone**, an investigative racing reporter, cares for his invalid wife while looking elsewhere for sexual gratification. Physics teacher **Jonathan Derry** (*Twice Shy*) has been trapped for years in the kind of marriage normally chronicled on the problem page of a women's magazine. Architect and builder **Lee Morris** (*Decider* 1993) has married

too young and grown apart from his wife, **Amanda Morris**. They continue to live together and even share the same bed, but marital relations are a fond memory. That leaves one solitary hero who is allowed to enjoy a relatively normal married life, film actor **Edward Lincoln** in *Smokescreen* (1972). But even he has endured a rocky patch with his wife, **Charlie Lincoln**, and it had taken an accident which left their young daughter brain damaged to bring them together as allies in adversity.

To this short list we must add damaged but durable racing investigator **Sid Halley** who, alone of Francis's heroes, appears in four novels: *Odds Against* (1965); *Whip Hand* (1979); *Come to Grief*; and *Under Orders*. Sid's tunnel vision in his quest to become champion jump jockey drives his wife, **Jenny Halley**, to force him to choose between her and his career. Jenny is runner-up by several lengths but, with a tongue like paint stripper, remains in the background to belittle Sid at every opportunity. Finally, at the end of *Under Orders*, Sid marries his girlfriend, **Marina van der Meer**, and threatens to sink inexorably into a life of domesticity.

Three more characters have been married and failed to stay the course. **Matt Shore**, the depressive, downwardly mobile air-taxi pilot in *Rat Race* (1970), had stayed married for twelve years but has been divorced for three. The twin burdens of being a husband at nineteen and spending most of his time flying to far-flung parts of the world finally put his marriage into a nosedive. In *Knock Down* (1974), bloodstock agent **Jonah Dereham** mentions a failed marriage without dwelling on the reasons why, whilst bohemian, aristocratic artist **Alexander Kinloch** (*To the Hilt* 1996) manages to last only four months with his new wife, **Emily Jane Cox**, in the racing village of **Lambourn**. By then he had realized that if he stayed there he would never again paint anything worth looking at. Decamping to the solitude of an isolated Scottish mountain, he happily rediscovers his muse. He remains, however, on speaking terms with his wife, who seems to have been quite content to see the back of him.

Ironically, the two characters who appear to have been happily married are both, at the start of their respective novels, widowers. In *Enquiry* (1969) a car crash had claimed the life of **Kelly Hughes**'s wife Rosalind four years previously, while Emma, the young wife of wine merchant **Tony Beach** (*Proof* 1984), has recently died in childbirth, and Tony is still grieving.

(d) Girlfriends/partners: Marriage may be a non-starter for most of Francis's heroes, but girlfriends and partners are by no means ruled out. In *Bonecrack* (1971) Neil Griffon is trying to run his ailing father's racing stable as well as deal with the madness of an Italian criminal obsessed with his son's desire to become a jockey. At the end of a hard day he at least has the consolation of going home to Gillie, the tenant of his Hampstead flat and his lover into the bargain. The well-connected Randall Drew, returning with a nasty chest infection from Moscow in *Trial Run* (1978), is possibly hoping for a bit of sympathy when he receives a visit from his posh girlfriend, Lady Emma Louders-Allen-Croft. Playing the ministering angel is not, however, Lady Emma's strong suit, and she wastes no time in letting Randall know how tedious she finds his illness. When, somewhat optimistically, Randall floats the idea of marriage, Lady Emma is characteristically dismissive.

More harmonious is the relationship in *Twice Shy* between William Derry, ex-amateur jockey turned racing manager, and his live-in girlfriend Cassie Morris. Cassie is undemanding, independent and—always a quality to be valued—possesses the presence of mind to defend William by knocking out a would-be assailant with a coalscuttle. In *Under Orders* Sid Halley's girlfriend Marina van der Meer is steadfastly supportive despite being beaten up and shot in the leg. Sid, recognizing a diamond when he sees one, promptly marries her. Multi-millionaire's son Ian Pembroke, who in *Hot Money* (1987) acts as his five-times married father's unofficial bodyguard, has made a conscious decision not to marry, since he does not trust himself to be faithful. Instead he has a mutually convenient arrangement with a married woman a decade or so older than him—a casual but satisfying relationship.

Several heroes, if not involved with someone at the outset, soon find themselves drawn into a web of emotional entanglement from which they rarely emerge unscathed. It is not long before *Dead Cert*'s Alan York realizes he has fallen for the delectable Kate Ellery-Penn. That a close relative of Kate's later proves to be responsible for most of the crimes committed on the racecourses of southern England does not help to smooth the path of true love.

Jockey Rob Finn (*Nerve* 1963) loves his cousin Joanna, and expends a considerable amount of energy trying to persuade her that, if inbreeding is good enough for the racehorse, it should be good enough for them. As for the aristocratic Lord

Henry Gray in *Flying Finish* (1966), he has never loved anyone, an upbringing devoid of real affection having failed to give him the necessary skills. Then one day, in his capacity of head traveling groom for a horse transport firm, he flies a load of broodmares to Milan. At the airport he meets Gabriella, a young trinket seller. In seconds Henry's repressions and hang-ups are forgotten, and it's not long before he and Gabriella are improving Anglo-Italian relations under a horse blanket in the back seat of Henry's DC4.

Falling for the wrong person is a regular occurrence in Francis's novels, as it is in life generally. Thirty-eight-year-old Gene Hawkins is attracted to Lynnie Keeble, the seventeen-year-old daughter of his boss. When, at the end of *Blood Sport*, Lynnie says she's prepared to wait for him until she's twenty-one, her dad isn't too worried. "She'll change her mind," he says. Knowing Hawkins' luck, she probably does.

For merchant banker Tim Ekaterin (*Banker* 1982) it's Judith Michaels, his boss's wife, whom he finds difficult to ignore. Judith reciprocates his feelings, but both are prevented by the respect and affection they share for Gordon Michaels, Judith's husband, from committing to each other—at least while Gordon is still alive. In *The Danger* (1983) Andrew Douglas, an expert in negotiating the release of kidnap victims, surprises himself by developing strong feelings for one of his clients, pretty Italian jockey Alessia Cenci. It's a relationship doomed to fail; Alessia's harrowing experiences have left her without the desire for physical love. In *Straight* jump jockey Derek Franklin goes to bed with Clarissa Williams, the titled, married ex-lover of his dead brother Greville Franklin, but he is under no illusions about what she really wants from him—to feel close again, through him, to Greville.

(e) Children: With marriage being the exception rather than the rule, children do not figure heavily in Francis's books. Of the nine heroes that are or have been married, only two have children—though *Decider*'s Lee Morris has, admittedly, taken the job seriously and is the proud father of six sons. This novel is a departure from Francis's normal modus operandi in that the boys and their relationship with their father play an important role in the story, and Lee Morris's character is the richer for being given extra definition by his interaction with his sons. In contrast, the three young children of movie actor Edward Lincoln are peripheral to the plot of *Smokescreen*. Libby,

Lincoln's five-year-old daughter, is brain damaged after being accidentally dropped by son **Peter** as a baby. This tragic event has, ironically, served to hold together Lincoln's marriage to **Charlie Lincoln**, which his frequent absences on location and burgeoning career were threatening to undermine. That apart, the children remain in the background.

Freddie Croft in *Driving Force* (1992) has a child out of wedlock. The mother, finding she is pregnant, is by this time in a relationship with another man. She does not see fit to disabuse her current partner of the mistaken notion that the child is his, and promptly marries him. Living nearby, and moving in the same circles as his ex-lover, Freddie occasionally sees his daughter **Cinders**, but she is oblivious of who her father really is, and Freddie has no intention of disturbing the status quo.

(f) **Vulnerability:** The first person narrative style that Francis adopts in all his novels demands protagonists whom the reader can care about. To achieve this Francis makes them admirable and, particularly in the earlier books, vulnerable. Until his form tailed off in the last few years, Francis rarely created heroes lacking in depth or human frailty. Certainly, they have heroic traits, among them modesty, physical courage and the ability to maintain an even temper in the face of extreme provocation. But they are human, and often it is the struggle with the less heroic side of their nature that is most compelling. In an article in the magazine *Book Collector*, the crime writer and reviewer HRF Keating pointed out that Francis's heroes are "not afraid of judging." But to hold clear views on the behavior of others demands from the hero a searching self-analysis in return. When a brutal evaluation of his own shortcomings is combined with adverse circumstances in his personal life, the result is a complex character whose sensitivity to the sharp edges of life is acute. In *Forfeit* James Tyrone faces an agonizing moral dilemma—how to keep faith with his polio-stricken, totally dependent wife **Elizabeth** while dealing with the occasional sexual temptations that present themselves in the course of his life as an investigative racing journalist. Leaving Elizabeth is a possibility that James does not entertain. But he is haunted by the compromises he allows himself to make, and is sharply aware of his weakness in taking lovers. Rather than submit to blackmail James is forced to tell Elizabeth that he has been sleeping with someone else, and hates himself for it.

The character that most clearly demonstrates a man struggling both with himself and with the malignity of fate is **Sid Halley**, particularly in the first two novels in which he appears (*Odds Against* and *Whip Hand*). Born without advantages, Sid's natural talent and sheer strength of will had combined to forge a brilliant career as a jump jockey. He became champion, but success had its price. His wife, **Jenny Halley**, walked out, no longer able to cope with his obsessive determination to be the best. Not long afterwards Sid took a heavy fall in a race. His horse's racing plate sliced through his wrist, and Sid's career was over. Reluctantly he became a racing investigator, but in his dreams he still saw himself in jockey's silks, heard the crowd shouting his name, and smelled the sweat of the horse beneath him as together they surged for the line.

In the opening chapter of *Odds Against*, Sid is on a seemingly routine surveillance assignment when he is shot in the stomach. Visiting Sid in hospital, his estranged wife's father shrewdly brings him a book on company law. As a result Sid becomes involved in a struggle to save a racecourse from a fraudulent take-over. Sid's dormant will to fight is re-awoken; the villains, however, exact their revenge by smashing his deformed hand to a pulp. The doctors have no choice but to amputate what remains.

In *Whip Hand* Sid is hired by the wife of a **Newmarket** trainer to safeguard their Two Thousand Guineas favorite, **Tri-Nitro**. Her fears are well-founded; the colt finishes last in the Guineas while Sid, forced to back down as a result of menaces and intimidation, sits of his own free will in an airport hotel room in Paris. Abducted before the big race, Sid had faced the threat of having his one good hand blown off with a shotgun. For the first time in his life he had known eviscerating fear; afterwards he can barely live with himself. Francis is at his best in his portrayal of the way Sid deals with his self-loathing and how he subsequently rediscovers his self-esteem.

Gene Hawkins (*Blood Sport*) is a flawed character, burdened by his past. Working in counter-espionage, he sleeps with a gun under his pillow, and has constantly to guard against the urge to put it in his mouth and pull the trigger. Early in the novel Gene dives into the Thames to save a man from drowning. Fighting his way back to the surface against a strong current, the thought of just letting himself die is seductive, but the responsibility he feels towards the man he is saving keeps him going.

Partly responsible for Gene's depression is the intense loneliness he has felt since Caroline, the woman he'd lived with for six years, left him the previous year. Without someone to love, he feels that his life is worthless. His spirits are at their lowest ebb when his friend and colleague, American **Walt Prensela**, dies while saving Hawkins' life: "Walt had taken what I wanted, stolen my death..."

Amidst the gloom there is a faint glow of hope for Hawkins. Seventeen-year-old **Lynnie Keeble**, his boss's daughter, has seen in him something that attracts her. Hawkins feels the same about her but tells her she's too young. When Lynnie says she'll wait for him till she's twenty-one Hawkins, finally, finds a reason to go on living.

In *Rat Race* the source of **Matt Shore**'s disillusionment is a career in flying that has stalled dramatically. Once a first officer and in line for captain with British Overseas Airways Corporation, Matt is now broke and divorced, with a conviction for gross negligence and a sacking for cowardice on his CV. As *Rat Race* opens he has just signed on with a small air-taxi firm whose finances are decidedly shaky. Matt describes himself as "negative as wallpaper"; certainly, he's got plenty to be negative about.

Lord Henry Gray, the protagonist of *Flying Finish*, has gone through prep school and **Eton** virtually unnoticed, and has grown into a secretive man who finds relationships difficult. He loves no-one, because he has never learned how. What Henry wants most is to be a professional jockey, but hasn't the talent to match his ambition; he rides as an amateur but lacks the social skills that would allow him to join in the camaraderie of the weighing room. On top of everything else, he hates his desk-bound job in London. One lunchtime he leaves his office and he doesn't go back. Instead he takes a job as a traveling groom, ferrying racehorses by plane in and out of Britain, and sets in motion a chain of events that will change him forever.

The family background of jump jockey **Kelly Hughes** (*Enquiry*) would have had lesser men reaching for the 1960's equivalent of Prozac. It was bad enough that four years previously his adored wife Rosalind had been killed in a car crash. But Kelly's problems had started in childhood. His father, working class and proud of it, had wanted nothing more for his son that a dead end job to match his own, and had considered Kelly's enjoyment of books and academic study a personal af-front. He was contemptuous when Kelly won a place at the London School of Economics, but at least it gave him a stick to beat his son with when Kelly subsequently decided to make racing his career; in his father's eyes, Kelly had misused public funds. When Kelly has his jockey's license withdrawn by the Stewards of the **Jockey Club** for allegedly not trying to win when riding the favorite in a big race, it never occurs to his disgusted parents that he may be innocent.

The characters with the heaviest crosses to bear appear in Francis's earlier novels. After *Rat Race* this trait becomes much less obvious. In the novels of the 1970's only **Jonah Dereham**, hero of *Knock Down* conforms to type. At the age of sixteen he is orphaned and left penniless when his mother is killed in a riding accident, and his father dies shortly afterwards. Jonah struggles to forge a career as a bloodstock agent whilst caring for an abusive alcoholic brother.

Burdened heroes make a bit of a comeback in the early 1980's, though their personal difficulties are not on the same scale as previously. In *Twice Shy*, teacher **Jonathan Derry** is trapped in a loveless marriage, owing to his wife's bitterness at being unable to have children. **Tim Ekaterin** (*Banker*) is deeply ashamed when his widowed mother, following the example set by her profligate late husband, manages to gamble away half a million pounds and is made bankrupt. This experience, however, strengthens Tim's resolve not to emulate his feckless parents.

The last of these emotionally troubled characters is **Tony Beach** (*Proof*). Tony was an only child and not much loved, his mother resenting the fact that his birth disrupted her hunting schedule. His father and grandfather were war heroes and dashing amateur jockeys. Tony himself, a wine merchant with little interest in horses and even less personal ambition, unsurprisingly considers himself a failure in comparison. The recent death of his pregnant, twenty-seven-year-old wife Emma has further depleted his reserves of optimism. Then Tony becomes embroiled in an investigation into stolen whisky, and his personal courage is put to the test. The realization that he possesses the same raw nerve as his illustrious forebears bolsters Tony's self-esteem and gives him the confidence to face the world.

By making his heroes vulnerable, Francis explores one of the essential elements of the human condition—endurance. He demonstrates how the unavoidable accidents of life—birth, childhood, family—create the background for a personal struggle for survival but also, ultimately, growth as a human being. Faced with a troubled past and an uncertain present, his heroes are forced to examine their deepest fears, to reveal the opaque facets of their innermost self, and often to draw on reserves of stamina and courage they didn't know they had.

(g) Equanimity: Calmness and placidity are traits common to many of Francis's heroes. They do not lose their tempers easily; they are restrained in the face of provocation. **Sid Halley**, for example, refuses to react when faced with the constant belittlement that his wife sustains in *Whip Hand*. **Lord Henry Gray** (*Flying Finish*) is philosophical about the frequent delays inherent in transporting horses around the world, shrugging off the frustrations of spending hours drinking tepid tea in draughty airports.

Architect **Lee Morris** (*Decider*) has a fragile marriage that causes him concern; he and his wife, **Amanda Morris**, had married young and produced six sons, but they have drifted apart emotionally. Though they still live together and even share a bed, they are no longer physically intimate. Yet Lee's essentially placid nature prevents the relationship from foundering completely, and the novel ends with a suggestion that reconciliation is a possibility.

Freddie Croft (*Driving Force*), ex-jump jockey and now owner of a horse transport firm, recognizes that his calmness is a definite advantage: "I was better at placating than confronting, at persuading than commanding; and I wasn't defeated much." Not that he wasn't capable of feeling anger: having survived an attempt to drown him, Freddie returns home to find his house ransacked and his prized Jaguar XJS a pile of tangled metal—someone had crashed it into his sister **Lizzie's** helicopter. Inside Freddie seethes, but his outward persona is more that of a man who has mislaid his fountain pen.

In *Twice Shy*, **Jonathan Derry** displays the lack of visible emotion typical of Francis's heroes. Nonconfrontational by nature, he possesses the teaching strategies—notably an ability not to rise to the bait—to defuse the combustible situations that can easily develop with adolescents. He uses these skills to deal with a pair of young thugs, one of whom is threatening him with a pistol. Using his quiet demeanor to lull them into thinking that he is not a threat, Jonathan is able to turn the odds in his favor by suddenly producing a high-powered rifle.

(h) Courage: Courage is a commodity that Francis's heroes possess without exception. In his second novel, *Nerve*, Francis explores the nature of courage, both physical and mental. When steeplechase jockey **Rob Finn** endures a sequence of twenty-eight consecutive losing rides and his horses run as if pulling a cartload of gravestones, racecourse rumor has it that his nerve has gone. Eventually his principal employer tells Rob he's going to find someone else to ride his horses. For a jockey this is the ultimate humiliation, and looks like putting an end to a promising career. But at his lowest point, when everyone in racing is writing him off, Rob shows the mental toughness to fight back. He knows he has not lost his nerve, and sets about proving that there is some other reason for his lack of success. When he finally gets a leg up on a horse that is fit and well, his almost reckless disregard for his own safety is matched only by the horse's, and the doubters are silenced.

If true courage is to struggle against fear and, ultimately, to conquer it, then **Sid Halley** is perhaps the most courageous of all Francis's heroes. In *Whip Hand*, Sid is forced to confront the most terrifying of all the demons that haunt him—the possibility of losing his one remaining hand. A villain scents Sid's fear, and uses it to make him abandon his role as protector of Two Thousand Guineas favorite **Tri-Nitro**. When Sid voluntarily absents himself from England, allowing Tri-Nitro to be "got at," his self-esteem plumbs previously unknown depths. Up till then his courage had been one of the few constants in his life he could rely on; now, it seemed, even that had deserted him. A few days later Sid finds himself an unexpected competitor in a hot air balloon race, partnering **John Viking**, a man for whom risking his life is a routine morning's work. Crashing through the tops of trees on take-off, they narrowly avoid a potentially fatal crash. Sid emerges smiling from the ordeal, his nerve as strong as ever, and determined never again to give in to threats.

Francis's heroes regularly exhibit unthinking, spur of the moment bravery. Merchant banker **Tim Ekaterin** (*Banker*) witnesses a stabbing attempt as he is leaving **Ascot** races. Regardless of the danger, he rushes at the assailant just before the blade finds its target. Bloodstock agent **Jonah Dereham** (*Knock Down*), arranges to meet a horse van driver in a rest area to collect a horse for a client; when he gets there two thugs are threatening the driver. Jonah does not stop to consider whether caution might be sensible. He picks up a thick branch and lays into them, despite the possible consequences to himself.

The possibility of being blown to bits by a variety of explosive devices tests the hero's courage in several novels. In *Rat Race* air-taxi pilot **Matt Shore**, bleeding from a knife wound, sees a young boy pick up a tin from the hood of a car. Realizing that the tin contains explosives that are about to be detonated by remote control, Matt urgently calls to the boy to throw the tin to him. As the tin reaches his hand he hurls it away behind a row of parked cars. The bomb explodes in the air, shattering car windows and knocking Matt off his feet.

In *Slay-Ride*, Jockey Club chief investigator **David Cleveland** displays bravery verging on the foolhardy. In Norway to look into the disappearance of an English jockey, David employs **Eric**, the brother of an Oslo policeman, as a driver. Eric's faithful dog **Odin** comes as part of the package. They return to the car to find that a bomb has been planted in the boot. Eric, distraught, has to be physically restrained by his brother from rushing to get Odin out. Unnoticed, David runs to the car, pulls open the back door and sprints for cover. Encouraged by a whistle from Eric, the dog follows. They manage to put a few yards between them and the car before the bomb rips it apart.

For Francis's heroes, the line between courage and bloody-mindedness is often a fine one, **Kelly Hughes**, the warned-off jump jockey in *Enquiry*, is laid up in his flat with his leg in plaster when he receives a visit from a villain demanding that he hand over incriminating evidence. Kelly's refusal to cooperate results in a relentless beating with his own crutch. The longer it goes on the more determined he is not to give in. He fights back as best he can, but eventually he is knocked unconscious. At no time does Kelly consider the line of least resistance an option.

In *To the Hilt* **Alexander Kinloch**, fourth son of the deceased Earl of Kinloch, recognizes the streak of obstinacy in his make-up and wonders at what point he would crack. He soon discovers the answer. A list of foreign bank accounts detailing the whereabouts of money embezzled from the family's brewing business has come into Alexander's possession. A villain, frantic to get his hands on the list, removes the red-hot grill from a garden barbecue and tells Alexander that if he does not talk, he will make him lie on it. Alexander knows he should tell the villain what he wants to know, but can't bring himself to do it. So he suffers for his stubbornness.

(i) The duds: In his book *Fiction First Aid*, Raymond Obstfeld makes a valid point about genre fiction. Because the structure of the plot tends to be relatively simple and the format doesn't vary a lot, it's vital to have a protagonist who is likeable or compelling or, preferably, both. This, after all, may be the only way of discriminating between similar novels. Inevitably, amongst Francis's many successfully drawn heroes there are some who are not sufficiently credible or interesting to make the reader care what happens to them. **Benedict Juliard (*10 lb. Penalty*)** is one such character. He has all the charisma of an over-serious actuarial student. He has no well-defined motivation for his actions. Worst of all, he is totally lacking in a sense of humor. In part this may be blamed on his age—he's just seventeen years old at the start of the book. At the end, though, he's twenty-one and still just as boring.

Charles Todd (*In the Frame* 1976) is twenty-nine and has no such excuse, though he's not helped by a weak plot and minor characters that are even more irritating than he is. Being an ex-real estate agent doesn't help. Now he's an artist, which is more promising, but he retains the aura of excitement and magnetism that surround his former employment. Nor does Charles act in a realistic way. At one point in the story, in which he investigates the fraudulent sale of valuable paintings, Charles is thrown from a hotel balcony by intruders and suffers a broken shoulder and ribs. The clear intention was to kill him; yet when, soon afterwards, he receives a message to meet friends outside the hotel, it never occurs to him to suspect that his attackers may have returned to finish the job. It's hard to sympathize with such naivety.

Diplomat **Peter Darwin (*Comeback* 1991)** is another protagonist who struggles to impress. In a story told from a first person viewpoint, that person must be at the heart of the action and emotionally involved in it. The reader, traveling with the narrator through the story, must want to know what is going to happen to him and, more importantly, must care. Peter, however, is not sufficiently involved in the plot. He's caught up by chance in the criminal activities affecting an equine veterinary practice and, for much of the novel, his role is merely to offer insight into the motives of the villains through having known their families as a child. It is further to his detriment as hero that Peter is party to improbable events—as when his mother, in the course of a routine telephone conversation with Peter, suddenly admits to a steamy affair twenty years before with the father of one of Peter's friends.

In *Second Wind* (1999) the hero again suffers owing to a feeble storyline. The plot requires meteorologist **Perry Stuart** to make questionable decisions without a credible motivation—like trust an unreliable friend to fly him through the eye of a hurricane and, on the way, to land on an uninhabited cay to check how someone's mushrooms are doing. Perry's behavior gets stranger as the novel progresses; in London he inexplicably bolts with a folder containing information vital to the plot. By this stage it's a major disappointment that he doesn't become completely unhinged and throw the wretched folder—and himself with it—into the Thames.

Herrick, Malcolm (*Trial Run* 1978)

Herrick, Moscow correspondent of English newspaper *The Watch*, is as close to being the villain of the piece as it is possible to get in this often impenetrable tale of murky goings-on in Communist Russia. Yet Herrick is no more than a minor player in the real game, which is a plan by two terrorists—unnamed, provenance unknown—to disrupt the forthcoming Olympic Games, to be held in Russia. Herrick has supplied the terrorists with a lethal substance and has charged them a lot of money for it—a piece of sharp business practice which subsequently proves detrimental to Herrick's health.

Randall Drew arrives in Moscow to investigate a possible relationship between **Johnny, Earl of Farringford**, and a German three-day-event rider, Hans Kramer, who has died in suspicious circumstances. Herrick, who knows more about Kramer than he should, uses his terrorist contacts in an attempt to prevent Randall from discovering anything. The terrorists however, by now realizing that Herrick has swindled them, have their own plans for Herrick.

Hertfordshire, England

Hertfordshire is one of the Home Counties which surround London. It lies to the north of the capital, and forms part of London's commuter belt. Despite its proximity to London, Hertfordshire has many areas of natural beauty and several pleasant country towns, including Hertford, **St. Albans**, Radlett and Berkhamstead.

Reflex (1980): the firm of solicitors for whom Jeremy Folk works is in St. Albans, Hertfordshire.

Twice Shy (1981): Bingo hall owner **Harry**

Gilbert lives in Welwyn Garden City, Hertfordshire.

Banker (1982): **Oliver Knowles'** stud farm is in Hertfordshire.

Break In (1985): **Major** and **Mrs. Clement Perryside**, former owners of **Metavane**, live in a retirement home in Hertfordshire.

Hewett, Carey (*Comeback* 1991)

Hewett is the senior partner in a veterinary practice in Cheltenham, **Gloucestershire**. Hewett's proclivity for getting involved in shady and financially ruinous deals belies his appearance of patrician calm and professional competence. When Hewett's carefully conceived plans run into serious difficulties he has no compunction about resorting to extreme measures in order to cover his tracks.

Hewlitt (*The Danger* 1983)

Hewlitt is one of the kidnappers of **Dominic Nerrity**. He has a long criminal record, mainly for stealing antiques and silver from houses. He is arrested by police after **Tony Vine** rescues Dominic.

Hexham, England

Hexham is a country market town in Northumberland, a large rural county which borders Scotland.

For Kicks (1965): After attending **Bogside** races, journalist **Tommy Stapleton** had stayed with friends near Hexham before being killed in a car crash whilst driving back to London.

Hialeah Turf Club, Florida

When **Miami** Jockey Club was established in 1924, a racetrack and grandstand were built adjacent to the already existing greyhound track. Massive damage was incurred during the Great Hurricane of 1926, and in 1930 Joseph E Widener bought the racetrack and completely rebuilt the 200 acre site. Known as Hialeah Park, the area was beautifully landscaped, and hundreds of royal palms and coconut trees planted. A lake was constructed in the infield and a flock of flamingos imported from Cuba. Hialeah Park became a magnet for the rich and famous who arrived on race trains from Palm Beach at the Park's own railway station.

Hialeah Park was widely considered to be the world's most beautiful racetrack. The standard of winter racing was high, with races such as the Flamingo, Widener and Turf Club attracting race goers in their thousands. However, no racing has taken place at Hialeah Park since 2001 owing to financial pressures and competition from neighboring tracks Gulfstream Park and Calder Racecourse. It seems highly unlikely that racing will resume at Hialeah.

High Stakes (1975): American racehorse owner **Warren Barbo** takes his cousin **Allie Ward** and toy maker **Steven Scott** to the races at Hialeah Turf Club, and afterwards to the bloodstock sales.

Hickory, John (*Shattered* 2000)

Hickory is **Gerard Logan**'s assistant in his glass-blowing business in **Broadway, Gloucestershire**. About thirty years old, he is a promising glass-blower and is popular with customers. He is considered by Gerard to be getting a bit above himself. He is given tasks to do to improve his skills, but when he makes mistakes he is reluctant to admit to them. When he does well he expects Gerard's admiration, and thinks that Gerard does not properly appreciate his talent. Gerard suspects, however, that Hickory will never be as good as he wants to be, and is becoming resentful as a result. When his attempt to make a perfect sailing boat breaks because he is distracted by colleagues he is angry; he finally succeeds with Gerard's help.

Gerard suspects an unhealthy alliance between Hickory and **Rose Payne**. When Gerard tackles him about it Hickory at first denies it, but then admits his guilt.

Hicks, Mrs. Loretta (*Field of 13* 1998: "The Gift")

Mrs. Hicks is the owner of Kentucky Derby entry **Salad Bowl**.

Higgins, Mr. (*Comeback* 1991)

Mr. Higgins works for an equine insurance company. He is introduced to **Peter Darwin** by **John Ambrose**. Higgins gives Peter general information about insuring horses. He subsequently discovers, via colleagues in the insurance world, that certain individuals had perpetrated a fraud involving dead horses.

Higgs, Lenny (*The Edge* 1988)

Higgs is the English stable lad in charge of **Laurentide Ice**, a horse belonging to **Daffodil Quentin**, on board the Great Transcontinental Mystery Race Train He is found moaning in terror among the hay bales on the train after **Winnipeg** races. He willingly accepts **Tor Kelsey**'s offer to get him off the train and to give him a rail ticket of his choice in return for telling Tor what is frightening him.

Higgs, Sir Owen (*The Danger* 1983)

Sir Owen Higgs is second in command, under Senior Steward **Morgan Freemantle**, at the **Jockey Club**. When Freemantle is kidnapped, Higgs engages the services of **Liberty Market Ltd.** to ensure his safe return.

High Stakes (1975)

In the winner's enclosure at **Sandown Park**, wealthy toy maker and racehorse owner **Steven Scott** tells his trainer, **Jody Leeds**, that he's taking his horses away. **Energise**, his best horse, has just won a race, which has hardened Steven's resolve. Leeds is furious, and creates a scene, but doesn't ask why Steven is doing it. Steven has finally discovered that Leeds has been systematically defrauding him for years. But Steven's hopes that simply finding a new trainer will bring closure to an unpleasant episode are sadly misplaced. Leeds vows to make life as difficult for Steven as he can, and starts by removing Energise from the racecourse stables and taking him home.

After suffering further humiliations at the hands of Leeds and his accomplice, bookmaker **Ganser Mays**, Steven is intent on getting his own back. In this context the portrayal of Steven as a mechanical toy maker is a nice touch; with the help of his friends he orchestrates a sting in which the villains are made to dance to his tune. The problem with *High Stakes* is that the sting itself is just too unlikely, and thus weakens the novel's credibility. The novel's strong points—the character of Steven himself and the tense dénouement in which the unhinged Ganser Mays meets a painful end—go some way to compensate.

Highbury, George (*Field of 13* 1998: "The Gift")

Highbury is an American racehorse trainer based at Somerset Farms, Kentucky. He has a low opinion of jockeys. He warns jockey **Piper Boles** to watch his weight as he is riding Highbury's horse, **Crinkle Cut**, in the Kentucky Derby.

Hillman, Dave (*Dead Cert* 1962)

Jump jockey Dave Hillman is an up and coming star of the **National Hunt** scene. He is a rival of **Alan York** for the affections of **Kate Ellery-Penn**.

Hillsborough (*Bolt* 1986)

Hillsborough is a steeplechaser owned by **Princess Casilia**. He runs a disappointing race at **Newbury** when ridden by **Kit Fielding**. Called in for an explanation by the stewards, one of whom is his arch-enemy **Maynard Allardeck**, Kit tells them that the Princess's horses are always trying, and the other stewards accept this.

Hirst, Hudson (*10 lb. Penalty* 1997)

Hirst, a politician, is appointed Minister of Defense in the Government, a post which **George Juliard**—given the post of Minister of Agriculture—would have preferred. Hirst is a bit of a thug whose rough edges have been smoothed by political manipulator **A.L. Wyvern**. He challenges the Prime Minister for leadership of the party, and is opposed by George Juliard when the Prime Minister decides to step down.

Hitchins, Billy (*Field of 13* 1998: "Blind Chance")

Aged twenty-seven, Hitchins is a racecourse bookmaker who also owns a betting shop in **Ascot**. At Ascot races, Hitchins takes several bets on a horse, **Jetset**, to win a photo-finish. When Jetset is announced the winner he pays out without worrying, having won overall on the race. Later, in conversation with his betting shop manager, he learns that a young blind boy, who lives near the track and who listens to radios, had backed Jetset on credit to win the photo-finish. Hitchins immediately suspects fraud.

Hodge, Roderick (*Smokescreen* 1972)

Hodge is the Features Editor of the *Rand Daily Star*. He is present at **Edward Lincoln**'s press conference in Johannesburg, South Africa. He is about forty years old, but dresses and speaks as if fifteen years younger. He introduces his girlfriend **Katya**, a radio journalist, to Edward. When Katya is electrocuted by a microphone he is panic-stricken; he is hugely relieved when her heart restarts. When she is clearly recovering Hodge rushes away to telephone the story to his newspaper.

Hodge gains permission from **Quentin Van Huren** to visit a goldmine with Edward, with a view to writing an article. He tells Edward that **Joe**, the technician in charge of the radio equipment at the press conference has discovered that the recorder, which was not his own, had been dangerously wired up.

Hodge invites Edward to dinner with him and Katya. He also invites a beautiful model, who unsuccessfully tries to compromise Edward so that waiting press photographers can photograph them together. He tries in vain to get Edward to express some newsworthy political opinions on apartheid, the political system in South Africa. When Edward phones him up to complain Hodge apologizes, claiming that **Clifford Wenkins** had put him up to it.

Hodges, Arnold Vincent (*Bolt* 1986)

Hodges, a middle-aged racegoer, accepts £10 from a man at **Bradbury** races to give **Prince Litsi** a message to meet **Danielle de Brescou** at the top of the grandstand, which is closed for refurbishment. A day or two later he sees **Kit Fielding**'s advert in the *Sporting Life* offering a reward for information, and arranges to meet Kit in a pub in Bradbury. He is initially wary, and gives a false name. From Kit's photos, he identifies the man who gave him the message. For an extra financial inducement he signs a statement to that effect, and gives his correct name and address.

Holth, Gunnar (*Slay-Ride* 1973)

Holth is a Norwegian racehorse trainer for whom English jockey **Bob Sherman** sometimes rode; his stable yard adjoins **Øvrevoll racecourse**. He speaks English with an Irish accent. Initially curt with **David Cleveland**, Holth relaxes when David asks to see his horses. He tells David that Sherman sometimes stayed in his lads' dormitory, and sometimes with his owners. He also tells David that Sherman's wife is in Oslo looking for him, and arranges for David to see her.

Hoopwestern, Dorset

Hoopwestern is a fictional town in **Dorset**, a beautiful, rural county on the south-west coast of England.

10 lb. Penalty (1997): **Benedict Juliard**'s father, **George**, is the successful candidate in a by-election in the political constituency of Hoopwestern.

Horfitz, Ivor J. (*The Edge* 1988)

Horfitz is an elderly former racehorse owner; he has been warned off for life for running a crooked stable. At **Nottingham** races, **Tor Kelsey** sees Horfitz accompanying a young man who passes a briefcase to **Julius Filmer**. Horfitz's stable is subsequently found to belong to Filmer.

Horfitz, Jason (*The Edge* 1988)

Jason is the son of warned-off owner **Ivor Horfitz**. According to **Val Catto,** Jason lacks the brain power to be anything more than a messenger for his father. He delivers a briefcase to **Julius Filmer** at **Nottingham racecourse,** to Filmer's annoyance. Later, when **John Millington** warns him that he should pass on any information he has, Jason says he doesn't want to end up dead, and runs away.

Horses

"Beautiful, marvellous creatures whose responses and instincts worked on a plane as different from humans as water and oil, not mingling even where they touched." (**Sid Halley,** *Whip Hand* 1979).

"The sight of a string of thoroughbreds winding slowly home through a village street on a summer morning is one of the pleasantest sights in English country life." (**John Hislop,** *The Turf* 1948).

When Francis writes about horses his touch, stemming from a deep affection and an inborn understanding, is unerring. As far as it is possible for a human to know the equine mind, Francis knows. The scenes in his novels that involve horses are invariably fresh, dramatic and credible. Horses have their own individual, sometimes unfathomable, personalities, and in Francis's novels they often exert a powerful influence on the plot. In Francis's first book, the excellent *Dead Cert* (1962), the chestnut hunter-chaser **Admiral** is as much a character as the hero, amateur jockey **Alan York.** A brilliant jumper, Admiral is deliberately brought down at **Maidenhead** races and crushes to death his owner-rider, **Major Bill Davidson.** When Davidson's friend Alan investigates the murder, Admiral's courage and jumping ability are instrumental in saving him from a violent death.

In *Nerve* (1964) the six-year-old chaser **Template,** owned by **Lord Tirrold,** is a racehorse of huge potential but he is not one that much likes the company of humans. He is cold and aloof, giving nothing of himself in his stable but everything on the racecourse. Jockey **Rob Finn** had won a big race on him on Boxing Day, but since then had endured a miserable three weeks in which everything he'd ridden had run as if wearing hobnailed boots. By the time Template lines up at **Ascot** to contest the Midwinter Cup Rob has discovered why the horses have been running badly. But he knows that Template is fit to run for his life. Rob has every faith in Template, who is clever and relishes a fight. Giving Rob the ride of a lifetime, Template wins the Midwinter Cup by two lengths.

Elderly aristocrat **Princess Casilia** owns a well-named steeplechaser in **North Face** (*Break In* 1985). The ten-year-old shares Mount Eiger's distinctive characteristics—bleak, forbidding, and often in the foulest of moods. On the racecourse, though, he's a formidable racing machine.

Template and North Face may not care for humans but at least they have proved themselves on the racecourse. In *Bonecrack* (1971), the two-year old colt **Traffic,** from **Neil Griffon**'s flat-racing **Newmarket** yard, lacks that—and every other—saving grace. Traffic is mulish, mean and intent on giving an unpleasant experience to anyone rash enough to sit on his back. On the Newmarket gallops he runs away with Italian apprentice **Alessandro Rivera,** and ends up careering along a busy road in the wrong direction . The next day, for good measure, he bucks Rivera off in the stable, knocking him senseless.

Racehorse trainer **William Finch** (*Risk* 1977) attempts to harness the uncertain temper and appalling jumping of his horse, **Notebook,** to incapacitate amateur jockey **Roland Britten,** an accountant who is due to check the stable's accounts. Roland endures a nightmare ride on the willful gelding at **Towcester races;** Notebook attempts to demolish every hurdle, finally ejecting Roland from the saddle. As he gallops away Notebook kicks Roland in the thigh.

In Francis's novels there are many examples of horses being directly or indirectly involved in corrupt or criminal acts perpetrated by those who train, own or ride them. In *Rat Race* (1970), a racehorse named **Rudiments** is prevented from winning his race at **Haydock Park** by his jockey, who gets him boxed in on the rails. Next time out, ridden by a different jockey, Rudiments bolts up, and is greeted in the winner's enclosure by a chorus of boos from the disgruntled punters.

In *Enquiry* (1969) **Squelsh,** hot favorite for a valuable steeplechase at **Oxford,** finishes second, beaten by his apparently unfancied stable companion, **Cherry Pie.** It looks bad, and at the subsequent enquiry into the running and riding of Squelsh trainer **Dexter Cranfield** and jockey **Kelly Hughes** have their licenses indefinitely suspended. The enquiry, though, does not reveal the fact that, on the day, Squelsh had simply not been good enough.

Knock Down (1974), set in the world of bloodstock dealing, has more than its fair share of nefarious schemes and fraudulent practices involving racehorses. A bloodstock agent had paid £60,000 for a stallion on behalf of a client who then inconveniently died, leaving the agent with the horse and no buyer. Worse, he discovered that the horse was incubating tetanus, rendering him worthless. Fortunately for the agent, he was at the time arranging the export to Japan of another, much more valuable, stallion whose markings were virtually identical to those of the first horse. The shipment went ahead, but it was the infected stallion that ended up on the boat to Japan. The horse died in transit, enabling the agent to collect a cool £115,000 in insurance. He then sold the healthy stallion, now masquerading as the one that died, to stand as a stallion in Ireland.

The plot of *For Kicks* (1965) hinges on an owner and trainer who devise a method of making slow horses run fast enough to win. They do this by terrifying the animals to such an extent that their natural flight instinct produces hitherto untapped reserves of speed.

In *Banker* (1982) **Indian Silk** is one of the best young steeplechasers in Britain, but earlier in his career he had been so sick, apparently suffering from a mystery virus, that he had looked unlikely ever to run again. With the vets' bills mounting and the horse deteriorating so fast that he seemed certain to be useless for racing, his owner-trainer had sold him on cheaply. The new owner sent Indian Silk to an equine herbalist and healer, and soon the horse was back in training, fit and healthy and looking like the top class horse he'd been before getting sick. It seemed that the healer, **Calder Jackson**, had performed a miracle cure on the horse, but the reality was very different. Subsequently Indian Silk was sold on for a large sum.

The **Newmarket**-trained racehorses in *Bonecrack* suffer various villain-engineered catastrophes. In order to bend trainer **Neil Griffon** to his will, Italian crime boss **Enso Rivera** has two of the horses injured beyond saving. Neil's father's hack **Moonrock** and **Indigo**, a gelding used as a schoolmaster for the yard's apprentices and to lead the two-year-olds, are both found in their boxes with one of their legs broken, and have to be destroyed.

Lancat, a promising three-year-old colt, is an unlucky victim when being ridden by Neil on Newmarket Heath. A sniper in Rivera's employ is about to shoot Rivera's son **Alessandro**, mistaking him for another jockey. In a desperate bid to save Alessandro's life, Neil gallops Lancat straight at Alessandro's horse **Lucky Lindsay**. Lancat takes the high velocity bullet meant for Alessandro in the neck and is killed instantly.

Black Fire (*High Stakes* 1975) is a five-year-old gelding with a handsome Arab profile but does not have the ability to match his looks. Racing in the United States, Black Fire had won as a three-year-old, but has since gone through an extended barren spell, and now finds himself plodding round the sales ring at **Hialeah**, South Florida. It is Black Fire's misfortune that he is a doppelganger for a useful hurdler named **Energise**, racing on the British tracks and owned by toy maker **Steven Scott**. Steven is concerned to keep Energise safe from harm at the hands of his former trainer, **Jody Leeds**, whom Steven has sacked.

Whilst in Florida Steven sees Black Fire at the sales and, struck by his likeness to Energise, buys him. Black Fire is flown to England and takes Energise's place at **Rupert Ramsey**'s racing stables whilst Energise is moved to a livery yard. Steven's precautions prove to be all too necessary, and Black Fire is the hapless victim.

In *Whip Hand* (1979), a lingering, drawn-out fate has befallen racehorses trained by **George Caspar** in Newmarket. **Gleaner** and **Bethesda** were top class two-year-olds who had failed miserably to give their running as three-year-olds, and had been packed off to stud as soon as was decently possible. Gleaner's career as a stallion was short; he collapsed and died after covering a mare. Bethesda, too, suffered an early death whilst foaling.

Now the very useful two-year-old winner **Tri-Nitro** is the latest from Caspar's yard to be humiliated. He starts even money favorite for the Two Thousand Guineas and finishes last. An investigation by **Sid Halley** reveals the cause of the horses' demise: their health has been deliberately compromised for financial gain.

In *Bolt* (1986), the horses belonging to **Princess Casilia** at the stables of veteran trainer **Wykeham Harlow** become the targets of a man obsessed with revenge. In the night he quietly enters the box where two-mile chaser **Cascade** is dozing on his feet, and puts a humane killer to the horse's head. Minutes later **Cotopaxi**, a staying chaser whose objective was to have been the Grand National, suffers the same fate. A few days later he returns to the stable and, despite increased security, kills **Col**, the stable's hope for the **Cheltenham** Gold Cup. His third visit to the yard is one too many; he is killed with his own gun.

Horse lovers the world over will have felt that

the villain got what he deserved. They may also have thought that such a death would have been far too quick and painless for the warped character in *Come to Grief* (1995), who takes pleasure in mutilating horses. His preferred method is to sever one foot with a pair of gardening shears; one of his victims is a grey pony named **Silverboy**, owned by **Rachel Ferns**, a nine-year-old girl who suffers from leukemia. Silverboy has to be put down. Eventually exposed and disgraced, the villain commits suicide, but this doesn't offer a sense of closure to the reader. The horrific nature of his cruelty makes *Come to Grief* a disturbing and unsatisfying novel.

Hot Money (1987)

Ian Pembroke has just resigned from his job as an assistant racehorse trainer. He and his father, **Malcolm Pembroke**, a wealthy gold trader, have not spoken to each other in the three years since Ian criticized **Moira**, Malcolm's fifth wife-to-be. When Moira is murdered Malcolm phones Ian, saying he needs his protection. Someone is out to murder Malcolm too, and the chief suspects are his own children. Malcolm has, besides Ian, five sons and two daughters. Two attempts on Malcolm's life have failed; then his country house is destroyed by a bomb. A second bomb, intended for Malcolm, instead kills the murderer.

Hot Money is a study of the psychology of the individual: the villain's emotional problems provide the motivation to kill. Its main weakness as a novel is its plethora of unsympathetic characters. There are too many family members for the reader to keep tabs on, and it is difficult to engage with the majority of them. Francis's treatment of Ian Pembroke is the most successful aspect of *Hot Money*. His role is that of bodyguard to his father and amateur detective, but his character develops as the novel progresses. His relationship with Malcolm changes from purely filial to one where Malcolm, to his surprise, is forced to accept Ian as an equal. At the same time Ian reassesses his own life, realizing that he has wasted years playing at being a trainer. When he makes the decision to become a professional jockey his life is fulfilled.

Houston, Luke (*Twice Shy* 1981)

Houston, a rich American, employs **William Derry** on a yearly contract to run his racing interest in England and Ireland; he had interviewed William for the job after meeting **Jonathan Derry**, William's brother, at a party. Houston runs his racing on commercial lines, profiting from selling on his successful racehorses as stallions. He allows William to spend large amounts of money at **Newmarket Yearling Sales**. When he comes over to England to inspect the yearlings that William has bought, he offers William a further year's employment.

Howard (*Proof* 1984)

Howard is the recently appointed head lad at **Jack Hawthorn**'s racing stables. During Jack's absence in hospital, Howard treats Jack's wife, **Flora Hawthorn**, with deference beyond the call of duty when she and **Tony Beach** are inspecting the horses at evening stables.

Hoylake, Tommy (*Bonecrack* 1971)

Hoylake is stable jockey to **Neville Griffon**. He rides Lincoln Handicap entry **Pease Pudding** in a trial in which a previously useless colt, **Lancat**, finishes close up, and is assured by Neville Griffon that Pease Pudding has no chance in the Lincoln. Hoylake is surprised when **Neil Griffon**, running the yard while his father is in hospital, says that he has backed Pease Pudding and to ride him positively or he will put someone else up. Hoylake does as Neil says and rides a fine race to win by a short head.

Hoylake's job as stable jockey is coveted by Italian apprentice **Alessandro Rivera**, which proves potentially dangerous to Hoylake's health.

Huggerneck, Bert (*High Stakes* 1975)

Huggerneck is a friend of **Charlie Canterfield**'s, and is introduced by Charlie to **Steven Scott**. He is built like a brick outhouse, and is militantly working class. He lives in Staines, **Middlesex**, and had worked as a bookmaker's clerk until made redundant when his boss went bankrupt through laying Steven's horse, **Energise**, which he believed wasn't trying but won. Huggerneck tells Steven that **Ganser Mays** had immediately phoned up to buy the lease on his boss's betting shop. At Charlie's request Huggerneck finds work in one of Mays' betting shops to help with Steven's sting against Mays and **Jody Leeds**. In this and other ways Huggerneck proves extremely useful. As a reward for his help, Steven gives him a share in Energise.

Hughes, Kelly (*Enquiry* 1969)

Top jump jockey Kelly Hughes is aware that the **Jockey Club's** view of discipline and its enforcement is, in many respects, archaic. But when he is wrongly accused by the local stewards of not trying to win on a beaten favorite at **Oxford** races he has no reason to believe that he won't receive a fair hearing. His case is referred to the disciplinary committee of the Jockey Club at **Portman Square**, London. There, to his astonishment, he finds that the Stewards, and the chairman of the committee in particular, have already decided he is guilty. They dismiss everything that Hughes says in his own defense—he is not legally represented, which would not be the case today—and they produce witnesses who either twist the truth or ignore it altogether. Hughes, together with the trainer of the horse, has his license withdrawn indefinitely, thus depriving him of the ability to earn a living at his chosen profession.

For most jockeys that would have been the end of it, since there was no right of appeal against the Stewards' decision. Kelly Hughes though, is not most jockeys. He is, for a start, well educated, with a degree in politics, philosophy and economics from the London School of Economics. Feeling in need of a break from books after graduating, he had worked for a farmer who also trained steeplechasers under permit. When the regular jockey was injured Kelly was given the job and was immediately successful. His career took off, and by the time he lost his license he was challenging for the title of champion jockey.

Kelly lives alone in a flat at the racing stables of his cousin, **Tony**. Four years previously his wife, Rosalind, had been killed in a car crash. He had loved her deeply but time had dulled the pain. He misses her company now, in the aftermath of the Jockey Club enquiry—particularly so since he gets no support from his parents. Welsh, working class and proud of it, they don't consider the possibility that the Stewards might have got it wrong. To them their son is an embarrassment and a disgrace to the family name.

Kelly is reticent about his romantic attachments since his wife died; perhaps he has had none, since he says that, among jockeys, he's an "also-ran as a bird attracter."

He may well be underestimating his appeal; at least one female he meets rates him "smashing looking and dead sexy." Posh girls fancy him too— namely, **Roberta Cranfield**, daughter of the trainer warned off at the same enquiry. Used to treating him as a social inferior when he was her father's jockey, Roberta sees a different side to Kelly when they are thrown together in adversity.

And she likes what she sees; Kelly is determined to get his license back, and impresses Roberta by the way he takes control of the situation.

Kelly's investigations into how and why he was framed bring him up against desperate men who are equally determined to stop him. A failed attempt on his life leaves him with leg injuries which render him immobile. Soon afterwards he is beaten up and knocked unconscious with his own crutch. But his courage is never if question. Undeterred, Kelly presses on until finally, he clears his name and wins back his jockey's license to ride. Meanwhile his feelings for Roberta have deepened; after riding the winner of the **Cheltenham** Gold Cup, he tells Roberta that it is no longer his dead wife that occupies his thoughts.

Hughes-Beckett, Rupert (*Trial Run* 1978)

Hughes-Beckett is a high-ranking civil servant in the Foreign Office. He attempts in vain to persuade **Randall Drew** to go to Moscow on a "delicate" investigation. He returns with the **Prince** to try again, this time successfully. Hughes-Beckett makes it clear to Randall before he goes to Moscow that his trip has a low priority with the Foreign Office, and he doesn't hide his contempt for anything to do with horses. Nevertheless he provides Randall with a short list of contacts in Moscow. He sends Randall, on request, detailed information on Hans Kramer and the three Russian observers at **Burghley**. He is subsequently impressed by Randall's achievements in Moscow.

Humber, Hedley (*For Kicks* 1965)

Racehorse trainer Hedley Humber is the employer from hell. A tyrant, Humber runs the worst racing yard in England. He starves his stable lads and knocks them about. Each lad has four or five horses to look after, and Humber has to pay over the odds to attract any staff at all. A large man with unsmiling eyes, Humber walks with a slight limp and uses a walking stick. His stable lads sleep in a hayloft above the horses and use a spare loose box as a kitchen. The food is worse than the accommodation. Humber demands long hours from his lads and gives extra work as punishment for the most trivial of misdemeanors. If a lad shows signs of staying more than three months Humber picks on him and physically bullies him until he leaves. With his owners Humber is plausible, and his training fees are lower than anyone else's.

Humber is always impeccably dressed. He

drives a huge Bentley, which is his pride and joy. Unmarried, Humber lives in a house adjoining the stables. He is in league with owner **Paul James Adams**; together they are inducing slow horses to run faster by illegal and, for the horses, terrifying means. When they discover that one of their stable lads, **Daniel Roke**, is not who he appears to be, Humber and Adams corner Daniel in the stable office and try to kill him. Daniel picks up a heavy glass paperweight from Humber's desk and throws it at him. It hits Humber between the eyes and knocks him unconscious.

Humphries, Rodney (*Under Orders* 2006)

Humphries is a neighbor of **Charles Roland's**. He goes with Charles to **Towcester** races to help **Sid Halley** feed information to **Paddy O'Fitch**. Humphries pretends to be a Professor of Ballistics, discussing with Sid the bullet that he found at **Bill Burton's** stables. Later, Sid tells O'Fitch that he was seeking the Professor's advice about the bullet.

Hunt Radnor Associates (*Odds Against* 1965; *Whip Hand* 1979)

Hunt Radnor Associates is a private investigation agency owned by **Radnor**. **Sid Halley** works for the Racing Section. Petty criminal **Thomas Andrews**, breaking into the Hunt Radnor offices, panics and shoots Sid. The offices are bombed by a villain who is attempting to destroy incriminating evidence. Sid buys a partnership in the agency.

Huntercombe, Antonia (*Knock Down* 1974)

Antonia Huntercombe is **Sophie Randolph's** aunt. About sixty years old and posh, Antonia owns a rundown stud farm at Paley, **Gloucestershire**. She is initially suspicious of **Jonah Dereham** because he's a bloodstock agent. She has recently lost a lot of money on her best yearling at **Newmarket Sales**; the yearling had cost £8,000 to produce, but because of an unfounded rumor that it had a heart murmur it had sold for only 1,800 guineas. According to Antonia, the rumor was started by a bloodstock agent because she had refused to give him a "kickback"—a share of the profit in return for bidding the horse up to a good price. Advised by Jonah to attend the Sales herself rather than send a groom, she complains that she's too old and not in the best of health.

Hunterson, Harry (*Forfeit* 1968)

Hunterson is the owner of racehorse **Egocentric**, which he won in a raffle. He lives in Virginia Water, **Surrey**, and is about sixty years old. Hunterson had risen from being a junior clerk in a finance company to joining the Board of Directors. He has made his money through share dealing. He had married young, but five years later his wife, daughter and mother had been killed in a car accident. Fifteen years afterwards he had met his wife, **Sarah Hunterson**, through the local Conservative Party and had married her three months later. Hunterson had never been interested in horses before but had found that owning Egocentric had increased his social standing locally. Hunterson is not a man to refuse a drink.

Hunterson, Sarah (*Forfeit* 1968)

Sarah is the wife of **Harry Hunterson**, owner of the raffle horse **Egocentric**. Conventional and conservative, Sarah struggles to overcome her instinctive prejudice about her niece **Gail Pominga's** skin color; the two women don't have a close relationship. Like her husband, Sarah is not averse to a drink.

Huntingdon racecourse

Racing has taken place in Huntingdon since 1603, when the uncle of Oliver Cromwell, future Lord Protector of the Commonwealth, owned the winner of a race for the "Silver Bell." In the 1880's the present course was laid out on land belonging to Lord Sandwich, but facilities were poor until improvements were made when the course reopened after the Second World War. The track is flat and left-handed, with the open ditch right in front of the stands. Although most of the racing is of a moderate standard, Huntingdon hosts a few valuable races which attract good horses.

Wild Horses (1994): Film director **Thomas Lyon** shoots scenes on Huntingdon racecourse. To prove himself to the jockeys he has hired for the shoot, Thomas rides in a race against two of them, acquitting himself creditably. While filming he receives death threats; the next day someone tries to kill him with a knife.

Hutchings, Fred (*Comeback* 1991)

Hutchings is the British consul in **Miami**; he had previously worked with **Peter Darwin** in Tokyo. He is about forty, slightly overweight and of a mildly nervous temperament. He invites Peter for dinner at a restaurant while he is passing through Miami. When his friends **Vicky Larch** and **Greg Wayfield** are attacked outside the restaurant Hutchings asks Peter to accompany them to hospital, since his children have chicken pox and he wants to get back to look after them. He persuades Peter to fly on the same plane to England with Vicky and Greg, and to go with them to **Gloucestershire**.

Huxford, Patricia (*Come to Grief* 1995)

Patricia Huxford is a weaver and fabric designer based in Chichester, West **Sussex**. She is petite, attractive and middle-aged. She confirms to **Sid Halley** that, thirty years before, she had woven the distinctive piece of cloth in which the shears used to mutilate a yearling colt were wrapped.

Note: Patricia Huxford is the name of an actual person who, in 1994, was successful in an "auction of opportunities that money can't buy." She won the right to have her name used as a character in *Come to Grief*.

I

Icefall (*Break In* 1985)

A six-year-old grey owned by **Princess Casilia**, Icefall is a top class hurdler; he is a front runner and straightforward in every way. He is a full brother to **Icicle**, a steeplechaser in the same ownership. Icefall wins a two-mile hurdle race for **Kit Fielding** at **Ascot** by eight lengths, jumping well.

Icicle (*Break In* 1985)

Icicle, an eight-year-old grey steeplechaser owned by **Princess Casilia**, is lengthy, angular, and good-natured. He is a full brother to **Icefall**. He is a former good class hurdler but is not proving a natural over fences. He finishes second under **Kit Fielding** at **Devon and Exeter**.

Idris, Owen (*High Stakes* 1975)

Idris is a Welshman who works for **Steven Scott** as a driver and general factotum. He has been in his post for less than a year, but his quiet, non-judgmental manner is highly valued by his employer. After collecting Steven from the magistrates' court he is concerned about Steven's missing Lamborghini, on which he lavishes loving care and attention. Collecting the car from the police pound, he is furious to discover that the bodywork has been deliberately damaged.

Idris plays a useful part in Steven's sting against **Jody Leeds** and **Ganser Mays**. As a reward for his help, Steven gives Idris a quarter share in his horse **Energise**.

In the Frame (1976)

Artist **Charles Todd** goes to **Shropshire** to stay with his cousin, wine merchant **Donald Stuart** and his wife **Regina**. He finds the police there; Regina has just been murdered by burglars, who have cleared the house of its valuable antiques and paintings. Regina's grieving husband mentions a missing painting by **Alfred Munnings** which he'd recently bought in Australia. At **Plumpton** races Charles meets **Maisie Matthews**, another art and antique collector, who had bought a Munnings in Australia and whose house had recently burned down.

Fearful for Donald's mental health, Charles decides to go to Australia. With the help of an old art school friend, **Jik Cassavetes**, Charles investigates a possible link between Regina's murder and the organized theft of valuable paintings and antiques; both Donald Stuart and Maisie Matthews had bought their paintings from the same fine art company.

Charles's determination to discover the truth proves hazardous to his health. Surviving more than one amateurish attempt to incapacitate him, he eventually tracks down the villains responsible and brings closure, of a kind, to Donald's nightmare.

When Francis strays from what he knows best—horse racing—the quality of his story-telling tends to plummet. *In the Frame* is set in Australia but at no stage does it convey the atmosphere of that country. If the reader wanted to know about the Sydney Opera House, Bring Your Own restaurants, Ayers Rock or the aboriginal artist Albert Narratjira, there are more appropriate places to find the information. None of this, interesting though it may be, advances the story in the slightest.

The shortcomings of *In the Frame* are exacerbated by a series of unconvincing incidents. The villains, recognizing that Charles is on their case, trap him behind a steel mesh gate, and then meekly let him go when he protests. Later Charles walks blindly into an obvious set-up when the hotel receptionist phones to tell him his friends are waiting outside for him in a car. This is poor, but it gets worse: the villains drive Charles to a beach, no doubt with violence in mind, and then tamely allow him to escape.

Nor is the characterization strong enough to compensate for these absurdities. Charles Todd has no past life to give him depth; his friend Jik is irritating, and Jik's wife Sarah is a shrew. It's hard not to feel exasperated with the villains for wasting their opportunities to do Charles, Jik and Sarah some serious mischief.

Indian Silk (*Banker* 1982)

Now a seven-year-old steeplechaser, Indian Silk was bought as a yearling and trained by **Fred Barnet**. At the age of five he won the Hermitage Chase at **Newbury**, and was considered a potential **Cheltenham** Gold Cup winner. Inexplicably, Indian Silk lost all form and became weak and useless for racing. He was sold cheaply to **Dinsdale Smith**, who sent him to equine healer **Calder Jackson**. Indian Silk regained his strength and his form, and was put back into training. He was sold on for a big profit and subsequently won the Cheltenham Gold Cup.

Indigo (*Bonecrack* 1971)

Indigo is a gelding trained by **Neville Griffon**, and subsequently by Griffon's son **Neil Griffon**, at **Newmarket**. He is used as a lead horse for the two-year-olds, and as a schoolmaster for the apprentices. Indigo is given to **Alessandro Rivera** to ride on his first day at the yard, which doesn't please him. When Alessandro is bucked off **Traffic**, in revenge **Enso Rivera** has Indigo's leg smashed. Indigo has to be destroyed.

Ingersoll, Tick-Tock (*Nerve* 1964)

Jump jockey Tick-Tock Ingersoll is a smart dresser and a happy-go-lucky character. He rides a winner at **Cheltenham** when **Peter Cloony** arrives too late for his ride owing to a tanker blocking the road near his house. With **Rob Finn**, Ingersoll buys a Mini Cooper to get to and from the races. He is unfairly labeled a non-trier by trainer **Corin Kellar**, and his rides begin to dry up.

Ingold, Superintendent (*Straight* 1989)

Ingold is an officer in London's Metropolitan Police. Summoned to **Greville Franklin**'s house, he finds a man shot dead and the murderer lying unconscious. Ingold sees no reason not to accept **Derek Franklin**'s story that he had knocked the villain out with his crutch. Ingold, however, has been misinformed.

Ingram, Eddie (*Knock Down* 1974)

Ingram is a wealthy client of bloodstock agent **Jonah Dereham**. He asks Jonah to buy him two good horses at **Newmarket Sales**, and invites him to dinner the next evening. When Jonah buys an Irish filly, Ingram believes a rival agent's false assertion that she is sterile and refuses to take her. Ingram alleges that Jonah is not acting in his best interests; he is disconcerted when Jonah does not react to the charge, but merely points to the four good winners he'd previously bought for Ingram.

When Ingram discovers that the Irish filly is not sterile he asks Jonah if he can have her, but Jonah has already passed her on to another client.

Injured Jockeys Fund (*Comeback* 1991)

This is a charitable organization which gives financial and other help to injured jockeys, those too badly hurt to ride again, and the dependants of jockeys and stable lads killed in accidents. The Fund had helped **Peter Darwin**'s mother to find a job as a secretary at **Cheltenham racecourse** after her husband Paul was killed in an accident on the road while riding out.

Inscombe, Mr. and Mrs. (*Break In* 1985)

The Inscombes are friends of **Princess Casilia**; they are guests in her box at **Devon and Exeter racecourse** on the day that **Kit Fielding** meets the Princess's niece **Danielle de Brescou**.

Inskip (*For Kicks* 1965)

Inskip trains the **Earl of October**'s racehorses. He is youngish, with sandy hair and a sharp voice. When **Daniel Roke** is falsely accused of sexual assault, Inskip tells him to pack his bags and get out of the yard.

Intramind Imaging Ltd. (*Come to Grief* 1995)

This is a Manchester-based firm which makes advertising films. It is employed by **Topline Foods** to advertise their horse cubes.

Ipswich, England

Ipswich is the county town of **Suffolk**, in the agricultural region of East Anglia. Its importance in medieval times stemmed from its position at the mouth of the River Orwell; it was the main port for the lucrative Suffolk wool trade.

Straight (1989): **Greville Franklin**, elder brother of steeplechase jockey **Derek**, is critically injured when scaffolding falls on him in an Ipswich street.

Ireland, Bunty

Break In (1985): Ireland is a racing journalist employed by *Sunday Towncrier* newspaper. He tells **Kit Fielding** at **Plumpton** races that the *Daily Flag*'s racing correspondent knows nothing about the Intimate Details column in which allegations have been made about **Bobby Allardeck** and his father **Maynard**.

Bolt (1986): Ireland agrees to run an advert on the *Sunday Towncrier*'s racing page for Kit Fielding, offering a reward to anyone who passed on a message to **Prince Litsi** at **Bradbury** races which resulted in him falling from the balcony of the grandstand. He gives Kit an envelope from **Lord Vaughnley** containing a photo of **Henri Nanterre** at a party in Monte Carlo. The date of the party has significance for Kit's investigation into the deaths of **Princess Casilia**'s horses.

Irestone, Detective Chief Superintendent (*Twice Shy* 1981)

Irestone is a **Newmarket**-based policeman; he is in charge of the investigation into **Chris Norwood**'s death. He tells **Jonathan Derry** that **Peter Keithley**'s death was an accident and not due to foul play. However, he takes seriously Jonathan's account of being threatened over cassette tapes containing a system for betting on horses.

Irish, John (*Shattered* 2000)

Irish is **Gerard Logan**'s assistant in his glass-blowing business. Aged forty, Irish is enthusiastic but only moderately talented.

Irkab Alhawa (*Driving Force* 1992)

Irkab Alhawa is a strongly-made three-year-old trained by **Michael Watermead**; he is winter favorite for the Derby after winning the Middle Park Stakes and the Dewhurst Stakes, both at **Newmarket**, as a two-year-old.

Ironside, Kris (*Second Wind* 1999)

Ironside is a meteorologist employed by the British Broadcasting Corporation. He is aged thirty-one and unmarried. Blond, pale and skinny, Ironside has a Norwegian mother. He is a specialist in giving advice on the weather to farmers and landowners. He is prone to unpredictable bouts of elation and depression, and autumn is a particularly bad time for him. His hobby is flying his own Piper Cherokee.

Ironside is the former lover of **Belladonna Harvey**, and is still in love with her despite a difficult relationship. According to Bell, he is an occasional poet but destroys his work, **Perry Stuart** considers this to be Ironside's alternative to suicide. Ironside goes with **Robin Darcy** and Perry to **Grand Cayman**, where Darcy has hired a plane for him to fulfill his wish to fly through the eye of a hurricane which is brewing. When the plane crashes into the sea Ironside is able to get into a dinghy, but Perry isn't. Ironside is rescued by a helicopter hired by Darcy to search for the two men.

Ironside gets engaged to Bell. He is flying from **Doncaster** races back to London with Perry when oil starts to leak from an engine and cover the windscreen. He manages to crash land the plane safely at Luton airport, just north of London.

He sends to **Oliver Quigley** a worthless list of horses instead of information about radioactive materials which **Glenda Loricroft** had taken from her husband **George Loricroft**. He claims he did it as a joke. Eventually Ironside is fired from his job with the BBC and becomes an actor.

Isabella (*Proof* 1984)

Isabella is **Orkney Swayle**'s attractive girlfriend, whom **Tony Beach** meets in Swayle's box at **Martineau Park** races.

Isle of Wight, England

The Isle of Wight is a small island off the south coast of England. It lies at the entrance to Southampton Water, separated from the mainland by the Solent. The island's beaches and landscape make it a popular holiday resort. The town of Cowes is host to the world-famous sailing regatta. Boat building has long been an important industry.

Risk (1977): **Roland Britten**'s mother had run a small hotel on the Isle of Wight. Roland goes to see boat builder **Johnny Frederick** on the island. He shows Frederick photos of the man who had abducted him and of the boat used in the abduction.

Twice Shy (1981): **Angelo Gilbert** is imprisoned for fourteen years in Albany Prison on the Isle of Wight.

Isobel (*Driving Force* 1992)

Isobel is the secretary at **Croft Raceways** horse transport firm. She is young, sweet and efficient. In one of the horse vans she finds a thermos flask containing a number of glass tubes with amber liquid in them. She tells **Freddie Croft** that the man who had come to repair the firm's computer had said that a virus had destroyed its memory. She apologizes to Freddie for not making back-up discs, unaware that Freddie had done so. She tells Freddie that the previous August **Jogger** had found a dead rabbit crawling with ticks in the inspection pit.

Ivan (*Wild Horses* 1994)

Ivan is the actor who "doubles" in riding scenes for star **Nash Rourke** in **Thomas Lyon's** film *Unstable Times*. He has a surly manner. He pretends to be on friendly terms with Rourke, although the two rarely meet. While filming on **Newmarket Heath**, Ivan is slashed by another rider with a knife but is unharmed; the rider escapes.

Ivanora, Olga (*Trial Run* 1978)

Olga Ivanora is the wife of **Evgeny Sergeevich Titov**; she works for the Russian Government in Cultural Relations, and is a friend of **Ian Young**. At Young's instigation **Randall Drew** meets **Boris Dmitrevich Telyatnikov** at Olga's apartment.

Ivansky (*Risk* 1977)

Ivansky, a steeplechaser trained by **William Finch** at **Axwood Stables**, runs in the Grand National at **Aintree**, finishing fifth.

Iverson, Vivian (*Risk* 1977)

Iverson is a racing acquaintance of **Roland Britten**. He is in his mid-thirties, and runs a successful gambling club in London. He is well informed about dubious goings-on in the world of racing. He arranges a meeting at his club between Roland and three fraudsters recently released from prison whom Roland's evidence had put there. He insists on being present to prevent them attacking Roland. At **Kempton Park** before the Oasthouse Cup, Iverson tells Roland that he overheard one of the ex-convicts on the phone at his club, talking about Roland.

J

Jacek (*Dead Heat* 2007)

Jacek is a kitchen porter at **The Hay Net**, **Max Moreton's** restaurant in **Newmarket**. Max, realizing that Jacek is watching him cook, wonders why. Jacek kills **Gary**, who is looking for **Caroline Aston**, with a kitchen knife; he is shot in the shoulder. When Max opens his new restaurant in London, Jacek is appointed assistant chef.

Jack (*Break In* 1985)

Jack is a guest in **Princess Casilia's** box at **Cheltenham racecourse**. He criticizes **Kit Fielding's** riding of the talented but wayward **North Face** despite Kit having won the race. He is put in his place by Princess Casilia and **Lord Vaughnley**, who stick up for Kit.

Jackson, Calder (*Banker* 1982)

Nowadays horse owners and trainers use complementary therapies such as chiropractic, acupuncture and hydrotherapy to assist in a horse's recovery from injury or illness. Back in the early 1980's such ideas were less accepted and, if Calder Jackson had been a typical practitioner, these therapies would have struggled to gain a foothold in the equine world. Jackson had set himself up as a horse healer, using herbal remedies and the "laying on of hands." Word had spread of his startling success, and now he is running a thriving business. Used by a skilled and knowledgeable person, herbal supplements may indeed have a part to play in the rehabilitation of horses. However, Jackson's apparently miraculous cures have a simple explanation, which has nothing to do with medicine and everything to do with his dubious alliance with a local veterinary surgeon. The two men eventually fall out, a parting of the ways which has immutable consequences for the vet. Jackson's business falters, and he hatches a desperate plan to restore his fortunes. A stallion's first crop of foals are the victims, soon to be followed by a stud owner's teenage daughter. When Jackson fails to prevent merchant banker **Tim Ekaterin** from exposing his crimes, he takes a coward's way out.

Jackson, Mrs. (*Reflex* 1980)

Mrs. Jackson is **Philip Nore's** next door neighbor in **Lambourn**. The wife of a horse van driver; she is friendly and misses nothing that goes on in the street. She tells Philip that an official from the local council had called at his house and she'd let him in, but had stayed with him while he counted the rooms. When Philip shows her photographs, she recognizes the man; he is not a council official.

Jackson, Wyoming

Jackson is a small town in Teton County, Wyoming, popular with tourists visiting nearby Yellowstone National Park.

Blood Sport (1967): Investigator **Gene Hawkins** visits Jackson when trying to trace the provenance of a handkerchief found in a punt on the River Thames, and the identities of the young couple in the punt. A shopkeeper in Jackson recognizes the pair as **Matt** and **Yola Clive**, proprietors of a nearby dude ranch.

Jacksy (*Whip Hand* 1979)

Jacksy is a crooked ex-jockey who has been warned off for taking bribes. **Sid Halley** offers him money for information about **Peter Rammileese**.

Jacobs, Margaret and Patrick (*Dead Heat* 2007)

The Jacobs run a saddlery business in **Newmarket**. They suffer food poisoning at a dinner at **Newmarket racecourse** on the night before the Two Thousand Guineas. Fortunately for them, they are too ill to go as guests of **Delafield Industries Inc.** to the Guineas the next day, when the Delafield guest boxes are bombed.

James, Ted (*Come to Grief* 1995)

James, a garage owner in **Lambourn**, had obtained a Range Rover for veterinary surgeon **Bill Ruskin** from English Sporting Motors, **Oxford**.

Janet (*Twice Shy* 1981)

Janet is a computer operator at **Angel Kitchens**, a **Newmarket** food production company. She tells **Jonathan Derry** that **Chris Norwood** wanted to know how the computer worked; she admits to having allowed Norwood to run his computer tapes on it.

Jardine, Jay (*Comeback* 1991)

Jardine is a partner in Hewett and Partners, veterinary surgeons of Cheltenham, **Gloucestershire**. He is not long out of veterinary college, and specializes in cattle. He is critical of **Carey Hewett**; he thinks that Hewett is too old to deal with the crisis at the practice and wants to see him retire. He is defensive when interviewed by the police as to his whereabouts on the evening of the fire at the veterinary practice.

Jason (*Straight* 1989)

Jason is an employee of the late **Greville Franklin** at **Saxony Franklin**, a firm which imports semi-precious stones. Young, with spiky orange hair, Jason does the heavy work and odd jobs. He is highly skeptical of **Derek Franklin**'s ability to keep the firm going. Subsequently it is discovered that Jason had been disloyal to his employer and,

after Greville Franklin's death, he had committed criminal acts. When this is revealed Jason doesn't return to Saxony Franklin; instead he is given full-time employment by **Prospero Jenks**.

Jazzo (*To the Hilt* 1996)

Jazzo is one of four London thugs hired to carry out an assault on **Norman Quorn**. They also assault **Alex Kinloch** at his remote cottage in the Scottish mountains and throw him over the edge of a cliff. Later, they use boxing gloves to beat Alex up and administer the same punishment to him as they did to Quorn.

Jean (*Dead Heat* 2007)

Jean is a waitress at **The Hay Net**, a Newmarket restaurant run by **Max Moreton**. After Max opens a new restaurant in London, Jean leaves.

Jenkins (*Decider* 1993)

Jenkins is a minor racecourse official at **Stratton Park racecourse**. He takes **Lee Morris**'s sons to collect jockeys' autographs while Lee is talking with **Oliver Wells** and **Roger Gardner**.

Jenkins (*Come to Grief* 1995)

Jenkins is a groom; he is mentioned by the owner of a mutilated two-year-old thoroughbred as having found the colt's severed foot, and being distressed by the discovery.

Jenkins, Mrs. (*Bolt* 1986)

Mrs. Jenkins, young and recently married, is secretary and personal assistant to **Princess Casilia** and her husband, **Roland de Brescou**.

Jenkins, Ralph (*Twice Shy* 1981)

Ralph Jenkins was the head of the Math department at East Middlesex Comprehensive School in North London when **Jonathan Derry** worked there. He was an unpleasant and unpopular man. **Ted Pitts** cites his dislike of Jenkins as one of his reasons for quitting his job.

Jenkinson, Charles (*Nerve* 1964)

Jenkinson is a **Jockey Club** handicapper who appears on **Maurice Kemp-Lore**'s TV show to explain how he builds a handicap. He is embarrassed when trainer **Corin Kellar** suggests that he should take a jockey's loss of nerve into account when handicapping future races; he refuses to be drawn on the issue.

Jenks, Prospero (*Straight* 1989)

Jenks is a London jewelry designer who had bought precious stones from recently-deceased dealer **Greville Franklin**. Jenks is not averse to a spot of chicanery when the opportunity arises, and he had seen his chance when Franklin showed him twenty-five uncut diamonds which he'd just bought. Franklin's death following a freak accident merely hardens Jenks' resolve to profit financially from the diamonds. However, in jockey **Derek Franklin**, Greville's brother, Jenks more than meets his match, and his schemes come to nothing.

Jennings, Elizabeth (*Dead Heat* 2007)

Elizabeth is the wife of **Newmarket** trainer **Neil Jennings**. She is killed when a bomb explodes in the grandstand boxes at **Newmarket racecourse**.

Jennings, Jimmy (*To the Hilt* 1996)

Jennings is a **Hampshire** racehorse trainer, and a friend of **Emily Cox**. Middle-aged and suffering from a possibly terminal illness, he has reduced his string of horses. He agrees to look after **Golden Malt** for **Alex Kinloch** and to train him for the King Alfred Gold Cup. Jennings owns a painting, by Alex, of a jockey. He tells Alex that he has drawn strength from the painting, which portrays the jockey's strength and endurance.

Jennings, Neil (*Dead Heat* 2007)

Jennings is a leading **Newmarket** racehorse trainer. His wife, **Elizabeth**, is killed when a bomb explodes during lunch on Two Thousand Guineas day in the grandstand boxes at **Newmarket racecourse**. Neil had not attended the function, having suffered food poisoning the previous evening.

Jetset (*Field of 13* 1998: "Blind Chance")

Jetset is a two-year-old colt that runs at **Ascot** and wins in a four-way photo-finish. He is fraudulently backed to win by associates of a racecourse official.

Jill (*Smokescreen* 1972)

Also known as "Handcuffs," Jill is an assistant on the film crew making *Man in a Car*. She is in charge of the keys to the handcuffs worn by **Edward Lincoln** in the film. She doesn't enjoy the location work in Southern Spain, complaining of the heat and lack of excitement.

Jim (*10 lb. Penalty* 1997)

Jim is assistant to racehorse trainer **Spencer Stallworthy**; he is a good horseman, who does most of the hands-on training. He collects **Benedict Juliard** from an **Exeter** hotel and drives him out into the **Devon** countryside to meet Stallworthy.

Jim (*Shattered* 2000)

Jim is a driver hired by **Gerard Logan**, who has lost his license, to take him to Taunton, **Somerset**, to meet **Victor Verity**, and to Lynton, **Devon**, to see **Dr. Force**. He is small, fat and unforthcoming. Jim believes in ghosts and at first refuses to drive up to Phoenix House nursing home in Lynton, which is said to be haunted. Later he overcomes his fear and collects Gerard from there. In the absence of **Worthington** and **Tom Pigeon**, Jim volunteers his services as a bodyguard. He becomes agitated when he sees Force approaching him while he is sitting in the car waiting for Gerard.

Jimmy (*For Kicks* 1965)

One of **Hedley Humber's** stable lads, Jimmy is an ex-prisoner, a bully and a liar. He walks out after Humber hits him with his stick.

Jimmy (*The Edge* 1988)

Jimmy is a character in the mystery play on board the Great Transcontinental Mystery Race Train; he is an employee of the railway company.

Jo (*Hot Money* 1987)

Jo is the wife of a respected **Newmarket** trainer; she keeps three horses to run in amateur races and gets **Ian Pembroke** to ride them. Ian rides her horse **Young Higgins** at **Sandown Park**. She is thrilled when Ian brings the horse in first at long odds in a three mile chase at **Kempton Park**.

Joanna (*Nerve* 1964)

Joanna is **Rob Finn's** cousin; Rob has been in love with Joanna since he was a child but Joanna doesn't reciprocate his feelings. She is a classical singer and amateur artist. She disapproves of Rob's career as a jump jockey, thinking that he'll be washed up at forty with only memories to live on. Joanna has a boyfriend, **Brian**, who wants to marry her and settle down, but Joanna refuses, knowing that she'll be miserable with him.

Joanna receives a phone call from Rob, who has just extricated himself from an abduction attempt. She goes to fetch him in a taxi with hot soup and warm clothes. She takes him back to her flat and resists his advances on the grounds that he is her cousin, even though her relationship with Brian is over. The next morning Joanna bandages Rob's injuries before he goes to **Ascot** to ride **Template** in the Midwinter Cup.

Joanna's feelings towards Rob begin to change, but she still has reservations because of their blood relationship. She asks him to stay on at her flat after he recovers from his exertions at Ascot and agrees to help Rob in his plan to inconvenience his abductor. Soon afterwards Joanna realizes that she can't live without Rob any longer, cousins or not. She allows Rob to persuade her that there is no barrier to their marrying.

Jobberson, Pelican (*Enquiry* 1969)

Bookmaker Pelican Jobberson is mentioned by colleague **George Newtonnards**, in conversation with jockey **Kelly Hughes**, as having a grudge against Kelly. Jobberson had laid a horse that Kelly had won on after telling the bookmaker that it had no chance.

Jockey Club

The English Jockey Club was founded in 1752 as a social club for wealthy horseracing enthusiasts. Gradually the Club assumed responsibility for the regulation of British racing—setting the rules of racing, licensing owners, trainers and jockeys, and protecting the integrity of the sport. In 1969 the Jockey Club amalgamated with the **National Hunt Committee**, which oversaw jump racing. In 1993 the Club's regulatory duties were taken over by the **British Horseracing Board**, and more recently the vital job of keeping the sport free of corruption has been assumed by the Horseracing Regulatory Authority. The Jockey Club now concentrates on managing thirteen racecourses and, via its Jockey Club Estates arm, some 4500 acres of land in **Newmarket** and **Lambourn**.

Jockeys

Of Francis's thirty-seven heroes, fifteen are, or have been, amateur or professional jockeys. Like Francis himself, they all are, or were, steeplechase jockeys, as are most of the jockeys, virtuous or otherwise, who appear in the novels. Francis writes about the jump jockey's life with a passion and a depth of knowledge that allow the reader to live that life with the character. The dilemmas, the flashes of pure joy, the pain, the mysterious telepathy between horse and rider—every feeling is explored and laid bare, revealing the pure essence of a tough, unforgiving sport and the men who risk their lives to make it happen. From **Alan York** (*Dead Cert* 1962) through to **Sid Halley** (*Under*

Orders 2006), these are Francis's jockey heroes: **Alan York** (*Dead Cert* 1962): amateur; **Rob Finn** (*Nerve* 1964): professional; **Sid Halley** (*Odds Against* 1965; *Whip Hand* 1979; *Come to Grief* 1995; *Under Orders* 2006): ex-professional; ex-champion jockey; **Lord Henry Gray** (*Flying Finish* 1966): amateur; **Kelly Hughes** (*Enquiry* 1969): professional; **Jonah Dereham** (*Knock Down* 1974): ex-professional; **Roland Britten** (*Risk* 1977): amateur; **Randall Drew** (*Trial Run* 1978): ex-amateur; **Philip Nore** (*Reflex* 1980): professional; **William Derry** (*Twice Shy* 1981): ex-amateur/professional; **Kit Fielding** (*Break In* 1985; *Bolt* 1986): professional; champion jockey; **Ian Pembroke** (*Hot Money* 1987): amateur; turns professional; **Derek Franklin** (*Straight* 1989): professional; **Freddie Croft** (*Driving Force* 1992): ex-professional; **Benedict Juliard** (*10 lb. Penalty* 1997): amateur.

All these men, despite their flaws, are fundamentally good and honest. The same comment does not apply to Francis's jockeys in general, a significant proportion of whom are shady, corruptible or otherwise felonious. Some uncharitable souls might say that this is an accurate reflection of reality, given the numerous opportunities for sharp practice inherent in racing. Crooked jump jockeys include **Raymond Child** (*High Stakes* 1975), who stops horses owned by **Steven Scott**; **Vernon Arkwright** (*Field of 13* 1998: "Haig's Death"), who is bribed by the owner of the favorite in a race at **Winchester** to hamper another fancied runner to prevent it from winning; **Sandy Mason** (*Dead Cert* 1962) who recruits colleague **Joe Nantwich** to stop horses for a sinister owner; and **Charlie West** (*Enquiry* 1969), who takes a bribe to lie about **Kelly Hughes** at an enquiry into the running and riding of a beaten favorite at **Oxford**.

Bob Sherman (*Slay-Ride* 1973) is an English jockey who rides a lot in Norway. Asked to deliver a packet when traveling from England to Oslo, he allows greed to get the better of him, and pays a heavy price for his duplicity. In *Longshot* (1990) the aggressive, short-tempered amateur rider **Everard Nolan** causes the death of a girl at a party. He maintains it was an accident but is given a suspended jail sentence. Another amateur, **Peter Enstone** (under orders), has had the advantages of a wealthy background and an expensive education. But he has failed to appreciate his good fortune, and instead chooses a path that is bound to lead to violent confrontation.

Rebecca Stratton is one of only two female

jockeys to feature in Francis's novels, possibly because he has been quoted as saying that he is not entirely comfortable about women putting their lives at risk riding racehorses. In *Decider* (1993) Rebecca is a tough cookie, and as unyielding in a race as any of her male colleagues. Away from the track she exhibits the same ruthless streak. The other female jockey is **Alessia Cenci**, a top Italian rider on the Flat, who is kidnapped in *The Danger* (1983) but released after a ransom is paid. She later goes on to ride the winner of the Washington International at **Laurel Park**.

Flat jockeys appear much less frequently in the novels that their jumping counterparts. In *Rat Race* (1970) Australian **Kenny Bayst** gets his mount boxed in during a race at **Haydock Park**. Later he is beaten up at **Redcar** races by hired thugs after winning a race he should have lost. *Bonecrack* (1971) is a novel set wholly in the flat racing world, and one of its main characters is **Alessandro Rivera**, a teenager taken on as an apprentice jockey by **Newmarket** trainer **Neil Griffon** as a result of threats by Rivera's father, a deranged Italian criminal. Difficult and arrogant but a talented rider, Alessandro gradually learns from Neil how to be a civilized human being.

In *Bonecrack* Griffon's experienced stable jockey **Tommy Hoylake** is implicitly cited as an example to Alessandro of how he should conduct himself. There are other examples, apart from the heroes, of honest jockeys, though they themselves may be the victims of crime. Leading amateur rider **Major Bill Davidson** (*Dead Cert*) is killed in a fall at **Maidenhead** races when his horse is deliberately brought down. The opening scene of *Nerve* sees a well-respected and popular jump jockey, **Art Matthews**, shoot himself in the paddock at **Dunstable** races. He has recently been sacked by his trainer after baseless rumors about his honesty are circulated.

After this litany of transgression and misfortune, the happy event befalling struggling Irish jump jockey **Dermot Finnegan** (*Forfeit* 1968) helps to restore the reader's faith in the riding fraternity. For years he's cheerfully ridden bad horses round low-grade tracks, his mounts more likely to bury him at the open ditch than to win a race. Then, unexpectedly, Dermot is given a ride on a good horse, **Rockville**, in the Grand National. Riding like a man possessed, he beats the favorite by three lengths.

Joe (*Rat Race* 1970)

Joe, Known as "Old Joe" is a mechanic for **Derrydown Air Transport**. He takes as a personal affront **Matt Shore**'s theory that a pulley on the elevator wires had come adrift during a return flight from **Haydock Park**, forcing Matt to land for a check-over. However, he grudgingly accepts that Matt doesn't abuse the plane.

Joe (*Smokescreen* 1972)

A technician at **Edward Lincoln**'s press conference in South Africa, Joe is in charge of the radio equipment used to interview Edward. He has a problem with his microphone so he uses an old one rather than wait for a replacement from the studio. After **Katya** is electrocuted Joe discovers that the recorder, which is not his own, has been wrongly wired up.

Joe (*Break In* 1985)

Joe is a news editor at the London-based American news-gathering agency where **Danielle de Brescou** works. He is black, around thirty years old, friendly and helpful. He edits **Kit Fielding**'s tapes of **Maynard Allardeck**'s interview on "How's Trade?" and Kit's interviews with the **Perrysides**, **George Tasker** and **Hugh Vaughnley**.

Joe (*Bolt* 1986)

Joe is a jump jockey who falls at the same hurdle as **Kit Fielding** in a novice race at **Sandown Park**. Knocked unconscious, he partly recovers during the ambulance ride back to the stands, and begins to groan. Joe's young, pregnant wife, who was watching the race, is distressed when she sees him and is comforted by Kit. Joe is transferred from the first-aid room to an ambulance and taken to hospital, where he makes a full recovery within a few days.

Jogger (*Driving Force* 1992)

Jogger is the company mechanic at **Croft Raceways** horse transport firm. In his early fifties and a former army truck driver, Jogger is solitary and parsimonious; he's a bow-legged Londoner with a distinctive way of walking, and he uses his own form of Cockney rhyming slang. He finds metal boxes stuck by magnets onto the undersides of three horse vans. He promises **Freddie Croft** not to talk about it in the pub, but he does so a day or two later. The next morning Jogger is found dead in the inspection pit with his neck broken. On the morning of his death Jogger had left an incomprehensible message in rhyming slang on Freddie's answer phone; it is later found to refer to his discovery of a dead rabbit, crawling with ticks, in the inspection pit.

John (*Flying Finish* 1966)

John works for **Yardman** Transport; he is about fifty years old, fat and balding. He refuses to make eye contact with **Henry Gray**. He is incompetent with horses, and frightens them when he tries to pull them up the airplane's ramp. He is equally hopeless at installing the horses and dismantling the boxes. In France, John has a row with **Billy Watkins**. On his second trip John disappears. Watkins says that John has gone to Paris to see a prostitute there and would return to England the following day on a regular airline.

John (*Banker* 1982)

An employee of merchant bank **Paul Ekaterin Ltd.**, John works in the Banking Department with **Tim Ekaterin**. He returns from his holidays with lurid and unlikely tales of his sexual conquests. He resents the fact that Tim is doing **Gordon Michael**'s job; he thinks that it is down to nepotism, and wastes no opportunity to undermine Tim's authority. He refuses to speak to Tim despite Tim's efforts to get along with him. John is subsequently transferred to another department; eventually he leaves to take up a partnership in a Stock Exchange broking firm.

Johnson (*The Edge* 1988)

An alias used by **Alex Mitchell McLachlan**.

Johnson, Inspector (*Under Orders* 2006)

Inspector Johnson, of Thames Valley police, investigates the death of trainer **Bill Burton**. He works on the assumption that Burton has committed suicide, but a copy of a videotape which he receives from **Sid Halley** makes him reconsider.

Johnston, Miss (*High Stakes* 1975)

Miss Johnson is one of two elderly sisters who own a somewhat run-down riding school and livery yard, Hantsford Manor in **Hampshire**. They also offer accommodation. She and her sister, **Mrs. Fairchild Smith,** look after **Black Fire** for **Steven Scott**. Steven's American friend, **Allie Ward,** stays at Hantsford Manor for one night, and takes Black Fire away in a horse van when Steven needs him.

Jonathan (*Come to Grief* 1995)

Jonathan is the fifteen-year-old nephew of **Mrs. Betty Bracken;** he is currently living with her after being expelled from his private school, and is on probation for stealing a car and crashing it. He tells **Sid Halley**, who is investigating the mutilation of Mrs. Bracken's colt, that he was returning home during the night after an illicit sexual liaison with a local woman when he saw a Land Rover in the lane next to the colt's paddock.

Jonathan breaks the lock on the boot of Sid's Mercedes to hide in it in order to get away from his family for a while. Forced by Sid to run after the car for a mile, Jonathan demonstrates impressive physical fitness. He notices a Land Rover with the same window transfer as the one he'd seen in the lane, allowing Sid to trace the Land Rover's owner.

Jonathan enjoys being taken out in a speedboat on a lake by **Norman Picton**'s wife. According to Sid, he needs a challenge. He shows a natural talent for water skiing; spending several weeks practicing has a beneficial effect on his character. Sid, recognizing a possible replacement for **Chico Barnes**, sends Jonathan to **Shropshire** to undertake a bit of detective work.

Jones, Frank (*Trial Run* 1978)

Jones, in his late twenties, is an English KGB agent living in Moscow. He was recruited to the communist cause by his Russian grandmother, who had married a British sailor. He is assigned to watch **Randall Drew** while he is in Moscow. Jones claims to have been a teacher at an **Essex** junior school, and that he is temporarily between jobs. He invites himself along when Randall says he is going to the Lenin Museum. He tails Randall when he is on his way to meet **Misha** but loses him. Following Randall again, Jones sees him thrown into a river and rescues him. Next day Randall returns to his room to find Jones inside, trying to open the Matrushka doll. Jones says he was worried when Randall didn't come to breakfast.

Jones, Max (*Hot Money* 1987)

Max Jones is mentioned by **Ian Pembroke**, while at **Newmarket Yearling Sales**, as being the owner of a lot of horses, and regularly bidding against an old lady with whom he was conducting a feud.

Jones, Priam (*Shattered* 2000)

Priam Jones is a racehorse trainer; his jockey, **Martin Stukely**, is killed during a race at **Chel-**

tenham when one of Jones's horses, **Talahassee**, falls on him. Jones is in late middle age; he has a high opinion of his own ability as a trainer, not totally substantiated by results. Though normally unemotional, he is in tears after Stukely's death. He tells **Gerard Logan** that Stukely's wife **Bon-Bon** wants no-one but him, Jones, to visit her after her husband's death, a claim subsequently denied by Bon-Bon. Jones reminds Gerard about a video-tape that he had given to Gerard. He says that Gerard had left the video in his raincoat in Stukely's car, and that he, Jones, had returned it to Gerard.

Jones is affronted when **Lloyd Baxter** transfers his horses to another stable. He doesn't deny it when Gerard asks him if he'd played the video before returning it. Jones says that racecourse valet **Eddie Payne** had asked him if he was sure that the tape he'd returned to Gerard was the same one that Eddie had given Gerard at **Cheltenham**, and Jones said it was. However, Jones later admits he had lied. Thinking that the tape showed the hiding place of a valuable necklace, he had kept it and switched it for a tape with racing on from Stukely's house. When he found it wasn't about the necklace, Jones had put it back in Stukely's car the following day. As a result Jones is charged and bailed by the police.

Jones-Boy (*Odds Against* 1965)

Jones-Boy is the office boy at **Hunt Radnor Associates**. He is a long-haired, irreverent, awkward teenager but is good at his job. He argues constantly with **Chico Barnes** and spends his free time chasing girls. He always arrives early at work, and so finds **Sid Halley** before he dies of gunshot wounds.

De Jong, Mike (*Forfeit* 1968)

De Jong, a South African reporter on the racing desk of a rival newspaper to *The Blaze*, is a friend of **James Tyrone**. He warns James about a dangerous villain who has a notorious reputation in South Africa.

Juliard, Benedict (*10 lb. Penalty* 1997)

To describe Benedict Juliard as the main character of *10 lb. Penalty* is stretching the truth, implying as it does that Benedict actually has a character. He is seventeen years old, untainted by experience, and less interesting than a tax return. Benedict is mild-mannered to the point of martyrdom: when George, his obnoxious father, engi-

neers his wrongful dismissal from a racing yard where he is employed as a lad and amateur jockey, so that Benedict can help him get elected as an MP, he endures the humiliation with hardly a murmur. Meekly acquiescing to George's bullying, Benedict sets off on the election trail. He is soon called upon to show a modicum of courage; when someone takes a shot at his father late at night after a political meeting, Benedict refuses to leave George's side while he may still be in danger. Benedict claims that he is committed to his father rather than to his father's party, which sounds like a statement of the obvious; no-one in his right mind would be willing to risk being shot dead for the sake of the Conservative party of the late 1990's, whose candidate George almost certainly is. In his political campaign George had envisioned for Benedict the role of "social asset" in order to make him more electable, which only goes to show how far those aspiring to be politicians are capable of losing the plot completely.

Benedict persuades his father that someone may just be trying to kill him, and assumes a new role, that of bodyguard. At **Dorset County racecourse** Benedict meets **Orinda Nagle**, widow of the MP whose death caused the by-election and who hoped to be selected to fight the seat. When she complains that George has ruined her life, Benedict whines, in similar vein, that his life-long ambition to be a jockey has been dashed. Orinda, mysteriously, is impressed; she soon decides to campaign on George's behalf, telling Benedict that he had showed her how it was possible to deal with a setback.

After a hiatus of three years during which nothing of moment happens, Benedict graduates from university with, predictably, a math and accounting degree, and lands a job with **Weatherbys**, the administrative arm of the horse racing industry. It is lucky the Benedict enjoys his job, since he appears not to pursue the other normal activities of a healthy young man. He complains that his sex life is virtually non-existent: For this unsatisfactory state of affairs he cites a pact with his father—now a prominent MP—that neither would do anything that might adversely affect the good reputation of the other. Meanwhile the villain who had tried to shoot George at the beginning of the story tries to do it again. This time he makes a better job of it—he manages to shoot Benedict. Sadly though, only in the leg.

Juliard, George (*10 lb. Penalty* 1997)

George is the father of **Benedict Juliard**, his son by a much older woman whom he had married as a teenager and who died in childbirth. Juliard fostered his baby with his dead wife's sister while he went off to make his fortune in the city. Juliard gets Benedict sacked from his job as a stable lad and amateur jockey so that Benedict can help him get elected as a Member of Parliament. Benedict, unaware of his father's duplicity, thinks him an honorable man with high standards of behavior. Juliard overrules Benedict's decision not to take up a place at **Exeter** University.

One night, after a political meeting in the constituency of **Hoopwestern**, someone takes shot at Juliard but misses. Soon Juliard upgrades his son's role to that of a bodyguard rather than merely a socially acceptable dogsbody.

Juliard wins the Hoopwestern by-election, and soon afterwards he is appointed Under-Secretary of State in the Department of Trade and Industry. After the General Election he is appointed Minister of State in the Ministry of Transport. Later he is given a Cabinet post as Minister of Agriculture. Showing Benedict round 10 Downing Street, he self-consciously sits in the Prime Minister's seat.

Juliard enhances his political reputation by his handling of an international fishery crisis. When the Prime Minister decides to step down as leader of the party, Juliard runs against **Hudson Hirst** for leader. Benedict is called upon to exercise his function as a bodyguard when Juliard is the subject of another murder attempt.

Julie (*Dead Heat* 2007)

Julie is a waitress at **The Hay Net**, a Newmarket restaurant run by **Max Moreton**.

June (*Straight* 1989)

June is an employee of **Greville Franklin** at his business, **Saxony Franklin**; she oversees the computers and stock control. She is energetic, proactive and a vital cog in the continuation of the business after Greville's death. Checking the computer for **Derek Franklin**, June discovers a secret file opened by Greville under the password "June." It is only a message to June giving her a raise if she finds the file. She is appointed Deputy Personal Assistant by Derek, and is helpful to him as he tries to learn the business. Derek subsequently promotes June to Merchandise Manager as he prepares to return to race riding.

Just the Thing (*Longshot* 1990)

Just the Thing is a hurdler trained by **Tremayne Vickers**. At **Windsor** races he runs green, finishing third under a sympathetic ride from stable jockey **Sam Yaeger**.

K

Kandersteg (*For Kicks* 1965)

Kandersteg is a steeplechaser in **Hedley Humber**'s yard. Owned by **Paul J. Adams**, he is a pale, washy chestnut. Kandersteg is taken to Adams's farm and subjected to a terrifying ordeal in order to prepare him for a future selling chase betting coup.

Katya (*Smokescreen* 1972)

Katya is a radio journalist and the girlfriend of **Roderick Hodge**, the features editor of the *Rand Daily Star*. She is present at **Edward Lincoln**'s Press reception in Johannesburg. She intends to interview Edward for a women's radio show but is electrocuted by a faulty microphone which had originally been handed to Edward. Her heart stops, and her life is saved by Edward, who gives her mouth-to-mouth resuscitation. She is detained in hospital overnight. When she recovers she helps Hodge in an unsuccessful attempt to set Edward up in a compromising situation with a beautiful model. This is at the request of **Clifford Wenkins**, who is trying to drum up publicity for Edward's new film.

Kealy, Emma (*Dead Heat* 2007)

Emma is the wife of **Newmarket** racehorse trainer **George Kealy**. She suffers food poisoning after a meal at **Newmarket racecourse** prepared by chef **Max Moreton** on the evening before the Two Thousand Guineas. Emma is too ill to go to the races the next day as a guest of **Delafield Industries Inc.**; if she had, she would have been in the grandstand box blown up by a bomb. Emma overrules her husband's decision to cancel their regular pre-booked table at Max's restaurant, **The Hay Net**.

Kealy, George (*Dead Heat* 2007)

George Kealy is a top **Newmarket** racehorse trainer whose wife, **Emma**, is the sister of trainer **Neil Jennings**. He suffers food poisoning at **Newmarket racecourse** on the evening before the running of the Two Thousand Guineas; as a result he doesn't go to the races the next day, when he would have been a guest of **Delafield Industries Inc.** He attends the funeral of **Elizabeth Jennings**. He cancels his pre-booked Saturday evening table at **Max Moreton**'s restaurant, **The Hay Net**, but Emma overrules his decision. After dining at The Hay Net Kealy deliberately leaves his cell phone behind. He returns to collect it after the restaurant is closed, bringing his criminal associate, **Pyotr Komarov**, with him. He goes outside to look for **Caroline Aston**. On returning he sees Komarov in the cold room; he goes in to investigate and is imprisoned there by Max. Arrested and charged with murder, he cooperates with police in return for a lesser charge.

Keeble, Joan (*Blood Sport* 1967)

Joan is the wife of **Sim Keeble, Gene Hawkins'** boss. She has no idea who Gene is when he arrives for a day's sailing on their boat, suggesting a lack of intimacy between her and her husband.

Keeble, Lynnie (*Blood Sport* 1967)

Lynnie is the teenage daughter of **Sim Keeble**. She is at finishing school in South **Kensington**, London, where she lives in a hostel with sixty other girls. She has just passed her driving test, and collects **Gene Hawkins** to take him to her father's boat on the Thames. Later, she goes back to Gene's flat for a meal, their relationship warming to friendship. She gives Gene a Yogi Bear handkerchief she'd found in the punt which had almost caused **Dave Teller**'s death.

Lynnie goes with Gene to **Eunice Teller**'s house in California. She is looking forward to meeting Eunice but is apprehensive when Gene tells her he thinks the real reason for their visit is to stop Eunice drinking too much when she is on her own. Stopping off in New York on the way, Lynnie and Gene go on an evening tour of the sights. She enjoys Gene's company and tells him as much, allowing him to kiss her goodnight.

In California Lynnie goes for a walk with Gene on the beach. When Gene kisses her Lynnie wants him to continue; but Gene, though he doesn't want to stop, makes a joke of it.

Lynnie is furious with Gene when she learns that he had deliberately put himself in danger in the course of his investigations into the disappearance of two stallions. She is very cool towards him when **Walt Prensela** explains Gene's absence by saying that he had been visiting a woman friend in

San Francisco. Later, when Gene tells her it was not true, she is relieved.

When she flies back to England with Gene she doesn't want to leave him at the airport. Gene says she's too young for him; Lynnie tells him she'll wait for him until she's twenty-one.

Keeble, Peter (*Blood Sport* 1967)

Peter is the son of **Sim Keeble, Gene Hawkins'** boss. About twelve years old, Peter enjoys photography, and takes lots of photos during a boat trip on the Thames.

Keeble, Sim (*Blood Sport* 1967)

Sim Keeble is a civil servant, working for a secret anti-infiltration department, and is **Gene Hawkins'** boss. He is thirty-five years old but looks fifty; an unassuming exterior conceals a sharp brain. He has two children, **Lynnie** and **Peter**. He invites Gene to spend the day on his boat on the Thames; he is worried that Gene might kill himself during his three weeks' leave from work. He wants to keep Gene occupied, so he introduces him to American racehorse owner **Dave Teller**. Keeble is keen for Gene to go to America to look for Teller's stallion, **Chrysalis**, which has gone missing. After Teller is almost killed in a punting incident, Keeble is skeptical of Gene's theory that it had been a deliberate attempt to murder Teller. However, he is happy to admit he was wrong when faced with incontrovertible evidence to the contrary.

When Gene and Lynnie return from America Keeble meets them at the airport. He sees how much Lynnie cares for Gene, but when she says she is prepared to wait for him until she's twenty-one, Keeble has no doubt that she'll change her mind.

Keene, Ziggy (*Wild Horses* 1994)

Keene is a highly regarded Ukrainian-born stuntman who specializes in stunts involving horses. He had trained at the Moscow Circus School, and then worked in America, where **Thomas Lyon** hired him for his rodeo film. Keene has a mercurial temperament. He goes to Norway for Thomas to find wild Viking horses for a dawn beach scene in the film *Unstable Times*; he stays in Norway to work with the horses' trainer before bringing them to England. He dresses as **Yvonne**, **Sonia Wells'** character in the film, to ride one of the wild horses when Thomas shoots the scene.

Keith, Eddy (*Whip Hand* 1979)

Ex-police superintendent Eddy Keith is Deputy Director of Security to the **Jockey Club**. He is the loud, hearty type. Keith is investigated by **Sid Halley** at the request of Commander **Lucas Wainwright**, Keith's boss. Wainwright tells Sid that he suspects Keith of taking bribes.

Keith meets Sid as he is leaving the Jockey Club's headquarters in **Portman Square**, London, and delivers an apparently friendly warning not to get involved with matters that concern the Security department. Keith asks **Sir Thomas Ullaston**, Senior Steward of the Jockey Club, to stop Sid operating on racecourses. Sir Thomas refuses.

Later, Sid discovers that Keith is not the corrupt employee in the Security department.

Keithley, Donna (*Twice Shy* 1981)

Donna Keithley used to share an apartment with **Sarah Derry**; now she lives in **Norwich, Norfolk**, with husband **Peter Keithley**. She is involuntarily childless. She steals a baby from its buggy and drives seventy miles to the coast. Abandoning car and baby, she walks away along the beach. The police soon find the baby and Donna is arrested. Freed on bail, she tries to commit suicide by plunging an electric hair dryer into her bath water; she is prevented from doing so in the nick of time by her husband. She is subsequently comforted and looked after by Sarah Derry.

Donna is at home with Sarah when villains break in and tie them up. She screams incessantly that she will report them to the police, and almost gets both of them killed as a result. After Peter is killed in an explosion on his boat, Donna stays with Sarah until she outstays her welcome and goes home.

Donna is placed on probation for stealing the baby. She tells Sarah that after she had stolen the baby she was ecstatically happy until the baby woke up. When it wouldn't stop crying and needed changing she got angry with it, dumped it on the back seat of the car and left it.

Keithley, Peter (*Twice Shy* 1981)

In his early thirties, Peter Keithley is an IT consultant to small businesses; he works for **Mason Miles Associates**. He lives in **Norwich, Norfolk**, with his wife **Donna**, who once shared an apartment with **Sarah Derry**. Peter phones Sarah to tell her that Donna has been arrested for stealing a baby. While she is on bail awaiting trial, he stops her from committing suicide.

Keithley gives cassette tapes containing a computer program for handicapping horses to **Jonathan Derry** for safekeeping. Two days later, working on his cabin cruiser, he is killed when the boat explodes. This subsequently proves to have been an accident.

Kelsey, Tor (*The Edge* 1988)

Tor was christened Torquil but it is kinder to draw a discreet veil over this. His father, a wealthy second-hand car dealer, was already sixty-five years old when he got married. Dead from cancer within five years of Tor's birth, he still managed to outlive his wife, a slip of a girl from an upper-class family that had fallen on hard times and needed an injection of hard cash. She was only twenty-two when she was killed out hunting, leaving the infant Tor to be reared by an elderly aunt who loved going racing and towed him along with her. Tor grew up to share her passion and, as soon as he was old enough, set off to travel the world working in studs and stables. Seven years later, aged twenty-five, Tor returned to the UK, having been left a fortune by his aunt and father. The family lawyer, no doubt keen that Tor should not fritter away his inheritance, recommended him to **Val Catto**, the **Jockey Club's** Director of Security, for a job as a racecourse investigator.

Catto asks Tor to fly to Canada to carry out covert surveillance on a known criminal who is to be traveling on the Great Transcontinental Mystery Race Train. The trip is for rich owners intending to race their horses at various race tracks across Canada, and includes an on-board mystery, performed by actors for the entertainment of the passengers. Tor travels on the train as a waiter called Tommy.

Travel company executive **Nell Richmond**, organizer of the trip, knows that Tor is working for the Jockey Club. She is young and pretty, and Tor wastes little time in inviting her to dinner. Nell suspects that Tor may be gay, but her female instinct, normally so finely tuned about these things, is wide of the mark in Tor's case. He is red-bloodedly heterosexual, though not in the least offended by Nell's conjecture.

Nell describes Tor as "light-hearted," but that doesn't stop him from taking his investigation seriously. When he sees the villain deep in conversation with a similarly unsavory character and misses an opportunity to photograph them together he is annoyed with himself, and frets that he isn't doing his job properly. He is worrying unnecessarily; he can only do his best with an unlikely, and, at times, barely credible storyline. Given the opportunity to write the script for the mystery being played out on board the train, he uses it to warn certain passengers that he is keeping an eye on their activities. He demonstrates his initiative by preventing a train crash, and displays courage when fighting off an attack that leaves him with a broken shoulder. When the train reaches Vancouver, the end of its journey, Tor is able to confront the villain with evidence of his wrongdoing.

A good result for Tor, then, especially when he persuades Nell to go on holiday with him, despite having known each other only a few days. But after a train journey as fraught as this one, who can begrudge them a bit of fun?

Kemp-Lore, Maurice (*Nerve* 1964)

Maurice Kemp-Lore draws the motivation for his actions from a well-tapped source—consuming envy of a lifestyle denied to him, and the resulting hatred for those who are lucky enough to enjoy it. In Kemp-Lore's case he is unable to uphold the family tradition of riding in steeplechases owing to a debilitating asthmatic reaction to horses. An even greater humiliation for Kemp-Lore is that riding frightens him so much that it focuses his spite on that group of men to whom the skill comes naturally—the professional jump jockeys with whom he mixes every day in his role as presenter of a TV racing show. His dark side is unsuspected; the public face he presents is one of good humor and compassion. Whilst Kemp-Lore's behavior is abhorrent, his feelings of inadequacy and his moral and physical frailty are understandable, and allow the reader to feel some sense of pity for him.

Kempton Park racecourse

Kempton Park is in **Middlesex**, fifteen miles from central London. Racing began here in 1878, and was soon patronized by the Prince of Wales and his set. In 1937, following the abdication of King Edward VIII in December of the previous year, the Kempton Park executive honored the new King with a race named for him, the King George VI Steeplechase. It remains one of the highlights of the jumping year. The immensely popular grey, Desert Orchid, won the King George three times in the 1980's and is commemorated with a life-size statue overlooking the parade ring. In 1997, £10 million was spent on upgrading the course's facilities, including the building of a new stand. Re-

cently an all-weather circuit has been added to the turf flat and jumping tracks.

Nerve (1964): Jockey **Rob Finn** wins Kempton Park's King Chase on **Template** on Boxing Day.

Risk (1977): Amateur jockey **Roland Britten** rides the **Binny Tomkins**–trained chaser **Tapestry**—winner of the **Cheltenham** Gold Cup—in the Oasthouse Cup at **Kempton Park**. Tomkins, in debt to bookmakers, doesn't want the horse to win and tampers with the bridle. Roland notices, has the bridle changed and wins the race.

Whip Hand (1979): Racehorse owner **Lord Friarly** asks **Sid Halley** to investigate some owners' syndicates whose horses don't run to form. Friarly has a share in one of these syndicates.

Reflex (1980): At **Kempton Park** jockey **Philip Nore** learns that the house of fellow-jockey **Steve Millace**'s mother has been burned down. He rides two winners at the meeting, **Pamphlet** and **Sharpener**.

Hot Money (1987): **Young Higgins**, a horse ridden by amateur jockey **Ian Pembroke**, wins at **Kempton Park**.

Kendall, John (*Longshot* 1990)

"It isn't important to come out on top," Bertolt Brecht wrote. "What matters is to come out alive." This is a theory with which John Kendall fully concurs, having written half a dozen books on how to survive in deserts, jungles and similar inhospitable places. He has recently given up his job with a travel company to become a full-time novelist. His first novel has been accepted for publication but he is broke and, to add to his problems, he has just been made homeless. So when the opportunity arises to write the biography of racehorse trainer **Tremayne Vickers**, board and lodging included, he ignores the advice of his agent and accepts the commission.

John's survival skills are called into play almost at once. The car ferrying him to Vickers' house in **Berkshire** on a freezing winter's afternoon skids into a water-filled ditch. Immediately recognizing that his fellow passengers are in danger of succumbing to hypothermia, John makes them strip off their wet clothes in exchange for the dry ones in his suitcase.

John had learned to ride when in Mexico, and is allowed to ride out with Vickers' string. Even before that he's proved his worth on the gallops, helping Vickers to catch a loose horse from someone else's yard.

John's Achilles heel is a self-acknowledged

tendency to leap in without weighing up the consequences. Misgivings kick in when he begins to plan his biography of Vickers: "I still hadn't put an actual sentence on paper ... and it was never easy, ever, to dig words and ideas from my brain..." John's sentiments sound suspiciously like Francis's own. In interviews that Francis has given over the years, his stance on the nitty-gritty of producing three hundred or so pages of writing has been contradictory. On occasions he has spoken of his love of writing, but more often he has admitted to finding it a difficult business, and has always been much happier describing himself as a jockey than a writer.

A stable girl's body is found in local woods, and the local tight-knit racing community is a whirlpool of rumor. One of Vickers' owners, whose husband is under suspicion, looks to John to help them and John is quick to oblige. He uses his survival training to rescue the man from drowning when someone sets a trap similar to one for catching animals that John himself had described in his survival guidebooks.

Working in a racing yard hones John's riding skills to the extent that Vickers applies for a permit for John to ride as an amateur. At the same time John hears from his literary agent that his novel is to be published in America. He is ecstatic and senses that his life is taking a new direction. Meanwhile the local police are impressed by John's amateur detective work. The policeman in charge of the investigation into the stable girl's murder asks John if he's ever considered police work. Modestly, John brushes aside the compliment: "Not good at that sort of discipline."

What John is good at is being shot twice in the back with arrows and living to tell the tale, putting him at least one rung up from General George Custer. Lost in dense woodland, John ignores the excruciating pain and, somewhat improbably, finds his way back to his car. Franklin D. Roosevelt would have been proud of him: "When you get to the end of your rope," he said, "tie a knot and hang on."

Kennet, Trevor (*High Stakes* 1975)

Newmarket trainer Trevor Kennet is sent three racehorses by **Steven Scott** after Steven sacks his trainer, **Jody Leeds**. Kennet is dour and uncommunicative. His stables are drab, possibly to discourage owners from visiting.

Kenny (*Reflex* 1980)

Kenny is a stable lad at **Harold Osborne's** yard in **Lambourn**. An unpleasant and shifty young man with no social graces, Kenny is an ex-employee of trainer **Bart Underfield**. He tells **Philip Nore** that he saw **Elgin Yaxley**, in a very angry state, at Underfield's yard.

Kensington, London

The Royal Borough of Kensington and Chelsea is in central London, west of the City of Westminster. Kensington is an affluent area with expensive residential districts as well as up-market shopping streets: Also in Kensington are the Royal Albert Hall, the Natural History and Science Museums and Imperial College, part of London University.

The Danger (1983): **Liberty Market Ltd.**, a firm specializing in negotiating the release of kidnap victims, has its offices in Kensington.

Kessel, Mr. (*Enquiry* 1969)

Kessel is the owner of **Squelsh**, favorite for the Lemonfizz Gold Cup at **Oxford**, over whose riding **Kelly Hughes** and **Dexter Cranfield** are warned off. As Kelly is leaving the enquiry Kessel tells him that he'll never ride for him again. At the Jockeys' Fund dance Kessel tells **Roberta Cranfield** that he's sent his horses to **Pat Nikita**, a great rival of Cranfield's.

After Kelly and Cranfield get their licenses back Kessel sees Kelly at **Reading** races. He just stares at Kelly and walks away. He is furious when Kelly, riding **Breadwinner**, beats Squelsh by a nostril in the **Cheltenham** Gold Cup.

Kevin (*The Danger* 1983)

Kevin is one of the men who kidnap **Dominic Nerrity** and hold him for ransom. He is suspicious when he sees **Andrew Douglas** sitting in a car nearby. He goes out to check on Andrew, who has overheard Kevin on his radio receiver and has moved his car. He is later arrested by the police, and found to have previous convictions for burglary.

Kiddo (*Blood Sport* 1967)

Kiddo is a young man who works for **Culham James Offen** as a stud groom. He had previously worked on stud farms in **Lexington**, Kentucky and in Maryland. He is good-natured, and an excellent horseman.

Kildare, Gordon (*Nerve* 1964)

Kildare is an associate TV producer at Universal Telecast Studios; he works on **Maurice Kemp-Lore**'s show, "Turf Talk." He welcomes **Rob Finn** to the studios and entertains him before the show.

King, Trevor (*Risk* 1977)

King is the senior partner at King and Britten, accountants of **Newbury, Berkshire**. He likes to see himself as a pillar of the community. He allows **Roland Britten** to work flexible hours in order to go racing as an amateur jockey. King had appointed Roland six years previously, accurately judging that he would attract more clients from the racing world. He cultivates the traditional image of the successful accountant—sober and authoritative; Roland, however, has his reservations about King and has found him difficult to get to know on a personal level.

King is on holiday in Spain when Roland is abducted. After Roland escapes, King sends a cable to say that his car has broken down and he will be returning later than expected. Back from holiday, he goes to the police station in Newbury to collect Roland after he is released from his second abduction. He appears shocked at Roland's loss of weight. When Roland goes to the office the next day King tries to persuade him to have a few days off, but Roland doesn't want to. He tells Roland he has signed lawyer **Denby Crest**'s Solicitor's Certificate, but prevaricates when Roland asks where he was making a mistake with Crest's accounts.

When Roland asks King if he knows "**Arthur Robinson**," King is shocked that Roland knows so much. Roland's long-standing misgivings about his partner prove to be well-founded.

King Alfred Brewery (*To the Hilt* 1996)

Based near Wantage, **Oxfordshire**, and owned by **Sir Ivan Westering**, the King Alfred Brewery is in deep financial trouble owing to the embezzlement of its funds by a trusted senior employee.

Kingdom Hill racecourse

Kingdom Hill is a fictional racecourse in England.

Field of 13 (1998): "**The Raid at Kingdom Hill**." At a race meeting at Kingdom Hill a bomb hoax provides the opportunity for the theft of money from the Tote building.

Kinley

Break In (1985): Kinley is a three-year-old grey novice hurdler trained by **Wykeham Harlow** and owned by **Princess Casilia**. He wins first time out at **Towcester**, impressing **Kit Fielding** with his ability.

Bolt (1986): Now a top class young hurdler and a brilliant jumper, Kinley wins at **Newbury** with his head in his chest. He is described by the Princess as being the equal of triple Champion Hurdle winner Sir Ken. Kinley narrowly avoids being deliberately killed in his box at Harlow's stables.

Kinloch, Alexander (*To the Hilt* 1998)

"Unlike the male codfish, which, suddenly finding itself the parent of three and a half million little codfish, cheerfully resolves to love them all, the British aristocracy is apt to look with a somewhat jaundiced eye on its younger sons."

P.G. Wodehouse's astute observation is one to which twenty-nine-year-old Alexander Kinloch, the grandson of an earl, readily subscribes—"My many and fairly noble relations," he says, "thought me weird." Alexander has long hair. He plays the bagpipes. He lives alone, in a shepherd's hut on the side of an isolated Scottish mountain. And he is an artist. This is a career, in the estimation of his relatives, for the seriously deranged. Not that the opinions of his family concern Alexander in the slightest. Indeed, he quite enjoys his reputation for eccentricity and happily ploughs his own furrow, painting mostly golf scenes and finding a buoyant market for them. He even pays rent on his hut to his Uncle **Robert, Earl of Kinloch**, in the form of a painting. His work, in its genre, is acclaimed.

Five years before, Alexander had left his wife **Emily Jane Cox**, a racehorse trainer in the racing village of **Lambourn, Berkshire**, after only four months of marriage. Realizing that he was unable to conjure up the inspiration to paint in Lambourn, he decamped to the Scottish Highlands. To her credit Emily Jane harbors no bitterness towards Alexander and they have remained friends.

One day, four men turn up at Alexander's hut, beat him up and throw him over the edge of an escarpment. This unkind treatment, Alexander later discovers, is connected to the financial troubles of the brewery owned by his stepfather, **Sir Ivan Westering**. He is fond of Ivan but is inclined to get exasperated with his vacillation and lack of backbone in dealing with the problems of his ailing brewery and the rapaciousness of his own family.

Alex feels a strong loyalty towards his Uncle

Robert who, after the death of Alexander's father in a shooting accident when Alexander was seventeen, had supplied the love and wise counsel that he needed. When Robert asks Alexander how much pain he would endure before telling anyone a secret that Robert had entrusted to him, Alex confesses that he doesn't know. This, in essence, is the central theme of *To the Hilt*: the extent to which a man's conduct and endurance in adversity are governed by the genes he has inherited from his family and by the codes to which he is expected to adhere. Alexander is fully conscious of his ancestral endowment: "I had inherited the mainstream Kinloch mind, stubbornness and all."

It isn't long before Alex has the chance to demonstrate his bloody-mindedness. A villain subjects him to an excruciating torture in order to extract information. Even then Alexander refuses to cooperate. He survives, but when the information proves valueless, he has to accept that he'd burned for no better reason than to preserve his own self-respect.

Kinloch, Andrew (*To the Hilt* 1996)

Andrew is the eleven-year-old son of **James Kinloch**, and the grandson of **Robert, Earl of Kinloch**. He is wild and a tough cookie. He uses the King Alfred Cup as a treasure to be guarded in a game with his brother and sister. Andrew's grandfather thinks Andrew had taken the Cup with him when he went home, but in fact **Alex Kinloch** had taken it.

Kinloch, James (*To the Hilt* 1996)

James is the eldest son of **Robert, Earl of Kinloch**. He has red hair and freckles. He is genial, garrulous and light-hearted. James has a wife and three children. He plays golf in Scotland with **Alex Kinloch**.

Kinloch, Robert, Earl of (*To the Hilt* 1996)

Robert, Earl of Kinloch, is the uncle of **Alexander Kinloch**. Aged sixty-five, he is tall and well-built. Though physically clumsy, Robert is mentally sharp and tough; however, he tends to be over-trusting. He had taken an interest in Alexander's welfare after the death of his father. He lives in Kinloch Castle, which is now the property of the nation. Robert has entrusted the ceremonial sword hilt of Bonny Prince Charlie to Alexander to hide from the castle's administrators, who believe it to be also now the property of Scotland; Robert

doesn't agree. He brings the King Alfred Cup north to Scotland at **Sir Ivan Westering**'s request. He is bequeathed the Cup by Sir Ivor in his will, and appointed by him as an executor of the will.

Kinser, Dennis (*Field of 13* 1998: "Collision Course")

Kinser is a thirty-year-old ex-stable lad. He is over-confident, and harbors unrealistic ambitions to be a champion trainer. To that end he gets his aunt to sell her house and buy a riverside restaurant near **Oxford**. He raises money by mortgaging the restaurant, with the intention of buying horses for syndication and training them himself. Kinser is worried that **Bill Williams**, a local newspaper editor who had received poor service at the restaurant, has the power to harm his putative business. He takes steps to ameliorate the situation.

Kinser, Pauline (*Field of 13* 1998: "Collision Course")

Pauline Kinser is the owner of the Mainstream Mile, a new riverside restaurant near **Oxford**. She had been persuaded by her nephew **Dennis Kinser** to sell her house and buy the restaurant, which he had mortgaged in order to raise money to set himself up as a racehorse trainer. Newspaper editor **Bill Williams** complains to Pauline about the poor service he had received at her restaurant. When Dennis finds out he is angry with his aunt, thinking that the editor could harm his fledgling business.

Kinship, Lance (*Reflex* 1980)

Lance Kinship is a film director who pursues a lucrative but illicit second career which provides him with a warped sense of prestige in his social set. Kinship goes to **Newbury racecourse** with a film crew to shoot a commercial. Though a bespectacled, unimposing man, Kinship has a self-important manner which does not impress jockey and gifted amateur photographer **Philip Nore**, whom Kinship has asked to photograph the crew while they are working. Kinship soon realizes, to his alarm, that Philip is taking a close interest in his extra-curricular activities, and takes steps to deal with the situation. Kinship, however, finds that Philip is not easily deterred. In the end, considering the nature of Kinship's non-cinematic occupation, he gets off lightly.

Kirk, Archie

Come to Grief (1995): Kirk is the brother of **Betty Bracken**, whose £¼million colt suffers a horrendous assault. He lives in **Berkshire**, and works for a small clandestine government department which forecasts the probable consequence of political appointments or proposed legislation. **Sid Halley** recognizes in Kirk qualities of leadership and authority, so automatically seeks his help in investigating the crime. Sid asks Kirk if he knows a reliable policeman, and Kirk introduces him to **Detective Inspector Picton**. He accompanies Sid and Picton when they search a suspect's Land Rover.

Kirk tells Sid he is always looking for high-quality investigators with no strongly-held political views. He checks Sid out with **Sir Thomas Ullaston**, former Senior Steward of the **Jockey Club**. He asks Sid if he'd consider working for him in the future.

Under Orders (2006): Over the years, Kirk has employed **Sid Halley** to investigate the influence of pressure groups and their members on the possible implementation of proposed Government legislation. He phones Sid to draw his attention to coverage, hostile to Sid, of the murder of a jockey in *The Pump* newspaper. Kirk is anxious to protect Sid's reputation. He arranges for Sid to come to his office; there he asks Sid to investigate possible links to organized crime connected with the forthcoming Gambling Bill which will lead to an increase in casino and on-line gambling.

After Sid has extracted a videotaped confession of race fixing from a suspect, he visits Kirk and gives him a copy of the video, as well as the interim results of his investigations into internet gaming.

Kitch, Jarvis (*Rat Race* 1970)

Kitch is a racehorse trainer who trains for owner **Dobson Ambrose**. He shares a **Derrydown** plane to **Haydock Park** races with **Annie Villars** and **Kenny Bayst**. He is killed in a traffic accident, along with Ambrose, outside **Newmarket**.

Kitchen, Sam (*Blood Sport* 1967)

Kitchen is a stable lad who looked after the stallion **Chrysalis** during the horse's racing career at the stables of trainer **Mr. Arkwright**. He remembers, when asked by **Gene Hawkins**, that Chrysalis likes sardines. When Gene locates Chrysalis in the USA, Kitchens accompanies **Walt Prensela** to a rendezvous with Gene in order to identify the stallion.

Kitchens, Leonard (*10 lb. Penalty* 1997)

Kitchens works in a plant nursery. He is on the selection panel which chooses **George Juliard** to be prospective Member of Parliament for **Hoopwestern, Dorset**; however, he had voted for **Orinda Nagle**, not Juliard. He is a spectator when Juliard's constituency offices go up in flames. He is unhappy when Orinda decides to support Juliard, accusing her of betrayal.

Kitchens is suspected by the police of shooting Juliard after a rifle is found in the guttering of a nearby hotel; he supplied the hotel with flowers. He denies any involvement in either the fire or the shooting.

Kitchens, Mrs. Leonard (*10 lb. Penalty* 1997)

Mrs. Kitchens is married to nurseryman **Leonard Kitchens**; she is active in the **Hoopwestern, Dorset**, constituency on behalf of the political party represented by recently deceased Member of Parliament Dennis Nagle. She is angry when her husband seems too enamored of **Orinda Nagle**. Years later, when visited by **Benedict Juliard**, she tells him she suspects that Leonard had been responsible for an arson attack at **George Juliard**'s constituency offices. However she rules out his possible involvement in the attempted shooting of Juliard on the grounds that he wouldn't have the ability to shoot a gun.

Klugvoïgt, Mr. (*Smokescreen* 1972)

Klugvoïgt is the Chairman of **Germiston** Race Club, South Africa. He is self-confident and authoritative. When visiting Germiston, **Edward Lincoln** is invited to lunch with Klugvoïgt and the **Van Huren** family.

Knightwood, Lady (*Straight* 1989)

Also known as **Clarissa Williams**.

Knightwood, Lord Henry (*Straight* 1989)

Lord Henry Knightwood is the supremo at the University of York in the county of **Yorkshire**. He attends **York** races to present the University of York Trophy to connections of the winning horse. He is married to **Clarissa Williams**, mistress of the late **Greville Franklin**.

Knock Down (1974)

Jonah Dereham, bloodstock agent and ex-steeplechase jockey, goes to **Ascot Bloodstock Sales** with a client, American **Kerry Sanders**, to buy a racehorse as a birthday present for the son of her husband-to-be. Later, in the parking lot, two men attack Jonah with an iron bar and force him to sell them the horse he has just bought. Jonah is at a loss to understand why, but over the next few weeks he finds himself under increasing pressure to conform to a culture of swindles, kickbacks and scams perpetrated by a group of rival bloodstock agents. At the same time Jonah has to deal with an alcoholic brother whose irrational behavior is a source of constant worry. The burgeoning violence that Jonah is subjected to spills over into his private life, and ultimately leads to unexpected tragedy.

Knock Down is a prime example of how strong characterization can turn a good basic storyline into a successful, well-crafted novel. Jonah Dereham is one of Francis's most interesting main characters. He is honest but not holier-than-thou, courageous in a bloody-minded sort of way, patient and impulsive in equal measure. The supporting cast is strong too: **Crispin Dereham**, Jonah's whining soak of a brother; the cynical, grasping cartel of bloodstock agents who see Jonah's straight dealing as a threat to their lucrative frauds; and Jonah's girlfriend, **Sophie Randolph**, who acts in a satisfyingly unpredictable way.

A further reason why *Knock Down* works as a novel is that Francis has woven the didactic element into the plot—the multitude of sharp practices that an unscrupulous bloodstock agent might employ to fleece his client—without a diminution of its pace. In fact these fiddles are central to the action, and their successful continuance is the prime motivation for the villains' attempts to neutralize Jonah's opposition to them. Francis is at his best when racing and the thoroughbred are at the heart of the plot, and *Knock Down* proves the point.

Knowles, Ginnie (*Banker* 1982)

Ginnie is the fifteen-year-old daughter of stud farm owner **Oliver Knowles**. She is at boarding school but comes home on weekend visits. She is self-conscious about her adolescence, though her father doesn't notice. She confides in **Tim Ekaterin** her teenage worries about her looks and her schoolwork. When the stallion **Sandcastle** bolts and escapes Ginnie is in despair, but points out to Tim a track that the horse might have taken. She's right, and tries to approach the horse slowly to catch him, but he knocks her over. Tim, however, manages to catch the horse.

When Tim visits the stud farm again Ginnie runs up to him and gives him a hug and a kiss, which Tim sees as a sign of increasing self-confidence. She tells him that she is looking forward, when she leaves school, to becoming her father's assistant.

As soon as she turns seventeen Ginnie leaves school and fulfills her dream. When several of Sandcastle's foals are born with deformities she is very upset. But at the height of the crisis she remains positive, telling Tim that if the stud fails, she and her father will start again.

Ginnie goes for a walk one evening and is later found unconscious on the drive by one of the stud grooms. On the way to hospital she dies of a fractured skull. The police tell her father she had been assaulted.

Knowles, Oliver (*Banker* 1982)

Oliver Knowles is a thoroughbred stud farm owner. In his early forties, Knowles is an efficient and highly competent businessman; he is polite, authoritative and cultured. His wife has recently left him, and he is bringing up his fifteen-year-old daughter, **Ginnie**, on his own. He successfully negotiates with merchant bank **Paul Ekaterin Ltd.** a loan of £5 million to buy top class racehorse **Sandcastle** to stand at his stud. Knowles is aware that he is taking a calculated gamble in buying Sandcastle in order to enhance the prestige of his stud farm; however, he has no trouble in selling nominations to Sandcastle. When Sandcastle bolts and **Tim Ekaterin** catches him without thought of personal danger Knowles berates him for risking his life but is relieved that his huge investment is safe.

As a father Knowles is loving but not fully aware of his adolescent daughter's feelings. He is surprised at her impulsiveness when she runs up to Tim and kisses him. He is much more at home dealing with the stallions and mares on the farm. He is extremely concerned when many of Sandcastle's foals are born with deformities. During the crisis he continues to run the stud with calm efficiency despite the knowledge that, not being a limited company, he might be bankrupted.

When Ginnie is killed Knowles is stunned and incredulous but, initially, shows little anger. Automatically he immerses himself in the work of the farm. His wife returns briefly, but Ginnie's death serves only to finalize their separation. Knowles is resigned to losing the farm even though Tim Ekaterin manages to secure a two-month moratorium on paying the interest on the loan. Before the bank forecloses, however, Knowles is handed a lifeline when Tim discovers why the foals had been born with deformities. Tim tells Knowles that if Sandcastle is given the all clear the bank will probably reschedule his debt repayments. Knowles is typically unemotional but clearly relieved.

Knut (*Slay-Ride* 1973)

Knut is an Oslo policeman; he is in charge of the investigation into the death of **Bob Sherman**. He is referred to initially as "**Lund**" in *Chapter Ten* of *Slay-Ride* and afterwards as "Knut," which is somewhat confusing. David asks him if he can recommend a driver, and Knut suggests his brother **Erik**.

When David suspects that his car has been booby-trapped, Knut refuses to allow Erik to rescue his dog **Odin** from the vehicle, physically holding him back. When David opens the car door to release Odin, narrowly avoiding death or serious injury, Knut criticizes his stupidity. Knut doesn't want Erik to drive David any more, but eventually relents.

Komarov, Pyotr (*Dead Heat* 2007)

In his mid-fifties and thick-set, Komarov is President of the St. Petersburg Polo Club in Russia. He runs a business importing polo ponies into the United Kingdom, mainly from South America. This is not his only source of income, though it may be his only legal one. He and his wife, Tatiana are guests of **Delafield Industries Inc.** at a dinner at **Newmarket racecourse** on the evening before the running of the Two Thousand Guineas. However, they do not attend the race meeting the next day, when a bomb explodes in the grandstand boxes, causing death and destruction. It transpires that this apparent piece of good fortune is not a coincidence.

Newmarket chef **Max Moreton** discovers a good deal more about Komarov's activities than Komarov is comfortable with. He goes to Max's restaurant with the intention of neutralizing the threat that Max poses; however, his plans do not meet with success.

Kraye, Doria (*Odds Against* 1965)

Doria is the third wife of **Howard Kraye**; she is dark, physically attractive and thoroughly nasty. She considers **Sid Halley** beneath her contempt because of his apparent spinelessness. Among her belongings in her bedroom Sid discovers pornographic books, a diary detailing sadomasochistic perversions, a leather strap and a gun.

Alone with Sid, Doria disparages him and mocks **Jenny Halley's** choice of him as a husband. When Kraye enters the room Sid insults Doria to distract his attention from a picture of Sid as a jockey on the back page of a newspaper. Doria and Kraye assault Sid, enjoying the infliction of pain.

When, at **Seabury racecourse**, **Oxon** says that jockeys can withstand a lot of pain, Doria derives pleasure from the anticipation of it. She kisses Sid, who is tied to a chair, long and hard on the lips, drawing blood.

Kraye, Howard (*Odds Against* 1965)

Kraye is a geologist by profession. Under his real name, **Wilbur Potter**, he had served four years in a U.S. jail for assaulting the father of a girl he had beaten. He is now on his third marriage. His first wife had committed suicide; his second had divorced him for cruelty. Now Kraye is married to **Doria**, a woman as unpleasant as Kraye himself. Kraye is superficially plausible but **Sid Halley**, on first meeting, is made aware of his nastiness. While a guest of Sid's father-in-law, **Charles Roland**, Kraye is contemptuous of Sid's disabled hand and takes pleasure in belittling him, unaware of Sid's former career as a champion jump jockey. When Sid is forced to insult Doria in order to distract Kraye from seeing a picture of him in a newspaper, Kraye's reaction is furious and immediate. He and Doria assault Sid and force him to show them his withered hand. Then Kraye hits Sid across the tenderest part of his damaged wrist.

Kraye is intent upon acquiring a controlling interest in run-down **Seabury racecourse**, and Sid is equally determined to prevent him from doing so. Sid eventually prevails, but at great personal cost.

Kristiansen, Arne (*Slay-Ride* 1973)

Kristiansen, who is in his forties, is chief investigating officer of the Norwegian Jockey Club; he is also in charge of security at Øvrevoll racecourse. He had spent three months in England learning his job under **David Cleveland**. He purports to have an irrational fear of being overheard—hence the meeting with David on a dinghy two miles outside Oslo harbor. He says he believes that missing English jockey **Bob Sherman** has stolen 16,000 kroner from Øvrevoll. When the outboard motor on the dinghy cuts out Kristiansen tries to wave down a passing speedboat, which apparently doesn't see him and smashes into the dinghy. Kristiansen jumps before the collision.

He is surprised and shocked—though his face

registers relief—when he finds that David has not drowned. According to his wife **Kari**, Kristiansen is an excellent swimmer and very fit. For his part, Kristiansen is inordinately proud of his beautiful wife.

Kristiansen and Kari have dinner at the restaurant at the Grand Hotel where David is staying. After dinner, when the singer and orchestra start, he says he needs some air and escapes outside. According to Kari he has a persecution complex which started during the Second World War. His grandfather had been shot by the Nazis; his father, a resistance fighter, sometimes used Arne to carry messages, and Arne was always terrified that he would be followed. Kari says that Arne has sought psychiatric help for his phobia.

David discovers that Kristiansen knows a good deal more than he should about Sherman's disappearance. This knowledge ultimately proves deleterious to Kristiansen's health.

Kristiansen, Kari (*Slay-Ride* 1973)

Kari is the wife of **Arne Kristiansen**, chief investigating officer of the Norwegian Jockey Club. She is slim, blonde and beautiful. She tells **David Cleveland** that she does not share Arne's love of sporty, outdoor pursuits. David, who fancies her, thinks she may not be totally in love with her husband. Flirting with David, she tells him he looks younger than his thirty-three years. She has dinner with David and her husband at the Grand Hotel in Oslo, where David is staying. After dinner Arne goes out for some air, and David asks Kari to dance. Dancing very close and erotically, Kari has an orgasm on the dance floor; afterwards she thanks David with a smile and acts as if nothing had happened.

David goes to Kari's home to look for Kristiansen, who has packed a suitcase and left without telling her where. When David tells her that her husband is implicated in the death of **Bob Sherman** she doesn't want to believe it, but accepts that it is true.

Kropotkin, Nikolai Alexandrovich (*Trial Run* 1978)

Kropotkin is a horse trainer with the Russian Olympic Three Day Event team. About sixty years old, he has the poker face common to many Muscovites in the Communist era. He agrees to meet **Randall Drew** and introduces him to **Misha**, a groom who had been near Hans Kramer when he died. He allows Randall to question Misha about

Kramer. He is relieved when Randall says he won't mention the horse van which had tried to run him down, and says that he will give Randall any help he can.

Kropotkin makes enquiries about "Alyosha." Someone sends him a piece of paper on which is written "For Alyosha" and **Johnny Farringford's** name; he passes it on to Randall, with the request that Randall doesn't mention where he got it from. With masterly understatement, Kropotkin tells Randall that "it is not possible for Soviet citizens to speak with total freedom."

Kruger National Park, South Africa

Situated in the north-east of the country, Kruger is the best-known of South Africa's National Parks, with 7,500 square miles of land which is home to a huge number of different species of mammals, birds, fish, reptiles and trees. Wilderness trails allow the visitor to trek across wide areas of unspoiled countryside, guided by trail rangers. There are numerous archaeological sites in the Park, dating from the Paleolithic and Iron Ages.

Smokescreen (1972): Film actor **Edward Lincoln** travels to the Kruger National Park with film director **Evan Pentelow**.

Kurt (*Dead Heat* 2007)

Kurt looks after **Pyotr Komarov's** polo ponies at the Lake Country Polo Club in Wisconsin. He is suspicious and aggressive when **Max Moreton** comes to the Club asking about Komarov. When Max shows him the metal ball he got from **Mrs. Schumann**, Kurt tries to snatch it from him. Kurt's henchman hits Max with a polo mallet, causing Max to drop the ball. Kurt picks it up.

Kyle, John (*Flying Finish* 1966)

Kyle, a pilot, flies horses abroad for **Yardman** Transport. He is on the Milan flight when **Simon Searle** disappears. A fan of racing, Kyle meets **Henry Gray** at **Cheltenham** races to give him what little information he can about Searle's disappearance.

L

Lagland, D.J. (*In the Frame* 1976)

Lagland is an area manager for Foundation Life and Surety Insurance Company. He is middle-aged, competent and unremarkable. He investigates the burning down of **Maisie Matthews'** house.

The Lake District, England

The Lake District is an area of great national beauty in Cumbria, a county in the north-west of England. John Constable, perhaps England's best landscape painter, said that the Lake District had "the finest scenery that ever was." The region's hills are the highest in England.

Bolt (1986): **Danielle de Brescou** goes with **Prince Litzi** for a cultural break in the Lake District.

Lake Louise, Alberta, Canada

Lake Louise, and the village of the same name, are in the Banff National Park, Alberta. They are named after Princess Louise, daughter of Queen Victoria, who was married to Sir John Campbell, Governor General of Canada from 1878 to 1883. The lake is surrounded by mountains and glaciers.

The Edge (1988): The Great Transcontinental Mystery Race Train stops at Lake Louise, where the passengers spend the night in a hotel.

Lambourn, Berkshire

The valley of Lambourn lies on the chalk downlands of **Berkshire**, where the springy, ancient turf provides an ideal location for the training of racehorses. There are over 2,000 horses in training in the Lambourn valley, which is known as the "Valley of the Racehorse."

Reflex (1980): In Lambourn, jockey **Philip Nore** meets trainer **Bart Underfield**, who gives him information about racehorse owner **Elgin Yaxley** and **Terence O'Tree**.

The Danger (1983): Italian jockey **Alessia Cenci**, after her release from captivity by kidnappers in Italy, flies to England to stay with **Popsy Teddington**, a friend who trains racehorses in Lambourn. **Andrew Douglas** visits her there.

Break In (1985): Jockey **Kit Fielding** takes **Danielle de Brescou** to Lambourn to see the house which he is having built.

Come to Grief (1995): **Sid Halley** arranges for a veterinary surgeon in Lambourn to reattach the foot of a mutilated colt.

To the Hilt (1996): **Alexander Kinloch's** wife **Emily Jane Cox**, from whom he is separated, is a racehorse trainer in Lambourn.

Under Orders 2006: **Sid Halley** goes to see trainer **Bill Burton** at his stables in Lambourn. He finds that Burton's wife **Kate** has just left him, taking their four children with her.

Lancaster, England

Lancaster is the county town of Lancashire in the north-west of England, though its population is only 45,000. Established by the Romans on a defensive site next to the River Lune, Lancaster attained prosperity in the eighteenth and nineteenth centuries largely through its involvement in the slave trade.

Straight (1989): **Derek Franklin** has a degree from Lancaster University.

Lancat (*Bonecrack* 1971)

Three-year-old colt Lancat did not show anything as a two-year-old but had started to work well at three. Ridden by **Alessandro Rivera** in a trial with **Archangel** and **Pease Pudding**, he shows improved form. Alessandro wins on him at **Teesside** at 25/1, and also at **Newmarket**. He is ridden by **Neil Griffon** to try to save Alessandro when the Italian apprentice is riding **Lucky Lindsay** on the gallops. Neil points Lancat straight at Lucky Lindsay; Lancat is hit by a bullet meant for Lucky Lindsay's jockey, and dies instantly.

Lancer (*Twice Shy* 1981)

Lancer, a racecourse bookmaker, is mentioned to **William Derry** by **Taff**, another bookmaker, as having taken a bet of £1,000 from **Angelo Gilbert** on a horse that lost. He works for "Honest" Joe Glickstein. He is a victim of a mugging by a group of youths outside his home.

Lane, Mrs. (*Come to Grief* 1995)

Mrs. Lane is an employee of a firm of interior decorators consulted by **Sid Halley** about the provenance of a piece of cloth wrapped round the shears found hidden on a stud farm where a yearling colt was mutilated. She is unhelpful to Sid, and disapproves of one of her juniors helping him.

Lang, Dr. Zoë (*To the Hilt* 1996)

Dr. Lang is an octogenarian retired lecturer in English at St Andrew's University, Scotland. Thin and feisty, Dr. Lang is an expert on early English gold artefacts. She is asked by **Robert, Earl of Kinloch**, to value the King Alfred Cup. She tells Robert that the Cup is Victorian, not early English and, though beautiful, not especially valuable. She asks to see the Kinloch hilt; Robert shows her a replica. Dr. Lang thinks that the hilt should be in national ownership. She joins the Board of Trustees who look after the castle and demands that the Earl hand over the hilt to them.

She is surprised when **Alexander Kinloch** asks if he can paint her, but agrees. Seeing the unfinished painting, she doesn't like his accurate depiction of her, considering it cruel. She goes to Alexander's cottage to search for the hilt; when she sees the finished painting she is moved, and tells Alexander that she will not look for the hilt any more.

Larch, Belinda (*Comeback* 1991)

Belinda is the snobbish, self-centered daughter of **Vicky Larch**. About thirty years old and quite pretty, Belinda lives in **Gloucestershire** and is about to marry equine veterinarian **Ken McClure**. When her mother and stepfather arrive for the wedding, after being mugged in **Miami**, she doesn't show them much sympathy or affection. She is off-hand with **Peter Darwin**, whom she mistakenly believes to be a general dogsbody her mother can't afford. She is bossy towards her mother, who comments that she and Belinda get on all right so long as they don't see too much of each other. Belinda is embarrassed that her mother still performs as a singer, telling her that she's past it.

When the office block of the veterinary practice burns down Belinda takes the three horse patients in the stable block to a nearby trainer's yard for safety. She resents Peter Darwin's growing friendship with Ken. At **Stratford** races, when Ken asks her to put a bet on for him, she backs a different horse, thinking her judgment superior. Ken's choice wins and he is angry with her.

Larch, Vicky (*Comeback* 1991)

Vicky Larch is a middle-aged singer. She is married to fellow-singer **Greg Wayfield**; it is her second marriage. A good natured woman, Vicky has four children by her first husband. She sings at the **Diving Pelican** restaurant in **Miami**. When she is attacked and robbed outside the restaurant she bravely fights back. She isn't badly hurt. Her youngest daughter, **Belinda Larch**, is about to marry an equine veterinary surgeon in **Gloucestershire**. Afraid that the robbers might turn up at their house, Vicky and Greg beg **Peter Darwin** to stay the night. They travel to England with Peter. Vicky is received with lukewarm affection by Belinda. Despite the chaos at the veterinary practice which has been partly destroyed by fire, Vicky soon recovers her health and strength. She enjoys a day out at **Stratford** races.

Laurel Park racecourse, Maryland

Situated midway between Baltimore and Washington D.C., Laurel Park racecourse has staged thoroughbred racing for almost a hundred years. Its best known race is the Washington D.C., International, run over twelve furlongs on turf. It also stages the Grade I Frank J De Francis Memorial Dash Stakes. Both the dirt and turf tracks have been widened in recent years.

The Danger (1983): Italian jockey **Alessia Cenci** rides **Brunelleschi** to win the Washington D.C. International.

Laurentide Ice (*The Edge* 1988)

Laurentide Ice is a Canadian racehorse traveling on the Great Transcontinental Mystery Race Train. **Julius Filmer** buys a half share in him from owner **Daffodil Quentin**. Laurentide Ice wins the Race Train's Special Race at Woodbine. Daffodil subsequently sells her share to Filmer.

Lavender (*10 lb. Penalty* 1997)

Lavender is a volunteer worker for **George Juliard** in the **Hoopwestern** by-election; she helps with door-to-door canvassing.

Lawson (*Dead Cert* 1962)

Lawson is a farmer from Washington, near Steyning, **Sussex**. While he is away in London appearing in a quiz show with his family, a horse van is taken from his farm. Subsequently the van is used during an attempt to intimidate **Alan York**.

Lawson-Young, Professor George (*Shattered* 2000)

A highly respected medical researcher, Lawson-Young heads a team which had once included **Dr. Force**. In a melodramatic and unconvincing scene, Lawson-Young helps **Gerard Logan** to escape via the roof of his building from villains who are waiting outside. After the death of a police officer at Gerard's workshop, Lawson-Young arrives and explains the background to the crime to **Superintendent Shepherd**, who is in charge of the investigation.

Leaded Light (*Under Orders* 2006)

Leaded light is a jumper trained by **Bill Burton** and due to be ridden by **Huw Walker** on Gold Cup day at the **Cheltenham** Festival. Walker can't be found, so Burton puts up another jockey. In the race, Leaded Light finishes a close second. After the race he has a bit of heat in his near-fore tendon.

Leeds, Felicity (*High Stakes* 1975)

Felicity is the wife of crooked racehorse trainer **Jody Leeds**; she is blonde, hard-working and opinionated. She is angry and abusive when **Steven Scott**, after sacking her husband, phones to arrange transport for his horses to new stables. When a load of manure is dropped in his driveway, Steven suspects Felicity's involvement. At **Stratford** races Steven repeatedly tackles her about this, as a ploy to stop her going to the racecourse stables and discovering the sting which is in progress. Finally Felicity grudgingly admits that the manure had come from the Leeds stables. She agrees to a written apology when Steven says he has involved the police.

At Stratford, Felicity has her own reasons for keeping Steven away from the horse that Jody is running. So she pretends to be conciliatory towards Steven, and invites him to have a drink with her. She keeps Steven in the bar until the horses are going out onto the course. When the stable's runner is beaten Felicity takes it badly, exhibiting the symptoms of severe shock.

Leeds, Jody (*High Stakes* 1975)

For years racehorse trainer Jody Leeds has colluded with bookmaker **Ganser Mays** to swindle his owners, among whom is wealthy toy maker **Steven Scott**. When Steven eventually realizes what Leeds has been doing, he tells Leeds he is going to take his horses away.

Leeds, young and pugnacious, takes his sacking as a personal insult and his only regret is being found out. Leeds trains nine horses for Steven, and when horse vans arrive at his yard to take them to other trainers Leeds has made his own arrangements for **Energise**, the best of Steven's horses. By underhand means he retains Energise in his stable and intends to use the horse to pull off a betting coup. Steven, however, has other ideas.

Leeds, Quintus (*High Stakes* 1975)

Quintus is the father of crooked trainer **Jody Leeds**. He is a member of the **Jockey Club** and is of aristocratic lineage. A physically imposing man with a confident manner, Leeds is thought by **Steven Scott** to be intellectually limited but fundamentally genuine, and proud of his son. He refuses to believe that Jody could have been guilty of defrauding Steven. He says that Steven would have been elected to the Jockey Club but for the disgraceful way he had treated Jody.

Quintus organizes the dumping of a pile of horse manure from Jody's stables on the driveway of Steven's London home. When Steven reports this to the police Quintus grudgingly admits his involvement and accedes to Steven's request for a written apology. Even when Quintus knows for certain that Jody is guilty of fraud he continues to hold Steven responsible for his son's actions.

Leeds, Dr. William (*Slay-Ride* 1973)

Dr. Leeds is the Managing Director of Wessex-Wells Research Laboratory. His establishment had prepared a geological core chart which was subsequently stolen. Leeds tells **David Cleveland** that the chart was worth £100,000 to someone in a position to exploit the information it contained. Concerned at the breach of security, Leeds asks David if he would investigate who had sold the chart; David, however, explains that he works for the **Jockey Club** and declines.

Lees, Wynn (*Comeback* 1991)

Lees is a bad-tempered bull of a man; he is the owner of a pregnant mare with colic successfully operated on by **Ken McClure**, who finds a needle and thread in the horse's intestine. Lees is remembered by **Peter Darwin** from his childhood as a frightening figure used by his mother to scare him into behaving himself. According to her, Lees was imprisoned as a young man for extreme cruelty to horses, and later served another sentence for assaulting a rival in love with a rivet gun, stapling the man's jeans to his skin.

Lees visits the pregnant mare and is left alone with her; the horse is later found dead. When Lees' criminal activities finally catch up with him, he leaves the country before he can be charged.

Leggatt, Sam (*Break In* 1985)

Leggatt, the editor of the *Daily Flag* newspaper, is under pressure from **Kit Fielding**, who has in his possession items belonging to two *Flag* journalists caught in the act of removing a bugging device from the roof of trainer **Bobby Allardeck**'s house. Leggatt is forced to promise to publish an apology for his newspaper's libelous attack on Allardeck. Later, he phones Kit to say that his lawyers have advised him not to publish an apology. He is alarmed when Kit says he will make the *Flag*'s phone-tapping of Bobby's house public, and decides, after all, to print the apology.

Leicester racecourse

There has been racing at Leicester since the beginning of the seventeenth century, and at the present location since 1884. The course is a severe one, providing a stiff test for mainly moderate animals, both Flat and *National Hunt*. It is easy to reach from most of the training centers and thus relatively popular with trainers.

Forfeit (1968): Investigative racing journalist **James Tyrone** goes to Leicester to watch Lamplighter Gold Cup entry **Egocentric** run. Returning to London on the race train, he is beaten up by two thugs.

Twice Shy (1981): **Angelo Gilbert** goes to Leicester races where, using **Liam O'Rorke**'s system, he bets heavily on an outsider which finishes unplaced. Gilbert goes berserk, punches a **Jockey Club** official, and is arrested.

Leicestershire, England

Leicestershire is a county in central England with a population of about one million. It is a diverse county, with busy towns and cities like Leicester, Ashby de la Zouche and Melton Mowbray, but also peaceful countryside, ancient woodland and pretty villages.

For Kicks (1965): **Daniel Roke** travels to Leicestershire to collect a horse, **Sparking Plug**, which has been bought by one of the Stewards of the National Hunt Committee.

Wild Horses (1994): **Alison Visborough** lives in Market Harborough, a town in Leicestershire.

To the Hilt (1996): The Leicestershire police phone **Sir Ivan Westering** to ask if he can go and identify a body. **Audrey Newton**, the sister of **Norman Quorn**, lives in Leicestershire.

Leigh Foods Ltd. (*Dead Heat* 2007)

This is the supplier used by **Max Moreton** for his **Newmarket** restaurant, **The Hay Net**.

Lenny (*For Kicks* 1965)

Lenny is one of **Hedley Humber**'s stable lads, and is a replacement for **Geoff**; he is a former inmate of young offenders' institutions, and needs money to repay what he stole from another employer.

Lenny (*Banker* 1982)

Lenny is a stud groom who works for **Oliver Knowles**. Middle-aged and highly experienced, Lenny is good with the stallions and considered by Knowles to be very reliable. Lenny is moving **Sandcastle** from his box to the paddock when the horse rears and escapes from his grasp.

Lester Piggott—The Official Biography

Francis published a biography of legendary jockey Lester Piggott in March 1986, a project he had been working on for several years. The book sold well, but was criticized by reviewers for its perceived lack of partiality. The general feeling was that the biography concentrated too heavily on Piggott's outstanding career in the saddle and minimized his undoubted character weaknesses. In mitigation it can be argued that Piggott, who is partially deaf and famously reticent, must have made a difficult subject for a biographer.

Lewis (*Driving Force* 1992)

Lewis is a driver with **Croft Raceways** horse transport firm. He is young, a good worker, and considered helpful and reliable. Trainer **Michael Watermead** prefers Lewis to drive his good horses to the races. Lewis drives to France to collect two two-year-olds to be trained by Watermead. Delayed, he arrives back suffering from flu so can't drive Watermead's horses to **Doncaster** races the next day.

Freddie Croft discovers that Lewis is using his horse vans for illegal purposes. Lewis admits it, saying he needed money to pay for his baby son's future education.

Lexington, Kentucky

Lexington is the second largest city in Kentucky after Louisville. It is located in the heart of the Bluegrass region, which gets its name from a favored lawn and pasture grass in the eastern USA, north of Tennessee. The underlying limestone and highly fertile soil of this region means that the pasture is ideal for horse breeding. However, some of the many horse farms are being lost to development.

Blood Sport (1967): Investigators **Gene Hawkins** and **Walt Prensela** fly to Lexington to interview the drivers of a hijacked horse van.

Leyhill Prison, Gloucestershire, England

Leyhill is a minimum security prison catering for about 500 prisoners at Wotton-under-Edge, **Gloucestershire**. An open prison, with no perimeter security, Leyhill has a special role in assessing and preparing life sentence prisoners for release.

Risk (1977): Accountant and amateur jockey **Roland Britten** asks **Peter**, his assistant, to ring

Leyhill Prison to see if fraudster **Connaught Powys** is still an inmate. Roland had been responsible for Powys being convicted.

Liberty Market Ltd. (*The Danger* 1983)

This is a firm, consisting of thirty-one partners, which specializes in all aspects of combating kidnappers; it conducts seminars on how to avoid being kidnapped, and negotiates with kidnappers to secure victims' release for the minimum cost. It has offices in **Kensington**, London. Most partners are ex-army, ex-police or ex-secret government departments. Fees are not excessive and sometimes the firm gives its services free of charge. It has a 95% success rate.

Lida (*Risk* 1977)

Lida is the girlfriend of **William Finch**. When Finch flees abroad, he takes Lida with him. She is disliked by Finch's daughter **Jossie Finch**.

Lillehammer, Norway

Lillehammer lies at the edge of Lake Mjoso in the Norwegian mountains. The town, which hosted the winter Olympics of 1994, has pretty wooden buildings and a rich cultural life, with museums, art galleries and music festivals. It is the birthplace of Nobel Prize winning poet and playwright Bjorn-Stjerne Martinus Bjornson.

Slay-Ride (1973): **Jockey Club** investigator **David Cleveland** and **Arne Kristiansen**, his opposite number at the Norwegian Jockey Club, travel by train to Lillehammer, where David claims to have arranged a meeting with a man who has information about jockey **Bob Sherman**.

Lily (*Straight* 1989)

Lily is an employee of the late **Greville Franklin** in his business importing semi-precious stones. She is old fashioned in dress and appearance. She deals with the orders, and is appointed stockroom manager by **Derek Franklin** at her own request.

Lilyglit (*Field of 13* 1998: "Haig's Death")

Lilyglit is a promising young hurdler, owned by **Jasper Billington Innes** and trained in **Lambourn** by champion trainer **Percy Driffield**. He is favorite for the valuable Cloister Handicap Hurdle at **Winchester**, and is due to be sold after the race to settle his owner's gambling debts. He comes to win the race but takes a crashing fall at the last hurdle. Lilyglit is badly winded but uninjured.

Linardi, Tomaso (*The Danger* 1983)

Linardi is the owner of the Milan Fine Leather Company; he had been held for ransom by kidnappers two years before **Alessia Cenci** was kidnapped. He owned a majority share in a racetrack which was sold to help fund his ransom. **Andrew Douglas** had negotiated with the kidnappers for his release. Linardi recommended **Liberty Market Ltd.** to Paolo Cenci.

Lincoln, Charlie (*Smokescreen* 1972)

Charlie is the wife of **Edward Lincoln**; she is intelligent, sensible and reliable. She has a formidable temper, but mostly she is calm and controlled. She does not show in public her deep affection for Edward. She has three children, one of whom is handicapped. At the request of Edward, who is in South Africa, Charlie goes to see **Nerissa Cavesey** to find out the terms of her will. She tells Edward that Nerissa has left her holding in "Rojedda" to Edward. Charlie doesn't know that Rojedda is a goldmine and that Edward is in danger because of this. She is upset at Nerissa's obvious deterioration in health.

Lincoln, Chris (*Smokescreen* 1972)

Chris is one of film actor **Edward Lincoln**'s three children.

Lincoln, Edward (*Smokescreen* 1972)

Film actor Edward Lincoln, contrary to the classic mould of early Dick Francis heroes, is happily married with three children. Edward's five-year-old daughter **Libby** is brain damaged, having been dropped on her head as a baby by her brother. At that time Edward's relationship with his wife, **Charlie Lincoln**, was deteriorating, just as his acting career was taking off. The accident to Libby might have made the rift unbridgeable; instead it pulled them together and saved their faltering marriage. They moved from London to the **Berkshire** countryside, where Edward shunned the celebrity lifestyle and found contentment in his family.

Edward's own childhood was unhappy. He had a stepmother who could have appeared in Christmas pantomimes without having to learn the lines. When she wasn't making life miserable for Edward's dad, a head-lad in a racing stable, she was starving Edward of affection.

Echoing Dick Francis's own early upbringing with horses, Edward says, "I could ride before I could walk." His ambition was to be a jockey, but increasing size and moderate talent necessitated a rethink. He found work as a film stuntman, falling off horses when required, and took drama classes in the hope they might lead to something better. Soon they did; a perceptive director gave him a few lines to say, and kick-started Edward's acting career. Now aged thirty-three, he is much in demand as the strong, laconic type. That kind of role suits Edward, who is uncomfortable with laying open his own private persona to public scrutiny. Off screen, he avoids publicity as much as possible. But he uses the need to promote his new film as an excuse to visit South Africa when asked by a dear friend, who is terminally ill, to find out, if he can, why her racehorses are running as if wearing hobnailed boots.

Edward represents a further departure from Francis's standard hero in that he has apparently, an explosive temper. Evidence of it is not conclusive; he doesn't exactly go around breathing fire. But in contrast with the habitual mildness of manner typical of the breed, he does actually get angry sometimes. One such occasion is when he is being hassled by promoters Worldis Cinemas to make personal appearances to stoke up interest in his film. "Stuff Worldis," I thought violently. "Personal appearances left me feeling invaded, battered and devoured."

In South Africa Edward finds that his life is in danger because he is heir to a share in a gold mine. In dealing with attempts to kill him Edward displays the recognizable facets of the hero: he is afraid, but is able to keep his fear in check whilst dealing practically with the immediate threat.

Lincoln, Libby (*Smokescreen* 1972)

Libby is the young daughter of film actor Edward Lincoln. When ten months old Libby had suffered a fractured skull when accidentally dropped by her brother Peter. As a result her mental and physical development has been retarded.

Lincoln, Peter (*Smokescreen* 1972)

Peter is the son of film actor Edward Lincoln. At the age of five Peter had been holding his baby sister Libby when, by accident, he had dropped her on her head. Libby had suffered brain damage as a result.

Lincolnshire, England

Lincolnshire is an agricultural county in the east of England, lying between South Yorkshire to the north and Cambridgeshire to the south. The fields of Lincolnshire produce wheat, barley, sugar beet and oilseed rape. The county town is Lincoln; other towns include Boston, Stamford, Grimsby and Grantham.

Flying Finish (1966): Tom Wells owns an air charter firm based on an airfield in Lincolnshire.

Trial Run (1978): A Russian observer named Chulitsky who had attended Burghley Horse Trials near Stamford, Lincolnshire, gives Randall Drew information about Johnny Farringford.

Litsi, Prince (*Bolt* 1986)

Prince Litsi is the nephew of Princess Casilia; he was brought up in England after his grandparents were forced to relinquish their Eastern European throne. He now lives in France. He is cultured, sophisticated, friendly and courteous. Separated from his wife, Litsi is attentive towards Kit Fielding's fiancée Danielle de Brescou, the niece of Princess Casilia's husband Roland de Brescou. He takes Danielle to a hotel in the Lake District to hear lectures on Renaissance painting. Litsi doesn't have a nine-to-five job, but is the part-owner of an art gallery. He says that he would like to have been an artist himself but lacked the talent.

At Bradbury races Litsi is given a message to meet Danielle on the viewing balcony at the top of the grandstand, which is closed for building work. While up there he stumbles on some planks and falls over the balcony. Hanging on by his fingertips, he is seen by Kit below, who gets racegoers to make a mattress of their coats. When Litsi can't hang on any longer, the coats break his fall. He is dazed and shaken but not seriously hurt.

Liv (*Slay-Ride* 1973)

Liv is a four-year-old girl who witnesses a man tampering with Erik's car. The man had told her to run home and not to play near the car. But she is still there when Knut, Erik and David Cleveland return to the car. A policeman ensures that she and other children move away to a safe distance. After the car is destroyed by an explosive device the police speak to her. She is able to give David a good description of the man.

Livingstone, Mr. (*Whip Hand* 1979)

Livingstone, a scientist at Tierson Pharmaceuticals Vaccine Laboratories, is elderly, sharp and voluble. He explains to Sid Halley how, in the 1940's, a mutant strain of swine erysipelas disease had been inadvertently injected into horses.

Lochs, George (*Under Orders* 2006)

George Lochs, who is in his thirties, has made a lot of money through internet betting via his betting exchange make-a-wager.com. He was born Clarence Lochstein, and came from a poor North London background. He won a scholarship to the prestigious **Harrow School; Sid Halley** subsequently discovers from Lochs' former housemaster that he had been disciplined for taking bets from other boys. When his housemaster had tried to cane him Lochs had broken his jaw with a single punch and had been expelled. However, Lochs had done sufficiently well in his exams to go to the London School of Economics.

Lochs is surprised when Sid Halley calls at the offices of make-a-wager.com's parent company, **Make A Wager Ltd.**, in **Wembley**. He shows Sid round but gets annoyed when Sid queries his admission that he had asked **Huw Walker** for information about his rides, and asks Sid to leave. Sid discovers that Lochs has been using inside information, illegally obtained, to manipulate the odds offered on his internet betting exchange. When this becomes public knowledge the betting exchange quickly loses its reputation and runs into financial difficulties. Lochs is not charged with any criminal offence but is banned from all racecourses.

Loder, Nicholas (*Straight* 1989)

Loder is the **Newmarket**-based trainer of gem trader **Greville Franklin**'s two horses. Not far off the top flight of trainers, Loder is charismatic but has a touch of arrogance. He is rumored to be a big gambler and to train for people who like a bet. When jockey **Derek Franklin** phones to tell him of his brother Greville's death in an accident, Loder appears anxious that Greville's horse **Dozen Roses** should still run at **York** that Saturday, and Derek is suspicious of his motives. Loder tells Derek that because he is himself a registered agent for Greville's company, he has the authority to run Dozen Roses and will do so at York, adding that he will sell Greville's horses at the end of the season.

When Loder sees Derek at York races he is angry and tells him he has no business to be there. Derek notices that Dozen Roses has been gelded by Loder against Greville's wishes. Loder, annoyed at being caught out, asks Derek how much he wants to keep quiet. When Derek tells him he's selling Dozen Roses to the **Ostermeyers**, an American couple, Loder presses Derek to leave the horse with him to train. He later phones to offer Derek double what the Ostermeyers are paying but Derek refuses and moves the horse to jumping trainer **Milo Shandy**.

Loder tells Derek that he has had an offer for **Gemstones**, Greville's other horse. He takes the prospective buyer to see Derek, and is astonished when the man attacks Derek. Bravely, Loder tries to prevent the man from shooting Derek, with tragic consequences for himself.

Lodge, Inspector (*Dead Cert* 1962)

Lodge is a policeman based at Maidenhead, **Berkshire**. He is in his late thirties, small and dark. Lodge leads the investigation into the death of **Major Bill Davidson**. He is efficient and methodical.

Lodovski, Chub (*Blood Sport* 1967)

Lodovski, a stud groom at Midway Farm, **Lexington**, Kentucky, works for **Dave Teller**. He is an excellent employee who takes pride in his work and keeps the stud in superb order. He tells **Gene Hawkins** about **Allyx** getting loose from the paddock during a fire at the stable block.

Logan, Gerard (*Shattered* 2000)

At another time, in another place, glass blower Gerard Logan might be the kind of man you'd want to know more about. The trouble is, Gerard's energies are fully engaged in unraveling *Shattered's* boring and largely pointless plot, and so none of the potentially interesting facets of his character is fully explored. The whereabouts of a missing videotape take up a disproportionate amount of his time. If he'd tried the local video store in the first place it might have saved us all from the tedium of ploughing through this turgid storyline. On the credit side, Gerard benefits from comparison with the other characters in *Shattered* who are, almost without exception, shallow caricatures or so thinly drawn as to be virtually transparent.

As a boy Gerard had spurned the normal childhood dreams of being a firefighter or a paratrooper in favor of following the calling of his uncle **Ron**, "a brilliant flame worker." Ron tutored Gerard, and when he died he left Gerard his detailed notebook, which he used to hone his developing skills. Now thirty years old, Gerard is making a good living, with a workshop and showroom in **Broadway**, a Cotswold village. Gerard is modest about his glass-blowing skills and realistic about his faults, one of which is his cavalier treatment of girlfriends. He fancies **Catherine Dodd,** a young policewoman who investigates a theft at his workshop, but acknowledges that in the past he has been guilty of heartlessness and a lack of fidelity towards previous girlfriends. Be that as it may, sex with Catherine advances the relationship satisfactorily; three weeks later, though, his appetite sated, the novelty appears to be wearing off, and feelings of incipient domestication begin to trouble him.

The wretched videotape stolen from Gerard had been passed on to him at **Cheltenham** races by the valet of his friend, jockey **Martin Stukely.** Later that afternoon, Stukely is killed in a fall. Gerard is deeply saddened at his death: "One had so few close friends in life. None to spare."

Few close friends but plenty of enemies is Gerard's lot as he suffers various assaults in the course of this implausible tale. In an unconvincing dénouement, Gerard, cornered in his workshop, causes a glass trophy he is making to explode; in the subsequent mayhem **Paul Cratchet,** a police colleague of Catherine's, is killed, for which Gerard feels some responsibility. After Cratchet's funeral Gerard goes to Catherine's house where they make love "in Paul's honor." If this all sounds unbearably contrived, that's because it is, and the feeling remains that Gerard Logan, though by no means one of Francis's most compelling characters, deserves better than this.

Lois (*To the Hilt* 1996)

Lois works as a cleaner for **Sir Ivan** and **Lady Westering;** she is the sister of **Edna,** the cook. She acts as a witness when Sir Ivan adds a codicil to his will. Lois is indignant when, after Sir Ivan's death, **Patsy Benchmark** criticizes her for throwing away an old tissue box for which Sir Ivan had been searching the rubbish bags.

Longchamp racecourse

Longchamp racecourse is situated in the Bois de Boulogne in Paris, on the banks of the River Seine. It is used for Flat racing only. The prestigious Prix de l'Arc de Triomphe, a race over twelve furlongs for three-year-olds and upwards, is held on the first weekend of October.

Hot Money (1987): **Blue Clancy,** a colt partly owned by **Malcolm Pembroke,** finishes third in the Prix de l'Arc de Triomphe.

Longerman, Mrs. Moira (*Risk* 1977)

Small, blonde and middle-aged, Mrs. Longerman is the owner of **Cheltenham** Gold Cup winner **Tapestry,** ridden to victory by **Roland Britten.** She is a client of Roland's, who is her accountant as well as her jockey. When **Binny Tomkins,** her trainer, had objected to Roland riding Tapestry, she told him that she would move the horse to another trainer. Roland had secured for her a large tax refund, and she'd given him the ride as a way of saying thank you.

When Roland returns after being abducted Mrs. Longerman insists on his riding Tapestry in all his races despite further objections from Tomkins. She doesn't trust Tomkins to run Tapestry on his merits, and knows that he had laid against the horse in the Gold Cup.

When Roland is abducted a second time she rings the editor of the *Sporting Life* newspaper, who publicizes his disappearance. The story is immediately picked up by the daily papers. She rings Roland after his release to insist that he rides Tapestry in the Oasthouse Cup at **Kempton Park.** She is beside herself with joy when Tapestry wins, though appalled that Tomkins had tampered with the bridle. When Tomkins won't let her into the stables to see Tapestry she phones Roland and tells him that Tomkins has gone mad.

Longshot (1990)

John Kendall, writer of six survival handbooks, has given up his job with a travel company to write novels full time, and is himself struggling to survive on little money. He goes to see his agent, **Ronnie Curzon,** and there meets **Tremayne Vickers,** a well-known **Berkshire** racehorse trainer, who has been looking, unsuccessfully, for someone to write his biography. When John has to move from his rented accommodation and finds himself homeless, he decides to offer his services to Vickers.

John travels to Berkshire, where he soon becomes involved in investigations into the death of a stable girl who had worked for Vickers. Her body is found in woods near the stables, and **Harry Goodhaven,** one of Vickers' owners, is the chief suspect. Not long afterwards John has to rescue Goodhaven when someone tries to kill him. The trap set for Goodhaven is similar to one which John had described in his survival guidebooks for catching animals.

It is John himself who has the greatest need of his survival skills when he is shot twice in the back with arrows, and loses his bearings in the woods. The death of the man whom John has identified as the stable girl's killer is a source of shock to

Tremayne Vickers, but confirms that John's suspicions were well-founded.

Loricroft, George (*Second Wind* 1999)

In his mid-forties, successful American racehorse trainer George Loricroft is a bully to his young wife **Glenda**. He is one of the **Unified Traders**, who buy and sell radioactive materials. He is suspected by **Perry Stuart** of removing the dipstick from **Kris Ironside**'s plane so that oil would escape. He lies to Glenda about his movements in Germany where he was meant to be running horses, when in fact he was using the racecourse as venues for his Unified Trader activities. When Glenda finds out the truth she reacts with disproportionate violence.

Loricroft, Glenda (*Second Wind* 1999)

Glenda is the young, blonde, attractive wife of top American racehorse trainer **George Loricroft**. She is dominated by George and resents it. She suspects her husband of seeing other women when he is supposed to be at racecourses in Germany and Poland. She asks **Perry Stuart** to check on the weather in those places to see if her husband is lying to her; Perry discovers that he is. When she finds out George is dealing in radioactive materials, Glenda pursues a course of action that ends tragically for them both.

Lorna (*Driving Force* 1992)

Lorna is the sister of **Maudie Watermead**. A tall, platinum blonde, Lorna resembles her sister physically. She is a worrier, and a supporter of good causes. She helps **John Tigwood** with **Centaur Care**, a dubious charity for retired horses. She disapproves of **Freddie Croft**'s skepticism about Tigwood.

Lorrimore, Bambi (*The Edge* 1988)

Bambi is the wife of Canadian banker and racehorse owner **Mercer Lorrimore**. Cold and haughty, Bambi adopts a head-in-the-sand approach to her son **Sheridan Lorrimore**'s appalling behavior. She doesn't kiss or hug **Xanthe Lorrimore**, her daughter, to comfort her when she is terrified by the uncoupling of their private car on the Great Transcontinental Mystery Race Train. Bambi receives awful news about her son without any display of emotion.

Lorrimore, Mercer (*The Edge* 1988)

Mercer Lorrimore is a rich, influential Canadian banker and racehorse owner, and a member of the Ontario Jockey Club. He is a decent man but strangely naive, thinking the best of everyone and blind to their faults. He has a private car on the Great Transcontinental Mystery Race Train. He is forced to apologize on a regular basis for his son **Sheridan Lorrimore**'s loutish behavior; he gives **Tor Kelsey** twenty dollars when Sheridan pushes him. He regularly has to pay off waiters and other staff when his son is rude or violent towards them.

After the train leaves **Banff**, Lorrimore is clearly troubled, and it later transpires that he is being blackmailed. Lorrimore is deeply shocked when he finds out that Sheridan has fallen from the rear platform of their private car into **Fraser Canyon**. However, when Sheridan's body is found in the river shortly afterwards, Lorrimore takes the news calmly. He is amazed when Tor Kelsey reveals himself as a **Jockey Club** investigator and is willing to cooperate fully in bringing his blackmailer to justice. He is emotionally overwhelmed when his horse **Voting Right** wins the Jockey Club Race Train Stakes at **Hastings Park**.

Lorrimore, Sheridan (*The Edge* 1988)

Sheridan is the son of Canadian banker and racehorse owner **Mercer Lorrimore**; he is a disturbed young man with a violent streak and psychopathic tendencies. At Toronto station, Sheridan punches the actor **Raoul** for no good reason; he is forced by his father to apologize. On the Great Transcontinental Mystery Race Train, he demands rudely that **Tor Kelsey**, a **Jockey Club** investigator working undercover as a waiter, bring him a double scotch. When Tor hesitates, Lorrimore pushes him. Again his father excuses him, and gives Tor twenty dollars. During a scene in the mystery play, Lorrimore tries to snatch a pistol from an actor playing a Royal Canadian Mounted policeman; he is furious when thwarted. During the next scene he shouts one of the actors down, grabs the wrist of travel company employee **Nell Richmond** and tries to pull her onto his lap.

According to his sister, **Xanthe Lorrimore**, Sheridan only avoided jail in England owing to his father's influence. He falls to his death from the rear platform of his car as the train passes through **Fraser Canyon**; his body is found in the river soon after. His father believes that he had jumped, perhaps on impulse; just before doing so he had apologized to his father for his behavior.

Lorrimore, Xanthe (*The Edge* 1988)

Xanthe is the sulky teenage daughter of Canadian banker and racehorse owner **Mercer Lorri-**

more. Xanthe is not enjoying her trip on the Great Transcontinental Mystery Race Train, owing partly to the crass behavior of her brother, **Sheridan Lorrimore**. She runs screaming into the dining car, saying she had nearly stepped off the speeding train because the Lorrimores' private car had been unhitched and was no longer at the rear of the train. When the train stops in the Rockies, Xanthe doesn't go on the organized coach trip to **Banff**. She meets **Jockey Club** investigator **Tor Kelsey** while out walking, and confides in him, despite believing she shouldn't talk to "servants" (Tor is working undercover as a waiter on the train). Xanthe tells Tor that she sometimes wished she was poor like him. Tor believes that she is basically a nice girl who lacks the support of a warm, happy family. She takes the news of Sheridan's death calmly, underlining their lack of a close sibling relationship. With Sheridan gone, Xanthe now has the opportunity to grow up and mature without the difficulties that Sheridan's presence within the family had caused.

Losenwoldt, Peter (*Smokescreen* 1972)

An Afrikaner mining engineer, Losenwoldt is an employee at **Quentin Van Huren**'s goldmine at **Welcom**, South Africa. He is instructed to show **Edward Lincoln** and his party around the mine. He considers this an unwelcome chore, and conducts the tour with bad grace. He discourages questions and answers only when he has to, in a surly manner, showing contempt for the lack of knowledge of his party. He takes an immediate dislike to **Danilo Cavesey** and refuses to answer any of his questions. After Edward goes missing underground and is eventually found by searchers, Losenwoldt is quick to shift any blame from himself and onto Edward.

Louders-Allen-Croft, Lady Emma (*Trial Run* 1978)

From a wealthy, aristocratic family, Lady Emma works as a bed linen buyer in a London department store. She is capable and competent, but touchy about her lack of formal educational qualifications. She is unsympathetic when her boyfriend, **Randall Drew**, returns from Moscow ill. When Randall suggests marriage she tells him crisply that it wouldn't work. Randall thinks that their relationship is unlikely to last.

Louisa (*Twice Shy* 1981)

Louisa is a laboratory technician in the physics department at East Middlesex Comprehensive School in North London. She is forty years old and good at her job but is resentful of her lack of a university education and feels that she has been denied the chance to fulfill her potential.

Louise (*Flying Finish* 1966)

The elder of **Lord Henry Gray**'s two sisters, Louise lives in a large house near Elgin in Scotland. She had pleased her parents by marrying a rich man, only to find her husband unwilling to part with a penny. Henry visits Louise when she is recovering from a hysterectomy, and she gives him her birth control pills to take to Italy.

Lubbock (*Nerve* 1964)

Lubbock, a professional gambler, had paid for information about trainer **James Axminster**'s horses, resulting in stable jockey **Grant Oldfield** being sacked by Axminster. Lubbock thinks that the information was coming from Oldfield, though he had to send the money to a man named Robinson at a London Post Office address. He makes a written statement to **Rob Finn** that he never knew for sure who was giving him the information.

Luccese, Silvio (*The Danger* 1983)

Luccese is the Italian trainer of **Brunelleschi**, a colt who runs fourth in the English Derby at **Epsom** and subsequently wins the Washington D.C. International at **Laurel Park**.

Luce, Stephen (*Trial Run* 1978)

Luce is an English exchange student at Moscow University. He is sponsored by the Foreign Office and recruited by them to act as interpreter for **Randall Drew**. Luce gives Randall advice about how to behave—advice which, by and large, Randall ignores. He arranges a meeting for Randall with **Kropotkin**, the Russian Olympic Three Day Event team trainer. He takes Randall to see **Misha** at Misha's sister's flat. He collects a telex from British Embassy for Randall, and lets him sleep in his room when Randall needs a safe place to stay. He shows courage when two thugs burst into Randall's room, fighting them off with a broken vodka bottle.

Lucky Lindsay (*Bonecrack* 1971)

Lucky Lindsay is a two-year-old chestnut colt; he cost 30,000 guineas, and is trained by **Neil Griffon**. He whips round and unseats his lad near the Warren Hill gallop in **Newmarket**, then knocks over a man riding a bicycle on the road nearby. A superficial cut on his leg is the horse's only injury. Lucky Lindsay continues to live up to his name; when shots are fired at his rider on the gallops on the morning of the Two Thousand Guineas, Lucky Lindsay escapes unscathed.

Ludville, Mrs. Angelina (*Field of 13* 1998: "The Raid at Kingdom Hill")

Mrs. Ludville is a Tote ticket seller at **Kingdom Hill racecourse**. She is in her fifties, divorced, childless and broke. During a race meeting there is a bomb hoax and the buildings have to be evacuated. On her way out Mrs. Ludville takes the opportunity to steal money from one of the Tote windows.

Luisa (*The Danger* 1983)

Luisa is the aunt of **Ilaria Cenci** and **Alessia Cenci**. She lives at Villa Francese with **Paolo Cenci**.

Lund (*Slay-Ride* 1973)

In *Chapter 10* of *Slay-Ride,* Lund is the name of the Oslo policeman in charge of the investigation into the death of **Bob Sherman**. From *Chapter 11* he is referred to as **Knut**.

Lymington, Hampshire

Lymington is a Georgian seaside town on the edge of the **New Forest** in **Hampshire**, on the south coast of England. The town is built on an estuary, and has a pleasant port and marina.

Risk (1977): **Roland Britten**'s friend, boat builder **Johnny Frederick**, phones with information about the boat on which Roland had been held a prisoner. It was built at Lymington for a client named **Arthur Robinson**.

Lyon, Thomas (*Wild Horses* 1994)

Someone once said—rather unkindly—about film director Otto Preminger that he couldn't direct his small nephew to the toilets. Thomas Lyon has so far avoided such a withering critique of his work, but there is unquestionably an element of hubris in his words when he says: "I'd begun to feel recently that I finally understood my trade..." After all, plenty of film directors work for forty years and never seem to understand their trade, which is to make films that will entertain the public. But maybe Thomas has real talent: in the USA at the age of twenty-six he directed a critically acclaimed film about a boy and a puma for a producer called O'Hara. Now he's in **Newmarket**,

working again with O'Hara, shooting a film about the unexplained death of a trainer's wife that had occurred a quarter of a century before. He has the self-confidence to rewrite swathes of the script to make it more exciting, but nothing is guaranteed to infuriate a scriptwriter more, and retaliation is inevitable. It's not long before he is reading misquotes in the newspapers, ostensibly from **Nash Rourke**, the star of the film, criticizing both the film and its director.

Where horses and racing are concerned, though, Thomas's pedigree makes him eminently suited to the job. His grandfather trained in Newmarket, and he himself rode as an amateur. Thomas's racing background helps to ensure O'Hara's support when the film's backers hear about the newspaper headlines and demand his sacking. Thomas holds on to his job, the condition for which is closer supervision by O'Hara.

The publicity hasn't done Thomas's reputation any favors with the professional jockeys hired to ride in the film; they view him with suspicion and promise to be unhelpful. In order to assert his authority he challenges them to ride against him over **Huntingdon racecourse**'s steeplechase fences. Foolhardy Thomas may be, but he doesn't lack courage, and he acquits himself well in the race against the two jockeys who have taken him up on his challenge, earning their respect and future cooperation. Thomas has volunteered to pay out of his own pocket the private nursing home bills of **Dorothea Pannier**, an elderly friend, rather than her being forced to go into a retirement home near her unpleasant son. It's impossible to fault Thomas's generosity, but he is apparently unaware how much nursing home fees are. Film directors may be well paid, but it is unlikely that his remuneration will cover such largesse indefinitely.

If the enemies that Thomas has made while investigating the violent background to the film have their way, his financial support of Dorothea will be posthumous. They are determined to prevent Thomas from discovering how and why the trainer's wife had died all those years ago. Thomas, however, refuses to be deterred.

M

Maarten-Pagnier (*Straight* 1989)

This is the Antwerp, Belgium, firm of diamond cutters to whom **Greville Franklin** had sent twenty-five rough diamonds for cutting on behalf of **Prospero Jenks**. One of the partners had arranged to hand over the cut diamonds in **Harwich**, but Greville was killed in **Ipswich** on the way to meet him.

Macclesfield, Sir Stuart (*For Kicks* 1965)

Sir Stuart is one of the three Stewards of the **National Hunt Committee**. He is elderly, stooping and white-haired. He has a piercing stare and a slow, rasping voice. He briefs **Daniel Roke** when Daniel arrives in England to investigate the possible doping of racehorses.

Mackintosh, Mac (*Comeback* 1991)

Mackintosh is an elderly racehorse trainer based in Riddlescombe, near Cheltenham. He is going senile, and the training license is now held by his daughter, **Zoë Mackintosh**. Long ago he was said to have lost a lot of money in a failed property deal, and to have resorted to illegal means to repair the financial damage.

Mackintosh, Zoë (*Comeback* 1991)

Zoë Mackintosh is a racehorse trainer based near Cheltenham. Her father, **Mac Mackintosh**, who had held the license before her and still lives at the yard, is rumored to have lost a substantial amount of money in a failed property speculation. Two of Zoë's horses had died when veterinary surgeon **Ken McClure** was operating on them. Zoë is not hostile to **Peter Darwin**'s questions about the two dead horses. She herself doesn't rule out the possibility that one of her stable lads had put poison in their feed.

Macrahinish (*High Stakes* 1975)

An ex-veterinary surgeon, Macrahinish had been struck off and jailed for doping and fraud. He suffers from a condition, ectropion, which causes his eyelids to be inflamed and swollen. He is referred to by **Steven Scott** as "Sunglasses" or "Muscles" until Steven discovers his identity. A big, well-built man, Macrahinish is an associate of crooked trainer **Jody Leeds**. He is a willing participant in Leeds' schemes, and has no compunction about resorting to violence when necessary.

Maggie (*Flying Finish* 1966)

Maggie works with **Lord Henry Gray** at the **Anglia Bloodstock Agency** in London. She is prone to saying unkind things about people, then pretending to regret having said them. She annoys Henry with her untidy habits. She holds a low opinion of Henry, thinks him lacking in brains and character.

Magic (*Field of 13* 1998: "Spring Fever")

An unprepossessing gelding, Magic is stabled in a rundown yard in **Yorkshire**. He is bought on behalf of owner **Mrs. Angela Hart** by jockey **Derek Roberts**, who deceives her over the price he paid. In his first race for new trainer **Clement Scott** at **Stratford**, Magic dives at a fence when Roberts asks him to quicken, and falls. In his next race, the valuable Whitbread Gold Cup at **Sandown Park**, Magic shows plenty of ability when running on to be third.

Maidenhead racecourse

Maidenhead is a fictional racecourse in the town of Maidenhead, **Berkshire**, about twenty-five miles west of London. Today the town has a population of about 60,000 and is part of the Royal Borough of Windsor and Maidenhead.

Dead Cert (1962): Amateur jockey **Major Bill Davidson** is killed at Maidenhead when his horse, **Admiral**, is deliberately brought down.

Major-General (*Trial Run* 1978)

The Major-General, whose name we do not learn, is an important man in the Soviet hierarchy, according to **Yuri Chulitsky**. He is put in touch with **Randall Drew** by Chulitsky. He speaks fluent English, and is clearly a man of prestige and power. At first he listens to Randall's story with skepticism, denying that there are any terrorists in Russia. Eventually, however, he is convinced, and takes steps to have the terrorists arrested.

Make-A-Wager Ltd. (*Under Orders* 2006)

This is the parent company, of which **George Lochs** and **Lord Enstone** are directors, of internet betting exchange make-a-wager.com. The firm has offices in **Wembley**, north London.

Manley, Fred (*Under Orders* 2006)

Manley is the head lad at **Bill Burton**'s stables. He is in his late forties but his tough outdoor life has aged him prematurely. He is polite and a hard worker. Manley is worried when Burton doesn't turn up to oversee the horses' morning work. When he learns what has happened to Burton and finds himself without a job, Manley tells **Sid Halley** that his heart is no longer in it, and that he's thinking of finding a job outside racing.

Marconicars (*Dead Cert* 1962)

This is a **Brighton** taxi firm whose drivers engage in criminal activities on behalf of their employer.

Marcus, Saul (*Come to Grief* 1995)

Saul Marcus is a weaver and fabric designer based in Chiswick, west London. He is consulted by **Sid Halley** over the provenance of a piece of cloth in which a pair of shears is found wrapped. Marcus suggests that Sid try **Patricia Huxford** in **Surrey** or **Sussex**.

Margaret (*Bonecrack* 1971)

Margaret, stable secretary to **Newmarket** trainer **Neville Griffon**, is a widow in her late thirties with two children. She is intelligent and self-contained. She remarks that **Alessandro Rivera** is rude but attractive and sexy. She discovers, via her daughter's friend's mother who is a receptionist at the Forbury Inn, that Alessandro is living there, and also that the address on his passport is Bastagnola, Switzerland. She is flattered and aroused when Alessandro makes time to chat to her; she is unaware that Alessandro merely wants information. After Neville Griffon's death, Margaret comments that, although it is disloyal to say it, she much prefers working for his son, **Neil Griffon**.

Marge (*10 lb. Penalty* 1997)

Marge is a volunteer worker for **George Juliard** in the **Hoopwestern** by-election. She helps with canvassing door-to-door.

Marguerite (*Dead Heat* 2007)

Marguerite was the head cook at the **Oxfordshire** restaurant owned by a distant relative of **Max Moreton**. She had taught Max how to cook. However, she had been sacked for using bad language, and Max had taken over.

Marigold (*Shattered* 2000)

Marigold is the wealthy mother of **Bon-Bon Stukely**, widow of steeplechase jockey **Martin Stukely**. She is energetic and amusing but argumentative when she's had a drink. She is gassed and loses consciousness when an intruder enters **Bon-Bon**'s house. Marigold asks **Gerard Logan** to make a copy of an ancient Cretan necklace of gold and glass for Bon-Bon; then she decides that the necklace will be a trophy to present each year at **Cheltenham** to the winning owner of a steeplechase run in honor of Martin. Marigold's relationship with **Worthington**, her chauffeur, changes from that of employer-employee to something more romantic.

Mark (*Decider* 1993)

Mark is **Mrs. Marjorie Binsham**'s chauffeur.

Marlborough racecourse

Marlborough is a fictional racecourse. The town of Marlborough is in **Wiltshire**, a rural county to the west of London.

Field of 13 (1998): "Collision Course." Fledgling trainer **Dennis Kinser** sponsors a race at Marlborough racecourse.

Marsh, Warrington (*Twice Shy* 1981)

Marsh is the former manager of American **Luke Houston**'s racing interests in England. He has suffered a stroke and is unfit for work. In his place Houston has employed **William Derry** temporarily. William has to cope with a lack of help and support from Marsh and his wife Nonie.

Martin (*Dead Heat* 2007)

Martin is the barman at **The Hay Net**, a **Newmarket** restaurant run by **Max Moreton**.

Martin, Zanna (*Odds Against* 1965)

Zanna Martin works as a secretary for stockbroker **Ellis Bolt**. At the age of sixteen Zanna was hit by a firework which caused serious burns to her face. She lost an eye and suffered fractures to her facial bones. Though plastic surgery has improved her disfigurement, the psychological wounds have not healed. Zanna keeps her desk facing the wall so that clients can't see her face. She is in her late thirties, and slender with straight dark hair. She wears no make up or jewelry, and has made no effort to make herself more attractive.

Sid Halley asks Zanna to go for a meal with him after she finishes work. Though Sid had said he'd meet her at the door of the office, she isn't expecting him to be there, and doesn't look round for him when she comes out. She answers Sid's questions about her work without suspecting that he is pumping her for information about **Seabury racecourse**. Later, in the restaurant, she tells Sid how her face was disfigured and says that she often wishes that the firework had killed her. Sid encourages her to move her office desk so that it faces the door; Zanna agrees, on condition that Sid doesn't hide his withered hand in his pocket.

When Zanna discovers by chance who Sid is, she bitterly accuses him of using her to find out about her employer. She says that when Sid persuaded her to move her desk he was just playing a cruel game. But, with time for reflection, Zanna decides to forgive Sid and voluntarily provides the information he needs.

When Sid is recovering in hospital after being assaulted, Zanna visits him. Her clothes are smart and fashionable, her hair is re-styled and she is wearing make-up. Zanna has at last come to terms with her scars. She tells Sid that she has a new and better job, and thanks Sid for helping her to change her life.

Martineau Park racecourse

Martineau Park is a fictional racecourse in the south of England.

Proof (1984): Wine merchant **Tony Beach** goes with trainer's wife **Flora Hawthorn** to Martineau Park as a guest of racehorse owner **Orkney Swayle**. Tony and private investigator **Gerard McGregor** confront **Vernon**, the catering manager at Martineau Park, about his extra-curricular activities.

Mary (*Dead Heat* 2007)

Mary is the owner of Mary's café, Delafield, Wisconsin. She tells **Max Moreton** that **Rolf Schumann** is in a mental hospital in Milwaukee.

Mason, Sandy (*Dead Cert* 1962)

Mason, a jump jockey in his thirties, is red-haired, tough and cheerful. He has a healthy disregard for rules and is a practical joker. He is not one of the top jockeys, and is thought to be willing to stop a horse if the money is right. Mason is uncompromising in a race, and doesn't hesitate to put rival jockey **Joe Nantwich** over the rails when the two fall out. **Alan York** has cause to suspect Mason of criminal activity, but Mason tells him that he can't prove a thing. He tries to put Alan over the rails in a race at **Maidenhead**, but suffers the same fate himself at Alan's hands.

Mason Miles Associates (*Twice Shy* 1981)

This is a computer consultancy firm in **Norwich** for whom **Peter Keithley** worked.

Matthew (*Rat Race* 1970)

Matthew is the young nephew of the **Duke of Wessex**. At **Redcar** races he is sent by his uncle to fetch **Matt Shore** from his plane to drink his health after **Rudiments** wins the big race. Matthew loves going racing with his uncle, and can't understand why people think that the Duke is dim. He is there when the Duke introduces Matt to **Charles Carthy-Todd**. Matthew accepts Carthy-Todd's offer of chocolate orange peel; afterwards, though, he tells Matt that he doesn't care much for Carthy-Todd.

In the car park of **Warwick racecourse** Matthew notices the tin that had contained the chocolate orange peel on the hood of his uncle's Rolls Royce, and picks it up. When Matt tells him to throw the tin to him, Matthew sensibly does so, and saves his life in the process.

Matthew (*Bolt* 1986)

Matthew is a small boy who is at **Bradbury racecourse** when **Prince Litsi** is hanging by his fingertips from the viewing balcony of the grandstand. He responds to **Kit Fielding's** pleas for racegoers to use their coats to make a mattress to break Litsi's fall. Matthew takes off his anorak and jersey, and shouts to other racegoers to do the same until there's a big pile.

Matthews, Art (*Nerve* 1964)

Art Matthews is a thirty-five-year-old jump jockey. He has a reputation for honesty, and is well respected in the weighing room. He has no close friends, though, and is never willing to admit to having lost a race through his own mistake. He is very bitter when sacked by trainer **Corin Kellar**. In the paddock at **Dunstable** races, Matthews shoots himself in front of Kellar.

Matthews, Maisie (*In the Frame* 1976)

Maisie Matthews, a wealthy widow, had married her late husband after nursing his first wife, who died of cancer. Her house in Worthing, **Sussex**, has recently burned down. Meeting artist **Charles Todd** at **Plumpton** races, she asks him to paint the ruins so that she can hang the painting in her new house. She takes Charles to see the ruins, where they find a man searching through the rubble. He claims to be from the insurance company. Maisie tells Charles that she had bought an **Alfred Munnings** painting in Australia while visiting her sister-in-law. She admits that she had smuggled the Munnings into Britain to avoid paying tax and had hidden it behind a radiator. She decides she doesn't want Charles to paint her ruined house after all, and pays him the sum they had agreed on if she hadn't liked the picture.

Maudsley, Russell (*Field of 13* 1998: "Collision Course")

Maudsley, the co-owner of Lionheart News Group, doesn't get on with his two other co-owners. Rows amongst them have led to financial difficulties at the Group. Maudsley interviews editor **Bill Williams** for a post with their organization. Initially Maudsley considers that Williams looks too young and is not impressed. Later, in discussion with colleague **Harold F. Field**, he is persuaded to change his mind.

Mays, Ganser (*High Stakes* 1975)

Mays is a bookmaker who for years has colluded with trainer **Jody Leeds** to swindle Leeds' owners, including wealthy toy maker **Steven Scott**. Mays has resorted to dubious tactics to build up his large string of betting shops. His unholy alliance with Leeds had worked well until Steven Scott, up till then a lucrative source of income for Leeds and Mays, discovers what the pair has been up to and sacks Leeds.

Mays is not slow to resort to violence when Steven continues to be a thorn in his flesh. When he finds himself humiliated and a good deal poorer as a result of Steven's sting, Mays loses control and seeks revenge. It's a bad call on Mays' part.

McClure, Josephine (*Comeback* 1991)

Josephine is **Ken McClure**'s widowed mother. She is unsubtly milked by **Peter Darwin** for her memories of various people presently involved in her son's troubles.

McClure, Ken (*Comeback* 1991)

McClure is an equine veterinary surgeon in a six-partner practice in **Gloucestershire**. He is in his mid-thirties, and is tall with fair, thinning hair. He is about to be married to the unpleasant **Belinda Larch**, daughter of **Vicky Larch**. Ken is out to dinner with Belinda, her mother and **Peter Darwin** when he gets a phone call to say that the practice's buildings are on fire. However, only the office block is destroyed.

McClure is worried because he has had four horses die under anesthetic during operations in the last two months; he is afraid that clients will stop sending their horses to the practice. He is called out during the night to see a mare with colic; he has to bring the mare in for an immediate operation. He removes a piece of twisted gut from the mare containing a needle and thread.

At **Stratford** races McClure is accused by trainer **J. Rolls Eaglewood** of causing the deaths of two of his horses during surgery. McClure, however, has his own theories—subsequently proven to be correct—as to why these horses, and two others, have died.

McGregor, Gerard (*Proof* 1984)

McGregor, a tall, middle-aged Scot, is intelligent and cultivated. He is the manager of **Deglet's**, a detective agency specializing in services to commercial clients. As a young man he had studied accountancy without much enthusiasm until a family friend had found him a job in an agency investigating business fraud. McGregor helps **Tony Beach** to rescue guests trapped beneath a marquee after a horse van crashes into it at **Jack Hawthorn**'s owners' party. Some time later, he goes to see Tony to ask him to act as a consultant to his firm, which is looking into the theft of three tankers of Scotch whisky. McGregor goes to phone the police when he and Tony disturb two men stealing wine from Tony's shop. Returning to his car, he is shot at by one of the men; the windscreen is shattered, and McGregor is injured in the shoulder. He is kept in hospital for only a couple of days but his recovery is slow.

McGregor's investigations into the whisky thefts prove even more hazardous to his health, and he has Tony Beach to thank for rescuing him from an unpleasant fate.

McGregor, Louise (*Whip Hand* 1979)

Louise McGregor once shared an apartment with **Jenny Halley** in Oxford. Mindful of Jenny's withering remarks about **Sid Halley**, Louise is on her guard when Sid comes to the apartment to ask about **Nicholas Ashe**. After meeting Sid, though, she is pleasantly surprised. Louise is doing research after taking a first class degree at **Cambridge**. According to Sid, she is sensible and practical although, like Jenny, she'd been taken in by Ashe. She says she will contact Sid if she can think of anything to help Jenny.

Jenny, suspecting that Sid and Louise had got on well, tells him that Louise is out of his class. But Louise is attracted to Sid and knows that he feels the same. She and Sid make love at a hotel, and she is surprised at his gentleness.

McGregor, Tina (*Proof* 1984)

Tina is the wife of investigative consultant **Gerard McGregor**. She calls, with **Flora Hawthorn**, at **Tony Beach**'s shop; she tells Tony that her husband, who is in hospital after being shot, wants to see him. She says that it's the third time that he's been shot. Tina does not give her feelings away, but McGregor admits to Tony that she has never been too keen on his job.

McLachlan, Alex Mitchell (*The Edge* 1988)

McLachlan, also known as "**Johnson**," is an associate of **Julius Filmer**; he is traveling on the Great Transcontinental Mystery Race Train. An ex-railway employee, McLachlan is considered by a former colleague to be unpopular and potentially violent. He commits a series of criminal acts for which he is subsequently imprisoned.

Medic (*Smokescreen* 1972)

Medic is a colt owned by **Nerissa Cavesey** and trained by **Greville Arknold** in South Africa. He had once been highly thought of, but had disappointed badly in all four of his starts.

Melanie (*Smokescreen* 1972)

Melanie is a top fashion model employed by the *Rand Daily Star*, a South African newspaper. She is used by **Roderick Hodge** and **Katya** in an unsuccessful attempt to compromise **Edward Lincoln** in order to get some "sensational" photos. Forgetting her intended role while talking to Edward about politics, Melanie animatedly defends the racially divisive apartheid system. Then, remembering that she is supposed to be seducing Edward she pretends to be a vacuous air-head whose opinions are worthless. She tries to get Edward to leave the apartment block with her so that the waiting photographers can snap them together but Edward, alive to her game, slips out alone.

Melanie (*Second Wind* 1999)

Melanie is a young assistant in a clandestine British civil service department involved in anti-criminal activities.

Melbourne-Smith, Mr. (*Field of 13* 1998: "Bright White Star")

Melbourne-Smith, a rich racehorse owner, goes to see the Director of the Racecourse Security Services at **Jockey Club** headquarters in **Portman Square**. He complains bitterly that an expensive yearling he had bought at the November Yearling Sales has been stolen. His trainer had received a clearly inferior colt from the Sales instead. He threatens to buy all his horses in France in future.

Mellit, Claudius (*Nerve* 1964)

Mellit, an eminent psychiatrist, lives in Wimpole Street, London. He is a friend of **Rob Finn**'s father. He delays his Saturday round of golf to advise Rob on a villain's possibly deranged state of mind. He accepts the possibility of Rob's theory about the reason behind the man's behavior, but won't commit himself without hard facts to work with.

Merry and Co. (*The Edge* 1988)

This is a Toronto-based travel company which organizes the Great Transcontinental Mystery Race Train trip.

Mervyn (*Proof* 1984)

Mervyn is employed in the catering department of **Martineau Park racecourse**, checking in deliveries of food and drink.

Metavane (*Break In* 1985)

Two Thousand Guineas winner Metavane was trained by **Maynard Allardeck**'s father and owned by Maynard. The horse was previously owned by **Major Clement Perryside** as an unraced two-year-old. Perryside had been duped by Maynard Allardeck into selling Metavane cheaply to pay off part of a loan.

Metrella (*Comeback* 1991)

Metrella, a chestnut mare with a white star, is trained by **Zoë Mackintosh** at Riddlescombe, near Cheltenham. At evening stables Zoë's father, **Mac Mackintosh**, confuses Metrella with Poverty, a horse he used to train himself years previously.

Mevagissey, Mrs. (*Second Wind* 1999)

Mrs. Mevagissey, **Perry Stuart**'s grandmother, brought Perry up after the death of his parents. She is eighty years old, confined to a wheelchair, and needs constant nursing, which Perry pays for. She lives in a flat overlooking the Thames. She had worked for many years for a travel company, touring the world on its behalf. At the age of seventy-four she had felt ill after white water rafting in Colorado; a benign spinal tumor had been diagnosed but the operation to remove it had not been successful and she had lost the use of her legs.

A mentally sharp, uncomplaining old lady, Mrs. Mevagissey has premonitions of impending misfortune, notably when Perry's parents were killed in a gas explosion. She warns Perry not to go to Florida chasing hurricanes. She is relieved and tearful when she learns that Perry is still alive after his plane crashes into the sea, though her instincts had told her that he'd survived.

Miami, Florida

Miami is a major American city in South Florida. Its metropolitan area has over 5,000,000 inhabitants. Miami is a cosmopolitan city with a large population of Latin Americans and West Indians. Among the thriving industries in Miami are tourism, banking, fashion, film making and music.

Comeback (1991): Diplomat **Peter Darwin**, en route from Mexico to London, stops off in Miami to visit a friend, British consul **Fred Hutchings**.

Second Wind (1999): Meteorologist **Perry Stuart** flies to Miami to visit his friend **Will** who works in the Hurricane Tracking Centre. **Robin Darcy** and his wife, **Evelyn Darcy**, live in Miami.

Michaels, Gordon (*Banker* 1982)

Gordon Michaels is in his fifties, and is a director of merchant bank **Paul Ekaterin Ltd**. He is bright, imaginative and well-off. He is in charge of the Banking arm of the bank, with **Tim Ekaterin** in his department. Michaels is found to be suffering from Parkinson's disease, and needs to take some time off work. On his return he invites Tim to Royal **Ascot**, where he has bought a half-share in a box for the day.

Michaels invites Tim to spend Christmas with him and his wife, **Judith Michaels**. Tim and Judith fancy each other but if Michaels suspects, he says nothing. His health problems gradually become worse; he is still mentally alert but is deteriorating physically.

As he approaches sixty Michaels makes plans for his retirement. He and Judith go on a world tour; in India he suffers a cerebral hemorrhage and dies.

Michaels, Judith (*Banker* 1982)

Judith is the wife of **Gordon Michaels**. She and Gordon live in a big house on Clapham Common, London. She is an energetic woman in her late thirties. Judith is greatly admired by **Tim Ekaterin**. She relays her attraction to Tim in the noncommittal, circumlocutory code favored by certain of the upper middle classes. Judith's husband invites Tim for Christmas. On Boxing Day Tim drives Judith across London to visit her mother's grave. She is tempted to go back to Tim's flat and make love to him but resists with difficulty. Their relationship consists of occasional meetings at

office parties or phone calls; they often don't see each other for weeks.

On a world tour after Gordon's retirement, Judith phones Tim for help after Gordon has a cerebral hemorrhage in India. Tim flies out, but Gordon dies. There is a strong implication that Judith and Tim finally get together.

Mickey (*For Kicks* 1965)

Mickey, also known as **Starlamp**, is a steeplechaser at **Hedley Humber's Durham** yard; he is looked after by stable lad **Jerry Webber**. Mickey disappears from the yard for three days; when he returns he is a savage, maddened by pain. He is given a powerful sedative until wounds on his legs begin to heal. However, Mickey begins to lose condition, and has to be continually sedated; he's dying on his feet. Undercover **Jockey Club** investigator **Daniel Roke** decides to try an experiment; as a result Mickey goes crazy, eventually breaking his neck in an attempt to escape from his tethering chain.

Middlesex, England

Middlesex was once one of the thirty-nine historic counties of England, but now the county does not officially exist, though the name is still included in postal addresses. In the 1960's Middlesex became part of the Greater London conurbation. Lying to the north and west of the capital, its towns include Harrow, Uxbridge, Ealing, Staines, Enfield and Hounslow.

High Stakes (1975): **Bert Huggerneck**, a friend of **Charlie Canterfield's** lives in Staines, Middlesex.

Twice Shy (1981): **Jonathan Derry** is Head of Physics in a Middlesex comprehensive School. Dick Francis's son Felix was educated at Mill Hill, an independent day and boarding school in Middlesex, and later became a physics teacher.

Mike (*Nerve* 1964)

Mike, known as "Young Mike," is **Rob Finn's** racecourse valet.

Mike (*The Edge* 1988)

Mike is an engine driver on the Great Transcontinental Mystery Race Train. He is the elder of the two drivers.

Miles, Mason (*Twice Shy* 1981)

Miles, a computer consultant, is the boss of **Mason Miles Associates, Norwich**, where **Peter Keithley** had been employed. He tells **Jonathan**

Derry that he was unaware that Keithley had been writing programs for **Chris Norwood**, but that what Keithley did in his free time was of no concern to him.

Millace, George (*Reflex* 1980)

Millace, recently deceased, was a racecourse photographer, and the father of jockey **Steve Millace**. He was a brilliant photographer but favored shots which did little to enhance the reputation of his subjects. As a result, Millace was unpopular, and unmourned after crashing his car into a tree. **Philip Nore** discovers that Millace had an agenda far beyond his photographic activities, and that the circumstances of his death were not as straightforward as they appeared.

Millace, Mrs. Marie (*Reflex* 1980)

Marie is the widow of **George Millace**. She had been assaulted when two burglars ransacked her house the day after her husband's funeral. She tells the police that the burglars demanded to know where the safe was. While she is in hospital her house is torched. Later she tells **Philip Nore** that the police had confirmed that it was arson, and she asked if George had any enemies. Philip finds it prudent to be less than frank with Mrs. Millace.

Millace, Steve (*Reflex* 1980)

Steve Millace is a jockey in his early twenties, and the son of racecourse photographer **George Millace**, who has recently been killed in a car crash. He is lacking in humor and inclined to dwell on perceived injustices. At **Sandown** races, he tells his fellow-jockeys about his mother's house being burgled while at his father's funeral. He breaks his collarbone in a racecourse fall and gets a lift home with **Philip Nore**, to find the police and an ambulance outside. His mother has been beaten up by burglars. When his mother's home is burnt down, he is near the end of his tether and asks Philip for help.

Millbrook, Red (*Field of 13* 1998: "Dead on Red")

Millbrook, a talented but inexperienced amateur steeplechase jockey, is the son of aristocratic parents. Out of the blue, he is offered the job of stable jockey to trainer "Gypsy Joe" Smith. To the surprise of the racing world Millbrook proves a resounding success; he rides winner after winner for his new stable. A few months later, however, the partnership comes to an abrupt and violent end.

Miller, Mort (*Twice Shy* 1981)

Newmarket trainer Mort Miller is in charge of a number of **Luke Houston**'s horses; he is a natural worrier. He has no problem with asking for **William Derry**'s opinions, and accepts William's selling of slow two-year-olds. Miller trains **Genotti**, a three-year-old colt entered for the St Leger at **Doncaster**. When Genotti wins the race Miller's joy is unbridled.

Miller, Suzanne (*Dead Heat* 2007)

Suzanne Miller is the managing director of a hospitality company that provides catering services to **Newmarket racecourse**. After a food poisoning incident at the course, Miller phones chef **Max Moreton**, who had prepared the meal, to say that one of the guests who had taken ill intends to take legal action. She agrees to provide Max with a list of the guests and of the catering staff working at the racecourse that evening. She is worried when the local District Council informs her that her company is to be prosecuted under the Food Safety Act.

Millington, John (*The Edge* 1988)

Millington is the Deputy Head of the **Jockey Club** Security Service. A retired police Chief Inspector, he is a large man but light on his feet. He is annoyed at the acquittal of **Julius Apollo Filmer** on a charge of conspiracy to murder; Millington had helped the police to put together the case against Filmer. Millington is not keen to lose the services of **Tor Kelsey** when Tor is sent to Canada to keep an eye on Filmer on the Great Transcontinental Mystery Race Train. At **Nottingham** races, he tells **Jason Horfitz** he should pass on to him any information he has.

Mills, Kevin (*Come to Grief* 1995)

Mills is a reporter on *The Pump* newspaper. He is middle-aged, running to fat, and going bald. He had covered the story about the mutilation of horses, and publishes a warning in *The Pump* to horse owners not to leave their animals unguarded in open fields. Mills sets up a "hotline" for readers to get in touch with **Sid Halley** if they have any information. He is promised an exclusive story by Sid, who in fact doesn't keep his side of the bargain. Mills is angry, and he vilifies Sid in *The Pump*. After several weeks of continuous anti–Halley vitriol Mills tells Sid that it is on the instructions of the proprietor, **Lord Tilepit**. Subsequently, however, Tilepit worries about the legal implications of what Mills had written, and instructs Mills to retract allegations he has made against Sid.

Milne, Angela (*Dead Heat* 2007)

Environmental health officer Angela Milne contacts **Max Moreton** after twenty-four people are treated at Addenbrooke's hospital, **Cambridge**, for food poisoning following a dinner prepared by Max at **Newmarket racecourse**. The next day she is unaware that **The Hay Net**, Max's Newmarket restaurant, has been closed and the kitchen sealed. She discovers that the Food Standards Agency had ordered its closure because someone had allegedly died as a result of the food poisoning. When Milne finds that the death was not connected, she gives Max permission to re-open the restaurant, subject to inspection.

Minchless, Mr. and Mrs. Wyatt L. (*In the Frame* 1976)

Mr. and Mrs. Minchless are a wealthy retired couple from Carter, Illinois. Both are racing fans. Minchless is pale, white-haired and pompous; his wife, Ruthie, wears her expensive jewelry ostentatiously, the hard lines of her face betraying an unsympathetic outlook on life. They are onlookers in **Victoria Arts Center**, Melbourne, when a young artist copying an **Alfred Munnings** painting is accused of being a fraud by **Jik Cassavetes**, and throws turpentine in Jik's eyes. Minchless tells **Charles Todd** that the artist had told them of a Munnings for sale at **Yarra River Fine Arts** gallery nearby.

Minor Characters

One of the ways in which Francis enriches his minor characters is by highlighting those elements of personality that truly define that character. In the case of **Toby Morris**, the twelve-year-old son of protagonist **Lee Morris** in *Decider* (1993), it is his natural rebelliousness that makes him stand out. Told to do something, the chances are that he will do exactly the opposite. Ignoring his father's urgent request over the public address system to evacuate the grandstand at **Stratton Park racecourse**, he almost gets both of them killed when there is an explosion. But the tap root which gives rise to Toby's instinctive lack of respect for authority nurtures also a spontaneous courage, bordering on recklessness, which ultimately is to save the lives of his brother and possibly his father too.

One important function of a minor character is to shed light on the major characters through his interaction with them. In *Twice Shy* (1981) **Cassie Morris**, girlfriend of **William Derry**, is affectionate, ironic, and fun to be with but she has her own life to live and just so happens to share part of it with William. That a girl like Cassie chooses to be with William informs the reader that William himself must be a decent sort of guy.

Cassie shares a rented cottage with William near **Newmarket**, and works in a building society in **Cambridge**. Despite spending most of the working day discussing mortgages with her clients, never once has Cassie suggested to William that they should get a mortgage themselves, and that suits William fine. What Cassie is much more likely to suggest is that William make love to her. She has just persuaded him to come to bed when a lunatic smashes in the door of the cottage with a baseball bat. Cassie rushes to help William but the flailing bat connects sickeningly with her forearm, snapping the bone. Expecting no more problems from Cassie, the thug concentrates on trying to smash William to a pulp. This is a bad call; Cassie picks up a brass coal scuttle and, swinging it like a mace, almost removes the man's head from his shoulders.

One of the techniques that writers employ to make their minor characters more memorable is to give them unusual names, and Francis certainly does not underplay his hand; among the more preposterous are **Bert Huggerneck** (*High Stakes*), **Lord Verney Tilepit** (*Come to Grief*), **Surtees Benchmark** (*To the Hilt*) and **Lady Emma Louders-Allen-Croft** (*Trial Run*). In *Twice Shy* Bananas Frisby, an innkeeper and restaurateur, gets his nickname from one of his delicious puddings, made from eggs, rum, bananas and orange. As a minor character, Bananas is no less of a fascinating concoction than his celebrated dessert. He's a fat man, but he has a cunning justification for his fatness; he tells William Derry that his more corpulent customers, seeing him, feel better about their own rotundity and therefore spend their money more freely. Though brimming with outward bonhomie towards his customers and his friends, Bananas is a deep thinker who cares about the state of the world and is prone to depression over mankind's inability to learn from its mistakes. Throughout *Twice Shy* Bananas is a loyal friend to William. When William is shot it is prompt action by Bananas that helps to save William's life.

Bananas' strongly idiosyncratic personality enhances the scenes he is in. So does that of racehorse trainer **Neville Griffon**, the father of *Bone-*

crack's hero **Neil Griffon**, though in his case it is his sheer unpleasantness that makes him memorable. Mean-spirited and incapable of affection, Griffon has resented Neil from the day of his birth. Throughout Neil's childhood Griffon has offered his son nothing but criticism and constant punishments for trivial misdemeanors, a cycle broken when he packs Neil off to boarding school. When Neil runs away from **Eton** at the age of sixteen, it provides Griffon with the excuse to sever all contact with his son, a state of affairs which lasts for fourteen years. When Neil, who by now has a successful career in business, finally goes to see his father, seeking a rapprochement, Griffon doesn't recognize him. Grudgingly, he allows Neil to visit him occasionally, though he remains distant and unbending. When Griffon is hospitalized after a car accident it is with the greatest reluctance that he allows Neil to take over temporarily the running of his Newmarket stable. He makes it clear that he has no faith whatsoever in Neil's ability to train horses and does everything within his power from his hospital bed to undermine his son's efforts.

Blood ties also feature strongly in *Knock Down* (1974), in which tensions exist between the hero, bloodstock agent **Jonah Dereham**, and **Crispin Dereham**, his alcoholic elder brother. Minor characters are enriched when the writer explores the internal conflict that drives their actions, and Crispin's dependency on drink makes him both more human and more real. Past experience, too, is important in explaining why a character behaves as he does; and the contrast between how Crispin and Jonah respond to difficulties in their childhood is striking. When their profligate parents die within months of each other the brothers have to leave their boarding school and fend for themselves. But whereas Jonah, by dint of sheer hard graft, forges for himself a career, first as a jockey and then as a bloodstock agent, Crispin's attempts to find employment in the City have foundered owing to his fondness for the bottle. Finally, jobless and broke, he moves into Jonah's house near **Gatwick** airport and concentrates solely on his drinking. Crispin isn't a happy drunk; he is verbally abusive, sometimes violent and always, afterwards, self-pitying. Crispin's life is a personal tragedy, and it is somehow inevitable that it will end tragically. Just too late comes redemption of a sort. The phone rings: with supreme irony, it is Alcoholics Anonymous, returning a call for help that Crispin had made earlier that evening.

Stockbroker's secretary **Zanna Martin** in *Odds Against* (1965) is, like Crispin Dereham, living in a private hell. Zanna had been a cheerful, pretty girl living an unexceptional life until, at the age of sixteen, a firework exploded in her face. Zanna lost an eye, as well as suffering severe burns and multiple fractures of her facial bones. With her self-confidence shattered, Zanna had resolved to hide her disfigured face from the world. Now in her late thirties, Zanna keeps her desk at work facing the wall. She wears no make up, nor any jewelry. She tells investigator **Sid Halley** that she wishes the firework had killed her.

Sid resolves to help Zanna adopt a more positive approach to life. He uses her reaction to his own withered, useless hand to demonstrate that while pity is a negative, even a bad-mannered response, sympathy is not. He promises not to keep his hand in his pocket if she will turn her desk to face the world. Bravely, Zanna does as Sid asks. Though angry when she discovers that Sid asked her out partly to pump her for information about her employer, Zanna's budding self-confidence has not been totally shattered. When she visits Sid in hospital after he has taken a beating, Zanna has dispensed with the dowdy clothes and the long hair designed to conceal her scars. She is fashionably dressed, her hair is cut stylishly and her body language speaks of her new-found self-assurance. She has a new job and she wants to thank Sid for providing the impetus she needed to change her life.

Minor characters like Zanna Martin play an enriching role in the novel by leading lives which go on beyond the strict confines of the plot. They also provide an insight into the motivations and personalities of the leading players. In *Forfeit* (1968), we learn, through the relationship between investigative racing journalist **James Tyrone** and his bedridden wife, **Elizabeth Tyrone**, that James is a caring and thoughtful husband. But we see, too, the flaws in his make-up and recognize that, in a marriage struggling to cope under difficult circumstances, loyalty has its limits. Elizabeth Tyrone's part in the plot of *Forfeit* is physically passive; three years into her marriage poliomyelitis leaves Elizabeth almost totally paralyzed and dependent on a mechanical pump to breathe. But it is Elizabeth's fragile emotional state, and how it affects the way James behaves, that defines her role. Elizabeth needs, above all else, to feel safe and secure and loved, and she becomes anxious if she suspects that anything is happening in James's life to compromise that. When James is forced to admit that he has been sleeping with a girl he'd met through his work, Elizabeth is shattered. She sees the stark inevitability of their situation in shocking clarity: she is no longer attractive, whereas James is still young and virile.

Whilst Elizabeth Tyrone's vulnerability and self-doubt define her as a character, with **Charles Roland** the emphasis is on the strength of his personality. Roland, who appears in *Odds Against* (1965), *Whip Hand* (1979), *Come to Grief* (1995) and *Under Orders* (2006), is the father-in-law of ex-champion jockey turned investigator **Sid Halley**, and he exerts a major influence on the decisions that Sid makes. The relationship between the two men, based as it is on a strong mutual respect, is the more interesting for having initially been colored by intense dislike and, on Charles's part, feelings of disdainful superiority. Charles is a retired rear admiral, and had considered Sid, a mere jockey from a working class background, on a par with the lowly naval ratings who had whistled him on board ships in the days when deference had come with his rank. The catalyst for change had been a rare visit by Sid and his wife, **Jenny Halley**, to Charles's imposing house in **Oxfordshire**. Forcing himself to be civil to Sid, Charles had suggested a game of chess, and, to his amazement, had been comprehensively outplayed. A second game, ending in a hard fought draw, proved Sid's skill to be no fluke, and Charles's opinion of his son-in-law underwent a radical reappraisal. He began to take an interest in Sid's career, and over the years he has provided both a staunch support and a shot across the bows when Sid has needed it.

Another character who plays a role in more than one novel is **Wykeham Harlow**, the octogenarian racehorse trainer who first appears briefly in *Break In* (1985) and who then plays a minor but crucial part in the plot of *Bolt* (1986). His is a character wonderfully redolent of the post–World War Two era of **National Hunt** training. Then it was less a business, more a way of life; trainers with a lifetime of experience carried on sending out runners and winners until they were physically incapable of doing so. In common with many trainers who are also true horsemen, Harlow prefers being at home with his horses, and thinks taking them to far-flung racecourses the least enjoyable part of the job. Based on the **Sussex** Downs, on the south coast of England, Harlow suffers badly from migraines which seem to occur on days when he has runners at north country courses like **Haydock**,

Newcastle or **Doncaster**; on those occasions his traveling head lad and **Kit Fielding**, his stable jockey, are left to get on with the job themselves.

Among Wykeham Harlow's most loyal owners is **Princess Casilia**, an old lady descended from one of Europe's dethroned royal families. When Harlow finds two of the Princess's horses dead in their boxes, deliberately killed, he is devastated. An opportunity to exact retribution presents itself, and Harlow does not hesitate. It is a mark of Francis's skill in establishing a likeable character that we can accept Harlow's transgression of the law without losing one iota of sympathy for him.

The personality of a man in his eighties is immutable and needs only to be demonstrated and confirmed by the action and dialogue. By contrast, a young person's personality is still evolving and susceptible to modification by new experiences and influences. Nineteen-year-old **Roberta Cranfield's** stunning good looks are frequently marred by expressions of disdain, irritation or boredom. Roberta has copied her unpleasant attitude from her snobbish father, racehorse trainer **Dexter Cranfield**, whose social prejudices are reflected in the master-servant relationship that, he likes to think, prevails between him and his stable jockey **Kelly Hughes**. Roberta, because of this, simply assumes that Kelly is not of her class and therefore devoid of interest.

Though in many ways her father's daughter, Roberta at least has a fighting spirit that he lacks. When Cranfield and Kelly lose their livelihoods after a **Jockey Club** enquiry finds them guilty of preventing a horse from winning, Roberta goes to see Kelly, hoping that he might be able to persuade her father to fight back. Roberta already has Kelly mentally pigeon-holed as bereft of social graces and, unless on the back of a racehorse, slow-witted. Instead she is reluctantly impressed by his calm self-assurance, and especially by his refusal to be intimidated, either by her or by the loss of his license to ride.

As Roberta gets to know Kelly better she finds herself questioning long-held assumptions and realizes that her father's view of the world is narrow-minded and ignorant.

A badly-drawn minor character can detract significantly from an otherwise well-told story. **Chanter**, for example, the pseudo-hippy art teacher in *Rat Race* (1970), is so stereotypical that virtually nothing he says or does is surprising. *10 lb. Penalty* (1997) is not a gripping story, and **George Juliard** does nothing to mitigate its weakness. The political ambitions of George, the father of vapid hero **Benedict Juliard**, play a crucial role in affecting the direction of his son's life. George's actions, however, serve only to highlight his own unattractive nature and Benedict's weakness in tamely giving up his life's ambition to be a jockey with barely a whimper. The problem with George Juliard is one of sympathy. Are we really expected to admire a man who, when his wife died in childbirth, palmed off his baby son with his wife's sister and slunk away to pursue a lucrative career in the City? Having made his fortune, Juliard turns his attention to becoming an MP, and decides that Benedict might be useful to him. So he effects Benedict's dismissal from his job as a stable lad and amateur jockey on spurious grounds. The reader is forced to endure Juliard's inexorable ascent up the political ladder until he is a powerful member of the Cabinet and a candidate to succeed the Prime Minister. It could be argued that there are parallels to be drawn with Juliard's despicable behavior in real political life. But in *10 lb. Penalty* George Juliard is supposed to be one of the good guys, and to expect the reader to buy that is a bridge too far.

Less contemptible than Juliard but still intensely irritating are painter **Jik Cassavetes** and his wife **Sarah** in *In the Frame* (1976). Cassavetes' role is to help his friend **Charles Todd** in tracking down the murderers of his cousin's wife. Cassavetes' erstwhile sense of adventure, however, appears to have deserted him since his recent marriage to Sarah, whose sole aim in life is to make sure that he does nothing more dangerous than trim his beard with a pair of blunt scissors. Sarah's later change of heart about allowing Jik to help Charles comes too late to matter; she is already established in the reader's mind as a sourpuss.

No matter how small their role in a novel, minor characters should still have aspects of their personality sufficiently striking or unusual to make the reader care what happens to them. Bland characters do not excite; and if, in the end, they turn out to have been crucial to the plot, the reader is left dissatisfied. In *Second Wind* (1999) **Robin Darcy** allegedly has a mind like a whetted knife but he does little to demonstrate it; indeed, allowing himself to be recognized by **Perry Stuart** on **Trox Island** is a singularly stupid thing to do.

Darcy is physically unremarkable—small, tubby, bespectacled—and his studied dullness may have been a useful cover for the potentially dangerous nature of his work. But these traits, combined with

the fact that he has little to say, means that he fails to establish himself as being important or interesting, and so when his true role is finally revealed the impact is weak and the reader has cause to feel cheated.

A similar criticism may be leveled at dishonest medical researcher **Dr. Adam Force** in *Shattered* (2000). With Force, though, not only is the character development sketchy, it is also barely credible and at times contradictory. We are told he is fifty-six years old—hardly ancient by today's standards of longevity—yet he is described elsewhere as elderly and white-bearded. That, too, is difficult to reconcile with protagonist **Gerard Logan**'s own assessment of Force as "powerfully attractive." Force is said to possess great charm yet shows no evidence of it; he is considered an intellectual giant but his actions are often ludicrous and unconvincing, none more so than when he threatens Gerard Logan with a hypodermic syringe.

Minorca, Balearic Islands

Minorca is the smallest of the three major Balearic Islands which lie off the coast of Spain between France and the North African coast; the others are Majorca and Ibiza. The quietest of the three, Minorca has not been developed so ruthlessly for the tourist trade as its larger neighbors. The island's main town is Mahon, which has one of Europe's largest natural harbors.

Risk (1977): Amateur jockey **Roland Britten**, abducted after winning the **Cheltenham** Gold Cup, ends up on the island of Minorca.

Miranda (*To the Hilt* 1996)

Miranda is assistant to solicitor **Oliver Grantchester**; she accompanies him when he visits **Sir Ivan Westering**.

Misha (*Trial Run* 1978)

Misha's real name is Mikhail Alexeevich Tarovsky; he is about nineteen years old and was a groom with the Russian Three Day Event team which competed at the International Horse Trials at **Burghley**. He was standing near Hans Kramer when Kramer died, apparently of a heart attack, and had heard Kramer's last words, spoken in German: "I am dying. It is Alyosha. Moscow." Misha reports this, on the instructions of trainer **Kropotkin**, to **Randall Drew**.

Leading a horse just behind Randall, Misha sees a horse van heading straight at them and jumps out of the way. He gives **Stephen Luce** a phone number so that Randall can ring him without Kropotkin knowing.

Mohammed (*Bolt* 1986)

Mohammed is a Middle Eastern arms dealer. At **Prince Litsi**'s request, Mohammed meets him and **Kit Fielding** in a London hotel. He shows them a plastic handgun, the Grock 17, and explains how a manufacturer can make a good profit, both legally and, via kickbacks, illegally. He admits that he has no moral scruples about selling guns to anyone who has the money to pay for them.

Moncrieff (*Wild Horses* 1994)

Moncrieff is the Director of Photography for the film company making *Unstable Times*. Gangling and scruffy, Moncrieff has a quirky sense of humor, and is brilliant at his job. He dislikes scriptwriter **Howard Tyler** for his attempts to influence director **Thomas Lyon**'s interpretation of the script.

Monga Vineyards Proprietary Ltd. (*In the Frame* 1976)

This is a firm of Australian vineyard owners and wine exporters, based in Adelaide, from whom **Donald Stuart** had bought wine. The company also has an office in Melbourne.

Moonrock (*Bonecrack* 1971)

Moonrock is **Newmarket** trainer **Neville Griffon**'s hack; he was formerly a top-class steeplechaser. Moonrock is found by his lad in his box with a smashed hock, and has to be put down. Later, **Neil Griffon** receives a model of Moonrock with a broken leg, suggesting that the injury had been deliberately inflicted.

Morden, Mrs. Margaret (*To the Hilt* 1996)

Mrs. Morden is an insolvency practitioner hired by accountant **Tobias Tollright** to try to save the **King Alfred Brewery**. She is in her forties, highly competent and intelligent. When **Sir Ivan Westering**'s assistant at the brewery, **Desmond Finch**, demands that he make any decisions on behalf of the brewery, Mrs. Morden tells him that **Alex Kinloch** has power of attorney. After Finch has gone she asks Alex for written assurance that she won't be held liable for anything she does on his behalf. She persuades the brewery's creditors not to make the brewery bankrupt straight away.

Moreton, Max (*Dead Heat* 2007)

Michelin-starred chef Max Moreton runs, though doesn't own, **The Hay Net** restaurant on the outskirts of **Newmarket**. Max's father, an ex-steeplechase jockey turned trainer, was killed in a road accident when Max was eighteen. He does not have a close relationship with his mother, who is vague and uninterested in Max's life. Max had ridden as a child but had no wish to make it a career. After boarding school he had deferred a place at university to take a gap year. Working in the **Oxfordshire** restaurant of a distant relative, he found that he enjoyed the life and stayed on to learn the trade, becoming the chef there before his twenty-first birthday. When the restaurant was sold Max left and did the catering for dinner parties organized by his mother. At one of these he met **Mark Winsome**, a wealthy young entrepreneur, who offered to set him up in the restaurant business. Six years on, Max is running the successful Hay Net restaurant, which is popular with the town's racing fraternity.

At the time of receiving his Michelin star Max was the youngest chef ever to do so. Now he is no longer up-and-coming; he is an established, if minor, "celebrity chef." Max would like to have a family but has not had a lasting relationship, partly due to the anti-social hours of his job.

A serious outbreak of food poisoning at a function where the catering was provided by Max leads to his meeting professional musician **Caroline Aston**, one of the victims, who threatens to sue him for loss of earnings. Max arranges to meet her for dinner; he finds her attractive and, despite their unpromising start, a relationship begins to develop. Max believes that the food poisoning incident, which took place at **Newmarket racecourse**, is somehow connected with the planting of a bomb that rips through the guest boxes at the course the following day, causing death and destruction.

Max's efforts to restore his professional reputation and to get to the bottom of the racecourse bombing put his life in danger. When his car's brakes mysteriously fail he crashes into a coach in Newmarket and loses consciousness. Waking up in hospital, he is comforted to find Caroline at his bedside. After a second attempt on his life Max admits to being afraid, but he pursues his investigations and, somewhat improbably, tracks down the criminal responsible for the bombing.

Max accepts an offer from Mark Winsome to open a new restaurant in London's smart Mayfair district. He and Caroline become engaged to be married.

Morris, Alan (*Decider* 1993)

Alan is one of **Lee Morris**'s six sons. He is cheerful, extrovert and brave. After a pile-up at a fence during a steeplechase at **Stratton Park**, Alan runs out onto the course to help the fallen jockeys.

Morris, Amanda (*Decider* 1993)

Amanda is the wife of **Lee Morris** and the mother of his six sons. She is still cohabiting with Lee but is leading a separate life. She had married Lee at the age of nineteen and had wanted lots of babies; however, she and Lee had gradually grown apart, and now she found little in common with her husband. She is fed up with moving from one shell of a house to another while Lee renovates them; she is surprised and pleased when he tells her they won't be moving from a recently converted barn on the **Surrey-Sussex** border.

Amanda is alerted by a newspaper to the explosion at **Stratton Park racecourse**. She phones Lee to berate him for putting the children in danger, but shows scant concern for his well-being. She doesn't demand to see the children, having made her own plans for the weekend. Later, she phones again to ask Lee to look after the boys for another two days, but doesn't say why. When Lee comes home with the boys she tells him she has a married lover but is willing to stay with Lee for the sake of the children. That night she allows Lee to make love to her. She falls pregnant and subsequently gives birth to a seventh boy.

Morris, Cassie (*Twice Shy* 1981)

Cassie is **William Derry**'s girlfriend; she is tall, thin and independent. She lives with William in a cottage in **Six Mile Bottom**, near **Newmarket**, and works in an office in **Cambridge**. She goes to William's aid when a deranged thug breaks into their cottage and attacks William with a baseball bat. He breaks her arm, but she knocks him out with a coal scuttle. Cassie agrees, together with William and **Bananas Frisby**, to use **Liam O'Rorke**'s betting system occasionally in order to supplement their income.

Morris, Christopher (*Decider* 1993)

Christopher, at fourteen years old, is the eldest son of **Lee Morris**. Tall, fair and reserved, Christopher looks after his five brothers. When a fence on **Stratton Park racecourse** is deliberately burnt down Christopher suggests that firelighters could have been used, which later proves to be correct. When a circus tent on the racecourse, with Lee, **Neil Morris** and **Toby Morris** inside, is set alight, Christopher has the presence of mind to turn on the makeshift sprinkler system to dowse the fires.

Morris, Edward (*Decider* 1993)

Edward is one of **Lee Morris**'s six sons. He is quiet, but possessed of a vivid imagination and a rich internal life; he has invisible friends with whom he has conversations.

Morris, James (*Decider* 1993)

James is the infant son of **Lee Morris**.

Morris, Lee (*Decider* 1993)

In *Decider* Francis develops a device begun tentatively in *Driving Force* (1992), that of using children in the plot. He certainly embraces the theme enthusiastically, given that Lee Morris and his wife **Amanda** have six children, all boys. Fatherhood adds an extra dimension to Lee's character; it makes him more human, more rounded and extends his range of motivations. Lee's problematic relationship with Amanda broadens the background further. His very weaknesses strengthen him as a character and contrast with his more admirable traits.

For years Lee, an architect and builder, and Amanda struggled financially, living in the houses he was renovating and moving on to the next after it was sold. Gradually they became better off but, ironically, their pleasure in each other's company dwindled at the same rate. They had met as students and married young. Amanda had developed a hunger for babies; but now that Lee had served his biological function Amanda had lost interest in him. They still share a bed, but nothing exciting goes on in it. Another man might have raised objections but, by his own admission, Lee is "too lazy to fight ... too placid." Lethargic is how Amanda describes him, and it's clear that she isn't really bothered whether the marriage survives or not.

The manager and the clerk of **Stratton Park racecourse** ask Lee to use voting shares he'd inherited from his late mother—who had been married to **Keith Stratton**, brother of **Lord Conrad Stratton**—to help stop the racecourse from being sold for building land. When Lee becomes embroiled in the feuding of his mother's relatives, both he and his children are exposed to danger. Lee is instrumental in resolving the uncertain future of

Stratton Park racecourse, but there is no such clear-cut resolution to the muddle that is Lee's marriage. Lee himself doesn't know his own mind. A few days previously he'd been wishing for a reconciliation with Amanda; then he meets an eighteen-year-old girl who reminds him so strongly of his wife when she was young that he would have taken her to bed if given half a chance. Amanda tells Lee she has a lover, but she's willing to stay married to him for the children's sake. Take it or leave it, she says. Lee, ever the pacifist, takes it. Feeling broody again, Amanda lets him make love to her, and in due course their seventh son is born.

Morris, Mrs. (*Risk* 1977)

Mrs. Morris lives near **Newbury, Berkshire,** in a cottage next door to **Roland Britten.** She is small, stout and elderly. She is suspicious when she hears noises in Roland's house while he is away, and goes to investigate. She finds three men there, who say they are Roland's friends and are waiting for him to return. Bravely, she tells them they shouldn't be in the house and to wait outside.

Morris, Neil (*Decider* 1993)

Neil, shy and cerebral, is the seven-year-old son of **Lee Morris.** While playing hide and seek in the stands at **Stratton Park racecourse,** he notices something he thinks is odd. He runs to tell his father, who uses the public address system to call his sons down from the stands.

Neil is lured into the circus tent on the racecourse by a villain who threatens to kill him. Neil is saved when **Toby Morris** knocks the man off balance, and he is rescued by Lee.

Morris, Toby (*Decider* 1993)

Toby is the twelve-year-old son of architect **Lee Morris.** His behavior has been of concern to Lee over the years; he is a natural rebel, awkward and obstinate. Lee fears that he will become a difficult teenager who will get into trouble.

Playing hide and seek in the stands of **Stratton Park racecourse,** Toby does not respond to his father's urgent warning over the public address system to leave the stands. He is found by his father hiding at the top of the stands, but they don't have time to get down before the stands explode. Toby, shielded by Lee's body, survives the explosion without injury. Afterwards he is subdued and thoughtful.

Toby goes reluctantly to the Easter Monday race meeting at Stratton Park. There he sees his brother,

Neil Morris, and his father in great danger. He launches himself at a villain who is holding Neil and, catching him unawares, knocks him off balance. This gives Lee the opportunity to save both Neil and Toby.

Morrison, Arthur (*Field of 13* 1998: "Carrot for a Chestnut")

Racehorse trainer Arthur Morrison is good at his job, and puts a higher value on success than on popularity. He has prepared his best horse, a chestnut steeplechaser, to win a big race at **Cheltenham.** When he is saddling up the chestnut before the race Morrison is concerned that the horse lacks its usual sparkle. Ridden by Morrison's son, **Toddy Morrison,** the horse falls at the first fence. He gets up but gallops blindly into the rails, and injures himself so badly that he has to be destroyed. In the next race Morrison's younger son, **Chick Morrison,** has a fall and crushes his spinal cord. Morrison, visiting Chick in hospital, is unaware that Chick knows why his father's chestnut had fallen.

Morrison, Chick (*Field of 13* 1998: "Carrot for a Chestnut")

Chick Morrison is a nineteen-year-old stable lad; he gets occasional rides as a jump jockey, though he is nowhere near as talented as he thinks he is. He lacks any clear moral code, and is inclined to blame anyone but himself if something goes wrong. That afternoon at **Cheltenham,** Chick's brother, **Toddy Morrison,** takes a horrendous fall at the first fence from a horse trained by his father. Toddy is not seriously injured but the horse, getting to its feet and racing on blindly, crashes into the rails and is so badly injured that it has to be put down. Chick knows why the horse had fallen but refuses to accept any responsibility for the horse's death. He takes a spare ride in the next race, a novice hurdle. Unable to concentrate, he gives his horse no help at the hurdles and takes a bad fall, crushing his spinal cord. He wakes up in hospital, his head and neck encased in plaster.

Morrison, Toddy *Field of 13* 1998: "Carrot for a Chestnut")

Steeplechase jockey Toddy Morrison is the son of trainer **Arthur Morrison.** In his late twenties, Toddy is good-natured, strong-minded and independent. He rides his father's best horse, a chestnut, in a big steeplechase at **Cheltenham.** However, the horse falls at the first fence and rolls on

Toddy, who is knocked unconscious. Toddy, though, recovers quickly and is able to walk away.

Morse, David (*Break In* 1985)

Morse is the head of the legal department at the *Daily Flag*, a national newspaper published in **Fleet Street**, London. He phones **Kit Fielding**, offering him a large sum of money to stop a horse. Later, when Kit meets Morse in the *Flag's* offices, he recognizes Morse's voice and tells him that his attempt to bribe him was unconvincing.

Morton, Luke-John (*Forfeit* 1968)

Morton, the Sports Editor on the *Sunday Blaze* newspaper, lives for his job; the needs of the newspaper always come first. He has no compunction about inconveniencing his reporters if it will benefit *The Blaze*. Morton is delighted with **James Tyrone**'s article on non-starting ante-post favorites, and has it cleared by the newspaper's libel lawyer. He readily endorses James's suggestion that *The Blaze* should guarantee that **Tiddely-Pom**, favorite for the Lamplighter Gold Cup at **Heathbury Park**, will run in the race. Thinking that James's follow-up article lacks "bite," Morton makes him spice it up, oblivious of the danger he's putting James in.

Morton, Mr. (*Reflex* 1980)

Morton, a racehorse trainer, had run a "ringer" in place of his horse **Amber Globe** at **Southwell** races. The ringer lost; Amber Globe subsequently won a race at **Fontwell Park** three months later.

Munnings, Alfred (*In the Frame* 1976)

Alfred Munnings was a celebrated English equestrian artist who was born in 1878 and died in 1959. He was brash and eccentric, but a brilliant painter of horses—from gypsies' ponies to Classic thoroughbreds—and of the English countryside. In *In the Frame* (1976), both **Donald Stuart** and **Maisie Matthews**, while in Australia, had bought paintings which they thought were by Munnings but were in fact expert copies.

Murder

Francis's novels contain many graphic accounts of murders and attempted murders. His description of violent crime is one of the strengths of his writing, and the death of amateur jockey **Bill Davidson** in Francis's first book *Dead Cert*, sets a high standard. Davidson's horse, winning a steeplechase with ease, is deliberately brought down. Crushed beneath half a ton of thoroughbred, Davidson dies in hospital of internal injuries.

Whilst guns, knives and blunt instruments figure prominently as weapons of choice, the murders are often, like Davidson's, out of the ordinary. In *Proof* (1984), a tale of theft and fraud in the wine trade, a villain who knows too much has a wet plaster of Paris bandage wrapped around his head, causing him to suffocate. In *Twice Shy* (1981), a man wrongly thought to have a computerized betting system is shot in both feet and left to bleed to death. An embezzler in *To the Hilt* (1996) meets an excruciating end when forced to lie on a hot barbecue grill. The shock and pain of doing so stops his heart. Technically manslaughter rather than murder, perhaps, but the distinction is lost on the victim. A similar legal nicety might be argued about the way policeman **Paul Cratchet** meets his death in *Shattered* (2000). He is in the workshop of glass-blower Gerard Logan when he is struck in the neck with a punty iron loaded with molten glass.

One murder that poses a moral dilemma is that of a psychopath in *Flying Finish* (1966). That he deserved his fate is easy to accept; he had shot two men in cold blood and had planned a horrific death for a third. His intended victim, however, turns the tables. He waits until the villain realizes what is about to happen to him before he shoots him dead. The reader's sympathies may be with the psychopath's killer, but it is still murder.

N

Nader, Aziz (*Driving Force* 1992)

Aziz Nader is in his late twenties and of Lebanese origin. He was raised in Quebec, and is a Canadian citizen. He speaks Arabic and French. He successfully applies for a horse van driver's job at **Croft Raceways** horse transport firm. He is disappointed with the first job that **Freddie Croft** gives him, to collect some old racehorses from **Yorkshire**. Freddie is not sure he believes Nader's assurances that he has driven racehorses before. Nader mildly flirts with **Lorna Watermead**, strengthening Freddie's suspicions that he is a jack-the-lad. He phones Freddie to tell him he doesn't think that the old horses he is transporting for **John Tigwood** are fit to travel.

When **Nina Young** phones Nader from France, Freddie finally realizes that Nader is using his driving job as a cover.

Nagle, Orinda (*10 lb. Penalty* 1997)

Orinda is the widow of recently deceased Dennis Nagle, Member of Parliament for **Hoopwestern, Dorset**. She is furious that she has been passed over for selection to fight the by-election caused by her husband's death in favor of **George Juliard**. At a political meeting in the constituency, Orinda is scathing about Juliard's lack of political experience. She is annoyed and hostile when, as a fellow-guest of the Stewards at **Dorset County** races, she is looked after by **Benedict Juliard**, who had wanted an opportunity to talk to her. She tells Benedict that she, not his father, should be the next Hoopwestern Member of Parliament.

She doesn't believe that George Juliard was shot at, thinking it to have been a publicity stunt. However, after Benedict and George escape the blazing constituency offices, she tells Benedict that she intends to support his father. She claims, somewhat implausibly, that Benedict has shown her how to deal with disappointment. While out canvassing with the Juliards, Orinda is physically assaulted. She is saved by Benedict from being run over by a truck when she stumbles into the road.

The Nagrebbs (*Comeback* 1991)

The Nagrebbs are a show jumping family. A horse of theirs had died in mysterious circumstances after a routine operation carried out by **Ken McClure**. The father, according to McClure's mother, **Josephine McClure**, had been in trouble for cruelty to his show jumpers. A second horse of the Nagrebbs' had to be destroyed by McClure after he diagnosed acute laminitis. **Peter Darwin** asks the Nagrebbs about the deaths; the son punches Peter in the stomach, and the father warns Peter not to come back. Subsequently Peter's suspicions about the family prove to have a strong foundation.

Nancy (*The Edge* 1988)

Nancy is a friend of **Bill Baudelaire**'s daughter Clarrie. At **Winnipeg** racetrack Nancy acts as a messenger for **Tor Kelsey**, taking water samples from horses' water buckets to Baudelaire for analysis. The next day, she delivers an undeveloped film to Baudelaire.

Nanterre, Henri (*Bolt* 1986)

For over a hundred years the Nanterre family have run a road construction company in France in partnership with the family of **M. Roland de Brescou**. The current representative of the Nan-terres, Henri, is a bad lot. He wants to make money quickly, and sees the manufacture and export of weapons as the way to do it. This, however, is a trade which M. de Brescou, the ancient and venerable head of the de Brescou family, considers dishonorable.

Nanterre is in his mid-thirties and has a domineering manner. Since inheriting his half of the company three years before he has sacked the auditors and appointed new ones, and dismissed many of the managerial staff. Now, in order to achieve his goal, he directs the force of his unpleasant character against **Princess Casilia**, the wife of M. de Brescou, and **Danielle de Brescou**, the Princess's pretty young niece. **Kit Fielding**, the Princess's jockey and friend, does all he can to protect them. Eventually he finds a way to neutralize the threat that Nanterre poses.

The Nantuckets (*Risk* 1977)

The Nantuckets, a rich American family, are the owners of **Axwood Stables Ltd.**, near **Newbury, Berkshire**. The yard was established by tycoon Naylor Nantucket, now deceased. The family continues to employ Naylor's salaried trainer, **William Finch**, but they take little interest in the horses and never visit the yard. This gives Finch the opportunity to follow his own agenda.

Nantwich, Joe (*Dead Cert* 1962)

Jump jockey Joe Nantwich is young, immature and dishonest; he is also a moaner. He complains to **Alan York** that **Sandy Mason** had put him over the rails at **Plumpton racecourse**. Nantwich is terrified when he gets anonymous, threatening notes. Soon afterwards Nantwich's worst fears are realized.

Natasha (*Trial Run* 1978)

Natasha is one of two Russian guides provided by **Intourist** for **Randall Drew**. She is attractive, but is intent only on acting as a chaperone. When Randall says he is planning to visit the Lenin museum she is pleased that he appears to be toeing the official tourist line. However, Natasha and her colleague **Anna** have their work cut out to prevent Randall from disappearing without telling them where he is going.

National Hunt

This term applies to racing which takes place, mostly over jumps, on commercial racetracks in Great Britain and Ireland. The obstacles are either hurdles or fences, and the horses known as hurdlers or (steeple)chasers. The sport of steeplechasing developed in the nineteenth century from the practice of gentlemen riders racing across country between the steeples of two churches.

There are two other types of National Hunt racing: Hunter Chases, which are weight-for-age steeplechases for good horses that have been hunted behind a pack of foxhounds in the current season and ridden by amateur riders; and National Hunt Flat races, or Bumpers, which aim to give racecourse experience to potential young hurdlers and chasers.

National Hunt Committee

This was the body in charge of the administration and regulation of racing under **National Hunt** rules until amalgamating with the **Jockey Club** in 1969. In turn, the Jockey Club was superseded by the **British Horseracing Board** in 1993.

Naylor, David (*Proof* 1984)

David is the son of **Stewart Naylor**. He is a friend of **Kenneth Charter Jnr.**; he and Charter are both keen on war gaming.

Naylor, Stewart (*Proof* 1984)

Stewart Naylor, also known as **Paul Young**, is the short, pugnacious, middle-aged owner of a bottling plant in Ealing, a suburb of North London. The business isn't making any money until Naylor decides to circumvent the law in order to boost the profits. Much of the money made illegally is laundered via the bloodstock market. **Larry Trent**, Naylor's half-brother and a good judge of horseflesh, buys horses at the sales and exports them abroad where they are sold at a profit.

Recently Naylor has spotted an ideal opportunity to expand his illicit operations. But things start to go wrong when Trent is killed by a runaway horse van at a garden party at the home of his racehorse trainer. The police, aided by local wine merchant **Tony Beach**, close in on Naylor, who adopts extreme measures in order to avoid detection.

Nerrity, Dominic (*The Danger* 1983)

Dominic is the three-year-old son of **John** and **Miranda Nerrity**, owners of **Epsom** Derby winner **Ordinand**. He is kidnapped while playing on the beach at **West Wittering, Sussex**. After being rescued by **Tony Vine**, Dominic reverts temporarily to babyhood—wanting his bottle, and clinging to his mother. Out of the blue, he hums "Il Tra-

vatore" and says "Ciao, bambino." This helps Andrew to identify the kidnapper. Dominic wakes up crying every night; a doctor recommended by Andrew gives him something to help him sleep.

Nerrity, John (*The Danger* 1983)

John Nerrity is the father of **Dominic Nerrity**, and the owner of **Epsom** Derby winner **Ordinand**. He had married Miranda, his former secretary, who is much younger than he is, and he is beginning to see it as a mistake. He lives in a large house on the edge of a golf course near Sutton, **Surrey**. Nerrity says he won't pay the £5 million ransom demand for his kidnapped son; his wholesale import business is in trouble, and he is selling Ordinand to clear his debts and start again. He says he can't afford to hire **Liberty Market Ltd. Andrew Douglas** thinks that it more likely a case of not loving his son enough; Nerrity complains that his wife had persuaded him to have the child because she was lonely. When **Tony Vine** and Andrew deliver Dominic safely to his house, Nerrity is grudgingly grateful.

Nerrity, Miranda (*The Danger* 1983)

Miranda is the former secretary and now wife of **John Nerrity**. She is blonde and in her mid-twenties. Her three-year-old son is kidnapped whilst on holiday in **West Wittering** near **Brighton**. Distressed, she explains to **Andrew Douglas** how **Dominic Nerrity** was taken when her attention was diverted by a boat burning on the beach. Her husband, who treats her with neither love nor respect, blames her lack of vigilance for the kidnap. Miranda is looked after by **Alessia Cenci** during the period of her son's kidnap; when he is rescued by **Tony Vine** and Andrew Douglas she is speechless with relief and gratitude. Later, however, Miranda is miserable because she is not getting on with her husband, and exhausted because Dominic is waking up crying every night. She goes to stay in **Lambourn**, close to Alessia.

Nerve (1964)

When a well-respected jockey takes his own life in the paddock at **Dunstable** races, the incident highlights a nebulous undercurrent of bad feeling and mistrust within the racing world. But for fellow-jockey **Rob Finn**, the tone-deaf son of musical parents and thus something of a disappointment to them, things seem to be looking up. He wins on an apparent no-hoper for top trainer **James Axminster**, which results in his being offered rides at other meetings. Rob is introduced to television personality **Maurice Kemp-Lore**, who invites Rob to appear on his TV show as an example of a jockey on the fringe of success. However, another of the guests is hostile towards Rob, who is obliged to make an impassioned defense of race-riding for its own sake.

Initially Rob's career prospers, but soon his luck changes. Every horse he rides over the next few weeks runs badly, and rumors begin to spread that Rob has lost his nerve. James Axminster, under pressure from his owners, puts other jockeys up on his horses. Rob is depressed, but he is certain that he is not to blame for his mounts running below form. He has a strong suspicion about who is behind this disaster, and how it has been engineered.

At **Stratford** races Rob rides a novice chaser which he knows is fit and well. He gives the horse a risky, almost reckless, ride, and would have won but for falling at the last fence. Everyone watching is convinced that Rob hasn't lost his nerve. Soon afterwards an unsuccessful attempt is made to incapacitate Rob permanently. Rob's recovery from the physical discomfort he suffers is speeded up by the solicitations of his cousin **Joanna**. Rob's emotional pain is almost as bad; his love for his cousin is, as always, unreciprocated owing to the closeness of their familial relationship.

Rob collects evidence of the suspect's involvement in ruining the careers of other jockeys. Then he hatches a plan to stop the villain once and for all. Again Joanna is there to lend a hand, and at last she realizes that she can't live without Rob any longer, cousins or not.

Nerve is a penetrating study of how one man deals with adversity; how he stands up to the constant psychological pressure of having his most precious possession—his courage as a jockey—systematically denigrated.Parallel with Rob Finn's mental anguish, Francis portrays the workings of a tortured mind driven to criminality by feelings of inadequacy, envy and spite. The villain is complex yet pitiable, and *Nerve* succeeds as an absorbing story of how two men are shaped by their past.

Nestegg (*Knock Down* 1974)

Nestegg was a stallion bought by **Vic Vincent** for a client for £10,000. Vincent was left with Nestegg when the client died suddenly. Realizing that Nestegg was incubating tetanus, he hatched a plan to make a healthy profit from the situation.

New Forest, England

The New Forest is a mixture of woodland, heathland and pasture land covering an area of almost 300 square kilometres in southern England. The New Forest is mostly in south-west **Hampshire**, but also in South **Wiltshire** and East **Dorset**. In 2005 much of the area was designated as a National Park. Towns and villages in or near the New Forest include Lyndhurst, Fordingbridge and **Lymington**.

Come to Grief (1995): A body is found in a car in the New Forest.

Newbury, Berkshire

Newbury is the main town in the west of **Berkshire**, a county lying to the west of London. The town is situated on the River Kennett and the Kennett and Avon Canal. It has a population of around 32,000 people. **Newbury racecourse** is one of the finest in the United Kingdom.

Risk (1977): **Roland Britten** is a partner in a firm of accountants in Newbury. **Axwood Stables Ltd.** are situated to the south-west of Newbury.

Straight (1989): Jockey **Derek Franklin** stays at the **Chequers Hotel** in Newbury, where he plays the micro-cassettes that he'd found in his late brother **Greville**'s house.

Driving Force (1992): **Kevin Keith Ogden** is hired to transport a thermos flask from **Pontefract** to Chieveley Service Station, near Newbury.

Newbury racecourse

Newbury racecourse is situated in the county of **Berkshire**, west of London. It is a flat, two mile circuit which stages top class racing, both Flat and **National Hunt**. The fences are stiff and beautifully presented, and the course is popular with racing's professionals. In recent years the paying customer has been well provided for, with a new Tattersall's stand and good bars, cafés and restaurants.

High Stakes (1975): Toy maker **Steven Scott**'s horse **Dial**, trained by **Rupert Ramsey**, wins a hurdle race at Newbury.

Reflex (1980): Jockey **Philip Nore** wins a valuable two mile chase on **Sharpener**. At another race meeting film director **Lance Kinship**, at Newbury racecourse to film an advertisement, sees Philip with his camera. He asks Philip to take photos of him and his crew at work. Philip takes a heavy fall from one of **Harold Osborne**'s hurdlers.

Banker (1982): At Newbury races merchant banker **Tim Ekaterin** recognizes the boy who had attacked equine healer **Calder Jackson**. **Fred**

Barnet's gelding **Zoomalong** finishes third in a hurdle race.

Bolt (1986): Champion jump jockey **Kit Fielding** wins a race at Newbury for owner **Princess Casilia**, giving her horse, **Cascade**, a hard ride. Meeting the Princess after racing, he finds her in a shocked state after a confrontation with Frenchman **Henri Nanterre**. On the second day of the Newbury meeting Kit wins on the Princess's brilliant novice hurdler, **Kinley**.

Straight (1989): After an attempt on his life **Derek Franklin** stays in **The Chequers Hotel** in Newbury.

Under Orders (2006): At Newbury **Andrew Woodward** asks for **Sid Halley**'s opinion of **Juliet Burns**, who has applied for an assistant trainer's job with him. **Peter Enstone** rides a ten-to-one winner. Sid has a drink with racing historian **Paddy O'Fitch**, who tells Sid about the relationship between **Lord Enstone** and **George Lochs**.

Newcastle racecourse

Racing at Newcastle, in the north-east of England, takes place at Gosforth Park racecourse, three miles to the north of the city. The course provides a good standard of racing under both codes. The one mile six furlong circuit favors resolute gallopers.

Forfeit (1968): At Newcastle races **Jockey Club** handicapper **Major Colly Gibbons** asks **James Tyrone** if he will swap his train ticket for Gibbons' plane ticket, since he has to attend a meeting at the course and will miss his plane.

Newmarket Bloodstock Sales

The first bloodstock sales were founded in Newmarket by auctioneer Richard Tattersall in 1766. Today Tattersalls run regular sales both in Newmarket and at Fairyhouse in Ireland, offering for sale up to 10,000 horses a year. Tattersalls have sold many Classic winners, as well as top class two-year-olds, broodmares and **National Hunt** horses, and are considered the leading auctioneers in Europe. The famous October Yearling Sale comprises the very best of Europe's young thoroughbreds, and is backed up by the Autumn Horses in Training Sale, the Breeze-Up Sale of two-year-olds in training and the July Sale of horses in training and breeding stock.

Knock Down (1974): Bloodstock agent **Jonah Dereham**, ignoring a warning from rival agents, buys **Antonia Huntercombe**'s yearling for 2000 guineas. He pays 11,000 guineas (though Francis says pounds) for a filly for client **Eddy Ingram**. He advises fellow-agent **Pauli Teksa** not to bid for a colt, alleged to be by a leading sire, whose parentage is doubtful.

Jonah buys a filly consigned by an Irish stud cheaply, despite being warned not to bid for her by rival agents. Client Eddy Ingram, however, refuses to take her.

Hot Money (1987): **Ian Pembroke** meets his father **Malcolm Pembroke** at Newmarket Sales. Despite knowing nothing about racing, Malcolm buys a colt for £2 million. As they are leaving the Sales a car tries to run Malcolm down.

Newmarket/Newmarket racecourse

The racing town of Newmarket is situated in the county of **Suffolk** in East Anglia. It boasts two of the finest Flat courses in Britain: the Rowley Mile and the July courses. Major races staged here include the first two Classics of the season, the One Thousand Guineas and the Two Thousand Guineas. Other important races are the Cesarewitch, the Cambridgeshire, the Craven Stakes, the Middle Park Stakes and the Dewhurst Stakes.

The two courses, which intersect and are separated by a medieval dyke, were constructed in the later years of the eighteenth century and viewing is somewhat restricted. This disadvantage is offset by the marvelous ambience of the winner's enclosure and weighing room area with its thatched roof and beautifully-tended lawns and flowerbeds.

Bonecrack (1971): **Neil Griffon** is working on the accounts at his father's Newmarket racing stables when two armed men burst in and abduct him. Apprentice jockey **Alessandro Rivera** rides a good race to win on **Lancat** at Newmarket.

Knock Down (1974): A colt belonging to owner **Wilton Young** beats another owned by rival **Constantine Brevett** in the day's big race at Newmarket.

Break In (1985): **Holly Allardeck**, twin sister of champion steeplechase jockey **Kit Fielding**, lives in Newmarket, where husband **Bobby Allardeck** is a racehorse trainer.

Wild Horses (1994): Director **Thomas Lyon** makes a film in Newmarket based on a crime committed in the racing world twenty-five years before.

Second Wind (1999): Meteorologist **Perry Stuart** and **Kris Ironside** fly in Kris's plane to have Sunday lunch at Newmarket with racehorse owner **Caspar Harvey**.

Dead Heat (2007): Chef **Max Moreton** runs

The Hay Net, a Newmarket restaurant popular with the town's racing fraternity. Many of the characters in *Dead Heat* live and work in Newmarket, and much of the action takes place in and around the town and its racecourse.

Newmarket racecourse, South Africa

Situated in Alberton, near Johannesburg, Newmarket racecourse is a right-handed turf track, and is considered to be one of the fairest tests of a racehorse in South Africa, giving a chance to both front runners and hold-up horses.

Smokescreen (1972): Film actor **Edward Lincoln**, in South Africa to investigate why his godmother's horses are running badly, goes to Newmarket races, where he meets her nephew, **Danilo Cavesey**.

Newton, Mrs. Audrey (*To the Hilt* 1996)

Mrs. Newton is the sister of **Norman Quorn**. She lives in Bloxham, **Oxfordshire**. She is given a list of names and numbers by her brother to look after. She passes on the list to **Lady Westering**. Mrs. Newton is persuaded by **Alex Kinloch**—who fears for her safety—to go away with Lady Westering and **Emily Jane Cox** for a few days to Paignton, **Devon**.

Newton Abbot racecourse

Newton Abbot is a jumping track near the seaside town of Teignmouth in **Devon**, south-west England. The course is flat with good viewing from the stands. It provides racing of a moderate nature but is popular with holidaymakers.

Bolt (1986): **Bernina**, a hurdler owned by **Princess Casilia** and ridden by **Kit Fielding**, wins a race at Newton Abbot.

Newtonnards, George (*Enquiry* 1969)

Newtonnards, a racecourse bookmaker, is at **Oxford** races on the day of the Lemonfizz Crystal Cup. Called as a witness at the enquiry into the race, Newtonnards says that an anonymous punter had backed the winner, **Cherry Pie**, to win £900, and that he'd seen the same punter talking to trainer **Dexter Cranfield** before the race.

He is not pleased to see **Kelly Hughes** at the front door of his home in Mill Hill, north-west London. However, he is forced to listen when Kelly parks his car across the entrance to his drive. Despite Kelly's denial, Newtonnards believes that he stopped **Squelsh** from winning. He advises

Kelly just to accept that he was caught and to take his punishment.

After Kelly gets his license back he phones Newtonnards and asks him if he will ask the bookmakers he told about Cranfield backing Cherry Pie if they can remember whom they told. Newtonnards says he'll see what he can do; in return, he asks Kelly to let him know when one of his rides is not fit or is unlikely to win.

Nigel (*Banker* 1982)

Nigel is a stud groom on **Oliver Knowles'** stud farm in **Hertfordshire**. He is promoted to stud manager after the purchase of the stallion **Sandcastle**. Nigel is helping **Lenny**, a groom, to move Sandcastle from his box to a paddock when he makes a sudden movement, causing the horse to rear and escape from Lenny's grasp. Knowles overlooks Nigel's occasional excessive drinking because he is good with the mares.

Nigel (*Break In* 1985)

Nigel is **Bobby Allardeck's** long-serving head lad. He is worried when, checking on the horses after leaving the pub, he finds that **Sooty**, one of the horses owned by **Jermyn Graves**, is not in his box. He is relieved when Allardeck tells him he had moved the horse to another box.

Nigel (*Driving Force* 1992)

Nigel is a driver with **Croft Raceway** horse transport firm. Young, fit and irreverent, he spends his free time chasing women. He is fancied by **Tessa Watermead**, who wants to go with him in a horse van to deliver some horses; Nigel, however, refuses. He is sent to France with **Nina Young** to collect **Jericho Rich's** daughter's horse.

"Nightmare" (*Field of 13* 1998)

Successful horse feed salesman **Martin Retsov** is haunted by a dark secret, and his nights are troubled by a recurring nightmare. When Retsov decides to revert to his previous criminal behavior he recruits a young hitchhiker to help him. But the young man triggers unpleasant memories for Retsov, and then provides him with an even more disagreeable reality check.

Noble, Gerry (*Under Orders* 2006)

Noble, a betting shop punter; recognizes **Sid Halley** when Sid comes into the shop. He discusses his betting habits with Sid.

Noland, Mike (*The Danger* 1983)

Noland is a **Lambourn** trainer for whom **Alessia Cenci** often rode when in England. After Alessia's rescue Noland, meeting her at **Brighton** races, tells her to come and ride out for him.

Nore, Amanda (*Reflex* 1980)

Amanda Nore is also known as **Mandy North**. **Philip Nore**, her half-brother, tracks her down to a religious sect, the Colleagues of Supreme Grace, based near Horley, **Surrey**. Philip is unable to see a resemblance between her and himself. She appears simple and immature, with expressionless eyes. Collecting on the street for the Colleagues, she sells Philip a polished stone. She is rebuked by other members of the sect for talking to Philip, and told she won't be allowed to collect again.

Nore, Caroline (*Reflex* 1980)

Caroline Nore, now deceased, was the mother of **Philip Nore**. She had been a pretty young woman but had completely messed up her life with drugs and had been an irresponsible mother. She had left Philip, as a boy, with a succession of friends to be brought up. She also had a daughter, **Amanda Nore**, by a different father. She had died as a result of her heroin addiction.

Nore, James (*Reflex* 1980)

James is the son of **Lavinia Nore** and the uncle of **Philip Nore**; Philip has never met James before, but goes to see him in London to find out why James has been disinherited. Angrily he tells Philip that it is because he is a homosexual and will therefore have no descendants. He is rude about his mother and Philip. He offers Philip money if he can prove that **Amanda Nore** is dead.

Nore, Mrs. Lavinia (*Reflex* 1980)

Lavinia Nore is **Philip Nore's** seventy-eight-year-old grandmother. Philip had never met her until she summoned him to her nursing home. She offers Philip £100,000 to find his half-sister, whom he hadn't known existed. She thinks Philip came only because of the money, but Philip hadn't been told about it, only that Mrs. Nore was dying. Philip's mother, **Caroline Nore**, had described Mrs. Nore to Philip, as a child, in unflattering terms; Caroline had written to her mother asking for an allowance to help some friends of hers to bring up her daughter, **Amanda Nore**, but Mrs. Nore had not replied to Caroline's letter.

Philip refuses the money that Mrs. Nore is offering, so she says that Amanda can have it if Philip finds her. To persuade him to cooperate she says she will tell Philip who his father is if he looks for Amanda. She tells Philip that she hated his father, who had been her lover but had made her daughter—Philip's mother—pregnant when she was seventeen.

Close to death, Mrs. Nore asks Philip if he's brought Amanda to see her but Philip says that "she's lost." In her will she leaves half her estate to her son whom she despised for not having given her a grandchild to continue her genes. The other half she leaves to Philip.

Nore, Philip (*Reflex* 1980)

Philip Nore is an interesting man with a fascinating past. Nowadays he's a half-decent jump jockey, no longer completely in love with the game, a bit tired of the petty corruptions inherent in racing, but realistic enough to accept that life isn't perfect. Considering his start in life, he knows he's done pretty well to forge any sort of career at all. Philip had never known who his father was, and life with his feckless, unstable mother was rootless and chaotic. Without a permanent home, Philip was farmed out to stoical friends for months, even years, on end while his mother pursued her own dubious agenda, which included ingesting as many chemical substances as she could lay her hands on. Philip, whose guardians could never be sure how long he was going to be with them, never attended school on a regular basis. When he was twelve he fetched up with a pair of kindly, gay photographers; at fifteen he was left with a **Hampshire** racehorse trainer, and after that he never saw his mother again. For a year or two he received a card on his birthday, a present at Christmas; and then nothing. Philip guessed she must have died of an overdose, but he had no way of knowing for sure.

So Philip got on with his life without complaint and, since he had learned to ride racehorses, becoming a jockey seemed a sensible move. By his own admission Philip is not a driven man, happy to finish the season in the top twenty on the jockeys' list. The fact that he can't ride at much less than eleven stones restricts his rides. He is considered a good horseman but not the strongest in a finish.

Unfortunately for Philip his duties as a stable jockey include stopping horses when he is required to do so by the trainer who employs him. Francis is sound on the compromises forced on a journeyman jockey. For every rider that refuses to stop a horse there is another who will do it simply to survive. Up till now Philip has accepted the trainer's demands; of late, though, being told that his mount is not trying is making Philip angry, a reaction which, for him, is out of character. He is reaching a turning point in his life; after a routine but painful fall at **Sandown Park** he wonders, for the first time, if there might not be an easier way to pay the rent. In his personal life, too, Philip is made to confront hitherto unacknowledged feelings when his autocratic grandmother, whom he'd never met, demands to see him; she wants to enlist his help in tracing **Amanda Nore**, the half-sister he never knew he had. Philip refuses to be either bullied or bribed, but is curious nonetheless.

Philip tells the trainer he works for that he isn't going to stop any more horses and accepts that, sooner or later, he's going to have to find another way of earning his living. Luckily there's something else he can do: he can take photographs. His guardians, **Charlie** and **Duncan**, had taken the time to nurture Philip's interest in photography, and he'd proved an able pupil. All through his riding career Philip had snapped away and now, facing up to a sea-change in his life, he contemplates a future behind a lens rather than in the saddle.

Meanwhile, Philip finally succumbs to his grandmother's inducements. She says that, if he looks for Amanda, she will tell him who his father is. This is a deal Philip can't ignore, but he would probably rather have been spared the ghastly details. Daddy, it turns out, was his grandmother's lover, which explains her tetchiness towards him. Eventually Philip tracks Amanda to a hippie-type commune, but he doesn't tell his grandmother.

Philip puts his knowledge of photography to good use when the suspicious death of a racecourse photographer lays bare a catalogue of crime within the racing community. Philip's involvement makes him a target for the villains seeking to gain possession of the incriminating evidence. After Philip is beaten up he recuperates at the house of **Samantha Bergen**, whom he had lived with on several occasions as a child. Samantha's daughter, **Clare Bergen**, who works in publishing, is selling Philip's photos on his behalf. Up to this point in his life Philip had deliberately avoided commitment; but when Clare goes with him to the races he is surprised at the satisfaction he feels at having a girl waiting for him at the weighing room door. They stay in a pub together, and afterwards, returning to his cottage alone does not hold quite

the same appeal as before. Philip asks Clare to live with him, and she agrees. Musing on the recent changes in his life, Philip is glad that he'd agreed to look for Amanda. It had put him in touch with his family, rum crew though they were. Re-establishing contact with Samantha had given him "a feeling of continuity, of belonging ... I had roots." Committing himself to Clare makes it easier for Philip to come to another life-changing decision; at the end of the jumping season he would retire from racing and become a photographer.

Norfolk, England

Norfolk is a largely flat, rural county in the East Anglia region of England. It is famous for its wetlands and inland waterways, known as The Broads. It has a picturesque coastline, most of which is designated an Area of Outstanding Natural Beauty.

Twice Shy (1981): **Donna Keithley**, a childless friend of **Jonathan Derry**'s wife, **Sarah Derry**, steals a baby and drives to the coast of North Norfolk. She abandons the car and baby and is later found sitting on the beach.

Wild Horses (1994): Film director **Thomas Lyon** goes to the North Norfolk coast to plan a shoot of wild horses running on the beach. Later, he returns to shoot the scene.

Norse, Trevor (*Enquiry* 1969)

Racehorse trainer Trevor Norse is better with his owners than with his horses; he is extremely hard to please from a jockey's point of view. When he sees **Kelly Hughes** at the Jockeys' Fund dance he demands to know why he's there, clearly believing that Kelly should not have shown his face after losing his license to ride.

North, Ronnie (*Knock Down* 1974)

Bloodstock dealer Ronnie North, in the estimation of **Jonah Dereham**, is trustworthy only so far as his judgment of a horse is concerned. Though amiable enough, North is determined to make the maximum possible profit from every deal. Asked by Jonah to find a replacement horse for **Hearse Puller**, he offers **River God** and demands a £500 commission on top of his profit, eventually settling for £250. At **Newmarket Sales** Jonah asks North to start the bidding for **Antonia Huntercombe**'s chestnut yearling colt. North checks with bloodstock agent **Vic Vincent**, who tells him not to bid.

North Face (*Break In* 1985)

North Face is a ten-year-old steeplechaser owned by **Princess Casilia** and trained by **Wykeham Harlow**. A liver chestnut, North Face would win no prizes in the show ring. He is ill-tempered, awkward and has his own ideas about the game; however, he is a brilliant jumper, tough, sound and the winner of thirty-eight races. He is in a foul mood during the *Sunday Towncrier* Trophy at **Cheltenham** and tails himself off; finally consenting to race for regular jockey **Kit Fielding,** he makes up the lost ground and gets up to win on the line.

Northamptonshire, England

Northamptonshire is a county in central England. Northampton, once the centre of the shoe-making industry, is its biggest town. Much of the county is rural, with many small villages. Two major canals, the Oxford and the Grand Union, flow through Northamptonshire. **Towcester racecourse** is in Northamptonshire.

Come to Grief (1995): A colt is cruelly attacked at Windward Stud Farm in Northamptonshire.

10 lb. Penalty (1997): **Benedict Juliard** gets a job with **Weatherbys**, the administrators of racing in the United Kingdom, who are based in Northamptonshire.

Norwich, Norfolk

Norwich was one of the most important cities in medieval England; today it is one of the major cities in the East Anglia region. The city has a magnificent 900 year old Norman cathedral; the Cathedral's library houses 7,000 rare books, including some of the earliest books printed in England. Norwich has had a busy, prosperous market since the twelfth century, and specialist shops of all sorts can be found in its maze of cobbled streets and alleys.

Twice Shy (1981): **Peter Keithley** works for **Mason Miles Associates,** a computer consultancy firm in Norwich. He and his wife **Donna** live in the city.

Norwood, Chris (*Twice Shy* 1981)

Norwood was a former employee of **Angel Kitchens,** a food production company in **Newmarket.** According to colleague **Vince Akkerton,** Norwood was dishonest and involved in all sorts of fiddles. He was suspected of stealing cash from girls in the office. Norwood had dishonestly acquired notes on handicapping horses, and had hoped to turn this to financial advantage. His possession of these notes had subsequently proved fatal.

Notebook (*Risk* 1977)

Notebook, a four-year-old chestnut gelding, is a novice hurdler trained by **William Finch** at **Axwood Stables**. He is described by Finch as promising but green. Ridden by **Roland Britten** at **Towcester,** he bucks down to the start. In the race Notebook proves willful and a bad jumper, and unseats Roland at the seventh flight.

Nottingham, England

Nottingham is the main city in the county of Nottinghamshire, in the East Midlands region of England. The city lies on the River Trent. It is well known for its lace-making industry and for its association with the legendary outlaw Robin Hood, who is said to have lived in nearby Sherwood Forest.

Driving Force (1992): The man who hitches a ride in one of **Freddie Croft**'s horse vans is identified as **Kevin Keith Ogden** from **Nottingham.**

Nottingham Airport

Nottingham airport is situated 3½ miles southeast of Nottingham city centre. Since 1963, the airport has been operated by Truman Aviation Limited. Aircraft maintenance, flying lessons and aircraft hire are available.

Rat Race (1970): Air taxi pilot **Matt Shore,** returning from **Haydock Park** races to **Newmarket,** realizes that the plane is not responding properly. He lands at Nottingham Airport to have the plane checked. This proves to be a sound decision.

Nottingham racecourse

Nottingham racecourse is a flat, left-handed twelve furlong circuit. To the disappointment of many regular racegoers, **National Hunt** racing was abandoned in 1996. The track's management team does a good job, but attendances are modest.

The Edge (1988): **Jockey Club** security service investigator **Tor Kelsey** is watching criminal **Julius Filmer** at Nottingham races when a young man tries to pass Filmer a briefcase. At first Filmer refuses to take it but later in the afternoon he does. Tor also sees racecourse bookmaker **Collie Goodboy** receiving information from an apprentice jockey.

Nutbourne, Annabel (*Comeback* 1991)

Annabel Nutbourne is a pretty young woman employed by the **Jockey Club** to look after visiting VIP's. She is the daughter of a bishop, and competent, but struggling with non–English speaking members of the Japanese Jockey Club at **Stratford** races. She gladly accepts **Peter Darwin**'s offer of assistance with translation, and subsequently meets him for dinner in London. She introduces Peter to **John Ambrose**, Deputy Director of Security for the Jockey Club. Annabel is concerned for Peter's safety after a murder at a veterinary practice, and tells him to stop his investigations, betraying her growing affection for him. She allows their relationship to develop slowly but surely, needing to be sure of her feelings. Annabel goes with Peter to the veterinary hospital; there she suffers a serious assault, but she recovers.

Nutbridge, Bob (*Field of 13* 1998: "Corkscrew")

Bob is the ten-year-old son of bloodstock salesman **Sandy Nutbridge**. He flies out from England to South Carolina with his grandmother and sister to visit his father. While he is there his father is arrested on tax and drug charges.

Nutbridge, Miranda (*Field of 13* 1998: "Corkscrew")

Miranda is the eight-year-old daughter of **Sandy Nutbridge**. She flies out from England to South Carolina with her grandmother and brother, **Bob Nutbridge**, to visit her father.

Nutbridge, Mrs. (*Field of 13* 1998: "Corkscrew")

Mrs. Nutbridge, the mother of **Sandy Nutbridge**, flies out from England with Sandy's two children to visit him. When he is arrested on tax and drug charges, she borrows money from her bank, her neighbors and Sandy's client, **Jules Harlow**, to pay for his bail. After Sandy's release, however, his lawyer, **Patrick Green**, refuses to return the bail money. Mrs. Nutbridge returns to America to give evidence against Green at a hearing before the South Carolina Bar Association's grievance committee

Nutbridge, Sandy (*Field of 13*: "Corkscrew")

Nutbridge, an American-based English bloodstock salesman, lives in South Carolina. He has a sleek and persuasive sales patter. He is employed by a local bloodstock agency, and works on commission. Nutbridge is divorced; his children live in England. He is mystified when he is arrested on tax and drug money laundering charges. With the help of lawyer **Patrick Green**, Nutbridge raises his bail money by borrowing from his mother, his employer and client **Jules Harlow**. The charges against him prove to be baseless, but when Green refuses to return the bail money Nutbridge's problems are only just beginning.

Nyembezi, Piano (*Smokescreen* 1972)

Nyembezi, a South African, is a checker at **Quentin Van Heuren**'s goldmine in **Welcom**. He insists that there is one person missing when **Edward Lincoln** is left down the mine, and instigates the search for Edward. Later, Edward signs a photo of himself in Nyembezi's film magazine; he writes that he owes his life to Piano Nyembezi.

O

Oakley, David (*Enquiry* 1969)

Oakley, a private enquiry agent based in **Birmingham**, is called as a witness at the enquiry into the running of **Squelsh** in the **Lemonfizz Crystal Cup** at **Oxford**. Oakley's evidence proves hostile to **Kelly Hughes**. When Kelly goes to Oakley's office, Oakley is contemptuous and threatening. Oakley breaks into Kelly's flat on a retrieval mission, and lives up to his reputation for ruthlessness and violence. Ultimately, however, his dubious activities catch up with him.

October, Earl of (*For Kicks* 1965)

In his mid-forties, Lord October is smooth, authoritative and tough. He is a member of the **National Hunt Committee**. While visiting racing and breeding centers in Australia, he hears about a homesick English groom who works for young stud farm owner **Daniel Roke**. He thinks he may be able to use the groom to investigate a possible doping scandal in England. He visits Daniel's farm and finds that the groom is unsuitable for his purpose; however he sees immediately that Daniel would be ideal. After checking on Daniel's background he returns to the farm and persuades Daniel to undertake the investigation. His relationship with Daniel is quickly soured, however, when his daughter, **Lady Patricia Tarren**, falsely accuses Daniel of sexually assaulting her. Eventually Lord October learns the truth, and gives Daniel crucial support when he needs it.

Odds Against (1965)

Sid Halley, ex-champion jump jockey, has been forced into retirement after a bad fall results in his losing the use of his hand. Now he is working without enthusiasm for **Hunt Radnor Associates**, an investigation agency. Shot by a petty criminal, Sid ends up in hospital with a bullet in his stomach. He is visited by **Rear Admiral Charles Roland**, RN, rtd., the father of his estranged wife. Roland had strongly disapproved of his daughter marrying a jockey and had virtually ostracized Sid. Then, on one of Sid's rare visits, Roland had invited him to play chess and lost. Realizing that there was more to Sid than met the eye, Roland began to take an interest in racing. The relationship between the two men slowly warmed, even surviving the break-up of Sid's marriage.

Roland lives near **Seabury racecourse**, which in recent years had suffered a run of misfortune. Roland brings Sid a book on Company Law without explaining why, and asks Sid to come and stay with him when he leaves hospital. Roland has an ulterior motive—to reawaken in Sid the zest for life that he has lost. Roland succeeds in that, but if he had foreseen the price that Sid would have to pay, he might have thought twice about it.

The inspiration for *Odds Against* came, according to Francis's biographer Graham Lord, from the demise of Hurst Park, a pretty racecourse near Hampton Court in west London which was sold off to property developers. The story moves at a good pace and is informative about the financial difficulties involved in running a small racecourse. There are no major surprises, no unexpected twists and turns to keep the reader guessing, though the ending is tense and gripping. But the relatively mundane nature of the plot is more than compensated for by the brilliant depiction of the main character. Sid Halley is the first of Francis's flawed heroes, and arguably his greatest invention. The focus of the book is not only on Seabury racecourse and the fight to save it; it is on Halley's inner turmoil—his weakness as a husband and his strength as a man; and on the intensity of the emotions that he hides behind an undemonstrative façade. Against the odds, Sid has made a success of two careers, but it has come at a heavy price—a broken marriage, a damaged body, and a troubled mind.

Odin (*Slay-Ride* 1973)

Odin is a Great Dane belonging to **Erik, David Cleveland's** driver in Oslo. A huge dog, Odin accompanies Eric everywhere in his old Volvo. The dog is in the car when a man tampers with the trunk. Odin is disturbed, knowing that something is wrong. David opens the car door and Erik whistles for Odin to jump out. David and Odin run from the car; it is not a moment too soon.

Offen, Culham James (*Blood Sport* 1967)

Offen is the owner of **Orpheus Stud Farm** in California. He stands two top class thoroughbred stallions there under false names. Their progeny have won plenty of races and the stud fees have risen accordingly. Offen employs his nephew **Matt Clive** and his niece, **Yola Clive**, to acquire **Chrysalis**, another young stallion, by unorthodox means.

Offen, known to the Clives as "Uncle Bark," is alarmed when **Dave Teller**, who has a financial interest in two of these horses, buys the stud farm next to his. Worried that Teller might recognize the stallions Offen attempts, unsuccessfully, to remove the risk.

When **Gene Hawkins** is hired by Teller to find Chrysalis, events move out of Offen's control, and he has to resign himself to losing all three stallions. Furthermore, **Jefferson Roots**, the Chairman of the **Bloodstock Breeders Association**, is determined to hold Offen to account for his activities.

O'Fitch, Paddy (*Under Orders* 2006)

O'Fitch is an ex-jockey whose real name is Harold Fitch. He was born in Liverpool but considers himself Irish. Extremely knowledgeable about all aspects of racing, O'Fitch is now a writer on racing history; his booklets are sold at racecourses in their hundreds. On behalf of the **Jockey Club**, O'Fitch oversees all the exhibits in racing museums around the country. At **Newbury** races, he is approached by **Sid Halley**, who buys him two pints of Guinness in return for information about the relationship between **Lord Enstone** and **George Lochs**. At **Towcester** races O'Fitch sees Sid discussing something, apparently confidentially, with **Charles Roland** and a man whom he wrongly takes to be a professor. He pesters Sid to tell him what the discussion was about. As Sid expects, O'Fitch shares this information with as many people as he can.

O'Flaherty, Paddy (*Slay-Ride* 1973)

O'Flaherty is a head lad employed by Norwegian trainer **Gunnar Holth** at **Øvrevoll racecourse**, Oslo. He is a friend of **Bob Sherman**'s—they had worked together in England when Sherman was an apprentice. He tells **David Cleveland** that Sherman had carried an envelope from England back to Norway in the summer but O'Flaherty did not know what is contained.

O'Flaherty admits to having exchanged his own damaged helmet for Sherman's. He loans it to David, who pulls out the lining but finds nothing.

Ogden, Kevin Keith (*Driving Force* 1992)

Middle-aged and overweight, Ogden is hitchhiking on the M25 motorway at **South Mimms** service station. His car has apparently broken down. He accepts a lift with **Croft Raceways** horse transport, in a horse van going to **Pixhill**, a village south of **Newbury**. Ogden dies during the journey, seemingly of natural causes. He lived in **Nottingham**. At the time of his death there was a warrant out for his arrest on petty fraud charges. A post-mortem confirms that he died of a heart attack. **Jockey Club** Director of Security **Patrick Venables** discovers that Ogden had placed an advert in *Horse and Hound* magazine offering "transport services."

Ogden, Lynn Melissa (*Driving Force* 1992)

Melissa is the widow of deceased hitch-hiker **Keith Ogden**. After the inquest into his death, she tells **Freddie Croft** that her husband had been unemployed for four years and was very hard up. She had lost her own job in a greengrocer's because he had stolen money from the till. She says that a woman had answered Ogden's advertisement in *Horse and Hound* magazine, and had asked him to deliver a thermos flask to Chieveley service station, near **Newbury**.

Okinawa (*Flying Finish* 1966)

Okinawa is a muscular three-year-old colt; he goes berserk when being transported by air to New York; with no humane killer on board, **Lord Henry Gray** has to kill the horse with a carving knife by piercing the carotid artery.

Oldejohn, Eric (*Break In* 1985)

Oldejohn is a racehorse owner for whom **Kit Fielding** rides a winner at **Towcester**. A senior civil servant, Oldejohn is undemonstrative but an effective facilitator. He agrees to try to find out for Kit if **Maynard Allardeck** is being considered for a knighthood. He invites Kit to his home and tells him that he has obtained information that may be helpful to Kit.

Oldfield Grant (*Nerve* 1964)

Grant, an ambitious and ruthless jockey with an aggressive style of riding, is volatile and bad-tempered. When he is sacked by trainer **James Axminster**, for whom Oldfield has only recently begun to ride regularly, he loses control completely. After finding a list of Axminster's horses in **Rob Finn**'s pocket in the weighing room, which Rob has been asked to ride, Oldfield punches Rob in the face. It subsequently transpires that Axminster had dismissed Oldfield for allegedly passing on stable information to a professional gambler.

As Rob's success grows Oldfield's fury steadily builds until, finally, he snaps. In the car park at **Warwick** races he smashes Rob's car window with a tire lever, then tries to do the same to Rob's head. Rob knocks Oldfield unconscious, takes him back to his filthy house—Oldfield's wife has left him—and goes to fetch the doctor. Returning, they find him in the garden in a withdrawn blank state, and put him to bed.

After spending time in a psychiatric hospital Oldfield makes a good recovery; his wife, realizing that he'd been mentally ill, returns to him. He decides to leave racing and sell toys for a living. He is grateful when Rob comes to see him, and says he will try to clear his name.

Oliver (*The Edge* 1988)

Oliver is dining-car waiter on board the Great Transcontinental Mystery Race Train.

Olympia (*Longshot* 1990)

Olympia is a girl who was killed at a party at **Tremayne Vickers'** home. In her early twenties, Olympia had ridden in ladies' races at point-to-points and worked as a riding instructor. When police drop the case through lack of evidence, her father brings a private prosecution against **Nolan Everard**, who subsequently receives a six month jail sentence, suspended for two years. Though portrayed as an innocent victim by her father, Olympia is considered by **Dee Dee**, Vickers' secretary, to have been sexually active and experienced.

Ondroy, Willy (*Forfeit* 1968)

In his mid-forties, Ondroy is an ex–Royal Air Force wing commander. He is a former member of the Red Arrows display team, and had been invalided out of the RAF after fracturing his skull when crash landing a bomber. He is now Clerk of the Course at **Heathbury Park** racecourse, and has used his organizational skills to transform Heathbury Park into one of the top racecourses.

Ondroy agrees to keep **Tiddely-Pom**, favorite for the Lamplighter Gold Cup, at the racecourse stables, after **James Tyrone** has to move the horse from **Norton Fox**'s yard, until the race is run the following day. On the morning of the Lamplighter he catches a villain trying to gain entry to the racecourse stables and turns him away.

Ordinand (*The Danger* 1983)

Ordinand, the winner of the **Epsom** Derby, is owned by **John** and **Miranda Nerrity**, whose three-year-old son, **Dominic Nerrity**, is kidnapped. The colt had won the Derby at odds of 33/1 and was not, according to **Alessia Cenci**, one of the best winners of the race.

O'Rorke, Liam (*Twice Shy* 1981)

O'Rorke was a professional gambler who used a successful statistical system of handicapping. He was negotiating to sell his system to bingo hall owner **Harry Gilbert** when he died, aged eighty-six. His papers were subsequently stolen from his home.

O'Rorke, Mrs. (*Twice Shy* 1981)

Now in her late eighties, Mrs. O'Rorke is the wife of the late professional gambler **Liam O'Rorke**. She lives in Stetchworth, **Cambridge-shire**. Mrs. O'Rorke is an educated woman, self-deprecating and greatly missing the company of her late husband. She tells **Jonathan Derry** that **Harry Gilbert** had arranged to buy Liam's methods but her husband's notes had been stolen before she could pass them on to Gilbert. Jonathan tells her that the system has been transcribed onto computer tapes, which he could obtain for her. Encouraged, she asks Jonathan to negotiate with Gilbert for her and offers him a commission. When Jonathan locates the tapes he sends them to Mrs. O'Rorke, but she dies before receiving them. Her solicitors return them to Jonathan.

Orpheus Stud Farm, California (*Blood Sport* 1967)

This is the farm owned by **Culham James Offen**.

Osborn, Ramsey (*Hot Money* 1987)

Osborn is a large, genial American from Stanford, Connecticut. He sells **Malcolm Pembroke** a half-share in his four-year-old colt **Blue Clancy** a few days before it runs third in the Prix de l'Arc de Triomphe at Longchamp. He and Pembroke get on well when they meet for the first time just before the Arc is run. Osborn arranges for Pembroke to stay with friends of his in **Lexington**, Kentucky en route to Los Angeles for the Breeders' Cup.

Osborne, Dr. (*Under Orders* 2006)

Dr. Osborne is the consultant on duty at the Accident and Emergency Department at St Thomas's Hospital, London, when **Marina van der Meer** is admitted. He tells **Sid Halley** that Marina is in theatre undergoing an emergency operation and that her condition is serious.

Osborne, Harold (*Reflex* 1980)

Racehorse trainer Harold Osborne is in his early fifties but looks younger. He has employed **Philip Nore** as his stable jockey for the past seven years. He is volatile and unpredictable, but has been loyal to Philip. Osborne tells Philip to lose a valuable steeplechase at **Sandown Park** on hot favorite **Daylight** for owner **Victor Briggs**. He is angry with Philip when he won't accept Briggs's cash for losing on Daylight. When Philip tells Osborne he won't stop any more horses, Osborne says he'll have to get someone who will. He makes it clear that his business relies more heavily on keeping Briggs sweet than on taking account of Philip's scruples. But he also tells Philip that he doesn't want to lose him.

Oscar (*Dead Heat* 2007)

Oscar is a temporary chef employed at **The Hay Net**, **Max Moreton**'s **Newmarket** restaurant, to cover for Max after he is hospitalized following a car crash. He is wrongly suspected by **Carl Walsh** of stealing petty cash. Oscar has a row with **Gary** and, in Max's absence, Walsh sacks him. He is subsequently reinstated and appointed as Walsh's assistant.

Osprey, Norman (*Shattered* 2000)

Osprey is a heavily-built, thuggish racecourse bookmaker trading under the name of **Arthur**

Robins. Twice, in the company of others, he assaults **Gerard Logan**. He is with **Rose Payne** and **Dr. Force** when they enter Gerard's workshop while he is making the leaping horse trophy. After the trophy explodes Osprey runs out of the workshop, pursued by **Tom Pigeon** and his dogs. He is soon caught and arrested by the police.

Ostermeyer, Harley and Martha (*Straight* 1989)

The Ostermeyers are the American owners of steeplechasers trained by **Milo Shandy**, though they have had no horses in training during the past year. Both are around sixty years old; Martha is the dominant partner. She and Harley are pleasant most of the time, though Harley occasionally displays an ill-tempered side to his character. Harley runs a supermarket chain, while Martha is from a multi-millionaire banking family.

The couple buy **Cheltenham** Gold Cup winner **Datepalm** from one of Shandy's other owners. They invite **Derek Franklin** to accompany them to **York** races to see his late brother **Greville Franklin**'s horse, **Dozen Roses**, run. Martha decides to buy Dozen Roses and send him jumping with Shandy.

While they are being driven back from Shandy's yard, someone in an overtaking car shoots at Derek but misses and instead kills the chauffeur, causing the car to crash. The Ostermeyers are badly shaken but suffer only shock, bruises and concussion.

O'Tree, Terence (*Reflex* 1980)

O'Tree shoots and kills steeplechasers out at summer grass belonging to **Elgin Yaxley**. Brought to court and convicted, O'Tree is sent to jail for nine months. Subsequently a collusive relationship between O'Tree and Yaxley is discovered.

Oven Cleaner (*Under Orders* 2006)

Oven Cleaner is a big, grey, top class steeplechaser. Tremendously popular with the public, he wins the **Cheltenham** Gold Cup for the third time, coming with a late run. He collapses in the unsaddling enclosure after the race, trapping his lady owner's ankle beneath him, and dies of a heart attack.

Øvrevoll racecourse, Norway

Øvrevoll racecourse, which opened in 1932, is situated at the head of the Oslo Fjord, to the west of the city. It is the only racecourse in Norway. Racing takes place between April and September on turf and dirt. On the flat the most important race is the Norwegian Derby, held in August. The jumping track is a figure of eight on the inside of the dirt track. The Norwegian Grand National is run in September.

Slay-Ride (1973): Jockey Club investigator **David Cleveland** goes to Norway to look into the disappearance of English jockey **Bob Sherman**. He focuses his enquiries around Øvrevoll racecourse.

Owners

"I'm glad I won, because if I hadn't I'd have taken my horses away from you."—Owner Lord Joicey to trainer Neville Crump after his horse Springbok had won the 1962 Hennessy Gold Cup at **Newbury**.

History doesn't record the choleric and combustible Crump's reply, but if it had been one of his less aristocratic owners that had made the remark it would probably have included a liberal sprinkling of expletives. It has been a regular and not unjustified gripe from trainers over the years that the owners require more training than the horses. **Bobby Allardeck** (*Break In* 1985) would doubtless agree; when rumors start to fly around **Newmarket** about Allardeck's stable being in financial trouble owner **Jermyn Graves** twice tries to remove his horses despite owing a huge amount in training fees. He is prevented from doing so by **Kit Fielding**, Allardeck's brother-in-law, who forces him to write a check and then stops him taking his horses away until it clears.

For sheer ingratitude millionaire owner **Ambrose Baxter** (*Shattered* 2000) is up there with Lord Joicey. When his horse **Tallahassee** falls at **Cheltenham**, killing jockey **Martin Stukely**, Baxter's principal emotion is not shock but irritation. He subsequently sacks his trainer for failing to school the horse properly. In *Enquiry* (1969) jockey **Kelly Hughes** and trainer **Dexter Cranfield** are warned off for allegedly stopping the favorite, **Squelsh**, from winning at **Oxford**. Squelsh's owner, a man named **Kessell**, is quick to tell Kelly that he'll never ride for him again and to take his horses away from Cranfield's yard. Kelly manages to restore his good name and is soon back riding. Kessell has cause to regret his lack of faith when Kelly, riding another horse, beats Squelsh by a nostril in the Cheltenham Gold Cup. Other owners quick to find fault when their horses are beaten include **Orkney Swayle** (*Proof* 1984), **Ralph Torp** (*Slay-Ride* 1973) and **John Ballerton** (*Nerve* 1964).

These owners are merely unpleasant; others are downright villainous. In *For Kicks* (1965) **Paul J. Adams** is a near-psychopath who likes nothing better than knocking the stable lads around. Suspected of killing his widowed mother as a young man, he has no compunction about resorting to extreme violence when his cruel and corrupt racecourse activities are about to be revealed. Owner **Thomas Rollway** (*Straight* 1989), fearing that jockey **Derek Franklin** knows too much about him, will stop at nothing to ensure Franklin's silence. He reckons without the intervention of the ex-lover of Derek's dead brother.

Elgin Yaxley (*Reflex* 1980), the owner of five talented steeplechasers, conspires with an accomplice to make a tidy capital sum out of them by illegal means. His plans backfire; not only does he end up considerably out of pocket, but he is forced to leave the country. Equally detestable is owner **Wynn Lees** (*Comeback* 1991). Lees was jailed as a young man for extreme cruelty to horses, but the experience has not proved salutary.

These rogues and cheats are, happily, balanced by a similar number of decent, caring owners who want only the best for their horses. Elderly European aristocrat **Princess Casilia** (*Break In* 1985; *Bolt* 1986) is reminiscent of the late Queen Elizabeth the Queen Mother in her love of steeplechasers and the pleasure she takes in seeing them run. **Lord Friarly** (*Whip Hand* 1979), a sporting owner of the old school, is appalled at becoming involved in syndicates whose activities appear not to be entirely above board. In *Risk* (1977) **Mrs. Moira Longerman**, owner of Cheltenham Gold Cup winner **Tapestry**, shows commendable loyalty to amateur jockey **Roland Britten** when her dishonest trainer wants him replaced. American owner **Mrs. Kerry Sanders** (*Knock Down* 1974) has a frightening experience at **Ascot Sales**; she is forced by two thugs to sell the horse that her bloodstock agent, **Jonah Dereham**, has just bought for her. Refusing to be deterred, Mrs. Sanders asks Jonah to buy her another horse. Easily the most attractive owner is the young and beautiful **Kate Ellery-Penn** (*Dead Cert* 1962). She is given a racehorse as a twenty-first birthday present by her seemingly affable and innocuous **Uncle George**.

Ownslow (*Risk* 1977)

Ownslow is a tough, burly ex-convict. With **Glitberg**, he was convicted on embezzlement charges on the evidence of **Roland Britten** and served a six-year sentence, reduced for good be-

havior. He and Glitberg had defrauded the local council on which they both served, by authorizing construction work that was never carried out and pocketing the money allocated to it.

Ownslow meets Roland in **Vivian Iverson**'s gambling club and warns him not to go near building sites on a dark night. With Glitberg and others, Ownslow exacts a painful revenge on Roland.

Oxford/Oxfordshire

Oxfordshire is a county in southern England, in the Thames valley to the west of London. It is a county of busy market towns and picturesque villages with houses built of honey-colored stone. The Oxfordshire Cotswold hills are a designated Area of Outstanding Natural Beauty. The city of Oxford, with its 800-year-old university, is a blend of ancient and modern, a busy cosmopolitan city built around the university's thirty-six colleges, with business and science parks on its outskirts.

Odds Against (1965): **Sid Halley** goes to stay with his father-in-law, Rear Admiral **Charles Roland**, RN. rtd. in Oxfordshire. There he meets **Howard Kraye**, who is trying to buy up shares in **Seabury racecourse**.

Whip Hand (1979): **Sid Halley** goes to his ex-father-in-law's house in **Aynsford**, Oxfordshire. He has an awkward meeting with his ex-wife **Jenny Halley**. Later, he goes to the apartment in Oxford which Jenny had shared with **Nicholas Ashe** and student **Louise McInnes**. Louise lets Sid see the things that Ashe has left behind.

Hot Money (1987): **Donald Pembroke**, eldest of **Malcolm Pembroke**'s nine children, lives in Henley-on-Thames, Oxfordshire.

Wild Horses (1994): Film director **Thomas Lyon** goes to see **Jackson Wells** on his farm near Oxford. The film that Thomas is making is based on a tragic incident in which Wells was involved twenty-five years before.

Come to Grief (1995): Investigating the mutilation of several colts, **Sid Halley** traces a transfer seen on a Land Rover parked near the scene of one of the crimes to English Sporting Motors, a car saleroom in Oxford.

Field of 13 (1998): "**Collision Course**": Editor **Bill Williams** has a meal with potential employers at a riverside restaurant in Oxford.

Dead Heat (2007): Chef **Max Moreton** learned his trade at the restaurant of a distant relative in Oxfordshire. Racehorse trainer **Toby Chambers**, Max's half-brother, lives in East Hendred, Oxfordshire.

Oxford racecourse

Oxford is a fictional racecourse situated near the ancient university city of Oxford in the Thames valley, west of London.

Enquiry (1969): Trainer **Dexter Cranfield**'s horse **Squelsh**, favorite for the Lemonfizz Crystal Cup at Oxford, is beaten into second place by an outsider from the same stable. Cranfield and jockey **Kelly Hughes** are subsequently warned off over the running and riding of Squelsh.

Oxon, Captain (*Odds Against* 1965)

Oxon is the manager of **Seabury racecourse**. He is ex-army, and in his fifties. He appears to be taking his time over repairs to Seabury after a tanker spillage, and resents **Sid Halley** bringing **Lord Hagbourne** to check progress. Oxon puts the general dilapidation of the course down to the "sea air." At first Sid thinks that Oxon is a fool and that he has a defeatist attitude. Subsequently Sid has good reason to revise his opinion of Oxon, which turns out to be over-generous.

P

Paddy (*For Kicks* 1965)

Paddy is a senior lad at **Inskip**'s racing stable. He is around forty years old, and an unofficial father to the younger lads. He immediately marks **Daniel Roke** down as a troublemaker. After Daniel is sacked from Inskip's, Paddy tells **Hedley Humber**'s head lad that he'd be a fool to take Daniel on. In fact this makes it easier for Daniel to get a job at Humber's stable.

Paget, Polly (*Trial Run* 1978)

Polly Paget is assistant to the cultural attaché at the British Embassy, Moscow. She phones **Randall Drew** to tell him that a telex is waiting for him at the Embassy.

Palindrome (*Dead Cert* 1962)

Palindrome, an eight-year-old bay gelding, is a steeplechaser owned and ridden by **Alan York**, and trained by **Peter Gregory**. Alan wins an amateur chase on Palindrome on Champion Hurdle day at **Cheltenham**. He is riding Palindrome at **Bristol** when the horse is deliberately brought down.

Palissey, Mrs. (*Proof* 1984)

Mrs. Palissey works in **Tony Beach**'s wine shop. She is good-natured, good at her job, and likes a gossip. She is dishonest in a minor way, helping herself to Tony's candy or coffee, but otherwise reliable. She is happy to work overtime while Tony is away working with **Gerard McGregor**.

Palmerstone, Cinders (*Driving Force* 1992)

Cinders is the nine-year-old daughter of **Freddie Croft** and **Susan Palmerstone**, but is accepted as his own child by Susan's husband, **Hugo Palmerstone**. Cinders is unaware that Freddie is her father. She is at the premises of **Centaur Care**, a dubious charity for retired horses, when a murderer is apprehended. Frightened, Cinders is told by Freddie to hide under the horse van. She allows Freddie to help her out from underneath, but immediately rushes to Hugo.

Palmerstone, Hugo (*Driving Force* 1992)

Hugo Palmerstone works in the City of London's financial sector. He is red-haired, and has a temper to match. He is married to **Freddie Croft**'s ex-lover, **Susan Palmerstone**. He is deeply agitated by the fact that his daughter, **Cinders Palmerstone**, is not his child biologically; Cinders was conceived by Susan to Freddie prior to her marrying Hugo. Because of this, Hugo hates Freddie.

Palmerstone, Susan (*Driving Force* 1992)

Blonde, cheerful, and in her late thirties, Susan Palmerstone is the ex-lover of **Freddie Croft** and the mother of his daughter, **Cinders Palmerstone**. She is married to city executive **Hugo Palmerstone**, who has accepted Cinders as his own child despite having recently realized that she isn't.

Pamela Jane (*Shattered* 2000)

Pamela Jane is an assistant in **Gerard Logan**'s glass-blowing workshop. She is concerned that her ability as a glass-blower does not match her ambitions and tends to put herself down. Outside Gerard's workshop she is assaulted by enemies of Gerard, taken inside and tied up. She is disappointed in Gerard's response, not realizing that he is engineering her escape, and says she'll never work for him again. However, Gerard frees Pamela Jane's ankles and tells her to run; when she doesn't Gerard carries her bodily to safety.

Pampering (*The Edge* 1988)

Pampering, a racehorse owned by Canadian **Daffodil Quentin**, is fifth in the Jockey Club Race Train Stakes at **Assiniboia Downs, Winnipeg**.

Pamphlet (*Reflex* 1980)

Pamphlet is a hurdler trained by **Harold Osborne**. He wins a race at **Kempton Park** ridden by **Philip Nore**.

Pandita, Mr. (*Under Orders* 2006)

Mr. Pandita, a surgeon at St Thomas's Hospital, London, operates on **Marina van der Meer**. He tells **Sid Halley** that the operation, though serious, had gone well.

Pankhurst, Pip (*Nerve* 1964)

Pankhurst is a steeplechase jockey employed by **James Axminster**. He breaks his leg badly in a fall, allowing **Rob Finn** the chance to ride the stable's best horses.

Pannier, Dorothea (*Wild Horses* 1994)

Dorothea Pannier, the sister of **Valentine Clark**, lives with him in **Newmarket** and nurses him through his last days when he is dying with bone cancer. She is in her late seventies but competent and independent. She is concerned at Valentine's desire to receive absolution from a priest since he is no longer a practicing Catholic, but is finally relieved when **Thomas Lyon** arranges it. When Valentine dies, Dorothea refuses to accede to the various demands of her pompous son, **Paul Pannier**. She takes Thomas's advice not to sign anything without consulting a solicitor.

Dorothea is found by her friend **Betty**, seriously injured after being assaulted at home. She gradually recovers in hospital. Dorothea is disturbed by her memories of the assault and by her suspicions about the identity of the perpetrators.

Pannier, Paul (*Wild Horses* 1994)

Paul Pannier, the son of **Dorothea Pannier**, is supercilious and unpleasant. Even his mother finds him pompous and bossy. He is podgy, with an undernourished moustache. He arrives immediately from his home in **Surrey** when Dorothea phones to say that his uncle, **Valentine Clark**, is dying. Pannier resents **Thomas Lyon**'s presence at his mother's house. When informed over the phone by Thomas of the serious assault on his mother, Pannier sounds genuinely upset. Ultimately, Pannier's knowledge of dark secrets from both the distant and recent past proves his undoing.

Parakeet (*Banker* 1982)

Parakeet is an eleven-year-old stallion standing at **Oliver Knowles'** stud farm in **Hertfordshire**. He is an influence for stamina and his progeny tend to be late-maturing. Disappointingly for Knowles, Parakeet is more popular with **National Hunt** breeders than with those who breed for the Flat.

Pargetter, Ian (*Banker* 1982)

Newmarket veterinary surgeon Ian Pargetter is an associate of equine healer **Calder Jackson**. According to Jackson, Pargetter is happy to refer horses to him.

Pargetter is subsequently found dead at his home; he has been hit on the back of his head with a brass lamp from his sitting room after returning late at night from treating a horse. His instrument case and a quantity of drugs are missing. He is subsequently found to have had a collusive relationship with Jackson.

Park Railings (*Hot Money* 1987)

Park Railings, a steeplechaser owned by **Jo**, the wife of a leading **Newmarket** trainer, is ridden by **Ian Pembroke** into fourth place in a race at **Cheltenham**. Ian comments that the horse was less tired than he was.

Parlane, Jed (*To the Hilt* 1996)

Parlane is the factor, or manager, on the Scottish estate of **Robert, Earl of Kinloch**. In his mid-forties, Parlane is a shrewd lowland Scot, and good with the tenant farmers. After **Alex Kinloch** is beaten up outside his cottage, Parlane lends him his train fare to London and some cash. He changes the lock on Alex's cottage, and looks after Alex's unfinished painting of **Zoë Lang** while he is in London. He is married to Flora, who is reputed to have the ability to foretell the future.

Parrott, Willy (*Come to Grief* 1995)

Parrott is the production manager at **Topline Foods, Frodsham**. Unaware of who **Sid Halley** is, he shows Sid round the horse cubes production line. He treats his boss, **Owen Yorkshire**, with a healthy respect bordering on fear.

Pat (*Driving Force* 1992)

Pat is a driver for **Croft Raceways** horse transport firm. He is considered reliable.

Patrick (*Flying Finish* 1966)

Patrick is the pilot of an elderly DC4 airplane used by **Yardman** Transport to carry broodmares to Milan. Around thirty years old, Patrick is pleasant, good-natured and a good pilot. He introduces **Lord Henry Gray** to **Gabriella**, with whose family Patrick stays when in Milan; he is amused to see the immediate spark of physical attraction between the two. He secures Henry a bed for the night with Gabriella's family.

On a flight from Milan to Britain Yardman forces Patrick to change course so that he can deliver an illicit cargo. Soon after Patrick has landed the plane he escapes a violent death by a miraculous twist of fate.

Patterson, Mrs. (*Straight* 1989)

Mrs. Patterson, **Greville Franklin**'s cleaner at his London home, is very upset when she learns of Greville's death and finds the house ransacked by a burglar.

Patty (*Banker* 1982)

Patty works in a clerical capacity at merchant bank **Paul Ekaterin Ltd.** She helps **Tim Ekaterin** to investigate the rumor—unfounded, as it turns out—that someone is working a fraud at the bank by paying himself loans at low interest. She explains to Tim how computers can check all transactions.

Paul Ekaterin Ltd. (*Banker* 1982)

Under the chairmanship of **Henry Shipton**, London-based merchant bank **Paul Ekaterin Ltd.** has achieved major-league status. Founded by the great-grandfather of **Tim Ekaterin**, the bank has three main departments: Corporate Finance, Banking and Investment Management. The bank is accused in a satirical magazine of insider trading. There is no hard evidence, but the directors are worried.

Pauline (*Nerve* 1964)

Pauline is a model, and **Rob Finn**'s ex-girlfriend. She informs Rob by letter that she is going to marry wealthy industrialist Sir Morton Henge.

Payne, Eddie (*Shattered* 2000)

Elderly racecourse valet Eddie Payne looks after jump jockey **Martin Stukely**, who is killed in a fall at **Cheltenham** races. He gives **Gerard Logan** a packet containing a videocassette; it had been given to Stukely to pass on to Gerard. Payne makes an excuse not to go to Stukely's funeral. With others, he assaults Gerard outside his workshop in **Broadway, Gloucestershire**. Later he is involved in a fracas in the workshop which ends tragically.

Payne, Rose (*Shattered* 2000)

Rose Payne, also known as **Rose Robins**, is the daughter of racecourse valet **Eddie Payne**. A vile-tempered and violent harridan, Payne works with racecourse bookmakers operating under the trading name of **Arthur Robins**. She has a domineering nature, and is charismatic in a repulsive sort of way. With others, including her father Eddie Payne, she attacks **Gerard Logan** outside his workshop, urging her accomplices to break Gerard's wrists so he can't work at his glass-blowing. Approached by Gerard at **Leicester** races for information about a stolen videotape, she exudes hatred of Gerard and tells him nothing. According to Eddie Payne, Rose is a man-hater but has the ability to manipulate them.

Rose is the sister of **Gina Verity**, mother of **Victor Verity**. According to Victor, Rose had tortured people in his attic, reputedly pulling out their teeth. She had assaulted Victor's father on more than one occasion. Payne is instrumental in provoking a violent confrontation in Gerard's workshop which ends tragically.

Payne-Percival, Fenella (*Rat Race* 1970)

Fenella Payne-Percival is in her thirties, but she acts and dresses like a teenager. She has a high opinion of her own attractiveness; this is not shared by jockey **Colin Ross**, whom she pursues optimistically.

Peaky (*Dead Cert* 1962)

Peaky is a taxi-driver employed by **Marconicars** taxi firm, **Brighton**. He is so-called because of a dark widow's peak growing down his forehead.

Pease Pudding (*Bonecrack* 1971)

Pease Pudding is a racehorse trained at **Newmarket** by **Neil Griffon**. He is entered in the Lincoln Handicap at **Doncaster**. Ridden by **Tommy Hoylake** in a pre–Lincoln trial, Pease Pudding seems to go well but Hoylake is worried by the proximity of the previously disappointing **Lancat**. Unexpected by everyone but Neil, Pease Pudding wins the Lincoln by a short head, given a positive ride by Hoylake.

Pedder, Neil (*Under Orders* 2006)

Lambourn racehorse trainer Neil Pedder gives **Sid Halley** information about the logistics of sending horses to run in the north of England, in particular the number of stable staff required to accompany them. As an ex-stable employee and jockey, Sid would have known this already.

Pembroke, Alicia (*Hot Money* 1987)

Alicia is the third of the five wives of **Malcolm Pembroke**, and mother of his children **Gervase Pembroke**, **Ferdinand Pembroke** and **Serena Pembroke**. She lives in an apartment in Windsor, **Berkshire**. According to Malcolm, she was "a great mistress but a rotten wife." Despite a generous divorce settlement she continually complains about Malcolm to her children. She hasn't remarried, not wishing to lose her alimony, but has a lover. According to **Ian Pembroke**, Alicia had been adequate as a stepmother for seven years, but he'd had no illusions that she loved him. Despite being in her fifties, Alicia still dresses and acts as if she were a teenager, at the same time stunting daughter Serena's emotional growth.

Pembroke, Berenice (*Hot Money* 1987)

Berenice is the wife of **Thomas Pembroke**. According to **Malcolm Pembroke**, she is "a five-star cow." She resents **Ian Pembroke**, thinking him Malcolm's favorite and only after his father's money. She never misses an opportunity to criticize her husband. When Thomas breaks a gin bottle while making a drink for Ian she makes one sarcastic comment too many; Thomas lunges at her with the broken bottle, wanting to kill her. Ian pushes her out of the way. She tells Ian that her dissatisfaction with Thomas stems from her desperately wanting a son. Thomas, considering two daughters quite enough, had had a vasectomy.

Pembroke, Coochie (*Hot Money* 1987)

Coochie was the fourth wife of **Malcolm Pembroke**. She had been a caring and supportive stepmother to **Ian Pembroke**, loving him as much as she did her own twin boys, **Robin Pembroke** and **Peter Pembroke**. At the age of forty, when the twins were eleven years old, a hit and run driver had killed her and Peter, and left Robin brain-damaged. The identity of the driver is subsequently revealed.

Pembroke, Deborah (*Hot Money* 1987)

Deborah, known as "Debs," is the second wife of **Ferdinand Pembroke**. She works as a photographic model, and is expecting a baby. She gives **Ian Pembroke** a mock-friendly but seriously-

meant warning not to entertain designs on **Malcolm Pembroke**'s money.

Pembroke, Donald (*Hot Money* 1987)

In his mid-forties, Donald is the eldest of **Malcolm Pembroke**'s nine children; he is the son of Malcolm's first wife **Vivien**. With his wife **Helen Pembroke** and their three children, Donald lives a conventional life at Henley-on-Thames, **Oxfordshire**. Donald's sons are at **Eton College**, which he can't afford. His job as secretary of a posh golf club gives him the social standing that is important to him but not the salary his outgoings require. He had hoped to inherit some money from his father before school fees became a major burden.

Donald goes to **Sandown Park** races to tell **Ian Pembroke** to persuade Malcolm to stop spending so much money. He admits to trying to trace Malcolm in **Cambridge** because he needed his signature on a loan guarantee.

Pembroke, Edwin (*Hot Money* 1987)

Formerly Edwin Bugg, he had changed his name to Pembroke after his marriage to **Lucy Pembroke**, the daughter of **Malcolm Pembroke**'s first wife **Vivien Pembroke**. Aged fifty-three, Edwin has one teenage son and no job; he spends hours reading in the public library. Edwin is a lazy scrounger who had married Lucy because he saw her as a meal ticket who would eventually inherit a lot of money. Edwin is unhappy that Malcolm is spending too much of his money; he is well aware that Malcolm has a low opinion of him.

Pembroke, Ferdinand (*Hot Money* 1987)

Aged thirty-two, Ferdinand is the son of **Malcolm Pembroke** and his third wife **Alicia Pembroke**. He physically resembles his father and has inherited some of his financial acumen. He works in insurance and is studying to be an actuary. Ferdinand was friends with **Ian Pembroke** when both were children, but over the years Ferdinand's mother Alicia had turned him against Ian by telling him that Ian wanted Ferdinand's share of Malcolm's money. Ferdinand has married twice; his first wife was American. He is now married to **Deborah Pembroke**; they have no children. According to private detective **Norman West**, Ferdinand is able and industrious and has a sense of humor, but can be moody. He follows Ian home from **Sandown Park** races, hoping to find Malcolm at Ian's flat.

Pembroke, Gervase (*Hot Money* 1987)

Gervase is the son of **Malcolm Pembroke** and his third wife **Alicia Pembroke**. Now in his mid-thirties, Gervase was born before his parents married and is keenly aware of this, considering it a humiliation. He is married to **Ursula Pembroke**; they have two small daughters. Gervase is a mean-minded, pompous bully who rejoices in the misfortunes of others. As a boy, Gervase burned **Ian Pembroke** with a cigarette in an attempt to discover where Ian's new cricket bat was hidden. According to the receptionist at the stockbroking firm where he works, Gervase is not as diligent as he used to be, and sometimes returns from lunch drunk.

Private detective **Norman West** considers Gervase's alcohol problem serious. Gervase phones Ian to say that their father must be prevented from spending the money which he sees as his inheritance. When Ian calls to see him, Gervase gets belligerent, blaming Ian for Malcolm buying racehorses and for what he perceives as Ian's air of superiority.

Pembroke, Helen (*Hot Money* 1987)

Helen is the wife of **Donald Pembroke**, **Malcolm Pembroke**'s eldest son. She is a beautiful woman with the poise and style of a model but, according to Malcolm, fairly dim. She works at home painting views of Henley-on-Thames, **Oxfordshire**, onto china cups and plates. She tells **Ian** that she and Donald had been hoping to inherit some of Malcolm's money before their sons started at **Eton**. Without it, their financial situation is critical. She is forced to pawn her jewelry to pay interest overdue on a loan.

Pembroke, Ian (*Hot Money* 1987)

Ian Pembroke's multi-millionaire father, **Malcolm Pembroke**, has had five wives and sired nine children. Ian is the only child of Malcolm's second wife, **Joyce Pembroke**. Ian's mother hadn't had much time for him so he'd been brought up by a succession of Malcolm's wives. The only one to have given Ian any love was **Coochie Pembroke**, Malcolm's fourth wife, who had been killed by a hit and run driver at the age of forty.

Ian had learned to ride at the local riding school during the summer holidays. Now, thirty-three years old, he rides in amateur steeplechases while working as an assistant racehorse trainer. He has just quit his latest job, partly because the trainer's daughter was making life awkward for him as she

wanted the job for her fiancé, but mainly because he'd had enough of working for someone else. Not that he could expect any help from his father in setting up as a trainer on his own. Malcolm hadn't spoken to Ian for three years after he had rashly drawn attention to the shortcomings of **Moira Pembroke**, then Malcolm's fiancée and now his fifth wife.

Out of the blue, though, Malcolm phones Ian, asking for help. Moira, whom Malcolm was in the process of divorcing, has been murdered and now someone is trying to kill him. He wants Ian to act as his bodyguard. With time on his hands, Ian agrees. Fearless as an amateur jockey, Ian is now called upon to put his life at risk in other ways. His brushes with death make Ian uncomfortable; he realizes that, if he was killed, no-one would mourn him. Certainly none of his half-brothers and sisters would lose any sleep, since he is making himself unpopular in trying to find out who is trying to kill Malcolm. The only person who might shed a tear is his girlfriend, but even then their relationship is more practical than deep. A lot older than Ian, she's a married woman who occasionally escapes from a husband she doesn't love to have sex at Ian's flat in Epsom, **Surrey**. But Ian knows that if he wasn't around she wouldn't take too long to find someone else. Malcolm, wondering why Ian hasn't married, asks him if he doesn't trust himself. Ian ruefully accepts the accuracy of his father's insight: "In inconstancy I felt I was very much his son."

If Ian feels himself inadequate as a potential husband, at least things are looking up in the sphere of his life that really matters to him—his riding. When he wins a race against professional jockeys at **Kempton Park**, he is elated. But there are regrets too; realization that he can hold his own with the best has come late, possibly too late. He feels that he has idled the time away.

Ian hasn't been idle, though, in his pursuit of whoever killed Moira and is trying to kill Malcolm. He sets a trap into which the murderer obligingly falls. Then Ian, acutely conscious that life isn't a rehearsal, moves to **Lambourn** and, despite his age, follows his dream.

Pembroke, Joyce (*Hot Money* 1987)

Joyce is the second of **Malcolm Pembroke**'s five wives and the mother of **Ian Pembroke**. She lives in **Surrey**. From a very old family, Joyce is unmaternal, and was happy for Malcolm to bring Ian up. She has not married again to protect her alimony. She admits to Ian that she regretted divorcing Malcolm because of his infidelity. Joyce is a bridge player of international standard, and when she isn't playing she is teaching the game or writing about it. Though she had shown little interest in Ian's upbringing, Joyce is adamant that Ian should dissuade Malcolm from being profligate with his money, which she sees as Ian's inheritance. She is angry when she reads in the newspapers that Malcolm has been buying racehorses. She agrees to help Ian to set a trap for the murderer of Malcolm's fifth wife, **Moira Pembroke**.

Pembroke, Lucy (*Hot Money* 1987)

Lucy, aged forty-two, is the daughter of **Malcolm Pembroke** and his first wife **Vivien Pembroke**. She is married to **Edwin Pembroke** (né **Bugg**). Lucy didn't like his surname, so Edwin changed his name to hers. They have one teenage son. Lucy tries to make a living as a poet but relies on the income from a small trust fund; her husband doesn't work. Lucy wants **Ian Pembroke** to persuade Malcolm to stop spending so much of his money. When Ian tells her that Malcolm is fair, and to leave him alone, Lucy admits to feeling ashamed of herself for feeling as she does, but says that her work as a poet has more or less stopped. She agrees to look after her brother, **Thomas Pembroke**, after Ian advises him to leave his wife, **Berenice Pembroke**. Subsequently Lucy starts work on a biography of the poet Thomas Stearns Eliot.

Pembroke, Malcolm (*Hot Money* 1987)

Malcolm Pembroke is a multi-millionaire gold trader. He is in his late sixties, has been married five times and has nine children. He is in the process of divorcing his last wife, **Moira Pembroke**, when she is murdered. The police suspect him but he has an unbreakable alibi. When Malcolm's son, **Ian Pembroke**, had criticized Moira before they married, Malcolm had knocked Ian down and hadn't spoken to him for three years until phoning him and asking for his help. He asks Ian to travel with him, saying that he needs someone he can trust; he believes someone is trying to kill him. Meanwhile his children, most of whom have designs on his money, are trying to track him down.

Malcolm decides to go to the Prix de l'Arc de Triomphe at **Longchamp** and gets Ian to buy him a half-share in **Blue Clancy**, one of the runners. Malcolm's interest in racing is strengthened when Blue Clancy is third in the Arc. Feeling cooped

up in London, he decides to return home. This proves to be a mistake. He takes Ian's advice to fly out to California, where Blue Clancy wins the Breeders' Cup Turf.

After Moira's murderer is revealed, Malcolm acts upon Ian's suggestion to make a generous financial settlement on all his children.

Pembroke, Moira (*Hot Money* 1987)

Moira was the fifth wife of **Malcolm Pembroke**. According to Malcolm's son, **Ian Pembroke**, she was unscrupulous, greedy and manipulative, and interested only in Malcolm's money. She was in the process of divorcing Malcolm after three years of marriage, and demanding half of his vast wealth as well as his house, when she was murdered. Moira was found suffocated in the garden, her head in a sack of potting compost.

Pembroke, Peter (*Hot Money* 1987)

Peter was the son of **Malcolm Pembroke's** fourth wife, **Coochie Pembroke**, and the twin of **Robin Pembroke**. He was killed in a hit and run incident at the age of eleven.

Pembroke, Robin (*Hot Money* 1987)

Robin is the son of **Malcolm Pembroke's** fourth wife, **Coochie Pembroke**; he is sixteen years old. At the age of eleven, he was badly injured in a hit and run incident in which Coochie's car had been forced off the road. His mother and brother were killed. Now Robin is brain-damaged and living in a nursing home. The perpetrator of the crime is subsequently revealed.

Pembroke, Serena (*Hot Money* 1987)

Parents in dysfunctional families generally have a lot to answer for, and wealthy gold trader **Malcolm Pembroke**, married five times and the father of nine children, has more to answer for than most. His cavalier attitude to wives, sons and daughters has left many of them with an assortment of neuroses and unhealthy behavior patterns, not least Serena, his twenty-six-year-old daughter by his third wife, **Alicia Pembroke**. On the surface Serena appears to suffer from nothing more than arrested development. She lives alone, works as an aerobics teacher and, as a substitute for sex, buys herself huge amounts of new clothes. Her emotional immaturity can be traced back to the way she was treated as a girl by her mother who, though now in her late fifties, still dresses like a teenager. Alicia had wanted Serena to remain a little girl, because it helped her to feel young herself.

Alicia was embittered by her divorce from Malcolm when Serena was six years old, and remained so ever after. Serena, taken away from **Quantum**, Malcolm's luxurious country house, when her parents split up, still cannot accept that her father didn't want her to live with him. Her mindset is stuck in the past; at her flat in **Berkshire** she fills exercise books with fantasies about living with Malcolm at Quantum. Unfortunately, her childlike imaginings have gradually grown into a dangerous obsession. Serena's subsequent behavior has tragic consequences.

Pembroke, Thomas (*Hot Money* 1987)

Thomas is the son of **Malcolm Pembroke** by his first wife, **Vivien Pembroke**. He is in his late thirties, and lives near **Reading** in **Berkshire**. He is unhappily married to **Berenice Pembroke**, who sees nothing to praise in her husband. Thomas, however, does not want a divorce, not wishing to behave like his father. He had been dismissed for incompetence from his job as a quantity surveyor, but hadn't immediately told Berenice and had continued to go off every morning as if to work. He and Berenice have two daughters; one of Berenice's long-held grudges against Thomas is that he hasn't given her a son, and having had a vasectomy, never will.

According to private detective **Norman West**, Thomas is severely depressed. While making **Ian Pembroke** a drink, he breaks a gin bottle. When Berenice makes a sarcastic comment he lunges at her with the broken bottle, wanting to kill her. Ian pushes her out of the way, getting cut in the process. Thomas moves out of the family home, but eventually he goes back to Berenice. However, he tells Ian that if Berenice doesn't change he will leave her for good.

Pembroke, Ursula (*Hot Money* 1987)

Ursula is the wife of **Gervase Pembroke**, Malcolm **Pembroke**'s son by his third wife, **Alicia Pembroke**. She is quiet and, according to private detective **Norman West**, in an unhappy marriage. She is dominated by her husband, who won't allow her to work. Ursula detests her mother-in-law, who is a malign influence on Gervase.

Pembroke, Vivien (*Hot Money* 1987)

Vivien is the first wife of **Malcolm Pembroke** and the mother of **Donald**, **Lucy** and **Thomas Pembroke**. Once a beautiful woman, her looks have suffered as a result of her continuing bitter-

ness at Malcolm's infidelity. According to **Ian Pembroke**, Vivien is the least bright of his father's five wives. Dissatisfaction with her lot is Vivien's preferred mindset, and she has influenced her children to adopt a similar view of life. She has not married again in order to protect her alimony. She blames Ian for influencing his father's decisions.

Pentelow, Evan (*Smokescreen* 1972)

Film director Evan Pentelow worked on the film *Man in a Car* with **Edward Lincoln**. Forty years old, Pentelow is talented, energetic, intense and autocratic. He likes to take the credit for an actor's performance. He and Edward do not get on. He goes to South Africa to make a film about elephants. Discovering that Edward is there too, ostensibly to promote *Man in a Car*, Pentelow insists that Edward turn up at the film's première.

To Edward's surprise, Pentelow invites him to the **Kruger Game Park** where he is shooting his new film. He underestimates how dangerous elephants can be, demanding to film them at close quarters. One elephant charges their jeep, and Pentelow urgently orders the park ranger to drive away. Pentelow shows great determination in searching for Edward when he goes missing in the Park. When, after Pentelow and **Conrad** have found him, Edward begs them not to leave him, Pentelow is visibly upset despite his dislike of Edward. When Edward says he wants to set a trap for his abductor, Pentelow is ready and willing to help.

Perelli, Antonio (*Forfeit* 1968)

Perelli is a young Italian doctor in private practice in London; **Elizabeth Tyrone** is one of his patients. He straps up **James Tyrone**'s ribs and gives him painkillers after he is beaten up on the race train while returning from **Leicester** races.

James phones Perelli to tell him that Elizabeth must go straight to a nursing home for her own safety. Perelli asks James to stop at his surgery on the way so he can see Elizabeth. From there, he drives Elizabeth to the nursing home.

Perkins, Fred (*Hot Money* 1987)

Perkins was the gardener at **Malcolm Pembroke**'s house, **Quantum**, before **Arthur Bellbrook** took over. When Malcolm's children were young, they had watched him blow up a tree stump, knocking himself flat in the blast. Malcolm had been furious with him for putting himself and his children in danger and had taken away the remaining detonators, which Perkins had acquired from a quarryman friend. Perkins had told Bellbrook that Mr. Pembroke's son had built a shed in the wall of the kitchen garden.

Perryside, Major Clement (*Break In* 1985)

An octogenarian, Major Perryside lives in straitened circumstances with his wife, **Lucy Perryside**, in a retirement home in **Hertfordshire**. About ten years previously he had owned **Metavane**, a promising unraced two-year-old colt, trained by **Maynard Allardeck's** father in **Newmarket**. Perryside had incurred heavy losses in the London insurance market, and had then been tricked by Maynard Allardeck into selling Metavane for a fraction of his value. The colt had subsequently won the Two Thousand Guineas at **Newmarket**.

Perryside, Lucy (*Break In* 1985)

Lucy is the wife of **Major Clement Perryside**. She is in her eighties, and lives with her husband in genteel poverty in a retirement home in **Hertfordshire**. Her husband had been duped by **Maynard Allardeck** into selling cheaply an unraced colt, **Metavane**, which subsequently won the Two Thousand Guineas at **Newmarket** as a three-year-old.

Peter (*Risk* 1977)

Peter is a young assistant at **King and Britten**, accountants, in **Newbury, Berkshire**. He feels he has to work too hard because of **Roland Britten** taking time off to go racing as an amateur jockey. He is not terribly bright but is good at his job, which requires him to be unimaginative but careful. He is considered by Roland to have homosexual tendencies. Peter carries out Roland's instructions as if he is doing him a favor, and tends to sulk if things are not going well.

Peter (*Proof* 1984)

Peter is the owner of a horse van which careers down a hill and crashes into a marquee at **Jack Hawthorn's** racing stables, killing eight people. He insists that he had left the van with the handbrake on and in gear, but hadn't locked the door. He is blamed for that omission by the parents of the small boy who had let the handbrake off.

Peterman (*Driving Force* 1992)

Peterman is an aged retired racehorse; in the past he had won over jumps, ridden by **Freddie Croft**. Freddie is surprised to see Peterman again when one of his horse vans transports the horse from **Yorkshire**, on behalf of retired racehorse charity **Centaur Care**, to a new home in **Pixhill, Hampshire**. Peterman is taken on by **Marigold English**, at Freddie's request. However, he won't eat and quickly loses condition. He is taken away by Freddie and dies shortly afterwards.

Peters (*Flying Finish* 1966)

Peters, the traveling head groom at **Yardman Transport**, does not return to England after a trip abroad. His job is given to **Lord Henry Gray**.

Petrovitch, Clay (*Field of 13* 1998: "The Gift")

Petrovitch is an American racing journalist, and a racecourse colleague of **Fred Collyer**. He is at **Churchill Downs** to cover the Kentucky Derby. He lends Collyer one hundred dollars, after Collyer's wallet is stolen, to back a horse in the last race. Petrovitch is unhappy, when the horse wins at odds of twelve to one, that Collyer hadn't shared the information.

Petrovitch, Mr. and Mrs. Howard K. (*In the Frame* 1976)

Mr. and Mrs. Petrovitch are a wealthy retired couple from Ridgeville, New Jersey. They are onlookers in the **Victoria Art Center** in Melbourne where a young artist is copying an **Alfred Munnings** painting. The Petrovitchs are keen on racing; they tell **Charles Todd** that the artist had mentioned a Munnings for sale at **Yarra River Fine Arts** gallery nearby. He had also advised them to visit the gallery nearby.

Phil (*Driving Force* 1992)

Phil is a driver for **Croft Raceways** horse transport firm. He is reliable but lacking in initiative.

Phil (*To the Hilt* 1996)

Phil, a racehorse trainer based in **East Ilsley, Berkshire**, looks after **Golden Malt** for **Alex Kinloch** until Alex can find a more permanent home for the horse.

Phoenix Fledgling (*Knock Down* 1974)

Phoenix Fledgling is a top class American two-year-old. **Wilton Young**, when he hears that rival owner **Constantine Brevett** is interested in Phoenix Fledgling, instructs **Jonah Dereham** to go to the USA to bid for the colt.

Picton, Norman (*Come to Grief* 1995)

Picton is a young, ambitious Detective Inspector with Thames Valley Police. He is confident and highly competent. Following his investigations into the mutilation of horses, Picton secures an arrest; however the suspect is freed in bail, and doubts over his guilt arise. Picton tells **Sid Halley** that he is being pressurized by his superintendent to drop the case.

Pierre (*The Edge* 1988)

Pierre, a character in the mystery play on the Great Transcontinental Mystery Race Train, is a compulsive gambler and is deeply in debt. In love with **Donna Bricknell**, Pierre is shot by mistake by **Giles**, who is aiming at Donna.

Pigeon, Tom (*Shattered* 2000)

Tom Pigeon is about thirty years old and lives in **Broadway**, a village in **Gloucestershire**; he is a near neighbor of **Gerard Logan**. He is nicknamed locally "The Backlash," owing to the speed of his fists and of his thinking. He has a chequered past, and has spent eighteen months in prison for breaking and entering. Pigeon is walking his three Dobermans one evening when he sees Gerard being assaulted by several people outside his workshop. He yells at the assailants, scaring them off, and helps Gerard into his workshop. He offers his help to Gerard as a bodyguard while **Worthington** is on holiday, and performs the task effectively.

Pincer Movement (*Field of 13* 1998: "The Gift")

Pincer Movement, an American racehorse trained by **Harbourne Cressie**, wins the Kentucky Derby at **Churchill Downs**.

Pine Woods Lodge, Sussex (*Reflex* 1980)

This is the last known address of **Caroline Nore**, **Philip Nore**'s mother. It is an old mansion, variously used in the past as a nursing home, convent, TV studios and residence of a religious sect.

Pinkeye (*Bolt* 1986)

Pinkeye, a jumper trained by **Wykeham Harlow**, is ridden to win at **Bradbury** races by **Kit Fielding**.

Pinlock, Hilary Margaret (*Risk* 1977)

In her mid-forties, Hilary Pinlock is a tall, thin, plain spinster, with wrinkles and glasses. She is headmistress of a girls' comprehensive school. She is on holiday on the island of **Minorca** and is sunbathing on the beach when **Roland Britten**, escaping from an abductor, swims to the shore and crouches down behind rocks close by. When the coast is clear Miss Pinlock takes Roland to her hotel room. She buys Roland new clothes and food, and that evening asks him if he will go to bed with her. She tells Roland she has never slept with a man. She'd been too busy establishing her career, and when, finally, she'd had the time for romance the opportunities had not been there. Miss Pinlock claims to have an ulterior motive for her desire to have sex with Roland; she wants to find out what it's like to help her deal with her teenage pupils. Feeling that he owes her a debt of gratitude Roland obliges, despite misgivings, and the experience is a most satisfactory one for Miss Pinlock.

She extends her stay in the Mediterranean to find out about Roland's abductor. Back in England she uses her intelligence and initiative, when concerned as to Roland's whereabouts, to track him down.

Pitts, Jane (*Twice Shy* 1981)

Jane, the wife of **Ted Pitts**, is small, dark and serious. She offers to put **Jonathan Derry** up on the sofa of the mobile home where she lives with Ted and her three daughters if he will pay in advance; the family is very hard-up.

Fourteen years later, Mrs. Pitts is rich after Ted successfully uses **Liam O'Rorke**'s betting system. She is furious with her husband when she finds he has tampered with the computer tapes he had given to **William Derry**, and makes him apologize. She plays William the correct tapes over the telephone so that he can record them.

Pitts, Ted (*Twice Shy* 1981)

Pitts is a math teacher and a colleague of **Jonathan Derry** at East **Middlesex** Comprehensive School. He agrees to try out cassette tapes given to Jonathan by **Peter Keithley** on the school's computer, and asks Jonathan if he can keep a copy of the tapes. Pitts has three children and little money; he lives in a mobile home on a caravan park. When Jonathan needs to keep a low profile Pitts lets him stay with him for the weekend, though Jonathan has to pay for the privilege. He tells Jonathan he can't risk the money to use **Liam O'Rorke**'s betting system even though he has the tapes. However the temptation is clearly too great: fourteen years later Pitts is living in a large, expensive house in North London. He sometimes teaches university courses in computer programming. He tells **William Derry** that he had borrowed a hundred pounds to start betting with and had been a winner from the outset. When William asks for copies of the tapes Pitts agrees to let him have them; but he fails to keep his word and acts dishonorably. For so doing Pitts incurs the wrath of his wife, **Jane Pitts**.

Pixhill, Hampshire

Pixhill is a fictional racing village in **Hampshire**, a county in the south of England.

Driving Force (1992): Ex-jump jockey **Freddie Croft** runs a fleet of horse vans out of Pixhill. Trainer **Michael Watermead's** yard is in Pixhill.

Plimbourne, Lord (*Enquiry* 1969)

Lord Plimbourne is an old and doddery member of the committee of disciplinary stewards of the **Jockey Club** who conduct the enquiry at which **Kelly Hughes** and **Dexter Cranfield** lose their licenses for allegedly stopping the favorite for the Lemonfizz Crystal Cup at **Oxford**. He sleeps through most of the enquiry; when awake he shows no interest but agrees with **Lord Gowery** when required to do so.

Plots

Between 1962 and 2000, Dick Francis wrote thirty-eight novels. He added another in 2006, and in 2007 he collaborated with his son Felix in the writing of a fortieth. By any standards this is a prodigious output and, inevitably, the quality of these novels varies from outstanding to execrable, stopping at every station in between. From the standpoint of plotting, there are two significant correlations to be noted: first, a line graph drawn to show the link between the passing of the years and the excellence of the plotting would clearly show a downward curve. Second, there is a strong relationship between the quality of the storyline and the centrality of English horse racing to the novel; as a general rule, the further that Francis strays away from what he knows best, the less sure is his touch.

From 1962, when he published *Dead Cert*, up to *Enquiry* in 1969, Francis's writing was of a consistently high standard. The opening of *Dead Cert*, describing a steeplechase in mid-winter from the jockey's viewpoint, takes the reader straight to the heart of what jump racing in Britain is all about.

The action of the novel is driven by the plot, as is the norm in crime genre stories, but the protagonist **Alan York** is no mere cipher; the reader cares about what happens to him. The plot conflict—the events that make it difficult for Alan to find out who killed his friend—creates an intensity of suspense that is maintained to the end.

In Francis's three subsequent novels—*Nerve* (1964), *For Kicks* and *Odds Against* 1965)—the action is motivated both by the plot and by the internal conflict within the personality of the main character. In *Nerve* jockey **Rob Finn** has to find the inner strength to fight back against the effects of public humiliation; everyone thinks he has lost his nerve as he rides loser after loser, and the agony of it drives him to consider suicide. For **Daniel Roke** in *For Kicks*, the internal struggle is more subtle but insidious. He feels that his life as a stud farmer in Australia, working long hours year after year to provide for his younger siblings, is stifling him. It's a jail term from which, ironically, he is released by swapping it for a job which entails working even longer hours and in a much more dangerous environment. Francis's depiction in *Odds Against* of the angst-ridden ex-jockey **Sid Halley** is masterful. His hand crippled by a racing fall two years before, Halley is, as the book opens, recovering in hospital from being shot in the stomach. Messily estranged from a wife he still loves, desperately missing his previous life as a jockey, and employed in a job that he has no interest in doing well, Sid is plumbing the depths of misery. Sid's gradual rehabilitation and eventual redemption are the engines that motivate the action and lift a conventional plot above the ordinary.

The novels of the 1960's are enhanced not only by the excellence of the characterization but also by their settings. In six of the eight books published in that decade horse racing is at the heart of the plot, and in the other two it is a significant element in it. More specifically, it is in the quintessential English sport of **National Hunt** racing over hurdles and fences that Francis sets the action of his books and it is hard to think of anyone better qualified to portray it. As a jump jockey Francis was at or near the top of his profession and in the course of a career spanning ten years, experienced all the highs and lows that make up a jockey's life. He is adept at transporting his readers into this world, allowing them to experience it vicariously and to understand what drives jockeys, trainers, owners, gamblers or stable lads to act as they do.

Francis develops his plots—and maintains the suspense—by increasing either the obstacles which stand in the way of the hero achieving success, or his motivation to succeed. In *Flying Finish* (1966) **Lord Henry Gray** realizes, just days into his job as a groom with a firm which ships horses all over the world, that scams are being worked. As Henry attempts to find out more, a young psychopath takes every opportunity he can to inflict physical pain on Henry as a deterrent. When Henry discovers that the crimes being perpetrated are more serious than he first thought, the level of physical violence steadily rises. In the pay-off scene, which is unpredictable and emotionally intense, Henry proves every bit as ruthless as his adversary.

Fiction coach Raymond Obstfeld, discussing in his book *Fiction First Aid* the importance of a novel's ending in its overall structure, says that it should be appropriate to the story, memorable and credible. It should tie up loose ends satisfactorily and avoid contrived twists. Any weaknesses in Francis's early novels are likely to be found in their endings. In both *Dead Cert* and *Nerve*, well plotted in most other respects, the behavior of the villains at the conclusion of these novels is unconvincing in terms of what we already know about them.

In contrast, the ending of *Bonecrack* (1971) is one of its most exciting elements. Set in **Newmarket**, the headquarters of flat racing, the story is driven by both its plot—full of conflict, high on suspense—and its acutely observed and convincing characters. From the first page the menace of Italian **Enso Rivera** colors the action, and violence or the threat of it is never far from the surface. Rivera's unpredictability ensures a plot where nothing can be anticipated with certainty except the fact that life will get progressively more difficult for the hero, **Neil Griffon**. Rivera's motivation is his obsession over the desire of his son, **Alessandro Rivera**, to be a top flat race jockey. Neil, temporarily overseeing a yard full of blue-blooded racehorses in place of his hospitalized father, is forced to accept Alessandro as an apprentice. *Bonecrack* excels in its perceptive exploration of the father-son relationship; neither Neil nor Alessandro can communicate with their fathers who are intent on pursuing their own selfish agenda. As the novel progresses a bond forms between Neil and the young Italian; when Rivera sees that Neil is becoming more of a father to Alessandro than he is himself, his reaction sets up a tense and chilling climax.

In the 1970's Francis no longer found it easy to maintain the quality of plotting that he achieved in the previous decade. He followed up *Bonecrack* with *Smokescreen*, a less than compelling story set in South Africa in which he first exhibited a weakness which is repeated in later novels, that of using a foreign background as a means of introducing unnecessary and often tedious information about the country.

In *Slay-Ride* (1973) Francis handles the foreign setting much better. The action takes place mostly in Norway, and the information given about the country is appropriate and relevant to the story. Hero **David Cleveland**, a **Jockey Club** investigator, is an adequate but unexciting main character in an otherwise absorbing, plot-driven story with satisfying pay-off scenes. The discovery of a body on **Øvrevoll racecourse** is particularly well written: a small boy, wet through and sobbing his heart out, speaks quietly to men who are searching the course, shocking them to the core. David, not understanding, asks what he had said:

"Baltzersen loosened his jaw with a visible effort, and translated:

"He said, 'I have found a hand.'"

Francis's best early novels—*Nerve, For Kicks, Odds Against, Forfeit and Bonecrack*—combine two kinds of conflict: plot conflict, which is external to the life of the protagonist and which provides him with a variety of critical situations to survive; and character conflict, where the protagonist is tested by struggles in his personal life that are preventing him from achieving contentment. Francis successfully repeats the formula in *Knock Down* (1974), set in the duplicitous world of bloodstock dealing. Ex-jockey **Jonah Dereham** is trying to build up his bloodstock agency without resorting to the sharp practices which many of his colleagues adopt. They see him as a threat, and when their attempts to bring him into line fail they adopt increasingly violent methods to put him out of business. At the same time Jonah has also to deal with **Crispin Dereham**, his alcoholic brother, who is seemingly intent on wrecking his own life as well as Jonah's.

The period between 1975 and 1979 is notable for the sheer variation in quality of Francis's plotting. In *High Stakes* (1975) a crooked racehorse trainer, in concert with a bookmaker, defrauds his richest owner, **Steven Scott**. The plot has interesting possibilities, but the book's chemistry just isn't right, owing partly to the unconvincing nature of the sting by means of which Scott retaliates against his trainer. *High Stakes* is moderate, but *In the Frame*, published the following year, is far worse. It is Francis's first novel in which horse racing is no more than a minor element in the plot. Without the secure background of a familiar setting, Francis produces a tedious Australian travelogue peopled by irritating characters. The plot, which revolves around a fine art scam, is unconvincing and lacking in suspense.

By contrast *Risk* (1977) is the complete antithesis—a gripping, fast-moving story with arguably the most chilling opening scene of any of Francis's novels. Imagine waking up in total darkness, in a space so small that you can't move more than a few inches in any direction. You're freezing cold, you feel sick and there's a barrage of noise assaulting your ears. It's like you've survived your own burial; the icy chains of terror are tightening around your stomach and there's no-one to hear your screams. This is the situation that protagonist **Roland Britten** is faced with; how he deals with it without losing his nerve or his sanity is an example of Francis's writing at its best. *Risk* will have won back for Francis any fans who were wavering after struggling through *In the Frame*.

Unfortunately he may well have lost them again when they read his 1978 novel, *Trial Run*. The background is Communist Russia, which was, in the 1970's, a grey, threatening place. Francis, though, succeeds only with the grey. There are lots of furtive types following each other and pretending to be someone they aren't, but it's hard to care who they really are. Humorless protagonist **Randall Drew** is an upper-class bore with a wheezy chest; his only saving grace is his feisty girlfriend, who treats him like a doormat, thus providing a bit of much needed, if inadvertent, amusement.

In 1979 **Sid Halley** is dusted down after fourteen years and pressed into service in aid of the party. Rarely has the return of a hero been more timely or more welcome; by sheer force of character Sid drives the plot and sub-plots of *Whip Hand*. He's everything that Randall Drew isn't— a multi-faceted and complex man who acts in a realistic way, backed up by strong minor characters who have credible lives of their own, and interwoven storylines that are never predictable. *Whip Hand* is the last novel where the horseracing background is central to the plot. From 1980 onwards his novels fall into two groups: those in which the racing element, though still important, exists more to provide a familiar setting than as a crucial part

of the story; and those where racing is relegated to an insignificant role.

Of the novels published in the 1980's, five fall into the first category and five into the second. The excellent *Reflex* (1980) derives its quality not least from having a jump jockey as its main character. **Philip Nore** is questioning whether he really wants to be a jockey any longer. Photography has supplanted race riding as his first love, and it is this interest that draws him into an attempt to resolve the mystery surrounding the death of a racecourse photographer. The plot is well-constructed and unpredictable, with strong minor characters and a satisfying conclusion.

Reflex is one of three superb novels written in the 1980's. The others are *Proof* (1984) and *Straight* (1989), both of high quality despite the sparing use of the horseracing milieu. *Proof*'s tight, pacey plot deals with fraudulent practices which lead to murder and mayhem in the wines and spirits business. **Tony Beach** is the owner of a wine shop who finds himself involved in sorting out the ensuing mess, but what makes him interesting are the conflicts within himself that he is forced to confront as a result.

Straight is almost as good. When jockey **Derek Franklin**'s brother **Greville** is killed in an accident, Derek tries to make sense of the complex and potentially dangerous business decisions that Greville's dealing in precious and semi-precious stones had led him into. As a main character Derek is easy to like, with realistic human strengths and weaknesses; the racing connection, concerned with the doping of racehorses, is, almost twenty years later, still as topical as it was then; and the plot is never predictable. *Straight*'s only weakness is that the villains are by no means as finely drawn as the protagonist.

The decade had started and ended well for Francis; much of what lay in between, though, was mediocre. *Twice Shy* (1981) has not one protagonist but two: in the first part of the novel it is physics teacher **Jonathan Derry**, and in the second it is Jonathan's younger brother **William**. The mechanics of the plot involve a brute of a man making life for the brothers miserable in his pursuit of a set of cassette tapes containing a computerized betting system. Part One of *Twice Shy* is inhabited by people in whom it is difficult to be interested: Jonathan is dull, his wife's a harridan, and the villain is a caricature. Little suspense is generated; the stakes of the plot remain low throughout. Part Two is an improvement in so far as William at least is a likeable character. The plot, however, remains unedifying; though it is fourteen years later, time seems to have largely stood still. There are no developments in computer technology, and no changes in the way racing is conducted. Francis did not have the benefit of hindsight, but he could perhaps have been more alert to the risks inherent in this kind of plotting format.

Francis's 1982 novel, *Banker*, suffers from similar problems to *Twice Shy*. The action, taking place over three years, lacks pace and dynamism, a comment which could be equally applied to protagonist **Tim Ekaterin**. Another unexciting character is **Andrew Douglas** in *The Danger* (1983), but the novel succeeds despite him owing to the tense, gripping nature of the plot. Andrew's job is to secure the safe release of kidnap victims, and in *The Danger* the reader is taken to the heart of how such negotiations are coordinated, and the risks inherent in dealing with the dangerous and unpredictable men who take hostages for mercenary or political ends. Francis gets the texture right, supplying plenty of informative detail about the effects of kidnap on both the victim and the perpetrators.

Break In (1985) and its sequel *Bolt* (1986) share the same protagonist in **Kit Fielding**, a conventional yet potentially engaging main character who struggles with plots containing flaws which ultimately render them unsatisfying. *Break In*'s plot concerns the attempted character assassination of Kit's brother-in-law, racehorse trainer **Bobby Allardeck**, whose family has been at odds with the Fieldings since racing first started in the seventeenth century. The storyline offers massive scope for the exploitation of conflict, but too often the villains act in an unrealistic way, lessening the impact and lowering the suspense. This weakness is also noticeable in *Bolt*, which features several of the same characters and has a rather predictable storyline.

Problems with characterization continued to adversely affect Francis's plotting. In *Hot Money* (1987) one of the children of **Malcolm Pembroke**, a multi-millionaire businessman, appears to want him dead, but the field resembles an end-of-season maiden race at Newmarket, i.e. hugely oversubscribed. Five-times married Malcolm has nine children, not to mention their assorted husbands and wives. Trying to keep track of them all proves a major stumbling block, especially since most of them are unlikeable and lack the saving grace of being interesting. Only **Ian Pembroke**, the son

charged with the task of keeping his father safe and identifying the rogue member of the family, emerges with any credit.

When Francis sets his story in a foreign country it usually results in a sub-standard plot— *Smokescreen* (South Africa); *In the Frame* (Australia); and *Trial Run* (Russia) all fall into this category, with *Slay-Ride* (Norway) being an honorable exception. In *The Edge* (1988) Francis avoids the mistake of including travel brochure-type descriptions of the scenery merely for the sake of it. But the plot itself is contrived and unconvincing. Skulduggery takes place on a train ferrying horses and their connections across Canada in order to race at various locations on the way. En route a mystery play is enacted for the delectation of the passengers—but not, sadly, of the reader. Nor is the characterization robust enough to carry the plot's deficiencies.

In 1989 *Straight* more than makes up for *The Edge*, and heralds a period of almost vintage Francis. *Longshot* (1990) is a conventional crime novel but with plenty of unexpected twists. Though racing isn't pivotal, there are some excellent snapshots of life in a racing stable and its attendant joys and frustrations. **John Kendall** is a writer of survival handbooks who takes on the task of writing the biography of a racehorse trainer. Immediately sucked in by the murky undercurrents of life in the trainer's family, John needs to use all his expertise to ensure his own survival.

Even better than *Longshot* is *Driving Force* (1992), set against the background of a racehorse transport firm. The novel's title refers to the influence that causes people to behave as they do, and Francis cleverly knits together a web of criminal activities for which the motivating factors spring from diverse sources. **Freddie Croft**, the proprietor of the firm and the main character, is an ex-jockey, which almost guarantees that he will be sympathetically drawn. The minor characters too, are fully developed and avoid the stereotyping that can flaw this aspect of the plot.

In his next novel, *Decider*, Francis breaks new ground by putting the family at the heart of the plot—its tensions, its machinations, its secrets. It's not so much the inner workings of architect **Lee Morris**'s own family that are scrutinized, though the relationships between Lee and his wife **Amanda** on the one hand, and his sons on the other, provide a parallel subtext. The plot of *Decider* spotlights the interactions between the members of a wealthy but dysfunctional family who are vying for control of a racecourse. Their devious tactics and willingness to exploit each other's hushed-up misdeeds in the pursuit of their own ends bring to mind the remark made by Harriet, Lady Ashburton to the effect that racing people stick together, each knowing something that might hang the others. *Decider*'s perceptive characterization and sustained level of suspense created by the elements of hope and fear within the structure of the plot combine to place the novel among Francis's best.

Sandwiched between these excellent novels is the disappointing *Comeback* (1991). The storyline involves crimes taking place at the present time which are similar to ones committed by the previous generation of the same families. However, the details of what went on then and what is going on now are obscured by the mists of time on the one hand and by a lack of clear motivation on the other. Diplomat **Peter Darwin**, roped in to shed light on matters, manages to obfuscate more than clarify, and his cause is not helped by the lack of a convincing interior life of his own.

Even when a novel just doesn't work, the quality of the research on which the story is based can rarely be faulted. *Comeback* is set in an equine veterinary practice, and the technical detail of how the business functions goes some way to ameliorating the difficulties inherent in the plot. Such meticulous preparation is also evident in *Wild Horses* (1994), the setting for which is the film industry. It is a surprisingly lurid tale of sexual deviation which has tragic consequences for the participants. The novel's racing background is a plus—protagonist **Thomas Lyon** is shooting a film in **Newmarket**—but, like *Comeback*, events which had occurred many years before are crucial to the storyline, and these are shrouded in uncertainty. *Wild Horses* is, despite its faults, a tour de force in comparison with the aptly named *Come to Grief* published in the following year. It is possible only to feel sympathy for Sid Halley, wheeled out again fully sixteen years after appearing in *Whip Hand* and forced to perform in a thoroughly dispiriting story of cruelty to horses perpetrated by a loathsome lunatic. The novel fails either to enhance or to illuminate Halley's own character, and the inconsistencies in the behavior of the villain reduce to a minimum the credibility of the plot.

The growing suspicion that Francis was running short of ideas was only partially allayed by *To the Hilt* in 1996. At least the novel's themes—family loyalty, the influences exerted on a man's conduct by the genes he inherits, and the lengths to which he is prepared to go to honor his commitments—are worth exploring, and their impact on the life of painter **Alexander Kinloch** is crucial in the development of his character within the structure of the plot. Alexander, a painter who lives on a Scottish mountainside, is asked by his mother to do what he can to save her husband's brewery business, which is about to go bust. He risks life and limb in the cause without demur, in the process suffering an excruciatingly painful assault. Francis has been criticized for glorifying violence, but he is merely reflecting what happens all too often in real life.

A nadir was reached in 1997 with the publication of the irredeemable *10 lb. Penalty*, a wretched tale of how an unpleasant nonentity coerces his shallow, vapid son into helping him to win a parliamentary seat—and they're the good guys. The superficiality of the characterization is matched only by the triviality of the plot. This is a book of limited literary merit, and it was no surprise that in 1998 Francis decided, for the first time in thirty-five years, not to produce a novel. Instead he released *Field of Thirteen*, a collection of short stories, some written years before, which served only to underline the fact that short-story writing was not his forte.

In 1999 Francis published *Second Wind*. Set in the Caribbean, where Francis had made his home, it is a confusing story concerning the machinations of a group of criminals who deal in the raw materials of weapons of mass destruction. It's a promising milieu given world conditions today, but spoilt by the impenetrability of the plot and the inconsistent behavior of the protagonist, meteorologist **Perry Stuart**.

At least the plot of *Second Wind* has a vaguely recognizable structure to it, even if it's hard to follow; Francis's next novel, *Shattered*, struggles with even that basic ingredient. Ostensibly about a stolen video containing information on a new treatment for cancer, *Shattered* has a bunch of characters who have apparently escaped from a Broadway farce. The plot is so insubstantial as to be almost non-existent; no suspense is generated at any stage and the only good thing about the ending is that the reader is spared further torture.

There is little point in speculating upon what possessed Francis to come out of retirement six years after writing *Shattered* and to resurrect his best-loved character, **Sid Halley**, in *Under Orders*. It could be argued that he was ill-advised to do so. Though partly redeemed by being set in the horseracing world, *Under Orders* suffers from a threadbare plotline and a hero who is a pale spectre of the character that enriched *Odds Against* and *Whip Hand*. In 2007 Francis co-wrote *Dead Heat* with his son Felix. How much of the actual writing of this novel Francis did is open to question. *Dead Heat* deals with the problems besetting a Newmarket-based chef, but its lack of a properly developed villain consigns the novel to mediocrity at best.

It would be unkind to dwell on the quality of Francis's later novels; much better to remember the pleasure he has given to millions with novels like *Bonecrack*, *Whip Hand*, *Reflex* and *Proof*, examples of crime fiction at its best. Of the thirty-nine novels he wrote over a similar period of years, fourteen can be rated outstanding, and another five are not far behind. How many writers as prolific as Francis can boast a strike rate of almost fifty per cent?

Plumpton racecourse

Opened in 1884, Plumpton racecourse is in east **Sussex**, not far from **Brighton**. Just over one mile round, it has tight turns and severe undulations. The clay subsoil means that the going is often bottomless. Not many jockeys would rate Plumpton as their favorite course; certainly, Dick Francis didn't much like it. According to John Tyrrel, in his book *Chasing Around Britain*, Francis frequently came to grief at the second fence in the downhill back straight, and ruefully concluded that his bad luck at Plumpton could be attributed to the fact that he was usually poorly mounted. The three jumping courses along Britain's south coast are referred to, somewhat irreverently, as the "three F's— **Folkestone**, **Fontwell** and f****ing Plumpton."

The jockeys may have reservations about Plumpton but racegoers are generally in favor. The train from London stops right next to the course, "so adjacent that a spark ejected from the funnel of the last steam train to travel the line set fire to the plain fence just before the home turn on the eve of the first fixture of the season" (Tyrrel). In his book *Racing Around Britain* Stephen Cartmell describes Plumpton as "small, compact, intimate and everything you need within a few strides ... the paddock is delightful—in its centre two large, leafy oaks." Times journalist Alan Lee, assessing the course in 2003, has a caveat: "This is not a great viewing track, especially on Bank Holidays when a funfair in centre course obscures the back straight."

Dead Cert (1962): Amateur jockey **Alan York** rides a horse at Plumpton for delectable owner **Kate Ellery-Penn**. The horse is her twenty-first birthday present.

Forfeit (1968): Investigative racing journalist **James Tyrone** receives information from a bookmaker's clerk at Plumpton about the two thugs who had beaten him up the previous day as he returned by train to London from **Leicester** races.

In the Frame (1976): A racecourse acquaintance introduces painter **Charles Todd** to wealthy widow **Maisie Matthews**, whose house in **Sussex** has recently burned down. Maisie is interested in having the ruins painted.

Police

In his biography of Dick Francis, *A Racing Life*, Graham Lord says that in *Driving Force* (1992) "there is a surprisingly strong anti-police tone, as there is in many of the Francis novels...." Certainly, **Freddie Croft** has a jaundiced view of the police, stemming from an incident in his youth when they failed to act on his warning about a violent husband who subsequently killed his wife. Freddie's opinion is not improved by their apparent lack of interest in finding out who tried to kill him. Police Constable **Sandy Smith**, who is a competent officer and supportive of Freddie, explains the police's unsympathetic attitude on the grounds that they see such a surfeit of violence that continually showing compassion becomes difficult. Francis may portray the police as overly formal, skeptical and uncommunicative, but it is only natural that they should be suspicious of untrained amateurs who want to interfere in their investigations. **Sid Halley**, in *Come to Grief* (1995), comments that the police did not, in general, approve of people like him. Nevertheless, in many novels the police, whilst initially unimpressed with the help offered by the hero, are willing to cooperate if the information received is shown to be useful.

Lord also cites police indifference in *Risk* (1977) to **Roland Britten's** kidnapping and incarceration as another example of their uncaring attitude. This may be so, but given the fact that Roland emerged unharmed from his ordeal, the police view that their time and resources would be better spent on unsolved crimes is understandable. Francis's depiction of police attitudes in *Driving Force* and *Risk* is realistic rather than antagonistic.

An analysis of the forty police officers of all ranks who appear in Francis's novels and short stories does not support Lord's view. Nineteen are portrayed in a favorable light; sixteen have such a minor role that their contribution to the plot is either neutral or insignificant; and only five are deemed worthy of criticism for their attitudes, character or lack of competence. In *Hot Money* (1987) the self-important **Superintendent Yale** initially refuses to believe that **Malcolm Pembroke's** life is in danger. Subsequent events compel him to change his mind, but then he doesn't make much progress with his investigation. **Detective Superintendent Rightsworth** (*The Danger* 1983) appears to have a jaundiced view of the general public and fails, in **Andrew Douglas's** opinion, to take seriously enough the threats issued by the kidnappers of **Dominic Nerrity**. In *Proof* (1984) **Detective Sergeant Ridger** lacks warmth and good manners; he asks for **Tony Beach's** help in testing the whisky at the **Silver Moondance** restaurant but goes off without a word of thanks. **Gloucestershire** policeman **Detective Inspector Ramsay** (*Comeback* 1991) is portrayed as lacking the sharpness of the city detective, and is not keen to share information with **Peter Darwin**. *To the Hilt's* **Detective Sergeant Berrick** is a bigoted Scot who dislikes Englishmen, Celtic Football Club and the Conservative Party.

All of this may be reprehensible, but is not evidence of anti-police bias on Francis's part. None of the five is shown to be dishonest or corrupt, and here Francis appears to be erring on the side of generosity. By contrast, several police officers are revealed by their actions to be not only highly competent but supportive of the main characters' attempts to solve a crime or hunt down a villain. **Detective Sergeant Eagler** in *The Danger*, unlike **Rightsworth**, his curmudgeonly superior officer, is calm, undemonstrative and highly effective. He agrees to go along with **Andrew Douglas's** plan to rescue **Dominic Nerrity** without demanding to know all the details, and is always willing to listen to the opinions of others. Italian police officer **Pucinelli** is courageous and competent; he works harmoniously with Andrew to track down and arrest members of the kidnap gang, as does Captain **Kent Wagner** of the Washington D.C. police. In *Come to Grief* the young, ambitious Detective Inspector **Picton** is helpful to **Sid Halley** in breaking the villain's alibi and proving his involvement in the mutilation of horses. Detective Chief Inspectors **Wygold** (*Banker* 1982) and **Carlisle** (*Under Orders* 2006) are both initially skeptical about the theories advanced by the main characters to explain the murders that occur in those nov-els, but subsequently show themselves willing to change their minds when presented with corrob-orative evidence.

Pollgate, Nestor (*Break In* 1985)

Pollgate is the owner of **Fleet Street** newspaper, the *Daily Flag*. He had bought the *Flag* for the power and influence its ownership conveyed. He is youngish, socially ambitious and unpleasant. In his dealings with **Kit Fielding** Pollgate uses threatening behavior and encourages the use of violence against him. Eventually Pollgate is compelled to come to an agreement with Kit which is satisfactory to both parties.

Polly (*10 lb. Penalty* 1997)

Polly, known as "Dearest Polly," is a hard-working constituency worker in **Hoopwestern, Dorset**. She works for **George Juliard** during his by-election campaign. In her mid-forties, Polly is kind, easy-going and independently wealthy. She is on the selection panel which chose Juliard as the party's candidate. She is jealous when **Orinda Nagle** comes over to Juliard's side, but puts up with it for the greater good of the party. Two years later, Polly marries George Juliard.

Polyplanes (*Rat Race* 1970)

Polyplanes is an air-taxi firm, and a rival to **Derrydown Air Transport**.

Polyprint (*Knock Down* 1974)

Polyprint was a stallion supposedly shipped out to Japan by agent **Vic Vincent** and which was said to have died of tetanus in transit. In fact an identical stallion, owned by Vincent and much less valuable, had been sent in Polyprint's place.

Pominga, Gail (*Forfeit* 1968)

Gail Pominga is the mixed race, beautiful niece of **Harry** and **Sarah Hunterson**, owners of racehorse **Egocentric**. She is the daughter of Harry's sister, who had married an African barrister. She teaches fashion design at the Western School of Art in London, and lives with Harry and Sarah in Virginia Water, **Surrey**. She does not enjoy a close relationship with her uncle and aunt, being self-centered and lacking in warmth. Gail fancies **James Tyrone** when he comes to interview Harry and Sarah, and lets James know it. She willingly accepts his invitation to have sex, though with no emotional involvement. Gail's relationship with James is fraught with difficulties, but the pair eventually arrive at a mutually satisfactory accommodation.

Pontefract, Yorkshire

Pontefract is a market town in West Yorkshire, near the A1 and M62 motorways. It has a racecourse on the outskirts of the town, used for flat racing only.

Driving Force (1992): Racehorse trainer Michael Watermead conveys to Freddie Croft his suspicions about how and why a thermos flask was transported from Pontefract to a motorway service station near Newbury.

Poole, Inky (*Whip Hand* 1979)

Poole is Tri-Nitro's work rider at George Caspar's Newmarket stables. He is a quiet, sympathetic horseman, but surly and unhelpful in his dealings with Sid Halley.

Popsy (*Whip Hand* 1979)

Popsy is a girl who had volunteered to be John Viking's passenger in a balloon race when his usual passenger broke his leg during a rough landing. Viking won't let her take her handbag because of the weight, so at the very last moment she refuses to go. Sid Halley, arriving at the moment of take-off, goes instead.

Porter (*In the Frame* 1976)

Porter, a plain-clothes officer with Melbourne city police, is a big, hard man with a voice and manner to match. He successfully sets up a trap at the Hilton Hotel, Melbourne, to catch a villain. Later he sends a message of thanks to Charles Todd in England via Inspector Frost.

Portman Square, London

Portman Square is the former central London home of the Jockey Club, once racing's regulatory body but now concentrating on racecourse and property management. Based at 42 Portman Square since the 1960's, the Jockey Club moved in 2004 to Shaftesbury Avenue. In 1993 the Jockey Club ceased to be racing's regulatory authority; this responsibility is now held by the Horseracing Regulatory Authority. Until 1993 the Jockey Club conducted hearings and appeals at Portman Square.

Enquiry (1969): Jockey Kelly Hughes and trainer Dexter Cranfield lose their licenses at a Jockey Club enquiry held at Portman Square.

Potter, Wilbur (*Odds Against* 1965)

Wilbur Potter is the real name of criminal Howard Kraye.

Powys, Connaught (*Risk* 1977)

Powys is a smooth city type; his manner is suggestive of wealth and influence but there is wariness in his eyes. He has recently been released from Leyhill Prison after serving a four year sentence for computer fraud, a crime uncovered by Roland Britten.

Powys meets Roland in Vivian Iverson's gambling club; he will not admit, in front of Iverson, to having harmed Roland, or to having the intention to do so. Subsequently, however, Powys exacts his revenge.

Premiere (*The Edge* 1988)

Premiere, a racehorse owned by Canadian Mercer Lorrimore, is favorite when a close second in the Jockey Club Race Train Stakes at Assiniboia Downs, Winnipeg.

Prensela, Walt (*Blood Sport* 1967)

Prensela is an insurance investigator for Buttress Life, New York. In his late thirties, he is short and powerfully built, and has a skeptical outlook on life. He is suitably impressed, though, by the feedback he receives from the FBI and the CIA about Gene Hawkins. Prensela is in charge of the investigation into the disappearance of a valuable stallion. He is not delighted to have to cooperate with Gene, but is resigned to it. He reluctantly helps with the legwork, but loses patience when Gene insists on following up what he considers flimsy evidence in Wyoming, considering it a waste of time.

Prensela comments that he's worked with people like Gene before, who are depressed and suicidal, and that he doesn't like it. Nevertheless their efforts together bear fruit, and a successful conclusion seems likely until circumstances move beyond their control, with tragic consequences for Prensela.

Preston, William (*Dead Heat* 2007)

Preston is the manager at Newmarket racecourse. He contracts food poisoning after a dinner on the course on the night before the Two Thousand Guineas is run.

The Prince (*Trial Run* 1978)

The Prince is a cousin of the reigning British monarch and an acquaintance, through a shared love of point-to-point racing, of **Randall Drew**. He is used to having his opinions listened to and acted upon. He persuades Randall to go to Moscow to investigate allegations involving his brother-in-law, **Johnny Farringford**. After Randall's return to England the Prince meets him at **Fontwell Park** to receive an update. He doesn't like what he hears.

The Princess (*Trial Run* 1978)

The Princess is the wife of the **Prince**, and the elder sister of **Johnny Farringford**. When Farringford crashes his car outside her house she deals competently with his minor injuries whilst telling him off in a sisterly way.

Proof (1984)

Wine merchant **Tony Beach** delivers drinks for racehorse trainer **Jack Hawthorn**'s annual owners' celebration in a marquee at his stables, and stays on as an invited guest. Assistant trainer **Jimmy D'Alban** tells Tony about a fraud that one of Hawthorn's owners is involved in. While getting supplies from his car Tony sees a horse van roll down the hill behind the stables and smash into the marquee. The dishonest owner and several other guests are killed. The repercussions of the accident stretch far beyond the immediate carnage and loss of loved ones. Tony, who is himself still grieving the death of his wife six months previously, finds himself called upon to use his expert knowledge of the wine trade to assist the police in their investigations into the fraud. The stakes escalate when a gruesome murder is discovered and Tony's own life is put in danger.

Proof fulfils all the prerequisites of a successful Dick Francis novel: a flawed protagonist who is the product of an unhappy childhood and who is currently struggling to cope with tragedy in his life; a credible plot, skillfully worked and satisfyingly resolved; and a setting—the wine trade—which is informative without being boring. Though racing is only touched upon there is just enough expert knowledge—for example, on the primeval instinct of horses to race, or on the physical development of young thoroughbreds—to keep the diehard turning the pages.

Tony Beach is a typical hero; undemonstrative he may be, but inside there is turmoil as he fails to come to terms with his young wife's death. Tony is burdened, too, by the weight of having illustrious forebears; he feels inadequate in comparison. But as the plot of *Proof* unfolds Tony discovers in himself unsuspected qualities amoung which personal courage is conspicuous. Knowing that his wife would have been proud of him allows Tony, finally, to find peace.

Pucinelli, Enrico (*The Danger* 1983)

Pucinelli, an officer in the Italian Carabinieri, is in charge of the official investigation into the kidnapping of **Alessia Cenci**. He is a communist and therefore ambivalent about the Cencis, a wealthy capitalist family. Pucinelli is rated by **Andrew Douglas** as a very good police officer, an assessment subsequently proven accurate by Pucinelli's painstaking and ultimately successful detective work.

Pullitzer (*Bonecrack* 1971)

Pullitzer is a racehorse trained at **Newmarket** by **Neil Griffon**, and is one of **Alessandra Rivera**'s regular morning rides. Pullitzer wins an apprentice race at **Catterick**, ridden by Rivera.

The Pump

Come to Grief (1995): *The Pump* is a national daily newspaper; owned by **Lord Tilepit**. *Pump* journalists **India Cathcart** and **Kevin Mills** write defamatory articles about **Sid Halley**.

Under Orders (2006): *Pump* racing journalist **Chris Beecher** writes a malicious article about Sid Halley.

Putney, London

Putney is a district in south-west London in the London Borough of Wandsworth. It is on the south bank of the Thames, opposite Fulham. The famous boat race between Oxford and Cambridge Universities has started at Putney Bridge since 1856.

Blood Sport (1967): Investigator **Gene Hawkins** lives in a dingy flat in Putney.

Pyle, Billy (*In the Frame* 1976)

Pyle is a racecourse acquaintance of **Charles Todd**; he is a former business associate of Charles's late father and claims to have been a friend, though Charles, who finds Pyle bogus and boring, has his doubts. Pyle is always accompanied on the racecourse by his **Auntie Sal**.

Q

Quantum (*Hot Money* 1987)

Quantum, **Malcolm Pembroke**'s house in Berkshire, is a large, comfortable Victorian family home, named after the Latin inscription carved over the front door: "Quantum in me fuit" ("As much as was in me"). In an attempt upon Pembroke's life it is the house that is the victim.

Quayle, Oliver (*Whip Hand* 1979)

Quayle is **Charles Roland**'s solicitor. He represents Roland's daughter **Jenny Halley**, who has got mixed up with a fraudster. Quayle tells **Sid Halley**, Jenny's ex-husband, that Jenny, having misguidedly signed all the relevant documents, is guilty of fraud in the eyes of the law.

Quentin, Daffodil (*The Edge* 1988)

Canadian racehorse owner Daffodil Quentin has recently been widowed. In recent weeks Mrs. Quentin has collected insurance on three racehorses that have died in accidents, but her insurance company is satisfied that she hasn't tried to cheat them. She sells **Julius Filmer** a half-share in her horse **Laurentide Ice** which is traveling on the Great Transcontinental Mystery Race Train. Mrs. Quentin sees a lot of Filmer while on board the train. However, she appears upset on the morning after the races at **Winnipeg**; she tells people that she's had a disagreement with Filmer and that she's going to leave the train and go home. At **Calgary** she does leave, having smashed the mirror in her bedroom with a vodka bottle.

She agrees to cooperate with the Canadian Jockey Club, who have Filmer in their sights.

Quest, Harold (*Decider* 1993)

Quest is a large, bearded, animal rights protester who demonstrates at the gates of **Stratton Park racecourse** after a horse is killed. He lodges a complaint with the police that the driver of a car identical to that belonging to **Dartington Stratton** had almost knocked him over. Quest is later unmasked as a fraud.

Quigley, Miles (*Proof* 1984)

Miles Quigley is the boss of the catering firm which supplies **Martineau Park racecourse**. He has a self-important manner. He is unaware, until informed by **Tony Beach** and **Gerard McGregor**, that one of his trusted staff has been defrauding the company. At first he refuses to believe it; when faced with the facts he sacks the employee on the spot. Subsequently Quigley offers the man's job at twice the salary to Tony Beach.

Quigley, Oliver (*Second Wind* 1999)

Newmarket racehorse trainer Oliver Quigley is a born worrier. He is overly deferential to owner **Caspar Harvey**, who has recruited him as a **Unified Trader**, dealing in radioactive materials. He is keen to pick **Perry Stuart**'s brain about the weather forecast, since Harvey's filly is due to run soon. Subsequently Quigley loses Harvey's horses to another Newmarket trainer, **George Loricroft**.

Quigley, Ruth (*Twice Shy* 1981)

Twenty-one-year-old Ruth Quigley, an ex-pupil of **Ted Pitts**, lives in **Cambridge**. She is the only child of a wealthy family and is formidably intelligent. She had completed her Master's degree at the age of twenty and is now studying for a Ph.D. Ruth writes programs for teaching machines. She allows **William Derry** to use her computer to check **Liam O'Rorke**'s betting system, which Ted Pitts has tampered with.

Quince, Rose (*Break In* 1985)

Rose Quince, an acerbic columnist on the *Sunday Towncrier* newspaper, is the daughter of Conn Quince, a former **Fleet Street** editor. She is very experienced and a well-respected journalist. She writes an article about **Maynard Allardeck**'s business practices. **Kit Fielding** suspects, from the way that Rose talks about **Lord Vaughnley**, that they had once been lovers. She helps Kit to get an interview with **Sam Leggatt**, editor of *The Flag* newspaper.

Quincy, Oliver (*Comeback* 1991)

Quincy is a partner in Hewett and Partners, veterinary surgeons of Cheltenham, **Gloucestershire**. He works mainly with large animals and doesn't do much major surgery. He is keen to see senior partner **Carey Hewett** retire and to take over as senior partner himself. He helps at one of **Ken McClure**'s operations, monitoring the electrograph. McClure thinks that one of the readings may have changed without Quincy informing him.

Quint, Ellis (*Come to Grief* 1995)

Quint is a former champion amateur jockey who, by virtue of his charisma, popularity and ability, has carved himself a niche in the media world as a TV chat show host. As a jockey he was addicted to the dangers inherent in his profession. Now the physical risks are missing but Quint still craves the buzz they gave him. So Quint finds his thrills elsewhere, but chooses a perverted and repellent means of satisfying his needs. The ever-present possibility of being found out gives Quint pleasure and excitement. But Quint's friend **Sid Halley** is aware of what Quint is doing, and is prepared to confront Quint's friends, family and associates, who rally round to protect him.

Quint, Ginnie (*Come to Grief* 1995)

Ginnie is the mother of **Ellis Quint**. Unable to face the shame and humiliation about to engulf her family, she commits suicide by jumping from the sixteenth floor of a hotel.

Quint, Gordon (*Come to Grief* 1995)

Wealthy land-owner Gordon Quint is the father of **Ellis Quint**. He has a high opinion of himself. After his wife, **Ginnie Quint**, kills herself, Quint attacks **Sid Halley** in the street with a metal rod, cracking a bone in Sid's arm. Sometime later he makes another attempt to do serious harm to Sid. He is subsequently arrested and charged. Quint's vendetta against Sid is motivated by revenge for Sid's disclosure of Ellis Quint's activities and Quint's own role in protecting his son.

Quipp, Professor (*Driving Force* 1992)

Quipp is a research scientist who works at **Edinburgh University**. He is an organic chemist, and the boyfriend of **Lizzie Croft**. He puts **Freddie Croft** in touch with his friend **Guggenheim**, an expert on ticks.

Quorn, Norman (*To the Hilt* 1996)

Quorn was the Finance Director of the **King Alfred Brewery**. According to **Tobias Tollright**, Quorn was a sober, careful accountant, who lacked a sense of humor. Approaching retirement, Quorn had made his own unorthodox arrangements for a comfortable old age, and had vanished. Not long afterwards, however, Quorn's body is found in **Leicestershire** on a rubbish dump. The cause of death is unknown, but he has burns on his back.

R

Races

The five UK Classic races, some of which are mentioned in Francis's novels, are the One Thousand Guineas, the Two Thousand Guineas, the Derby, the Oaks and the St Leger. They are for three-year-old colts and fillies. The One Thou-

sand Guineas (for fillies) and the Two Thousand Guineas (for colts) are run at **Newmarket** over one mile in May. In *Bonecrack* (1971) trainer **Neil Griffon's Archangel** wins the Two Thousand Guineas, ridden by **Tommy Hoylake**. Prior to that Griffon, who has just taken over the running of his father's Newmarket stable, wins the first important handicap race of the Flat season, the Lincoln Handicap at **Doncaster**, with **Pease Pudding**. In *Whip Hand* (1979) Two Thousand Guineas favorite **Tri-Nitro** flops badly in the race after being "got at." **Maynard Allardeck** (*Break In* 1985) had owned Two Thousand Guineas winner **Metavane**, a horse which he'd obtained fraudulently from its previous owners as an unraced two-year-old. In *Dead Heat* (2007) a bomb explodes in the guest boxes at **Newmarket racecourse** during the running of the Two Thousand Guineas.

The Oaks (for fillies) and the Derby (for colts and fillies) take place on the Epsom Downs in June, over a distance of one mile, four furlongs. The Oaks, first run in 1779, is named after the 12th Earl of Derby's estate near Epsom, **Surrey**. The Derby, established a year later, was named after the Earl, who tossed a coin with Sir Charles Bunbury to decide on the new race's name. In *The Danger* (1983) the parents of kidnap victim **Dominic Nerrity** own Derby winner **Ordinand**, and Italian colt **Brunelleschi** runs well in the Derby, then wins the Washington International. **Irkab Alhawa** (*Driving Force* 1992), trained by **Michael Watermead**, is winter favorite for the Derby after winning two valuable races at Newmarket as a two year old, the Middle Park Stakes and the Dewhurst Stakes. The final Classic race of the season, the St Leger, is run at **Doncaster** in September over one mile, six furlongs. It is open to colts and fillies, and is the oldest, though the least prestigious owing to its extended distance, of the five Classics, being first run in 1776. American owner **Luke Houston** wins the St Leger with **Genotti**, trained by **Mort Miller** (*Twice Shy* 1981).

As a former steeplechase jockey Francis naturally favors the jumping game in his books. **Cheltenham racecourse**, which hosts the annual Cheltenham Festival held in March, provides a marvelous backdrop to four days of top class racing. The best hurdlers and steeplechasers from the UK and Ireland—geldings, mares and entire horses—meet to contest over twenty races. The winner of the Cheltenham Gold Cup, run over three miles, two and a half furlongs and twenty-two fences, decides the year's champion steeplechaser, while the two mile Champion Hurdle provides a similar test for the best hurdlers. Both of these races are run at level weights. Francis's novels mention no less than six (fictional) winners of the Gold Cup: **Breadwinner** (*Enquiry* 1969); **Tapestry** (*Risk* 1977); **Indian Silk** (*Banker* 1982); **Datepalm** (*Straight* 1989); **Touchy** (*Longshot* 1990); and the ill-fated triple Gold Cup winner **Oven Cleaner** (*Under Orders* 2006). Another of the Festival races mentioned is the Triumph Hurdle, contested by the best four-year-old hurdlers and won in *Under Orders* by **Candlestick**.

Magic, the horse for which **Mrs. Angela Hart** paid jockey **Derek Roberts** a great deal more than she should have, runs well in the Whitbread Gold Cup at **Sandown Park. (Field of 13 1998**: "**Spring Fever**"). This three mile steeplechase, though no longer sponsored by brewers Whitbread, is one of the most prestigious in the jumping calendar.

The Liverpool suburb of **Aintree** is the setting for the world's most famous handicap steeplechase, the Grand National. First run in 1806, the race sets a stiff test of stamina and jumping ability. The course is four and a half miles, and there are sixteen fences of which fourteen are jumped twice. Francis himself came heartbreakingly close to winning the Grand National; he was well out in front and coasting home on the Queen Mother's Devon Loch when, inexplicably, the horse collapsed on the run in. Clearly not Francis's favorite race, the Grand National rarely features in his books. In **Risk**, **Ivansky**, trained by **William Finch**, finishes fifth, while **Haunted House** (*Field of 13*: "**The Day of the Losers**") wins after being promoted from second place on the disqualification of the winner. **Cotopaxi**, owned by **Princess Casilia**, is being aimed at the Grand National when deliberately killed in his box.

Apart from **Brunelleschi's** victory in the Washington International, American racing features in *Hot Money* (1987) via **Malcolm Pembroke's** half-share in four-year-old colt **Blue Clancy**. After finishing third in Europe's premier all-aged twelve furlong race, the Prix de l'Arc de Triomphe at **Longchamp**, Blue Clancy wins the Breeders Cup Turf at Santa Anita. Francis's short story "**The Gift**" (*Field of 13*) takes place on Kentucky Derby day. The big race is won by trainer **Harbourne Cressie's Pincer Movement**.

Many of the races mentioned are, of course, fictional; examples are the Midwinter Cup at **Ascot** (*Nerve* 1964); the Oasthouse Cup (*Risk*); and the King Chase (*Nerve*) at **Kempton**; and the Cloister Handicap Hurdle at **Windsor** (*Field of 13*: "**Haig's Death**"). The King Chase, however, which takes place on December 26th, is clearly the King George V1 Steeplechase, one of the highlights of the steeplechasing calendar.

Radnor (*Odds Against* 1965)

Radnor is the owner of **Hunt Radnor Associates**, a private investigation agency. He bought the agency with his army gratuity after the Second World War, and has built it up from nothing into a high profile and successful business. Radnor's background in point-to-point racing led him to start a Racing Section which has done well, with work for the **Jockey Club** and the **National Hunt Committee** as well as providing pre-race security for horses and running checks on owners, trainers and bookmakers.

Radnor is also **Sid Halley's** boss. He is reluctant to have Sid back after his release from hospital, as Sid had done very little worthwhile in the two years he'd been at the agency. Radnor is delighted, however, when Sid says he wants the chance to earn his money properly; he remarks that it is like a zombie waking up.

Radnor is interested in Sid's discovery of **Howard Kraye's** dealings in **Seabury racecourse's** shares, and gives him permission to investigate, if he can find a client to pay for it. When the Racing Section of Hunt Radnor is destroyed by an explosion, Radnor is devastated. He tells Sid that, at the age of seventy-one, he's too old to start again. Sid persuades him to keep the agency going, and it restarts the next morning in Radnor's own house.

Rae, Sonny (*Second Wind* 1999)

Rae is mentioned by **Perry Stuart** as being a colleague at the BBC weather center who specializes in giving advice on weather to builders and decorators.

"Raid at Kingdom Hill" (*Field of 13* 1998)

Petty criminal **Tricksy Wilcox**, watching racing on TV from **Kingdom Hill racecourse**, has an idea that he thinks will make him rich. When he puts his plan into operation, Wilcox is not the only one to see the opportunity for illicit financial gain.

Ramekin (*Proof* 1984)

Ramekin is a racehorse bought, according to **Flora Hawthorn**, by **Larry Trent** at **Doncaster**

Sales for 30,000 guineas but never put into training. **Tony Beach** suspects that Ramekin was bought with the proceeds of crime, then shipped abroad and sold. The Doncaster auctioneer later confirms that Ramekin was sold for cash and transported to California by Larry Trent.

Rammileese, Mark (*Whip Hand* 1979)

Mark is the small son of farmer and horse dealer **Peter Rammileese**. He is with his mother in the indoor school when she is thrown from her horse and knocked unconscious. Mark phones the emergency services but forgets to tell them where he lives. He enlists **Sid Halley**'s help when Sid calls to see his father, who is away. He tells **Chico Barnes** that his dad has a bad temper. Mark has moved house three times, and wants to be a furniture removal man when he grows up.

Mark innocently points Sid out to his father at a county fair. He tells Sid that his father's friends intend to take Sid for a ride in their car, giving Sid the opportunity to avoid that dubious pleasure. He inadvertently helps Sid and Chico to extricate themselves from a tricky situation in his father's indoor school.

Rammileese, Peter (*Whip Hand* 1979)

Rammileese, a farmer and horse dealer, farms near **Tunbridge Wells** in **Kent**. He is involved in racehorse syndicates whose horses are not running true to form. He tries to have **Sid Halley** abducted at a county fair when he realizes that Sid is investigating him. He is unsuccessful on this occasion, but he doesn't give up. Sid and **Chico Barnes** find themselves in Rammileese's indoor school; it's a place they don't want to be, especially in the company of two Scottish thugs.

Ramsey, Detective Superintendent (*Comeback* 1991)

Gloucestershire policeman D.S. Ramsey looks and sounds bucolic. He investigates a murder at veterinary practice Hewett and Partners. He is content to listen to **Peter Darwin**'s theories and information, but not so keen to share his own.

Ramsey, Rupert (*High Stakes* 1975)

Ramsey is a racehorse trainer with a large, successful yard in **Sussex**. He is in his mid-forties; his laid-back manner belies his ambition and drive. He takes in **Energise** and two other horses belonging to **Steven Scott** after Steven removes them from **Jody Leeds**' stable. Initially, Ramsey is suspicious of Steven and his possible expectations. Ramsey wants to know if Steven expects him to get better results than Leeds, and why Steven left Leeds. He asks Steven if he was always satisfied with the running of his horses. Steven's reply that he can't answer in case Leeds sues him for slander satisfies Ramsey, and he becomes friendlier.

He is worried when Energise does not show him much ability at home, and is relieved when Steven says he doesn't want the horse to run. At this point Ramsey doesn't know what Steven knows. When Steven finally puts him in the picture, Ramsey agrees to help set a trap for Leeds. Afterwards, Ramsey agrees to teach Steven how to ride racehorses.

Randolph, Sophie (*Knock Down* 1974)

Sophie Randolph, aged thirty-two and unmarried, lives in Esher, **Surrey**. She is an air traffic controller at Heathrow airport. She crashes her car when she has to swerve to avoid a horse deliberately released from **Jonah Dereham**'s stables. With minor cuts to her head, she goes home with Jonah and demands an alcoholic drink to cover up the fact that she's over the drink-driving limit. Jonah hasn't any alcohol but rinses out an empty whisky bottle to make a glass smell as if she's just had a drink. The police arrive and breathalyse Sophie; she narrowly fails the test (The reader is left with the impression that she is not prosecuted, but we are not told).

Sophie stays at Jonah's house overnight. The next morning she is composed and in control. She asks Jonah to go and see her aunt, who owns a stud farm and give her his advice. When Jonah impulsively proposes marriage to Sophie on the telephone she accepts, then says she didn't mean it. She is angry on her aunt's behalf when she finds out that she has been swindled. She again rejects Jonah's offer of marriage; she wears a little gold airplane around her neck in memory of her long standing boyfriend, a pilot who had died in Karachi, Pakistan, of a virus.

After Jonah's stables are destroyed and his house damaged by fire she comes to see him; she is no longer wearing the gold airplane. She goes out and gets drunk with Jonah; later they go to bed together. When Jonah is assaulted at **Ascot Sales**, she raises the alarm, probably saving Jonah's life. She takes him to the doctors and, later, to the police station. Jonah realizes that he probably loves Sophie but that she is solitary by nature and will never marry him.

Sophie is shocked when Jonah, attempting to prevent a murderer from escaping, wrenches his arm from its socket. When he asks her to put it back she is appalled and refuses; finally, though, she summons up the courage and manages it with Jonah's guidance. After Jonah takes her home she is exhausted; she is relieved when Jonah, noticing, prepares to leave.

Ranger, Rinty (*Slay-Ride* 1973)

Ranger is an English jockey who rides occasionally in Norway. He knows **Bob Sherman**, though they weren't good friends. He tells **David Cleveland** that Sherman had stayed with **Per Bjorn Sandvick** a couple of times, and was friendly with Sandvik's son, **Mikkel Sandvic**. He says that Sherman was also a friend of **Paddy O'Flaherty**, one of **Gunnar Holth**'s grooms, and that he sometimes stayed in the grooms' dormitory at Holth's yard. Ranger remembers that Sherman had left his saddle and helmet in the jockeys' changing room.

On the day that David is investigating at **Øvrevoll racecourse**, Ranger wins the Norsk Grand National. At David's request he asks around in the weighing room at **Plumpton** races, to see if any jockeys had been asked to carry any papers to Norway; no-one had.

Raoul (*The Edge* 1988)

Raoul is a character in the mystery play on the Great Transcontinental Mystery Race Train. He is a racehorse trainer falsely accused of doping the **Bricknells**' horses, and the husband of murdered **Angelica Standish**.

Rat Race (1970)

Matt Shore's life and career have hit rock bottom, and for a long time now depression has settled over him like a shroud. He's divorced, broke and his job as a first officer with British Overseas Airways Corporation, with a captain's post just around the corner, is a distant memory. His descent through the ranks has been rapid, and now he is three days into a new job as a pilot for modest air-taxi firm **Derrydown Air Transport**.

Matt picks up four passengers at **White Waltham**, near London, and takes them to **Haydock Park** races. In the racecourse bar he meets a large Australian with his leg in plaster, loudly extolling the virtues of his insurance policy which had paid him £1,000. From this point on Matt's already troubled life becomes a lot more difficult. His new set of problems stems entirely from his unsought-for connection with the horse racing world and the devious and downright criminal individuals who inhabit it. Their schemes and scams spell danger for Matt, who also has to contend with Board of Trade investigators turning the spotlight on his past flying record. But it's not all bad news; one of his clients is top flat race jockey **Colin Ross**, whose sister, **Nancy Ross**, sees beyond the gloomy persona that Matt presents to the world. Adversity throws them together, and by the time that Matt has dealt with a villain intent on murder in his quest for financial gain, Matt's future is looking a little rosier.

In 1969 Mary Francis, herself a qualified pilot, had set up a small air-taxi business, Merlix Air, primarily to ferry racing people to and from racecourses. Francis used the knowledge gleaned from Mary's involvement with flying to give a ring of authenticity to the setting of *Rat Race*. In the novel Francis weaves together, via Matt Shore, two separate strands: the solving of a massive fraud perpetrated by dangerous men who will stop at nothing to achieve their ends; and the redemption, through love, of a life gone badly wrong.

Reading, Berkshire

Reading is an unexciting town in the Thames Valley midway between London and Oxford. Several large computer companies have offices in or near the town.

Odds Against (1965): **Mervyn Brinton**, brother of the late William Brinton, who was Clerk of the Course at **Dunstable racecourse**, retired to Reading.

Proof (1984): The Peverill Arms, a pub managed by **Mrs. Alexis**, is near Reading.

Longshot (1990): Writer **John Kendall** goes to **Berkshire** to write the biography of racehorse trainer **Tremayne Vickers**. He is met at Reading bus station by Vickers' daughter-in-law **Mackie Vickers**.

Reading racecourse

Reading is a fictional racecourse in or near **Reading, Berkshire**.

Enquiry (1969): At the enquiry into **Squelsh**'s defeat in the Lemonfizz Gold Cup at **Oxford**, **Lord Gowery** shows a videotape of **Wanderlust**, not **Squelsh**, winning at Reading races. **Jack Roxford** is at Reading races when he unburdens himself to **Lord Ferth**.

Redcar racecourse

Redcar racecourse is on the coast of North Yorkshire, and it has seen better days. Refurbishment would appear to be essential if the course is to survive in the modern era.

Rat Race (1970): At Redcar races **Rudiments**, owned by the **Duke of Wessex** and trained by **Annie Villars**, wins a valuable race.

Redi-Hot (*The Edge* 1988)

Redi-Hot is a dark bay racehorse on board the Great Transcontinental Mystery Race Train.

Reflex (1980)

Steeplechase jockey **Philip Nore**, picking himself off the turf after a routine fall at **Sandown Park**, wonders, for the first time, whether he really wants to be doing this any longer. His disillusionment is compounded by the fact that he is fed up with having to stop horses on the orders of the trainer who employs him as stable jockey. Outside the weighing room he is approached by solicitor **Jeremy Folk** acting for Philip's grandmother, a hard, malicious old woman whom Philip has never met. She wants Philip to find his half-sister, **Amanda Nore**, whom Philip didn't know existed. Philip himself had been abandoned as a child with a succession of friends of his feckless, drug-dependent mother. He had not seen her since he was fifteen years old and assumed that she was dead.

But Philip has more on his mind than a long-lost relative. Fellow-jockey **Steve Millace**'s father, **George Millace**, who worked as a racecourse photographer, had recently died in a car crash. Giving Steve a lift home after he had broken his collar bone, Philip arrives at Steve's house to find the police and an ambulance there. Steve's mother has been roughed up by two thugs and the house ransacked. Philip, an amateur photographer, takes away some photographic rubbish which Steve's father had kept; Philip is curious as to the reason why. That decision proves momentous; Philip discovers that there was a lot more to George Millace than met the eye, and that his photographic detritus is dynamite. Despite the risks to his own health Philip ensures that what George Millace had started is carried through to the conclusion that he would have wished.

Meanwhile Philip's search for Amanda ends in an anti-climax; but in the course of it he re-establishes contact with **Samantha Bergen**, one of his mother's friends with whom he had lived as a child. Philip and Samantha's daughter, **Clare Bergen**, find that they have much in common.

Reflex succeeds as a novel largely because of its main character, Philip Nore. He is one of Francis's most realistic creations, with perhaps the most interesting, if dysfunctional, upbringing of them all. His childhood experiences mould his character: he takes what comes without demur, plying his trade as a journeyman jockey contentedly and unambitiously, stopping the odd horse here and there when it is expedient to do so. The Horseracing Regulatory Authority may not like to acknowledge it, but Philip is representative of the kind of jockey who has a mortgage to pay and is not over-burdened with guilt about how he earns the money to pay it. .

What makes Philip different is that, finally, he begins to question whether he really wants to do it any more. The acquiescence and agreeability which had governed his life are no longer his preferred options. His becoming involved in the investigation into George Millace's death obliquely provides the impetus for a change of direction in his life. The subplot by which Philip searches for his half-sister is interesting in so far as it sheds light on Philip's chaotic childhood, but it fizzles out rather tamely. This weakness apart, *Reflex* is an excellent novel.

Reg (*Comeback* 1991)

Reg is head lad to trainer **Zoë Mackintosh**. He is said by Zoë to be honest and reliable, but **Peter Darwin** doubts this. Reg claims never to have heard of **Wynn Lees**.

Reggie (*For Kicks* 1965)

Reggie, a groom at **Hedley Humber**'s racing stable in **County Durham**, is a food stealer. He is thin, white-faced, and has a twitch in his left eyelid.

Reilly, Moggie (*Field of 13* 1998: "Haig's Death")

Reilly, a successful steeplechase jockey, rides for trainer **John Chester**. On the night before **Winchester** races he sleeps with trainer's daughter **Sarah Driffield**. He is due to ride fancied runner **Storm Cone** for Chester in a valuable hurdle race at Winchester. He is offered money not to try on Storm Cone. Reilly rejects the offer, but the result of the race is affected by a one in a million occurrence.

Den Relgan, Dana (*Reflex* 1980)

Dana is a pretty young woman whom **Ivor den Relgan** introduces to everyone as his daughter. At **Kempton** races she is talking to film director and drugs dealer **Lance Kinship** when den Relgan intervenes and punches Kinship, warning him to stay away from Dana. **Lord White** flirts with Dana; Ivor den Relgan encourages the relationship to secure his own advancement in the **Jockey Club**.

Philip Nore, however, discovers evidence which puts a different complexion on Dana's situation.

Den Relgan, Ivor (*Reflex* 1980)

Den Relgan is a wealthy man of uncertain, but allegedly Dutch, extraction who has a high opinion of himself and is easy to dislike. He is elected to the **Jockey Club** through the influence of the powerful but naive **Lord White**, who is infatuated with **Dana den Relgan**. He sponsors a race at **Kempton Park**, won by **Victor Briggs'** horse **Sharpener**. When he sees **Lance Kinship** talking to Dana, he assaults him and threatens further violence if Kinship doesn't stay away from Dana. Den Relgan's behavior shocks onlookers and tarnishes his reputation.

Lord White secures den Relgan's appointment to head an important committee charged with looking into the possibility of having paid stewards. However, when **Philip Nore** brings information about den Relgan and Dana to Lord White's attention, White is obliged to reconsider his decision. Furious with Philip, den Relgan seeks revenge.

Renbo, Harvey (*In the Frame* 1976)

Renbo is the manager of **Yarra River Fine Arts**, a gallery in **Alice Springs**, Australia. He is an expert copier of **Alfred Munnings** and other celebrated equine artists.

Retsov, Martin (*Field of 13* 1988: "Nightmare")

Retsov, a well-built American in his late thirties, gets a job as a salesman with Thoroughbred Foodstuffs Incorporated. He is very knowledgeable about horses, and after three years with the company is its most successful salesman. Retsov's previous career had not been so reputable, and after an encounter with a young hitchhiker he is tempted to revert to his former activities. The hitchhiker, however, is not who he appears to be.

Revelation (*Odds Against* 1965)

Revelation, an ex–**Cheltenham** Gold Cup winner, is trainer **Mark Witney's** hack. **Sid Halley** borrows him to mount a guard at **Seabury racecourse** before the race meeting so that he does not look conspicuous. Sid rides him over the Seabury fences; he falls when blinded by a dazzling flash caused by a mirror placed in a tree, but is uninjured.

Reynolds, Detective Chief Inspector (*To the Hilt* 1996)

D.C.I. Reynolds, of **Leicestershire** police, asks **Sir Ivan Westering** to identify a body.

Rich, Detective Constable (*Longshot* 1990)

D.C. Rich, of Thames Valley police, assists **Detective Chief Inspector Doone** with the investigation into the death of a stable girl who worked for **Tremayne Vickers**.

Rich, Jericho (*Driving Force* 1992)

Racehorse owner Jericho Rich, according to trainer **Michael Watermead**, is an ill-tempered, unpleasant man. The horse van which picked up hitch-hiker **Kevin Keith Ogden** had just transferred nine two-year-olds belonging to Rich from Watermead's yard in **Pixhill, Hampshire**, to **Newmarket**. Rich phones **Freddie Croft**, who had ridden for Rich in his previous career as a jockey, to complain about his employees picking up the hitch-hiker. He asks Freddie to collect a horse from France for his daughter.

Richard (*Dead Heat* 2007)

Richard is the maître d' at **The Hay Net**, a **Newmarket** restaurant run by **Max Moreton**. He is extremely upset at the death of **Louisa Whitworth** in the explosion at **Newmarket racecourse**; she was the best friend of Richard's teenage daughter. Richard is shot dead at the restaurant by the perpetrator of the bombing.

Richardson, Miss (*Come to Grief* 1995)

Miss Richardson is the joint owner, with **Miss Bethany**, of Windward Stud Farm, **Northamptonshire**. She is middle-aged, and masculine in appearance and manner. According to **Sid Halley**, she dislikes men. A yearling colt on her farm is cruelly attacked.

Richmond, Nell (*The Edge* 1988)

Nell Richmond is an employee of **Merry and Co.**, a Toronto travel company which is overseeing arrangements for the Great Transcontinental Mystery Race Train. She is young, pretty and good at her job. She has dinner with **Tor Kelsey**; she tells him she'd first of all tried to follow the family tradition and become a writer, but didn't enjoy it and is much happier working for Merry and Co. She lives in a small lakeside apartment in Toronto. Accompanying the trip on the Race Train, Nell habitually holds a clipboard to her chest, having once been sexually assaulted by a man in an office. She wonders about Tor's sexuality and probes to find out if he's gay. Nell is furious when **Sheridan Lorrimore** tries to pull her onto his lap. When Tor asks her to go to Hawaii with him after the trip she says she'll let him know after the Vancouver race; as a reply she gives Tor a telex showing that she'd booked two weeks' holiday.

Rickenbacker, Eric (*The Danger* 1983)

Rickenbacker is the president of **Laurel racecourse**, Washington D.C. He tells **Andrew Douglas** what he knows about the circumstances of **Morgan Freemantle**'s kidnapping. He assures Andrew that he will cooperate fully with the investigation.

Ricky (*The Edge* 1988)

Ricky is a groom in the mystery play on the Great Transcontinental Mystery Race Train. He is murdered, and his body left lying next to railway lines near Thunder Bay, Ontario.

Ridger, Detective Sergeant (*Proof* 1984)

D.S. Ridger, of Thames Valley police, is in his thirties and married with two daughters. Stiff and formal in manner, he is prickly and naturally suspicious. He asks for **Tony Beach**'s help in an inspection of the **Silver Moondance** restaurant; Tony tastes the whisky to see if it is the genuine article. When **Paul Young**, purporting to be from head office, objects to the restaurant being closed down Ridger's hackles rise, unhappy to have his authority questioned. Reluctantly he gives Tony a receipt for the wine bottles that Tony had bought and tested in the bar; then he drives off without thanking Tony for his help.

Ridger continues to be involved in the investigation until he is sent up north to deal with illegal picketing; after that he takes no further part.

The Ridgeway

The Ridgeway is a National Trail that begins near Avebury in **Wiltshire** and ends eighty-five miles away near Tring in **Hertfordshire**. For the most part the Ridgeway follows a prehistoric pathway along the ridge of the north-west Downs and the Chiltern hills.

To the Hilt (1996): **Alex Kinloch** rides **Sir Ivan Westering**'s chaser **Golden Malt** along the Ridgeway to a livery yard in **Foxhill, Wiltshire**.

Rightsworth, Detective Superintendent (*The Danger* 1983)

Rightsworth is a policeman based at Sutton, **Surrey**, where **John Nerrity** and his family live. He appears to have no liking or respect for the general public. He is not rated highly as a detective by **Andrew Douglas**, who thinks that Rightsworth is not taking the threats made by **Dominic Nerrity**'s kidnappers seriously enough. Rightsworth needs **Tony Vine**'s assistance to set up a phone tap in the Nerritys' house. He plans, with **John Nerrity**, to ambush the kidnappers when they try to collect a bogus ransom.

Risk (1977)

Roland Britten wakes up in the pitch dark. He is freezing cold, frightened, unable to move, nauseous and totally disorientated. Loud engine noises batter his ears. He has no idea where he is or how he got there.

Roland, an accountant and amateur jockey, thinks back to how the day—Thursday, March 17—began. Due to ride in the **Cheltenham** Gold Cup that afternoon, he had had to go in to work to apply for routine postponements for two clients who had to appear before the Tax Commissioners. Delayed by an anxious client, he had arrived just in time for the race. The first and second favorites had fallen and his horse, **Tapestry**, a long-priced outsider, had run on to win.

Still euphoric after winning steeplechasing's greatest prize, Roland had answered a summons from a man in a St John's Ambulance uniform to go and talk to an injured jockey in an ambulance. There had been no jockey; Roland had been attacked by two men who had held a chloroform rag over his face.

So begins a prolonged incarceration from which Roland, using all his reserves of courage and ingenuity, eventually escapes. But someone wants him out of the way, and Roland has to be constantly vigilant in order to preserve his freedom while at the same time trying to discover the reason behind the attempts to abduct him. Roland suspects that his job as an accountant for numerous clients in the horse racing world holds the key. But the closer he gets to the villains, the greater the risk that they will find a way to silence him.

Risk is one of Francis's best novels. Its plot is tightly woven, tense and finely crafted. The ending is not the strongest, but the rest of the story more than makes up for it. The opening pages are superbly written and—for anyone who has a fear of being confined in a tiny space, in the dark and unable to move—absolutely terrifying. Right from the opening scenes the story moves along at a cracking pace, with well-drawn minor characters who contribute to the high level of dramatic energy that the plot generates. Francis's biographer Graham Lord tells us that the details of the financial frauds used in the plot were meticulously researched by Mary Francis, who spent a lot of time with their own accountants—one a paralyzed ex-jockey.

Rivera, Alessandro (*Bonecrack* 1971)

Alessandro is the eighteen-year-old son of Italian criminal **Enso Rivera**. Enso compels **Neil Griffon** to accept Alessandro as a jockey at **Rowley Lodge**, the racing stables run by Neil's hospitalized father, **Neville Griffon**. When Alessandro turns up at evening stables he is surprised that Neil does not grovel to him. He tells Neil he will only ride, not muck out or feed. He reluctantly signs a Deed of Apprenticeship. He demands to ride the classy three-year-old colt **Archangel**, and says he will not accept orders from a woman, head lass **Etty Craig**. When Neil says he must prove he can ride on lesser horses and that he must obey Etty's instructions, he is furious and tells his father, who demands that Neil show due deference to Alessandro.

Alessandro rides **Traffic**, a difficult colt, and the horse runs away with him. Angrily, Alessandro insists on riding Traffic again the next day. Traffic unseats him in the paddock; Alessandro hits his head on the fence and is knocked out.

Alessandro's riding improves until he is better than the other apprentices. When Neil sees Alessandro starving himself to keep his weight down, he realizes that Alessandro is ambitious to the point of fanaticism. Alessandro skillfully rides Archangel in his work and gives an intelligent assessment of his mount in a trial. However he reacts with hate towards Neil and jockey **Tommy Hoylake** when Neil tells him that Hoylake will be first jockey to the stable. He says, in bewilderment, that no-one disobeys his father except Neil. He complains that he is merely a pawn in a power struggle between his father and Neil.

Alessandro goes to **Doncaster** races with Neil to watch the stable's horse **Pease Pudding** win the Lincoln Handicap, brilliantly ridden by Hoylake. He has the courage to admit that he couldn't have won on Pease Pudding; Neil tells him that his turn will come. Alessandro tells Neil that he never went to school. Instead he'd had tutors and then, when he was fifteen, only a riding master. One day, without really thinking, he'd said he wanted to win the English Derby on Archangel, and his father had told him he would.

At **Catterick** races Alessandro rides a well-judged race to win on **Pullitzer**. Over the next two weeks he rides three more winners. The racing journalists start to take notice, and he answers their questions quietly and civilly. He begins to chat with Neil on journeys to racecourses in a natural, relaxed manner. He tells Neil he has not seen his mother since he was six years old; she had left after a violent row with his father after taunting him with being sterile. When Alessandro rides a good race to win on **Lancat** at **Newmarket** he gives Neil a warm smile which turns to apprehension when he sees Enso glaring at them.

Alessandro tells Enso it is right that he doesn't ride Archangel in the Guineas and that he wants to be left alone to get on with his life. But that is the one thing that Enso cannot do, and his obsession with getting his own way leads inexorably to his death. Finally free of his father's malign influence, Alessandro tells Neil he still wants to be a jockey. When Neil offers him a job as second jockey to Tommy Hoylake he is ecstatic.

Rivera, Enso (*Bonecrack* 1971)

Rivera is one of Francis's most dangerous, unpredictable and menacing villains. Driven by obsession and mental instability, Rivera is like a badly broken colt with no brakes and no steering. Unhampered by conscience, he sees no variety of evil-doing as being off-limits. He has lived in Switzerland for fifteen years where he has got rich by acting as a middleman in the exchange of stolen currency and precious stones.

When his son **Alessandro** expresses a wish to be a jockey, Rivera violently sweeps aside any obstacles in the way of fulfilling that aspiration. He forces **Neil Griffon**, standing in as trainer for his father **Neville Griffon**, who is in hospital, to take Alessandro on as a stable jockey.

Rivera's relationship with his son is fatally

flawed. He gives Alessandro anything he wants, but he can't talk to him as a father or offer him affection. What makes the situation worse for Rivera is that he can see Alessandro gradually forming the kind of relationship with Neil that he is unable himself to have with his son. Noticing the mutual pleasure that Alessandro and Neil derive from winning a race at **Newmarket**, he glares at Neil "with the venom of the dispossessed."

An undiagnosed illness, which had caused him to become sterile after fathering Alessandro, exacerbates Rivera's megalomaniac behavior. He and his henchmen violently assault Neil and promise that more will follow if Alessandro is not allowed to ride stable star **Archangel** in the Two Thousand Guineas, the first Classic race of the season.

When he discovers that Neil intends to put stable jockey **Tommy Hoylake** up on Archangel, Rivera opts for an extreme solution to the problem. But his plans go dramatically awry, and it is Rivera who pays the ultimate price.

River God (*Knock Down* 1974)

River God is a jumper bought by **Jonah Dereham** on behalf of **Kerry Sanders** as a replacement for **Hearse Puller**. Previously owned by a **Devon** farmer, River God has plenty of ability and jumps well but his early schooling had not been good and he is a difficult ride.

River God is sent up from Devon in a hired van to rendezvous with Jonah in **Gloucestershire**. Jonah foils an attempt to abduct the horse. When River God's new owner **Nicol Brevett**, watches him walk and trot, he's impressed.

Roach, Al (*Enquiry* 1969)

Irishman Al Roach is stable jockey to **Pat Nikita**, a rival trainer to **Dexter Cranfield**. He rides **Squelsh** for owner **Mr. Kessel**, who had transferred his horses to Nikita after Cranfield was warned off. Roach should have won the **Cheltenham** Gold Cup on Squelsh but gives him two cracks of the whip after the last fence, which Squelsh resents. The horse stops and is beaten a short head by **Kelly Hughes** on **Breadwinner**.

Roadtrain (*Under Orders* 2006)

Roadtrain, a jumper, wins at **Newbury** races at odds of ten to one. Roadtrain's chances had, before the race, been put at zero by his amateur jockey, **Peter Enstone**.

Robbie (*The Edge* 1988)

Robbie, a gay actor, shares a house with **Tor Kelsey** in London; he shows Tor how to disguise himself by changing his hair style.

Robbiston, Dr. Keith (*To the Hilt* 1996)

Robbiston is **Sir Ivan Westering**'s doctor. He is in his fifties and has a brisk manner. He gives **Alex Kinloch** some painkillers when he visits Sir Ivan, noticing that Alex is suffering after being beaten up. He gives Alex more pills after he has another brush with villains, warning him not to get addicted to the morphine they contain.

Robert (*The Edge* 1988)

Robert is an engine driver on the Great Transcontinental Mystery Race Train. He is the younger of the two drivers.

Robert (*Dead Heat* 2007)

Robert is one of **Max Moreton**'s catering staff; he is working in the grandstand boxes at **Newmarket racecourse** when a bomb explodes. He is uninjured.

Roberts, Derek (*Field of 13* 1988: "Spring Fever")

Journeyman steeplechase jockey Derek Roberts makes a habit of being optimistic about the chances of the horses he rides in order to keep the owners sweet. He is surprised when one of them, a middle-aged lady named **Mrs. Angela Hart**, asks him to go with her to buy a horse. His employer, trainer **Clement Scott**, tells him that Mrs. Hart has a crush on him. Roberts agrees with Scott to use this fact to make some quick money for them both. His dishonesty, however, is soon exposed.

Robins, Rose (*Shattered* 2000)

Rose Robins is also known as **Rose Payne**.

Robinson, Arthur (*Risk* 1977)

Arthur Robinson is a pseudonym used on one occasion by **William Finch** when he wished his true identity to be concealed.

Robinson, Bill (*Wild Horses* 1994)

Bill Robinson is a young motorbike mechanic who works for Wrigley's garage on Exning Road, **Newmarket**. He is a friend of **Dorothea Pannier**, who asks him to look after the books which her brother, **Valentine Clark**, had left to **Thomas**

Lyon. Robinson delivers the books to Thomas's hotel. He is pleased to accept Thomas's offer of a small non-speaking part in Thomas's film.

Robinson, D.F. (*Twice Shy* 1981)

D.F. Robinson is a young man who arrives late for an interview for the late **Peter Keithley**'s job at **Mason Miles Associates. Jonathan Derry** is there, enquiring about Keithley.

Robinson, Gary (*In the Frame* 1976)

Gary Robinson is an employee of insurance company Foundation Life and Surety. He is assistant to the Area Manager, **D.J. Lagland**. Robinson investigates the burning down of **Maisie Matthews**' house.

Robson, Detective Inspector John (*Twice Shy* 1981)

Robson, a **Newmarket** policeman, is assistant to **Detective Chief Superintendent Irestone** on the investigation into the death of **Chris Norwood**. **Jonathan Derry** gives Robson information about **Angelo Gilbert** and **Eddy** after they leave **Donna Keithley**'s house.

Rockman, Davey (*Field of 13* 1998: "Dead on Red")

Rockman is stable jockey to trainer "**Gypsy Joe**" Smith. He is good looking, volatile and a sexual predator. He loses his job with Smith when the trainer employs a young, inexperienced amateur, **Red Millbrook**. Rockman, furious at his drop in income and the dent in his reputation, resorts to extreme measures to restore his fortunes. He succeeds, but only temporarily. Rockman is bent on revenge, and only an unforeseen disaster prevents his plans from coming to fruition.

Rockville (*Forfeit* 1968)

Rockville, a steeplechaser; is not an easy ride, but is well handled by Irish jockey **Dermot Finnegan** to win the Lamplighter Gold Cup Steeplechase at **Heathbury Park**.

Roke, Belinda (*For Kicks* 1965)

Belinda is the elder of **Daniel Roke**'s two sisters. She is a boarder at Frensham, a top private school in Australia. She wants to go to medical school. She is upset when Daniel decides to go to England, but understands his need to do so.

Roke, Daniel (*For Kicks* 1965)

Daniel, born in Australia of English parents, had hoped to become a barrister, like his father. But his parents were killed in a sailing accident, and at the age of eighteen Daniel was left to provide for his younger brother and sisters. He starts dealing in and breeding horses, and, nine years on, his stud farm is thriving. But Daniel is working every waking hour; he's miserable and badly in need of a change. The opportunity arises for him to go to England and assist the **Jockey Club** in investigating a doping scandal that is threatening the integrity of English racing. With his siblings away at boarding school, Daniel is attracted by the challenge. There is the added incentive of a large fee which will help to put his brother and sisters through university when the time comes.

The influence of his father had instilled in Daniel a respect for the law. The chance to help catch criminals appeals to his sense of justice, though he knows that the prime motivating factor for him is temporary escape from the chains of his own life.

To work undercover in English racing yards, Daniel assumes the guise of a disreputable and unreliable stable lad. He proves adept at this, adjusting his accent, manners and egalitarian view of the world.

Trouble arises in the shapely form of **Lady Patricia Tarren**, the highly-sexed daughter of Daniel's employer, Jockey Club steward **Lord October**. Daniel rejects Patricia's offer of sex. In revenge, she accuses Daniel of indecent assault, which, not surprisingly, sours the relationship between Daniel and her father.

Daniel lands a new job in a racing yard where he suspects that horses are being abused so that fear will make them run faster. Daniel has to play the part of a shiftless, craven, not too bright groom. At the same time he has to endure beatings at the hands of a near psychopathic owner for as long as it takes to gather evidence against him.

Only once does Geelong-educated Daniel let his pretence slip: in conversation with Lord October's daughter, **Lady Elinor Tarren**, as thoroughly nice as Patricia is tricky, he comes out with a quotation from Marcus Aurelius about learning to be content with one's lot.

Daniel's lot soon becomes a good deal more uncomfortable. His cover blown, he is forced to fight for his life against the men whose criminal activities he has laid bare. Arrested and charged with murder when one of his assailants dies, Daniel has to work hard to persuade skeptical detectives that he is not the shifty, grudge-bearing stable lad that he appears.

When Lord October hands over a substantial check as fee for services rendered, Daniel tears it up. Daniel had done it, as he tells Lord October with a wry smile, "for kicks." Daniel's experiences in England have taught him much about himself—too much to allow him to return peacefully to a life in Australia that he sees, more clearly than ever, as a prison sentence.

Roke, Helen (*For Kicks* 1965)

Helen is the younger of **Daniel Roke**'s two sisters. Like her sister, **Belinda Roke**, she is away at Frensham boarding school in Australia. Almost sixteen years old, Helen is gentle and graceful. She wants to go to art school. A sensitive girl, she has suffered most from not having a mother.

Roland, Charles

Odds Against (1965): Rear Admiral Charles Roland, RN (retired) is **Sid Halley**'s father-in-law. He is sixty-six years old but looks younger. His usual charm and good manners are occasionally spoilt by extreme rudeness. At first he thoroughly disapproved of his daughter, **Jenny Halley**, marrying Sid, a mere jockey, and refused to go to the wedding. For months he rarely spoke to Sid; but when Sid and Jenny made a rare visit to his home in the village of **Aynsford, Oxfordshire**, he challenged Sid to a game of chess and lost. A second game ended in a draw, and after that Sid was invited more and more often to his house. Even Sid and Jenny's separation did not destroy the regard the two men had for each other. Roland's interest in racing, previously non-existent, grew stronger every year, and he had recently been asked to act as a steward at one or two courses.

Roland is concerned about Sid, who has been forced to retire from race riding after a horrific injury to his hand. Now Sid is working for a detective agency, but is currently in hospital after a surveillance job goes badly wrong. To combat Sid's low morale, Roland engineers a situation which gets Sid involved in a bid to prevent a villain gaining control of **Seabury racecourse**.

When Roland's daughter Jenny rings him from Athens to ask him to tell Sid that she wants a divorce, he tells Sid that his daughter is a fool.

Roland visits Sid in hospital again after he has suffered a savage assault. He tells Sid that he had not got him the job at **Hunt Radnor** detective agency, as Sid suspected, but had merely recommended him when **Radnor**, the owner, had asked his opinion.

Whip Hand (1979): Roland is now Sid Halley's ex–father-in-law. He regularly lunches with Sid despite the marriage break-up. He asks Sid if he will help Jenny, who has become involved with a fraudster. Roland acts as a referee between Sid and Jenny when they meet. He doesn't approve when Jenny is nasty to Sid, but on the whole he allows Sid to deal with it himself.

Roland is unaware, until Sid points it out, that Jenny is still besotted with the fraudster, and that she doesn't want Sid to pursue him. He is unhappy with Sid when he disappears for six days and won't say where he's been, though he can see that Sid has suffered. He tries to galvanize Sid with insults, accusing Sid of having been on a drinking binge, but Sid doesn't respond. Sid goes to stay with Roland, who makes no further reference to Sid's disappearance. He is embarrassed by Jenny's vitriolic outburst at Sid, and assures him that he is always welcome to stay. Roland helps Sid with his investigations into the fraudster's activities.

Come to Grief (1995): Roland keeps his own counsel and does not show much emotion, but is supportive of Sid and allows him to stay at his house in **Aynsford** when he needs to. After Sid is attacked in the street, he invites Sid to stay with him. On Sid's behalf, Roland checks with his friend **Sir Thomas Ullaston**, the former Senior Steward of the **Jockey Club**, that he had passed on information about Sid to **Archie Kirk**. When the case that Sid is working on is over, he tells Sid that the **British Horseracing Board** wants Sid to do some work for them.

Under Orders (2006): In *Under Orders* Roland's name is spelled "Rowland," apparently in error. He goes with Sid to the **Cheltenham** Festival and introduces him to **Lord Enstone**. Somewhat reluctantly, he gives permission for Sid and his girlfriend, **Marina van der Meer**, to stay with him at **Aynsford**; Sid's ex-wife Jenny, now **Lady Wingham** and her husband, **Sir Anthony Wingham**, are also due to visit. Over a bottle of whisky, Roland discusses with Sid the recent deaths of a jockey and a trainer, and warns him of the danger that Sid, in investigating them, is putting himself in. Roland takes to Marina immediately, and talks with her about Sid's determined approach to taking on dangerous criminals. He shocks Marina when he asks her and Sid when they are going to get married. He goes to **Towcester** races with a neighbor, **Rodney Humphries**, to help Sid feed information to **Paddy O'Fitch**.

Roland receives a phone call from Sid who, worried about his ex–father-in-law, warns him to leave his house. At first Roland stays with Jenny, and then moves to his club, the Army and Navy. He sits with Marina, who has been injured, at Sid's apartment while Sid and **Chris Beecher** are setting a trap for a suspect. He falls asleep, having had one whisky too many; this initially annoys Sid, who quickly regrets his irritation.

Rollway, Thomas (*Straight* 1989)

Rollway is a racehorse owner who has horses with trainer **Nicholas Loder**. The recently deceased **Greville Franklin**, a dealer in semi-precious stones, had also had horses—**Dozen Roses** and **Gemstones**—with Loder. Rollway has his own ideas about how the horses in Loder's stable should run.

On the Saturday after Greville Franklin dies Rollway is with Loder at **York** races when Loder is saddling Dozen Roses. Walking to the parade ring Dozen Roses swings around and bumps Rollway, who drops a piece of equipment not normally employed in tacking up a horse prior to a race. He snatches it back from **Martha Ostermeyer**, an American lady who has stepped forward to pick it up. Rollway's temper isn't soothed when he sees Greville's brother, jockey **Derek Franklin**; he knows that Greville had owned Dozen Roses and that Derek, as executor of his brother's will, would now have charge of the horse. He decides to prevent Derek from working out what is going on with Dozen Roses. When Derek refuses to sell him the horse Rollway resorts to drastic measures, and the true extent of his desperate and callous amorality becomes starkly evident.

Romney, William (*Slay-Ride* 1973)

William Romney, **Emma Sherman**'s grandfather, is a pleasant and intelligent man. He meets Emma on her return from Norway and takes her to her cottage near **Newbury, Berkshire**. There they disturb two Norwegians who are ransacking the cottage. They knock William down and assault Emma. Shocked, William phones **David Cleveland**, who goes to the cottage. Furious when Emma miscarries her unborn child, William volunteers to go to Norway to look at police photos to try to identify their attackers. He spends two days in Oslo but has no success.

Ron, Uncle (*Shattered* 2000)

Ron, the deceased uncle of **Gerard Logan**, is mentioned by Gerard as having taught him everything he knew about the glass-blowing trade.

Roncey, Madge (*Forfeit* 1968)

Madge is the wife of **Victor Roncey**, an **Essex** farmer and the owner of **Tiddely-Pom**, ante-post favorite for the Lamplighter Gold Cup at **Heathbury Park**. Three stones overweight and a dreamer, Madge has a slovenly attitude to housework, tidying any mess out of sight behind the sofa. She jumps at the chance of a holiday when **James Tyrone** suggests it for security's sake in the week prior to the Lamplighter. **Derry Clark** takes Madge and her sons to the **Isle of Wight**. On Lamplighter Gold Cup day Madge, showing unexpected presence of mind, stops a villain from harming Tiddely-Pom by picking the man up, carrying him away, and then sitting on him with her sons.

Roncey, Pat (*Forfeit* 1968)

Pat, the son of **Victor Roncey**, is an amateur jockey; he rides his father's horses but, when they start to improve, Pat is often removed in favor of more experienced pilots. This causes Pat to be resentful of his father. He complains to **James Tyrone** that his father treats him like a child, only allowing him to ride in point-to-points. When James comes to take Lamplighter Gold Cup favourite **Tiddely-Pom** to **Norton Fox**'s yard for the sake of security Pat is not unhappy that his father is losing control of the horse.

Roncey, Peter (*Forfeit* 1968)

Peter is one of **Victor Roncey**'s five sons. Despite being only sixteen years old, Peter runs the family farm. Though he appears calm and cheerful, **James Tyrone** notices that he is resentful of his father's brusque manner towards him and his brothers.

Roncey, Victor (*Forfeit* 1968)

Essex farmer Victor Roncey is the owner and trainer of **Tiddely-Pom**, ante-post favorite for the Lamplighter Gold Cup at **Heathbury Park**. He is in his forties, and has a brisk, no-nonsense manner. He is hard on his five sons. His farm is neglected, but the stable block is in good repair.

Roncey is furious when he reads **James Tyrone**'s article in *The Blaze*, suggesting that punters should not back Tiddely-Pom ante-post in case he doesn't run. He phones James and complains bitterly that no-one is going to put any pressure on him to withdraw the horse. Against his will, Roncey agrees that Tiddely-Pom should leave his yard and go to another trainer until the day of the race, and that his wife and three youngest children should go away on holiday to keep them safe from harm.

Tiddely-Pom gets colic, and trainer **Norton Fox**, who is looking after the horse, phones Roncey. He in turn tells his son, **Pat Roncey**, causing James to have to move the horse again in order to keep his whereabouts secret. After thugs try to get at Tiddely-Pom on the way to Heathbury Park, Roncey apologizes to James for being skeptical of the danger.

Roots, Jefferson L. (*Blood Sport* 1967)

Roots is Chairman of the American Bloodstock Breeders Association, and owner of Perry Stud Farm, Kentucky. His gentle, easy-going manner conceals a steely core. **Gene Hawkins** goes to see Roots to enlist his help in finding two missing stallions. Roots contacts the publishers of a leading horse journal so that Gene can use their files and staff. When Gene traces the stallions, Roots is keen to prosecute the villain who stole them. He is surprised when Gene tells him he's not interested in punishment, only prevention. However Roots is determined, despite the difficulties involved in making a charge stick, to pursue it, though he accepts it could take years.

Roper, Arnold (*Field of 13* 1998: "Blind Chance")

Roper, aged forty-five, lives alone. His bedroom wardrobes are stuffed full of banknotes that he has won by betting on certainties at the racetrack. Roper employs a small army of men to do his betting for him, since his own job at the track—the source of his success—keeps him fully occupied.

Roqueville, Bernard (*Bolt* 1986)

Roqueville, a French owner who has a horse with **Basil Clutter**, is an acquaintance of **Henri Nanterre**. He tells **Kit Fielding** that he knows Nanterre slightly. Roqueville goes to **Ascot** with a friend, **Mme. Madeleine Darcy**, who also knows Nanterre. Basil Clutter introduces Kit to her.

Rose (*Driving Force* 1992)

Rose is the secretary at **Croft Raceways** horse transport firm. She oversees the financial records and customers' bills. She is middle-aged and slightly overweight.

Rosemary (*The Danger* 1983)

Rosemary is the mother of **Miranda Nerrity**. She comes to look after Miranda after her son **Dominic** is kidnapped.

Rosie (*Under Orders* 2006)

Rosie is a friend and colleague of **Marina van der Meer** at Cancer Research UK's London Research Institute. She produces for Marina a DNA profile of Marina's attacker. When she realizes that Marina might still be in danger, Rosie takes it upon herself to keep an eye on her. She phones **Sid Halley** in great distress, to tell him that Marina has been the victim of a shooting outside the Research Institute. At the hospital she tells Sid that a motorcyclist, pretending to be lost and in need of help, had shot Marina. Rosie had done what she could to stem the flow of blood until the ambulance arrived. She spends a lot of time at the hospital until Marina's condition improves. When an envelope arrives at Sid's apartment containing a threat against Marina, Rosie takes a DNA sample from the saliva on the gum; she subsequently finds a match between the DNA on the envelope and that previously taken from a suspect's hairbrush.

Ross (*Forfeit* 1968)

Ross is **Vjoersterod**'s chauffeur. He is an ex–South African prison guard, and used to administering beatings and torture. He employs his expertise in this field on **James Tyrone**. Ross's relationship with Vjoersterod is not totally employer-employee, though Vjoersterod is certainly the boss. Ross drives Vjoersterod's Rolls-Royce when following James to **Dr. Pirelli's** consulting rooms. This journey culminates in a fatal accident.

Ross, Colin (*Rat Race* 1970)

Champion flat jockey Colin Ross is twenty-six years old. He has younger twin sisters, **Nancy** and **Midge Ross**. He flies with pilot **Matt Shore** to **Haydock Park** races, where he rides three winners. Exhausted, he goes straight to sleep on the return flight to **Newmarket**, but wakes up when the other passengers are complaining about Matt landing at **Nottingham** to have the plane checked over. Ross supports Matt's decision, which proves eminently sensible.

Ross tells Matt that he was married for two years but had divorced three years ago. His ex-wife, a wealthy, older woman, had not appreciated the privations to which a top jockey had to subject himself, and had left him for an actor. Ross invites Matt to stay the night at his Newmarket home when Matt is feeling the worse for wear after helping **Kenny Bayst**. He tells Matt he is terrified of Nancy getting leukemia, like her sister Midge.

Ross flies to Haydock Park with Nancy piloting the plan; he is pleased to give her the practice, and is proud of her. Nancy gets lost on the way back to **Cambridge Airport** through no fault of her own, and they are in grave danger until Matt finds them and guides them home. Ross, however, shows no sign of having been worried when he gets out; he grins and waves at Matt.

A few days later Ross flies to **Folkestone** races with **Polyplanes**, a rival to **Derrydown Air Transport**, the firm that Matt works for. When challenged by Matt, Ross angrily shows him an old newspaper cutting of Matt's trial for negligence, and says he's been told that Matt had been sacked from another airline for cowardice. He is angry on Nancy's behalf because she was already talking of marrying Matt. When Matt tells him the report wasn't true, and that he was unaware of Nancy's plans Ross is apologetic and realizes that Matt is telling the truth; he tells Matt that Nancy has gone to see her irritating hippy friend, **Chanter**.

At **Warwick** races Ross tells Matt that he should marry Nancy, and not to worry about having no money. When a villain runs out in front of the horses during the last race at Warwick and is killed, Ross is brought down along with several other riders, but is unhurt.

Ross, Midge (*Rat Race* 1970)

Midge, the twin sister of **Nancy Ross**, suffers from leukemia. She lives with Nancy and her brother **Colin Ross**, the champion flat jockey, on the outskirts of **Newmarket**. Midge is afraid that Nancy might get leukemia too. At **Warwick** races, Midge sees **Matt Shore** in the car park when she returns, tired, to her car. At Matt's urgent request she goes to find the **Duke of Wessex**, whose life is in danger.

Ross, Nancy (*Rat Race* 1970)

Nancy is the dark, attractive sister of champion flat jockey **Colin Ross**. She is in her early twenties, and has a twin sister, **Midge Ross**, who has leukemia. The three of them live together, and are a close family. At **Haydock Park** races, mistaking **Matt Shore** for the pilot whose job Matt has taken, Nancy calls him a skunk and is apologetic when she realizes she has the wrong man. She per-

suades Matt to go with her to the race meeting, and explains what's happening to him, since he's never been racing before. She asks Matt to protect her from **Chanter**, an old college acquaintance who continually pesters her, but she treats Chanter with good-natured resignation.

Nancy has a pilot's license but limited experience. She flies Colin to Haydock Park races. When Matt says he hopes that Nancy will know him for the second half of her life Nancy asks him what he means but he won't say. She's pleased when Matt says he hopes Chanter won't be at the races. But Chanter is there, and makes a nuisance of himself; Nancy, though, is indulgent towards him.

On her flight back to **Cambridge** Nancy gets lost above the heavy cloud cover. Matt locates her with the help of the Royal Air Force's radar and guides her home. When she gets out of the plane she runs to Matt, flings her arms around him and kisses him, hugely relieved to be home safely.

According to Colin, Nancy and Midge have been talking about Nancy and Matt getting married; but when a rival **Polyplanes** pilot shows Nancy an old newspaper cutting of Matt's trial for negligence and his sacking for alleged cowardice, she is very upset and walks out of the house, apparently to go to Chanter.

After four days Nancy rings Midge to say she hasn't been with Chanter, and that it isn't Chanter she wants. In fact she had met an old friend and gone camping with her near Stratford-upon-Avon.

At **Warwick** races, following an incident in which Matt displays conspicuous courage, he asks Nancy to marry him, and she says yes.

Rossellini (*The Danger* 1983)

Patrolman Rossellini, of Washington D.C. police, translates the audio tape sent by the kidnappers of **Morgan Freemantle**. He is embarrassed by the crudity of the threats on the tape.

Rotaboy (*Banker* 1982)

Rotaboy is a nineteen-year-old stallion standing at stud at **Oliver Knowles'** stud farm in **Hertfordshire**. He has been a superb stallion, but has only one or two seasons left.

Rourke, Nash (*Wild Horses* 1994)

Nash Rourke is the American star of British director **Thomas Lyon's** film, *Unstable Times*. He is an ex–fighter pilot in the United States Air Force. Rourke is fifty years old, but looks ten years younger;

he is tall and good looking and a talented actor. He proves easy to work with, getting on with his job without fuss. He meets Thomas at the film set in **Newmarket** to rehearse alone; his desire to play the scene differently from the way it has been written is supported by Thomas.

Rourke is angry when he reads a tabloid newspaper report falsely quoting him as criticizing both the film and Thomas. He appears on TV at **Doncaster** races to refute the report so that Thomas is not sacked by the film's American backers. When someone tries to murder his stand-in on **Newmarket** Heath he is not unduly concerned for his own safety, but acquiesces in Thomas's insistence on a bodyguard.

Rous-Wheeler, John (*Flying Finish* 1966)

Rous-Wheeler is a civil servant in the Treasury Department of the British Government. In his mid-thirties, he is pompous, petty-minded, and has an exaggerated sense of his own importance and talent. Thinking himself undervalued in his job, Rous-Wheeler decides to defect to Russia. However, his arrangements for leaving Britain go badly wrong.

Rowland, Charles (*Under Orders* 2006)

Rowland is **Sid Halley**'s ex–father-in-law. This is presumably a mis-spelling of **Roland**.

Rowley Lodge, Newmarket (*Bonecrack* 1971)

This is the name of **Neville Griffon**'s racing stables. One of **Newmarket**'s two racecourses is called the Rowley Mile course, after "Old Rowley," the nickname of King Charles II.

Rowse, Miss Marsha (*Come to Grief* 1995)

Marsha Rowse is a teenage employee of **Topline Foods, Frodsham**. She has just started working for the firm in Customer Relations. She chats with **Sid Halley** when he goes to Topline Foods seeking information about **Owen Yorkshire**.

Roxford, Grace (*Enquiry* 1969)

Grace is the wife of trainer **Jack Roxford**, whose wealthy owner **Edwin Byler** had been intending to transfer his horses to **Dexter Cranfield** before Cranfield lost his license to train. At the Jockeys' Fund dance Grace, the worse for drink, accosts **Roberta Cranfield** and **Kelly Hughes**. She is ver-

bally abusive to Roberta, saying that her father got what he deserved, and rubbishes Kelly's assertion that he was framed. Subsequently Grace Roxford's behavior deteriorates further, to the point where she becomes a danger to herself and others.

Roxford, Jack (*Enquiry* 1969)

Roxford is a middle-of-the-road racehorse trainer and a natural worrier. One of his principal reasons for anxiety is the fear that owner **Edwin Byler** is about to remove his horses and send them to rival trainer **Dexter Cranfield**. This leads Roxford to take steps to retain the horses which are wholly disproportionate to the problems that the horses' loss would cause him.

Roydale (*Longshot* 1990)

Roydale, a jumper trained by **Tremayne Vickers**, is a new arrival in the yard. Though speedy, he is spooky and obstinate.

Ruapehu Fine Arts (*In the Frame* 1976)

This is an art gallery in Wellington, New Zealand. It is also a front for illegal activities.

Rudd, Basil (*10 lb. Penalty* 1997)

Basil Rudd is the cousin of local muck-raking newspaper reporter **Bobby "Usher" Rudd**. He is the manager of Rudd's Repair Garage in **Hoopwestern, Dorset**. Skinny and ginger-haired, Basil strongly resembles his cousin, whom he dislikes. He tries to locate Bobby for **Benedict Juliard**.

Rudd, Bobby "Usher" (*10 lb. Penalty* 1997)

Bobby Rudd, known as "Usher," is a reporter for two local newspapers, the *Hoopwestern Gazette* and the *Quindle Diary*. He is young and thin, with a pale, freckly complexion. He likes to think of himself as an investigative journalist but his reputation is that of a troublemaker. His family owns a chain of garages. Rudd pumps **Benedict Juliard**, unsuccessfully, for information about his dead mother. He tells **George Juliard** that he will secure his deselection as candidate for the **Hoopwestern** constituency. He spreads a rumor that Benedict is George's rent boy.

About two years later Rudd is sacked by the *Gazette* for fabricating salacious stories. He hounds an adulterous opposition Member of Parliament until the man commits suicide. Dismissed from a job with *SHOUT!* magazine after Benedict disproves Rudd's story about his taking drugs, Rudd tries to persuade Samson Frazer at the *Gazette* to claim in print that the drug allegation is true. When Frazer refuses Rudd react violently.

Rudiments (*Rat Race* 1970)

Rudiments is a flat racehorse owned by the **Duke of Wessex** and trained by **Annie Villars**. Ridden by **Kenny Bayst** at **Haydock Park**, he finishes third after being boxed in on the rails. With a different jockey up, Rudiments wins a valuable race at **Redcar**.

Rupert (*Banker* 1982)

Rupert, an employee of merchant bank **Paul Ekaterin Ltd.**, works in the Banking Department with **Tim Ekaterin**. His wife has recently died at the age of twenty-six; he is back at work but still grieving.

Rupert, John (*Second Wind* 1999)

John Rupert is a text-book publisher who also works in a clandestine civil service department dealing with anti-terrorist activities. He flies his own plane as a hobby at weekends. He interviews **Perry Stuart** on his return from **Trox Island**; he is interested in Perry's discovery of a folder of potentially important documents. He is disappointed that Perry says he has no idea where the folder is now, and thinks that Perry is being less than candid.

Ruskin, Bill (*Come to Grief* 1995)

Ruskin, a veterinary surgeon at an equine hospital in **Lambourn**, is a friend of **Sid Halley's**. At Sid's request he operates on a colt whose foot has been deliberately severed. He manages to reattach the foot.

S

St Albans, Hertfordshire

St Albans is a busy, historic market town a few miles north of London. It was an important Roman settlement, established soon after the invasion of Britain in AD 43. Its impressive cathedral, dating from the 11th century, commemorates St Alban, executed by the Romans for giving shelter to a priest.

Reflex (1980): Solicitor **Jeremy Folk** works for the firm of **Folk, Langley, Son and Folk** of St Albans.

Sal, Auntie (*In the Frame* 1976)

Billy Pyle's Auntie Sal is in her seventies. She loves her racing, and is always to be found on the racecourse with her nephew. She is never without a cigarette and her form book.

Salad Bowl (*Field of 13* 1998: "The Gift")

American racehorse Salad Bowl is second favorite for the Kentucky Derby at **Churchill Downs**. During the race Salad Bowl receives a deliberate bump, causing him to collide with another horse, stumble and fall.

Sally (*Proof* 1984)

Sally is the wife of **Peter**, the owner of the runaway horse van which causes carnage at **Jack Hawthorn's** racing stables. She and Peter had come to Jack's party in the horse van because they'd just bought a new hunter. Sally is so distressed that she leaves the horse at Hawthorn's stables, saying that she never wants to see it again. She is worried about the financial implications if the insurance companies can prove negligence. She is angry when the parents of the little boy who had let off the brake blame Peter for not locking the door. According to **Flora Hawthorn**, Sally retorts that they should have been supervising their son.

Sammy (*Bolt* 1986)

Sammy is a twenty-year-old karate expert hired by **Kit Fielding** to act as a guard in **Princess Casilia's** house. When nothing happens for a few days, Sammy begins to get bored. He insults **Beatrice de Brescou Bunt** with his familiarity. Sammy helps Kit to set a trap for a villain in the alley behind the Princess's house.

Sandcastle

Banker (1982): Sandcastle, a well grown, rangy three-year-old colt, is fourth in the **Epsom Derby**. He wins the King Edward VII Stakes at Royal **Ascot**. He is acquired by **Oliver Knowles**, with a substantial loan from merchant bankers **Paul Ekaterin Ltd.** and other private sources to stand at his stud farm in **Hertfordshire**. Sandcastle breaks free from his groom when being led from his box to the paddock, but is caught by **Tim Ekaterin**. Many of Sandcastle's first crop of foals are born with physical problems. This is subsequently discovered to have nothing to do with Sandcastle.

Under Orders (2006): Sandcastle is mentioned in conversation at **Cheltenham** races; one of his expensive sons, now in training, had broken his hock on the gallops and had had to be destroyed.

Sanders, Mrs. Kerry (*Knock Down* 1974)

Forty-year-old American Mrs. Kerry Sanders is soon to be married to British businessman **Constantine Brevett**. She engages bloodstock agent **Jonah Dereham** to buy a hurdler at **Ascot Sales** for Constantine's son, **Nicol Brevett**, as a birthday present. She is unwilling to tell Jonah who the horse—which is not an easy ride—is for; Jonah says he won't buy it for her unless she does. Mrs. Sanders is waiting in her car in the parking lot after the Sales when Jonah is attacked by two men, who demand to buy the horse, **Hearse Puller**, from her. To save Jonah from further injury Mrs. Sanders capitulates and takes the money. Furious, she demands to know why the men wanted the horse, but Jonah has no idea. She insists that they inform the police, who aren't very interested. She asks Jonah to find her another horse, and is pleased when he phones to tell her about **River God**. She asks Jonah to be there when she gives the horse to Nicol. She is delighted when Nicol declares himself very pleased with River God.

Sandlache (*Twice Shy* 1981)

Sandlache is one of **Luke Houston**'s trainers; he is based on the **Berkshire** Downs. He has no problem working with **William Derry**, Houston's racing manager.

Sandown Park racecourse

Sandown Park is at Esher, **Surrey**, fifteen miles from the centre of London. It is one of Britain's premier racecourses for flat and jumps, imaginatively run and attracting high class horses. The track itself is superb, the spectacle of top class steeplechasers flying over the seven fences down the back straight unmatched by any other course: "Any horse meeting (the fences) on a good stride evokes the tingling, uncertain sensation experienced on honeymoon or when jumping out of an aircraft" (Guinness Book of Steeplechasing 1988).

The site of the racecourse was originally an Augustine priory built by King Henry II in the 13th century. The monks, however, didn't get on with each other, and then the Black Death finished them off. The priory was finally pulled down in the mid 1700's. A hundred years later the land was bought by Lt. Col. Owen Williams, a racehorse owner, gambler and friend of the Prince of Wales. Williams set about creating the first enclosed "Park" course with separate enclosures for Club members and the public, and modern catering fa-

cilities. Tyrell, in *Chasing Around Britain*, comments; "For the first time, women could go racing and be entertained in complete safety and comfort, and Williams' concept of the Park course changed the face of British racing."

Patronized by the future King Edward VII, Sandown's success was assured. Hurdle racing, previously considered the poor relation of steeplechasing, was given a boost by the introduction of the Imperial Cup in 1907, and it remains an important race today. Sandown's management has always been innovative: in 1947–48 the first televised racing was transmitted from the course. Sandown was also the first to embrace race sponsorship: in 1957 the brewing firm Whitbread sponsored the Whitbread Gold Cup. This famous steeplechase is still run today, though now the sponsorship has been taken over by a bookmaking firm.

Odds Against (1965): At Sandown Park **Sid Halley** tells **Lord Hagbourne**, Senior Steward of the **National Hunt Committee**, that **Seabury racecourse** is under threat from an unscrupulous villain.

High Stakes (1975): In the winner's enclosure at Sandown Park, racehorse owner **Steven Scott** tells his trainer, **Jody Leeds**, that he is removing his horse from Leeds' stable.

Reflex (1980): Steeplechase jockey **Philip Nore** is approached at Sandown by solicitor **Jeremy Folk**, who tells Philip that his dying grandmother wants to see him. The following day Philip, due to ride the favorite in the day's big race, is ordered by the horse's connections to lose the race. Later, Philip tells the owner and trainer he won't stop any more horses for them. At another meeting at Sandown Park he does his best on one of their horses, finishing second.

Bolt (1986): Champion jump jockey **Kit Fielding** narrowly wins on **Princess Casilia**'s horse Abseil. The Princess dismisses racecourse steward **Maynard Allardeck**'s suggestion that Kit had ridden a poorly judged race.

Hot Money (1987): Amateur jockey **Ian Pembroke** goes to ride at Sandown Park, accompanied—unwisely in Ian's view—by his father **Malcolm**, who has recently survived an attempt on his life. Ian finishes third in the amateur chase on **Young Higgins**.

Longshot (1990): Jockey **Nolan Everard** rides a superb race to win the hunter chase on **Chickweed** for trainer **Tremayne Vickers**.

Field of 13 (1998): "Spring Fever": Magic,

owned by **Mrs. Angela Hart**, finishes third in the valuable Whitbread Gold Cup.

Under Orders (2006): At Sandown races **Sid Halley** disseminates his theories about **Bill Burton**'s death.

Sandvik, Mikkel (*Slay-Ride* 1973)

Mikkel is the seventeen-year-old son of **Per Bjorn Sandvik**. He is well mannered but slightly nervous. After witnessing a murder Mikkel is removed from his boarding school and sent to the Norwegian mountains to prevent **David Cleveland** from interviewing him. This decision leads to further violence and fatalities.

Sandvik, Per Bjorn (*Slay-Ride* 1973)

During the Second World War Norwegian Per Bjorn Sandvik had been a courageous fighter against the Nazis who had invaded his country. His experiences in the Resistance have left him with a deeply anti-authoritarian view of life, which he nevertheless keeps well hidden beneath his urbane exterior. He is now head of a Norwegian oil company, though tight government regulation leaves Sandvik little room to exercise initiative or real decision-making. He still craves the buzz that his war-time clandestine operations provided, but now he gets it from other sources. Nor has he lost that essential element in the armory of a Resistance fighter—ruthlessness. An added ingredient in the make-up of this complex man is greed; without this vice Sandvik might not have chosen the path he did.

Sandvik has identified an opportunity to enrich himself by virtue of his involvement in the oil industry. He enlists the help of an acquaintance made as a result of his directorship of **Øvrevoll racecourse** in Oslo. It is when this relationship turns sour that Sandvik's plans go awry, and he is forced to adopt desperate measures in an attempt to cover his tracks.

Santo, Giovanni (*The Danger* 1983)

Santo is a minor figure in the gang that kidnaps **Alessia Cenci**. He is arrested when his jealous wife reveals the location of her husband's share of the ransom money and the names of the other six kidnappers.

Sarah's Future (*10 lb. Penalty* 1997)

Sarah's Future is an eight-year-old chestnut gelding bought by **George Julliard** for his son **Benedict** to ride in amateur races. He is trained by **Spencer Stallworthy** near **Exeter**, **Devon**. A tough steeplechaser with good conformation, Sarah's Future wins novice chases, ridden by Benedict, at **Wincanton** and **Exeter**. Three years later, by now in another stable, Sarah's Future breaks a leg in a chase at **Towcester** and has to be destroyed.

Savile Row, London

Savile Row is in central London, in the City of Westminster. It is the center of bespoke tailoring in the capital.

High Stakes (1975): Toy maker **Steven Scott** is removed by police from a **Soho** street, blind drunk. He is taken to Savile Row police station to sleep it off.

Saxony Franklin (*Straight* 1989)

This is the name of a firm, owned by **Greville Franklin**, which imports and sells semi-precious stones.

Schultz, Blisters (*Field of 13* 1998: "The Gift")

Schulz is an American pickpocket. In the era of credit cards, Schultz is finding it tough to make a living at his trade. He goes to **Churchill Downs** on Kentucky Derby day, where he steals the wallet of racing journalist **Fred Collyer**.

Schumann, Dorothy (*Dead Heat* 2007)

Dorothy, the wife of **Rolf Schumann**, lives in Delafield, Wisconsin. She is very upset at the injuries sustained by her husband in the bombing of the grandstand boxes at **Newmarket racecourse**, and the mental problems that he has suffered as a result. Mrs. Schumann receives a visit from **Max Moreton**; she tells Max what she knows about **Pyotr Komarov** and his connection with the Lake Country Polo Club. She gives Max a metal ball, one of many belonging to her husband. She doesn't know what it is, but Max tells her that it may help him to find out why her husband was injured. When Max returns to ask for another ball, she gives him one, albeit reluctantly.

Schumann, Rolf (*Dead Heat* 2007)

Schumann is the Chairman of **Delafield Industries Inc.**, tractor manufacturers of Wisconsin and sponsors of the Two Thousand Guineas, the first Classic race of the British flat racing season. He is also Vice-President of the Lake Country Polo Club in Wisconsin. Schumann is tall, well-built and about sixty years old. He is severely injured when a bomb explodes in the grandstand boxes at **Newmarket racecourse**. Trauma to his brain causes mental problems, as a result of which he is committed to hospital. It later transpires that Schumann was the intended target of the bomb; he had diverted money, procured by illicit means in concert with an accomplice, to his financially troubled company.

Scott, Clement (*Field of 13* 1998: "Spring Fever")

Racehorse trainer Clement Scott is not especially talented but is charming and plausible with his owners. He is, however, essentially a cold man, lacking in human feeling and with an eye to the main chance. When he sees that one of his owners, **Mrs. Angela Hart**, has a crush on young jockey **Derek Roberts**, he suggest to Roberts a ploy to relieve her of a good deal of money. But Scott has seriously underestimated Mrs. Hart.

Scott, Steven (*High Stakes* 1975)

£35,000 was a lot of money in 1975. To be swindled out of such a sum by a man you have always considered a friend is particularly galling, and you would have to be a half-brother to St Francis of Assisi to turn the other cheek. Steven Scott is a rich man, but he's worked hard for his money and being defrauded still rankles. Steven owns racehorses as a hobby. He is no horseman, and his trainer **Jody Leeds**, in concert with bookmaker **Ganser Mays**, has taken him for a mug. Steven has, not before time, cottoned on to Leeds' duplicity, and has sacked him.

From the basement of his home in London's Regent's Park Steven runs a successful business, inventing and patenting toys. Not just any toys, but the celebrated mechanical *Rola* toys, a brand-name known world-wide for originality of design and ingenuity. As a child he'd been taught how to use tools by an uncle who was a welder, and he'd made his first *Rola* when he was fifteen. His uncle, recognizing potential, had loaned him the cash to take out a patent, and Steven had never looked back.

Steven is six feet tall, muscular and darkly good-looking. Making his business a priority, Steven has had plenty of girlfriends but no one serious; at thirty-five he is unmarried but beginning to wish he wasn't. One evening he comes to the assistance of a pretty American girl in difficulties in central London. **Alexandra Ward**, known as "Allie," is stranded outside a restaurant, having abandoned her partner for dinner when she realized that the deal did not end with the nougatine glacé. Reluctantly she asks Steven if she can borrow the taxi fare to **Hampstead**. When she repays the money by post, Steven writes to her, asking her to dinner and enclosing her taxi fare in advance. Undeterred by her previous experience, Allie accepts.

Visiting his best horse, **Energise**, in its new yard, Steven strongly suspects that not all is as it should be. However, his attempts to clarify the situation prove unexpectedly painful. The adage that suggests getting even, not angry, is not one that Steven subscribes to. He does not see the two options as being mutually exclusive, and exercises both. In pursuit of the former, he plans in meticulous detail a sting against his former trainer. One of the friends whose help Steven enlists comments that the scheme reminds him of Steven's own *Rola* toys: "There you are, turning the single handle, and all the little pieces will rotate on their spindle and go through their allotted acts."

When Allie returns home to New York, Steven finds her absence strangely disconcerting. He writes to her, asking her to dinner. She accepts, naming the date—January 5th—and the place—**Miami** Beach. Steven, no doubt reflecting that it's a tough call but someone has to do it, flies out. Sex with Allie on a deserted beach in the Florida Keys is, for Steven, a pleasant corollary.

Arriving home, Steven finds the stakes raised to dangerous heights, and a frenzied attack puts Steven's life in the balance. His experiences make Steven re-evaluate his involvement in the racing game. Disillusioned with ownership, he gives Energise to the friends who had helped him take his revenge. But opting for a more direct participation, he asks his trainer if he will teach him to ride racehorses.

Seabury racecourse

Seabury is a fictional racecourse on the south coast of England. The town of Seabury is also invented. Francis's biographer, Graham Lord, tells us that Francis had the idea for the plot of *Odds Against* from the closure of Hurst Park racecourse in west London, which was sold to property developers.

Odds Against (1965): Seabury racecourse is becoming badly run down—a circumstance which, given its potential as valuable building land, may not be coincidental. Ex-champion jockey **Sid Halley**, now an investigator with **Hunt Radnor Associates**, takes on the case.

Searle, Simon (*Flying Finish* 1966)

Searle, an employee of **Yardman** Transport, is about forty years old. He sometimes goes to the pub with **Lord Henry Gray**. He expresses surprise at Henry, an Earl's son, wanting to work for Yardman; he recognizes that Henry's unassuming persona may conceal a strong character. Searle is not above bending the rules in order to line his own pockets. He takes Henry's place on a flight to Italy when Henry is unable to go owing to his father's death. He promises to deliver some birth control pills to **Gabriella** on Henry's behalf. However, Searle does not return from Italy, and Henry suspects that Searle's disappearance may not be of his own volition.

Seb (*Break In* 1985)

Seb is one of racehorse trainer **Bobby Allardeck**'s owners. He phones Bobby to tell him he's received a newspaper clipping from the *Daily Flag* suggesting that Bobby is in a lot of debt, and wants to know if it's true. Bobby's wife, **Holly Allardeck**, thinks Seb has a nerve, since he hasn't paid last month's training fees. After receiving confirmation from Bobby's creditors that they'd been paid, Seb pays his fees.

Second Wind (1999)

Meteorologists **Perry Stuart** and **Kris Ironside** fly in Ironside's plane for Sunday lunch in **Newmarket** with **Caspar Harvey**, a wealthy farmer and racehorse owner. There Perry meets American couple **Robin** and **Evelyn Darcy**, who invite him and Kris to visit them in Florida. A hurricane is brewing, and Ironside asks Perry to fly with him through the eye of the hurricane. Darcy suggests that they go to **Grand Cayman Island** for a few days; he has arranged a small plane for them to fly through the hurricane. Perry discovers that Ironside and Darcy have another reason for wanting to make the flight; Darcy wants Ironside to land on a small island in the western Caribbean called **Trox Island**, apparently to check on some mushrooms growing there. The flight ends in disaster; both men survive but Perry finds himself floundering in the murky waters of international terrorism, and up against a group of men who control the illicit trade in radioactive materials.

A hurricane which had recently caused widespread damage to Grand Cayman Island, to where Dick and Mary Francis had moved from Florida in 1993, prompted Francis to write *Second Wind*. The storyline has a contemporary resonance; pinning down the shadowy characters involved in terrorism in the early years of the twenty-first century has proved tricky for western intelligence agencies. But understanding what is happening in *Second Wind* is at times similarly perplexing. The novel suffers from the lack of a racing background, though the meteorological setting is moderately interesting and there are tenuous racing links. As a protagonist Perry Stuart doesn't inspire confidence, and his judgment is suspect. A routine visit to a photographic shop in London, for instance, assumes for Perry the significance of St. Paul's conversion on the road to Tarsus. Similarly odd is his proposal of marriage to a girl he knows only slightly better than his dental hygienist. When, as a reader, you have to keep checking back in order to reconcile what is happening with what has gone before, you know that there is something amiss.

Servi, Guy (*Straight* 1989)

Servi is an Antwerp, Belgium, diamond dealer. **Greville Franklin** bought one hundred diamonds from Servi, at a cost of $1½ million, on behalf of **Prospero Jenks**, a London jewelry designer.

Sex

A consideration of the part that sex plays in Francis's novels must distinguish between that which takes place between the hero and his girlfriend or partner, and the rougher or more deviant sexual practices that occur between other characters, invariably the villains. Descriptions of the hero having sex are mostly understated, rarely explicit, and concentrate on the feelings and emotions that arise during a close physical relationship. The sex scene in *Knock Down* (1975) between **Jonah Dereham** and **Sophie Randolph** is typical: "a matter of small movements, not gymnastics." In *Flying Finish* (1966) the cold embers of **Lord Henry Gray**'s heart are kindled by a chance meeting with **Gabriella**, an Italian trinket seller. But the fierceness of their need for each other, which is satisfied in the unromantic surroundings of an aircraft's luggage bay, is reflected in Francis's description, not of the sexual act, but of the sheer joy and contentment that accompany and follow their lovemaking.

If Francis prefers to leave the detail of his characters' intercourse to the reader's imagination, he is not averse, as in *Flying Finish*, to providing a setting that is slightly uncomfortable. **Steven Scott** (*High Stakes* 1975) has sex with pretty young American **Alexandra Ward** on a Florida beach;

Kit Fielding's relationship with Princess Casilia's niece, **Danielle de Brescou**, is consummated on the bare floor of Kit's new house in **Lambourn**, with dustsheets for a bed. One of Francis's more erotic scenes takes place on the dance floor in an Oslo hotel: in *Slay-Ride* (1973), **Kari Kristiansen**, the attractive wife of a Norwegian Jockey Club investigator, gets close up and intimate with **David Cleveland**, her husband's opposite number from the English **Jockey Club**. Whatever chemicals of sexual arousal David's scent exudes, they're enough to bring Kari to orgasm as they dance.

The motivation for plain, unmarried headmistress **Hilary Pinlock** to have sex with amateur jockey **Roland Britten** is considerably more prosaic. Hilary is a virgin whose desire for carnal knowledge overcomes any feelings of delicacy she may have about asking Roland to assist. Hilary is in a strong bargaining position, having just helped Roland to escape from a man whose aim is to incarcerate him. Many men would think Hilary's request to be above and beyond the call of duty, but Roland is made of sterner stuff. Francis deals with the physical act in an economical five lines of prose; let's hope that Roland took longer.

Biographer Graham Lord, in *Dick Francis: A Racing Life*, quotes Francis as saying, in an interview with journalist Corinna Honan, that when writing about sex he was conscious of the fact that Queen Elizabeth the Queen Mother read his books. Whether she approved of the sexual proclivities of some of Francis's less salubrious characters, we can only surmise. *Enquiry* (1969) features an aristocratic member of the Jockey Club whose favorite way of spending an evening is being whipped by a leather-clad madam. In *Wild Horses* (1994) a sex game played by a group of young people had lead to a tragic death. And a villain in *Odds Against* (1979) has a wife who derives sexual pleasure from the infliction of pain.

Such references to sexual deviance, however, are very much in the minority and confined, in the main, to deeply unpleasant people. The morality of Francis's heroes may occasionally be questionable—**James Tyrone** (*Forfeit* 1968) is unfaithful to his bedridden wife, and **Ian Pembroke** (*Hot Money* 1987) regularly visits an older married woman for mutual gratification—but their preference for straightforward sex is never in doubt.

Shacklebury, Paul (*The Edge* 1988)

Shacklebury, a **Newmarket** stable lad, is murdered after threatening in a pub to reveal things he knew about a crooked owner. At the time of his death Shacklebury is working for a trainer employed by **Ivor Horfitz**.

Shankerton, Arnold (*Forfeit* 1968)

Shankerton is the Features Editor on *Tally*, a glossy racing magazine. He commissions **James Tyrone** to write an article on the forthcoming Lamplighter Gold Cup at **Heathbury Park**. He declares himself satisfied with James's finished article, which concentrates on the usually unpublicized backroom characters of racing rather than the top owners, trainers and jockeys.

Shantytown (*Nerve* 1964)

A big chestnut gelding owned by **John Ballerton**, Shantytown is ill tempered, hard-mouthed and a poor jumper. He is normally a hard puller but, when ridden by **Rob Finn** at **Dunstable** races, is never on the bit and hardly picks his feet up, finishing last. He is subsequently found to have been doped.

Sharpener (*Reflex* 1980)

Sharpener, a steeplechaser trained by **Harold Osborne**, wins a race sponsored by **Ivor den Relgan** at **Kempton Park**. He goes on to win a valuable two mile chase at **Newbury**.

Shattered (2000)

On the last day of the millennium glass-blower **Gerard Logan** is at **Cheltenham** races when his friend, jockey **Martin Stukely**, is killed in a crashing fall. Stukely's valet gives Gerard a package containing a videotape that someone had given Stukely to pass on to Gerard. That evening the package is stolen from Gerard's workshop in the **Gloucestershire** village of **Broadway**. When Gerard goes to see Stukely's wife **Bon-Bon Stukely**, he finds her and the rest of her family unconscious on the floor. Gerard himself is attacked and knocked out. When they recover they find that video equipment has been stolen. Bon-Bon tells Gerard that her husband had entrusted a secret to Gerard on the videotape. Gerard stays at Bon-Bon's that night; on his return home he finds that someone has broken into his house and stolen all his videotapes.

Confused yet? Already fed up with videotapes? If not, you probably soon will be. The wretched tape is the focus of a story at best banal, at worst ludicrous to the point of farce. The novel is peopled by characters for whom it is difficult to feel any sympathy and who act in barely credible ways. *Shattered* is one of several less than gripping novels that Francis wrote at the tail-end of his career. The title, some may think, adequately describes Francis's own levels of energy and enthusiasm at this point in his life.

Shawn, Silva (*Wild Horses* 1994)

Silva Shawn is the beautiful and beguiling female star of the film, *Unstable Times*, which **Thomas Lyon** is directing in **Newmarket**. Thomas is impressed by her acting skills, as is the producer, O'Hara, who is sleeping with her.

The Sheikh (*Proof* 1984)

The Sheik owns horses trained by **Jack Hawthorne**. According to **Flora**, Hawthorne's wife, he is a deeply unpleasant man. Hawthorne's assistant, **Jimmy d'Alban**, considers him uncouth and terrified of being assassinated. He is, however, knowledgeable about horses. He arrives at Hawthorne's party with a full car of unsmiling minders. He is killed when a runaway horse van crashes into the marquee.

Shell, Simpson (*Twice Shy* 1981)

Shell is one of **Luke Houston**'s four racehorse trainers in England; he is based in **Newmarket**. He resents **William Derry**'s appointment as racing manager to Houston and especially William's policy of selling unsuccessful two-year-olds. Shell has to bite his lip, however, since he can't afford to lose Houston's horses. After **Newmarket Yearling Sales** he surprises William by asking him to help him saddle his runner at **Doncaster** on St Leger day. The filly wins, and William thinks that Shell is beginning to accept that he can do the job.

Shellerton, Berkshire

Shellerton is a fictional village near **Reading**, in **Berkshire**.

Longshot (1990): Racehorse trainer **Tremayne Vickers** lives in Shellerton.

Shepherd, Superintendent (*Shattered* 2000)

Shepherd, of West Mercia police, is the senior officer in attendance at **Gerard Logan**'s workshop when several villains are arrested.

Sherman, Bob (*Slay-Ride* 1973)

Sherman was an English jump jockey who had ridden regularly in Norway. His disappearance, along with 16,000 kroner from the racecourse office on race day, casts suspicion on him. But **Jockey Club** investigator **David Cleveland** can unearth neither a motive for theft nor, initially, any trace of Sherman. However it is not long before Sherman's disappearance is explained.

Sherman, Emma (*Slay-Ride* 1973)

Emma is the young wife of jockey **Bob Sherman**; they have been married for nearly two years and Emma is expecting their first child. She searches in vain for her husband in Oslo for three weeks. She is in a distressed state when **David Cleveland** meets her, and faints in the street. She doesn't believe her husband can be a thief, but has no idea why he has disappeared. She agrees to go back to England when David suggests it.

Arriving at her cottage, she and her grandfather disturb two men who are ransacking it. They assault Emma and her grandfather, and demand to know where her husband might have hidden papers. That night she loses the baby she is carrying and almost dies herself. Bravely, she returns home from hospital to put her house in order and rebuild her life. Under David's skillful prompting she remembers significant details about her attackers.

Shipton, Henry (*Banker* 1982)

Shipton is the chairman of merchant bank **Paul Ekaterin Ltd**. He is a successful businessman with a gambler's streak, which he uses to the benefit of the bank. In twenty years at the bank, ten of them as chairman, he has grown an unexceptional, medium-sized concern into one of the country's leading merchant banks. Shipton deals calmly with **Gordon Michaels**' aberrant behavior, giving him time off work to recover and asking **Tim Ekaterin** to do Michaels' job in the meantime. Shipton and **Uncle Freddie** offer Tim a directorship.

Shipton asks Tim to investigate reports in a muck-raking magazine of someone in the bank loaning money to himself at low interest. A horseracing enthusiast, Shipton sanctions a substantial loan to breeder **Oliver Knowles** to buy top racehorse **Sandcastle**. When many of Sandcastle's foals are born with physical problems he is supportive of Tim, who had been instrumental in agreeing the loan.

Shipton, Lorna (*Banker* 1982)

Lorna is the wife of **Henry Shipton**, chairman of merchant bank **Paul Ekaterin Ltd**. She is over-critical, acerbic and sharp-tongued. She berates

Tim Ekaterin for being at the races, and says she'll tell Tim's Uncle Freddie. She warns Tim not to bet.

Shore, Matt (*Rat Race* 1970)

Pilot Matt Shore's career has fallen apart in dramatic fashion. He had given up his job as a first officer with British Overseas Airways Corporation in an unsuccessful bid to save his ailing marriage, and taken a much less prestigious job with a small airline, British Interport. When a colleague made an error and lied about it, Matt was held responsible and found guilty by an enquiry of gross negligence. A year later British Interport went bust. Matt moved on to a South American airline, flying supplies in and refugees out of a war-torn African country. Sacked for refusing to ignore basic safety procedures, Matt returned to England to a short spell of crop-spraying, and then finally to his present job, with a small air-taxi firm. He lives in a scruffy caravan on the airfield, broke after paying off his fine for negligence and the costs of his divorce.

Matt's disinclination to take avoidable risks, always a comforting attribute in a pilot, is instrumental in saving his life and those of his passengers. Unhappy with the lack of response from the controls of his plane on a return journey from Haydock Park races, he insists on landing to check it out. It is a sound decision.

At Redcar races Matt doesn't think twice about intervening when he sees two heavyweight thugs beating up a jockey. He fights dirty, kicking and gouging, and somewhat improbably, the pair skulk away. His bravery earns him an offer from champion flat jockey Colin Ross to stay the night with him and his twin sisters Midge and Nancy Ross. It's just what Matt needs to alleviate his chronic depression. Though he is wary of involvement after an acrimonious divorce, the more he sees of Nancy the more he is attracted to her. The time he spends with her and Colin and Midge, who is battling against leukemia, becomes precious to him. The Ross family is a close one, and Matt desperately wants to be part of it. But he is afraid to make a claim on Nancy while Midge needs her more, and holds back from revealing how he feels about her.

It takes a near-disaster to jolt Matt out of his over-cautious approach to romantic involvement. Nancy, piloting a small plane, loses radio contact in deteriorating weather. She is in grave danger until Matt, searching for her in his own plane, locates her and guides her down safely. The kiss that

Nancy gives Matt is heartfelt and motivated by more than just relief at her rescue. Recognizing this, Matt returns her kiss, but then, soon afterwards, Nancy is given inaccurate information about the negligence and cowardice charges that Matt had faced earlier in his career. Devastated, she packs her bags and leaves home. Matt is astounded to learn from her brother Colin that Nancy had been talking of marrying him; He realizes, belatedly, that he loves her.

Matt suspects that the problems with both his plane and Nancy's have been engineered by a dangerous and unpredictable villain. Surviving one attempt to kill him, Matt shrugs off the real possibility of losing his life in order to protect innocent victims. The payback for his bravery is immediate. Before passing out from pain and loss of blood, Matt hears Nancy, now safely returned to the fold, agree to his proposal of marriage.

Showman (*Blood Sport* 1967)

Showman is an American stallion that had disappeared ten years before after getting loose from his groom, and was supposedly found dead two years later in the Appalachian mountains; however, the horse was not identified beyond doubt. In reality, Showman is alive and well, and serving mares under a different name.

Shropshire, England

Shropshire is a rural county in the west of England. One of the least populous and most peaceful parts of Britain, it is the largest inland county in England, with market towns such as Ludlow and Shrewsbury surrounded by unspoilt countryside.

Flying Finish (1966): Mr. Thackery, who farms in Shropshire, trains his own hunter-chasers. His horse Clobber finishes fourth in the Cheltenham Gold Cup.

In the Frame (1976): Artist Charles Todd goes to Shropshire to stay with his friends, wine merchant Donald Stuart and his wife, Regina Stuart. On his arrival he finds the police there; Regina has been murdered after disturbing burglars in the house.

Whip Hand (1979): Lord Friarly has a country estate in Shropshire.

Come to Grief (1995): Lawyers acting for a suspect in a case of horrific cruelty to horses claim that at the time of one of these crimes he was at a private dance in Shropshire. Later, Sid Halley asks Jonathan, the nephew of one of the horses' owners, to go to Shropshire to check out the alibi, which proves to be solid.

Shummock, Barry (*Whip Hand* 1979)

Shummock is the brother of **Trevor Deansgate**. He is a scientist, specializing in mutant strains at Tierson Pharmaceuticals vaccine laboratories. According to colleague **Mr. Livingstone**, Shummock is from a poor background, and used to be resentful of that fact. He is, however, considered a competent scientist. Unfortunately his scruples do not match up to his ability.

Silver Moondance Restaurant (*Proof* 1984)

This is a restaurant in **Berkshire** run by **Larry Trent**, who is killed in a horse van accident at **Jack Hawthorne**'s racing stables. The bar is temporarily closed by the police after it is discovered that a fraud has been committed. Subsequently a wine waiter is found murdered in the manager's office.

Silverboy (*Come to Grief* 1995)

Silverboy, a grey pony owned by nine-year-old leukemia sufferer **Rachel Ferns**, suffers an act of appalling cruelty. The pony cannot be saved.

Simms (*Straight* 1989)

Simms, a chauffeur, drives the **Ostermeyers** and **Derek Franklin** to **York** races in a hired Daimler. He is employed part-time by a luxury hire car company; during the week he works in a one-hour photo shop. He drives the Ostermeyers and Derek to **Milo Shandy**'s stables; on the return journey to London unforeseen carnage ensues, of which Simms is the principal victim.

Simon (*Smokescreen* 1972)

Simon, who is in his early twenties, is an assistant to the camera crew working on the film *Man in a Car*. He is immature and rather dim.

Simone (*The Edge* 1988)

Simone is an assistant chef on the Great Transcontinental Mystery Race Train; she is employed by the railway company. She would have preferred to be in charge but has to defer to **Angus**, the chef provided by the outside firm of caterers providing food for the journey. By the end of the trip Simone is being awkward and is resentful of Angus's proficiency. She sulks in the kitchen when Angus receives applause from the passengers for the standard of the food.

Simpson, Greg (*Field of 13* 1998: "Blind Chance")

Simpson is in his early fifties. Two years before, he had been made redundant from his managerial job; he had been unable to find employment and had become depressed. Then, answering an advertisement, he had met **Arnold Roper**, who had offered him a job betting at the racecourse on Roper's behalf. Now Simpson is once more financially secure and happy, since he only bets on horses that win. He sends Roper part of the winnings and keeps the rest for himself.

Sims, Bernard (*Dead Heat* 2007)

Sims, a large, cheerful man, is **Mark Winsome**'s lawyer. He provides **Max Moreton** with information on the guest at the dinner at **Newmarket racecourse** who had suffered food poisoning and who now intended to sue Max. At Max's request, Sims meets him at **Toby Chambers**' house in **Oxfordshire** to discuss the attempts on Max's life and the reasons behind them.

Singeling (*Knock Down* 1974)

A two-year-old colt by the sire Scorchmark, Singeling was bought at **Newmarket Bloodstock Sales** by **Jonah Dereham** on behalf of **Wilton Young**. He was unplaced in three races as a two-year-old but, according to Jonah, is from a late-maturing family and a certain future winner. Unimpressed, Young sells him on at a profit to a man who tells him that any horse selected by Jonah is good enough for him.

Six Mile Bottom

Six Mile Bottom is a small village on the **Suffolk-Cambridgeshire** border, about six miles from the racing town of **Newmarket**.

Twice Shy (1981): **William Derry** shares a rented cottage in Six Mile Bottom with his girlfriend **Cassie Morris**.

Slaw

Slaw is a fictional village in North **Yorkshire**.

For Kicks (1965): Racehorse trainer **Inskip**'s yard is in the village of Slaw.

Slay-Ride (1973)

On a dinghy an hour out of Oslo harbor **David Cleveland**, chief investigating officer of the **Jockey Club**, meets **Arne Kristiansen**, his opposite number in Norway and also security officer for Norwegian racecourse **Øvrevoll**. The isolated venue is due, so Kristiansen claims, to his over-developed fear of being overheard whilst he and David discuss missing English jockey **Bob Sherman** and 16,000 kroner which has also disappeared from the racecourse. David has come to Norway at the request of the racecourse's chairman to see if he can help.

The problem, as David is soon to find, is that his help is not welcomed in all quarters, and he is seriously hampered in his investigations by having constantly to watch his back. David discovers that Sherman's involvement with the Norwegian racing scene was not confined to riding the horses, and that his extra-curricular activities had cost him dearly.

A visit in 1972 to the Norsk Grand National gave Francis the idea for *Slay-Ride*. As regards geographical setting, he manages to find the balance between education and entertainment which had eluded him in *Smokescreen* and would do so again in *In the Frame*. His descriptions of the Norwegian climate, countryside and racing scene color and enhance the narrative without being a distraction from it. However, both the disappearance of Bob Sherman and David Cleveland's subsequent investigation into the reasons for it are predicated upon a somewhat unlikely event: Sherman had confided his plans to the seventeen-year-old son of a man with whom he'd stayed only a couple of times. In other respects the storyline is convincing, and there are some nice touches. As writer and critic H.R.F. Keating noted in a review for *Book and Magazine Collector* (November 1994), Francis creates a chilling and realistic moment of suspense just at the point where the search of Øvrevoll racecourse for a body seems to have drawn a blank. A little Norwegian boy, looking for dropped coins after a race meeting, is standing near the Tote building, tears on his cheeks. His few brief words shock the searchers near enough to hear him. David Cleveland asks them what he'd said. "He said," they tell him, "'I have found a hand.'"

For Keating, one of the strengths of *Slay-Ride*'s plot—though more of a subtext here—is the relationship between a son and his father. This is one of Francis's favorite themes, already explored in *Enquiry* and *Bonecrack* and returned to in later novels. In *Slay-Ride* Mikkel Sandvik is a bewildered, unremarkable adolescent who is caught up in a dangerous game in which his father is one of the players. A lack of communication between the two leaves Mikkel struggling to deal with the horrors of the events he witnesses.

Slipperclub (*The Edge* 1988)

Slipperclub, a racehorse owned by Canadians **Mr. and Mrs. Young**, runs third in the Jockey Club Race Train Stakes at **Assiniboia Downs, Winnipeg**.

Smith, Bettina (*Banker* 1982)

Bettina, the third wife of **Dinsdale Smith**, is much younger than her husband; she works as a model. According to **Judith Michaels**, Bettina is more intelligent than she looks.

Smith, Chris (*Enquiry* 1969)

Steeplechase jockey Chris Smith is mentioned by bookmaker **George Newtonnards**, in conversation with **Kelly Hughes**, as having a reputation for stopping horses.

Smith, Detective Sergeant (*Twice Shy* 1981)

D.S. Smith works out of **Newmarket** police station. He takes **Jonathan Derry**'s name and address when Jonathan phones to tell police what he knows about the death of a local man. Smith promises to pass the information on the **Detective Chief Inspector Irestone**.

Smith, Dinsdale (*Banker* 1982)

Car dealer Dinsdale Smith has a box at Royal **Ascot**, and has sold a half-share in it for the day to **Gordon Michaels**. He is a friend of horse healer **Calder Jackson**, who is a guest in the box. He is married to his third wife **Bettina**, a model. According to **Judith Michaels**, Smith likes to give the impression of being a high roller, but is not as successful as he appears to be. Smith backs Two Thousand Guineas winner **Sandcastle** heavily for the King Edward VII Stakes at Royal Ascot. **Tim Ekaterin** suspects that he has gambled more than he can afford. Smith can hardly bear to watch the race, and his relief when Sandcastle wins is palpable.

Smith buys steeplechaser **Indian Silk** very cheaply from small trainer **Fred Barnet**. The horse, once a potential champion, had inexplicably lost its form and become useless for racing. Smith sends it to Calder Jackson, who apparently revitalizes it; Smith subsequently sells the horse on for a big profit. He offers **Oliver Knowles** £25,000 for Sandcastle after the stallion's foals are born with physical problems. He claims that he wants to put Sandcastle back into training.

Smith, Frederick (*Knock Down* 1974)

Frederick Smith, also known as "Frizzy Hair" by **Jonah Dereham**, is a thuggish bruiser, and is in the pay of a crooked bloodstock agent. He attacks Jonah Dereham in the parking lot at **Ascot Sales** and demands to buy the horse Jonah had just bought for American **Mrs. Kerry Sanders**. Smith clearly knows about the webbing that Jonah wears to keep his shoulder in place; so Mrs. Sanders, afraid for Jonah, reluctantly takes Smith's money. Smith takes the horse away.

With an accomplice, Smith turns up at the roadside rest area where Jonah had arranged to meet the horse van bringing **River God** from **Devon**. He is about to force the driver to hand over River God when Jonah arrives and attacks him with a branch, breaking Smith's elbow. Smith and his henchman beat a hasty retreat.

Smith is seen by a boy setting fire to Jonah's stables. He is forced to abandon his car in the village. The police trace the car to him and he is arrested. Identified by Jonah, he is unrepentant and defiant, and tells the police nothing.

Smith, Geoff (*For Kicks* 1965)

Geoff Smith is one of **Hedley Humber's** stable lads. He has a habit of looking over his shoulder in a furtive manner, and mention of prison by any of the other lads upsets him. When he's been at the yard for three months Humber begins to knock him about with his walking stick. While Geoff is doing extra jobs the other lads eat his food. Eventually he quits his job on the advice of **Cass**, the head lad, who says that Humber has taken against him.

Smith, John (*Field of 13* 1998: "Dead on Red")

John Smith is a racehorse trainer; he is referred to in "**Dead on Red**" as Gypsy Joe.

Smith, Lew (*Proof* 1984)

Lew Smith is an employee of **Stewart Naylor** at his bottling plant. With **Denny**, he attempts to recover wine from the **Silver Moondance** restaurant; however, the wine had already been removed by **Tony Beach**. Either he or Denny shoots **Gerard McGregor** when they are disturbed; both men escape.

Smith, Mr. (*Hot Money* 1987)

Mr. Smith is an explosives expert; he is in his late forties and is of military bearing. He assists the police in investigating an explosion at **Malcolm Pembroke's** house. He suspects that the explosive responsible is ammonium nitrate fuel oil. Smith makes a discovery among the debris which sheds light on the cause of the explosion.

Smith, Sandy (*Driving Force* 1992)

Police constable Sandy Smith is based in the racing village of **Pixhill, Hampshire**. He is forty years old, and more intelligent than first appearances would suggest. He is good at his job, especially crime prevention. Smith is called by **Freddie Croft** to **Croft Raceways** to deal with a dead body in one of his horse vans. He defends the unsympathetic attitude of the police when Freddie is knocked unconscious and dumped in **Southampton** docks; he tells Freddie that the police see so much violence that it's hard always to feel sympathy for the victim.

Smith, Sergeant (*Come to Grief* 1995)

Sergeant Smith is a policeman who, while searching the grounds of Windward Stud Farm, **Northamptonshire**, finds hidden in a hedge the shears used in a cruel attack on a yearling colt.

Smokescreen (1972)

Film actor **Edward Lincoln** goes to see his terminally ill aunt, who has a favor to ask of him. She wants him to go to South Africa and find out why her string of racehorses is running so badly. Edward's father had been a head lad, and Edward had been brought up with horses; also, Nerissa had seen Edward performing miracles in films. Nerissa had inherited the horses from her sister who had died in South Africa; expensive when bought as yearlings, their stud value had plummeted. Nerissa wants to leave the horses to her nephew **Danilo Cavesey**, and she doesn't want to pass on a worthless inheritance.

Edward goes to South Africa on the pretext of promoting one of his films. It doesn't take long for his suspicions about the underperforming racehorses to take shape. It takes even less time for someone to make a determined effort to prevent Edward from acting on those suspicions. When that attempt is unsuccessful, the villain has other, more imaginative deterrents to fall back on.

The idea for *Smokescreen* was sown as a result of a visit by Dick and Mary Francis to South Africa in 1971, where Dick had been invited to judge at the Johannesburg Horse Show. The story, however, fails to set the pulse racing. Parts, such as

Edward's tribulations in a mine and in the desert, are well-written. But there are several unconvincing minor characters, and Francis rarely manages to get into the skin of 1960's South Africa or convey a sense of what that country was really like under the apartheid system. There is a feeling, too, that some of the information contained in *Smokescreen*, particularly about the mechanics of gold mining, is there to serve a didactic function rather than to advance the plot. Edward Lincoln is a credible main character, though he lacks the complexity of Francis's most successful heroes.

Snell (*In the Frame* 1976)

Snell, also referred to as "Beetle Brows," is a powerful thug of limited intelligence. He is part of an Australian criminal organization, and participates in acts of threatening behavior and in an abduction.

Snow, Frank (*Under Orders* 2006)

Snow is the secretary of the Old Boys Association of **Harrow School**. He tells **Sid Halley** that **George Lochs**, then known as **Clarence Lochstein**, and **Peter Enstone** had been disciplined for taking bets from other boys. When Snow, Lochs' housemaster, had tried to administer a caning, which was permitted in those days, Lochs had swung a punch and broken Snow's jaw. Lochs had been expelled from Harrow.

Snowline (*Break In* 1985)

Snowline is a mare owned by **Princess Casilia**. She was a winner on the flat, but hadn't taken to jumping. She was sold as a broodmare; two of her foals subsequently won races on the flat.

Soho, London

Soho is an area of central London bordered by Oxford Street, Regent Street and Charing Cross Road. One of its most well-known streets, Greek Street, is named for the Greek Christians who fled persecution in the Ottoman Empire. Later, French Huguenots sought sanctuary here from France's Catholic King Louis XIV. In the 1950's there was an influx of Chinese from Hong Kong. In the second half of the twentieth century Soho became known for its cheap restaurants, jazz clubs and sex shops.

High Stakes (1975): Toy maker **Steven Scott** is picked up at 4 AM, drunk and incapable, by the police from a Soho street and taken to **Savile Row** police station.

Soluble (*The Edge* 1988)

Soluble, a racehorse owned by Canadians **Mr. and Mrs. Young,** runs unplaced in the Jockey Club Race Train Stakes at **Assiniboia Downs, Winnipeg**.

Somerset, England

Somerset is a rural county in the south-west of England. It has borders with **Gloucestershire, Wiltshire, Dorset** and **Devon**. Its county town is Taunton. Better known are the Roman city of Bath and the seaside resort of Weston-super-Mare. The Somerset town of Glastonbury is steeped in legend, notably that of King Arthur; Glastonbury has been identified in some versions as the island of Avalon.

Shattered (2000): **Victor Verity** lives in Taunton, Somerset.

"Song for Mona" (*Field of 13* 1998)

Olympic rider **Oliver Bolingbroke** and his famous country and western singer wife, **Cassidy Lovelace Ward,** engage **Mona Watkins**, a kindly, down-to-earth Welsh woman, to look after their show jumpers. Gradually Mona becomes a valued part of their family; however, while both Oliver and Cassidy are away working, Mona contracts a nasty virus. **Joanie Vine,** Mona's snobbish daughter, ignores calls from the doctor to care for Mona who, neglecting to eat or drink, dies. The Bolingbrokes resolve to ensure that Mona's life is celebrated, rather than conveniently forgotten as Joanie would have preferred.

Going through Mona's few possessions, the Bolingbrokes find old newspaper clippings that shed light on Joanie's attitude to her late mother.

Sonny (*Dead Cert* 1962)

Sonny is a taxi driver employed by **Marconicars** of **Brighton**. He threatens **Alan York** with a knife when delivering a warning to Alan not to ask questions about **Major Bill Davidson**'s death.

Sooty (*Break In* 1985)

Sooty is a racehorse owned by **Jermyn Graves** and trained by **Bobby Allardeck**. **Nigel**, Allardeck's head lad, is concerned when Sooty is not in his box; he is relieved when he finds that Allardeck has moved the horse to another box.

South Mimms, Hertfordshire

South Mimms is a village in **Hertfordshire**, a county immediately to the north of London. It is near to the junction of the M25 and A1 (M) motorways.

Driving Force (1992): **Kevin Keith Ogden** hitches a lift in one of **Freddie Croft**'s horse vans at South Mimms service station.

Southampton, Hampshire

Southampton is a city on the south coast of England, in the county of **Hampshire**. Its port handles both luxury liners and container traffic.

Driving Force (1992): **Freddie Croft** is assaulted and knocked unconscious at his farmyard in **Pixhill, Hampshire**. He is taken to Southampton docks and thrown into the water.

Southwell racecourse

Southwell racecourse in Nottinghamshire stages low-grade flat racing on its dirt track and, less frequently, jumping fixtures on turf.

Reflex (1980): **Morton**, a racehorse trainer, had run a ringer at Southwell in place of a racehorse named **Amber Globe**. This deception is discovered by racecourse photographer **George Millace**.

Driving Force (1992): Trainer **Larry Dell**, a client of **Freddie Croft**'s, rings to cancel a trip to Southwell for a horse which has injured itself in its box.

Sparking Plug (*For Kicks* 1965)

Sparking Plug is a useful hurdler and promising novice chaser trained by a man named **Inskip**. He is bought by **Colonel Beckett** with all engagements to give **Daniel Roke** the opportunity to stay overnight at various racecourses and thus mix with lads from other yards. He has a hard mouth but a good action. He wins at **Bristol** and is second at **Cheltenham**. Daniel agrees to stop Sparking Plug winning its next race in order to convince people of his corruptibility. He keeps the horse thirsty the day before, and then gives it two buckets of water before the race. The horse finishes last.

Sparrowgrass (*The Edge* 1988)

Sparrowgrass is a racehorse owned by Canadians **Mr.** and **Mrs. Young** and traveling on board the Great Transcontinental Mystery Race Train. He finishes second to **Voting Right** in the Jockey Club Race Train Stakes at **Exhibition Park**, Vancouver.

The Sport of Queens

Dick Francis's autobiography *The Sport of Queens* was first published in 1957; a revised edition came out in 1974. In the book Francis briefly describes his career as a novelist up to that year. He says that he started writing novels out of financial necessity, and that he finds the actual task of getting words down on paper a demanding one.

Sporting Life

Sporting Life was a much-loved daily racing newspaper, now sadly defunct.

Bolt (1986): **Kit Fielding** places an advert in *Sporting Life*, offering a reward for information about the attempt on **Prince Litsi**'s life at **Bradbury** races.

"Spring Fever" (*Field of 13* 1998)

Middle-aged racehorse owner **Mrs. Angela Hart**, a widow, develops a schoolgirl crush on **Derek Roberts**, the young jockey who rides her two horses. So that she can see more of him, she asks Roberts to buy her another horse. Her trainer, **Clement Scott**, realizing that she is besotted with Roberts, phones him up and suggests a course of action which would line the pockets of the two men. At first Mrs. Hart is blissfully ignorant of what her trainer and jockey have done. When she does find out, her way of dealing with the situation demonstrates that she is more than a match for them.

Springwood, Jerry (*Field of 13* 1998: "The Day of the Losers")

Thirty-two-year-old Jerry Springwood is a popular steeplechase jockey who has lost his nerve and is dreading having to ride in the Grand National at **Aintree** that afternoon. So far he has managed to disguise his fear of injury by relying on his instinctive skills. Somehow Springwood manages to get down to the start on third favorite **Haunted House** and jump off. He is unable to give the horse any help at the fences and is last for a long way. When the situation improves beyond his wildest expectations, Springwood is more ashamed than pleased, knowing he had little or nothing to do with it. Interviewed on TV, he announces his retirement from the saddle.

Squelsh (*Enquiry* 1969)

Squelsh, a steeplechaser trained by **Dexter Cranfield**, is favorite for the Lemonfizz Crystal Cup at **Oxford** but is beaten into second place by **Cherry Pie**, an outsider from the same stable. Needing to be ridden sympathetically, Squelsh had refused to run on when his jockey had given him a smack. Cranfield later admits that he had over-trained Squelsh for the Lemonfizz.

Stable Staff

The caliber of Britain's stable staff should not be judged by the bunch of rogues, losers and assorted riff-raff employed at trainer **Hedley Humber's** yard in *For Kicks* (1965). They represent the dregs of the country's racing yards, recruited by Humber because he knows they won't stay long enough to realize what's going on. There's **Jimmy** and **Charlie**, both bullies, liars and ex-prisoners; half-witted **Jerry Webber**, the butt of physical abuse; **Reggie**, who steals food off other lads' plates; **Cecil**, an alcoholic who's been sacked from more yards that he can remember; **Bert**, a bedwetter whose deafness is due to the beatings he took from his father as a boy; and **Lenny**, an ex-offender, whose wages go to repay money he's stolen from a former employer. The head lad and traveling head lad are even worse; they are conspiring with their employers to terrify slow horses into running faster.

In reality the grooms who work in Britain's stables are the unsung foot soldiers of the racing game, working long hours for a meager pay packet and often exploited for their love of horses. Jockey **Philip Nore** (*Reflex* 1980) takes a less charitable view, complaining of their habit of leaving their jobs without notice and turning up, unapologetic, at another yard. Overall, though, Francis's portrayal of stable staff is realistic and not unsympathetic. Apart from the rum crew at Humber's yard in *For Kicks*, only two other novels feature stable staff who are involved in criminal activity. In *Flying Finish* (1966) **Alf**, a deaf, elderly groom who works for **Yardman** Transport has no scruples about breaking the law on a regular basis. **Juliet Burns** (*Under Orders* 2006), in her first assistant trainer's job after years of working in **Lambourn** stables, betrays the faith placed in her.

Most of the jobs in racing that are done behind the scenes can be found in Francis's novels. At the bottom of the pyramid are the ordinary stable lads and girls: looking after their three or four horses, grooming, riding out, cleaning tack and taking their horses racing. In the UK horses are not trained on the racetrack as is common in America; they are stabled at the trainer's own yard and taken by horse van to the racecourse on the morning of the race or, if it's a long journey, the day before. Some of the bigger yards use only the best riders to exercise the horses, and employ non-riding grooms. In *Whip Hand* (1979) **Inky Poole** is a work rider for **Newmarket** trainer **George Caspar**.

Overseeing the horses at home, and reporting directly to the trainer, are the head lads or girls, and assistant trainers. **Etty Craig** (*Bonecrack* 1971) is head groom in **Neville Griffon's** Newmarket stable. She is a recognizable type: from a well-off background, Etty is middle-aged and unmarried, preferring horses to men. Most yards also have a traveling head lad, in charge of taking the horses racing. Many head lads, whether traveling or stay-at-home, are fiercely loyal to and protective of the horses in their yard. **Dusty**, who works for veteran trainer **Wykeham Harlow** (*Break In* 1985; *Bolt* 1986) is an example: when jockey **Kit Fielding** gives **Cascade** a hard ride to win at **Newbury**, Dusty is annoyed.

Finally, there are the horse van drivers (horse vans are called horseboxes in the UK); the stable secretaries; and the yardmen, whose responsibility is to keep the stable looking tidy. **Old George**, Neville Griffon's yardman in *Bonecrack*, had once been deputy head gardener at the Viceroy's palace in India. In *Banker* (1982) **Nigel** is a stud groom, working for stud owner **Oliver Knowles**. He sometimes drinks too much, but is good with the mares.

If stable staff are not often the criminals in Francis's novels, neither are they the victims of crime. One exception is **Angela Brickell** (*Longshot* 1990), a groom who had worked for trainer **Tremayne Vickers**. The subsequent explanation for her disappearance results in a criminal investigation. The only other groom to suffer an unenviable fate is Paul Shacklebury (*The Edge* 1988). Employed by trainer **Ivor Horfitz**, Shacklebury had threatened to reveal what he knew about the criminal activities of the principal owner, and had paid accordingly.

Stafford racecourse

Stafford is a fictional racecourse. The town of Stafford is in the county of Staffordshire in the West Midlands, to the north-west of **Birmingham**. Originally a Saxon stronghold, after the Norman Conquest the town grew up around a Norman castle. Today it has a population of 120,000, mainly employed in service industries.

For Kicks (1965): **Jockey Club** investigator **Daniel Roke** is at **Stafford** races when he sees one of the runners in the selling steeplechase, **Superman**, crash through the rails, unseat his jockey and bolt after landing over the last fence. Daniel thinks that Superman must have been doped.

Staines, Middlesex

Staines is a somewhat nondescript town in **Middlesex**, once a county in its own right but now part of the Greater London conurbation.

High Stakes (1975): The owner of a betting shop in **Staines**, who has incurred substantial losses laying a horse that won, is forced to sell the lease on his shop to crooked bookmaker **Ganser Mays**.

Stallworthy, Spencer (*10 lb. Penalty* 1997)

Stallworthy, a racehorse trainer based near **Exeter, Devon**, has had plenty of success at local courses. He does most of his training from the office while **Jim**, his assistant, oversees the horses' work. He agrees to train a horse for **George Juliard** which Juliard's son **Benedict** can ride in amateur races. Stallworthy sells Juliard a chestnut gelding named **Sarah's Future**. He has a moan when Benedict eventually moves his horse to another trainer when he gets a job with **Weatherbys** in **Northamptonshire**. Years later, when Benedict is libeled in the magazine *SHOUT!* Stallworthy provides a reference for Benedict.

Stampe, Sir Creswell (*Dead Cert* 1962)

Stampe, the Senior Steward of the **National Hunt Committee**, is consulted by **Inspector Lodge** about the possibility that **Major Bill Davidson's** death was caused deliberately. Stampe relays the view of the committee that it was most probably an accident.

Standish, Angelica (*The Edge* 1988)

Angelica Standish is a character in the play on board the Great Transcontinental Mystery Race Train. She is the first murder victim, found dead with head wounds on the floor of the rest room.

Stapleton, Tommy (*For Kicks* 1965)

Stapleton was a journalist investigating the unexplained doping of horses on behalf of the stewards of the **National Hunt Committee**. He died in mysterious circumstances when his car left the road on the **Yorkshire** moors one night and caught fire as it plunged into a valley. The last nine hours of his life were unaccounted for, but it was known that he had been staying with friends near **Hexham** and was returning to London after attending **Bogside** races.

Stavoski, Lieutenant (*The Danger* 1983)

Stavoski, of Washington D.C. police, works with **Captain Kent Wagner** on the kidnapping of **Morgan Freemantle**.

Stirling, Charles V. (*Slay-Ride* 1973)

Stirling, an ear, nose and throat surgeon, is a neighbor of **David Cleveland's**; he lives in the downstairs apartment. Reserved and fastidious, he is quick to complain if David makes a noise. He responds immediately when David turns the volume on his TV up to maximum while being attacked by a man with a knife. Stirling's unexpected appearance scares off the assailant. He stitches David's minor chest wound. He accepts the offer of a meal with David at a local restaurant, and the two become friends.

Storm Cone (*Field of 13* 1998: "Haig's Death")

Storm Cone, a useful hurdler trained by **John Chester**, is a fancied runner in the valuable Cloister Handicap Hurdle at **Winchester**. During the race Storm Cone's jockey, **Moggy Reilly**, is almost unseated by another rider but manages to cling on. Storm Cone contests a close finish and appears to have won; however, the race is declared void.

Straight (1989)

Steeplechase jockey **Derek Franklin** is currently on crutches with an ankle injury. He receives a phone call from a hospital in **Ipswich** to say his elder brother **Greville** has been critically injured and is on life support. He finds Greville, who works as a dealer in precious stones, on the point of death. There is no sign of activity in Greville's brain, so Derek gives permission for the life support machine to be switched off. The doctors tell Derek that scaffolding had fallen on Greville as he was walking down the street. As Derek is leaving the hospital he is attacked, and the bag in which he was taking away Greville's clothes is stolen.

Next day Derek goes to the offices of **Saxony Franklin**, Greville's business in London. He finds the police there, investigating a break-in. No stones have been stolen. The staff looks to Derek to make decisions. Derek phones Greville's lawyer, who tells him that he is the executor of his brother's will.

Derek quickly familiarizes himself with his dead brother's business. He calls the trainer of Greville's two racehorses, **Nicholas Loder**, who is anxious that one of them, **Dozen Roses**, should run at **York** that Saturday. Derek watches videos of Dozen Roses' races, which confirm the impression he had already got from reading the form book that the horse is not being run on its merits. Greville's bank manager tells Derek that Greville had recently borrowed $1½ million to buy diamonds. A Mrs. Williams phones the office to speak to Greville and hangs up on being told of his death. Derek discovers that **Clarissa Williams** is Greville's married lover. The staff, discovering that Derek is a jockey, have misgivings about his running the business; Derek tells them it's either that or their being unemployed.

Derek has a good deal more to concern him than the future careers of Greville's staff as he sets about investigating the whereabouts of the missing diamonds and the handling of Greville's horses by trainer Nicholas Loder. In both cases Derek finds himself up against desperate men determined to prevent him from spoiling their plans. He finds an unlikely ally in Clarissa Williams who, badly missing Greville, sees in Derek a means of remaining close to her dead lover. In mortal danger, Derek has reason to be grateful for Clarissa's stout support.

Straight is a well-plotted novel that keeps the reader guessing. The opening is shocking in an understated way, and from then on Derek's path to the truth is twisty, treacherous and strewn with unsuspected dangers. Francis provides just enough information about the sometimes arcane world of dealing in precious stones without resorting to superfluous technical jargon. The racing interest derives from the ever-present threat of drugs being administered to racehorses to affect their performance. This aspect of *Straight* was given deeper resonance by revelations in 2002 about the infiltration into racing of major figures in the drug-smuggling world intent on money laundering, the corruption of jockeys and the doping of horses to lose. The disgraced Irish jump jockey Dermot Browne has admitted to his active involvement in using drugs to slow horses down.

Derek Franklin is a strong main character and satisfyingly normal; by no means a paragon of virtue but intelligent and courageous. His relationship with his dead brother's lover has an unusual poignancy, and is sympathetically handled. *Straight* is an excellent read, and Francis's best novel since *Proof* in 1984.

Stratford racecourse

Stratford racecourse is one mile to the southwest of Stratford-upon-Avon, in the West Midlands. The course stages decent jump racing, including the Horse and Hound Cup, a valuable hunter chase. Stratford is popular with **Lambourn** trainers.

Nerve (1964): **Rob Finn** rides **Turniptop**, a novice chaser, for trainer **James Axminster** at Stratford. The bold ride that he gives the horse convinces Axminster that Rob hasn't lost his nerve.

High Stakes (1975): Trainer **Jody Leeds** set up a major gamble at Stratford. Things do not go according to plan.

Comeback (1991): Diplomat **Peter Darwin** goes to Stratford races with vet **Ken McClure** and his fiancée **Belinda**. There he meets **Jockey Club** employee **Annabel Nutbourne**, who is escorting a party from the Japanese Jockey Club.

Field of 13 (1998): "Spring Fever": Magic, a steeplechaser owned by **Mrs. Angela Hart**, falls at Stratford in a prep race for the Whitbread Gold Cup at **Sandown Park**.

Stratton, Lord Conrad (*Decider* 1993)

Conrad, who is in his mid-sixties, is the son and heir of **William, Lord Stratton**, deceased. He has a twin brother, **Keith Stratton**, who is resentful of the fact that Conrad was born first and thus inherited the title. Conrad is elected a director of **Stratton Park racecourse**; he commissions an architect, **Wilson Yarrow**, to design new stands. He is unhappy when his aunt, **Marjorie Binsham**, taking **Lee Morris**'s advice, proposes an architectural competition so that they can choose the best design. However, Conrad has to accept the proposal when it is passed by a majority of the racecourse's directors. According to racecourse shareholder **Perdita Faulds**, Conrad was addicted to heroin as a student; this was hushed up by his father, who sent him to an expensive clinic for treatment.

Conrad is furious with Lee for delving into Keith's past, and threatens him with violence. When, however, Conrad learns the truth about Keith he accepts Marjorie's advice and asks Lee to join the board of directors of the racecourse.

Stratton, Dartington (*Decider* 1993)

Dartington is the indolent, easy-going son of **Conrad, Lord Stratton**. About thirty years old, he is unhappy about going bald, and starting to put on weight. He is elected a director of **Stratton Park racecourse**. Notionally in charge of running the family estate, Dartington is bored by the job and leaves it to his farm manager and land agent. He is wealthy in his own right after receiving millions from his late grandfather, and lacks the motivation to make something of himself. He lives in a wing of Stratton Hays, his grandfather's house. He denies being the driver of the car which almost knocks over an animal rights protester at the gates of the racecourse. The police suspect him of withholding information about an explosion at the course.

Stratton, Forsyth (*Decider* 1993)

Forsyth is the son of **Ivan Stratton**. He is dim, jobless and unpopular within the family. His opinions are ignored. He turns up at the racecourse while a tent is being erected as temporary accommodation for a race meeting, but at first remains in his car, watching. Eventually he tackles **Lee Morris** about his involvement in the racecourse's preparations; he says that none of the family wants Lee there. He is furious when Lee asks him what he has done that the family has covered up. Later Lee discovers that Forsyth had been guilty of an attempted fraud. His grandfather, **William, Lord Stratton**, had smoothed things over at great expense, to the annoyance of the rest of the family.

Stratton, Hannah (*Decider* 1993)

Hannah is the tall, blonde daughter of **Keith Stratton**, brother of **Conrad, Lord Stratton**; she is **Lee Morris**'s half-sister and not pleased about it. As a child—according to **Perdita Faulds**, former mistress of **William, Lord Stratton**, Keith's father—Hannah was sulky and spiteful. As a result of Keith's repeated sexual assaults on her, Hannah's mother had rejected her baby daughter. Keith had told Hannah that her mother had wanted to abort her. Hannah hates Lee, who was not rejected by his mother, Keith's first wife.

Hannah is unmarried, but has a son, **Jack**, said to be the result of a casual liaison with a gypsy. Keith had savagely beaten up the gypsy, and his father had had to pay the gypsy off to ensure his silence. It is later revealed that the gypsy is not Jack's father. After an explosion in the stands at **Stratton Park**, Hannah goes with Keith and Jack to racecourse manager **Roger Gardiner**'s office, where she joins in a physical assault on Lee.

Stratton, Ivan (*Decider* 1993)

Ivan is the youngest brother of **Conrad, Lord Stratton**. Stolid and unremarkable, Ivan owns a garden centre. He initially takes the family's side against **Lee Morris**, believing them when they say that Lee intends somehow to blackmail them.

When he sees Lee doing all he can to stage the Easter race meeting after the stands are badly damaged, Ivan changes his mind about Lee and apologizes for his behavior. He provides plants and flowers for the temporary tented accommodation.

Stratton, Jack (*Decider* 1993)

The son of **Hannah Stratton**, Jack is an awkward teenager. After the racecourse stands suffer serious damage, Jack goes with **Keith Stratton** and **Hannah Stratton** to **Roger Gardner**'s office and physically assaults **Lee Morris**. He comes off worse, however, when Lee breaks his nose. Jack is thought by most members of the family to be the illegitimate son of a gypsy who had tried to extort money from Keith for his silence. This subsequently proves to be untrue; the reality is more shocking.

Stratton, Keith (*Decider* 1993)

Keith is the younger twin of **Conrad, Lord Stratton**, whose family own **Stratton Park racecourse**. Conrad had inherited the title, the family mansion and most of the money, which has fostered in Keith a burning sense of injustice. Keith possesses a deeply unpleasant nature, one of the most frightening aspects of which is his unpredictable and violent temper. He had been married to his first wife, Madeleine, for less than six months when he broke her arm and knocked out her front teeth. His second wife committed suicide, his third left him and his fourth and present wife is an alcoholic.

Now in his mid-sixties, Keith purports to have a job in the City but is a gambler and heavily in debt. As a major shareholder in Stratton Park racecourse he is keen to see the land sold off to developers as a means of solving his financial problems. He is incensed when **Lee Morris**, Madeleine's son by her second husband, turns up at a shareholders' meeting; Madeleine had died and passed on to Lee in her will shares she had been given to hush up the physical abuse she had suffered at Keith's hands. At the meeting Keith argues for the sale of the racecourse but Conrad, who is having plans drawn up for a new stand, disagrees.

Soon afterwards Keith goes to the racecourse with daughter **Hannah Stratton** and her son **Jack Stratton**. They are furious to see Lee Morris there and physically assault him. Keith is prevented from causing Lee serious harm only by the arrival of **Marjorie Binsham**, Keith's aunt, who tells the racecourse manager to phone the police. Lee doesn't press charges, but he takes it seriously when Keith vows to kill him.

When Keith discovers that Lee has unearthed dark secrets from his past he is incandescent. He goes to the racecourse where, losing control completely, he threatens the lives of both Lee and one of Lee's sons. He has reckoned, though, without the courage and resourcefulness of another of Lee's children.

Stratton, Rebecca (*Decider* 1993)

Rebecca, the daughter of **Conrad, Lord Stratton**, is an amateur jump jockey. Tall, thin and masculine in appearance, Rebecca is abrupt to the point of rudeness. She is focused on winning at all costs. After a pile up at a fence during a race at **Stratton Park**, she angrily refuses help from **Lee Morris**'s son **Alan Morris**, and then berates the jockey whose horse had caused the fall.

Rebecca wants new stands to be built at the racecourse, and the dismissal of both **Oliver Wells** and **Roger Gardner**. After the explosion in the stands she arrives to inspect the damage and bossily tells Lee to leave the racecourse even though, through his voting shares, he has more right to be there than she has. She tells Lee she wants to run the racecourse herself when she stops riding. At the Easter Monday race meeting she wins the first race.

When Rebecca realizes that Lee knows a good deal more about her activities than she would prefer, she reacts in an extreme and potentially dangerous manner.

Stratton, Lady Victoria (*Decider* 1993)

Lady Victoria, the wife of **Conrad, Lord Stratton**, is slender and dresses immaculately.

Stratton, Lord William (*Decider* 1993)

William, Lord Stratton, was the father, now deceased, of **Conrad, Keith** and **Ivan Stratton**, and the brother of **Marjorie Binsham**. On his death his title passed to Conrad. He appears to have spent a considerable amount of time, energy and money in covering up for the indiscretions of his family.

Stratton Park racecourse

Stratton Park is a fictional racecourse to the north-east of Swindon, in **Wiltshire**. It is a private limited company; the majority of the shares were owned until his death by **William, Lord Stratton**. The shares have now passed to his heirs who are feuding over the course's future.

Decider (**1993**): Stratton Park racecourse is the subject of a bitter row among members of the aristocratic **Stratton** family. Some want it to continue to stage racing; others want to sell the course for building land.

Strepson (*Enquiry* 1969)

Strepson, referred to as "Old Strepson," is the owner of **Breadwinner**, the horse on whom **Kelly Hughes** wins the **Cheltenham** Gold Cup.

Stress-Free Catering (*Dead Heat* 2007)

This is a catering equipment hire company used by chef **Max Moreton**.

Stuart, Donald (*In the Frame* 1976)

Thirty-seven-year-old wine merchant Donald Stuart lives in **Shropshire**. He comes home one evening to find his young wife, **Regina Stuart**, dead and his home burgled. Antiques, paintings and wine have been stolen. He is looked after by his cousin, painter **Charles Todd**, who arrives the same evening. Stuart is suspected of involvement in the crimes by the police, since his business has cash flow problems.

Shattered by his wife's death and exhausted by the police's persistent questioning, Stuart tells Charles that he hasn't the energy to defend himself. He is upset when the police tell him that Regina's funeral can't take place until their enquiries are completed.

Over the next two weeks Stuart's health deteriorates; he loses a stone in weight and, more seriously, the will to live. When Charles tells him that wealthy widow **Maisie Matthews** had, like Stuart, bought a painting by **Alfred Munnings** in Australia and then had it stolen in England, he is too tired to care. He asks Charles not to go to the police about it since he feels unable to face further police interviews. He tells Charles that he spends his time sitting looking at a portrait that Charles had painted of Regina.

Five weeks later, when Charles returns from Australia, Stuart remains severely depressed. He is shocked when Charles tells him to stop brooding over his dead wife, and is alarmed to hear that Charles is taking the picture of Regina with him to London to be framed. Finally he is persuaded to go to London with Charles. He starts to cry—possibly the first stage of his eventual recovery.

Stuart, Perry (*Second Wind* 1999)

Thirty-one-year-old Perry Stuart is doing rather well for himself as a television weather presenter.

He got his big break fortuitously; at the age of twenty-two and working in the BBC's meteorology department, he stood in at short notice when a colleague was indisposed and proved popular with the viewers. Seven years later he was deputy head of the department, by which time he was Dr. Stuart, having completed a PhD in physics. Apart from his work for the BBC, Perry gives after dinner talks and lectures on physics, mostly to young audiences: "I had always found it extraordinary," he comments, "that people turned their back on physics as a subject at school and university..." Not so strange, Perry: it's a lot harder than media studies.

TV weathermen apparently, have their own set of fans. Perry's are mostly racehorse trainers who treat his forecasts as gospel when deciding, for example, whether to declare at **Cheltenham** with a horse that needs the going hock deep. If Perry says there is a deluge imminent in **Gloucestershire**, the horse duly runs. Presumably if the rain fails to materialize, the going is like concrete and the horse breaks down jumping the second fence, Perry has a bit of explaining to do.

When a hurricane begins to form in the Caribbean, Perry can't resist an invitation from a colleague, **Kris Ironside**, to fly with him through its eye. He is suspicious, however, about the motives of the American, **Robin Darcy**, who hires the plane on their behalf and has asked Kris to land on tiny **Trox Island** to check on his mushrooms. Predictably Kris ditches the plane and Perry ends up in the sea. Luckily Perry, an ex-surfer, is a strong swimmer and is eventually cast upon Trox Island. Perry's survival tests his resources to the limit, but he is strengthened by the example of his eighty-year-old grandmother, who had brought him up single-handedly after his parents were killed in a gas explosion. At the age of seventy-four, with a lifetime traveling the world behind her, she'd fallen ill after a white water rafting holiday in Colorado. Having lost the use of her legs she was now in a wheelchair and needed twenty-four-hour care, but not once had Perry heard her complain. It is Perry's money that buys the round-the-clock nursing that his grandmother needs. His generosity has an unexpected bonus when Perry develops a strong attraction to her new carer, **Jett Van Els**.

By now Perry has a good idea of the criminal activity being carried out by various racing people of his acquaintance. This is more than can be said for the average reader attempting to get to grips with *Second Wind*'s convoluted and unlikely storyline, which concerns illegal trading in radioactive material. At a crucial point in the story Perry seems to lose his marbles, and for no apparent reason absconds with a folder of vital information. Perry later admits that his aberration was due to temporary madness. Presumably Perry's mental faculties are still in a state of disorder when he asks Jett Van Els, whom he barely knows, to marry him. And, judging by the alacrity with which she accepts his proposal, Van Els's sanity must also be in serious doubt.

Stuart, Regina (*In the Frame* 1976)

Twenty-two-year-old Regina, the wife of wine merchant **Donald Stuart**, returns home early one evening after an argument at the flower shop where she works. She disturbs burglars, who kill her with a bronze statuette. Her body is found by her husband on his return from work. She is described by **Charles Todd**, Stuart's cousin, as a sociable, light-hearted girl.

Stukely, Bon-Bon (*Shattered* 2000)

Bon-Bon is the plump, pretty wife of jockey **Martin Stukely**; she is widowed when Martin is killed in a fall at **Cheltenham** races on New Year's Eve 1999. She is well-off financially, enjoys a gossip, and has four small children. Immediately after Martin's death she asks **Gerard Logan** if he will come and help her out. She is gassed and loses consciousness when an intruder steals videotapes from her house. She keeps asking Gerard to stay, subconsciously wanting Gerard to replace Martin in her life. She confides in Gerard that she and Martin argued constantly, but that they loved each other. She tells Gerard that Martin had recorded a secret on a videotape, which has now gone missing.

Stukely, Daniel (*Shattered* 2000)

Daniel is the eldest of the four young children of steeplechase jockey **Martin Stukely** and his wife **Bon-Bon**. He is able to give the police a description of the intruder who gassed him, his siblings, his mother and his grandmother and stole videotapes from the family home. During a game organized by **Gerard Logan** at Daniel's house, Daniel finds a letter sent by **Dr. Force** to his late father. Daniel is an intelligent boy, though of a mercenary disposition: he demands payment from Gerard for any help he might give him. He points out a pair of trainers in a shop in **Broadway** similar to those worn by the man who gassed them. He tells Gerard that there is a videotape in his father's car; however it turns out to be of no importance.

Stukely, Martin (*Shattered* 2000)

Martin Stukely is a brave and talented steeplechase jockey. He is married to **Bon-Bon** and has four young children. He is killed on New Year's Eve 1999 when his horse, **Tallahassee**, falls at **Cheltenham** races and crushes him. Prior to the race he had been given a packet containing a videotape to pass on to his friend, glass-blower **Gerard Logan**. After his death, Stukely's racecourse valet gives the tape to Gerard.

Suffolk, England

Suffolk, along with neighboring **Norfolk**, **Essex** and **Cambridgeshire**, is one of the counties that make up the essentially rural region of East Anglia, in the south-east of England. With its fertile, gently rolling countryside and its charming seaside towns such as Southwold and Aldeburgh, Suffolk represents the English countryside at its best. The Suffolk-Essex border was the home of artist John Constable, and the inspiration for many of his best-known paintings. The famous racing town of **Newmarket** is in Suffolk.

Straight (1989): **Greville Franklin**, elder brother of jockey **Derek Franklin**, is in **Ipswich**, Suffolk, when scaffolding falls on him, causing injuries which prove fatal.

Sunday Blaze (*Forfeit* 1968)

Investigative racing reporter **James Tyrone** works for the *Sunday Blaze*, a **Fleet Street** national newspaper.

Sunday Towncrier (*Break In* 1985)

This is a national newspaper whose proprietor, **Lord Vaughnley**, sponsors the *Sunday Towncrier* Trophy, a steeplechase at **Cheltenham**. Vaughnley has launched a daily version of the *Towncrier*, which is doing well. *Towncrier* columnist **Rose Quince** writes an article exposing **Maynard Allardeck**'s business methods.

Sung Li (*Proof* 1984)

Sung Li owns the Chinese restaurant next door to **Tony Beach**'s wine shop. Finding Tony and **Gerard McGregor** injured outside the shop, he calls for an ambulance. After Tony returns from hospital he has a meal at Sung Li's restaurant, for which Sung Li refuses payment.

Superman (*For Kicks* 1965)

Moderate steeplechaser Superman is an inmate of **Hedley Humber**'s racing stable. He is readied for a betting coup on Boxing Day at **Stafford** races; however, he goes berserk when landing over the last fence. He unseats his jockey, crashes through the rails and bolts. When eventually caught Superman is dripping with sweat; his eyes are rolling, his ears are flat back and he is lashing out.

Surrey, England

Surrey is a prosperous county in south-east England with a population of about one million. One of the Home Counties, Surrey's proximity to London means that many of its residents work in the capital. Its county town is Guildford. **Epsom racecourse**, home of the Derby, is in Surrey. **Sandown Park racecourse** is in Esher, Surrey.

Forfeit (1968): **Gail Pominga** lives with her uncle and aunt, **Harry** and **Sarah Hunterson**, in Virginia Water, Surrey.

Knock Down (1974): Bloodstock agent **Jonah Dereham** lives near Gatwick, Surrey. Air traffic controller **Sophie Randolph** lives in Esher, Surrey.

High Stakes (1975): Merchant banker **Charlie Canterfield** lives in Surrey.

Risk (1977): **Hilary Pinlock**, who hides **Roland Britten** in her hotel room in **Minorca** after he escapes from captivity, lives in Surrey. Roland visits her there to ask her to keep a parcel of documents safe for him.

Reflex (1980): **Philip Nore**, trying to trace his half-sister **Amanda Nore**, places a photo of her as a little girl on a pony in *Horse and Hound* magazine. A lady who sees the photo recognizes the stables as being in Surrey, where Philip's mother had lived for a while.

Twice Shy (1981): **Jonathon Derry** practices his rifle shooting at **Bisley**, Surrey.

The Danger (1983): **John Nerrity**, owner of **Epsom** Derby winner **Ordinand**, lives near Sutton, Surrey.

Hot Money (1987): **Joyce Pembroke**, the second of **Malcolm Pembroke**'s five wives, lives in Surrey. **Ian Pembroke** has a flat in Epsom, Surrey.

Wild Horses (1994): **Dorothea Pannier**'s unpleasant son **Paul** lives in Surrey.

To the Hilt (1996): Private detective **Chris Young** tells **Alexander Kinloch** that **Surtees Benchmark** visits a prostitute in Guildford, Surrey.

Susan, Aunt (*10 lb. Penalty* 1997)

Benedict Juliard's Aunt Susan brought him up after his mother died in childbirth. She is not happy when his father sends him to the fee-paying Marlborough College when her own four sons had gone to the local comprehensive school.

Sussex, England

Sussex is a rural county on the south-east coast of England. Geographically, Sussex has a ridge of high land running from east to west, known as the Weald. Between the Weald and the sea are the beautiful South Downs. On the Sussex coast are the resort towns of **Brighton** and Eastbourne.

In the Frame (1976): Maisie Matthews's house, which has burnt down, is in Hastings, a town on the coast of Sussex.

Reflex (1980): **Pine Woods Lodge**, the last known address of **Philip Nore's** mother **Caroline**, is in Sussex.

The Danger (1983): Mrs. **Blackett**, a former employee of **Paolo Cenci**, now lives with her brother in Sussex.

Break In (1985): Mr. **Davies**, one of **Wykeham Harlow's** owners, lives in Sussex.

Straight (1989): **Saul Bradley**, former sports editor of the *Sunday Towncrier*, lives in Selsey, Sussex.

Come to Grief (1995): **Sid Halley** tracks down the provenance of a piece of material in which shears used to injure horses were wrapped. The cloth was woven by **Patricia Huxford**, whose business is in Chichester, West Sussex.

Swann, Lida (*Risk* 1977)

The girlfriend of trainer **William Finch**, Lida Swann is of ravishing appearance, and is thoroughly disliked by Finch's daughter **Jossie**. When Finch decamps to France he takes Lida with him, annoying Jossie even more.

Swayle, Orkney (*Proof* 1984)

Swayle, one of trainer **Jack Hawthorn's** more awkward owners, has four two-year-olds in training. He has recently lost his driving license for drink-driving. He has a box at **Martineau Park racecourse**, where he shows his lack of good manners when a delay to the previous race means that saddling his own runner in the next race has to be hurried. He is unpleasant to the jockey before the race; when his horse is beaten he blames the horse, the jockey and the trainer.

Sylvester, Scott (*Comeback* 1991)

Scott is a veterinary nurse at Hewett and Partners, a large practice in Cheltenham, **Gloucestershire**. About forty years old, he is considered a good nurse, and veterinary surgeon **Yvonne Floyd** thinks him kind. He is called in during the night to assist in an operation on a pregnant mare with colic. He spends a night at the hospital checking on convalescing horses; the next morning he is found dead in gruesome circumstances.

T

Tables Turned (*Smokescreen* 1972)

Tables Turned is a racehorse owned by **Nerissa Cavesey** and trained by **Greville Arnold** in South Africa. He looks well before his race at **Germiston** races but weakens two furlongs out and finishes well beaten. Arnold is angry; he thinks the horse had the ability to win easily.

Taff (*Twice Shy* 1981)

Taff is a veteran racecourse bookmaker. He tells **William Derry** that **Angelo Gilbert** is boasting about how he's going to take the bookies to the cleaners with **Liam O'Rorke's** system. He refuses to give Gilbert a fair price against the horse he wants to back. Not long afterwards, Taff tells William that Gilbert is losing a lot of money using the system, and the bookies are allowing him to bet at fair odds.

Tallahassee (*Shattered* 2000)

Tallahassee is a steeplechaser trained by **Priam Jones**. He is leading at the last fence in the Coffee Forever Gold Trophy at **Cheltenham**, but falls and crushes jockey **Martin Stukely** to death.

Tally (*Forfeit* 1968)

Tally is a racing magazine; the Features Editor, **Arnold Shankerton**, commissions **James Tyrone** to write an article on the Lamplighter Gold Cup at **Heathbury Park**.

Tansing, Colonel (*The Danger* 1983)

Colonel Tansing is the Deputy Licensing Officer of the **Jockey Club**. He is informed by Mrs. **Berkeley** of a phone call from kidnappers to say that Senior Steward **Morgan Freemantle** has been abducted. He phones **Eric Rickenbacker**, President of **Laurel racecourse**, Washington D.C., to tell him the news.

Tansy (*Longshot* 1990)

Tansy is a teenage stable girl employed by **Tremayne Vickers**. She is routinely interviewed by **Detective Chief Inspector Doone** in connection with the death of a girl who worked in the same stable.

Tape, Nigel (*Field of 13* 1998: "Dead on Red")

Tape, a steeplechase jockey of moderate ability, is second jockey to "Gypsy Joe" Smith's stable. He is in awe of the stable's first jockey **Davey Rockman**, and is resentful when Gypsy Joe appoints the young and inexperienced **Red Millbrook** as first jockey in Rockman's place. Tape recruits his brother, who has criminal contacts, to assist Rockman with his plans to get his job back.

Tapestry (*Risk* 1977)

Tapestry is a steeplechaser trained by **Binny Tomkins** and owned by **Moira Longerman**. An outsider, he wins the **Cheltenham** Gold Cup ridden by **Roland Britten**. Held up to stay the trip, Tapestry takes advantage of the falls of the first and second favorites to come through and win. He also wins the Oasthouse Cup at **Kempton Park**, again ridden by Roland.

Tarleton, Thomas Nathaniel (*For Kicks* 1965)

Tarleton, known as "Soupy," is a stable lad at **Granger**'s racing stable in North **Yorkshire**. He wears a gold ring, an expensive watch and sharp clothes. He is seen as untrustworthy by **Inskip**'s lads. When he realizes that **Daniel Roke** is corruptible, Tarleton tries to procure him for a doper who wants Daniel to give **Sparking Plug** something to stop him winning. Tarleton is later charged by the police for this offence.

Tarren, Lady Elinor (*For Kicks* 1965)

Lady Elinor is **Lord October**'s elder daughter. She is blonde, graceful, well-mannered and charming; in character, she is the antithesis of her sister, **Lady Patricia Tarren**. She meets **Daniel Roke** at Inskip's training stables, where she rides out. Elinor is a student at nearby **Durham** University. After Daniel has been sacked from Inskip's for allegedly sexually assaulting Patricia and is working at **Hedley Humber**'s yard, Elinor writes to him, asking him to visit her at Durham. There she apologizes for her sister's behavior; Patricia has told her what really happened. Elinor finds herself attracted to Daniel's dark good looks, saying shyly that she could see why Patricia acted as she did. When Daniel asks to borrow an old silent dog whistle to try an experiment Elinor agrees, but doesn't ask what he intends to do with it. A few days later Elinor calls in at Humber's yard to collect the dog whistle from Daniel. She has, unwittingly, put herself in grave danger.

Some time later, at her home in London, Elinor meets Daniel again. At first she barely recognizes him, and is slightly put out that Daniel had not told her what he was up to.

Tarren, Lady Patricia (*For Kicks* 1965)

Lady Patricia, known as "Patty," is the younger daughter of **Lord October**; she is beautiful, wild and manipulative. She digs her nails into **Daniel Roke**'s ear lobe when he's giving her a leg up onto her horse to see how he reacts. The next time she rides out at **Inskip**'s yard she kicks Daniel in the ribs while he is shortening her stirrups, and calls him a coward when he refuses to react.

One afternoon Patty sees Daniel working on extra duties in the yard. She lures him into the hay barn and tries to seduce him. When Daniel rejects her advances she tells her father that Daniel has sexually assaulted her. Lord October is furious, and feels that he has to believe her story even though Daniel denies it. Later, Patty tells her sister, **Lady Elinor Tarren**, the truth; Elinor tells her father, who is ashamed of his lack of trust in Daniel.

When Lord October introduces the real Daniel to his two daughters, Patty doesn't recognize him at first and blushes when she realizes who he is. She calls him a beast for deceiving her.

Tasker, George (*Break In* 1985)

Tasker is an elderly man who runs a boat repair yard on the Thames estuary. He is deeply distressed after the suicide of his son, also named George, who had borrowed money to expand his electronics business from **Maynard Allardeck**. Without warning Allardeck had demanded early repayment of the money, taken over the business when George could not repay, sold the assets and put the workforce on the dole.

Tatum, Davis (*Come to Grief* 1995)

Tatum is a senior barrister in chambers where a colleague is acting as prosecuting counsel in a trial involving extreme cruelty to horses. His corpulence belies a sharp brain. He informs **Sid Halley** that the suspect has changed his plea from not guilty to guilty on grounds of diminished responsibility. Later, Tatum tells Sid that the suspect has retracted his guilty plea and that his lawyers are confident of an acquittal. After speaking with **Archie Kirk**, Tatum has reason to believe that there is a powerful unseen presence manipulating the case behind the scenes. He asks Sid to look into the background of **Owen Yorkshire**, owner of **Topline Foods**.

Taunton racecourse

Taunton is a small, rural jumping track in the county of **Somerset**, south-west England. The setting is picturesque but viewing of the racing for the paying customer is partially restricted by the undulating nature of the home straight.

10 lb. Penalty (1997): Racehorse owner **Mrs. Courtney Young** is upset when her horse is killed in a race at Taunton. The main reasons for her grief are that she has let the insurance lapse on the horse, and that she owes her trainer a lot of money for training fees.

Tavel, Henri (*Proof* 1984)

Tavel is a Bordeaux-based wine shipper; **Tony Beach** had stayed with Tavel as a paying guest in order to learn about the wine trade. Tony consults Tavel about the Bordeaux wine labels on bottles sold at the **Silver Moondance** restaurant.

Taylor, Hudson (*In the Frame* 1976)

Hudson is an Adelaide-based vineyard owner and wine exporter. He had sold wine to English wine merchant **Donald Stuart**, who was vacationing in Australia. Taylor also controls a network of art galleries across Australia, the raison d'être for which is not primarily cultural. He had loaned Stuart money to buy a painting, supposedly by **Alfred Munnings**.

Stuart's cousin, painter **Charles Todd**, arrives in Australia to investigate a burglary at Stuart's house which had resulted in the death of Stuart's wife. He contacts Taylor, who arranges to meet him at Melbourne races. Taylor tells Charles that Stuart had bought his Munnings at **Yarra River Fine Arts** gallery in Melbourne. Subsequently the gallery's manager, **Ivor Wexford**, is arrested, but is allowed to contact Taylor. Wexford has been fed false information about the whereabouts of some copies of Munnings' paintings which Charles had removed from the gallery in Melbourne. Taylor goes to collect them from a deposit box at the airport, where a reception party awaits him.

Teck, Mervyn (*10 lb. Penalty* 1997)

Teck is a political agent who works for **George Juliard** during the **Hoopwestern** by-election. According to his secretary **Crystal Harley**, Teck had favored **Orinda Nagle** to run as the candidate, but he is nevertheless efficient on Juliard's behalf. He is annoyed when Juliard neglects door-to-door canvassing in favor of a day at **Dorset County** races, but uses his personal and political connections to organize lunch with the Stewards for Juliard and his son.

Teddington, Popsy (*The Danger* 1983)

Popsy Teddington is a widowed **Lambourn** racehorse trainer. She is in her mid-forties, and is large and ebullient. She is a friend of **Alessia Cenci**, who stays with Popsy after her release by her kidnappers. According to Alessia, Popsy is a good, perceptive trainer. She worries that Alessia has become insecure; she makes Alessia get back up on a horse on the Lambourn gallops to restore her confidence. After the rescue of **Dominic Nerrity**, Popsy invites the Nerrity family to Lambourn for the day, together with Alessia and **Andrew Douglas**.

Teesside racecourse

Teesside is a now defunct racecourse on the banks of the River Tees in north-east England. It was formerly known as Stockton racecourse. The last meeting took place in 1981. The site was developed as a shopping complex, and the stands remain as part of a leisure centre.

Bonecrack (1971): Apprentice jockey **Alessandro Rivera** wins on **Lancat** at 25/1 for trainer **Neil Griffon** at Teesside.

Teksa, Pauli (*Knock Down* 1974)

American Pauli Teksa is the main player in an informal grouping of bloodstock agents. To the casual observer Teksa appears ambitious, energetic and friendly, but he is ruthless in his quest for the financial edge.

Ex-jockey turned bloodstock agent **Jonah Dereham** finds the practices employed by his colleagues unethical, and is building a thriving business through his reputation for straight dealing. Teksa is prepared to give Jonah the chance to be one of the boys; he advises wealthy American **Kerry Sanders** to use Jonah to buy a horse for her. The deal completed, Teksa phones Jonah to negotiate a cut of Jonah's commission for himself. At **Newmarket Sales** Teksa bids for a seemingly well-bred colt but withdraws when Jonah throws doubt on the colt's paternity. When Jonah refuses payment for the information Teksa calls him a fool. Later, over a drink, Teksa gives Jonah a friendly warning to go along with the crowd if he wants to avoid trouble for himself. When Teksa realizes that Jonah has no intention of following his advice, he takes steps to bring Jonah into line. This course of action has dreadful consequences.

Telebiddy (*Longshot* 1990)

Telebiddy, a steeplechaser trained by **Tremayne Vickers**, is a trier, but is one-paced. He finishes fourth at **Windsor** races, ridden by stable jockey **Sam Yaeger**.

Teller, Dave (*Blood Sport* 1967)

Teller is an American friend of **Sim Keeble**, **Gene Hawkins'** boss. He is in his late forties, well-educated and wealthy. On his father's death Teller had inherited his money and his racehorses. He owns a one-eighth share in a missing stallion. He asks Gene to go to America to find the horse.

On Keeble's cruiser on the Thames, Teller is knocked into the river by a punt pole when they go to the help of a young couple in difficulties near a lock. Swept under the lock gates by the strong current, Teller is saved by Gene, who dives in after him, but suffers a broken leg.

Teller doesn't trust his wife, **Eunice Teller**; when Gene returns from America he wants to know what she's been doing. He receives a phone call from Gene, who is back in America, saying that he's found the stallion and asking if Teller wants him to look for another missing stallion in which Teller has an interest. Despite having to repay the insurance money and losing three crops of foals, Teller gives Gene a free hand.

Teller, Eunice (*Blood Sport* 1967)

Eunice is the English wife of **Dave Teller**. She is in her forties, slim and petite. In the manner of rich, bored housewives, Eunice always has a drink near to hand but never gets properly drunk. Finding **Gene Hawkins'** Luger in his clothes by the swimming pool, she points it at him, and then throws it away. The gun goes off, the bullet just missing her. At dinner she tells Gene that she lacks for nothing, but it is obvious that she is unsatisfied with her life. She asks Gene to stay the night but he declines the invitation.

Eunice is happy to have **Lynnie Keeble** stay with her in Kentucky, and the two get on well.

After Gene again refuses her offer of sex she tells him she's bored. Gene suggests she make a business out of her hobby, interior decorating. Scornfully, Eunice says it would just be a substitute for sex for a woman whose appeal was fading, but Gene tells her that the need for casual sex is a sublimation of a deeper need.

Eunice surprises Gene by revealing that the stud farm that she and Dave are buying in California is next door to **Culham James Offen's** farm. At Gene's request, she visits Offen, shows him photos of Gene and tells him about Gene rescuing her husband from drowning.

Lynnie's stay with Eunice has a beneficial effect; she virtually gives up drinking. Taking Gene's advice, Eunice decides to buy a business in Santa Monica, importing luxury household items.

Telyatnikov, Boris Dmitrevich (*Trial Run* 1978)

Telyatnikov is a member of the Russian Three Day Event team which competed in the International Horse Trials at **Burghley**, where German rider Hans Kramer died of a heart attack. On a train journey to London, Telyatnikov overhears a conversation in Russian about Kramer's death. Telyatnikov's friend, **Evgeny Titov**, asks **Ian Young** to arrange for **Randall Drew** to speak to Telyatnikov about what he had heard. Telyatnikov's own trip to London was illicit; he was going to deliver personal letters and messages from home to Russians who had defected to the west.

Tempesterai (*Decider* 1993)

Tempesterai is a chestnut gelding owned by **Conrad, Lord Stratton**. Ridden by Conrad's daughter, **Rebecca Stratton**, he wins a two mile hurdle race at **Stratton Park**.

Template (*Nerve* 1964)

Template, a six-year-old brown gelding, is a steeplechaser of great potential owned by **Lord Tirrold**. He is not a good looker but is clever, brave and fast. Ridden by **Rob Finn**, Template wins the King Chase at **Kempton Park** on Boxing Day, and the Midwinter Cup at **Ascot** in January.

10 lb. Penalty (1997)

Seventeen-year-old **Benedict Juliard** is sacked from his job as stable lad and amateur jockey in **Sir Vivian Durridge's** stable after Sir Vivian accuses him of drug taking. Benedict's father, **George**

Juliard, sends a car to the yard to take Benedict to meet him in **Brighton**. Benedict realizes that George has engineered his dismissal so that Benedict can help him win a political by-election at **Hoopwestern** in **Dorset**.

Benedict goes to the constituency with his father, and attends a dinner and public meeting. He is seated next to **Orinda Nagle**, the hostile widow of the previous Member of Parliament, who had expected to be chosen as the party's candidate in her dead husband's place. Returning to his apartment, George is apparently shot at in the town square. When a second attempt is made on George's life Benedict assumes the role of bodyguard to his father. Orinda Nagle, who had been initially antagonistic towards George Juliard, has a change of heart and decides to support him. This does not please political fixer **Alderney Wyvern**, who had been a close friend of Orinda's late husband.

Polling day at Hoopwestern arrives; George wins the seat and begins his climb up the political ladder. When, years later, George is appointed Minister of Agriculture, Alderney Wyvern is still around, his hostility no less virulent, and Benedict is called upon to protect his undeserving father.

The chief problem with *10 lb. Penalty* is the main character, since character is the very quality that he lacks. It is virtually impossible for a vapid, naive ingénu like Benedict Juliard to engage the sympathy of the reader. His father, George Juliard, is even more difficult to like. What father who loves his son, as Juliard apparently does, would stoop so low as to have his name falsely besmirched for drug abuse and sacked from the only job he's ever wanted to do? What son, having suffered such unspeakable nastiness, would meekly submit to his father's selfish plans without even a mild reproof? This is an infelicitous start, but a pacey, entertaining storyline could have partially diverted attention from the inadequacy of the principal characters. Instead the action regularly grinds to a halt in order to allow Benedict to bore the reader with his own perspective on events. One example will suffice: Benedict and George are, at one point, trapped in a burning building. But the dramatic tension is dissipated by Benedict's prolonged speculation on the nature of panic in life-or-death situations. After that, nothing happens at all for two years, which reflects the novel's lack of energy and immediacy. Graham Lord, Francis's biographer, tells us that the inspiration for *10 lb.*

Penalty was a meeting with the then Prime Minister, John Major. Enough said.

Terry (*Smokescreen* 1972)

Terry is a film cameraman working on *Man in a Car*. He is unflappable and an excellent technician.

Terry (*10 lb. Penalty* 1997)

Terry, a mechanic, works for Rudd's Repair Garage in **Hoopwestern, Dorset**. He services and checks **George Juliard's** Range Rover. He dislikes **Bobby Rudd**, who had engineered his sacking from his job at Bobby's father's garage in nearby Quindle.

Thackery, Mr. (*Flying Finish* 1966)

Thackery, a wealthy Shropshire farmer, is the father of a well-known amateur jockey. He owns and trains half a dozen good hunter chasers. He is a good trainer, but doesn't want the worry of training other people's horses. He offers **Lord Henry Gray** the rides on all his horses till the end of the season because his son has jaundice. Thackery runs **Clobber**, his chestnut hunter, in the **Cheltenham** Gold Cup purely for the prestige and enjoyment. He is delighted when Henry, making the most of the running, finishes fourth.

The Dream (*Bolt* 1986)

The Dream, a winning racehorse on the flat, is fast but hasn't yet got the hang of jumping. On his first run over hurdles at **Newbury**, he falls at the first hurdle when ridden by **Kit Fielding**.

Thiveridge, Claude (*Dead Cert* 1962)

Claude Thiveridge is the pseudonym of **Uncle George**. The shadowy owner of **Marconicars** taxi firm, Thiveridge communicates by phone with manager **Mr. Fielder**.

Thomas (*Break In* 1985; *Bolt* 1986)

Break In: Thomas, a Londoner, is **Princess Casilia's** chauffeur. He is a long-serving, devoted employee. He is not really interested in racing and doesn't bet but enjoys his job. Leaving **Towcester** racecourse, Thomas sees **Kit Fielding** with two men and suspects that he is in trouble. He stops the Princess's Rolls-Royce, allowing Kit to dive in and escape from the men who are attempting to abduct him.

Bolt: Thomas is worried when Kit tells him that the Princess didn't watch one of her horses run at **Newbury**. After the Princess is threatened, Thomas acts as her bodyguard at Newbury races. He helps Kit to confront the villain responsible, and acts as a witness to a written contract designed to neutralize the threat.

Thompkins (*Dead Cert* 1962)

Thompkins, the landlord of the Blue Duck pub in **Brighton**, resists attempts by **Marconicars** taxi drivers to extort protection money. An ex–Regimental Sergeant Major, Thompkins had bought the pub with his savings and retirement pay. He organizes the fight against Marconicars by other small businessmen, persuading them to get guard dogs and helping to train them.

Thompson, Detective Constable (*To the Hilt* 1996)

D.C. Thompson, of **Leicestershire** police, phones **Sir Ivan Westering** to report the death of a former employee.

Thomson (*Twice Shy* 1981)

Thomson is one of **Luke Houston's** trainers; he is based on the **Berkshire** Downs. He gets on reasonably well with **William Derry**, Houston's racing manager.

Thrace, Henry (*Whip Hand* 1979)

Newmarket stud owner Henry Thrace stands the **George Caspar**–trained colts **Zingaloo** and **Gleaner** as stallions at his stud. He had been up half the night when visited by **Sid Halley** during the foaling season. He tells Sid that the two stallions tire easily, and may not have the energy to cover all the mares booked to them. Later, Thrace calls Sid to tell him that Gleaner had collapsed and died after covering a mare on a hot day.

Tiddely-Pom (*Forfeit* 1968)

Tiddely-Pom, the ante-post favorite for the Lamplighter Gold Cup at **Heathbury Park**, is owned and trained by **Essex** farmer **Victor Roncey**. Tiddely-Pom's looks belie his ability: he is a plain horse with a poorly-developed neck and shoulder. His dam was a hunter, but despite his ordinary pedigree he is fast and an excellent jumper. He had won the Foxhunters' steeplechase at **Cheltenham**, and the following year four out of six handicaps.

The week before the Lamplighter he is sent secretly to **Norton Fox's** yard to prevent anything happening to him. However, while he is there he develops violent colic. He recovers quickly but for reasons of security he is taken by horse van to Heathbury Park stables. He has an eventful journey but arrives unhurt. In the Lamplighter Tiddely-Pom finishes second, three lengths behind the winner.

Tigwood, John (*Driving Force* 1992)

Tigwood is the director of **Centaur Care**, a charity for old horses which Tigwood runs for his own benefit rather than that of the horses. He is thought to charge the owners of the horses for looking after them while passing on the horses to other people willing to give the horses homes for free. This, however, is not Tigwood's only source of income. He also provides horses for purposes which are harmful to both their health and that of other horses. He is prepared to go to extreme lengths to ensure that his activities remain secret.

Tilepit, Lord Verney (*Come to Grief* 1995)

Tilepit is the owner of *The Pump* newspaper and a director of **Topline Foods**, producers of animal foodstuffs. Topline Foods have spent huge sums of money on TV advertisements using a well-known racing personality. However, they can't use the adverts, since the man is on trial for allegedly treating horses with extreme cruelty. Tilepit therefore directs his newspaper's journalists to vilify **Sid Halley**, who uncovered the crime, in order to discredit him in the eyes of the public. Tilepit is uncomfortable with the level of violence which his associates subsequently use against Sid.

Timmie (*Flying Finish* 1966)

Timmie works for **Yardman** Transport. A stocky, dark Welshman, he suffers from chronic catarrh, an affliction which, he claims, has stopped him following his father down the coalmines.

Timpson, Tommy (*Enquiry* 1969)

Timpson is an eighteen-year-old stable lad and occasional jockey for **Dexter Cranfield**. He rides **Cherry Pie** to win the Lemonfizz Gold Cup at **Oxford**. He is nervous when called to give evidence at the enquiry into the race. He says, mistakenly, that Cranfield had told him to try to pass **Squelsh** after the last fence. When Cranfield denies it, Timpson says that Cranfield had just told him to win if he could.

Tina (*Straight* 1989)

Tina is an employee of **Greville Franklin** at his gem dealing business, **Saxony Franklin**. She checks and sorts the new gems as they arrive. She is appointed Enabling Manager by **Derek Franklin**.

Tirrold, Lord (*Nerve* 1964)

Lord Tirrold, a steward at **Dunstable** races, is on duty in the paddock when jockey **Art Matthews** shoots himself. He is the owner of **Template**, trained by **James Axminster**. When **Pip Pankhurst** breaks his leg, Tirrold puts **Rob Finn** up on Template. He is somewhat surprised when Rob wins on Template.

Tishoo (*Reflex* 1980)

Tishoo, a jumper trained by **Harold Osborne**, runs unplaced at **Kempton Park**.

Titov, Evgeny Sergeevich (*Trial Run* 1978)

Titov, a middle-aged Russian, is a friend of **Ian Young**. **Randall Drew** meets **Boris Telyatnikov** at Titov's apartment. According to Young, Titov is a patriotic man who holds the reputation of his country dear. He is keen that Randall should investigate Hans Kramer's death.

To the Hilt (1996)

Artist **Alexander Kinloch** lives in a remote mountain cottage in the Scottish Highlands, on the estate of his uncle **Robert, Earl of Kinloch**. Alex's mother, who lives in London, contacts him to say that his stepfather, **Sir Ivan Westering**, has had a heart attack. Returning to his cottage Alex finds four men there. They beat him up and throw him over the edge of a sharp drop. Not badly hurt, Alex painfully returns to the cottage to find it trashed and his jeep and paintings gone.

In London Sir Ivan's accountant, **Tobias Tollright**, tells Alex that Sir Ivan's **King Alfred Brewery** is on the verge of bankruptcy. Sir Ivan, seemingly resigned to dying, asks Alex to hide a horse for him which belongs to the brewery. When it comes to hiding things, Alex has form: at his Uncle Robert's request, Alex has hidden the most precious Kinloch treasure, the gold hilt of the ceremonial sword of Bonnie Prince Charlie. The Prince had given it to Robert's ancestor, the Earl of Kinloch, during his retreat northwards. Robert believes the hilt to be his personal property, but his castle is now owned by a "conservation organization," whose administrators consider the hilt to belong to the public, and are looking for it. Alex has also concealed from the brewery's creditors a

cup, thought to be medieval and valuable, which is presented annually to the winner of the steeplechase that the brewery sponsors.

Alex becomes the focus of the fury of **Patsy Benchmark**, Sir Ivan's daughter, who considers her position in the household to have been usurped by Alex. This, together with his involvement in tracing substantial funds missing from the brewery, makes life painful and unpleasant for Alex.

The issues that *To the Hilt* raises are interesting: up to what point can a man endure pain and hardship in the defense of what has been entrusted to him? To what extent are his actions the result of his upbringing and background? The character of Alex Kinloch is central to the plot; his family rely on him to do the right thing on their behalf despite seeing him as something of an oddball. Obliged to involve himself in the financial troubles of his stepfather's brewery, Alex doesn't hesitate to answer the call despite a strong preference for peace and solitude. In doing so he subjects himself to acts of violence which might be considered disproportionate to the crimes with which they are connected. Francis has been criticized for glorifying gratuitous violence in his novels; however his graphic descriptions of violence and its often unusual nature constitute one of his strengths as a crime writer.

Toby (*Whip Hand* 1979)

Toby is a close friend of **Jenny Halley**, **Sid Halley**'s ex-wife. He has a low opinion of Sid and is barely polite to him. Toby is considered by Sid to be fairly dim but to be providing a reassuring dullness in Jenny's life. Jenny has been thinking of marrying Toby, but Sid thinks it unlikely.

Todd, Charles (*In the Frame* 1976)

Charles Todd's background—often a useful starting point in defining a character's motivations—is less than riveting. His parents had died when he was twenty-two—a promising piece of information, but we are not told the cause of their demise, an omission more irritating than tantalizing. Charles's reaction to his parents' death is not to rail against life's injustices, nor to drink too much absinthe. Instead he takes a job selling real estate. In his free time he sketches the racehorses working on the nearby **Sussex** Downs, continuing a hobby he had started as a boy. Finding that his talent for drawing thoroughbreds outweighs that of selling houses, Charles takes up painting full time. To go with his artistic ability, Charles has a modicum of the artist's temperament, though it may only be a touch of Seasonal Affective Depression syndrome. Whatever the cause, Charles professes to hate autumn. He could use some female companionship to jolly him along but, at the age of twenty-nine, unmarried and apparently unattached, the signs aren't encouraging.

But Charles has more pressing concerns, notably the mental and physical health of his cousin **Donald Stuart**, whose wife, **Regina Stuart**, has been killed during the theft of antiques and paintings at their home in **Shropshire**. Charles discovers from a client of his, **Maisie Matthews**, who had had her house similarly robbed of antiques, that both she and Donald had recently been in Australia, where they had bought paintings by the English equine artist **Alfred Munnings**. Donald's health is deteriorating so rapidly that Charles decides he must fly to Australia to investigate the matter himself.

In Australia Charles enlists the help of an old art school friend, **Jik Cassavetes**. Jik's new wife, **Sarah Cassavetes**, is angry that Charles has involved Jik in his search for the truth. When she calls Charles a fool for pursuing his inquiries he is provoked into a reaction: "I see the hell [Donald's] in. How can I just turn my back?"

Admitting to being afraid is not something that Francis's heroes have a problem with. When Charles is trapped in an art gallery behind a steel mesh gate, he has never felt more frightened. He has good reason to be, given the violence of Regina's death; but, implausibly, Charles persuades the villains that his presence at the gallery is just a coincidence and they meekly let him go.

As Charles continues to collect evidence of complicity in robbery and murder, the villains step up their efforts to do Charles some serious damage. For his part, Charles is insufficiently suspicious of offers to meet unnamed third parties in exposed locations. Fortunately for him, the villains have not totally abandoned their unconvincing generosity of spirit.

Tollman, Marius (*Field of 13* 1998: "The Gift")

American Marius Tollman, an illegal bookmaker, bribes jockey **Piper Boles** to fix a race at **Churchill Downs** on Kentucky Derby day, and also to stop his mount, **Crinkle Cut**, in the Derby.

Tollright, Tobias (*To the Hilt* 1996)

Tollright is a partner in the firm of chartered accountants, Pierce, Tollright and Simmonds, in **Reading, Berkshire**; they are the auditors of the **King Alfred Brewery** accounts. Tollright phones **Sir Ivan Westering** to remind him that it is illegal for the brewery to trade if it is insolvent. He is helpful to **Alex Kinloch** when Alex is appointed an Alternate Director of the brewery. He explains how a trusted employee had embezzled the brewery's funds and suggests hiring an insolvency practitioner. He initially traces the funds to a bank in Panama, but doesn't know the account number. When he obtains further information he tracks the money down to a bank in Colombia.

Tom (*Under Orders* 2006)

Tom, the gateman at **Cheltenham racecourse**, doesn't check whether **Sid Halley**'s badge is valid for entry.

Tomkins, Binny (*Risk* 1977)

Tomkins, an averagely successful racehorse trainer, trains **Cheltenham** Gold Cup contender **Tapestry**, due to be ridden by **Roland Britten**. He doesn't want Roland, who is an amateur, to ride the horse in the Gold Cup despite having won on him at **Newbury**. He acquiesces with bad grace when owner **Moira Longerman** threatens to take the horse away. Expecting Tapestry to lose, Tomkins can scarcely believe it when he wins. He objects when Mrs. Longerman insists on retaining Roland to ride Tapestry in all his races; she tells him that she's heard that Tomkins had laid against Tapestry in the Gold Cup, and makes it clear that she doesn't trust him to run the horse on his merits. Before the Oasthouse Cup at **Kempton Park**, Tomkins begs Roland to give Tapestry an easy race; he says that he'll lose everything if he wins, since he is deeply in debt to bookmakers. He is furious when Roland refuses; in desperation he tampers with the bridle so it will break during the race. Roland notices and has the bridle changed before the race starts. After Tapestry has won Tomkins is nowhere to be seen; later he refuses to let Mrs. Longerman into his yard to visit Tapestry.

Tony (*Enquiry* 1969)

Kelly Hughes's cousin Tony trains around thirty horses at a stable in **Berkshire**, where Kelly has an apartment. When Kelly is released from hospital after a serious incident, Tony has some bad news for him; he has had a letter from the **Jockey Club** to say that Kelly, as a warned off person, must leave the stables, otherwise Tony's license to train may be reviewed.

When Kelly discovers that **Grace Roxford** is sitting outside **Dexter Cranfield**'s house in her car, in a disturbed mental state, Tony takes him there, since Kelly has a broken leg and can't drive. Later, Tony helps to subdue Grace until a doctor arrives to sedate her.

Tony (*Under Orders* 2006)

Tony is a security guard at St Thomas's Hospital, London. He attempts to stop **Sid Halley** entering a restricted section of the Accident and Emergency Department when **Marina van der Meer** arrives for treatment.

Top Spin Lob (*Longshot* 1990)

Top Spin Lob, a steeplechaser trained by **Tremayne Vickers**, is a former winner of the Grand National at **Aintree**.

Topline Foods (*Come to Grief* 1995)

This is an animal feed company based in **Frodsham**, near Liverpool, and run by **Owen Yorkshire**.

Torp, Ralph (*Slay-Ride* 1973)

Norwegian racehorse owner Ralph Torp is small, belligerent, demanding and clever. He runs Torp-Nord Associates, a titanium mining company. He thinks that it is a waste of time for **David Cleveland** to return to Norway to investigate the **Bob Sherman** case. He grudgingly agrees to speak to David, but gives him only ten minutes. He tells David that he was unhappy with the ride Sherman had given a horse of his which subsequently won the Norsk Grand National. David guesses that any time the jockey didn't win Torp would think he had ridden badly.

Touchy (*Longshot* 1990)

Touchy, a former winner of the **Cheltenham Gold Cup**, is now **Tremayne Vickers'** hack. He is ridden on the gallops by **John Kendall**.

Towcester racecourse

Racing at Towcester in **Northamptonshire** has taken place on the estate of Lord Hesketh of Easton Neston since the early years of the twentieth century. The present course, built in 1928, is right-handed with a grueling climb to the finishing post. Attendances at this rural course suffered in the aftermath of the 2001 foot and mouth epidemic, and the grandstand was condemned. Towcester closed for redevelopment in 2002 and reopened the following year, complete with new stabling block but still no new stand. That followed in 2004, at a cost of £5 million.

Risk (1977): **Roland Britten** rides **Notebook** for crooked trainer **William Finch**, who knows the horse can't jump. Roland is unseated at the seventh flight.

Break In (1985): **Kit Fielding** rides four winners on one day at Towcester. In the parking lot after racing two men try to abduct him but he is rescued by **Princess Casilia**'s chauffeur, and escapes in her Rolls-Royce.

10 lb. Penalty (1997): **Benedict Juliard** breaks his collarbone when falling from his horse **Sarah's Future** at Towcester. The horse breaks a leg and has to be destroyed.

Under Orders (2006): **Sid Halley** goes to Towcester, where he feeds **Paddy O'Fitch** information, knowing that O'Fitch will be unable to keep it to himself.

Tracker, Bill (*Smokescreen* 1972)

Berkshire racehorse trainer Bill Tracker trains **Edward Lincoln**'s steeplechaser, and allows him to ride out with the string.

Traffic (*Bonecrack* 1971)

Traffic, an awkward two-year-old colt, is ill-tempered and a difficult ride. He runs away with **Alessandro Rivera** on Warren Hill gallops in **Newmarket**; the next day he bucks Alessandro off in the paddock. Alessandro is knocked unconscious when his head hits the paddock rail.

Trainers

"[Training] is a competitive profession in every way. If you want to succeed in life you need to take things from other people." French trainer André Fabre, quoted in the now defunct racing newspaper *Sporting Life*, 1993.

The legendary Fabre's assessment of what it takes to make it as a racehorse trainer is harsh but, as a man of integrity, he undoubtedly meant that success should be achieved by acting within the rules. A significant number of the trainers in Francis's novels would clearly agree with Fabre's sentiments but do not feel a similar constraint to observe the law. Their ranks include fraudsters, cheats, thieves, drug addicts, perverts and at least one villain who would have committed murder if he could. **Hedley Humber** (*For Kicks* 1965) is a tyrant who runs what must be the worst racing stable in Britain. His miserable collection of virtually unemployable lads endures starvation rations, long hours and living accommodation little better than that of the horses. If they look like staying too long Humber or his psychopathic owner **Paul J. Adams** knocks them about until they leave; that way the lads never find out the pair's cruel method of getting slow horses to run faster. Undercover **Jockey Club** investigator **Daniel Roke** does, so Humber and Adams attempt to silence him for good.

Scarcely less vicious than Humber is **Jody Leeds** (*High Stakes* 1975). For years he has colluded with bookmaker **Ganser Mays** in swindling his owners, including toy maker **Steven Scott**. When Steven realizes what's been happening he takes his horses away, When Leeds loses heavily after a planned betting coup goes wrong he has no compunction about exacting revenge.

William Finch (*Risk* 1977) is a top trainer under both codes of racing but his wealthy lifestyle is no more than a veneer; he is a paid employee of the American **Nantucket** family and has no capital of his own. Finch needs the cash to keep rolling in, and so he adopts unorthodox methods of so doing. Equally important to Finch is to ensure that these methods do not become public knowledge.

Finch is not the only trainer in *Risk* with his own agenda. When Roland unexpectedly wins the **Cheltenham** Gold Cup on **Tapestry**, winning trainer **Binny Tomkins** had decidedly mixed feelings, having betted against his own horse. Heavily in debt to bookmakers, he wants to stop Tapestry winning at **Kempton Park** but Roland refuses to comply. In desperation Tomkins sabotages the horse's bridle so that it will break during the race, but Roland notices and has it changed.

Talented but arrogant **Newmarket** trainer **Nicholas Loder** (*Straight* 1989) is rumored to be a heavy gambler. He has an unhealthy relationship with one of his owners, who is prepared to use Loder for his own ends. Too late, Loder realizes what he has got himself into. No one, however, needed to manipulate veteran trainers **J. Rolls Eaglewood**, **Fitzwalter** and **Mac Mackintosh** in *Comeback* (1991). All three willingly entered upon their nefarious course of action purely for financial gain.

In Francis's short story "**Bright White Star**" (*Field of 13* 1998) **Jim Turner** is a dishonest jump jockey recently turned dishonest trainer. At the bloodstock sales he steals a valuable yearling and switches it for a cheap look-alike. He might well have got away with it but for the intervention of a wandering tramp. In "**Spring Fever,**" another story in the collection, **Clement Scott**—a cold, calculating man and a moderate trainer—conspires with jockey **Derek Roberts** to make money out of owner **Mrs. Angela Hart**.

Millionaire owner-trainer **Benjy Usher** (*Driving Force* 1992) is not content with trying to win races fairly against rival trainers; he comes up with an unusual plan to give him an edge. Almost as strange are the activities of the two trainers— **George Loricroft** and **Oliver Quigley**—who belong to a clandestine grouping known as the **Unified Traders**, dealers in radioactive materials. The motivation for trainer **Jack Roxford**'s behavior in *Enquiry* (1969) is not financial gain but the fear of losing the horses he trains for owner **Edwin Byler** to rival trainer **Dexter Cranfield**.

To correct the impression that the profession of racehorse training is peopled entirely by crooks of various hues, Francis also gives us a representative sample of men and women who are decent, hardworking and fundamentally honest. One is **Tremayne Vickers** (*Longshot* 1990), a distinguished trainer approaching the end of his career, who employs **John Kendall** to write his biography. From a wealthy but eccentric family, Vickers has experienced a harsh upbringing which, perversely, he had enjoyed. He had taken over the stable from his father's private trainer and, over the years, had won every race worth winning in the jumping calendar. Vickers is forceful and assertive, but has never lost his capacity for compassion.

Another veteran trainer portrayed sympathetically is **Wykeham Harlow** (*Break In* 1985; *Bolt* 1986). He clings to his old-fashioned but highly successful methods of training, and hates traveling, preferring to stay at home with his beloved horses. He is devastated when two of them are deliberately killed in their boxes, and is prepared to resort to drastic measures to prevent it happening a third time.

The few women trainers in Francis's novels tend to have admirable qualities. **Emily Jane Cox**, the estranged wife of artist **Alex Kinloch** in *To the Hilt* (1996) is energetic, capable and considered to be an excellent trainer. Despite their separation she remains on good terms with her husband. **Marigold English** (*Driving Force*) is a forthright woman in her fifties, perhaps modeled on Grand National winning trainer and now best-selling author, Jenny Pitman. Beneath her sometimes forbidding exterior Marigold conceals a kind heart. At **Freddie Croft's** request she gives a home to an elderly racehorse, but subsequently voices her concern at the horse's condition. In *Rat Race* (1970) **Annie Villars** is a highly competent handler; she is a disciplinarian but sympathetic with her horses and good with her owners.

The strength of character of these women contrasts with the weakness of trainers like Dexter Cranfield and **Sir Vivian Durridge** (*10 lb. Penalty* 1991). Cranfield, a snobbish, mean-spirited social climber, sinks into depression when he is warned off, and is close to suicide. He is shamed by Kelly Hughes into keeping his staff on for two more weeks while Kelly fights to clear their names. He is delighted when they get their licenses back but, typically, is unwilling to believe that Kelly could have been responsible. Durridge, a wealthy establishment figure, employs seventeen-year-old **Benedict Juliard** as a stable lad and amateur jockey. At the instigation of Benedict's father, who has other plans for his son, Durridge falsely accuses Benedict of taking drugs and summarily sacks him.

The only novel that has a trainer—and then a reluctant one—as a main character is *Bonecrack* (1971). While his unpleasant and obstructive father, **Newmarket** trainer **Neville Griffon**, is in hospital, **Neil Griffon**—a financial troubleshooter—proves adept at training. When his father dies suddenly, Neil decides to become a trainer on a permanent basis. Another Newmarket trainer is jockey **Kit Fielding's** awkward, grumpy grandfather (*Break In*), in his eighties but still training a few horses and harboring an intense hatred of the **Allardecks**, a rival training family. The old man has never forgiven his grand-daughter, Kit's twin sister **Holly Allardeck**, for marrying trainer **Bobby Allardeck**. Intensely jealous of Kit's close relationship with Holly, Bobby is sorely tempted, at one point, to shoot Kit. Fortunately for Kit, good sense prevails.

Traventi, Georgio (*The Danger* 1983)

Georgio Traventi is a lawyer who acts for **Paolo Cenci** when his daughter, **Alessia Cenci**, is kidnapped. His son, **Lorenzo Traventi**, suffers serious injury when acting as driver when the ransom is being delivered to the kidnappers. Traventi acts as a negotiator between Paolo Cenci and the kidnappers, taking messages and passing on the replies. He shows dogged determination in representing his client.

Traventi, Lorenzo (*The Danger* 1983)

Lorenzo is the son of **Georgio Traventi**, the lawyer acting for **Paoli Cenci**. He drives the car delivering a ransom to the kidnappers of **Alessia Cenci** but is critically injured when Italian police attempt to arrest the kidnappers. His life hangs in the balance, but he eventually pulls through. When fully recovered, Lorenzo starts seeing a lot of Alessia on her return to Italy from England.

Traventi, Ricardo (*The Danger* 1983)

Ricardo is the son of **Georgio Traventi** and the younger brother of **Lorenzo Traventi**. After Lorenzo is injured, Ricardo takes **Paolo Cenci** to a motorway restaurant outside **Bologna**, where messages are passed between Cenci and the kidnappers.

Travers, Mr. (*Comeback* 1991)

According to **Josephine McClure**, Travers had been a business partner of **Ronnie Upjohn's** father; he was wealthy, and untrustworthy around women. He had lost his money when guaranteeing loans for Porphyry Place, a failed leisure centre.

Travers, Theodore (*Comeback* 1991)

Theodore is the grandson of **Mr. Travers**. He is in his early thirties and an insurance agent. His body is found in the burnt-out office block of Hewett and Partners veterinary practice in Cheltenham, **Gloucestershire**.

Trelawney, Eliot (*Straight* 1989)

Magistrate Eliot Trelawney was a colleague of the late **Greville Franklin** at West London Magistrates' Court. He contacts **Derek Franklin** to request Greville's notes on a gaming club license application which Greville intended to advise turning down; Greville had heard allegations against one of the organizers, a man named **Vaccaro**. Trelawney rings Derek up to remind him, when Derek forgets, having been concussed when the victim of an assault. Later, he calls Derek to tell him that Vaccaro has been arrested for drug smuggling and faces extradition to America on murder charges.

Trial Run (1978)

Farmer and ex-amateur jockey **Randall Drew** is persuaded by a royal acquaintance, the **Prince**, to go to Moscow to investigate rumors concerning **Johnny Farringford**, the Prince's brother-in-law, who wants to compete in the Three Day Event at the Moscow Olympics. Farringford tells Randall that two men had come to his stables, beat him up and told him to keep away from "Alyosha." He says that a German event rider called Hans Kramer had died at **Burghley Horse Trials**, apparently of a heart attack, and it had something to do with Alyosha. Kramer had taken Farringford to a transvestite club in London, which had embarrassed Farringford, and rumors were circulating that he and Kramer were gay. Farringford tells Randall that the rumors are unfounded. But the Prince wants Randall to prove that there is no truth in them since anyone suspected of being a homosexual would be a political liability in Russia, where homosexuality is illegal.

Armed with a short list of contacts, Randall flies to Moscow. Investigating the background to Farringford's embarrassing situation proves far from easy for Randall. He meets obstruction and obfuscation at every turn, as well as determined threats to his life. What soon becomes clear to Randall is that Kramer's death is part of a pattern of events much more serious than Farringford has suggested, and with the potential to disrupt the forthcoming Olympic Games.

Trial Run has suffered more than most of Francis's novels from the passing of the years. Only aficionados of the Cold War era, when Russia was still a huge, slavering bear and its people trampled beneath the jackboot of communism, would make *Trial Run* their first choice of bedtime reading. Francis, for all his strengths, is no John le Carré; his depiction of pre–Gorbachev Moscow fails to chill the heart, and the plot of *Trial Run* consists largely of boring people arranging clandestine meetings in uninspiring locations. It doesn't help that Randall Drew, the main character, is a representative of that class of Englishman who once, by virtue of his wealth and aristocratic connections, may have been respected but who, these days, would be the man most likely to be avoided at social functions. Short-sighted and consumptive, Randall is not a character many people would be keen to identify with. It's not hard to feel sympathy with Randall's acerbic girlfriend, who treats him with the same warm affection that a farrier might show to an apprentice who'd just dropped an anvil on his toe.

Tring, Andrew (*Enquiry* 1969)

Tring, a Disciplinary Steward of the **Jockey Club**, is one of the four stewards who conduct the enquiry at which trainer **Dexter Cranfield** and jockey **Kelly Hughes** lose their licenses for al-

legedly stopping **Squelsh**, favorite for the Lemon-fizz Crystal Cup at **Oxford**. Tring is a young man who has recently inherited a baronetcy and been appointed Steward. He knows Kelly quite well, having ridden against him as an amateur. He acts in an embarrassed manner at the enquiry, refusing to meet Kelly's eyes. He makes no contribution to the enquiry, and is seemingly overawed by **Lord Gowery**.

Tring is annoyed when later challenged by Kelly as to why he'd been so spineless. Finally he admits, guiltily, that his hands were tied; it was vital for him to keep in with Gowery, who owns the freehold of the land on which the Tring family's pottery factory is built. If Gowery chose to terminate the leasehold agreement when it came up for renewal in three years' time, they would lose the factory.

Tri-Nitro (*Whip Hand* 1979)

Tri-Nitro is a top two-year-old colt trained by **George Caspar** at **Newmarket**. He is the winner of the Middle Park Stakes and is strongly fancied to win the following year's Two Thousand Guineas. He is a good-looking colt with excellent conformation; according to Caspar's vet, Tri-Nitro's heart is loud and strong. He starts at even money for the Guineas and finishes last. He is subsequently shown to have been suffering from a disease which horses do not normally contract. Tri-Nitro is treated with antibiotics and is expected to recover.

Trox Island

Trox Island is a fictional island in the Western Caribbean, not far from **Grand Cayman**.

Second Wind (1999): Meteorologists **Perry Stuart** and **Kris Ironside** fly in a small plane to Trox Island to check on some mushrooms allegedly growing there on behalf of Ironside's friend **Robin Darcy**. However, there are no mushrooms. After taking off the plane comes down in the sea during a hurricane. Perry is washed up on Trox Island. After drinking milk from the herd of cows there, he subsequently contracts a rare form of tuberculosis.

Trubshaw, Kenneth (*Shattered* 2000)

Trubshaw is a member of the **Cheltenham Racecourse** Committee. At the request of **Marigold**, **Bon-Bon Stukely**'s mother, Trubshaw visits **Gerard Logan** to discuss her idea of presenting annually a copy of an antique necklace to the winner of a steeplechase run in memory of her late son-in-law, jockey **Martin Stukely**. Trubshaw is not enthusiastic, and asks Gerard to suggest something more suitable. From Gerard's design book he chooses a leaping horse on a crystal ball. He tells Gerard that the Cheltenham stewards believe that Stukely may have been aware that the information on a videotape, which he'd given to his valet to pass on to Gerard, was stolen. He asks Gerard to find the missing tape and prove Stukely innocent.

Tudor (*Dead Cert* 1962)

Tudor is a racehorse owner and a **Brighton** businessman. Of Greek origin, he is a large, powerful man with a forceful manner. After the Second World War, he had bought an ailing taxi firm in Brighton, which he'd sold at a profit; he has subsequently bought the Pavilion Plaza hotel. Unable to get a taxi back from **Plumpton racecourse** owing to a gang fight among the taxi drivers, Tudor commandeers a lift with **Alan York**.

Tunbridge Wells, Kent

Royal Tunbridge Wells lies in the wealthy "stockbroker belt" which includes parts of **Surrey** and Kent within easy commuting distance of London. The town has a population of about 50,000. It became a spa town, popular with royalty, after mineral springs were discovered in the early 1600's.

Whip Hand (1979): **Sid Halley**, with his assistant **Chico Barnes**, goes to the farm of **Peter Rammileese**, near Tunbridge Wells. They find his wife lying unconscious in the indoor riding school after being thrown from her horse.

Tunny, Tug (*Break In* 1985)

Tunny is the editor of the *Intimate Details* column in the *Daily Flag*, a **Fleet Street** newspaper. He is a veteran gossip columnist with a formidable memory and no pity for his victims.

Turner, Detective Chief Inspector (*Dead Heat* 2007)

D.C.I. Turner, of the Metropolitan Police's Special Branch, provides **Max Moreton** with a guest list from the **Delafield Industries Inc.** dinner at **Newmarket racecourse** on the evening before the running of the Two Thousand Guineas. Later, he gives Max the names of the guests who didn't go to the race the next day because they were suffering from food poisoning.

Turner, Jim and Vivi (*Field of 13* 1998: "Bright White Star")

The Turners are a married couple who have just started training racehorses. Jim is an ex–jump jockey who, with Vivi, steals a valuable yearling from the stables at the November Sales and switches it for a worthless colt of the same color and with the same white star on its forehead. Despite the theft being reported in the newspapers they are convinced that they will get away with it. A passing tramp, however, unwittingly throws the Turners' plans into disarray.

Turniptop (*Nerve* 1964)

Turniptop is a novice chaser belonging to **James Axminster**. He is promising, but is an untidy jumper. **Rob Finn** gives Turniptop a reckless but courageous ride at **Stratford** races, proving that he has not lost his nerve. Prior to the race, an unsuccessful attempt had been made to dope Turniptop in the saddling box.

Twice Shy (1981)

Part One: Jonathan: Physics teacher **Jonathan Derry** is stuck in a loveless marriage with wife **Sarah Derry**, who is permanently depressed because she can't have children. The husband of Sarah's friend, **Donna Keithley**, phones to say that Donna has been arrested for stealing a baby. Despite Jonathan's reluctance Sarah demands that they go to **Norwich** to comfort her. Released on bail, Donna has attempted suicide. Her husband, **Peter Keithley**, tells Jonathan of his own problems: he'd been approached by a man in a pub to use his knowledge of computers to produce a program for handicapping horses. He had done so and been paid for it. Then two other men had turned up, demanding the program and threatening to harm Donna if he didn't comply. He'd given them some unusable first drafts.

Jonathan decides to return home while Sarah stays on to look after Donna. Peter gives Jonathan the computer program, recorded on audiotapes for safe keeping, while he takes Donna away on holiday on his boat. Two days later he is checking the boat's battery when the boat explodes, killing him.

Accepting the tapes was not a wise move on Jonathan's part. A dimly-functioning lunatic is intent on gaining possession of the handicapping system and is not concerned about hurting anyone who gets in his way. He has already killed once, a crime which, fortunately for Jonathan and Sarah, catches up with him. Whilst Jonathan and Sarah move to America in the hope of patching up their marriage, the lunatic is jailed for life. Fourteen years later the jail's governor expresses reservations about the man's imminent release on parole.

Part Two: William: Jonathan Derry's younger brother, **William Derry**, had seen his short career as a jump jockey curtailed by injury and increasing weight. Now in his late twenties, he is employed as a racing manager to **Luke Houston**, a wealthy American whose horses in England are spread among several trainers. He shares a cottage in **Six Mile Bottom**, near **Newmarket**, with his girlfriend **Cassie Morris**. He is attacked in the garden and knocked unconscious by a man with a baseball bat, who is seen speeding away in his car immediately afterwards. When William later mentions on the telephone to Jonathan in America what has happened, and describes his attacker, Jonathan tells him it sounds like the same thug that had pursued him so obsessively.

William quickly decides that locating the computer tapes and handing them over to this dangerous hoodlum is the only way to stay healthy. All might have been well if the betting system had still worked. When things go wrong, the infuriated thug goes on the rampage, and William's life is on the line.

In *Twice Shy* Francis adopts a somewhat risky format by focusing his plot through the eyes of two brothers, with a second set of events occurring fourteen years after the first. Risky, because the subject matter of the plot is largely concerned with information technology, specifically the use of a computer program to predict the outcome of horse races. Francis is writing in 1980, when personal computers were still not widely used and program design unsophisticated. He then fast forwards to, presumably, the mid 1990's, but in *Twice Shy* computers are still as scarce as hairs on a boiled egg; William Derry is still using Neanderthal computer language and still loading programs from cassette tapes. A further problem arises owing to alterations to the Racing Calendar in the intervening years since 1980. The advent of summer jump racing, a huge increase in evening meetings, and racing on dirt as well as turf are only some of the changes that had taken place. As a result, the likelihood of a system designed to select winners in 1980 still doing so fourteen years later is minimal to zero.

There was, of course, no way that Francis could have foreseen the rapid developments that were to take place, either in the field of information technology or in the administration of racing. Reading *Twice Shy* in the early 1980's, Francis's public would have been blissfully unaware of how anachronistic the second part of the novel was to sound in later years. Nevertheless, this weakness in the plot has prevented *Twice Shy* from standing the test of time.

According to Graham Lord *(Dick Francis: A Racing Life)* the idea for *Twice Shy* came to Francis when, on a visit to Gulfstream Park racecourse in Florida, he saw on sale a miniature calculator purporting to select winners if the correct data were fed in. Francis's inspiration for Jonathan Derry's occupation came from that of his own son Felix, who was a teacher. As a character Jonathan is a disappointment; earnest and hardworking he may be but not, it has to be said, scintillating company; typical is his admission that he'd always seen headmasters as god-like figures of authority. He doesn't even have the sense in the end, to sever links with his appalling wife, a ball and chain if ever there was one.

William Derry can only be an improvement on his brother. Whereas Jonathan values safety and security, William abhors it. He's insouciant, irreverent, and he's got a feisty girlfriend. Even so, the change of focus onto William halfway through *Twice Shy* isn't enough to divert attention from the unedifying antics of the cerebrally-challenged villain. The reader may feel a mixture of horror and fascination as the thug blunders through life, but it is debatable whether his acts of gross stupidity are enough to sustain interest.

Twinkletoes (*The Danger* 1983)

Twinkletoes is the nickname for the partner at **Liberty Market Ltd.** who is in charge of internal discipline.

Tyderman, Major (*Rat Race* 1970)

Tyderman is an associate of Australian **Charles Carthy-Todd**. In his late sixties, he is a wiry little man with a wary and suspicious air. During the Second World War he had been a bomb disposal expert. He is one of **Matt Shore**'s air-taxi passengers on the flight to **Haydock Park** races. There is a palpably hostile atmosphere between Tyderman and another passenger, **Kenny Bayst**. At the races he tells Matt that he's left his *Sporting Life* newspaper in the plane. Matt gives him the keys to the plane so that he can fetch it. Tyderman, however, has another motive for wanting to return to the plane.

According to trainer **Annie Villars**, Tyderman had been wild and dishonest as a young man; he had had a good war, but had subsequently been forced to resign his commission for cashing dud checks in the officers' mess. Through Annie Villars, Tyderman had engineered an introduction to the simple but trusting **Duke of Wessex**; he and owner **Eric Goldenberg** had had a big say in the management of Wessex's horse **Rudiments**.

At the next meeting at Haydock Park Tyderman has good reason to be disturbed when he finds out that **Nancy** and **Colin Ross** have flown back to **Cambridge** in a different plane to Matt. Shortly afterwards, Tyderman disappears. Subsequently his body is found beside the main London to South Wales railway line. He has been stabbed.

Tyler, Howard (*Wild Horses* 1994)

Acclaimed author Howard Tyler wrote the book on which *Unstable Times*, the film that **Thomas Lyon** is directing, is based. Tyler also wrote the film script, and complains without success of changes that Thomas has made; he thinks that Thomas has sensationalized his script, over-emphasizing the sex and violence. Tyler is warned by Thomas that he is contractually obliged not to criticize the film until after its release. However, Tyler feeds an untrue report to a national newspaper that the film's star, **Nash Rourke**, had criticized the film and Thomas. The film's American backers are incensed and threaten to sue Tyler for breach of contract. Tyler is furious with Thomas when he discovers that **Cibber**—in real life, **Rupert Visborough**, Alison's late father—is portrayed as **Yvonne**'s murderer. He demands that Thomas stop filming.

Tyrone, Elizabeth (*Forfeit* 1968)

Racing reporter **James Tyrone**'s wife, Elizabeth, is almost completely paralyzed by polio; she is bedridden, and dependent upon an artificial pump to breathe. Elizabeth had been married for three years when she contracted polio, falling ill on a flight to Heathrow from Singapore, where James was working for Reuter's news agency. She had collapsed on the tarmac and had never walked again. Elizabeth's marriage to James, based on a deep mutual affection, remained strong, but her condition had meant that sex was no longer part of the relationship. She'd been brought up by a man-hating mother with a deep distaste for the physical side of marriage. As a result Elizabeth did not miss sex, unlike James, whose appetites were undiminished.

Elizabeth's self-confidence is low; she needs James's assurance that she is loved and wanted. For his part, James does all he can to prevent her worrying about him, as it affects her fragile health. Elizabeth is concerned when a neighbor reads to her James's tough magazine article about non-starting favorites. When James is forced to admit that he has slept with **Gail Pominga** Elizabeth is devastated. She doesn't cry for long because physically she can't, but the realization that she is starting to look old, whereas James is still young and vigorous, depresses her utterly. Rationally, she can see that it is a lot to ask of James to remain celibate, but emotionally his cheating is hard to bear. Nevertheless she begins to try harder to look pretty for James.

Elizabeth is terrified when villains burst in to her apartment and threaten to turn off her breathing pump. After they've gone James persuades Elizabeth, against her will, to leave the apartment. She is afraid when James disconnects her breathing pump to move her, and her breathing is beginning to labor when James finally gets her into their van and reconnects the pump. James drives her to her doctor, **Antonio Perelli**, who takes her to a nursing home.

Tonio convinces Elizabeth that James will always protect her and will never leave her. She tells James that she doesn't mind if, sometimes, he goes elsewhere for sex.

Tyrone, James (*Forfeit* 1968)

James Tyrone, a racing reporter on a down-market newspaper, has cared devotedly for his invalid wife Elizabeth for the past eleven years, relying on a mercenary daily help when he is at work. There is never enough money, but James battles on without complaint. He is fiercely protective of Elizabeth who was almost totally paralyzed after contracting polio three years into their marriage, and who relies upon a breathing pump for survival. The sexual side of their relationship—never without inhibitions on Elizabeth's part even in the early years of their marriage—had quickly died after her illness. So James, who is not a man who can sublimate his physical needs, takes lovers. Not very often: **Gail Pominga**, a mixed-race beauty whom he has sex with on her living room floor, is only the fourth since Elizabeth caught polio. Afterwards his emotions are a mixture of guilt at his treachery, and euphoria at the release of pent-up frustration. The sheer pleasure of illicit lovemaking leaves him wanting more. He arranges a second meeting with Gail; afterwards, she wants to know why James stays with his wife if, as he says, they don't sleep together. She assumes that Elizabeth must be a wealthy woman, and James does not correct her misconception.

The complications in James's personal life are matched by his problems at work. In the course of researching a magazine article on a forthcoming important steeplechase, he has discovered that a significant proportion of ante-post favorites for big races turn out to be non-runners. Under the Rules of Racing such bets are lost, thus benefiting the bookmakers who have laid the bets. James's determination to ensure that the favorite lines up for the Lamplighter Gold Cup at **Heathbury Park** puts both himself and Elizabeth in mortal danger. James has hurt Elizabeth dreadfully by admitting that he has been unfaithful, but he partially atones by displaying selfless courage in protecting her from villains who would not think twice about harming her.

James had never told Gail about Elizabeth's illness—but someone else does. Meeting James at the races, Gail demands to know why he had kept the truth from her. "I didn't want consolation prizes," he tells her. But James still wants Gail, consolation or not. When Elizabeth, accepting at last that James will never leave her, tells him that she can put up with his occasional dalliances, he is content.

U

Ullaston, Sir Thomas (*Whip Hand* 1979)

Ullaston, the Senior Steward of the **Jockey Club**, is considered hard but fair, and is well-respected. He tells **Sid Halley** that **Eddy Keith** has been complaining about him, and asking that Sid be banned from operating on racecourses. Ullaston had refused, considering that Sid was doing a good job on behalf of racing. He is amazed at Sid's thoroughness when Sid presents the evidence to him of the criminal activities of a seemingly respectable figure in the racing world. Up to that point he had thought of Sid as simply an ex-jockey but now recognizes that he is a highly competent investigator. But when Sid tells him that there is corruption within the Jockey Club's Security Service, Ullaston is highly skeptical. Sid, however, convinces him, and the suspect, when challenged, fails to

deny his wrongdoing with any conviction. Ullaston accepts Sid's advice to seek the man's resignation in return for no prosecution or publicity.

Under Orders (2006)

Sid Halley goes to the **Cheltenham** Festival with his ex-father-in-law, **Charles Roland**, who wants Sid to speak with his friend, **Lord Enstone**. Enstone asks Sid to investigate why his horses are running badly; he suspects that his trainer and jockey are stopping them. Later that afternoon the same jockey is found dead, with three bullets in his chest.

When the trainer arrested on suspicion of murder is himself found dead, apparently by his own hand, Sid's task becomes at once more complex and more dangerous. Not only Sid but also his girlfriend, **Marina van der Meer**, are in the firing line of those desperate to deter Sid's enquiries. .

Dick Francis's decision to put pen to paper at the age of eighty-five, after an absence of six years, was something of a gamble. His previous three novels—*10 lb. Penalty*, *Second Wind* and *Shattered*—were well short of his best, and many of his admirers would have breathed a sigh of relief at his apparent retirement. Those same admirers would have anticipated his new offering, *Under Orders*, with trepidation, and their nervousness has proved not to be misplaced. The plot of *Under Orders*, though promisingly set in the horseracing world, is mundane and devoid of dramatic tension. Worse, it has so much padding that it could be wearing a fat suit. It is full of unnecessary detail and tangential information which serve to slow the pace to that of an elderly steeplechaser plodding round one of the more bucolic tracks.

Most of the irrelevant verbiage is introduced via the musings of the main character, Sid Halley. Random examples include: the nature of legislation in a democracy; the danger of fire in a stable; the distribution of National Lottery funds; ruminations on rural life, including a quotation from the poet Browning; and the decline of the Church of England in modern Britain. I could go on; Sid, unfortunately, does. What happened to the tough, vulnerable, many-faceted character so skillfully drawn in *Odds Against* and *Whip Hand*? In *Under Orders* he has lost the edginess and inner emotional conflict that defined him; he has become, in a word, dull.

A point of detail, minor but telling, exemplifies the unsatisfactory nature of *Under Orders*. Charles Roland, Sid's ex-father-in-law and a veteran, like

Sid, of *Odds Against*, *Whip Hand* and *Come to Grief*, is spelled, presumably in error, Charles Rowland.

Underfield, Bart (*Reflex* 1980)

Underfield, a **Lambourn** racehorse trainer of middling ability, is not as good as he thinks he is. One of Underfield's more dubious owners, **Elgin Yaxley**, had been forced to withdraw from racing, but the two are seen together at **Ascot**, clearly on good terms with themselves. At **Newbury** races Underfield, slightly drunk, tells **Philip Nore** that Yaxley is a man who has good ideas. After Philip persuades Yaxley to quit the racing scene once again, Underfield is bitter, and threatens Philip with retribution.

Unified Traders (*Second Wind* 1999)

The Unified Traders are a group which has formed to buy and sell radioactive material for criminal purposes. Their number includes owners and trainers of racehorses as well as others unconnected with racing. The activities of the Unified Traders are investigated by meteorologist **Perry Stuart**, who obtains information about the radioactive materials available for sale. Eventually the Traders disband, though a similar group takes their place.

Unwin (*Second Wind* 1999)

Unwin is the pilot of the weekly plane which supplied the residents of **Trox Island**. He gives **Perry Stuart** information about Trox, and identifies the boat hired to evacuate the residents of the island. He sends to Perry in the UK the camera that Perry had left on Trox. Unwin flies Perry and **Robin Darcy** to Trox to recover the folder of information on the Unified Traders' deals; later, he flies them through the eye of Hurricane Sheila.

Unwin, Bobby (*Whip Hand* 1979)

Bobby Unwin is a hard-hitting racing journalist on the *Daily Planet*. He is a good writer, and popular with his readers but not with the racing fraternity. At **Kempton Park** races, Unwin gives **Sid Halley** a copy of a recent piece he had written about top **Newmarket** trainer **George Caspar**. When Sid returns from Paris after the running of the Two Thousand Guineas, Unwin asks him what he knows about the Caspars, **Gleaner** and **Zingaloo**. Sid says he knows nothing; Unwin doesn't believe him, and Sid knows that Unwin won't be quick to help him in the future.

Unwin, Mr. and Mrs. Harvey (*The Edge* 1988)

Mr. and Mrs. Unwin are the Australian owners of **Upper Gumtree**, a racehorse traveling on board the Great Transcontinental Mystery Race Train. They are delighted when their horse wins the Jockey Club Race Train Stakes at **Assiniboia Downs, Winnipeg**.

Updike, Mr. and Mrs. (*In the Frame* 1976)

Norman and "Chuckles" Updike live in Auckland, New Zealand, in a house overlooking the bay. They had bought a painting, apparently by the artist Herring, from **Ruapehu Fine Arts** gallery in Wellington. They are visited by **Charles Todd** and **Jik** and **Sarah Cassavetes**, who pretend to be professional artists sent by the gallery to admire the painting. Chuckles is suspicious and unwelcoming; Norman, though, is happy to show off his painting, as well as his valuable collection of jade. He too becomes suspicious when Charles can't remember the name of the gallery. Charles, abandoning the pretence, explains the true reason for his visit.

Upjohn, Ronnie (*Comeback* 1991)

Upjohn is mentioned by vet **Ken McClure** as having threatened to sue over an injured horse which he'd sold cheaply to McClure and which had subsequently won a race. Upjohn is heard at **Stratford** races, where he is a steward, criticizing McClure. For his part, McClure considers Upjohn to be of limited intelligence. There is no love lost between Upjohn and **Mac Mackintosh**, whom Upjohn had accused of taking bribes from bookmakers. Upjohn is said by Mackintosh to have lost a lot of money over Porphyry Place, a failed leisure centre.

Upper Gumtree (*The Edge* 1988)

Upper Gumtree, an Australian racehorse traveling on board the Great Transcontinental Mystery Race Train, is owned by **Mr. and Mrs. Harvey Unwin**. He wins the Jockey Club Race Train Stakes at **Assiniboia Downs, Winnipeg**.

Upton, Erica (*Longshot* 1990)

Erica Upton is the nom de plume of literary novelist **Erica Goodhaven**.

Urquhart, Phil (*Straight* 1989)

Urquhart is a youngish, well-respected veterinary surgeon; **Lambourn** trainer **Milo Shandy** is one of his clients. Urquhart dope tests **Dozen Roses**, who appears excessively docile, when he arrives from **Nicholas Loder**'s yard. The horse tests negative for tranquillizers. At **Derek Franklin**'s request, Urquhart tests for other illegal substances.

Usher, Benjy (*Driving Force* 1992)

Usher, a multi-millionaire racehorse owner-trainer, is married to **Dot Usher**, with whom he argues constantly. He is ill-tempered, and often yells at his lads. Training is no more than a hobby to Usher; he doesn't adopt a hands-on approach, never saddling his own runners; he has been known to send the wrong horse to the races. Usher owns good horses which are trained overseas. He uses **Freddie Croft**'s horse vans and prefers **Lewis** to drive them. Usher is subsequently discovered to be using his stable in southern France for purposes other than merely training racehorses.

Usher, Dot (*Driving Force* 1992)

Dot, the wife of **Benjy Usher**, is unhappy with her lot, and quarrels continuously with her husband. She is in her forties, attractive and intelligent. She tells **Freddie Croft** that an old horse that **John Tigwood** had given them had died of a fever of some kind. She is unaware of what is going on at her husband's stable in France.

V

Vaccaro, Ramon (*Straight* 1989)

Wanted by the police for drug smuggling in Florida, Vaccaro is suspected of murdering several pilots who had worked for him in order to silence them. Now in England, Vaccaro has applied to local magistrates for a gaming license. **Greville Franklin** was a magistrate, and in notes found by **Derek Franklin** in Greville's car after his death, he advises turning down the application.

Valery (*Bolt* 1986)

Valery is a young lawyer who is working for **Henri Nanterre**. He accompanies Nanterre to **Princess Casilia**'s house; there he inspects the documents by which **Roland de Brescou** has given up his right to make independent decisions on company matters and declares it legal.

Van der Meer, Marina (*Under Orders* 2006)

Marina is the Dutch girlfriend of **Sid Halley**; she is from the province of Friesland. She took her first degree in Amsterdam and studied for a Ph.D. at **Cambridge**. Marina shares an apartment in central London with Sid. Blonde and highly intelligent, she works as a research chemist at the Cancer Research UK Laboratories in London.

On her way home from work Marina is attacked, suffering superficial cuts and bruising to her face. Her assailant tells her to warn Sid to drop his investigations into a jockey's death. She refuses to involve the police or go to hospital. She is patched up by Sid's doctor. Using the facilities at Cancer Research UK, she extracts a sample of her attacker's DNA from skin under her fingernails. She goes with Sid to stay with **Charles Roland** at **Aynsford**. She gets on well with Charles; together they persuade Sid to continue his investigation and not to worry about putting her in danger. At the laboratories where she works Marina enlists the help of a colleague, **Rosie**, to produce a DNA profile of her attacker.

Marina, however, suffers a second and much more serious injury as a result of ignoring the warning. She is rushed to hospital where she undergoes an emergency operation. For a while her survival is in the balance; however her condition stabilizes, and then starts to improve. When Sid visits her in hospital and asks her to marry him, she teases him by saying she'll think about it. She is released from hospital and returns home. She and Sid are married in a West **Oxfordshire** registry office.

Van Dysart, Mrs. (*Odds Against* 1965)

Dumpy and frizzy-haired, Mrs. Van Dysart specializes in cutting remarks. She is invited to **Charles Roland**'s house specifically to humiliate **Sid Halley** in front of **Howard** and **Doria Kraye**. She asks Sid to take some pieces of quartz from her, knowing that he wouldn't be able to manage them. Mrs. Van Dysart says that Sid owes it to Charles, his father-in-law, to get some treatment on his hand. She demands to see his hand; when Sid refuses she comments that Sid doesn't want to get better.

Van Dysart, Rex (*Odds Against* 1965)

Van Dysart is on a visit to England from South Africa; **Charles Roland** invites him to his house because of his wife's cruel tongue. He is a large man with a domineering manner.

Van Ekeren, Hans (*Straight* 1989)

Van Ekeren is an Antwerp-based diamond cutter. He tells **Derek Franklin** over the phone that he has done no business with **Greville Franklin** within the last six or seven years, since he took the business over from his uncle. He rings Derek a few days later to say that Greville had phoned his uncle for advice about whom to buy diamonds from; he gives Derek the name of a dealer, **Guy Servi**.

Van Els, Jet (*Second Wind* 1999)

Jet Van Els is an attractive nurse who looks after **Perry Stuart**'s grandmother, **Mrs. Mevagissey**. When Perry returns from America he visits his grandmother; Jet sits on the porch with him and they kiss. Jet goes out for lunch with Perry; she tells him that Mrs. Mevagissey had warned her about falling for him. She goes with Perry to **George Loricroft**'s yard in **Newmarket**. When Perry asks her on impulse to be his wife, Jet says yes, and they soon marry.

Van Huren, Jonathan (*Smokescreen* 1972)

Jonathan is the son of **Quentin van Huren**. Aged about twenty, he is sulky and a bit of a brat. He tells **Edward Lincoln** that he never goes to see the sort of film that Edward is in. He boasts to Edward that his family owns a gold mine. At **Germiston** races, he comments on trainer **Greville Arnold**'s lack of manners.

Van Huren, Quentin (*Smokescreen* 1972)

Quentin Van Huren is the brother of the late husband of Portia, **Nerissa Cavesey**'s late sister. He is part-owner of Rojedda gold mine in the town of **Welkom**, and a director of a mining company. A very wealthy man, Van Huren lives in a big house in Johannesberg. At Nerissa's request, he unenthusiastically invites **Edward Lincoln** to dinner. Initially he is polite but reserved; however, as the two men get to know each other their relationship becomes more cordial. Van Huren is shocked to hear that Nerissa is dying. He invites Edward to visit his gold mine.

When Edward phones him for information about Nerissa's holdings in the gold mine, Van Huren tells him that it is equal to his own.

Van Huren, Sally (*Smokescreen* 1972)

Sally is the pretty daughter of **Quentin Van Huren**. She is a nice, straightforward girl who loves horses. She asks **Edward Lincoln** about his riding in one of his films. Sally develops a crush on **Danilo Cavesey**, and agrees to play tennis with him. She is impressed when Danilo bets ten rand on a horse, which Edward finds reassuringly innocent.

Van Huren, Vivi (*Smokescreen* 1972)

Vivi is the wife of **Quentin Van Huren**. She has the polish and veneer of sophistication that go with her wealth and social standing, but lacks both warmth and perceptiveness. She is impressed by **Danilo Cavesey**'s manners, which are even more superficial than her own.

Vaughnley, Hugh (*Break In* 1985)

Hugh, the son of **Lord Vaughnley**, is in his early twenties; he is pleasant but immature. He has fallen out with his father, who has thrown him out of the family home. Hugh turns up at **Ascot** races, at his father's private box. He tells **Kit Fielding** to stay, as he is afraid that his father will be furious with him.

Hugh allows Kit to make a video of him explaining how he was inveigled into selling his shares in his father's newspaper, the *Sunday Towncrier*, to **Maynard Allardeck**. Lord Vaughnley had found out what Hugh had done and thrown him out.

Vaughnley, Lady (*Break In* 1985)

Lady Vaughnley, the wife of **Lord Vaughnley**, is close to tears when **Kit Fielding** comments on the absence of her son, **Hugh Vaughnley**, from **Cheltenham** races; Kit assumes a family rift.

Vaughnley, Lord (*Break In* 1985; *Bolt* 1986)

Break In (1985): Lord Vaughnley is the proprietor of the *Sunday Towncrier* newspaper, and the sponsor of big race at **Cheltenham** won by **North Face**. He took over the *Towncrier* from his father, who had transformed an ailing weekly provincial newspaper into a nationwide success. When **Kit Fielding** wants information about **Maynard Allardeck**, Vaughnley introduces him to *Towncrier* columnist **Rose Quince**

Vaughnley has fallen out with his son, **Hugh Vaughnley**, and thrown him out of the house; he is alarmed when Hugh turns up at **Ascot** and talks to Kit; Vaughnley doesn't want Kit to know the reason for the rift. Knowing that Kit is going to be at a race sponsors' lunch in London, Vaughnley arranges for himself, **Nestor Pollgate** and **Jay**

Erskine to be there as well. He agrees to go to Newmarket with Kit, who promises to give him information about Allardeck; both Vaughnley and Pollgate, editor of the rival newspaper *The Daily Flag*, are at odds with Allardeck, who had tried to take over both the *Flag* and the *Towncrier*. Vaughnley watches a video made by Kit of Allardeck's business practices.

Bolt (1986): Vaughnley agrees to check the *Towncrier*'s computer files for Kit to see if they have any information on French businessman Henri Nanterre. At Sandown races, he passes on to Kit newspaper cuttings and a photo of Nanterre racing in France. The next day at Sandown, Vaughnley warns Kit that Maynard Allardeck knows that Kit had sent a copy of the video about his business practices to the government's honors committee.

Venables, Patrick (*Driving Force* 1992)

Venables, the Director of Security at the Jockey Club, is a former member of MI5, the British government's counter-espionage department. He is wary of getting too friendly with his contacts within the racing world. Asked for advice by racehorse transport firm owner Freddie Croft, Venables sends one of his operatives, Nina Young, to work as a horse van driver. He also sends undercover agent Aziz as back-up, without informing Freddie.

Vera (*Second Wind* 1999)

Vera is a research vet at the Equine Research Establishment, Newmarket, and a specialist in colic. She thinks that Caspar Harvey's filly could be suffering from radiation sickness, but test results are inconclusive. She gives Perry Stuart a sample of the filly's droppings.

Verity, Gina Waltman (*Shattered* 2000)

Gina Verity, the sister of Rose Payne, lives in Taunton, Somerset. She has a fifteen-year-old son, Victor Verity, who had sent a letter to Martin Stukeley about a videotape allegedly containing highly sensitive information. She is initially friendly when Gerard Logan questions Victor, but gets annoyed when she wrongly thinks Gerard is accusing Victor of theft. Gina has a brief affair with Dr. Adam Force. Her husband, informed by Rose, beats her up and is imprisoned for assault. Rose subsequently moves in with Gina, who allows Victor to go away for the weekend to stay with Gerard.

Verity, Victor Waltman (*Shattered* 2000)

Victor, the fifteen-year-old son of Gina Verity, is an internet expert. He is tracked down by Gerard Logan, who has found a letter written by Victor to Martin Stukeley about a video containing valuable information. Victor's father is in jail for assaulting his mother, who had had an affair. Victor phones Gerard to ask him to go to Taunton, Somerset, to see him; he is concerned about his family's violent behavior. He tells Gerard that when he sent the letter to Stukeley he had just appended his own name to letters written by someone else. Now that his aunt, Rose Payne, had moved in with his mother, Victor is desperate to leave, and he asks Gerard to take him away.

Vernon (*Proof* 1984)

In his late forties, Vernon is based at Martineau Park racecourse, where he works as the stores manager in the catering department. He is an associate of Paul Young, who suspects that Vernon is cheating him.

When Vernon sees Tony Beach in the catering department his suspicions are aroused, and he challenges him. Tony disappears, and Vernon and Young spend two hours searching for him. The next day Vernon is shocked to find Tony and Gerard McGregor with his boss, Miles Quigley. After Quigley hears what McGregor has to say he sacks Vernon on the spot.

Vernon, Detective Inspector (*To the Hilt* 1996)

Small and overweight, D.I. Vernon is not destined for great things in the police force, but is persistent and reliable. He is one of the policemen called to Oliver Grantchester's house by Chris Jones when Alex is in difficulties.

Vernonside Stud (*Comeback* 1991)

This is a thoroughbred stud near Cheltenham, Gloucestershire. The owners are clients of the veterinary practice where Ken McClure is the equine specialist. A heavily pregnant mare with colic is taken from the stud to be operated on by McClure on the night that the office block at the practice burns down.

Vic (*Driving Force* 1992)

Vic is a driver for Croft Raceways horse transport firm.

Vickers, Gareth (*Longshot* 1990)

Gareth, the fifteen-year-old son of **Tremayne Vickers**, is much loved by his father. Confident and willful, Gareth is a day pupil at a nearby boarding school. He is fascinated by **John Kendall**'s survival skills, including his ability to cook. He has a different mother to **Perkin Vickers** and his half-sister Jane, who lives near Paris. His mother is a celebrity cook on TV. Gareth shows John the workroom where Perkin makes furniture. He asks John to teach him how to cook since his mother, he says, wouldn't allow him in the kitchen while she was working.

Gareth goes on an afternoon's survival course on his father's land with John. On a second survival trip in the woods he tells John that **Angela Brickell** had wanted to kiss him, and he had told his father about it. When John goes missing, Gareth helps to search for him in the woods. After John is found, badly injured, he fears for his life, and pleads with Gareth to stay with him.

Vickers, Mackie (*Longshot* 1990)

Mackie is the sweet-natured daughter-in-law of racehorse trainer **Tremayne Vickers**; she works as his assistant. She is married to Vickers' son, **Perkin Vickers**. Mackie collects **John Kendall** from **Reading** bus station and drives him to the **Berkshire** village where they live. On an icy road she loses control of her jeep when a horse appears on the road and skids into a water-filled ditch. Dazed and semi-conscious, Mackie is hauled out of the car by John Kendall and carried towards the village by John and **Harry Goodhaven** until she recovers.

Mackie was briefly engaged to **Nolan Everard** but called off the wedding when she realized that she wouldn't be able to live with his uncertain temper. She faints when about to ride work on the gallops; when she discovers she is pregnant she is delighted.

Mackie finds John badly injured in the woods; she ensures that John's desperate instruction that he should not be touched is complied with.

Vickers, Perkin (*Longshot* 1990)

The son of racehorse trainer **Tremayne Vickers**, Perkin still lives, with his wife **Mackie Vickers**, in the family home where he works as a furniture designer. According to his father, he lacks business acumen. Perkin resembles his father physically—both are big and well-built—but lacks Tremayne's self-assuredness and his practical, down-

to-earth approach to life. However Perkin's wishy-washy exterior gives no clue to his true nature. Perkin has a dark side which he has kept well hidden but which causes him to choose a course of action that leads inexorably to grief and loss of life.

Vickers, Tremayne (*Longshot* 1990)

Berkshire racehorse trainer Tremayne Vickers is approaching the evening of a distinguished career. He has trained almost 1000 winners, including the winners of the **Cheltenham** Gold Cup, Champion Hurdle and Grand National. Looking for someone to write his biography, he offers the job to **John Kendall**, whom he meets in the offices of literary agent **Ronnie Curzon**. Vickers' wife has left him years before. He has a daughter who lives near Paris and two sons, **Perkin** and **Gareth Vickers**, at home. Vickers is voluble, decisive and practical; as John gets to know him he recognizes that Vickers is also a sympathetic and compassionate man. His father had inherited a great deal of money; described by Vickers as a lunatic, he'd lived a life of idleness and gambling, employing a private trainer for his racehorses. Vickers' mother had died when he was ten years old. Deciding that one member of the family at least should learn the value of hard work, his father had sent him to be a tack-cleaner for a fox-hunting family, and later to be a groom for a polo player in Argentina. Perversely, he had enjoyed the experience, and had eventually taken over the training of his father's horses.

The previous year Vickers had been fined by the Stewards of the **National Hunt Committee** when a horse tested positive for stimulants; according to Tremayne it had been given chocolate by a stable girl who is now missing. He is shocked when the police tell him that her body has been found.

Vickers accepts a Lifetime Award at a race-course dinner-dance, where he tells John that he'll apply for an amateur jockey's permit on his behalf. Later in the evening he is angry when **Sam Yaeger** and **Nolan Everard** come to blows, and goes home early.

After Perkin's death, Vickers is reluctant to continue with his biography, but John persuades him it is worthwhile.

Victoria Arts Center

In the Frame (1976): The Victoria Arts Center is a fictional art gallery in Melbourne, Australia; **Charles Todd** and **Jik Cassavetes** see a young man at the gallery copying an **Alfred Munnings** painting. Jik calls him a fraud; he throws turpentine in Jik's eyes and runs away.

Viking, John (*Whip Hand* 1979)

Hot air balloon racer John Viking is tall, thin and highly eccentric. He is a cousin of **Norris Abbott**. When his passenger refuses to fly with him, Viking allows **Sid Halley** to accompany him, as he has no alternative. He is annoyed with Sid for almost falling out of the balloon when it hits the tops of some trees. Viking is renowned for taking risks as a balloon racer; with Sid, he flies illegally at 15,000 feet, in the airways, to win the race. He almost sets the balloon on fire when his cigarette ignites a spurt of propane gas. Impressed by Sid's lack of fear, Viking asks him what he's doing next Saturday.

Villains

"I do not say that all those who go racing are rogues and vagabonds, but I do say that all rogues and vagabonds seem to go racing." (Sir Abe Bailey, Gimcrack Speech, 1937)

Francis has written all his novels from the viewpoint of the hero. However, using a first person narrator has implications for the way that the villain is depicted. Because the spotlight is on the main character, it can prove difficult for the writer to develop the villain's character enough to create believable conflict between the two. Francis encountered this difficulty in later books, but his early novels give no indication of it. Indeed, the covert yet malign influence that the villain exerts throughout *Dead Cert* (1962) is a paradigm of how he can be strongly drawn without necessarily being as prominent in the story as the protagonist.

The villain's descent into race fixing, protection rackets and murder is due to his own unhealthy fascination with violence, as well as the need to provide financially for his dependants. He is comfortable with playing the role of sinister puppetmaster, but when it comes actually to carrying out acts of violence he much prefers the contemplation of it to the execution.

In Francis's second book, *Nerve* (1964), the villain is a man with the outward trappings of success, who is nonetheless eaten away by hatred of those whose way of life he envies. He uses the influence that his job gives him to destroy the careers of professional jockeys. Such is his veneer of good humor that no-one suspects him. Then jump jockey **Rob Finn**, one of his victims, sets out to save his career. Identified as the culprit by Rob, the villain consents—unsatisfactorily from the point of view of his credibility—to go abroad and start a new life.

The unwaveringly malevolent villain in *For Kicks* (1965) is wholly committed to his evil doing, and has a motivation for his actions deeply rooted in his psychological make-up and in his desire for financial gain. In order to land successful betting coups he and his trainer devise a barbaric method of making their horses run faster. His psychopathic appetites are whetted by the use of his fists, his boots or his stick to encourage a rapid turnover of stable staff.

Enjoyment of cruelty for its own sake is a trait possessed by several of Francis's villains. **Sid Halley**'s adversary in *Odds Against* (1966), succeeds in repulsing the reader by his barely disguised contempt for Sid's disabled hand and his readiness to inflict excruciating pain. In *Flying Finish* (1966) a young criminal's hatred of the upper classes gives his capacity for violence an extra edge. His particular bête noire is fellow horse transport firm employee **Lord Henry Gray**. He makes Henry's life a misery in the hope that he will quit his job and so fail to discover the crimes that he and the owner of the firm are perpetrating. When that doesn't work he escalates the level of violence but finds, to his horror, that he has met his match in Henry.

Whereas *Odds Against* and *Flying Finish* feature villains with a psychopathic dimension to their propensity for violence, in the case of the criminal in *Bonecrack* (1971) the underlying cause is physical: his hold on reality has been progressively weakened by an undiagnosed disease. Obsessed with realizing his son's desire to be a top jockey, he forces **Newmarket** trainer **Neil Griffon**, on pain of death, to take his son on and to groom him for instant stardom. When a mutual respect grows between the trainer and his apprentice the father feels sidelined, and views this burgeoning relationship—which he has never had with his son—with impotent fury. It is the tension engendered by this emotional conflict that gives *Bonecrack* its hard edge and unpredictability.

In *Twice Shy* (1981) there is another character of Italian origin with a huge capacity for creating chaos. His motivations, though, are not so finely drawn as those of *Bonecrack*'s villain. He is just a dimly-functioning thug whose lack of brainpower makes him a highly dangerous man. He wants a computerized horse racing system which he thinks will make him rich. Intimidation and murder follow in the wake of his search for the system; but when he eventually has it in his grasp he finds no contentment. He looks to violence as the answer to his problems but it ultimately proves to be his undoing.

In contrast to *Twice Shy*'s villain, whose family background and lack of education are predisposing influences towards a life of crime, Francis has also created evil men from the higher levels of society. In *Decider* (1993) the twin brother of a Lord of the realm harbors bitter resentment about being born a few minutes later than his twin. In his eyes he has missed out, through a quirk of fate, on most of life's prizes: the family title, the mansion, the bulk of the inheritance. This sense of grievance only serves to exacerbate a naturally vile temper. His anger frequently spills over into physical violence, notably against his wives—he's now on his fourth, two having left him and one having killed herself. A dissolute lifestyle has left him with a burden of debt and he sees the sale of the family racecourse, **Stratton Park**, as a means of restoring his fortunes. Standing in his way is shareholder **Lee Morris**, the son by her second husband of the villain's first wife. When he discovers that Lee has unearthed dark secrets about his past, the villain's tenuous hold on self-control is broken.

The Allardecks (*Break In* 1985; *Bolt* 1986), are a famous **Newmarket** racing family. Nowadays they are known less for training classic winners than for their bitter and ancient feud with their rivals, the **Fieldings**. A rapprochement of sorts had been made when trainer **Bobby Allardeck** had married Holly Fielding, sister of champion jockey **Kit Fielding**. But this liaison had not gone down well with his father **Maynard Allardeck**, whose hatred of all things Fielding had continued undiminished. Allardeck is a wealthy man whose fortune is derived not from training, but from ruthless business deals in the City. He demonstrates a similar implacability in his dealings with Kit Fielding.

Cruelty to horses is a theme that Francis explores in *Bolt* and returns to in *Come to Grief* (1995). For the perpetrator, the mutilation of horses provides a thrill that his life has lacked since he stopped being a jockey. It provides him with the element of risk that his present career lacks—the risk of being caught. On one level he is a charming, intelligent and charismatic man; on another a perverted monster whose unspeakable cruelty is almost too awful to contemplate. To exploit the pathetic helplessness of animals in this way is so beyond the pale that it is very difficult for the reader to empathize with such behavior.

Immeasurably better is the conflict, in *Whip Hand* (1979, between **Sid Halley** and the villain, who has left behind a childhood of deprivation, and determinedly climbed the social ladder. Outwardly he is indistinguishable from the men of wealth and privilege with whom he loves to mix. But his success is built on a ruthless ambition fuelled by a total lack of moral conscience. As an owner with a top Newmarket trainer, he uses his access to other horses in the yard to stop them winning. When he learns that Sid Halley has been hired to guard a horse he has targeted, he moves swiftly to eliminate the threat. The battle of wills between the villain and Halley, who has also risen from an under-privileged background, is one of the strengths of *Whip Hand*.

In *High Stakes* (1975) Francis creates two villains of more or less equal stature who act in concert. A racehorse trainer and a bookmaker have for several years conspired to defraud wealthy owner **Steven Scott**. Finally rumbled and summarily sacked, the trainer refuses to accept the inevitable and continues, with his accomplice, to make life unpleasant for Steven. A violent confrontation in Steven's toy factory provides an exciting climax to the book.

The gulf between Francis's most thoughtfully drawn villains and his least successful is significant. The best have the attributes required of an involving antagonist. They are neither stereotypical nor one-dimensional. They have a clear, well-defined motivation for their actions. Their characters are developed to the extent that they provide a credible opposition to the protagonist. In fact the villain often seems to be stronger and more in control than the hero, thus heightening the suspense about how the hero will finally prevail.

In contrast, Francis's more notable duds lack power, menace and credibility. Often the problem is invisibility: the villain is neither developed nor compelling enough to involve the reader. Insipid, anonymous villains in *In the Frame* (1976), *Trial Run* (1978), and *Blood Sport* (1967) do not heighten the impact of even the scenes they are in. *In the Frame*'s crime boss makes only fleeting appearances and most of the criminal acts are carried out by his generally incompetent lackeys. He is finally trapped by a plot device similar to one previously used in *Slay-Ride* (1973), and the reader is unable to feel any interest in his fate.

In *Trial Run* an Englishman living in Moscow is involved with a pair of foreign terrorists. Since we never discover the names of these terrorists, and their motivation in unclear, the responsibility of fulfilling the role of the villain falls on the Englishman, who is not up to the job. He bumbles incompetently through the book, and his eventual fate at the hands of his associates makes no impact on this tedious and often unintelligible tale of foul play in Communist Russia.

The villain in *Blood Sport* similarly fails to set the pulse racing. His character remains unsubstantial throughout and the reader cannot build up antipathy towards such a nebulous figure. He employs relatives to do his dirty work for him, with the result that the minor characters become more important than he is. Allowing the hero—in this case morose investigator **Gene Hawkins**—to deal with the villain's henchmen should set up a critical confrontation between the villain himself and the hero. Instead the question of whether or not the criminal is brought to justice is not addressed.

The villain in Francis's 2006 novel, *Under Orders*, is another who is inadequately developed. He flits in and out of the story, scarcely more substantial than a spectral wraith, until finally named by his lover as a double murderer. At that point he turns up at Sid Halley's apartment and behaves in a manner both incompetent and implausible; first he fails to kill Sid, then he fails to kill himself.

A nadir is reached in *Dead Heat* (2007), the novel written as a result of a collaboration between Dick Francis and his son Felix. Here the villain scarcely exists as a functioning character, and plays no real part in the story until making a long-overdue appearance in the penultimate chapter. By this time the reader has long since ceased to care about him.

Unlike the well-handled pairing of villains in *High Stakes*, the two in *Straight* (1989) aren't working together, nor even known to each other, and the divided focus weakens the structure of an otherwise excellent story. The villains are tenuously connected through the recently deceased diamond merchant **Greville Franklin**. One has already stolen diamonds from Franklin and is now trying to steal more from Franklin's brother, **Derek Franklin**, who is working to keep Greville's business afloat. When confronted by Derek with his crimes, a grudging apology on the villain's part is enough to absolve him and deflect any further punishment.

The other villain in *Straight* is a racehorse owner who uses his access to his trainer's other horses for criminal ends. For sheer nastiness he is up there with Francis's most frightening villains,

but because we have a minimal amount of background information about him, he is a far less compelling character.

The problem of diluted focus reoccurs in *Second Wind* (1999). The villains are known as the **Unified Traders**, but this is a misnomer which belies the fragmented and disparate nature of the group. Ostensibly they exist to trade in nuclear materials, but so unfathomable is *Second Wind*'s plot structure that the Traders' role in it becomes almost irrelevant. The novel's conclusion leaves the reader feeling unsatisfied. Only one of the villains ends up in jail; the Unified Traders disband but another group takes their place.

Villars, Annie (*Rat Race* 1970)

Racehorse trainer Annie Villars is around fifty years old, and is considered to be an excellent trainer. She is strict with her stable lads but sympathetic to the needs of her horses and good with her owners. She is one of the passengers on **Matt Shore**'s air-taxi flight to **Haydock Park**. She is angry at the hostility between jockey **Kenny Bayst** and owner **Eric Goldenberg**. At the races she and Bayst fall out over his riding of **Rudiments**, who finishes third after being boxed in. She is further irritated when Matt has to land at **Nottingham Airport** to have the plane checked over.

On the return flight to **Cambridge** after another Haydock Park race meeting, Annie realizes that Matt is looking for **Nancy Ross**'s plane. She tells Matt that the passengers will do anything to help.

When Matt asks her about her friend, **Major Tyderman**, she is at first unwilling to divulge any information about him, but then relents out of her regard for Nancy and **Midge Ross**.

Vincent, Vic (*Knock Down* 1974)

Bloodstock agent Vic Vincent is about forty years old; he is bluff and superficially genial. He demands a share of the profits from **Antonia Huntercombe** when she submits a good filly at the Sales. When she refuses, Vincent ensures that the filly sells cheaply. At **Newmarket Sales**, he warns **Jonah Dereham** to leave it to him to buy horses for **Mrs. Kerry Sanders**, and not to bid for Antonia Huntercombe's yearling colt. When Jonah buys the colt Vincent is furious. He tells Jonah that all the bloodstock agents should stick together. Soon realizing that Jonah has no intention of heeding this advice, Vincent and his cronies take steps to bring him into line. However, Vincent becomes aware that, far from being in a position of strength, he has to do what Jonah wants. The result is a major fall-out between Vincent and his former associate which ends in violence and death.

Vine, George (*High Stakes* 1975)

Vine is one of trainer **Rupert Ramsey**'s owners. He meets **Steven Scott** at Ramsey's yard, where Vine's wife, **Poppet**, tells Steven that **Felicity Leeds** had introduced them to bookmaker **Ganser Mays**. When Poppet says that Mays gives them much better odds than the Tote, Vine remarks that, as a result, Poppet bets more heavily.

Vine, Joanie (*Field of 13* 1998: "Song for Mona")

Joanie Vine is the daughter of stable employee **Mona Watkins**. She is a snobbish social climber and ashamed of her working class mother. She is married to the equally stuck-up auctioneer's assistant **Peregrine Vine**. Joanie didn't invite Mona to her wedding and virtually shuts Mona out of her life. When Mona is ill, Joanie makes no effort to visit her despite Mona's doctor asking her do so. When Mona dies Joanie and Peregrine arrange a cheap, basic funeral for Mona on the only day that Mona's employers, **Oliver Bolingbroke** and **Cassidy Lovelace Ward**, can't attend. Joanie is acutely embarrassed by Cassidy's efforts to keep Mona's memory alive.

Vine, Peregrine (*Field of 13* 1998: "Song for Mona")

Thirty-year-old Peregrine Vine is pompous and self-satisfied. He works as an assistant to auctioneers of antiques and fine arts. He is married to Joanie, who is working class but even more of a snob than Peregrine. Both of them treat Joanie's mother with contempt; they don't bother to visit Mona when she is ill. When Peregrine hears that Mona has died he send a van to her house to take away her belongings, but is prevented from doing so by Mona's employer **Oliver Bolingbroke**. He and Joanie arrange Mona's funeral for the only day that Oliver and his wife, **Cassidy Lovelace Ward**, can't be there. However, Cassidy's actions in honor of Mona's memory finally prick Peregrine's conscience, and he begins to wonder if his selfish wife is worth the trouble.

Vine, Poppet (*High Stakes* 1975)

Poppet is the wife of **George Vine**, one of trainer **Rupert Ramsey**'s owners. At Ramsey's

yard, she mentions to **Steven Scott** that bookmaker **Ganser Mays** gives her more favorable odds than the Tote does. However, she won't tell Steven whether, on balance, she wins or loses.

Vine, Tony (*The Danger* 1983)

Tony Vine is a partner in **Liberty Market Ltd.** In his late thirties, Vine is a former sergeant in the Special Air Services; he is very fit, and an expert in undercover work. He has limited social skills, and is at his best among soldiers. He works with **Andrew Douglas** to locate **Dominic Nerrity**, a child kidnapped from the beach at **West Wittering**.

Vinicheck, Jill (*10 lb. Penalty* 1997)

Jill Vinicheck is Minister of Education in the British Government; she is a colleague of **George Juliard**. At a reception at 10 Downing Street, she suggests to **Benedict Juliard** that his stepmother **Polly** should dress more fashionably to avoid adverse newspaper comment. She suggests that Polly consult **Alderney Wyvern**, who advised Vinicheck and others on their presentation. A candidate for Prime Minister, Vinicheck stands against George Juliard and **Hudson Hirst**; she is eliminated in the first ballot.

Vintners Incorporated (*Proof* 1984)

This is a respectable firm of suppliers of wines and spirits whose name is fraudulently stamped on boxes of wine and whisky not supplied by them.

Viola (*Odds Against* 1965)

Viola is the elderly widowed cousin of **Charles Roland**. She is fond of **Sid Halley**, and concerned at Charles's apparent nastiness towards him in front of his guests. Sid tells her it's a game of Charles's that he is playing along with, and asks Viola not to mention anything about his past.

Viralto, Italy

Viralto is a fictional village in the Italian Alps. *The Danger* (1983): Kidnap victim **Alessia Cenci** is held near the village of Viralto.

Visborough, Alison (*Wild Horses* 1994)

Alison, the middle-aged daughter of **Audrey** and the late **Rupert Visborough**, lives in Market Harborough, **Leicestershire**. Formidable and forthright, she is an expert horsewoman. She is friendly with writer **Howard Tyler**, author of a book based on the death of her aunt, **Sonia Wells**. She is angry that **Thomas Lyon** has changed many of the details for the film of the book, especially those concerning her father. On the death of her father—renamed "**Cibber**" in Thomas's film—Alison had written his obituary, which had attracted Tyler's attention in the first place. Alison defends her late father to Thomas; she is annoyed that in the film he has not been portrayed as an honorable man.

Visborough, Audrey (*Wild Horses* 1994)

Audrey is the wife of the late **Rupert Visborough**, alias "**Cibber**" in **Thomas Lyon**'s film, *Unstable Times*. In the film the character based on Audrey has an affair with racehorse trainer **Jackson Wells**. Audrey takes great exception to this. She tells Thomas that Wells was twenty years younger than her and that she had disliked him intensely. She is angry that Thomas's film, in her eyes, fails to do justice to her husband's character and achievements. She goes to **Huntingdon racecourse** when Thomas is filming; she tells O'Hara, the producer, to stop the film.

Visborough, Rodbury (*Wild Horses* 1994)

Rodbury, the brother of **Alison Visborough**, teaches equestrian skills and prepares horses for eventing. Twenty-six years before, Visborough was one of a group of young friends that included **Sonia Wells**, the wife of **Newmarket** trainer **Jackson Wells**. Sonia had died in mysterious circumstances, and when film director **Thomas Lyon** arrives in **Newmarket** to shoot a film based on the incident, Visborough is a worried man. He resolves to deter Thomas from delving into the historical background to Sonia's death.

Vittorio (*Flying Finish* 1966)

Vittorio, an Italian, drives the taxi which is waiting outside the hospital in Milan for **Lord Henry Gray**. He takes Henry to **Billy Watkins**.

Viv, Aunt (*The Edge* 1988)

Aunt Viv is the sister of **Tor Kelsey**'s father. When her brother died, Viv took Tor in, then aged five, and brought him up. She is about sixty years old and unmarried, but is young at heart.

Vivat Club (*Risk* 1977)

This is a London gambling club run by **Vivian Iverson**. **Roland Britten** has a meeting there with ex-convicts **Connaught Powys, Glitberg and Ownslow**.

Vjoersterod (*Forfeit* 1968)

Vjoersterod is a blond South African who dresses well, has the stamp of an educated man, and travels in a chauffeur-driven Rolls Royce. He controls a string of betting shops in the **Birmingham** area, using a nominal owner, bookmaker **Charlie Boston**, as a front man. Vjoersterod runs his business aggressively, employing large men to expedite the payment of debts. He also successfully manipulates the ante-post betting market so that large sums of money wagered on horses in the weeks prior to a big race are lost as soon as the bets are laid.

Vjoersterod is not pleased to learn that **James Tyrone**, an investigative racing reporter, has written an article on the subject for his newspaper, the *Sunday Blaze*. He takes what he considers to be appropriate action to warn James off. When that doesn't work Vjoersterod adopts more extreme measures. These do not have the effect that Vjoersterod is anticipating.

Voting Right (*The Edge* 1988)

Voting Right, a Canadian racehorse traveling on board the Great Transcontinental Mystery Race Train, is owned by **Mercer Lorrimore**. He wins the Jockey Club Race Train Stakes at **Hastings Park**, Vancouver.

W

Wagner, Captain Kent (*The Danger* 1983)

Wagner is a Captain of Detectives in Washington D.C. police. Undemonstrative but highly competent, he liaises with **Andrew Douglas** in the search for the kidnappers of **Morgan Freemantle**. When events reach a dramatic climax Wagner acts with conspicuous bravery in confronting the chief villain.

Wainwright, Commander Lucas (*Whip Hand* 1979)

Wainwright is the Director of Security at the **Jockey Club**. At **Kempton Park**, he asks **Sid Halley** to make unofficial enquiries into the background of one of his deputies, **Eddy Keith**, who had given the green light for several undesirables to form syndicates to own horses. When Sid goes to **Portman Square** in Keith's absence to look at the syndicate files, Wainwright tells him that the last person to investigate the syndicates was attacked in the street and left blind and in a vegetative state. Subsequently Wainwright's own connections with the syndicates become the focus of Sid's enquiries.

Wakefield, Inspector (*Dead Cert* 1962)

Inspector Wakefield is the policeman called to **West Sussex racecourse** after the death of jockey **Joe Nantwich**.

Walker, Evan (*Under Orders* 2006)

Evan Walker, a Welsh farmer from **Brecon**, is the father of murdered jockey **Huw Walker**. After his son's death, he is telephoned by a journalist on *The Pump* newspaper, who accuses **Sid Halley** of involvement. In distress, Walker takes a shotgun and drives to London to confront Sid, but on the way he realizes that Sid has been falsely accused.

Walker is now the only member of his family still alive; he had lost his wife to cancer the previous year, and his eldest son had been killed in a hit-and-run road incident on his fifteenth birthday. He asks Sid to investigate his son's death.

Subsequently Walker asks Sid to send his bill for the work he's done and is offended when Sid says there's no charge. He is placated when Sid tells him that *The Pump* has already paid for the investigation.

Walker, Huw (*Under Orders* 2006)

Jump jockey Huw Walker is not top class, but is always high in the jockeys' list for winners ridden each year. The son of a Welsh farmer, Walker is said to enjoy fast cars and to have an eye for the ladies. Looking worried at **Cheltenham** races, Walker asks **Sid Halley** if he's listened to the message he'd left on Sid's answering machine; he says he'll phone Sid later as he can't talk at the races. He wins the Triumph Hurdle by a head on **Candlestick** for trainer **Bill Burton**; after the race, in the unsaddling enclosure, he is seen arguing vehemently with Burton. He doesn't show up for his ride in the fifth race on the card; he is later found dead among the rows of outside broadcast TV vans, with three bullets in his chest.

Wall, Superintendent (*In the Frame* 1976)

Wall, of **Shropshire** police, is a colleague of **Inspector Frost**. He tells **Charles Todd** that **Donald Stuart** has been informed by the police that they are satisfied he had nothing to do with his wife **Regina Stuart**'s death.

Wallis, Mr. (*Bonecrack* 1971)

Wallis is a young deputy sales manager of an electrical firm which **Neil Griffon** had advised on reorganization. He meets Neil to demonstrate how to install a security system at his father's stables. He tells Neil he owes his elevated position in the firm to Neil's reorganization.

Wally (*For Kicks* 1965)

Wally is head lad at **Inskip's** racing stable. He is shocked at **Daniel Roke**'s casual way of speaking to Inskip and **Lord October**. He tells Daniel that if he's a communist he can clear off.

Walsh, Carl (*Dead Heat* 2007)

Walsh is **Max Moreton**'s assistant chef at **The Hay Net** restaurant, **Newmarket**. He is separated from his wife, and lives alone in Kentford, near Newmarket. He doesn't like the fact that Max is ten years younger than him, and is generally unsympathetic with Max's problems. Walsh helps Max prepare dinner for guests at **Newmarket racecourse** on Two Thousand Guineas day. He is uninjured when a bomb explodes in the grandstand boxes while the race is being run. He lets Max stay for a couple of nights after Max's cottage is burnt down. After Max opens a new restaurant in London, he puts Walsh in charge of The Hay Net.

Walters, Brian and June (*Dead Heat* 2007)

Brian Walters is an ex–steeplechase jockey and a recently-retired sales manager for Tattersalls horse sales company. He and his wife June are guests of **Delafield Industries Inc.** at **Newmarket racecourse** on Two Thousand Guineas day. They are killed when a bomb explodes in the grandstand boxes.

Wanderlust (*Enquiry* 1969)

Wanderlust is a steeplechaser trained by **Dexter Cranfield**. At the enquiry at which **Kelly Hughes** and Cranfield are warned off, a videotape is shown of **Wanderlust** winning a race at **Reading**. The tape should have been of **Squelsh**, who is in the same ownership. Unlike Squelsh, Wanderlust responds well to vigorous riding.

Wangen, Sven (*Slay-Ride* 1973)

Wangen, the owner of Øvrevoll racecourse, is overweight, prematurely balding and unpleasant. According to **Eric**, **David Cleveland**'s driver, Wangen's late father had been a collaborator during the Second World War and had made a lot of money with the Nazis' help.

Bob Sherman had ridden a winner for Wangen on the day he disappeared. David is sufficiently unimpressed with Wangen to consider him capable of complicity in Sherman's disappearance.

Ward, Alexandra (*High Stakes* 1975)

Alexandra, known as "Allie" and in her early twenties, is a pretty American girl from Westchester, near New York. She works as a caterer for weddings and parties, and is staying with her sister in London. By chance, she meets **Steven Scott** and **Charlie Canterfield** after she walks out on an unsatisfactory date. She accepts their offer of a loan for her taxi fare home. She sends the money back and accepts Steven's subsequent invitation to dinner.

Allie goes with Steven to **Newmarket** to see his racehorses. Returning to Steven's apartment in London, she is impressed to find that he is the inventor of the *Rola t*oys which she had played with as a child. She kisses Steven goodnight in a friendly manner, without romantic implications.

Allie returns to the USA. Jokingly, in answer to Steven's question by letter as to when she'd be free for dinner, she replies: January 5th, in **Miami**. When Steven turns up there she is pleased. She takes Steven to a secluded beach in the Florida Keys for a swim and a picnic. There she allows herself to be persuaded to make love; she is a little apprehensive, since her only previous experience, at college, had been less than satisfactory. This time, though, it's a memorable experience.

Allie flies to England to help with Steven's sting against **Jody Leeds** and **Ganser Mays**. As a token of his gratitude, Steven gives Allie a quarter share in **Energise**.

Ward, Cassidy Lovelace (*Field of 13* 1998: "Song for Mona")

Cassidy, a glamorous American country-and-western singing star, is married to Olympic rider **Oliver Bolingbroke**. She is appalled by the rudeness of **Joanie Vine** to her mother, **Mona Watkins**, who is groom to Oliver's show jumpers. When Mona dies, Cassidy writes and records a song in her memory.

Ward, James (*Dead Heat* 2007)

Ward is a Health and Safety Inspector with **Cambridgeshire** County Council. He inspects the kitchen at **The Hay Net** restaurant in **Newmarket**.

He allows the restaurant to reopen after the kitchen was sealed following a food poisoning incident at **Newmarket racecourse**.

Warwick racecourse

Warwick racecourse, in the West Midlands, is a mundane jumping track with little to set the heart racing. It does, however, stage annually the Crudwell Cup, named for a high-class steeplechaser of the 1950's whose regular jockey was Dick Francis.

(*Field of 13* 1998: "**Dead on Red**"): At Warwick, trainer "**Gypsy Joe**" Smith sacks stable jockey **Davey Rockman**, whose riding has deteriorated.

The Watch (*Trial Run* 1978)

Malcolm Herrick is Moscow correspondent of *The Watch*, a national daily newspaper.

Watcherley, Bob and Maggie (*Banker* 1982)

The Watcherleys are a husband and wife team who run a hospital for sick horses on land next to **Oliver Knowles'** stud farm in **Hertfordshire**. Though untidy and rather disorganized, the hospital had prospered until **Calder Jackson's** popularity increased and he took much of their business. When Knowles buys **Sandcastle** he rents the Watcherleys' place and employs them to look after any mares which are ill or vulnerable.

Waterman, Oliver (*Trial Run* 1978)

Waterman is the cultural attaché at the British Embassy, Moscow. He is tall and grey, with a patrician air. He is not overly impressed by the brouhaha over **Johnnie Farringford**. He offers **Randall Drew** telex facilities while in Moscow.

Watermead, Ed (*Driving Force* 1992)

Ed, the sixteen-year-old son of **Michael** and **Maudie Watermead**, is a bit dim, according to **Freddie Croft**. At his father's lunch party, Ed tells people that **Jericho Rich** had wanted sex with his sister, **Tessa Watermead**. When she refused, Rich had removed his horses from Watermead's stables.

Watermead, Maudie (*Driving Force* 1992)

Maudie is the wife of racehorse trainer **Michael Watermead**. She is attractive and fun to be with. She firmly resists **Freddie Croft's** half-serious attempts at seduction.

Watermead, Michael (*Driving Force* 1992)

Watermead is a flat trainer with a sixty box yard in **Pixhill, Hampshire**. Tall, blond and middle-aged, he is seemingly indecisive but is successful and has an affinity with horses. He comes from an aristocratic background. He is on good terms with **Freddie Croft**; Freddie's firm had transported nine of owner **Jericho Rich**'s two-year-olds to **Newmarket** after Rich removes them from Watermead's yard.

Watermead is irritated when Freddie's horse van bringing two-year-olds from France is delayed, and more so when **Lewis**, the driver, arrives back with flu and can't drive Watermead's horses to **Doncaster** races. He is angry with Freddie and doesn't want to believe him when Freddie tells him what his daughter, **Tessa Watermead**, has been up to.

Watermead, Tessa (*Driving Force* 1992)

Tessa is the seventeen-year-old daughter of **Michael** and **Maudie Watermead**. She is a bit of a madam, and dissatisfied with her privileged lot; according to local policeman **Sandy Smith**, Tessa is close to being out of control. At her father's lunch party, she flirts with **Benjy Usher**. She had refused to have sex with owner **Jericho Rich**, who had taken his horses away from Watermead as a result. Subsequently she tells **Freddie Croft** what she had done in response to Rich's actions.

Watkins, Billy (*Flying Finish* 1966)

Nineteen-year-old Billy Watkins works for **Yardman** Transport, a firm transporting horses overseas. He is of slight build, but his cold eyes are a better indication than his physique of the menace he exudes, especially towards new employee **Lord Henry Gray**. Watkins is immediately antagonistic and deliberately unhelpful during trips abroad, making Henry's work as difficult as he can. During a delay over paperwork in France Watkins goes drinking; when Henry tells him the plane is ready to leave, Watkins pours his beer over Henry's feet. On the trip home he starts a fight with Henry, and is surprised to find that Henry is handy with his fists. After taking a beating Watkins locks himself in the toilet and refuses to help with the unloading of the horses.

On a flight to New York Watkins deliberately drops a metal box onto Henry's fingers. On the return flight a thoroughbred colt goes berserk in mid-air; Watkins suddenly produces a pistol and is about to shoot the horse, seemingly unaware of the danger of using a gun in an aircraft. Henry and the co-pilot urgently talk Watkins out of it, and Henry kills the colt with a knife.

Realizing that Henry is gathering evidence of Yardman's activities, Watkins raises significantly the level of violence. This proves to be a costly mistake.

Watkins, Mona (*Field of 13* 1998: "Song for Mona")

Sixty-year-old Mona Watkins, a Welsh stable employee, has a rough exterior but a heart of gold. She has a snobbish daughter, **Joanie Vine**, who is ashamed of her. She works in a riding school until it is burned to the ground; Mona acts heroically to save the ponies. She is offered a job by Olympic rider **Oliver Bolingbroke** and his American wife, singer **Cassidy Lovelace Ward**. An excellent groom, Mona soon becomes a valued member of the family. When her employers are away in America Mona becomes ill with a bad dose of flu. Joanie, though aware of her mother's illness, makes no effort to visit Mona who, neglecting to eat or drink, dies of kidney failure. After her death Oliver finds newspaper cuttings among her belongings which shed light on a family secret. The Bolingbrokes ensure that Mona's goodness is not forgotten.

Watson, Bob (*Longshot* 1990)

Watson, who is head lad to racehorse trainer **Tremayne Vickers**, is highly rated by his employer. He is a passenger in the jeep driven by **Mackie Vickers** which skids into a water-filled ditch. He is helped out of the jeep by **John Kendall**.

Watson, Ingrid (*Longshot* 1990)

Ingrid is the wife of **Bob Watson, Tremayne Vickers**' head lad. She is in the jeep which ends up in a ditch after skidding on an icy road. She is extremely cold, so **John Kendall** gets **Fiona Goodhaven** to take Ingrid's wet clothes off and lends her dry clothes. Lacking in self-confidence, Ingrid gives Tremayne Vickers the impression that she's scared of him.

Watts, Owen (*Break In* 1985)

Watts is an employee of the *Daily Flag* newspaper. He attaches an electronic bugging device to the telephone wires on the roof of **Bobby Allar-**

deck's house. He is surprised by **Kit Fielding** and Bobby one night when he is either removing the bug or changing its battery. He is badly beaten by Bobby, but manages to escape, leaving behind his jacket with his ID in it.

Wayfield, Greg (*Comeback* 1991)

Singer Greg Wayfield has been married for eighteen months to **Vicky Larch**. A middle-aged American, Wayfield sings at the **Diving Pelican** restaurant in **Miami**. He had trained as an opera singer, but had made his career in banking and sings semi-professionally. Attacked and robbed outside the restaurant, Wayfield is knocked unconscious but otherwise not badly hurt. He travels to **Gloucestershire** with Vicky and **Peter Darwin** to attend the wedding of Vicky's daughter, **Belinda Larch**.

Wayne, Noel (*Odds Against* 1965)

Wayne is **Sid Halley**'s accountant. He advises Sid on his purchase of a partnership in **Hunt Radnor Associates**. Asked by Sid to look at the photographs of **Howard Kraye**'s papers, Wayne eventually realizes the significance of Kraye's five bank accounts.

Weatherbys

Weatherbys is racing's administrative body. Its offices are in Wellingborough, **Northamptonshire**. Weatherbys began in 1770 as a family partnership; now it is a limited company, owned by the Weatherby family. Amongst other services Weatherbys maintains the General Stud Book, provides banking and financial services, arranges bloodstock insurance and publishes The Racing Calendar, Programme Book and European Pattern Book.

10 lb. Penalty (1997): **Benedict Juliard** gets a job in the insurance department at Weatherbys after he graduates from **Exeter** University.

Welfram, Derry (*The Edge* 1988)

Welfram is a common or garden thug. He dies, apparently of natural causes, at **York** races. He was an associate of **Julius Apollo Filmer**.

Welkom, South Africa

In South Africa's Free State, Welkom has grown over the last sixty years into the State's second largest town, after the discovery of gold on a local farm. It is the centre of the country's gold mining industry.

Smokescreen (1972): Film actor **Edward Lincoln** visits a gold mine at Welkom with **Danilo**

Cavesey, **Evan Pentelow** and others. Four thousand feet underground, Edward becomes separated from his group and is knocked unconscious by an unknown assailant.

Weller, Sharon (*The Danger* 1983)

Sharon is a seven-year-old girl who is on holiday in **West Wittering, Sussex**. While playing on the beach, she is given a note by one of **Dominic Nerrity**'s kidnappers to deliver to his mother, **Miranda Nerrity**.

Wells, Jackson (*Wild Horses* 1994)

Ex-**Newmarket** trainer Jackson Wells now lives near **Oxford**. He is middle-aged but still young-looking, and is good-natured. Twenty-six years previously Wells was suspected of murdering his wife, Sonia. He was never charged, but his training business folded as a result of the rumors. **Thomas Lyon**'s film, based on the unsolved crime, does not concern Wells unduly; he has been re-married for twenty-three years and has consigned the tragic incident to the past. Nowadays he makes a living by growing willows on his farm for making cricket bats.

When Wells says he doesn't know why Sonia died, Thomas is skeptical. Later, when tackled by Thomas, who by now has a good idea what happened to Sonia, Wells confirms Thomas's suspicions.

Wells, Jason (*Second Wind* 1999)

Wells is a teenage boy who works in a photographer's shop near Paddington station in London. Despite his unpromising appearance, he proves to be good at his job; he develops the negatives from the camera that **Unwin** had rescued from **Trox Island** on **Perry Stuart**'s behalf. Somewhat implausibly, Perry credits Wells' high standards of customer service as being the catalyst for restoring Perry's own feelings of self-worth which had lain dormant while he was ill.

Wells, Lucy (*Wild Horses* 1994)

Lucy is the teenage daughter of **Jackson Wells**. She is blonde, intelligent and possessed of a cheerful disposition like her father. She eagerly accepts Thomas's offer for her and her family to be extras in his film, *Unstable Times*. She refuses to have dinner with Thomas unaccompanied. She works for Thomas for two weeks, cataloguing **Valentine Clark**'s books; inside one she finds some old clippings about the death of her father's first wife,

Sonia. When Thomas offers her a holiday in California after the film is completed, Lucy says yes.

Wells, Mr. (*Risk* 1977)

Wells is a new client of accountant and amateur jockey **Roland Britten**. He has been ruined financially by a fraudulent advisor; having heard of Roland's reputation, Wells has engaged him to sort out the mess. In a fragile state of mind, Wells is reluctant to let Roland get away to ride in the **Cheltenham** Gold Cup.

While Roland is away Wells calls his office to say that one of his creditors is applying to have him made bankrupt, and demands some action from Roland. When, subsequently, Wells is about to be prosecuted for writing a dud check, Roland persuades the recipient of the check not to press charges. When Wells complains that he is penniless, Roland suspects he is selling his assets clandestinely to avoid the bailiffs taking them.

Wells, Mrs. (*10 lb. Penalty* 1997)

Mrs. Wells was **Benedict Juliard**'s landlady while he worked at **Sir Vivian Durridge**'s racing stable.

Wells, Oliver (*Decider* 1993)

Oliver Wells is Clerk of the Course at **Stratton Park racecourse**. With racecourse manager **Roger Gardner**, goes to see **Lee Morris** to ask him to use his voting shares to vote against those of the late **Lord William Stratton**'s heirs who want to sell the course for building land. Like Gardner, Wells is worried about finding alternative employment. He deals competently with the emergency services after the racecourse stands are badly damaged in an explosion. He loses his temper when stopped at the racecourse gates by animal rights protesters, revealing a less pleasant side to his outwardly civilized exterior.

Wells, Ridley (*Wild Horses* 1994)

Ridley is the brother of **Jackson Wells**; he lives in **Newmarket**, where he makes a living breaking in horses and performing other equine services for local trainers. According to **Thomas Lyon**, Ridley is less interesting and intelligent than his brother. At **Huntingdon racecourse**, where Thomas is shooting a scene for his film, Wells asks O'Hara, the producer, for a job; when O'Hara says no, Wells is unhappy about it.

Thomas offers Wells a morning's work on the film, which Wells accepts. Thomas asks him to re-construct the attack, on Newmarket Heath, on **Nash Rourke**'s stand-in. Wells is shocked to be asked, but does it, with Thomas acting as Rourke's stand-in.

Wells, Tom (*Flying Finish* 1966)

Tom Wells, formerly of the Royal Air Force, is amicable and unfussy. He owns and runs a small air charter firm based on the airfield in **Lincolnshire** where **Lord Henry Gray** flies from. He enlists Henry to work for him when he is a pilot short. He offers Henry a full-time job, which Henry turns down. After winning a lucrative contract ferrying businessmen around Europe, Wells again tries to persuade Henry to work for him. At dawn one day, Wells is amazed to be woken by a DC4 landing on his airstrip, accompanied by a U.S. fighter plane circling above.

Welwyn Garden City, Hertfordshire

Welwyn Garden city is a town in **Hertfordshire**, a county in the south-east of England. The town was established in the 1920's to ease the overcrowded areas of London. One of England's best examples of a new town, Welwyn Garden City's houses and businesses are laid out along tree-lined avenues, and the town has a neo–Georgian centre.

Twice Shy (1981): **Jonathan Derry** goes to Welwyn Garden City to offer computer tapes containing a horserace betting system to bingo hall owner **Harry Gilbert**.

Wembley, London

Wembley is a suburb of north London, in the London Borough of Brent. It is the home of the English national football stadium which has recently been rebuilt at enormous cost and has enhanced the profits of a phalanx of litigation lawyers.

Under Orders (2006): Sid Halley calls at the offices of **Make A Wager Ltd.**, which are located in Wembley.

Wenkins, Clifford (*Smokescreen* 1972)

Wenkins is the distribution manager for Worldic Cinemas in South Africa. He is around forty years old, nervous and voluble, and has reached the limit of his career. He arranges for the media to be at Johannesburg airport to meet **Edward Lincoln**, despite Edward's request for no publicity. At a press conference, Wenkins hands Edward a microphone to do an interview. The microphone, which is faulty, electrocutes not Edward but **Katya**, the interviewer. When he sees what has happened Wenkins visibly blanches.

At **Germiston** races Wenkins tells Edward that Worldic have arranged various personal appearances. When Edward firmly refuses to cooperate Wenkins panics, saying that Worldic might fire him; Edward, however, won't budge. Soon afterwards Wenkins is drowned in what at first appears to be a boating accident. Later, however, foul play is strongly suspected.

Wessex, Duke of (*Rat Race* 1970)

The Duke of Wessex is generous and good-natured but lacking in brain power. He acts as an insurance underwriter with Lloyds of London. The Duke owns **Rudiments**, but is not present at **Haydock Park** when the horse is third after getting boxed in. However, he sees Rudiments win at **Redcar**. He derives great pleasure from watching his horses. He asks if he can sit next to **Matt Shore** on the flight back to **Cambridge**, and shows a childlike interest in how the instruments work. He tells Matt proudly that his young nephew **Matthew** is his heir.

After he is introduced to **Charles Carthy-Todd** by his friend **Major Tydeman**, the Duke agrees to sponsor the Racegoers Accident Fund insurance scheme, and guarantees the compensation payments to the tune of £100,000. The Duke introduces Matt to Carthy-Todd at the Accident Fund's office in Warwick.

Owing to Matt's quick thinking, the Duke narrowly averts death at **Warwick racecourse**. Grateful to Matt, he responds positively to **Colin Ross's** suggestion that he set Matt up in an air-taxi business.

West, Charlie (*Enquiry* 1969)

Jump jockey Charlie West is a young and talented rider but is lacking in self-discipline. He rode in the Lemonfizz Crystal Cup at **Oxford**. Called as a witness at the enquiry into the race, West says that during the race **Kelly Hughes** had said that he wasn't trying to win, and claims that Kelly often didn't try.

When he sees Kelly at his front door, West jumps out of his living-room window and runs away. Unable to escape when Kelly returns later that day, West is forced to admit that he had lied at the enquiry. He is frightened and miserable when Kelly says he'll see to it that he loses his license to ride.

West, Mrs. (*Enquiry* 1969)

Mrs. West is the teenage wife of jump jockey **Charlie West**. She tries unsuccessfully to prevent Kelly from confronting her husband.

West, Norman (*Hot Money* 1987)

Norman West is an elderly private detective hired by **Malcolm Pembroke** to account for the whereabouts of all his family on the two days when attempts were made on his life. He was previously employed, twenty-eight years before, by **Joyce Pembroke**, to gather evidence of Malcolm's infidelity. Of unprepossessing appearance, West has an incongruous upper-middle class accent.

In his progress report, West tells Malcolm that he has met with no success in checking alibis, since the family has been uncooperative. **Ian Pembroke** is not impressed with West, thinking him too old. When Ian asks him to visit all the family again to establish their alibis, West feels it would be unproductive and should be left to the police.

West Sussex racecourse

West Sussex is a fictional racecourse, no doubt modeled on **Fontwell Park**, which is in West Sussex.

Dead Cert (1962): **Alan York** finds fellow-jockey **Joe Nantwich** dying of a knife wound behind the Tote building at West Sussex racecourse.

West Wittering, Sussex

West Wittering is a seaside village near Chichester in the county of **Sussex** on the south coast of England.

The Danger (1983): A child, **Dominic Nerrity**, is kidnapped while playing on the beach at West Wittering. He is the son of the owner of **Epsom** Derby winner **Ordinand**.

Westering, Sir Ivan George (*To the Hilt* 1996)

Sir Ivan Westering is a distinguished member of the **Jockey Club** and the stepfather of **Alexander Kinloch**. He is good-hearted and fair, but does not like Alex's bohemian lifestyle. Sir Ivan had inherited his baronetcy from a cousin and the family business, the **King Alfred Brewery**, from his father. He suffers a heart attack while clinically depressed owing to the imminent bankruptcy of the brewery. He has resigned himself to dying and seems unwilling to fight on. He asks Alex to hide **Golden Malt**, a racehorse owned by the brewery, so that the creditors won't get their hands on it.

He gives Alex power of attorney to administer his affairs and appoints him Alternate Director of the brewery despite opposition from his daughter **Patsy Benchmark** and solicitor **Oliver Grantchester**.

Sir Ivan gives the King Alfred Cup to **Robert, Earl of Kinloch**, to pass on to Alex for safekeeping. His depression deepens and he suffers from mood swings. After a second heart attack Sir Ivan dies. In a codicil to his will Sir Ivan leaves his horses to Alex's estranged wife, **Emily Cox**, and the King Alfred Cup to the Earl of Kinloch; he appoints Alex as an executor of the will.

Westering, Lady Vivienne (*To the Hilt* 1996)

Lady Vivienne is the mother of **Alexander Kinloch** and wife of **Sir Ivan Westering**. She lives near Regent's Park, London. She had lost her first husband, Alex's father, in a shooting accident; according to Alex, she showed no outward grief, owing to her rigid self-control. She calls Alex to tell him that Sir Ivan has had a heart attack; she is concerned that he is clinically depressed. She is appreciative of Alex's help in sorting out the **King Alfred Brewery**'s affairs. When Sir Ivan dies after a second heart attack, she is devastated.

Westerland, Sir William (*Field of 13* 1998: "The Day of the Losers")

Sir William Westerland is the Senior Steward of the **Jockey Club**. He is at **Aintree racecourse** on Grand National day, when stolen bank notes are used to buy a Tote ticket on the race, Westerland is asked by the local police chief to sanction the fixing of the race so that the man who placed the bet can be arrested when he collects his winnings. After consulting with his fellow stewards, Westerland rejects the request on both practical and moral grounds.

Wexford, Ivor (*In the Frame* 1976)

Wexford is the manager of the **Yarra River Fine Arts** gallery, Melbourne. He detains **Charles Todd** in the gallery and questions him after he is recognized by **Mr. Greene** and the young artist who had thrown turpentine in **Jik Cassavetes'** eyes. Incredibly, Wexford accepts Charles's lame explanation that his being there is a coincidence, and lets him go.

In Wellington, New Zealand, Wexford is deliberately alerted by Charles to the fact that he, Jik and **Sarah Cassavetes** are in town. Wexford finds out where they are staying and leaves a message for Charles with the hotel receptionist, saying that Jik and Sarah are waiting downstairs in the car. Wexford is being economical with the truth.

Whip Hand (1979)

Trainer's wife **Rosemary Caspar** asks investigator **Sid Halley**, without her husband's knowledge, to guard outstanding three-year-old colt **Tri-Nitro** before the running of the Two Thousand Guineas at **Newmarket**. In the past other top two-year-olds of theirs had failed miserably as three-year-olds, and she doesn't want the same thing to happen to Tri-Nitro.

Sid's ex–father-in-law, **Charles Roland**, asks him to come to his house for the weekend to speak to his ex-wife, **Jenny Halley**. She has become involved with a fraudster running a mail-order business selling expensive wax polish, ostensibly for charity. Sid agrees with reluctance, as he and Jenny don't get on. At **Kempton Park** races **Lord Friarly**, for whom Sid used to ride, asks him to investigate some racehorse-owning syndicates whose horses don't run to form; Lord Friarly is an owner in one of the syndicates.

Francis's biographer Graham Lord tells us that *Whip Hand* was a result of the friendship that developed between Dick and Mary Francis and actor Mike Gwilym, who had played Sid Halley in a television adaptation of *Odds Against*. Whatever Francis's motivation was for re-inventing Halley fourteen years after his first appearance, it was undoubtedly a master stroke. In Sid Halley Francis had a protagonist whose character could be developed still further and who, by virtue of his strengths and weaknesses, had the ability to drive the plot forward.

Francis skillfully uses the conflicting elements in Sid Halley's complex make-up to weave together three discrete storylines—the dubious syndicates, the under-performing Classic colts, and the wax polish fraud, each strand revealing different facets of his character. In the first, Sid's skills at crime detection are seen in his tenacity, his investigative ability and his insight into how the criminal mind works. Through his involvement with Tri-Nitro, Sid is forced to overcome pain and fear, and to confront his self-loathing for having buckled before the horror of a villain's threat to blow his hand off. By contrast, Sid's investigation of fraudster **Nicholas Ashe** serves a different purpose within the structure of the novel. Sid is once more in conflict with ex-wife Jenny, who resents his interference and refuses to cooperate. Eventually, though, Sid is able to negotiate, if not a cessation of hostilities, then at least a tenuous truce with Jenny.

In *Whip Hand* we see Francis in commanding form. This is a crime novel that measures up to the best of the genre, and it won two prestigious awards: the Crime Writers' Association's Gold Dagger Award and the Mystery Writers of America's Edgar Allen Poe Award.

White, Lady (*Reflex* 1980)

The wife of **Lord White**, Lady White bravely tries to maintain her dignity while tongues wag behind her back about her husband's infatuation with **Dana den Relgan**. She is a friend of **Marie Millace**, in whom she confides her despair at his behavior. She is willing to forgive her husband when he tells her his affair is over, accepting that he is having a mid-life crisis.

White, Lord (*Reflex* 1980)

Nicknamed "Driven Snow," Lord White is an influential member of the **Jockey Club**; he is held in great respect, and is a natural leader of men. He shows naivety, however, in sponsoring **Ivor den Relgan** for election to the Jockey Club, owing to his infatuation with **Dana den Relgan**. At **Kempton Park** races he flirts with Dana, and continues to do so even more openly at **Ascot**. Flirtation turns into an affair, and White promotes Ivor den Relgan to head an important committee to expedite the appointment of paid stewards.

When **Philip Nore** reveals to White how he has been duped, White cancels den Relgan's committee and demands his resignation from the Jockey Club. White admits his unfaithfulness and apologizes to his wife, confident that that will be the end of the matter.

White Waltham airfield, North London

White Waltham is one of Britain's oldest airfields. Situated close to the London Heathrow Central Zone, White Waltham was bought in 1928 by the De Havilland family and run as a flying school. During the Second World War it was the headquarters of the Air Transport Auxiliary. Until recently the home of Fairey aviation, White Waltham has been used by the West London Aero Club for almost sixty years. It is one of the few remaining grass airfields.

Rat Race (1970): Air taxi pilot **Matt Shore** picks up four passengers at White Waltham airfield and flies them to **Haydock Park** races.

Whitworth, Louisa (*Dead Heat* 2007)

Nineteen-year-old Louisa Whitworth is one of chef **Max Moreton**'s catering staff. She is killed when a bomb explodes in the grandstand boxes at **Newmarket racecourse**.

Wichelsea, Ray (*Field of 13* 1998: "Corkscrew")

Wichelsea is the owner of a South Carolina bloodstock agency. He employs salesman **Sandy Nutbridge** on commission. When Nutbridge is arrested on tax and drug charges, Wichelsea stands part of Nutbridge's $100,000 bail. Eventually the charges are dropped and Wichelsea, unlike the other guarantors, receives his money back from the U.S. District Clerk. Months later Nutbridge is re-arrested, tried on other minor charges and spends a short time in jail. Wichelsea, however, valuing Nutbridge's ability as a salesman, re-employs him.

Wickens, Janey (*Proof* 1984)

Recently married to **Tom Wickens**, Janey is a waitress at the end-of-season party at trainer **Jack Hawthorn**'s stables. She is killed when a horse van crashes into the marquee.

Wickens, Tom (*Proof* 1984)

Stable lad Tom Wickens works for trainer **Jack Hawthorn**. He is married to **Janey Wickens**, who is killed by the runaway horse van at Hawthorn's owners' party. Unaware of her death, Wickens asks **Tony Beach** if he had seen Janey while he was rescuing guests. He is devastated when he learns she is dead, and is comforted by **Flora Hawthorn**.

Wilcox, Tricksy (*Field of 13* 1998: "The Raid at Kingdom Hill")

Petty criminal Tricksy Wilcox phones the racecourse at **Kingdom Hill** during a race meeting and claims that he has planted a bomb in the stands. When the stands have been evacuated Wilcox goes around the bars, robbing the tills. However, he is spotted and arrested by the police.

Wild Horses (1994)

An old man is dying, blind and confused. **Valentine Clark**, former **Newmarket** farrier and journalist, mistakes his young friend **Thomas Lyon** for a priest and begs for absolution for killing "the

Cornish boy." Thomas is in Newmarket to direct a horse racing film based on a tragedy that had occurred in the racing world a quarter of a century before but had never been satisfactorily resolved. Sonia Wells, the young wife of trainer **Jackson Wells**, had been found dead, in an apparent suicide.

Thomas soon realizes that there are individuals determined to ensure that the veil of secrecy that has concealed the circumstances of Sonia's death for so many years remains undisturbed. But despite taking seriously the threats to his life, Thomas perseveres with the film and unflinchingly pursues the truth.

Sexual deviation, which is not a subject normally associated with a Dick Francis novel, plays its part in *Wild Horses*. It is likely that the research on this was conducted by Mary Francis, who would have brought a disinterested and academic rigor to the task. The reader is also regaled with a plethora—some would say a surfeit—of detail about film-making, the result, says Francis's biographer Graham Lord, of Mary's fascination with the subject.

As a character Thomas displays a credible human mixture of youthful ambition, impulsive generosity and impetuosity. The resolution of the plot, however, depends heavily on Thomas's inspired guesswork about what had happened twenty-five years before, and on those involved in Sonia's death conveniently falling for his stratagems to discover the truth. This, combined with the weakness of the villain and several of the minor characters, resulted in *Wild Horses* receiving a lukewarm reception from the critics.

Wilfred (*Proof* 1984)

Wilfred is the hen-pecked husband of **Mrs. Alexis**, landlady of the Peverill Arms, near **Reading**. He is ordered to use bellows to get the pub's fire going. After Mrs. Alexis fires a shotgun up the chimney, soot drops on Wilfred's head.

Wilfred (*To the Hilt* 1996)

Wilfred, a male nurse, looks after **Sir Ivan Westering** after his heart attack. **Lady Westering** considers Wilfred to be too deferential. He acts as a witness when Sir Ivan adds a codicil to his will. He doesn't think that **Alex Kinloch** values sufficiently what he, Wilfred, has done for Sir Ivan.

Wilkerson, Betty-Ann (*Blood Sport* 1967)

Betty-Ann, the wife of **Quintus L. Wilkerson**, is staying with her husband at **Matt** and **Yola**

Clive's Wyoming dude ranch. Unbeknown to Quintus, Betty-Ann begins to show more than a friendly interest in **Gene Hawkins**.

Wilkerson, Mickey (*Blood Sport* 1967)

Mickey is the son of **Quintus** and **Betty Ann Wilkerson**. After **Gene Hawkins** escapes from his burning cabin at **Matt** and **Yola Clive's** dude ranch Mickey, together with his sister **Samantha Wilkerson**, unknowingly saves Gene from further confrontation with Yola by walking with him to his car.

Wilkerson, Quintus L., III (*Blood Sport* 1967)

Wilkerson is staying with his family at **Matt** and **Yola Clive's** dude ranch in Wyoming. He rides out with **Gene Hawkins**, and explains how the horses are turned out on the hills to graze every night and herded down in the morning.

Wilkerson, Samantha (*Blood Sport* 1967)

Samantha is the daughter of **Quintus** and **Betty-Ann Wilkerson**. With her brother, **Mickey Wilkerson**, she walks with **Gene Hawkins** to his car after he escapes from his burning cabin.

Wilkins, Ted (*Odds Against* 1965)

Wilkins is the foreman at **Seabury racecourse**. He gives **Sid Halley** information about the tanker spillage of chemicals on the track.

Wilkinson, Mr. and Mrs. (*Trial Run* 1978)

The Wilkinsons are British tourists who are staying at the same hotel in Moscow as **Randall Drew**. At dinner they share a table with Randall, who gets the impression that Mr. Wilkerson would rather be at home watching football on TV with a can of beer in his hand.

Will (*Second Wind* 1999)

Will, an American meteorologist, is a friend of **Perry Stuart**. He works at the **Miami Hurricane Center**. He arranges for Perry to meet **Unwin**, a pilot with knowledge of **Trox Island**.

Williams, Absalom Elvis da Vinci (*Field of 13* 1998: "Collision Course")

Williams, known as Bill, is the editor of the *Cotswold Voice* newspaper. Aged twenty-nine, he was educated at a state school and **Cambridge**. He is solitary by nature and fiery-tempered. Given notice of dismissal by the new owners of the newspaper, Williams sends out his CV to potential employers. Before he leaves the *Voice* he takes a week's holiday, telling his racing reporter to follow up a story about **Denis Kinser,** who is selling shares in syndicated horses which he intends to train himself.

Williams hires a punt on the upper Thames and steers it down to **Oxford,** where he meets the owners of a newspaper group at a riverside restaurant to discuss possible employment. His experiences at the restaurant have an unforeseen impact on his future.

Williams, Clarissa (*Straight* 1989)

Clarissa Williams, also known as **Lady Knightwood,** is the wife of **Lord Henry Knightwood,** and for four years was **Greville Franklin's** lover. Around forty years old, she is attractive, sophisticated and capable. Clarissa married Lord Knightwood when she was eighteen and has two grown-up children. She phones Greville's office to speak to him; when she is told he has died in an accident, she rings off without replying. She goes to Greville's house to retrieve love letters; finding **Derek Franklin** there, she mistakes him for a burglar and attacks him with a cosh given to her by Greville to protect herself.

Clarissa meets Derek at **York** races when she is with her husband. She tells him that she finds comfort in being near him, as he is Greville's brother. They have dinner and go back to Greville's flat where they make love.

The following day, as she is going into Greville's flat to meet Derek, she finds him in serious danger. She acts quickly and decisively to save his life. Then, taking Derek's advice, she disappears before the police arrive.

Williams, Jason (*Banker* 1982)

Jason Williams, also known as Shane, Brett, Clint and Dean, works for **Calder Jackson.** When **Tim Ekaterin** meets Jackson for dinner in London, Jackson tells him that Jason no longer works for him. Williams, it later transpires, has a lot of question to answer, and the police are keen to interview him. He is caught because of his physical similarity to **Ricky Barnet,** whose photo Tim and **Ursula Young** had circulated to trainers. He is arrested in Malton, North **Yorkshire.**

Willis, Sandy (*Forfeit* 1968)

Sandy Willis is a groom who looks after **Zig Zag** at **Norton Fox's** yard in **Berkshire.** She is not over-endowed with brains but, according to Fox, her horses are always fit and healthy. She is thrilled to have her photo taken for **James Tyrone's** magazine article.

Wilson, Detective Chief Superintendent (*Proof* 1984)

D.C.S. Wilson is the first police officer on the scene after eight people are killed by a runaway horse van at **Jack Hawthorn's** owners' party. He is close to retirement; his movements are slow and deliberate, and his demeanor professionally unemotional. He questions **Tony Beach** about the identity of the victims. Later, he goes to see Tony at his shop and asks him if he saw anyone near the horse van before it rolled down the hill. On another occasion, he asks Tony to describe **Paul Young.** He receives a phone call from Tony to tell him where to find Young.

Wilson, Jud (*For Kicks* 1965)

Jud Wilson is traveling head lad at **Hedley Humber's** racing stable. He helps to terrify the horses which are being prepared to win future races.

Wiltshire, England

Wiltshire is a rural county situated to the west of London. It has vast areas of windswept chalk and limestone downland, as well as charming river valleys. Stonehenge, England's most famous prehistoric monument, is on Wiltshire's Salisbury plain. Swindon is Wiltshire's largest town.

Driving Force (1992): **Freddie Croft** moves **Marigold English's** racehorses from her stables on the Wiltshire downs to a new yard in **Pixhill, Hampshire.**

Decider (1993): **Stratton Park racecourse** is situated in north-east Wiltshire. **Perdita Faulds,** a shareholder in the racecourse, runs a hairdressing salon in Swindon, Wiltshire.

To the Hilt (1996): **Alex Kinloch** rides chaser **Golden Malt** along the **Ridgeway** to a livery yard at Foxhill, Wiltshire.

Wincanton racecourse

Wincanton is a jumping track in rural **Somerset,** a county in south-west England. It is a welcoming and well-run racecourse which attracts good horses to its feature races, especially those run in the weeks prior to the **Cheltenham** Festival in March. The Kingwell Pattern Hurdle is an established trial for Cheltenham's Champion Hurdle, and Wincanton's testing fences present a serious challenge to good steeplechasers.

10 lb. Penalty (1997): Amateur jockey **Benedict Juliard** rides his horse **Sarah's Future** to win at Wincanton.

Winchester racecourse

Winchester is a fictional racecourse in the county of **Hampshire**. The town has a cathedral dating back to the 12th century and a famous boarding school for boys, founded in 1382.

Field of 13 (1998): "Haig's Death": Racecourse judge **Christopher Haig** suffers a heart attack and dies whilst judging the finish of a race at Winchester.

Windsor racecourse

A few miles west of London, Windsor hosts summer evening Flat meetings which are very popular with the metropolis's racing public. Jump racing was discontinued in 1998. The most pleasant way to arrive is by Thames river bus, enjoying the view of Windsor Castle as the ferry docks at the racecourse jetty. For races longer than a mile the course is a figure of eight, and viewing is restricted to the last two furlongs. To compensate, the tree-lined parade ring, bedecked with flowers, is a delight.

Bolt (1986): **Danielle de Brescou** goes to Windsor races with jockey **Kit Fielding**, who is riding at the meeting. After racing she tells Kit that she wants to marry him.

Longshot (1990): Writer **John Kendall** goes to Windsor races with trainer **Tremayne Vickers**. Jockeys **Nolan Everard** (**Telebiddy**) and **Sam Yaeger** (**Bluecheesecake**) both ride winners at the meeting.

Wingham, Lady

Come to Grief (1995): Lady Wingham, formerly **Jenny Halley**, is the ex-wife of **Sid Halley**; she has recently married **Sir Anthony Wingham**. Meeting Sid at her father's house, at first she addresses him in her habitually scornful way. She complains that **India Cathcart** had tried to pump her for information about him, and that Cathcart had subsequently written that not only was Sid crippled, but he was unable to satisfy Jenny physically. Jenny's attitude towards Sid softens; she tells him she hadn't said that, and urges Sid not to let

Cathcart get to him. Smiling, she says goodbye to Sid, who recognizes that Jenny has finally rid herself of the anger and resentment that their failed marriage had caused her.

Under Orders (2006): Jenny Wingham goes with her husband to visit her father, **Charles Roland**, with whom she has a dutiful rather than loving relationship. Because Charles had been away at sea for much of Jenny's childhood, father and daughter had not become close. She meets Sid and **Marina van der Meer** at Charles's house, and is not pleased when Sir Anthony shows concern about Marina's injured face. Before she leaves she tells Sid she's happy with Sir Anthony, though life was more predictable than with Sid. When Sid kisses her goodbye, there is a tear in her eye.

After Marina is injured, Jenny meets her father in London to support Sid. She tells Sid that now that he and Marina are together, she no longer feels guilty about the break-up of their marriage. Later she surprises Sid even more when she admits that she has found recent events exciting. She implies that she is bored with life with Sir Anthony, saying that he often came home late from work after going out for a meal or a drink with colleagues. After Marina is released from hospital Jenny goes out for lunch with her, accompanied by a bodyguard arranged by Sid.

Wingham, Sir Anthony (*Under Orders* 2006)

Sir Anthony is the husband of **Jenny, Lady Wingham**, Sid Halley's ex-wife. He is a wealthy man who works in the City of London. He meets Sid at **Charles Roland**'s house, treating him with a noticeable lack of warmth. He is much more solicitous towards Sid's girlfriend **Marina van der Meer**, which doesn't please Jenny. Wingham was educated at **Harrow School** and **Oxford**; he tells Sid he didn't know **George Lochs** at Harrow, and advises him to contact the secretary of the Old Boys' Association if he wants information about Lochs.

Winnipeg, Canada

Winnipeg is a city in Western Canada. It is the provincial capital of Manitoba. The city lies on a flood plain at the confluence of the Red and Assiniboine rivers. The climate is one of extremes: mostly below freezing from mid–November to March, and often about 30°C between May and September.

The Edge (1988): The Great Transcontinental

Mystery Race Train arrives at Winnipeg, where the passengers make an overnight stop to go to the races.

Winsome, Mark (*Dead Heat* 2007)

Winsome, who is in his thirties, has made a fortune in the cell phone business. Six years ago he had set **Max Moreton** up as a chef after opening a restaurant, **The Hay Net**, in **Newmarket**. He splits the profits 50–50 with Max. He offers Max the opportunity to open a restaurant in London. He invites Max to London to discuss it, and over a meal they come to an agreement. Subsequently, with Max, he opens a restaurant in London's exclusive Mayfair district.

Winterbourne, James (*The Edge* 1988)

Winterbourne is a character in the mystery play on the Great Transcontinental Mystery Race Train; he plays an important member of the Ontario Jockey Club. He is slightly put out when the real Chairman of Ontario Jockey Club turns up at Toronto railway station at the start of the trip to wish the travelers a good journey.

Witney, Mark (*Odds Against* 1965)

Ex-jump jockey Mark Witney is now a racehorse trainer and a friend of **Sid Halley**. He tells Sid that he is finding it difficult to persuade his owners to run their horses at **Seabury racecourse** because it is so run-down and prone to abandonments. Asked by Sid if **Dunstable racecourse** had had problems before its closure, Witney reminds him that the Clerk of the Course was suffering from mental illness and had been making bad decisions.

Witney lends Sid his hack, ex–**Cheltenham Gold Cup** winner **Revelation**, to mount a guard on Seabury racecourse before the race meeting.

Women

Graham Lord, in *Dick Francis: A Racing Life*, says that Francis was well regarded by American feminist literary critics of the 1980's for his sympathetic portrayal of women. They felt that, unlike most crime writers, he depicted fully-developed, three-dimensional characters rather than stereotypical cardboard cut-outs that existed only to fulfill a specific function within the plot.

Zanna Martin (*Odds Against* 1965) is a good example from one of the early books of how Francis uses an event from a woman's background to define her and explain her motivation. Badly scarred in an accident as a teenager, Zanna has hidden her face from the world, her self-confidence shattered. A chance meeting with **Sid Halley**, whose hand has been crippled in a racing fall, starts Zanna on a hesitant and painful road to recovery. Francis again uses emotional fragility caused by disability to inform a female character in *Forfeit* (1968). **Elizabeth Tyrone**, wife of investigative racing journalist **James Tyrone**, is a polio victim, bedridden and unable to breathe unaided. Elizabeth's equanimity depends upon her feeling secure and loved, but when James admits his infidelity those crutches are swept away, and Elizabeth is forced to re-evaluate her life.

Jenny Halley is a powerfully-drawn character who appears in three novels (*Whip Hand* 1979; *Come to Grief* 1995; *Under Orders* 2006). As Sid Halley's ex-wife, her past is strongly linked with his and defines both her actions and her view of life. She is waspish and bitter, blaming Sid for the break-up of their marriage and for his shortcomings as a husband. It is only when she is remarried to a wealthy but boring baronet that she starts to appreciate Sid's qualities.

There are several women whose role in the novel, like Jenny Halley's, arises from a background shared with the main character. **Joanna** (*Nerve* 1964) is a classically trained singer who gradually overcomes her unease about having a physical relationship with her cousin, **Rob Finn**, whom she has grown to love. **Samantha Bergen** (*Reflex* 1980) had looked after jockey **Philip Nore** as a child when his drug-addicted, hippy mother had abandoned him. Kind and warm-hearted, Samantha comes back into Philip's life when he is looking for his half-sister. In *To the Hilt* (1996) racehorse trainer **Emily Jane Cox** is the estranged wife of artist **Alex Kinloch**. Independent and energetic, Emily maintains a good relationship with Alex despite their inability to live together, and is on hand to render valuable assistance when needed. So is **Clarissa Williams**, the former lover of jockey **Derek Franklin's** recently deceased brother **Greville Franklin** (*Straight* 1989). She makes love to Derek because it makes her feel closer to Greville; later, she saves his life by the judicious use of a cosh.

Capability and courage are qualities that are frequently found in Francis's female characters. **Mrs. Marjorie Binsham** (*Decider* 1993), a director of **Stratton Park racecourse**, is in her eighties but is still a formidable and efficient organizer. So is

Mrs. Baudelaire, the bedridden mother of Canadian Jockey Club Director of Security Bill Baudelaire (*The Edge* 1988). Despite failing health she acts as an intermediary between her son and his British counterpart, Tor Kelsey. Princess Casilia (*Bolt* 1986), a middle-aged European aristocrat, bravely struggles to protect her elderly husband who is being threatened by an unscrupulous business partner. Cassie Morris, William Derry's feisty girlfriend in *Twice Shy* (1981) comes to William's aid when he is attacked by a deranged thug. A broken arm doesn't stop her from knocking him out with a coal scuttle.

Francis does not shrink from depicting the less attractive aspects of the female character. Mrs. Van Dysart, with her unkind tongue, tries to humiliate Sid Halley in *Odds Against*, but she's a novice in comparison with Doria Kraye, a virago with a predilection for violence and sado-masochism. She relishes the opportunity to help her husband assault Sid; later, with Sid tied to a chair, Doria kisses him hard on the lips, drawing blood. In *Blood Sport* (1967) Yola Clive combines friendly efficiency in running a dude ranch in Wyoming with a calculated ruthlessness when dealing with individuals who stand in the way of her plans. Patsy Benchmark, the greedy and scheming daughter of Sir Ivan Westering (*To the Hilt*) has no compunction about employing violence as a means to an end. Equally callous is the filthy-tempered Rose Payne (*Shattered* 2000), a manipulative man-hater whose propensity for violence results in a fatality. In *Hot Money* (1987) the roots of Serena Pembroke's bizarre personality and subsequent actions lie in her upbringing; her emotional growth was stunted by a mother who refused to let her grow up. Certain female members of the Stratton family (*Decider*) exhibit a markedly violent streak. Hannah Stratton, the unpleasant daughter of Keith Stratton, helps to beat up Lee Morris, whilst Conrad Stratton's daughter, amateur jockey Rebecca Stratton, prefers to use a gun, though not with any degree of skill.

Rebecca is not typical of Francis's usual portrayal of women who work with horses. Most are sympathetic, competent, energetic and law-abiding. Emily Jane Cox, Marigold English (*Driving Force* 1992), Etty Craig (*Bonecrack* 1971), Mona Watkins (*Field of 13* 1998: "Song for Mona"), Annie Villars (*Rat Race* 1970), Popsy Teddington (*The Danger* 1983) and Ginny Knowles (*Banker* 1982) all conform to a type of horsewoman, caring and committed, that can be found in livery and racing yards the length and breadth of Great Britain.

Ginny, the seventeen-year-old daughter of stud farm owner Oliver Knowles, develops a close relationship with Tim Ekaterin, the hero of *Banker*, whom she has cast in the role of a caring uncle or elder brother. Biographer Graham Lord comments on similar relationships between young women and the hero in *Wild Horses* (Lucy Wells and Thomas Lyons), *Decider* (Penelope Faulds and Lee Morris), *Enquiry* (Roberta Cranfield and Kelly Hughes) and *Blood Sport* (Lynnie Keeble and Gene Hawkins). Lord sees a pattern here, and speculates that Francis or his wife Mary may have wished for a teenage daughter themselves. In *Decider*, *Enquiry* and *Blood Sport* the relationships are, putatively, of a romantic nature. However, relationships between young women and older men, though vaguely distasteful unless of the platonic type portrayed in *Banker*, are not uncommon. To identify from these examples a particular theme, intended or otherwise, seems to be reading too much into it.

One type of woman that does appear regularly—unsurprisingly, given the class-conscious nature of English society—is the snob. In *Dead Cert* (1962) Aunt Deb, wife of Uncle George, has an acute sense of her social position, and it is in order to maintain it that George acts as he does. Rosemary Caspar (*Whip Hand*), the wife of a grand Newmarket trainer, considers jockeys to be of inferior social status; her attitude is a throwback to the nineteenth century, when servants rode racehorses for their aristocratic masters. Trainer's daughter Robert Cranfield (*Enquiry*) has inherited the snobbish attitudes of her parents, and is taken aback to discover that jockey Kelly Hughes is both intelligent and well-educated. Grace Roxford tells Mrs. Cranfield to get rid of Kelly, who has come to the front door. Kelly sees a strange car parked outside, which Mrs. Cranfield says belongs to her gardener. Kelly knows immediately that she's lying—Mrs. Cranfield would never have allowed her gardener to park outside her front door.

Particularly unpleasant are two women who, owing to their snobbish attitudes, are disparaging towards their own mothers. Belinda Larch (*Comeback* 1991), soon to marry a veterinary surgeon, is embarrassed by her mother, Vicky Larch, who sings in a nightclub for a living. In the short story "Song for Mona" (*Field of 13*) social climber Joanie Vine is ashamed of her working class mother, stable groom Mona Watkins. Joanie fails to visit her when she's ill and, on Mona's death, arranges the cheapest possible funeral.

It isn't often that women in Francis's novels act in an unrealistic way. It is arguable, however, that middle-aged, virginal spinster **Hilary Pinlock's** quest for carnal knowledge in *Risk* (1977) lacks the ring of authenticity. So does **Orinda Nagle's** change of heart in *10 lb. Penalty* (1997). The widow of a recently deceased Member of Parliament, Orinda is furious when she is passed over for selection to fight the resulting by-election in favor of **George Juliard**. Yet soon afterwards, after a short conversation with Juliard's insipid son **Benedict**, she becomes one of Juliard's most ardent supporters. Most unlikely of all is the scene in *Comeback* in which **Peter Darwin's** mother confesses to him, in a telephone conversation and completely out of the blue, that as a young widow she had an affair with a vet who subsequently died in suspicious circumstances. *Comeback* may well be responsible for young men thinking twice before calling their mother for a routine chat.

Woodbine racecourse, Canada

Woodbine racecourse is on the north-western outskirts of Toronto. It hosts the Queen's Plate, the Canadian International and the North America Cup for Standardbreds, all valuable and prestigious races. Top class horses to have raced at Woodbine include Secretariat, French champion Dahlia and **Epsom** Derby winner Snow Knight.

The Edge (1988): At Woodbine **Daffodil Quentin's** horse wins the Great Transcontinental Mystery Race Train's special race.

Woodward, Andrew (*Under Orders* 2006)

Lambourn racehorse trainer Andrew Woodward is very good at his job but is reputed to hate all jockeys; he was too heavy to ride himself. At **Cheltenham** races, he is heard criticizing a jockey who had recently ridden for him. He has a conviction for assault on an apprentice jockey whom he had caught with his daughter in the feed store.

When **Lord Enstone** removes his horses from **Bill Burton's** yard he sends them to Woodward. At **Newbury** races, Woodward asks **Sid Halley** for his opinion of **Juliet Burns**, who has applied for an assistant's job with him. Unimpressed by Sid's cautious reply, he dismisses Sid as being nothing more than an ex-jockey. When Sid says that he knows that Woodward, contrary to the Rules of Racing,

uses the names of two lady owners to publicize his yard who don't in fact have any horses with him, Woodward is furious; he warns Sid that he'll regret it if he makes the deceit public. Later that afternoon Woodward wins the day's big race with a horse, supposedly belonging to one of the ladies, which he owns himself. Sid knows that Woodward is having an affair with one of these ladies.

Woodward, Mrs. (*Forfeit* 1968)

Mrs. Woodward is polio victim **Elizabeth Tyrone's** carer. She is a widow with a teenage son whose ambition is to be a doctor. She is capable and efficient but extremely businesslike in charging for her overtime. She stays with Elizabeth overnight when **James Tyrone** says he's in Newcastle but is actually in London with **Gail Pominga**.

Wordmaster (*The Edge* 1988)

Wordmaster is a racehorse traveling on board the Great Transcontinental Mystery Race Train.

Worthing, Sussex

Worthing is a seaside resort in West **Sussex**. In Victorian times it was patronized by the Royal Family, especially Princess Amelia, younger sister of the Prince Regent. In 1894 Oscar Wilde wrote *The Importance of Being Earnest* while on holiday in Worthing.

In the Frame (1976): At **Plumpton** races **Charles Todd** meets **Maisie Matthews**, whose house in Worthing has recently burnt down. She asks Charles to have a look at the ruins with a view to painting them.

Worthington (*Shattered* 2000)

Worthington is chauffeur to **Marigold**, mother of **Bon-Bon Stukely**. He is middle-aged but strong and fit. He is gassed and rendered unconscious by an intruder at Bon-Bon's house. He ferries **Gerard Logan** around in Marigold's Rolls Royce when she doesn't need it and acts as self-appointed bodyguard to Gerard. Walking into Gerard's workshop, he finds Gerard, **Pamela Jane** and **John Hickory** being threatened by criminals. He runs out immediately and returns with **Tom Pigeon**, **Jim**, **Catherine Dodd** and **Paul Cratchet**. After Marigold wrongly assumes that Worthington has been killed, their relationship becomes more romantic.

Wrecker (*High Stakes* 1975)

Wrecker is a nervous bay yearling colt owned by **Steven Scott**. He was to be trained by **Jody**

Leeds, but is transferred to **Trevor Kennet** after Steven sacks Leeds.

Wyfold, Detective Chief Inspector (*Banker* 1982)

D.C.I. Wyfold is an experienced policeman inured to all kinds of criminal depravity; he follows closely police procedures laid down in the rule book. Investigating the death of a young girl, he believes there may have been a sexual motive, though she had not been sexually assaulted. Wyfold initiates a search for **Jason Williams,** an employee of **Calder Jackson.** He finds Williams two weeks later in North **Yorkshire** and arrests him.

Wyvern, Alderney (*10 lb. Penalty* 1997)

Wyvern is a political fixer; a man who doesn't seek overt power for himself but is content to manipulate those who do. He had found himself a niche as the guiding influence behind **Hoopwestern** Member of Parliament Denis Nagle. When Nagle dies unexpectedly Wyvern immediately latches on to Nagle's wife, **Orinda Nagle,** who has designs on becoming the next Member for Hoopwestern. This suits Wyvern's own ambitions, and he soon forms what is rumored to be more than just a political alliance with Orinda. But Orinda's hopes of fighting the seat are dashed when wealthy City businessman **George Juliard** is selected as the party's candidate in the forthcoming by-election. Discontented, Wyvern settles on a simple but drastic solution to the problem.

However, Wyvern's plans are thwarted, and he drops out of sight for four years, re-emerging at a Downing Street reception attended by Juliard, now Minister of Agriculture. In the intervening years Wyvern has built himself a reputation for advising politicians on their dress-sense. He is considered an asset by the Prime Minister, but is rumored to wield a heavy behind-the-scenes influence over at least two Cabinet ministers.

When the Prime Minister decides to step down Wyvern attempts to undermine Juliard's campaign for election as party leader. When his efforts are unsuccessful he decides, once again, to adopt extreme measures. And, once again, his judgment is badly flawed.

Y

Yaeger, Sam (*Longshot* 1990)

Yaeger, stable jockey to **Tremayne Vickers'** yard, is young, self-confident and irreverent; he had finished third in the previous year's jockeys' championship. He doesn't get on with **Nolan Everard,** whom he sees as a rival for both rides and women. Yaeger buys antique boats, refurbishes them and sells them on; he is intent on building up a business in anticipation of his eventual retirement from the saddle.

At **Windsor** races Yaeger rides a winner, **Bluecheesecake.** He is annoyed when **Detective Chief Inspector Doone** questions him about his movements on the day that a stable girl had disappeared. Yaeger fights with Everard at Tremayne Vickers' award dinner.

Yale, Superintendent (*Hot Money* 1987)

Paunchy and self-important, Yale had investigated the murder of **Moira Pembroke,** and now inquires into the attempted murder of **Malcolm Pembroke.** Initially he doesn't believe Malcolm's account of the attempt on his life, but subsequent events change his mind. York, however, doesn't make much progress with his investigation.

Yardley, Alistair (*Risk* 1977)

Yardley, a tall, tough man in his early thirties, makes his living by looking after boats in the Mediterranean while their owners are at home. He has been around boats all his life—his father worked in a boat-building yard—and is considered a good sailor. He is not thought of as a crook, but has a mercenary approach to life and, if the money is right, is willing to bend the rules. This he does, with mixed results, in the case of **Roland Britten.**

Yardman (*Flying Finish* 1966)

Yardman is the owner of horse transport firm Yardman Transport. A habitually lugubrious expression belies a determined and ruthless character. Yardman tries to dissuade **Lord Henry Gray** from applying for a job with his firm, but reluctantly says that Henry can give it a try if he wants to. He is annoyed by the instant antagonism between **Billy Watkins** and Henry; he warns Henry not to allow it to interfere with his job. When **Simon Searle** disappears, Yardman is sure that Henry will want to leave but, short of staff, is content to keep him on when Henry says he wants to stay. Henry says he'll resign immediately if Watkins continues to aggravate him, and Yardman promises to speak to Watkins.

Both Yardman Transport and its owner prove to be very different from what they appear to be on the surface.

Yarra River Fine Arts (*In the Frame* 1976)

This is an art gallery in Sydney, Australia, where **Charles Todd** recognizes an **Alfred Munnings** painting belonging to **Maisie Matthews**. The manager, **Mr. Greene**, is suspicious of Charles and temporarily detains him. There are other branches of the gallery in Melbourne and **Alice Springs**.

Yarrow, Wilson (*Decider* 1993)

Architect Wilson Yarrow is retained by **Conrad, Lord Stratton** to design a new grandstand for **Stratton Park racecourse**. He is supercilious, condescending and arrogant. He trained, like **Lee Morris**, at the Architectural Association, but doesn't recognize Lee, who was three years below him. Yarrow is unhappy when, on Lee's advice, **Marjorie Binsham** proposes an architectural competition so that they can choose from several different designs for the stands. According to the diaries of Lee's friend **Carteret**, Yarrow had fraudulently won a prestigious prize while at the Association with a design he had plagiarized. However, he had been allowed to complete his diploma, the college deeming it an error of judgment rather than deliberate cheating. According to **Rebecca Stratton**, she had met Yarrow at a party, where he told her he was strapped for cash, and she had decided to use him to get the stands built.

Yates, Dave (*Driving Force* 1992)

Dave Yates is a driver with **Croft Raceways** horse transport firm. He is generally happy-go-lucky, but gets belligerent when drunk. He likes a bet on the greyhounds. Disobeying the firm's regulations, Yates picks up hitchhiker **Kevin Keith Ogden**, who dies during the journey. He is sent with Phil, another driver, to France to collect a show jumper for **Jericho Rich**'s daughter. Tackled by **Freddie Croft**, Yates admits that he was offered payment by a woman on the telephone to pick up Ogden at **South Mimms** service station, but claims he was never paid.

Yates, Mr. (*Smokescreen* 1972)

Mr. Yates is a young miner employed in **Quentin Van Huren**'s gold mine. He is instructed by **Peter Losenwoldt** to show **Edward Lincoln** the gold-bearing rock. He tells Edward he isn't used to showing people around; as soon as he can he excuses himself to go to another job, and asks Edward if he can find his own way back up the tunnel.

Yaxley, Elgin (*Reflex* 1980)

Yaxley is the owner of five valuable steeplechasers in trainer **Bart Underfield**'s **Lambourn** yard. While out at summer grass all five are apparently shot and killed. Yaxley claims £150,000 from a reluctant insurance company. Subsequently **Terence O'Tree** is sent to jail for the crime. After receiving the insurance pay-out Yaxley drops out of racing. Three weeks after the death of racecourse photographer **George Millace**, **Philip Nore** sees Yaxley at **Ascot** looking content with life. However, after a conversation with Philip, Yaxley is considerably less happy.

Yellowstone National Park

Yellowstone is the oldest National Park in the world, established in 1872. It is located in the states of Idaho, Montana and Wyoming. Most of its 3,470 square miles are in the north-west corner of Wyoming. The largest volcanic system in North America, the Yellowstone area is famous for its geysers and hot springs, as well as its abundant wildlife, including grizzly bears, wolves, pumas, bison and elk.

Blood Sport (1967): Investigator **Gene Hawkins** flies to Yellowstone National Park to try to trace the provenance of a handkerchief found in a punt on the river Thames, and the identities of the young couple who were on the punt.

York, Alan (*Dead Cert* 1962)

Amateur steeplechase jockey Alan York was born in the former Southern Rhodesia—now Zimbabwe—and brought up by his widowed millionaire father on a cattle station so vast that even back then a youthful Robert Mugabe must have been eyeing it with interest. Now twenty-four, Alan combines racing with working in London, representing his father's commodity trading empire. From an early age Alan's education had focused, at his father's insistence, more on how to read a company's year-end accounts than how to conjugate Latin verbs. This, together with tuition from a math teacher with a penchant for solving problems from a limited amount of information, has developed in Alan a nose for detecting frauds, a skill which serves him well after the death of his friend, **Major Bill Davidson**. Alan lived with Davidson and his family, and together the two men had indulged their passion for riding racehorses over fences. Davidson was champion amateur jockey and Alan, after his first season riding in England, was not far behind him. For Alan, the thrills and dangers of racing are an antidote to the routines of everyday life. As a boy he'd spent his weekends hunting crocodiles with his dad, so being a jump jockey must have seemed tame in comparison. If your horse falls and you end up in the open ditch, you're not likely to get your foot bitten off.

Alan's carefree existence is shattered when Davidson is killed, his horse deliberately brought down during a race. "The callousness [of the act] awoke a slow anger which, though I did not then know it, was to remain a spur for many weeks to come."

Alan proves to be a consummate gentleman, as well as a master of self-control, when Davidson's pretty widow, **Scilla Davidson**, comes to his bedroom at 2 AM, drowsy with the effects of sleeping pills. Alan comforts her in her grief and lets her sleep with him in his bed, but does not take advantage of her vulnerability. It is not long, though, before other opportunities arise. As Alan begins to retrace the path that had led to Davidson's death, he meets **Kate Ellery-Penn**, a gorgeous young racehorse owner, and knows within minutes that he wants to marry her. Unsurprisingly Kate wants to keep her options open. When Alan tells her he loves her Kate, innocent and inexperienced, says she isn't ready for love.

Alan's ability to woo Kate may be questionable, but his courage is not. Lured into a horse van and warned by three men not to pursue his enquires, he fights back, albeit unsuccessfully, and is in no way deterred. Neither are the villains; they try repeatedly to neutralize the threat that Alan poses. Nothing if not relentless, Alan finally runs to ground the sinister puppet-master responsible for Davidson's death and a host of other crimes. Alan's persistence pays dividends in other ways too; Kate, despite initial reservations, opts for a life of married bliss.

York racecourse

York is a well-run racecourse hosting top-class racing; it is situated a mile outside the cathedral city of York in North **Yorkshire**. The August Ebor Festival (Eboracum was the Roman name for York) attracts the best flat horses in Britain. When **Ascot** was closed for development in 2005, York was chosen to stage its Royal meeting.

The recently opened £20 million Ebor grandstand is considered a masterpiece of design and construction; the lawns, flower beds and hanging baskets combine to make racing here a visual pleasure.

The Edge (1988): Thug **Derry Welfram** dies at York racecourse, apparently of natural causes.

Straight (1989): **Derek Franklin** goes to York races where he is introduced to **Lord Knightwood** and his wife, who turns out to be his late brother's mistress, **Clarissa Williams**.

Yorkshire, England

Yorkshire is a large county in northern England, once comprising three counties or "ridings." The rural peace of nineteenth century Yorkshire was broken by the coming of the Industrial Revolution, with textiles, mining and fishing predominant. The Roman city of York—also a Viking capital—boasts the biggest Gothic cathedral in northern Europe. The Yorkshire Dales National Park is an area of outstanding natural beauty.

Blood Sport (1967): **Mr. Arkwright**, a neighbor of **Gene Hawkins**' father, trains racehorses in Yorkshire.

Knock Down (1974): Bloodstock agent **Fynedale** comes from Yorkshire, as does his principal client, **Wilton Young**.

In the Frame (1976): Artist **Charles Todd** goes to Yorkshire to paint a client's horse.

Banker (1982): **Jason Williams**, **Calder Jackson**'s former employee, is arrested in Malton, North Yorkshire.

Driving Force (1992): **Aziz**, **Freddie Croft**'s new driver, takes a horse van to Yorkshire to collect some old horses for **John Tigwood**'s charity, **Centaur Care**.

Field of 13 (1998): "Spring Fever": Jockey **Derek Roberts** goes to Yorkshire to buy a horse for **Mrs. Angela Hart**.

Youll, Eric (*Forfeit* 1968)

Youll, in his thirties, is the youngest and most recently appointed of the three Stewards of the **National Hunt Committee**, steeplechasing's ruling body. An ex-amateur jockey, he is on friendly terms with **James Tyrone**. He is willing to speak off the record about the Stewards' suspicions of a particular villain and to cooperate with *The Blaze* newspaper to force him out of English racing.

Young, Chris (*To the Hilt* 1996)

Chris Young is a private investigator, and a former inmate of young offenders' institution and prisons. Hired by **Alex Kinloch** to tail **Surtees Benchmark**, he discovers that Benchmark visits a prostitute in Guildford, **Surrey**, for sado-masochism. He undertakes research into Maxim, the maker of the King Alfred Gold Cup and into the Cup's provenance.

Young dresses as a woman when acting as Alex's bodyguard at **Sir Ivan Westering**'s funeral. He chauffeurs **Lady Westering, Emily Cox** and **Audrey Newton** to a **Devon** hotel when Alex fears for their safety. Again in female attire, he accompanies Alex to see **Patsy Benchmark**. When Alex gets into difficulties, Young uses his initiative to extricate him.

Young, Mrs. Courtney (*10 lb. Penalty* 1997)

Mrs. Young has racehorses with trainer **Spencer Stallworthy**. A heavy gambler, she is in tears when her horse is killed in a race at **Taunton racecourse**. The main reason for her grief is that she has let her insurance lapse and owes Stallworthy a lot of money for training fees.

Young, Ian (*Trial Run* 1978)

Ian Young is assistant to the cultural attaché at the British Embassy, Moscow. In his mid-thirties and unremarkable, he could easily be mistaken for a native Muscovite. He tells **Randall Drew** he's looked for "Alyosha" without success. He offers Randall a lift back to his hotel from the Embassy; instead he takes him to meet some Russian friends, one of whom has information about Hans Kramer. Young threatens to kill Randall if he betrays the trust of his friends, and warns him not to mention the visit to anyone from the Embassy.

Randall invites Young round to his room when he sets up a meeting with **Malcolm Herrick**. Young opens the door to two thugs, who knock him unconscious with a riot stick.

Young, Mr. and Mrs. (*The Edge* 1988)

Cumber and Rose Young are elderly passengers on board the Great Transcontinental Mystery Race Train. They are the owners of **Sparrowhawk**, a racehorse traveling on the train with them. Rose pays for **Xanthe Lorrimore**'s drink and listens to her complaints about her brother, **Sheridan Lorrimore**. The Youngs had been friends of the late **Ezra Gideon**.

The Youngs ship in two runners for the race at **Winnipeg**; their horse **Slipperclub** finishes third. According to Xanthe, Rose Young is nicer than Cumber, who is not so sympathetic. When one of the characters in the mystery play says that he'd rather die if he couldn't go racing—as Ezra Gideon had once said—Cumber wants to know where the actor got the idea from. Later, when one character blackmails another into giving him his horse, Cumber wants to know who has Gideon's horses now.

Young, Ursula (*Banker* 1982)

Successful bloodstock agent Ursula Young is knowledgeable and opinionated. She is approached at **Doncaster** races by **Tim Ekaterin**, who wants to find out more about the economics of bloodstock breeding. She asks **Calder Jackson** if one of her clients can send him a sick horse. Later she tells Tim that Jackson's business depended more on his relationship with the media than his medical ability. At **Newbury** races she introduces Tim to a client of hers, small trainer **Fred Barnet**.

Young, Vic (*Bonecrack* 1971)

Vic Young is the traveling head lad at **Neville Griffon**'s racing stable in **Newmarket**. He is now too heavy to ride most of the young horses, but is loyal and good at his job. When he sees **Alessandro Rivera**'s lack of emotion before his first race, Vic thinks he doesn't really care. After Alessandro wins on **Pullitzer** at **Catterick** Vic tells the lads at home that Alessandro hadn't ridden to instructions, and that the horse must have improved over the winter. When Alessandro wins on **Lancat** at **Teesside** Vic again gives the credit to the horse. However, Vic is soon forced to acknowledge Alessandro's ability. When Alessandro rides **Buckram** to finish second at Catterick Vic concedes that he had ridden an intelligent race and that it was not his fault that he'd lost.

Young, Wilton (*Knock Down* 1974)

Wilton Young, a wealthy racehorse owner from **Yorkshire**, is a business rival of **Constantine Brevett**. He is loud, opinionated and conceited. He spends large sums on yearlings on the dubious advice of **Fynedale**, his bloodstock agent. At **Doncaster** races Young has a blazing row with Fynedale, sacking him on the spot. He asks **Jonah**

Dereham to buy him a horse; however he doesn't like the horse, and sells it on immediately at a profit. Realizing that he'd been hasty, Young tells Jonah to buy him another horse and promises to keep it this time. Despite his experience with Fynedale, Young still wants to buy expensive horses. So Jonah buys him a good horse which he considers slightly over-priced, and Young is delighted with it.

Hearing that Constantine Brevett wants a top class American two-year-old named **Phoenix Fledgling**, Young instructs Jonah to go to the States and bid for it, simply to frustrate his rival.

Young Higgins (*Hot Money* 1987)

Young Higgins, a thirteen-year-old steeplechaser, is a genuine sort. Ridden by **Ian Pembroke**, he jumps well and finishes third in an amateur chase at **Sandown Park**. Fitter next time out, he wins a three mile chase at **Kempton Park**, again ridden by Ian.

Z

Zaracievesa, Feydor (*Proof* 1984)

Known as "Zarac" and of Polish extraction, Zaracievesa is a wine waiter at the **Silver Moondance** restaurant. He meets an untimely and unusual end.

Zeissen, Paul M. (*Blood Sport* 1967)

Zeissen, an insurance executive at Buttress Life, New York, puts **Gene Hawkins** in contact with **Walt Prensela**, the investigator in charge of the **Chrysalis** case.

Zephyr Farm Stables (*Reflex* 1980)

This is the headquarters of a dubious religious sect, the Colleagues of Supreme Grace, based near Horley, **Surrey**. **Amanda Nore**, **Philip Nore's** half-sister, is a member of the sect.

Zig Zag (*Forfeit* 1968)

Zig Zag, a former top class steeplechaser, is now approaching veteran stage and is not quite as good as he was. He is trained by **Norton Fox** in **Berkshire**. Zig Zag falls at the last fence when leading in the Lamplighter Gold Cup at **Heathbury Park**.

Zingaloo (*Whip Hand* 1979)

Zingaloo is a top two-year-old colt trained at **Newmarket** by **George Caspar**. He fails to train on as a three-year-old, and is subsequently found to have a heart murmur. According to Caspar's head lad, Zingaloo has had a virus. He is retired to **Henry Thrace's** stud outside Newmarket. Exercise exhausts him owing to his heart condition. **Sid Halley** subsequently discovers the true reason for Zingaloo's problems.

Zinnia (*Second Wind* 1999)

Zinnia, a research vet at the Equine Research Establishment, **Newmarket**, specializes in poisonous plants. She is about fifty years old, and always looks as if she needs a good night's sleep. She treats **Caspar Harvey's** sick filly, but is unable to pinpoint the cause of her illness.

Zoomalong (*Banker* 1982)

Zoomalong, a five-year-old gelding trained by **Fred Barnet**, finishes third in a hurdle race at **Newbury**. Barnet tries to persuade bloodstock agent **Ursula Young** to buy him for a client, saying that he would be a good ride for an amateur.

Appendix 1.
The Works of Dick Francis

Novels

All of Francis's novels have been published in the UK by Michael Joseph. In the USA *Dead Cert* was published by Holt Rinehart. From 1964 to 1979 Francis's publishers were Harper and Row. Since then Putnam Publishing Group have published his novels.

Dead Cert (1962)
Nerve (1964)
For Kicks (1965)
Odds Against (1965)
Flying Finish (1966)
Blood Sport (1967)
Forfeit (1968)
Enquiry (1969)
Rat Race (1970)
Bonecrack (1971)
Smokescreen (1972)
Slay-Ride (1973)
Knock Down (1974)
High Stakes (1975)
In the Frame 1976)
Risk (1977)
Trial Run (1978)
Whip Hand (1979)
Reflex (1980)
Twice Shy (1981)
Banker (1982)
The Danger (1983)
Proof (1984)
Break In (1985)
Bolt (1986)
Hot Money (1987)
The Edge (1988)
Straight (1989)
Longshot (1990)
Comeback (1991)
Driving Force (1992)
Decider (1993)

Wild Horses (1994)
Come to Grief (1995)
To the Hilt (1996)
10 lb. Penalty (1997)
Second Wind (1999)
Shattered (2000)
Under Orders (2006)
Dead Heat (2007): (Dick Francis and
 Felix Francis)

Omnibus Editions

*Four Complete Novels: Odds Against, Flying Finish,
 Blood Sport, Rat Race* (1988)
*The Dick Francis Collection: Odds Against, Knock
 Down, Comeback* (1992)
*Three Favorites: Odds Against, Flying Finish, Blood
 Sport* (1994)
Dick Francis Omnibus: Risk, Enquiry, The Danger
 (1994)
Dick Francis Double: Reflex, Comeback (1995)
*Dead Cert, Nerve, For Kicks: The First Three Dick
 Francis Novels* (1996)
*Dick Francis: Three Complete Novels: Decider, Wild
 Horses, Come to Grief* (1997)
*Dick Francis Omnibus: Enquiry, Rat Race, Smoke-
 screen* (1999)
Dick Francis Omnibus: Forfeit, Risk, Reflex (1999)
Longshot, Straight, High Stakes (1999)
Dick Francis Omnibus: Slay-Ride, Banker, Proof
 (2000)
*Dick Francis Giftset: Shattered, Second Wind, 10 lb.
 Penalty* (2001)
*The Sid Halley Omnibus: Odds Against, Whip Hand,
 Come to Grief* (2002)
Twice Shy, The Danger (2002)
The Kit Fielding Omnibus: Break In, Bolt (2003)
*Win, Place and Show: Odds Against, Whip Hand,
 Come to Grief* (2004)
*Dick Francis Omnibus: Blood Sport, Nerve, In the
 Frame* (2004)

Triple Crown: Dead Cert, Nerve, For Kicks (2005)
Field of Thirteen, Shattered (2005)

Short Story Collection

Field of Thirteen 1998 (Putnam):
  "Raid at Kingdom Hill"
  "Dead on Red"
  "Song for Mona"
  "Bright White Star"
  "Collision Course"
  "Nightmare"
  "Carrot for a Chestnut"
  "The Gift"
  "Spring Fever"
  "Blind Chance"
  "Corkscrew"
  "The Day of the Losers"
  "Haig's Death"

Anthologies Edited

Best Racing and Chasing Stories (with John Welcome)
(Faber & Faber 1966)

Best Racing and Chasing Stories 2 (with John Welcome
(Faber & Faber 1969)
Great Racing Stories (with John Welcome) (Bellew
Publishing 1989)
*Dick Francis Treasury of Great Racing Stories (with
John Welcome)* (Galahad Books 1989)
*The Dick Francis Complete Treasury of Great Racing
Stories* (with John Welcome) (Galahad 1989)
Classic Lines: More Great Racing Stories (Bellew Pub-
lishing 1991)
*The New Treasury of Great Racing Stories (with John
Welcome)* (W.W. Norton & Co. Inc. 1992)

Non-Fiction

*The Sport of Queens: The Autobiography of Dick Fran-
cis* (Michael Joseph 1957; revised 1968, 1974,
1982, 1988; Pan Books 1995; Harper 1969)
The Racing Man's Bedside Book (with John Welcome)
(Faber & Faber 1969)
Lester: The Official Biography (1986); published in
USA as *A Jockey's Life: The Biography of Lester Pig-
gott* (Putnam 1986)

Appendix 2.
Television and
Movie Adaptations

Dead Cert (1974, United Artists/Woodfall Film Productions)
Screenplay by Tony Richardson and John Oaksey.
Directed by Tony Richardson.
Produced by Neil Hartley.
Starring Scott Antony as Alan York; Judi Dench as Laura Davidson; Michael Williams as Sandy Mason.

Much was expected of *Dead Cert*, the only movie adaptation of Dick Francis's books to go on general release in cinemas. However the movie was, almost without exception, panned by the critics for its lack of realism and its deviations from the original story. Too many of the actors lacked confidence around thoroughbred racehorses, and it would be fair to say that the horses themselves weren't too keen to stick to the script.

The Dick Francis Thriller: The Racing Game (1979–80, Yorkshire Television)
Screenplay by Terence Feely.
Directed by Colin Buckley and Lawrence Gordon Clark.
Produced by Jackie Stoller.
Starring Mike Gwilym as Sid Halley; Mick Ford as Chico Barnes; James Maxwell as Charles Roland; Susan Woodbridge as Jenny Halley.

Yorkshire Television produced a series of six episodes entitled *The Racing Game* featuring Sid Halley, who was played by actor Mike Gwilym. The episodes were entitled: *Odds Against*; *Needle*; *Horsenap*; *Horses for Courses*; *Gambling Lady*; and *Trackdown*. Only *Odds Against* was based on a Dick Francis novel; the rest were the work of scriptwriters. The critical and public responses to the series in the UK were lukewarm at best. However, in 1980–

81 the series was shown in the USA, where it helped to boost the sale of Francis's novels.

Dick Francis Mysteries (1989, Comedia Entertainment Inc/Raidio Teilifis Eireann)

Blood Sport
Screenplay by Andrew Payne.
Directed by Harvey Hart.
Produced by Jonathan Hackett.
Executive Producers: Dennis E. Doty and Jackie Stoller.
Starring Ian McShane as David Cleveland; Heath Lamberts as Walt Prensela; Patrick McNee as Geoffrey Keeble.

In the Frame
Screenplay by Andrew Payne.
Directed by Wigbert Wicker.
Produced by Mathias Wittich.
Executive Producers: Dennis E. Doty and Jackie Stoller.
Starring Ian McShane as David Cleveland; Lyman Ward as Don Stuart; Amadeus August as Hermann Forster.

Twice Shy
Screenplay by Miles Henderson.
Directed by Deidre Friel.
Produced by W. Paterson Ferns.
Executive Producers: Dennis E. Doty and Jackie Stoller.
Starring Ian McShane as David Cleveland; Kate McKenzie as Cassie Donovan, Karl Hayden as William Derry; Patrick McNee as Geoffrey Keeble.

These three made-for-TV movies starred Ian

McShane as the Dick Francis hero David Cleveland. Reaction to the movies was generally critical, citing the absence of important characters, changes in location and over-simplification of the plots as problems that detracted from the quality of the finished product. One major problem with the movies is that Jockey Club investigator David Cleveland does not in fact appear in any of the three novels on which the movies are based. He was, in fact, the protagonist of *Slay-Ride* (1973). In *Blood Sport* it is Cleveland, rather than Gene Hawkins, who is on the trial of a kidnapped stallion in the Canadian Rockies. In *In the Frame* Cleveland takes the place of artist Charles Todd in pursuing a gang who use paintings and fine wine as a front for their criminal activities. The movie is set in Canada, England and Germany, rather than Australia, where the novel's action takes place. The book isn't very good, but the movie is, by general consent, a whole lot worse. Significant liberties are taken with the original plot of *Twice Shy* in the movie adaptation, which is considered to be marginally the best of the three. Here Cleveland is the hero rather than the Derry brothers, Jonathan and William. He investigates the death in a rock climbing incident of an I.T. expert who had in his possession computer discs containing a horserace betting system. In all three movies Ian McShane does his best with mediocre scripts, but the odds are stacked against him.

Bibliography

Andrews, Robert: *The New Penguin Dictionary of Modern Quotations* (Penguin Books 2000).

Barnes, Melvin: *Dick Francis* (Ungar 1986).

Bedford Julian: *The World Atlas of Horse Racing* (The Hamlyn Publishing Group 1989).

Blunt, Noel: *Horse Racing: The Inside Story* (The Hamlyn Publishing Group 1977).

Cartmell, Stephen: *Racing Around Britain* (Aesculus Press Ltd. 2002).

Chalmers, Patrick: *Racing England* (B.T. Batsford Ltd. 1939).

Churchill, Peter: *The Sporting Horse* (Marshall Cavendish Ltd. 1976).

Cranham, Gerry; Pitman, Richard; Oaksey, John: *The Guinness Guide to Steeplechasing* (Guinness Superlatives Ltd. 1979).

Cranham, Gerry and Pitman, Richard: *The Guinness Guide to Steeplechasing* (Guinness Publishing Ltd. 1988).

Davis, J. Madison: *Dick Francis* (Twayne 1989).

Dorling Kindersley Travel Guides: *Great Britain* (1995, reprinted 2002).

Fairley, John: *Racing in Art* (John Murray 1990).

Fitzgeorge-Parker, Tim: *Flat Race Jockeys: The Great Ones* (Pelham Books 1973).

Francis, Dick: *The Sport of Queens* (1957); *Dead Cert* (1962); *Nerve* (1964); *For Kicks* (1965); *Odds Against* (1965); *Flying Finish* (1966); *Blood Sport* (1967); *Forfeit* (1968); *Enquiry* (1969); *Rat Race* (1970); *Bonecrack* (1971); *Smokescreen* (1972); *Slay-Ride* (1973); *Knock Down* (1974); *High Stakes* (1975); *In the Frame* (1976); *Risk* (1977); *Trial Run* (1978); *Whip Hand* (1979); *Reflex* (1980); *Twice Shy* (1981); *Banker* (1982); *The Danger* (1983); *Proof* (1984); *Break In* (1985); *Bolt* (1986); *Lester: The Official Biography* (1986); *Hot Money* 1987); *The Edge* (1988); *Straight* (1989); *Longshot* (1990); *Comeback* (1991); *Driving Force* (1992); *Decider* (1993); *Wild Horses* (1994); *Come to Grief* (1995); *To the Hilt* (1996); *10 lb. Penalty* (1997); *Field of 13* (1998); *Second Wind* (1999); *Shattered* (2000); *Under Orders* (2006); *Dead Heat* (2007). All the above were published in the UK by Michael Joseph.

Fuller, Bryony: *Dick Francis: Steeplechase Jockey* (Michael Joseph 1994).

Gilbey, Quintin: *Champions All* (Hutchinson & Co. Ltd. 1971).

Goodman, Jean: *What a Go! The Life of Alfred Munnings* (Collins 1988).

Herbert, Ivor: *Red Rum* (William Luscombe Ltd. 1974).

Herbert, Ivor: *Six at the Top* (William Heinemann Ltd. 1977).

Hislop, John: *Racing Reflections* (Hutchinson & Co. Ltd. 1955).

Holloway, David: *Derby Day* (Michael Joseph 1975).

Hislop, John: *The Turf* (Collins 1948).

Leigh and Woodhouse: *Racing Lexicon* (Faber and Faber 2005).

Keating, H.R.F.: *Dick Francis* (article in Book and Magazine Collector No. 128 November 1994).

Lee, Alan: *An Inspector Calls* (racecourse reviews in www.timesonline.co.uk).

Lord, Graham: *Dick Francis: A Racing Life* (Little, Brown and Company 1999).

Morris, Tony (Ed.): *Great Moments in Racing* (Queen Anne Press 1976).

Mortimer, Roger: *The History of the Derby Stakes* (Michael Joseph 1973).

Obstfeld, Raymond: *Fiction First Aid* (Writers Digest Books 2002).

Ross, Alan (compiler): *The Turf* (Oxford University Press 1982).

Sharpe, Graham: *The William Hill Book of Racing Quotations* (Stanley Paul and Co. Ltd. 1994).

Tyrrel, John: *Chasing Around Britain* (The Crowood Press 1990).

West, Julian (Ed.): *Travelling the Turf* (Kensington West Productions Ltd. 1977).

Index

275